Women, Men and Persons

Women, Men and Persons

Managing Gender Meanings in Middle Class Madrid

Britt-Marie Thurén

Automatiserad teknik vilken används för att analysera text och data i digital form i syfte att generera information, enligt 15a, 15b och 15c §§ upphovsrättslagen (text- och datautvinning), är förbjuden.

© 2025 Britt-Marie Thurén
Cover drawing by Ylva López Campos
Publisher: Books on Demand, Östermalmstorg 1, 114 42 Stockholm,
Sverige, bod@bod.se
Print: Libri Plureos GmbH, Friedensallee 273, 22763 Hamburg, Tyskland

ISBN: 978-91-8080-976-4

For Louise

THANK YOU:

After thirty years, expressions of gratitude may seem out of place. They are overdue, evidently. But I do want to thank everybody who made this book possible.

Above all I am thinking of all the individuals and groups who admitted me into their everyday lives or let me interview them. They are many and I am deeply sorry I have not been able to thank them personally earlier. If any of you read this, please feel assured that I have been thinking of you all through the years.

Special thanks to the social club I have called Aguafría. And to the colleagues and friends who have read and commented earlier versions of this book.

The fieldwork period was financed by the Swedish Research Council for the Humanities and Social Sciences, HSFR.

As always, the closest circle of family and friends have meant so incredibly much. My dear sister Louise has offered constant support and practical help. So the book is dedicated to her.

Is this book thirty years late? If so, why?

This book is about gender and change in a big European city. Madrid was where I did anthropological fieldwork in the early 1990s and this book presents ethnography and analysis of what was a crucial period in the cultural and social history of Spain.

A first version of it was finished in 1994. So, yes, in a sense it is late in coming.

Life came into the picture. Private life, professional life... so much happened that I had no time to finish the book. "When I retire," was my excuse and hope until retirement came in 2007. But there were still tasks and duties that had to be finished. And health problems. The years slipped by.

In March 2024, I happened to see the manuscript lying there, in a dark corner of a bookshelf. I decided to at least read it through a last time.

And I liked it! It seemed it could still be a contribution. To gender theory above all, and to the ethnography of urban life in Spain. And to the always discussed but usually postponed anthropological goal of "studying up", i.e. focus on powerful sectors of society, not just poor or marginal people.

Local circumstances change. Descriptions of them, once written down, stay the same. So a certain imbalance is introduced by time. Theoretical thinking, however, builds on both old and new data.

Since I wrote the first version of this book, lots of issues have slid around on the cultural map, gaining or losing in contentiousness. But most of those I described are still there and in similar relations to each other. Still debated, still moving, still in search of useful explanations. My intention is to offer a moving picture of interest for the analysis of gender in Spain and in other countries, especially in similar periods of change.

CONTENTS

Comments

Part I: Questions: About gender in Madrid in the 1990s

Chapter 1. Introduction

Spain went through a dramatic process of change during the last half of the 20th century. Between approximately 1960 and 1980, "everything" happened. Basic economic and social structures were transformed, so that a rural society living mainly on agriculture became an industrial society where most people lived in big cities. High rates of illiteracy were transformed to a surplus of university educated persons. Not to speak of the transition from a long-lasting dictatorship to something quite similar to other Western European parliamentary democracies.

In such a conjuncture, ideas must change too. Even ideas on gender, which are usually among the deep and resistant ones. Few things were taken for granted in Spain around 1990, and this was perhaps especially true for gender. Issues like "the couple", women's work outside the home, divorce, abortion, sexuality, and so on were constantly on the agenda, in parliament, on TV debates and in friendly conversations at the corner bar.

It was, in other words, a situation of general cultural insecurity.

Shared ideas, i.e. culture, are always continually negotiated in any society. That is, they are talked about and thus reproduced with whatever adjustments to changing circumstances are called for. More or less, directly or indirectly, with words or other symbols, in the mode of debate or in other ways but handled and modified in interaction. Culture would not be shared, and thus not culture, if it was not communicated. and communication is never unproblematic, there are always differences of positions and opinions, that is why there is change. But in a situation like the one Spain found itself in, more negotiation was called for. And gender had become an especially prominent theme in those cultural negotiations.

Such a situation is strategic to describe, if we are interested in how cultural and social constructions of gender in any society might change. Anthropology offers the necessary tools for a detailed description. So, for a feminist anthropologist with a long-standing interest in Spain, like myself, to study gender in Spain becomes an intellectual and political requirement.

This book is about the gender order in middle class Madrid in the early 1990s.[1] It was changing, and people had opinions on it. They discussed it, and their discussions influenced what happened. The book is about how these cultural negotiations worked, who took part, where they took place and what was said. The purpose of this description is to scrutinize processes of change in the gender order, both social and cultural aspects, and especially the power relationships involved.[2]

The title of the book refers to an idea that cropped up very often in Madrilenian conversations at the time of my field study, both on gender and other topics. The idea was that men and women used to be very different sorts of creatures but that they were now becoming, or should now become, more similar to each other. They should not be women and men, they should just be persons. A "person" was implicitly thought of as a human being who takes on or is given rights and duties mainly according to other criteria than gender. A "person" is a social actor, a human being with sufficient dignity and resources to be able to occupy a place in society and be recognized in a way that she or he considers correct and fair. The idea of "person" was a key symbol in Madrilenian conversations, especially in the context of gender where it referred to a change away from rigidly dualist gender definitions.

Gender in Spain has been much more studied in rural than in urban contexts. For a few decades now, however, a majority of Spaniards had been living in cities. Therefore, I set out to do two studies of the Spanish urban gender order, with similar questions and methods, one in a working class environment, one in a middle class one. As it turned out, it was not possible to use exactly the same methods nor to ask the same questions, because the circumstances to be described were not similar enough. Reality tends to destroy systematic research plans. With all due consideration of the differences, however, the results of the two studies do speak to each other.

In the first project (Thurén 1987, 1988), I endeavored to describe the gender order in a peripheral working class area of the city of Valencia. I called the area Benituria. The focus of that study was on the contradictions inside the gender order – contradictions among different ideas as well as contradictions between ideas and social organization. There were also great variations in opinions on gender issues among the people of Benituria. The situation was dynamic, so gender had to change. The important difference of opinion for my informants was whether one saw all change as improvement and desired more of it, or whether one wanted things to calm down a bit or even return to "normal".

In Benituria, too, "person" was a key symbol related to change in the gender order. Both in middle class and working class discourses, there were constant references to Enlightenment values like "rationality", "justice", "self-realization" and "progress" and together they defined the idea of "person". Yet, there were also clear differences according to class.

10

The present book reports on the middle class project. It can be read by itself, but the design of the study is related to the Benituria one, and in the conclusions I will make some comparisons. The point of comparison is the difference in class, but the focus is on gender, not on class. Class, like the city, is part of the background.[3]

Madrid is a big city. It is impossible to say anything about it focusing on one small group or even a few key informants, as anthropologists do in small scale societies. To concentrate on discourses is, apart from other advantages, a way of partially solving the difficulty inherent in studying a big city; discourses and contexts are not infinitely many. People have criteria for recognizing and classifying discourses, and the anthropologist can learn them.

But on one condition – she has to move around. That is difficult, because middle class people do not just get to know each other, one has to have introductions. And moving a lot between contexts entails a risk: one may never get to know people well enough to be able to interpret correctly. On the other hand, anthropology has to develop methods that suit the conditions of big cities, and of studying up, and in my case, I had lived in Madrid for many years, so I had contacts I knew my way around and I had ways of judging where I was. I could gain breadth without losing too much depth.

And moving around in middle class Madrid, from an elegant restaurant to a meeting in some more or less revolutionary association, from the university to a gym class, from a tennis club to a department store, etc., I did what all anthropologists are supposed to do, namely do the same things the people they study do. Middle class Madrilenians move all around their city, they weave in and out of varied contexts. Urban life is like that, therefore that is what one has to know and describe.

But the natives usually also have some social context they return to often and feel at home in. I found such a context in a social club of the kind many Madrilenians belong to in order to have precisely that stable circle of friends that urban life does not automatically offer. Some long-time friends introduced me to their club, which I will call Club Aguafría. During the first half of fieldwork, approximately from June 1990 to March 1991, the club was my main field. Then, and until the end of fieldwork in January 1992, I moved out in widening circles, using old friends and the snowball method to obtain contacts and introductions. There were all sorts of events – dinners with groups of friends, art shows, weddings, and so on. I also participated in more long-lasting contexts, such as a book club, a gym class, a group of women who visited museums, and a group which had originally been a religious so called base community but where all the members had stopped being Catholics but nevertheless wanted to continue as a group.

In all of these contexts I learned what middle class Madrilenians usually talked about and how, in mixed company as well as in women-only groups. I also organized and taped some group discussions and a number of life history interviews.[4]

I found that the theme of gender was present in most conversations, organized or spontaneous. It was plain that gender was a prominent issue on the cultural agenda. The negotiation was usually centered around the themes of "work" (especially whether women should work outside the home or not) and "sexuality" (is it good or bad? how much should be allowed to whom? what problems are being created by the ongoing changes in attitudes? etc.). Power was seldom discussed head-on, but I found that it was the controversy around actually changing power relationships between the gender categories that made other gender themes so prominent and sensitive.

The main purpose of this book is to describe the ways in which gender was handled in different discourses and how these were related to the power structure of the gender order.

1990 – and 1965

To understand Madrilenian life in 1990, it is necessary to have some idea of the range and depth of recent changes. They will be further described in chapter 2. But as an appetizer, to give a feeling for it, let me sketch a scene from 1990, and compare it with some facts and images from the mid-1960s.

Imagine a street in downtown Madrid. It is in the afternoon according to Spanish definitions, around seven PM; there are people walking briskly on errands and leisurely with friends, as usual, outside buildings that house apartments, offices and shops. Along one block is a brick wall surrounding a school. A large group of festively dressed people is standing on the sidewalk there. More people arrive. Cars stop, letting out middle-aged women, then the men drive off to find parking space. The men are at the wheel unless there are compelling reasons for letting a woman drive, and the women prefer not to have to walk very far, since they are wearing high-heeled shoes and light jackets, and it is a cold and windy day in March. Some couples stand together, some groups consist of only women or only men. The young people stand off to one side. All are chatting eagerly. One young man in an impeccable grey suit and shoulder-length black hair dashes about video-filming. Some adults remark that he looks very nice in a suit. One can presume that they mean this as criticism, in spite of their smiles. They think the young man usually dresses too sloppily, and his long hair worries them because they interpret it as an ambiguous gender symbol. He himself interprets it more as a symbol of youth and "progressive" opinions.

Julia and Angel are celebrating their 25th wedding anniversary, "the silver wedding". There will be a religious ceremony and a dinner. Julia and Angel have four daughters who have all attended the same private religious school, and they know the school priest well, that is why they have chosen the school chapel for the ceremony.

About fifty persons file into the chapel in no special order. There is some music, a regular Mass and a few speeches. Angel himself makes a speech to Julia with a few light jokes and many but undogmatic references to marriage as a sacrament. The eldest daughter, Ana, twenty-four years old, also goes up to the microphone and makes a short speech to thank her parents "for having managed to construct a marriage that has lasted for a quarter of a century. That is quite a feat. And if it weren't for that marriage, we would not exist." A giggle and a glance at her sisters. The priest kisses her cheeks.

The ceremony lasts for almost an hour, so people get impatient, squirm, cough. About half take the communion. Finally the crowd is let out into the fading sunshine that still seems to give some warmth after the damp cold of the chapel. The mood changes instantly from restrained comportment to festive expectation. Off to the cars, to drive to the restaurant!

There, hot and cold appetizers are served in generous quantities along with a free selection of drinks, while people stand around chatting, waiting for everyone to arrive. Over an hour passes between the arrival of the first and the arrival of the last – the usual problems of traffic and parking space hit unevenly. All the men are in dark suits and white shirts. The women wear mostly suits, too, but of a festive and feminine kind, in light colors and soft materials, and they all wear big earrings.

Everybody sits down at one long table. There is plenty of food, much is left on the plates. The quality is good, but the quantity is also important to make the occasion festive.

There are no speeches during the dinner, only some joking verses, composed collectively during the dinner at one corner of the table and read aloud. The women comment on each other's dresses and talk about their children. Some of the men make jokes with a sexual innuendo of the type that are made at weddings, and Angel says in a loud voice that he is having a lot more fun today than twenty-five years ago, because he was too nervous then.

As soon as the dessert has been served, the young people get up to leave for "their atmosphere", i.e. bars and discotheques. Unlike the others, Ana walks around the table to kiss all the guests good-bye and say she is so happy to see them there. The women comment that she is such a nice girl, and someone says that she is planning to get married soon. Her courteous behavior and the women's comments help to establish her as almost-adult.

Ana is studying engineering and has one year to go. Her sisters study business administration and medicine. All four plan to work, and all four plan to get married and have children. The three oldest go out almost every night and sometimes stay out until early morning. Julia and Angel do not like that at all, but they cannot stop them, they say, because all young people do that nowadays.

Julia and Angel give me a ride home. At one thirty there is still heavy traffic, but at least it is fluid. We move between high office buildings, beneath many-colored neon signs, we drive past groups of youngsters standing outside bars with liter-sized beer glasses in their hands; we talk of drug problems and robberies, and we comment the latest Woody Allen film.

And I remember when I first came to Madrid 26 years earlier, in 1964. It was a dimly lit city, then, with little traffic. Hardly any private cars at all, as a matter of fact, only taxis and buses and some government cars with flags on the hood. There were no drugs and few robberies but policemen everywhere. Young couples who tried to steal a kiss in the street were promptly admonished. The parks were fenced and locked at night. The back streets were usually not asphalted. Neither was elegant Plaza de España.

The city has become hotter in the summer with all the asphalt. And it has become warmer in the winter, too, with all the central heating. I remember back in 1965 that one could tell when one walked past a building with central heating, because there would be like a breath of warm air across the sidewalk in front of it. In those days I was almost always late for work, since it was hard for me, one of the very few women at the bus stop, to scuffle with the men. Noone stood in line. One bus after the other would fill up and drive off and those of us left on the side-walk would get more and more nervous and wonder if our bosses would discount the day's salary.

Now, in 1990, there are enough buses so that people can await more or less calmly their turn. There are plenty of women working and studying. All middle class dwellings are heated and so are all office buildings. Better quality stores and offices even have air conditioning.

Ana would never sit at home waiting for her boyfriend to call to check if she is there, the way Julia did when she was young. The first woman engineer in electronics (Ana's specialty) graduated in 1965.

Julia comes from an upper class family. Her father was a prominent businessman in a coastal town, and they lived in one of the best houses of that town. Still, she remembers that she had only two summer dresses and two winter dresses, besides the school uniform. Angel comes from a middle class family, rural civil servants. All his brothers got to study at university (not the sisters), but for this to be possible the family had to make many sacrifices, such as eating meat and drinking wine only on Sundays.

In 1965, middle class and working class lives were more different from each other than they are now, and the long term security for a middle class family then was much better than that of a working class family in 1990. But the material comforts were less. There were no washing-machines. There were few refrigerators (and usually ice-boxes, not electric ones), and no canned food, so women of all classes (or their maids) went to market every day. Canned food and central heating were things that symbolized the good life in those foreign countries all the tourists came from and that hardly any Spaniard had visited. "Spanish cans!" people laughed when they cracked eggs to make dinner. "Spanish central heating!" said people when they had a shot of red wine or anis-flavored spirits before going to work on a cold morning.

They joked about it, yes. "One must laugh in order not to cry" was a common saying. I never hear it any more.

In 1965, Franco's portrait was everywhere. A small greyish picture behind glass in a narrow frame hung from the walls of bars and school rooms, offices and hospital entrances. In 1990, socialist prime minister Felipe González gave paternal explanations of the country's ills on the TV news almost every day. But in public places, his portrait appeared mainly on posters around election time. In government offices, there was sometimes a big color photograph of King Juan Carlos I.

When I first came to Madrid in 1964, it was months before I met anyone who had ever heard of Picasso. In 1990, middle class people had to be able to talk about Ingmar Bergman in order not to risk social ridicule, and they had to at least pretend they had been to Paris or London.

In 1965, a good middle class life was to be able to let your children study beyond primary school (at least the boys), and to have a maid dressed in a uniform. In 1990, a good middle class life was to be able to send each one of your children, boys and girls, to study abroad for at least one year, preferably to the United States, and to have a well-equipped home to which you could invite your friends with pride. Impeccable clothing was as important in 1990 as it was in 1965.

In 1965, the University of Madrid had a cafeteria which served cheap meals, where you could have as many helpings as you wished of the first course, which was always a nourishing soup with cheap vegetable ingredients, so you would not go away hungry, but you could only have one serving of the main course, which was usually one fried egg or a small piece of unaccompanied meat or fish. Water was served in metal pitchers. In 1990, students sat in the bars all around the university areas eating pizzas, fried shrimp or cuttlefish and drinking beer.

In 1965, a daring thing to do for young middle class people was to go to a "club", which was a dark place where the waiters would not say anything if couples kissed. But the girls had to be home before ten o'clock. In 1990, a daring thing to do for young middle class people was to get a part time job while studying in order to move in with a boyfriend or girlfriend in spite of parents' protests.

Julia had never worked outside the home. When she got married, she took it for granted that a woman's role was to be a good mother and a good wife. She still said so in 1990, if asked, but she took it for granted, too, that her daughters would get good jobs and earn good money.

In 1965, an average Spanish woman would give birth to around four children during her lifetime. In 1990, she would have fewer than two.

In 1965, a married Spanish woman could not, by law, sign a contract, open a bank account or obtain a passport without her husband's explicit permission. Abortions and contraceptives were forbidden, and many women did not know they existed. The law said that a married man's duties were to provide for his wife and children, and a married woman's duties were to obey her husband and live where he established the family residence. A woman who had a lover could be sent to prison, but a man who had a lover could only be taken to court if he had taken his lover home and made his wife wait on her. Divorce did not exist; separations were rare and very difficult to legalize.

In 1990, the laws on marriage were approximately the same as in other European countries, and close to 30% of adult women had a job or a business of their own. Rape was no longer a "crime against honor" but a "crime against sexual liberty", which meant among other things that a victim did not have to claim virginity in order to prove rape.

During the Franco regime, homosexuality was included in a law on vagrancy and socially dangerous behavior that permitted preventive detention. In the early 1990s, a law on homosexual marriage was proposed. The public debate included some thorny religious issues around marriage as a sacrament, but by 1994 the attention focused more on whether homosexual couples should be allowed to adopt children or not.

Spain had become a different country in the 1990s. Madrid was a different city. Young people did not know very much about those old hardships, even though many of the changes were quite recent. But Julia and Angel and their friends had lived in both worlds. They were only about fifty years old, but during their adult life, the last quarter century, their surroundings had changed as much as things changed in Sweden or England in, say, a hundred years.

Ana cannot be understood without understanding Julia. Nor can Julia, as she is today, be understood without knowing something about Ana. This book will be mainly about women of Julia's age, because they spanned the period of the changes that were ever present in anything Madrilenians said or did, but we must keep in mind that women of Ana's age were already coming into adult life and beginning to change major structures in it.

To describe a gender order

I do not pretend to describe "the situation of women in Madrid." Such a goal would be theoretically untenable. Around 1990, after about two decades of intense work,[2] anthropology of gender had arrived at a point where it was no longer considered useful to ask sweeping questions about conditions that might influence women's status overall. There was growing consensus that all gender orders are shaped by many specific local conditions, that they are varied and that they must be described in painstaking detail before we can return to generalizing and hypothesis-building. The theoretical challenge now was to develop methods and concepts for better descriptions and finer-grained analyses.

But if we are feminists, and if feminism means to criticize and try to change such parts of the gender order that we consider negative, then we must not abandon the goal of understanding the social processes that produce differences in power.

The focus must then be on relationships between women and men, and possible other gender categories, not on any category by itself. The first step is to identify asymmetries, imbalances, hierarchies. We cannot assume a priori that there is any hierarchy. But as soon as social categories are defined in a society, we can take the contrast as a starting point for asking questions about criteria, relationships, reasons and consequences, experiences, perspectives, etc. The fact that there is a categorization indicates that something important happens along the border, i.e. at the place of the defined difference. It is quite probable that it has to do with the distribution of resources of some kind. So we need descriptions of the categorization and the consequences of it, both as they are interpreted in the society in question and as they might be interpreted looking in from the outside. Studying only one of the categories can give other kinds of information, but no information on why the categorization exists and what social effects it has.[6]

Only when we have reliable empirical knowledge about the various categorizations that occur in a society, can we try to draw conclusions about their relationship to each other. That is why gender, not women, should be the focus of any study with a feminist-critical intent. And that is why any other hierarchies in the society studied should also be taken into account.

In most gender orders, especially in the Mediterranean area, there is an ideology of complementarity. Women and men are different (by nature, by education, by experience, or whatever) but equal in worth, as Spaniards often express it. But such difference-cum-equality is rare in practice. To the extent that the gender categories are placed so that they have different possibilities and are constrained by different limitations, some sort of hierarchy between them will be the almost inevitable outcome. A perfect balance in a complex system of differences (and all gender orders are complex) is an imaginable but not very probable possibility, and it is even less probable in complex societies, where myriads of other factors would also have to be in balance or compensate each other.

Since Spain is a society with a deeply rooted class hierarchy, gender works differently according to class context, and the interaction between the two hierarchies must be taken into account to understand either. There are differences in the gender order according to class, just like there are differences between village and city life, between different regions and different moments in time.

Gender as well as class and other social categorizations or organizational principles can be seen as structures that shape social practice. They can also be seen as results of social practice. The emerging theory of practice is making it unnecessary to choose between these two ways of seeing.[2] My focus is on discourse as practice. It is necessary to keep both structure and process in view, simultaneously, if we are to understand relations of power in a dynamic situation.

The Madrilenian middle class

In Spain, class is an emic category in the sense that it is part of daily experience. This is more consciously so for the lower classes, and perhaps for the highest ones. In the middle

17

sectors, it is more confusingly so and often denied. But it is there. Middle class Madrilenians can hardly generalize about their situation or even describe their daily life without running into the need to refer to class, and since they usually do not want to,[8] their discourse abounds in expressions like "people like... you know, like us...", "those who... let us say with a different background...", "people with... well, with very little education" and so on.

The most interesting class category to compare with the working class was the new middle class that based its position on educational merits and that came into its own during the 1970s.

It is interesting, first, because it was the emically salient sector of the middle class in Spain during the following decades. The traditional petite bourgeoisie of small businessmen had been rather impoverished. The narrow sector that could be called a technical intelligentsia[9] before 1970, i.e. whose work consisted of applying knowledge gained from university studies, consisted mainly of state employees, *funcionarios*, who had formal education but were notoriously poor, and lawyers and doctors with their own practices. To live on a salary was equal to being poor in those days, whether or not one had a high education. To belong securely to the middle class, one had to have a business of one's own, and in order to obtain that, it was all but necessary to be well situated by birth.

But starting in the 1960s, the economic structure of Spain had changed thoroughly. As the country industrialized and as big firms and transnational companies took over ever greater parts of the production, there was a growing need for specialists: engineers, lawyers, economists and the like. But it took some time before the universities produced as many as the country needed. The generation that graduated from university between approximately 1965 and 1975 could command high salaries, because they were in great demand.[10]

By the 1990s, the structure of the labor market was similar to that of other European countries, i.e. a majority of the economically active were salaried. It was now possible to live quite well on a salary in Spain. Many of the members of the new middle class also had considerable power of decision in spite of being employees, because they were in executive positions, and most of them had a higher standard of living than did small businessmen. This was especially true of the generation born between 1940 and 1950, again. They graduated at a propicious moment, and by 1990 their careers had had time to mature.

After slowly emerging for a decade or two, the new middle class was discovered by Spanish mass media, and during the 1980s it was talked about, debated, portrayed, caricaturized and stereotyped. This was another reason for choosing it for this study: the new middle class was an emically interesting phenomenon. It was obvious that its members had a very different life style from the older type of middle class. They were said to be given to a high level of consumption of luxuries, to be interested in obtaining power, to live above their means and to have extremely high ambitions for their children. Not a few of them had leftist opinions in their youth and many still voted socialist. All of this in contrast to the habits and values of the petite bourgeoisie and also to the older kind of middle class.

In other words: salaried employees could now lead non-proletarian lives in Spain, and this was a new phenomenon. But the pre-condition was advanced education, and earlier class conditions determined to a high (but not absolute) degree the access to education. There had been social mobility, but the really important fact was the shift from status to merit as the basis for a career. This had consequences for the gender order, and that was a third reason for focusing on the salaried sector of the middle class.

A fourth reason was that it seemed interesting to concentrate on a sector of the population that led very different lives in comparison to their parents. In this conjuncture of change, they ought to be the ones who noticed the changes most profoundly.

In Benituria, when I did fieldwork there in 1983, gender had become a key symbol for change. Change was usually felt to be something very good, even a prerequisite for a good life. The common interpretation was that "change" in the abstract was what had diminished poverty and increased freedom and personal autonomy. This was something most Beniturians had experienced concretely in their own lives. To be against "change" was therefore close to impossible. Those who had doubts or felt confused had to find excuses. For most, it was a good thing to "have an open mentality" and to "be ready to learn." And Beniturians who wanted to prove that they were really "progressive", i.e. not afraid of change, were especially careful to express "modern" opinions on gender issues (for instance being pro-abortion and pro-divorce, using contraceptives, criticizing traditional marriage, insisting on the need for "justice" and "equality" for women in the labor market, etc.).

Others were unsure of what "all these new ideas" would comport and preferred to make conservative choices in their own lives. But for them, too, gender was a salient symbol of ongoing social and cultural changes. For good and for bad, but mostly for good, they said, even when they did not act accordingly. And those who expressed clear opposition to what was happening almost always chose metaphors from the gender order to argue that change was leading to disorder and unhappiness: young girls do not guard their innocence any longer, they don't realize what they are losing, families are breaking up, children are left uncared for because selfish mothers prefer their careers, people are obsessed by sexuality...

Against that backdrop, it became interesting to see to what extent gender was a key symbol for the new middle class, too. It would be logical for it to be, since gender has often been used as a key symbol of almost anything in Mediterranean societies and since social change was a condition for the living standard of the new middle class. But it was predictable that the issues would be different ones to some extent, and that the controversies around them would be expressed differently. The objective situation of women would probably be quite different, and more contradictory, since they would not be forced by material needs to enter the labor market, but if they participated in the ideology of education and merit, they would want to.

For all of these reasons, the new middle class seemed to be the most interesting social sector to focus this study on. It was also possible to obtain access to them, since I belong to the same generation and had lived in Madrid during most of the 1970s as a typical middle class housewife (even though of foreign origin), married to an engineer who had graduated in 1965.

The Madrilenian middle class was culturally hegemonic, its ideas and actions influenced the whole country. Its gender order could certainly be described as gender orders are usually described: division of tasks between husbands and wives, daughters and sons, women and men in the office, differential access to resources and so on. Data of this type will be included in this book, as necessary background. But the most fundamental feature of this gender order was variation. Since doxa was breaking up, and new orthodoxies were being created[11] but were as yet not clearly demarcated nor firmly established, everything was up for discussion. Debate was the order of the day.

The object of study

In such a situation, then, the first step towards a useful portrait is to describe the discourses. What was the debate about? What did women and men in middle class Madrid find it worthwhile to discuss? What aspects of the gender order stood out in their discussions? What did they take to be rhetorically effective? Were these references really effective? Or was there perhaps a meta-debate about which references can function as legitimations?

Was there a feeling that something important was happening in the relationships between women and men? And if so, how was that conceptualized? Was it interesting to talk about, or not, or was it perhaps too controversial? What metaphors were used to grasp the process? Was the process used as a source of metaphors to discuss other things? What kinds of people talked in what ways about it? Could different discourses be distinguished? Did they refer to each other? Can we describe a dynamic field of discourses on gender in middle class Madrid?

Discourses constitute only one part of a gender order. But it is a part that represents the whole.

The exact formulation of the object of study is: the cultural negotiation of changes in the gender order in the Madrilenian middle class. The focus will be on which major themes came up, how the arguments were formulated, how different standpoints were related to each other, where most of the cultural negotiations took place, who took part in them and to what extent the gender categories had different access to crucial discourses, passively (reading, listening) or actively (writing, speaking). I also pay attention to the power aspect involved in the fact that women and men had different access to strategic fora for all kinds of cultural negotiation and the fact that the access to such fora was one of the topics in the negotiations on gender.

The legitimation of social hierarchies can always be described as symbolic violence.[12] This becomes especially visible to the participants in places and periods where doxa is breaking up, that is, in periods when things that used to be taken for granted no longer fit the situation; they become visible and can be criticized. That was exactly the kind of process Spain had gone through during the last half of the 20th century. When everything around you changes, you might applaud the changes, or you might wish them away. To have to have opinions on everything is tiresome, and you may long for a more comfortable state where there are not so many choices and decisions to be made at every step. When a large amount of taken-for-grantedness breaks up, the defense of doxa can no longer be doxic, because in the very moment you realize that it exists and has to be defended, it is no longer doxa but orthodoxy.

That does not mean that there is no doxa. There are always many things that remain invisibly accepted by all, and these are the very things that can most fruitfully be referred to in the debate. An argument is most effective if it can be built on something that even the opponents must accept.

In an anthropological study of change, then, it is interesting to find and describe on the one hand those things that are still taken for granted, and therefore not debated, and on the other those that are very much talked about and seen to be problematic and controversial precisely because they have until recently been invisible.

Things do not just change by themselves. People make them change, and they do so through their actions, and actions include talk, so what people say is one of the things that change the world. And there is also change in what many people say and slowly come to agree about. That is what cultural negotiation is about. Some people are usually more influential than others in such processes.

Gender and discourse

The discourses were varied, of course, just like all the other features of Madrilenian life. But they addressed each other. There was a field of gender discourse, a common field of debate. It was a field in Bourdieu's sense, a social game in which all participants felt they had something to gain and something to lose, so that it was necessary for them to participate; it was a game in that it had certain rules and certain things taken for granted; and these rules were more or less invisible, i.e. quite doxic.[13]

The game metaphor is limited, however, as is that of negotiation. When people participate in cultural negotiations, which is most of the time, in general they do not feel that they play a game or draw up a contract. The things to be won are not immediate individual advantages. But then neither can culture be described simply in terms of what ideas it "contains". This is true of all types of culture but the difficulties multiply when we try to describe what happens in complex societies. In his book about cultural complexity, Hannerz (1992) describes the forms and channels and other characteristics of the cultural flow and repeatedly says that all of this has to be "handled" or "managed" by people. Especially so, the more complexly organized it is. This is my point of departure, also.

To study the forms and contents of discourses is to catch cultural negotiation in flight, so to speak. The process is about moving meanings from one state to another. To describe the process, one has to have some approximate idea about the previous state and one may obtain a better understanding of the nature of the state that is being constructed, but the process itself is neither state. Cultural reality is always in movement, never perfectly reproduced, but always in the process of being recreated. Some values and images and definitions seem more or less stable, because they are frequently communicated and seldom opposed or contrasted. But they, too, are made and remade in the process of communication.

The process can be called cultural construction or cultural negotiation. I use the two terms as approximate synonyms. When I use the word negotiation, I place a somewhat stronger emphasis on the provisional nature of the results. I do not imply any given level of awareness or purposefulness. The term management of meaning has a similar referent, too, but it focuses more on the culturally specific styles of negotiation.[14]

By discourse I mean what is usually said about something in a given social context. The emphasis can be on the contents – a conservative discourse on gender, for example. Or it can be on the social contexts – the discourse of Club Aguafría women, for example. But the important thing to remember is that discourses are channels in which the process of cultural negotiation flows. They are vehicles more than results. Things happen in and through them.

To describe verbal cultural negotiation one should ideally include: the situational parameters of the process (not just of each communicative event or each communicative situation, but the social and cultural circumstances in general); the focused themes of the process (for instance gender, or, specifying a bit more, nature-versus-culture, work, sexuality...); the goals of the process, at whatever level of consciousness (for middle class Madrilenians, for instance, to resolve some of the intellectual, existential and practical dilemmas caused by the contradictions in the gender order); the participants in the process and the various positions they can take (emically relevant categories of participants, e.g. women and men, progressives and traditionalists, educated and not-so-educated, etc. and their social roles, e.g. housewife or teacher or politician, and also their positions in the communicative situations, such as interested-in-feminist-issues, defender of "nature", out-to-provoke-husband, etc.).

The forms and arenas must also be described. By forms I mean different types of verbal face-to-face negotiation (friendly chats, friendly discussions, spontaneous unorganized debate, formal debate, political debate...), the various uses of media, manipulation of space and other symbols, practical challenges and breaking of norms. By arenas I mean contexts defined by purpose, participants and places, e.g. a work place, a coffee party, an associational meeting.

If people say something, it is a fact that they say it, whatever we may think about the veracity of the contents. To speak is a social act. Discourse is connected to the gender order in two ways: different gender categories participate in different discourses, and participate in different ways and degrees; and some discourses are about the gender order or gender-related issues. In both these ways, the features of the field of discourses constitute a set of constraints and possibilities that work in different ways for men and women. Therefore, analyzing discourse is much more than analyzing texts or symbols. It is about real power relationships.[15]

Since talking is the major symbolic type of activity of human beings, talking has a privileged relationship to the reproduction of ideas. Talking is individual action, but it always contains references to other individuals (listeners), it takes the form of conversation more often than soliloquy, it usually concerns the actions of other individuals (gossip, narrative, joking, etc.) and it usually contains or leads up to some evaluation of events and interpretations of events, i.e. it interlocks with the chain of events. The analysis of discourse is therefore one way to disclose decisive processes of cultural reproduction.

In anthropology, what informants say is sometimes taken at face value, as information; sometimes it is systematically doubted and contextualized, to be treated as information more about constraints and strategies than about the contents as such. But there is a third way to treat what informants say, namely just like any other kind of social activity, something that happens and must therefore be described and then analysed in relation to everything else that happens. In this study, what is said is treated neither as true nor false, nor as indices of world view, nor as conscious strategies. The contents of what is said, generalized into discourses, and the circumstances in which certain discourses can be heard, and the access of women and men to certain discourses are all treated as social facts that interlock with other social facts.

Discourse is not just a strategic study object, it is also a strategic political instrument. And in view of this, it is possible to transcend the paralyzing relativism that anthropological analysis often condemns us to, and that makes feminist or any kind of critical anthropology look like a contradiction in terms. Participation in discourse is one possibly universal criterion for measuring power.

This includes all kinds of written text and other symbolic production. In urbanized, complex societies, extra-local discourses intersect constantly and intimately with face-to-face interaction.

Or, expressed in Dorothy Smith's terms, power is always a mobilization of people's concerted activities, and "objectified" knowledge is one crucial factor in the whole field

23

of factors that determine how such mobilization is effectuated. Therefore, it is dangerous for any category of people in any society to remain outside the spaces where objectified knowledge is produced and collective decisions are negotiated, honed and shaped.[16]

In my terms, for critical social analysis it is necessary to make a social map of discourses. Both written and spoken, but with special focus on what is spoken in everyday social situations. My intention is to draw such a map in order to suggest how feminist anthropology can be de-relativized without losing sight of real sociocultural variations.

Discourse and genderized space

Space is both material and symbolic, so it should be included in the description of discourses on gender as well as in other analyses of power.

It can never be fair to place certain categories of people in delimited places (for instance the home), to give them certain privileges (for instance the right to be supported or the monopoly over certain, also important, types of knowledge, for example about emotion) in exchange for their renouncing participation in other spaces. It is dangerous for the so placed. This is an objective fact, independent of what interpretations the so placed develop of the situation and the cultural plausibility and psychological defenses that such interpretations may contain.

Middle aged Madrilenians in the early 1990s had lived a good deal of their lives in a world where women and men were seen as very different kinds of people. The division of tasks kept women away from crucial social spaces, but most people, including some foreign anthropologists, felt that this was compensated for, or more than compensated for, by the fact that the home was also a crucial social space, and that women were perhaps more powerful than men there.

Now, they lived in a different world. Those who interpreted that old arrangement as irrational and unfair had gained the edge in public discourse. They made their voices heard in the schools, in the media, in legislation. That does not mean that all teachers, writers and politicians were wholly convinced or that they convinced all their listeners. Far from it. But it means that those who subscribed to the older discourses must develop new arguments and some differentiation between what to say in public and what in private. Besides, actual social arrangements varied much more than they used to. So arguments and discourses and roles multiplied, and the multiplication fed on itself and grew.

As complexification increases, textual realities become more and more prominent. Where the differentiation of roles is deep and wide, face-to-face interaction can only cover small areas of social life. What is learned from immediate experience is a diminishing proportion of everything that is necessary to know in order to manage one's life rationally and safely.

This had been a salient new experience for middle class Madrilenians. Necessary knowledge had become depersonalized. However, it was partially compensated for by the importance of personal relations. At least people had that impression. They valued their families, they found time for their friends, they cultivated friendly interaction with lots of people. Rules and regulations were not trusted to the same extent as personally known individuals. Someone you have met, even if you have no special knowledge of his or her trustworthiness and no special connection that would make her or him obliged to defend your interests, is like a safe sign-post in a jungle of complexity. Someone you have met is someone who knows who you are, someone who will therefore answer your questions and help you. Perhaps not beyond what her or his position requires, but at least that. You do not have to understand everything yourself. And that which is beyond one's own knowledge, yet cannot be left to experts, can be learnt via personal interaction.

There were many occasions for personal encounters in Madrid. And almost all interaction was strongly verbal. All those strange people who lived in the city, whose actions might seem incomprehensible and whom one had no chance of getting to know, could be brought close through the tales of friends and acquaintances, and thanks to conversation their actions took on meaning. The jumble of strange opinions that reached one through the media could be sorted out and interpreted.

So verbal face-to-face interaction was one place where people taught and learned, reflected and negotiated, attacked and defended – in one word, acted.

The analysis of discourse describes what is said in a given situation. It relates key themes to places, and places to the people who are usually present or are allowed to be present or are present on certain conditions. It relates places to the consequences of what is said there. It is a way, therefore, of relating the immediate and verbal to practice and to the results of practice in concentric circles of mediation. In other words, it is a way of relating the symbolic action in micro processes to material results in macro spaces.

What is described?

What kind of an ethnography is this?

It is urban. The people in its pages are of many kinds, and they are found in many places, and the events described are rather independent of each other, since that is what urban life is like. Monographs describing slices of human life as organic wholes cannot cover but small pieces of city life, and they are inevitably incomplete because no single small piece sets much of its own conditions in a complex reality. Further, such monographs are not very necessary since the knowledge that the classical anthropologist gathered about demography, economics, world-view and kinship systems in the classical anthropological field, is better rendered by a number of specialists when it comes to complex urban fields: demographers, economists, sociologists, etc. The anthropological task there must be to try to combine all those different kinds of information to a backdrop that more or less hangs together, and then formulate more intricate questions. For instance about change.

Benituria was an urban field, too. The informants lived in a big city, and to some extent they moved around all across the city and used its facilities. They would go outside their own area for purposes such as seeing a doctor, visiting relatives, or work. Yet, it was possible to describe the area as something similar to a village, because there was social life *of* the area. Most people had most of their friends and often many relatives living nearby. The area, *barrio*, was seen to have a personality of its own, like a village. Many personal relationships were multiplex, i.e. social roles overlapped. For example, one's neighbor could also be one's children's teacher, one's preferred conversational partner in the bar and a member of one's choir.

That was not so for the Madrilenian middle class. The people of the present study moved around Madrid for purposes of schooling, working, political and religious life, shopping, and so forth, and they had friends and relatives all over the city. They had different contexts for different purposes, and many contexts were narrow in purpose. Their networks were extensive but loose-knit, and few relationships were multiplex.

Thus, the situations chosen as illustrations of Madrilenian life must be manifold and varied. But they have been selected so as to complement each other and together give a reasonably complete picture of the object of study: the cultural negotiation of the changes in the gender order in the Madrilenian middle class.

This is not a "postmodern" or "reflective" ethnography. The anthropologist is present in the description, to be sure, but as I see it, that is simply because the anthropologist was present in the situations described, and her presence could not be totally inconsequential, so the reader has a right to know something about how she entered the interaction: how much, in what ways, how other persons present reacted. This would be true for all ethnography. It is perhaps especially necessary in an ethnography of discourse, where the anthropologist's expressed or presumed opinions inevitably form part of the situation. And it is even more so in a cultural context like the Madrilenian one where it was not licit to try to fade into the wallpaper, be "discrete", "neutral", etc. Such behavior was culturally ungrammatical in Madrid. Or even worse: a person who behaved in such a way would be seen as untrustworthy, provocative, pretentious, smug, selfish, uncooperative... all the things an anthropologist must not be if she wants to establish rapport, and interpretations that would definitely influence the situation more than "normal" participation. So I participated more or less as I would have done when I was a middle class Madrilenian housewife myself a few years earlier − except that I listened to everyone and did not try to win all the arguments, as most Madrilenians did. And since my actions formed part of the situations, I describe them.

Naturally, an anthropologist reflects and interprets. By choosing the situations I have chosen and not others, I present Madrilenian life from a certain angle. For this reason, too, it is only fair to give the reader some information on the anthropologist so that the

26

reader can place her in the field of opinions. But the purpose of the study is objectivist. The gender order is a political fact. It distributes crucial resources, it shapes social life, it channels communication and ideas, it influences personalities. Therefore it must be scrutinized. The reflexivity of the anthropologist is placed at the service of this purpose, it is not a purpose in itself.[17]

The description of situations is meant to give the reader a chance to do some interpreting of her/his own. It is impossible to include all the theoretically relevant facts, but the intention has been to come close to that goal, first by describing, as densely (cf Geertz 1973) as possible, and then presenting my own analysis separately.

The ethnographic information is of several kinds. There is a background picture of Madrilenian life, calling upon the knowledge I had not just from fieldwork and literature but from some fifteen years of living there and over thirty years of being involved with it in one way or another. The basic points of the background are in chapters 2 (space, class characteristics, clusters of opinions) and 14 (labor market, domestic tasks), and the rest is presented in footnotes as the need arises to explain details I presume non-Spanish readers would not know.

Then there are data that together make up an outline of the accepted middle class discourses on gender and related issues. Much of this is presented as summaries derived from analysis, especially in chapters 14, 17, 18 and 20. But since "discourse" is such an abstract object, and since the term "cultural negotiations" lends itself to different interpretations, it is necessary to present some thick descriptions of situated discourse in representative situations. This is done mainly in chapters 5-13 but also in chapter 19 and parts of chapters 14, 16, 17 and 18.

Parts II, III, IV and V are preceded by short introductions explaining what the material has been selected to illustrate.

Outline of the book

Chapter 2 offers the necessary general backdrop, centered on the relations between class, education and space, and on the relations between certain key symbols and opinions

In chapter 3 we get a first look at women's everyday life and verbal practice. It describes a typical day in the life of two women, both of them representative but chosen to be as different from each other as possible within that representativeness. It also situates them in relation to different types of discourses and discusses what this means for the distribution of power between women and men.

Chapter 4 elaborates further on the themes of complex culture and urban anthropology in the context of recent Spanish history. This leads up to the presentation of a key concept: mode of management of meaning.

In part II there are four ethnographic chapters from Club Aguafría. In part III we move outside the Club and sample other middle class contexts.

Two substantial topics recur in these mainly empirical chapters. They polarize people, and are therefore uncomfortable but ever present. Part IV is about the first one, "work". Part V is about the other one, "sexuality". In both parts, there are examples of situated discourse on the topics and also examples of how they appear in other than face-to-face situations.

After analyzing other people's words, the anthropologist presents her own in part VI. In chapter 20, the styles of interaction and the fora of debate are summed up and compared to those of the Benituria study. The key themes of the discourses on gender are lifted to a more abstract level in order to connect discourse and social reality. Chapter 21 places the results of this study in the light of historical processes of Enlightenment, individuation and industrialization in Europe. The changes in the Madrilenian gender order can be summarized as "modernization" and that is how Madrilenians themselves talk about them. The change is away from something called "traditional", and I propose a model for what that can be taken to mean, especially in the light of common features in many gender orders around the Mediterranean.

Chapter 22, finally, discusses what an ethnography of discursive practice can tell us about the power aspect of the gender order.

The three appendixes are placed at the end, since the reading of them is not absolutely required for an understanding of the rest. The group discussion in appendix A exemplifies many things, apart from giving a good idea of how a representative Madrilenian social conversation is woven together. It is especially interesting to compare it to chapter 13 for differences and similarities. Appendix B is a brief presentation of practice theory and shows how my ethnographic questions on gender can constitute a bridge between description and comparison. It also discusses the difficulties of "studying up" and describes the data gathering techniques used. Appendix C is especially recommended for people interested in group discussions as a method or in Spanish verbal behavior in general.

Chapter 2. The City, the Middle Class and the Women

This chapter contains background facts on the city of Madrid and on its new middle class. The purpose is to enable the reader unfamiliar with Spanish reality to contextualize the data and the interpretations in the rest of the book. Where did the protagonists live and why, what did they do for a living and in their leisure, what was their economic situation and what were the most important differences in opinion among them?

The reader should bear in mind that the description refers mostly to the 1990s.

City space

During the 1940s Madrid was still a small city, and recovering from the demographic effects of the civil war. In the late 1950s immigrants from rural areas started to arrive, and during the 1960s they flooded the city, building huge shanty towns all around it. There were jobs for all.

The 1970s was the decade when most of these shanty towns disappeared, because some of their inhabitants could now afford to buy apartments on the open market and because cheap dwellings were built for most of the rest of them. During this decade, especially towards the end of it, the flow of immigrants to the cities diminished, since there were fewer job opportunities. In the eighties there was little in-migration and some out-migration, as unemployment soared.[18]

The result was that downtown Madrid was under-sized for its population. This became ever more noticeable as the former shanty town paupers bought cars and could afford to come downtown for recreation and as they also demanded access to city facilities such as schools, universities and hospitals.

It also meant that most of the outlying residential areas were relatively recent, of low quality and inhabited by people of rural origin. And it meant that public transportation was inadequate there at the same time as private transportation clogged the streets that were built for a population for whom the dream of a car seemed light-years away. Other public facilities also lagged far behind private consumption: schools, health care, post offices and parks were scarce and low quality, and libraries and facilities for recreational activities hardly existed at all. The brutal unemployment of the 1980s concentrated here.

All of this in turn meant that these areas were infested with social problems, especially drug addiction and small-time but tenacious criminality.

From the point of view of the Madrilenian middle class, this used to mean that one had to live in the downtown area; anything else was unthinkable. But the downtown area was much too small and the middle class had exploded in size. The consequence was that middle class apartments in downtown Madrid had reached impossible price levels. The middle class had to find other places to live. As the downtown area during the eighties was invaded by the general social ills of the city, they also wanted to move out.

Starting on a small scale during the 1970s and gathering speed during the 1980s, middle class residential areas were built on the outskirts of Madrid. But these areas were clearly segregated according to income levels.[19]

The outlying middle class areas were better quality and offered larger apartments than the working class areas. In accordance with capitalist logic, they offered more local services for pay to the residents. They also featured such symbolic markings as entrances outfitted with wooden panels, potted green plants and always a counter for the door watchman, whether one was actually in residence or not, and perhaps a narrow lawn outside.

The environment outside the buildings was not beautiful; the price level of land permitted neither one family dwellings nor creative town planning for middle-middle class areas. Typically, streets were straight, parking space scarce and buildings high and built close together. However, the further out you went, the lower the land prices and therefore the more "green space" (as the advertisements called it). Thus there was a tension in middle class residential choice. To live far from the city center permitted more comfortable dwellings and surroundings, but the really elegant thing was still to live as close to downtown as possible.

One rather new type of solution for the middle class was to move even further out and buy one family houses in small villages or in "urbanizations"[20] in the midst of the previously rather empty Madrilenian hinterland. A life style reminiscent of British, American or Scandinavian residential area living was being formed.

It was considered elegant, but most Madrilenians were not convinced, probably because this life style goes counter to old dispositions. In these new areas, busy street life is absent, for good as well as bad, and downtown Madrid, with its socially and culturally lively environment, is so far away and transportation is usually so bad that it becomes in practice inaccessible. In other words, there is very little *ambiente*.[21] The disposition for certain kinds of sociability[22] was starved. Family togetherness tended to become an overwhelming fact of life. One might think that this would be one motive for the move, seeing that "the family" is an important ideological value. But that did not seem to be the case. "The family" in everyday discourse referred to solidarity, permanence, unquestioning love. Not to daily interaction with specific nuclear family members. When it came to leisure, the preference was for socializing in categories according to age and gender.

However, these outlying urbanizations were still a minority phenomenon. Most middle class families lived in apartments on the outskirts of the city, in middle class areas.

Even in reasonably urban areas, however, a common feeling was that social life was not what it used to be. There was a feeling that Madrid offers a lot in the way of cultural activities of high prestige, like theaters, cinemas and concerts, and a lively night life in the form of restaurants, bars, pubs, outdoor terraces and sidewalk cafés open almost all night in summer, and that not to take part in all of that is to lose something important. That night life and all those places were certainly crowded in Madrid. And the people crowding them were mostly middle class. Even so, a majority of middle aged middle class persons did not go out very much at all. And they felt they should. (Cf Carlota in chapter 3.)[23] They were missing out on one of the important pleasures of life, they thought, and also on the prestige points such a life can give. Yet, it was difficult. "One feels too lazy," was a common explanation, and it would then be filled in with details: one wants to be at home to be sure the youngsters get home safe, and if you have small children it is hard to find a babysitter now that you don't have a maid, and after fighting your way through the traffic to get back home from work you don't feel like getting into the car and fight your way back downtown again, and once there it is so hard to find a parking place, and expensive too, you might as well rent a video film...

These arguments were stronger, the farther away from downtown the speaker lived. It was true that Madrilenian traffic had become insufferable, but even so moving out from the downtown area was increasingly seen as a good alternative. One looses things, true. But central Madrid had become so "uncomfortable" that "it does not compensate" as the phrase went. The ones who moved out talked of breathing cleaner air (just cleaner, not clean – everyone was aware that the air was not very clean anywhere near Madrid), suffering a smaller risk of burglaries and robberies, having a garden, having your neighbors farther away, being able to hear birds and see stars. The difference in prestige between living downtown or in outlying areas was diminishing; it was coming to be more of a question of which area and which street.

Obviously, the spatial organization of Madrid affects women and men in different ways. And husbands and wives often have different ideas about where they want to live and what sort of dwelling to buy.

Class insecurity

The status of this middle class was uncertain, objectively, in that it was new and not yet clearly defined. It was being negotiated, it was on the cultural agenda. For many or most of its members, the uncertainty was also individual. In all probability, a person (or a family, as was usually the case) had changed position in society in recent decades. The movement may have been upwards or downwards in terms of money and general prestige, and it had probably been upwards in terms of education, at least for the men.

These facts were enough in themselves to create a feeling of insecurity. Looking closer at the distribution of incomes and the structure of the labor market, we find more reasons.

First of all the proportions of different middle class categories had been reshuffled. According to Lacalle (1990a), the salaried part of the economically active population in Spain had grown continually in recent decades.[24] Between 1979 and 1987, the structure of the salaried classes changed. Professionals and technicians increased slightly, administrators increased somewhat more, industrial workers decreased somewhat, service workers and others increased. All of these tendencies were more pronounced in big enterprises. By the 1990s more than half of salaried employees were not manual workers, but office workers, technicians, foremen and service personnel. Some of the changes had slowed down, others seemed to continue accelerating. Between 1984 and 1987, the groups of non-manual salaried employees increased with 75%. Within the dominant class, what grew both absolutely and relatively was the sub-class of managers, administrators and highly placed bureaucrats, as compared to traditional businessmen who own their businesses.

Income differentials had diminished. This had given many manual workers a feeling of having moved into the middle class, because they could now attain a material standard that was equal to or higher than what the middle class enjoyed twenty years ago. And this had given some middle class persons a feeling of loss, even though their material well-being had increased, too.

High executives often earned several times the minimum salary, but the total range had decreased (Lacalle 1990a:18-19). On the other hand, there were substantial differences within each group according to age, gender, economic sector and so on. The new middle class was spread thinly on the continuum of incomes. So each family or individual knew that its current living standard might well change, and that other middle class families might well earn a lot more or a lot less. Consequently, there was a felt need to signal symbolically the differences among themselves.

As to rate of employment, middle class people were better off than average (less unemployment) but they were losing ground. This also caused feelings of loss and anxiety.

Some conservatives in the new middle class tended to emulate old elite life styles. But for those who neither opted for the aristocratic model, nor felt radical enough to oppose it openly, there was little else to choose from, and this increased cultural insecurity. The working class was perceived as uneducated, which was strongly negative for all, even for middle class persons of leftist inclinations, and by these latter often also as regrettably conservative. Foreign middle classes, especially French and North American, were possible models, and eager comments about their life styles abounded when the conversation turned to traveling. But for one thing there was not enough information on them in order to set them up as models, and for another, there were certain stereotypical views of cultural differences, such as "coldness", social clumsiness, "lack of a sense of fun" and so on, i.e. negative images that probably constituted a brake on the tendency to consider foreign things more "modern". However, all in all, the general insecurity made for a lot of uncritical imitation of detextualized fragments of foreign life styles.

The generalized feeling of existential and status insecurity meant different things for women and men. Men felt the burden of being successful (according to the new middle class definitions). Women felt the burden of seeing to it that their husbands and children got all the emotional and practical service they needed in order to be successful. Some women also wished to be successful themselves, but that did not exempt them from the supportive and symbolic duties. (More on this in chapter 14) They tried to escape from the dilemma by saying they wanted to "be persons, too". But the emphasis on the individual robbed them of some of the prestige that used to accrue to women who lived only for their families, i.e. the ascription of women to certain roles.

Education

Education was a theme that bristled with contradictions and ambiguities for middle class Madrilenians.

The generation that was between 40 and 55 years old during my fieldwork believed in education and individual merits. They had accordingly prioritized education for their children, but the children did not have the same opportunities as their parents did. This caused conflicts. Some parents were disappointed in the positions the children managed to obtain in the labor market and the salaries they earned. Others would search for culprits. But the children worked hard, because they too believed in individual merit and conceptualized their failures as the result of individual shortcomings. Some of them did after all manage to obtain very good positions. They tended not to see that their parents had had an especially lucky conjuncture, or that their own position was especially unlucky in a period of economic downturn, or that their sheer number made for very harsh competition. So the theme of education produced tension between generations.

Another important imbalance was found in the couples where the husband had a university education and a good professional position that he had obtained thanks to his education, but where the wife had little schooling. This was unusual among people below forty, but among those older than that it was more the rule than the exception.[25] Couples in this situation shared the general idea of the wife/mother as the central pillar of family life, and they usually shared, at least to some extent, the growing idea of the couple as the most important relationship inside the family (and not mother-children, as it used to be). These two ideas demanded a measure of equality of worth between husband and wife. If their educational level was dissimilar, the solution must be to place worth elsewhere (usually "personality" and amount of "work" and "dedication to the family"), but this was difficult for people who had such a big stake in education. One solution that went against the grain of the "progressive" ideas but that was nevertheless common, was for the couple to show a united front to the rest of the world but live rather separate lives inside the family. At Club Aguafría, the form this took was that the couples arrived together but then either sat in separate groups or sat together but splitting the conversational interaction according to gender lines. At many dinner parties, the interaction similarly split.

These contradictions were producing situations that were experienced as difficult to manage and perhaps even conceptualize, and they were bound to increase. So far it had been possible for some young women to combine career with family, to some extent, because most of their mothers had been housewives and had been willing and able to help their daughters out, but as the generation of professional women become grandmothers, this possibility will disappear.[26] The clashes between women and men had been mitigated by their agreement around other important changes, but as economic and political change slows down, the tensions in the gender order will become more visible. And they cause suffering because they strike at a most vulnerable spot; they strike inside that culturally emphasized place of rest and protection, the couple.

Education must also be analyzed as a new kind of property. It is property in the sense that it is a necessary means of production in the kind of society Spain has become, and it is property also for the individual in the sense that investing it in the organization of production renders a return. More education means higher wages (and less risk for unemployment). But it is unlike capital or land in that it cannot easily be transferred to other individuals, i.e. wives or children. It cannot be inherited directly. If the head of a family dies or leaves, he cannot leave behind to the wife or the children this kind of property in such a way that they can use it directly to go on living as before (Durán 1987).

The children can inherit the father's education indirectly, in the sense that he can use part of the resources obtained with his own education to pay for the children's studies. But there is no guarantee that the children will be able to convert this investment to "profitable education" (as parents usually call it, "*educación de provecho*"). At Club Aguafría the reference was especially to engineering, law, business administration and computer careers, in contrast to "non-profitable education" such as art, humanities, social sciences, or non-careers, such as "irresponsible" living, i.e. drinks, drugs, early sex life and possibly early family responsibilities, which constitute the parents' main fears, and that is logical in that they do cut short the possibilities for the children to convert the parents' investment in their education into economic resources of their own.

Education is a fragile investment, even if invested in oneself, since one might not be intellectually fit for competition, or one might become ill, or in other ways incapable of using it. But it is more fragile yet when invested in other persons. In this sense it is not at all comparable to tangible property. But it is a crucial means of production in industrial society and becoming even more so as industrial society transforms itself into something else.

In such a situation one would expect education to be a central symbolic value. One would expect parents to be very worried about how their children are doing in their studies. One would expect parents to invest a lot in their children's education. One might expect competition between families as to what the children are studying and how well they are doing. One would expect a lot of conversation about these matters, and a lot of sensitivity and personal conflict around signs of fragility of the investment. All of these things were clearly visible at Club Aguafría, and common in other middle class contexts, too.

The principle of gender did not sort people into educational categories in the way it used to do. By 1990, young middle class women studied as much as young middle class men, and to a large extent they studied the same things. But gender influenced what they would be able to do with that education later on in life. And the relationship between gender and education strongly influenced daily life and long term life planning through the construction of motherhood: what mothers are supposed to want and supposed to do, and what mothers actually do.

In most families the pressures on the children were channeled through the mothers. In the division of tasks, the supervision of children's education had become a central one for mothers, and so important a task that it could be adduced as a reason for a woman to remain a housewife even when the children reached mature ages. (More on this in chapter 14.) In the middle class, almost all young people go to university. And as long as they study, they live at home and are largely exempted from domestic tasks because of the importance of education. This means that mothers shop, cook, wash dishes and clothes, iron, make beds, run errands, etc. for their children until they are close to thirty years old.

The centrality and legitimacy of education meant that it could be referred to in order to mask less legitimate circumstances, especially class. The most common designation for the middle class was "educated people" and the most common euphemism for lower classes was "uneducated people." In this usage, there was a convenient slippage from education = schooling to education = refinement, good behavior. So people with schooling and a comfortable living standard were seen to be morally superior. However, most of the middle class women over forty did not have much schooling, as we have seen. So they had to do what they could to decorate themselves with other types of "culture" (cf chapter 7) and in conversations and competition among themselves they emphasized money and innate taste rather than schooling.

In a situation like the Spanish one, where personal merit has only recently, and so far incompletely, replaced ascribed or inherited status as a basis for a person's incorporation into productive relationships, one would also expect that a class of persons heavily dependent on achieved status (especially education) would have strong opinions about the importance of merit and would tend to deemphasize ascribed status. This was not true of the women of Club Aguafría. Possibly it was true of their husbands and quite clearly it

35

was true of their children, daughters as well as sons. It was not true for the middle age women because history had placed them in a contradictory situation. The standard of living and personal prestige of a wife depended on her husband's income, i.e. her civil status, much more than on her personal merits. But the husband's income depended (largely) on his merits.

Family corporateness

In Western capitalist societies, it is taken for granted that a wage is paid to an individual as an individual. True, the workers of the 19th century fought for a "family wage", meaning a wage that covered the cost of reproduction of more than one individual. But even when they got it, it was still paid to the man as an individual, for him to distribute among his dependents. Today, Western states differ as to the degree to which this "family wage" is paid "indirectly", through the benefits of the welfare state, or "directly" to the man. For dependents, it is indirect in either case. That is, individuals have certain rights not defined by the wage value of their work but by their needs, which is what the family wage debate, at least ostensibly, was about. But the wage as such is always defined as payment for work done by one individual, and this individual determines its use and is also the one who accrues certain other benefits in terms of the wages earned (i.e. sick benefits, vacations, old age pensions). (Durán 1987, Fraser 1989.)

If the wage is defined as individual, but people continue to live in families, a contradiction obtains.

The main trends in Spain in the 1990s were clearly away from the family and towards the individual. The state defined itself as a welfare state, with responsibilities towards its citizens. The discourses of politicians of most political parties and of most mass media insisted that individuals should be paid for their productive work in such a way that they should not have to enter personal hierarchical arrangements in order to obtain security in case of illness or for old age. "Feudal" relationships of dependence between e.g. landowners and agricultural workers were being replaced by state payments to agricultural workers without work; the "charity" of giving alms to beggars on the street was increasingly seen as undignified, and state and local administrations built overnight lodgings and debated the possibility of a "social minimum wage" for everyone; the "paternalistic" relationship in which an old faithful worker received "what he needed" in his old age as "gifts" from former employers was practically replaced already by pension systems. And so on.

But Spain was far from an accomplished welfare state. The family had to deliver basic services. Few parents could afford to send their children to daycare centers with such hours and resources in personnel, learning materials, space and comfort as to give the children everything the parents felt they needed. So mothers had to stay at home with their small children. Most shops did not have hours that permitted shopping for basic necessities when factories and offices were closed, so shopping was a problem :f all adults in a family had jobs. The wage relationship did not officially give the employee much room for attending to persoral affairs (although many employers were liberal in their interpretations), and one mus: remember that other aspects of social organization were such that attending to perscnal affairs took an inordinate amount of time (in comparison to other European countries). For instance, the problems of finding schools for one's children could take weeks of a person's time, and obtaining necessary documents, such as passports, drivers' licenses, tax receipts, voters' credentials, or :itles to the family apartment, contracts for gas and electricity, home and car insurance, etc. usually entailed at least two or three full mornings of personal standing in line somewhere for each one. Very few of these necessities of modern urban society could be arranged over the telephone. These facts influenced the gender order, because they increased the need for a full time housewife in each home.[22]

If a person had an accident or became seriously ill, the quality of hospital service was such that some family member must usually be in attendance at all hours in the hospital. And after the immediate emergency was over, the patient would be dispatched to the home. There were few nursing homes and they were far too expensive for all but a small minority. The same was true for residences for the elderly, and they were furthermore considered by almost all to be an indignity that it was shameful for people to impose on their parents. So women had to stay at home with the incapacitated child, with the husband with a broken leg, with old parents or parents-in-law...

For over ten years, the rate of unemployment had been over 20%, and unemployment social security payments covered less than one third of the unemployed individuals, which meant that "the family" (the Spanish term *familia* includes relatives outside the nuclear family) had to step in and sustain the others (and their dependents, if they had them.

For all of these reasons, the family could not just stop functioning. So the contradictions between individual wages and family organization were strong and material, much more than a question of ideas. But of course ideas accompanied them. For some persons this turned into perscnal confusion, an uncomfortable feeling of not being able to get their opinions in line with what was happening. For others, their opinions were clear, and the main contradiction seen as one between people who thought like themselves and people who had the opposite kind of opinions. This can be observed in the various dichotomies that were debated in mass media and private conversations: left versus right, feminists versus ant:-feminists, progressives versus traditionalists, rural versus urban, and so on. All of these dichotomies can be reduced for most purposes to one: the family versus the individual.

Conservative parties in Spair argued explicitly for family solidarity, values, togetherness, and also indirectly, in defending all sorts of measures that strengthen the corporateness of the family and opposing measures that would augment individual freedom from family ties. The leftists too lived in families and usually argued for the emotional importance of families, but they defended measures that would make the state take over security such as old age pensions for all independently of kind and amount of wage work done, all sorts of measures that possibilitate women's wage work, and so on. Naturally, from a leftist point of view, social security based on the family can never be "fair" as long as families command very different amounts of resources. From a feminist point of view, family life can never be fair as long as most of the heavy duties fall on women. Feminist interpretations of recent changes were very varied, but most agreed that demographic changes had meant that women had increased their chances to shape their lives.[28]

Thus the historical situation was one where the corporate family was still necessary, but it was an embattled bastion. It was not as secure as it used to be. And if the family had to be redefined, the same was true for the individual. In such a situation, it seemed logical for "person" to be a key word for change. It was also logical for "woman" to be a concept related to women's "old roles" and therefore, in some sense, opposed to the concept of "person". I will come back to this.

Class and opinion: background

The period between 1965 and 1980 was a period of optimism on all fronts. The change from poverty, rural life and dictatorship to affluence, urban life and a new hegemonic discourse of democracy, freedom, justice, and so on, was conceptualized as evolution or progress. But it was also a period of ideological confrontation. This confrontation followed class lines to some degree, so that a "red duchess" was exciting news, and so were "red priests", while conservative bankers were not. The working class was divided but had voted socialist in overwhelming numbers ever since that became possible in 1977.

The new middle class, however, had no predefined ideological heritage. Its members came both "down", losing privileges, and "up", gaining new ground. One can presume that social origin and own experiences often pointed in opposite political directions.

There were several ideological polarizations in middle class circles in Madrid. On the scale of party politics, some people were very conservative, others revolutionaries or little less. Some were ecologists, pacifists and/or feminists (three sets of ideas that often coincided in the same individuals and definitely were associated in the public mind), while others subscribed to a world view where competition and efficiency overrode all other concerns. Some were atheists and some devote Catholics. And so on. Middle class Madrid was as polarized as all of Spain. Or more so. One could say that at no other point on the Spanish sociological map did so many different opinions meet and clash. They were all there. It was the central traffic intersection of the ideological road map of the country.

It was not all a wild traffic jam, however; there was some consensus about the main bearings. There were a couple of overriding metaphors that sorted opinions in clusters. And it is hardly surprising, in a Mediterranean country, that the dominant metaphor should be sexuality. Honor and shame were not key symbols in the Spanish debate by this time, far from it. But sexuality, in one ideological dress or another, has been culturally central in the Mediterranean area for several thousand years, and such old ideas die hard. They were changing both in form and content, but they remained pivotal. They continued to direct the ideological traffic (cf part V). Other dominant themes were nature versus culture, education and merit, women's work. They will recur throughout the empirical material of this book. But in order to understand the significance of the discourses to be described, it is necessary for the reader to have an overview, a vision of the landscape as a whole.

The dimensions of left versus right and gender change versus gender conservatism were the most fundamental ones in the sense that they were the most talked about and people classified each other according to them.

The Benituria study showed that working class women in general tended to approve of the changes in the gender order. There was not much practical change in their everyday lives, but they realized in which direction the larger changes pointed, and they saw them as promises, even though many also had mixed feelings and fear of vulnerability due to perceived own incompetence and ignorance.

The same feelings could be found in middle class Madrid. But they were not at all as pervasive. Middle class women tended not to express much open ambivalence. They tended instead to take a stand, for or against the changes they saw. Some of them placed their opinion in a more general framework of ideas, especially political left or right, and most found arguments that fitted their personal situation. The clearest division was between housewives and women with employment. Housewives[22] tended to refer to their family's needs for service and affection, and the material impossibility of combining such service with other activities, while working women and students tended to point to the material need for an income and the cultural need for "self-realization". Whatever they said and thought about change, it had to be related to gender. That was inescapable, even for those who might wish it was not so.

Middle class men, like working class men, seemed much less interested in the gender aspect of ongoing changes.

Merit was the factor that most middle class men saw as decisive, and most middle class women agreed. The fact that few working class persons obtained top positions was construed as social injustice by the leftists and as proof of the inherited qualities of the upper classes by the rightists, but they all agreed that society needs to assign individuals to positions in a "rational" way. Achievement was the order of the day, ascription was branded old-fashioned, irrational and inefficient. This did not mean that people did not try to help their friends and kin when they could. But such help was legitimized as necessary measures to overcome faults in the system, such as unfair teachers having given unfair grades, or irrational employers not realizing the special merits of a given person. The rationality of the social system was not taken for granted, the rationality of merit was.

In general, the ideological climate was confrontational, and the view of society pessimistic, seeing merciless competition, lies and treason everywhere. With such a view of reality, one easily reaches the conclusion that it must be softened. Something must be found to balance competition and rationality or they will cause more pain than efficiency. For the leftists, the compensation was found in the ideas of justice and solidarity. Justice was construed not only as a matter of equal opportunities to compete against each other, but in the sense of elimination of the many system faults that made the results of equal efforts unequal. Solidarity must be injected in all parts of the social system to make it livable.

For the conservatives, ascription of roles according to gender was the main albeit partial remedy. One gender category was called into the service of love, so that the other would be able to continue its non-love. "Women have to take care of the family, or everyone will suffer," people said. Or, in the phrase of the Franco regime, "A woman should be the soldier's resting place." In a situation of general change, it was difficult to legitimize non-change in the gender system. One solution was to declare it the only defense against chaos, or the only way to assure love a place in a society that must, inevitably, be harsh. Another way was to appeal to "tradition". It was a risky way for a class that did not have any traditions as a class, and it was not the choice of many, but for those to whom it did appeal, it appealed strongly.

Non-conservatives also considered gender change risky. The gender order was too important and much too closely connected with love and solidarity for it to be treated carelessly. To be legitimate, change in the gender order must be seen as necessary in order to wipe out injustice, i.e. as part of the more general process of improvement.

Let us now see what opinion surveys can tell us about who thinks what and what opinions tend to go with what others.

Class and opinion according to surveys

For the reasons just given, the opposition between "progressives" and "conservatives" was often expressed in the medium of gender. There were other emically central themes, above all religion and politics, and they too had a gender dimension.

According to many surveys, there was a relationship between opinions, class and education that indicated that well-educated urban upper middle class Spaniards were not conservative at all on many of these counts. The following statistical relationships have been shown for the period around 1980-1990:[30]

1) The higher the level of education attained, the higher the income, and the higher a person's professional prestige, the lower the church attendance. On the level of incomes and education that most of my informants had, some 35-40% never go to church. Furthermore, the interest in religion had declined over time for two or three decades. The sector of the population that had the largest incidence of religious indifference or non-belief were women who worked in their own business or as liberal professionals or non-manual salaried employees.

2) When it comes to interest in politics, we get the opposite picture: the higher the education, or the income, or the prestige, the greater the interest in politics. This was true for both women and men, but more true for women. This is because the traditional view had been that politics is a male area, so education, that tends to relativize such views, has more of an effect on women. The view that religion is for women what politics is for men was common in Benituria and was quite true for the conservative sectors of the Madrilenian middle class, for example Club Aguafría. But it was not at all true for the progressive sectors of the middle class, where both genders were about equally interested in politics. Both genders were also much more interested in politics and much less interested in religion than what used to be common. Many individuals described their personal history along the same lines: "I used to be very religious, but it was because of my family and the small town we lived in and everything. Once I started secondary school, I began to change, and in university I became interested in politics, and then when I moved to Madrid..."

3) Urban residence points in the same direction as high income, education and prestige, and residence in big cities even more so.

4) In all of these surveys, however, it is women's employment that makes the largest difference. Men's high incomes, education and prestige point in the same direction, but less clearly so. The women who were least interested in religion and most interested in politics, i.e. the least "feminine" ones according to traditional parameters, were those who had employment outside the home, independently of their income or education or the circumstances of their husbands

5) The same result shows up where the sociologists have tried to measure equality inside marriage, i.e. how decision-making is distributed between husband and wife. Higher education, higher incomes, higher prestige and urban residence mean more balanced power relations, but the factor that gives the largest indication is the wife's work outside the home.

Naturally it is an open question what these surveys really measure. They probably tell us more about what is considered correct to say than about what people actually do. But that too is an interesting result.

Is it a contradiction that surveys show that most indicators of middle class status tend to go with non-conservative opinions, while my study uncovers deep ambivalences and a lot of conservatism? No, it is just a question of range and distribution. The outstanding feature of the field of opinions in the Madrilenian middle class was that it was varied and polarized. So people had to discuss a lot. Opinions must be handled: debated, opposed, reinforced, clarified, sharpened, graded, and so on. And this constant handling or managing in itself erected barriers. There were styles or modes of management of meaning.

Class and opinion: clusters

In order to orient ourselves in this field of opinions, it is necessary to simplify a little. And it is possible, to do so, because a number of opinions in different areas tended to cluster and coincide in the same persons. We can distinguish six major groupings. They will be described here as ideal types, for the purpose of orientation, not exact description.

First, there was a very conservative category where many belonged to Opus Dei[21] and where one could find ex-members of the only party of the Franco regime, the Falange, and where people often expressed their belief that a similar regime is the only solution for Spain's long-lasting problems. Most people in this category were practicing Catholics and tended to prefer the contents and symbols that dominated before the Vatican II council. The human body was considered an enemy. It should be hidden and disciplined. Sexuality should not be talked about. Clothes should be strictly anti-sensual and of good quality, but not necessarily elegant. Family and Tradition are the most important things in life. Women should be Mothers and Wives, anything else is against nature.

The mode of cultural management in this first category was generally cautious.[22] Their attitude was that roles ought to be ascribed, because a person's characteristics were thought to be mostly inherited. What counts is what one is born with, who one "is". Merits are important, too, however. They were interpreted as signs of inborn capacity. And vice versa, of course: social or individual failures were considered to be due to inherited weaknesses.

Second, there was a category very similar to the first one, but more practical, less ideological. Their discourse expressed a wish for traditional privileges and old forms of social organization to be maintained as far as practical, where the first group was set on defending them at almost any cost. The second group was larger. (My group at Club Aguafría was a good example.) They were politically conservative enough not to talk about political parties unless it was to be against them all. They were practicing Catholics. The women hid the body and practiced no sports except, to some extent, sunbathing. Their clothes were meant to hide the body, and they ought not to attract the attention, but they ought to be nice-looking, decent and fresh. Socially, both men's and women's clothes expressed distinction rather than elegance. Their discourse stressed Family and Tradition, but also adaptation to circumstances. Women ought to be Mothers and Wives, anything else was unnatural and impractical.

Their mode of management of meaning was cautious, full of restraint. Women's roles were seen as mostly ascribed, men's as achieved.

In the third category, people would vote for the conservative party, Partido Popular, and saw this as desirable participation in the democratic game and as a defense against the undermining of values. Most were practicing Catholics, but they approved of new forms of practice. The body should be cared for: tennis, massage, physical exercise, make-up, to a certain extent fashion. But it should not be emphasized. So clothes became very important and must be very carefully adapted to each context. They should be relaxed for sports and among friends, but they should always measure up to class standards. The family was important. Divorces and abortions were not accepted in theory, but when concrete examples were discussed, it could be admitted that "circumstances might require it". Women should choose domestic work, "dedication to the family", before professional work, but if the two did not collide, it was acceptable, perhaps even a bit elegant, if they were successful in the labor market, too. (Many members of Club Aguafría would fit into this category.)

The mode of management of meaning was restrained and cautious, but adaptation to circumstances was a basic requirement here as well. Merit and achieved roles were more important than inherited characteristics and ascribed roles.

The fourth category could be called "ordinary people". They were probably a majority within the Madrilenian middle class, and they were seen as "normal" by themselves and by many in the other categories. Most of them voted for the socialist party, PSOE. Most of them said they were Catholics, but they did not practice much. Their style of appearance was cautiously modernizing. Many of the men sported beards, for example, but short and well trimmed ones. Both women and men liked to wear blue jeans for leisure, but always clean and ironed and combined with ironed blouses and shirts The men wore suits, long-sleeved shirts and ties to work. Professional women wore fresh blouses, suits with either skirts or pants, pumps. The body should be cared for and could be emphasized around swimming pools and at parties through elegant, slightly revealing clothes that could be just a bit original but not provocative. Family life was important, but it ought to be built on love more than duty, and the rights of individuals were also important. Women ought to strive to become "persons" and "realize" themselves, but it would be selfish of them if other individuals, especially their family members, had to sacrifice anything to that end.

The mode of management of meaning stressed criticism. Cultural negotiations referred often to naturalness and normality and above all to rationality. Merits and achieved roles were seen as the only rational, normal and natural grounds for organizing the division of tasks in society. A very important value word was progress. Time was usually thought to produce "evolution" and "development" by itself, unless obstacles were erected. Such obstacles were then "irrational", of course.

The fifth category consisted of people who were seen as and saw themselves as radical. They voted for leftist parties or they were anarchists. They were non-Catholics or anti-Catholics. Their rhetoric sounded a lot like that of the Enlightenment. (So did that of the fourth group, much of the time, but the ideological stress was stronger for the fifth group.) They spoke of the rights of the individual as against the totalitarianism of ascribed roles of any kind, and freedom was the foremost value word. They expressed a lot of pessimism about Spain and about present circumstances, but they shared with the fourth category a belief in progress as something that would be produced by time if unhindered. Change was often interpreted as synonymous with improvement. The body was important, as a source of expressivity and pleasure. Clothes should be relaxed or original, social distinction was found silly. Both women and men wore blue jeans and all kinds of slacks, but the women liked to stress their femininity with big earrings, original belts, colorful scarves, etc. and in summer they wore as little as possible. They believed in sexual education, the more the better. Most of them lived in nuclear families and enjoyed that, but they rejected anything that they saw as hindering individual growth, freedom, self-realization. Women and men were considered to be equal by nature and therefore both should work both inside and outside the home. But for many, it was a more practical arrangement for the woman to take on the responsibility for domestic work and children, since she had been educated for it, so it was easier for her. This was called "the roles", however, and seen as something that can and should be changed with time.

The mode of management of meaning was critical and expansive. Anything ascribed was anathema. There was a constant search for new goals, utopias (even though the word utopia was not much used and usually interpreted negatively as "that which cannot be", while what was desired were realizable goals).

The sixth category was the most radical when it comes to gender. They were feminists. Most of them were anti-Catholics, since they found the Catholic church anti-feminist. Some of them found other forms of spirituality, many had no religious belief. They saw sexuality as something very important that one must struggle for: such things as sexual freedom of choice, "options", both as to partners and activities, have been hidden and forbidden by evil forces, so now they must be not only legitimized but discovered, explored, made known as possibilities. The value stress was on freedom and on the individual. Experiments of all kinds were good, especially as to forms for living together and ways of sharing tasks. The cultural negotiations were merciless, and the goal was to take absolutely nothing for granted. Rationality was an important value, but new forms of mysticism were also accepted and cultivated. One should not only dream of utopias but actively try to create them. Practice was seldom as radical as theory, but one tried to close the gap as far as possible. The gap was called *incoherencia* (lack of coherence or logic) and there was much self-criticism and much discussion about how one can learn to live "coherently".

The mode of management of meaning was obviously critical and expansive.

Besides feminists, there were similar radicals in the peace movement and among ecologists. The three movements were often mentioned in parallel in Spanish conversations. They represented the same type of radicalism, even though individuals chose to stress different aspects of their critique. Many individuals belonged to two or all three, however, and others oscillated between them. Within all three movements, middle class persons dominated. But this radicalism did not dominate the middle class.

With this map of opinions in our hand, we can now move closer to real situations.

Chapter 3. Women's Days and Places

What were average days like in the life of the Madrilenian middle class women? It is hardly possible to generalize, except perhaps about the meal times.[33] I will present two reasonably representative days, chosen neither to be contrasts to each other or to be similar, just two normal possibilities.[34] Together they include most of the contexts of discourse, both written and oral, direct and mediated, with which Madrilenian middle class women normally came into contact.

Carlota and María had many things in common. They were both married housewives with no income of their own. They had both had the approximate number of children that was normal for their generation. They were both middle age and middle class. Their backgrounds were different: Carlota came from a well-to-do semi-urban family, María from a so called humble family that made it to a lower middle class status while she was growing up. But both these kinds of background were normal in the new Madrilenian middle class.

I will focus on factors shaping the lives of women like them: their husbands'good salaries offered them good living standards and little incentive to work outside the home unless for reasons other than money; they had usually not had any professional preparation, and even for those who did, like Carlota, or managed to obtain one later in life, as María was trying to do, the labor market was not receptive; the number and ages of their children shaped both their everyday tasks and their possibilities in life, since there were few acceptable childcare facilities and since their class norms made it unpalatable for them to leave the children in the care of maids; besides maids were getting scarce; the organization of time in everyday life made the coordination tasks of housewives formidable,[35] and so on.

These structural factors affected women and men differently and are thus gender relevant. But discourses must also be taken into account. Both as to their contents, i. e. discourses as cultural negotiation, and discourses as social contexts for action to which women and men had differential access (Cf chapters 4, 20, and Thurén 1998, 2002b).

If a person's habitus is composed of her experiences, and if receiving and formulating messages is an important part of one's experience, then the discourse contexts one enters determine partly who one is and what one can and wants to do. Furthermore, in a situation of change, cultural negotiation has important effects. Some people take a more active part than others in these negotiations, and some people do their negotiating in more influential contexts than others. This has consequences for power relationships. If there are differences between women and men as to what contexts of discourse they participate in, or come into more passive contact with, then this has consequences for the power aspect of the gender order.

After describing a day in the life of Carlota and María, I will analyze the contexts of discourse they contain and what consequences they have for the gender order.

A day in the life of Carlota

Carlota is up before eight to see to it that husband and children wake up, have breakfast and get on their way. Then she goes back to bed to read for a while. She often does, "it is a wonderful moment." But today she is tired and falls asleep again. She got to bed late last night.

Her husband Arturo was up at eight and off at eight thirty as usual in order to be at his office at nine. When he left, he ushered their two youngest children out the door. They are old enough now so that Carlota does not have to get dressed and take them down to the corner where their school bus stops. The oldest son, José Arturo, took his car around nine and drove to the university where he studies engineering, the same specialty as his father. About the same time, Catalina, the oldest daughter, left for her school, a religious secondary school.

Carlota often gets to bed late. For example, yesterday she and Arturo drove three hundred kilometers, to make a courtesy visit to an area coordinator of the company where Arturo works with sales organization, and then three hundred kilometers back again. The salesman's parents had just died in a car accident, and Arturo felt it his duty to make this visit. "You can't just send a card when something like that happens to a subordinate.' And his wife had to go, too, for the visit to appear personal. They do not usually have personal relations with this salesman, but they have visited once in a while, with the children, on their way to their summer residence on the coast.

Carlota has a shower and a cup of coffee with milk, then she gets dressed to go to the city. She walks to a metro station and takes the train downtown. She has never learnt how to drive. She is only forty-two years old, but she says that when she was young, women were not expected to drive, and later she has not felt like learning.

She has to buy summer clothes for the two youngest, and it is too complicated to take them along; to do that it would have to be a Saturday, when the stores are crowded, because Arturo would have to drive them all, and it is so hard to find parking space, and the kids get impatient, and Arturo prefers to do other things on his free days. She buys a few things and takes them home, and if they do not fit, she goes back and changes them the next day. She also looks for clothes for herself but does not feel inspired and decides to come back another day with some woman friend. Shopping is more fun in company. In passing she buys two shirts for Arturo, too, even though he says he prefers to do his own shopping, "but in the end he never does, so I have to do it."

Carlota used to go downtown more often than she does now. "I get more and more lazy about it." Since she no longer has a full time maid, and there are six members in her family, most of her days are filled with housework.

47

Just before lunch she drops in at María José's small business. María José used to be Carlota's next door neighbor and best friend. When she separated from her husband, she had to move, but they are still close friends. Carlota even worked for a while in María José's office. That was when her youngest child started school, a couple of years ago.

I asked if she was bored and wanted to "realize herself" as the phrase goes. It is a very common expression, especially among educated women, and Carlota does have a semi-academic professional preparation. But no, that is not Carlota's type of discourse. "I hate that word, «realize». I started to work for no special reason. Things have usually come easily for me in life, not traumatically, so it was just something that came naturally, I did not need it, I did not look for it, and it was absolutely not in order to realize myself. I think it is ridiculous that they say that only about work and only about women. You realize yourself, whether you are a man or a woman, if you carry out your projects according to your wishes. So I suppose a man with poetic tastes who has to work in the store of his father-in-law, for example, would feel just as little realized as a woman who has studied and wishes to work in public relations, for example, and has to stay at home."

But Carlota did not find work in her own profession, just office work. And she worked for less than a year. Working only five hours a day, it took over seven hours of her time, with the transportation. The children had lunch in school, and she was back before they got home in the afternoon, but she was tired then, and still had to do the shopping and cooking and planning, so she felt she had no time for them, for all those little extras she has always loved: arranging birthday parties for them, driving them to ballet and judo and swimming, reading to them, playing with them... There was no time to shop for clothes at all, and hardly time to take them to the doctor and to the dentist. Carlota felt like a bad mother. It worked out more or less as long as Tina, the maid, worked full time, but when she got married and wanted to come in only a few hours a day, Carlota felt she could not cope. Nor could she find a new maid. Tina had been with her for years, she knew what had to be done and how. Carlota did not feel she could trust a new employee with everything and anything for seven hours a day. Arturo also felt Carlota had too little time for him. So she quit, and she is happy with her decision. Now she has time to do fun things, like ceramics and visits to museums with a group of women friends, play tennis to keep in shape, and pamper her family, create a good home atmosphere. Working was just not worth the high price, and her income was of course negligible compared to Arturo's.

Another reason she quit just when she did was that her father was sick, and her mother was too old to nurse him alone, so Carlota had to spend a week or a month now and then with her parents, who live in another part of the country.

So today Carlota goes to see María José, and they go to a restaurant to have lunch together. Not a leisurely lunch, as they would have liked, because María José has to be back at her office at four o'clock. They talk about María José's business mostly: her economic worries, the substantial success of her business idea, and the details of competition and taxes that make it almost impossible for her to make a profit. They also talk about their children and how they ought to get together soon, all of them, so that the children can meet again; they used to be friends when they lived in the same building, but now they never see each other. María José's two children are the same age as Carlota's two oldest. Carlota decides to talk to Arturo about inviting María José and her family for a Sunday dinner soon.

María José returns to her office and Carlota rushes to the metro. She gets home just in time to meet the two youngest at the school bus, then she gives them their afternoon snack and changes into jeans and a shirt. To go downtown she had dressed up a bit, but she does not like to walk around her neighborhood in a fur coat and pearls, the way most of her neighbors do.

Catalina comes home and leaves again for her afternoon job at a pizza place. She is working to save money to be able to go to the United States this summer – she has friends there, because she spent last year studying there. Her parents paid for that, but they have told her that if she wants to go back, she has to pay for it herself. Actually Catalina even has a boyfriend in the United States whom she wants to visit, and her parents know about that and accept it, but they hope she will not marry him. They want her closer to home. Catalina laughs about their worries and says she does not plan to get married for many years.

José Arturo comes home and says he would like to play a game of tennis, so Carlota says she would too, and they go together to the club. After the game, they do not stay to chat. Carlota and Arturo have friends at the club, but they are not the kind to go there mainly to sit with friends; they mostly just use the sports facilities.

Back home, Carlota busies herself with the two youngest ones. She helps them with their homework and also to make a cardboard cut-out castle, and somehow she manages to make the homework feel like play, too. Then she sees to it that they have their bath and makes dinner for them. The two oldest decide to have a bite, too, before they go out with their friends for a beer or two, as they do practically every day. Carlota too eats a little, she can't help herself, she gets hungry when she sees the kids eat, it is the same thing every day, even though she really wants to wait for Arturo. He usually does not get home until after ten. When he does, she serves him dinner and tries to eat herself, too, again. They hardly ever watch television, says Carlota, "and never together, we don't like the same programs at all."

A day in the life of María

María gets up very early, between six and seven, most mornings. She does not usually stay up very late, but in Madrid that means around midnight, anyway, so she seldom gets as much as seven hours of sleep. She thinks that is a lot, however, and attributes her energy to the fact that she sleeps well. She likes to get up early in the morning, because that is when she feels most awake, and when she can study without being interrupted.

She has only a glass of juice and studies for an hour or two before she wakes up her youngest children and her husband and fixes breakfast for everyone.

She has five children but only the two youngest are still living at home. Her oldest moved out recently, since he found a job and a girl-friend. He lives in an apartment he shares with two other young men in downtown Madrid. He has gone to a trade school and now has a low level administrative job. María is worried about his future and wonders if her husband's high expectations for his oldest son has somehow caused his aversion against studying. But he has what most young Madrilenians can only dream of: a job, a girl-friend and a place of his own to live. And all of this even though he is only twenty-two years old.

Next come a girl of twenty-one and a boy of twenty. Both of them have clear intellectual ambitions and both of them have been studying abroad for a couple of years. María misses them but is proud of them and very much convinced that parents have to make sacrifices (emotional sacrifice, and also economic sacrifice, because they are paying for tuition and living expenses for both of them) in order to assure a future for their children. She is also convinced they deserve not just a livable wage in the future but a chance to develop their talents, which is very difficult in Spain, where, according to her view, state universities offer little knowledge and even smaller chances to find a good job, and where private universities mix better quality teaching with reactionary ideology.

This is the great dilemma she herself has faced now that the years of heavy family obligations are over. The two youngest boys are only twelve and thirteen and still take a lot of her time, especially since her maternal ambitions are high and cast in an exacting modern-psychological shape, but she also says that the fourth and the fifth are easier, she has practiced a lot on the first three, and she has an *asistenta*[36] for six hours a week.

Enrique, her husband, has mellowed with time in his resistance to help with household chores. He still knows nothing about cooking or washing, but he enjoys helping her to fix breakfast, he always plays an excellent host when they have guests, serving the wine, making drinks, making coffee, even emptying ashtrays. He takes the garbage out every day. He also takes a more practical interest in the children than he used to with the older ones, such as sometimes driving them to language classes and soccer practice.

Their family life is gravitating towards something like an American style,[37] in fact: they live in a house with a yard, thirty kilometers from Madrid, and Enrique has taken on some chores that are considered masculine in American suburban living, like watering the lawn, picking up guests at the train station and driving wife and children to a shopping center on Saturdays, where they shop for everything they need for the week, food and clothes as well as objects for the house. María does the planning for all the shopping, but Enrique takes an interest in what is chosen and he helps to carry everything from the car into the house when they get back. That is, unless he has to spend Saturday at the office, which happens frequently since he has a high level executive job.

So María feels she can finally think of her own future. Not that she has ever been the "typical housewife" (as she expresses it, ironically) who lives only for her family. She was elected president of a parent-teacher-association when her three oldest were not yet teenagers, later she participated in pacifist and feminist groups as well as some church work and in recent years she has been very active in a human rights organization. But all along she has had a feeling that everything she did was only makeshift or make-believe. A "real life", to her, implies working for an income. She had only primary schooling, but before the two youngest were born she prepared for and took the university entrance examination for people over twenty-five. She began studying history, but had to interrupt her studies after only one year, because she became pregnant with her fourth child and when she got pregnant for the fifth time immediately after the fourth one, she gave up. Five years later, just when the two youngest had started school, and María had begun to make new plans for herself, Enrique got a chance to work abroad for two years. It entailed a promotion and a challenge for him, so of course they went, and María does not regret it, for it was good for the children, too, and if she had refused to go it would have spoiled their marriage. But for her it meant four more years (the stay was prolonged) of postponing her own "real life" and four years of isolation from her friends and associational work.

But her moment has finally arrived. She is now forty-eight and thinks it is too late to study for the normal five years for a university degree, so she has decided to become a social worker, which takes only three years. The problem was what university to choose. She could not risk a state university, she thought; she wanted to be sure of being able to get a job, and employers prefer graduates of private universities when they can choose. Private universities are thought to have better teachers and more advanced courses, and the high dropout rates are construed as effective selection of the best. That did not worry María, she trusts her intelligence and her self-discipline. Neither was the cost of tuition any problem. Still, she doubted. In Spain, private universities are Catholic universities. María does not consider herself a Catholic. She has been, but she takes religion very seriously and therefore has had a lot of quarrels with priests and parish organizations and also personal crises of conscience. Later, through her associational work, she has come to know many non-Catholics and turned critical of the Church as an institution. As a feminist she feels alienated and hurt by the Christian conception of women. Her personal experience has been that Catholic teachings on sexuality can be pernicious to marital happiness. So, all in all, she did not feel she would agree with the ideology of a private university. Still, she thought that the ideology could not really interfere too much with the contents of the studies, which she imagined as a mostly technical preparation, and she thought that after all she still considers herself a Christian. So when she gained admittance to a high status Catholic university, she chose to go there.

Now, towards the end of the first course, she deeply regrets her choice. Hardly a day has passed when she has not had a quarrel with someone, teachers or fellow students. She is constantly upset over what she sees as reactionary nonsense and seriously worried about the future of Spain seeing that this nonsense, and not what she sees as necessary knowledge, is what is taught at the universities whose graduates will occupy the positions of influence in society. She is also worried about her own future. She has had to compromise on important issues; for example she had to fake an argument against abortion in order to pass one examination. She does not know whether she will be able to, or want to, keep up such a game of deceit for two more years, and if she does not, she knows she will not graduate. "My God, if they knew that I have been in demonstrations *for* abortion!"[38]

After breakfast Enrique drives to his office downtown. María studies for another hour or so, and then does housework or receives the asistenta and gives her the directions for the day. Then she takes her car to a nearby village to shop for fresh fruits and vegetables. She also attends to other family matters, like writing letters to the two children abroad, calling the psychotherapist who treats the youngest boy for his obesity and calls her sister and mother and mother-in-law to make sure they are fine and ask if they need any help.

Coming back from shopping this day, she runs into two women neighbors who are also friends and they want her to come with them to play cards at the area club, but María explains, as she has to do almost every day, that she must study. They say they understand. But María imagines that they think her strange and anti-sociable.

She worries about that while she prepares lunch and dinner. Dinner has to be made now, there is no time later. The boys come home for lunch, Enrique does not. So María and the boys have lunch together, and then María drives to her university, some thirty kilometers, where the afternoon classes (there are morning and afternoon groups) start at four.

Between four and eight, she suffers in anguish the strange mixture of ideological suffocation and intellectual stimulation that the classes are to her. At eight thirty or a quarter to nine, depending on traffic, she is back home, and soon afterwards Enrique arrives, too. The boys have come home from school before six, but they manage on their own, they are used to it and they have many friends in the neighborhood, friends whose parents are also friends of María and Enrique, so María feels they are safe. "But I would never have dreamed of leaving the first three alone like that every day, at such an age!" María changes into a home dress and sees to it that the boys have their bath, and then heats the food. By ten they sit down to dinner. The boys watch some television, María and Enrique do too, sometimes, usually not.

This has been a normal calm day. María has given up most of her associational work, but she still has an occasional meeting after classes, and then does not get home until eleven or later. Enrique may have a business dinner. They have to plan carefully so that at least one of them has dinner with the boys. Before they moved to this house, they could leave the boys with María's sister or mother, so that she could go with Enrique to business dinners or they could go to a theater or a movie once in a while. That is no longer possible. Only about once a month do they go out together, usually to have dinner with friends.[39]

Moving through worlds of words

Let us now look closer at the types of messages that surrounded the two women. There were a number of discourses (discourses in the sense of sets of messages defined by both medium and contents) that they encountered each day, whether they wanted to or not and others that they sought out because they were interested in them.

María might buy a newspaper, but she seldom had time to read it. Enrique would almost always buy one, and whenever he went to the office by train, he would read it during the ride.[40] The paper he preferred was El País, but at the office he sometimes looked through a colleague's copy of the conservative ABC.[41] In the evening he would comment major general news and issues of human rights with María. He himself paid more attention to business news, but in recent years he had made a real effort to understand and keep up on the matters that interested María.

There were no billboards in the immediate vicinity of their housing area, but there were in the village, where María did her shopping, and of course on the way to the university, so she could not avoid the messages of publicity. (More about the contents of them below, on Carlota.)

In the village she would encounter a very different world from her own present one – the grocer and the fruit and vegetable vendor, the parents of the classmates of her boys (who went to the village state school), the jobless young hanging out at the street corners and the pensioners at the bar. It was a world of manual work, little or no reading, some illiteracy even, and also a world of suspicion against the rich Madrilenians who had bought houses nearby and changed village life. But María liked the village. She found the traditional rustic architecture beautiful, and she said she might well someday become active in the village neighborhood association in order to save the village center from being torn down. She got along very well with the people in the shops, and she believed this was because she herself grew up in a village, even though a much bigger village in another part of the country. She found her asistenta through the grocer and she enjoyed gossiping with her about village events. The village discourses included references to discourses beyond the village, but indirectly so, via television, the only mass medium of general reference in village life. Village communication referred to the world beyond the village, and set village events against the background of that world, but it was almost wholly face-to-face (little use of telephone, practically none of written messages) and it concerned mostly matters of daily village life.

María thought it was a good thing for the village that there were now so many urban middle class persons present there. The new residents, she said, "are usually very interesting persons, with medium or high intellectual levels and with social interests, people who try to do things."

The only problem was the parent-teacher association at the school. So many "Madrilenian" children now went to the village school, that the villagers felt it had been taken over. There were many confrontations over educational methods. The "Madrilenians" believed in high ambitions and subtle manipulation, while the villagers believed in strict discipline, including thrashings, and a strict separation of chores and symbols according to gender. The teachers tended to agree more with the Madrilenians, being usually city persons themselves, but there were other conflicts on that front, since, unlike María and Enrique, most of the "Madrilenians" were Catholic and politically conservative, which young teachers tended not to be. There were no good private schools nearby, but even so, more and more "Madrilenians" transferred their children to private schools, because they found the state school teachers too "radical" and the village children too "lazy" to suit their own children's needs.

I have already described María's interpretation of the discourse at her university. It was in total confrontation with the discourse she encountered – and approved of – in her associational work. If there were "two Spains",[42] María lived in both of them. I would rather say there were more than two. The village religiosity was hardly that of the Catholic university, and the political conservativeness of her neighbors was different from that of her parents. In both cases, class entered as one important differentiating factor, along with age and rural/urban habitat. Talking about one of her associations, María said: "This is really atypical, I don't think you can imagine the type of discourse these women have. All of them consider themselves feminists and consider this the central point in how they construe themselves as persons. I cannot go along with all their arguments, they do not have families like I do. Some of them have a child, and that makes a difference for them."

During or after dinner, if they watched television, María and Enrique would probably connect the midnight news, where the anchor person might be a man or a woman, in either case good-looking although the men were older, and the contents of the news were similar to the newspaper front page or the news magazine covers (cf below on Carlota). They might also have watched some debating program. But if they were tired, they might prefer an entertainment program. They avoided the otherwise popular contest programs, like "All in the Family" where whole families of varying sizes competed with each other. They also avoided the private Channel Five, where practically all the entertainment programs featured hordes of pretty girls in bathing suits. They also found that the channel conveyed a reactionary message in sly ways. There were other, better, private channels and two state channels. If María and Enrique felt like staying up a bit longer they would almost certainly watch a movie. There were plenty to choose from each night; most of them were either Spanish or American, the latter dubbed in Spanish. (When they were younger they used to go to filmclubs, since that was where one could catch glimpses of issues that were otherwise censored in Spanish media during Franco times.)

If Enrique and María watched television, this is the fare they got. But they usually did not.

Instead they read books and professional magazines. And that was the most important kind of text in their lives, especially for María. And through these texts they entered into dialogue with a world of discourse that was different in every way from all the others. It was written. It was intellectually exacting. It was usually neither Catholic nor outrightly oppositional. It had very little to do with village life or with the life in central Madrid that both Enrique and María used to live and their parents still lived. It was a discourse with rather abstract middle class references. Some of María's textbooks and much of Enrique's professional, technical reading, had been translated from English. Together, these texts afforded them access to "intellectual" discourse, and since intellectuals define themselves in relation to texts, these reading habits gave María and Enrique the right to label themselves "intellectuals", they felt.

Through neighbors and a group of old friends, they kept in touch with "progressive" Catholic circles, even though they no longer attended mass. They kept up to date on what issues were under debate in such circles, but they did not find it terribly important to have an opinion on them. For example, they could not be bothered with subtle ways of legitimating an anti-abortionist stand so that it would not sound anti-feminist, since they firmly believed a woman should make her own choice. Nor did they worry about how to make sexual abstinence palatable to today's youngsters, since they thought the important thing was that their children learnt to enjoy their bodies and were careful to use contraceptives. They did not only say such things, they practiced them, for example receiving their two "foreign" children along with their respective girlfriend and boyfriend, foreigners both, during the summer holidays, letting the couples sleep where they wished. (But María said this fact of life had been harder on Enrique than on her, and that Enrique did not want the neighbors to know about the sleeping arrangements. "But I am sure they can guess.")

They sometimes hosted business dinners, but in her letter María commented that they had tried to eliminate representation from their life as much as possible. "That has been so for a long time. I have to play a role I don't like to play, and Enrique, too, and neither one of us likes to waste our time with stupidities." This isolated Enrique to some degree and María almost totally from the type of discourse I would label "conservative leisure". It was a discourse that was very cautious in style, that pretended to be politically neutral, but that took quite a lot for granted in order to avoid debate. It was most important in shaping "moral" and political opinions for the whole of the middle class. Most of its members, whether they agreed or not, found themselves immersed in it frequently, at their clubs and in friendship groups. These places were usually not as cautious in their modes of management of meaning as Club Aguafría, but neither were they freely expansive.[43] The Book Club and the work-out class are representative examples, and the friendship group Nosotros is representative for the type of context that consciously tried to make itself more expansive than its members might be on their own.[44] Women like Carlota got a lot of the conservative leisure discourse, furthermore, through women friends, playing cards, sitting with their children in play grounds, or in the "cultural" contexts that had become very popular with middle class housewives, such as gardening courses or visits to museums. María participated in no such activities. Enrique's glimpses of the conservative leisure discourse came from business lunches and professional meetings and the occasional dinner with colleagues he could not avoid. Both María and Enrique also heard some of it from their neighbors, but they did not socialize very much with them. This created a dilemma for María, as we saw, since she met her neighbors in one context or another almost daily, whereas Enrique did not see much of them except on weekends.

What were the texts Carlota met during her day? And what image did they give of gender?

She tried to read a little every morning, novels mostly, sometimes books on current social issues and perhaps something on children's education that the teachers had recommended at the parent-teacher association meetings, which Carlota always tried to attend. She might have bought a newspaper and flipped it through while she waited for María José at her office. In the metro she would not have been able to escape the advertisements, and along the road she walked between the metro station and her neighborhood likewise, and of course there were huge billboards and signs of all kinds all over downtown Madrid.

In all media, the advertisements reflected what Carlota called traditional roles. Stout women in aprons recommended brands of soap or canned soup, while slender women in evening dress were associated with cosmetics and elegant stores. Slender but curvy women in bathing suits or wispy déshabillés illustrated ads for brandy and sportscars, i.e. "masculine" products. Beautiful maternal women of indefinite age hugged their beautiful and charmingly rebellious children (usually blond) who had wisely chosen – or been wisely manipulated by their mother to choose – the right brand of chocolate snack or breakfast cereal. Authoritative men in white coats explained to grateful mothers the technicalities of the right brand of toothpaste and the correct way to get spots of grass and juice out of children's clothing. Magic men swirled in through the window to teach housewives how to clean a kitchen in no time, when the husband had called to announce his immediate arrival with an important guest. In other words, the ads were clearly divided into women's and men's ads, according to product. The ads directed to men were about luxury (brandy, perfume for both men and women, traveling) and major investments (cars, housing, stocks and bonds). The ads directed to women were mostly about housekeeping and childcare. The men in women's ads appeared knowledgeable and helpful but never, never sexy, while the women in men's ads were tremendously seductive and had nothing to say about the product itself.

Carlota and Arturo had no special preference as to which newspaper to buy, "any one of the major ones." If Carlota bought El País, she would have seen two major headlines and one major photo on the first page. The photo would probably be either of men in suits (political or economic decision-making) or violence (accident or war). The headlines would in all probability have had some names of important agents in them and these agents would be men in at least 91 % of the cases.[45] The gossip column, the interview and the personal column on the last page (which a lot of people read first) would be by and about both women and men, although not in equal proportions. Most politicians were men, while popular entertainers were about equally often of either sex. The famous columnists of El País were all men except two.

If Carlota stopped by the newsstand to look at the magazines, she would have seen a most colorful collection of covers.[46] Computers, sports equipment and beautiful landscapes abounded on the many specialty magazines. Famous actresses, princesses and singers dominated the covers of "traditional" women's magazines (known as "the press of the heart"), usually as close-up portraits. Some of the new women's magazines might feature a well-dressed upper class Spanish woman (the "elegant" women's magazines) or an anonymous youngish woman with a professional-cum-daring look (e.g. Cosmopolitan, cf chapter 18, note 218). The weekly newsmagazines would have had either a straight from front portrait of some famous male politician – e.g. a Spanish banker, an Italian party leader or the president of France or the United States – or a picture of some situation involving a group of men in business suits – e.g. union leaders around a negotiating table or the heads of state of the Common Market countries posing in one of their regular meetings. Exceptionally there might be a picture of a building, such as the Supreme Court, or of a disaster site. One of the newsmagazines, Interviú, which had a light touch but considered itself serious and even critical-minded, always had a photograph of a lightly clad anonymous woman on its cover; this had become the signum of the magazine.[47]

In the stores where she shopped for children's clothes, Carlota will have met only women: mothers shopping and women attendants. At most there may have been a male head of a department. Any signs giving messages to customers would have addressed the customers as mothers. These texts would not usually consider the existence of aunts, grandmothers, nurses, etc., much less any male relationships with children. If she went to one of the big department stores (which she probably did, because Carlota was a practical woman, and shopping there took less time), the male employees would have been in business suits and the women employees in the department store uniform. These uniforms changed every so often, to follow the seasons and the fashion, but they always involved skirts or dresses, never slacks, and they were never evidently fashionable but rather meant to be discrete.

If she took a taxi at some point, the driver would have been a man, and in all probability he would have been listening to sports news on the car radio; that is unless he tried to flirt with her, but that did not happen as often as it used to, even though Carlota looked much younger than her years. Taxi drivers were men and taxi-driving a male occupation, since it was construed as involving both technical knowledge and danger.[48] The sports programs on the radio constituted the purest kind of "male" discourse that could be found in Spanish mass media. They were about sports, which was mainly a male domain to begin with, they were by men, since sports journalists were almost always men, and they were aggressively "male" (and also "working class") in their style, since they were mainly about leadership, physical strength and intricate non-sport conflicts between clubs and stars.

The waiters in the restaurant will have been perfectly courteous and correct, treating women customers in exactly the same way as men customers. Only waiters in cheap places tended to banter seductively with unescorted female customers. One could say that one tacit but well-known measure of the social status of a bar or restaurant was the degree to which women could enter it in the assurance of having a right to be there. The gender message was: women are welcome where men (waiters, owners, other customers) so decide. The class message was: middle and higher class women have a freedom of movement that lower class women cannot expect.

The book on children's education will have addressed Carlota as mother, taking for granted that it is mothers who read such books. But at the same time it will in all probability have stressed strongly that it is "no longer" "necessary" to exempt boys from household duties and it might well have a special chapter on how to help girls escape from "too rigid sex roles" and learn to believe that they too have a right to "realize themselves" in the form of a career of some kind.

Carlota and Arturo did not watch television together, but separately and sometimes with the children they did. They hardly ever went to the theater; they went somewhat more, but not much, to movies or concerts. Arturo got home too late, they lived too far out, it was too hard to find parking space...

Discourse as space

Carlota and María thus encountered and more or less participated in many kinds of discourses during a normal day in life. They received passively, but rather critically, the discourses of advertising. They received passively, and more or less distractedly, but sometimes critically, the various categories of messages from television and radio. They read newspapers and magazines, if at all, in a rather superficial way, glancing through them. But they did obtain an idea of the public discourses of the media. During a normal day, they usually had a number of fleeting encounters with women in social situations similar to their own, and in these meetings they usually entered a discourse of family practicalities: cooking, shopping, health, schooling, planning for old age, the problems of coordinating the complicated schedules of big families leading city lives.

They did not pay much attention to the "male" discourse of sports, that took up so much room in media and in conversations among men in Spain,[42] except that Carlota liked to have some idea of the soccer news, mainly because both her husband and oldest son were very interested and sometimes played the soccer pools.

We have already seen that the two women stood in a very different relationship to the ubiquitous discourse of conservative leisure, and that this discourse had a wider socio-spatial distribution than one would conclude from the distribution of cautious and expansive modes of management of meaning. Most expansivists adapted to this rather cautious discourse whenever they were not sure that everyone present would accept the expansive mode. In that sense, the cautious mode was still hegemonic, even though the expansive one had come to dominate quantitatively and in the media.

María's encountered discourses were more varied than Carlota's, and she entered most of them actively. To the villagers she was an outsider, but she was under the impression that she was well accepted and that she knew how to interact with them according to their habits and norms. She gossiped with her asistenta about village matters, like weddings, baptisms, local festivities, unemployment, school dropouts... To some degree she did know about these things and was therefore able to participate in the village everyday life discourse. As an active member of the parent-teacher-association she deepened her understanding of village attitudes. There, she also got a rather good view of the clash between two very different social worlds, the village and the "Madrilenians" living in her urbanization, a view not all her neighbors had or cared to obtain access to.

The university was a place for a very special type of discourse, or rather two types. For one thing it afforded María access to academic debates, and in these she took the kind of active part that was possible for a student, discussing orally and writing papers, but of course she had no power to influence the major outlines of that discourse. Since her university was a Catholic one, its academic discourse was shot through with a religious or moral discourse. The syllabus was not only about what "is" but about what "ought to be". This was a discourse María suffered rather than received, and she suffered it actively, putting up strong resistance.

To the extent that she still had time for work in pacifist, feminist or human rights organizations, she had access to and participated very actively in another kind of moral discourse, another kind of "ought to" with the explicit purpose of trying to change things. It was a discourse of politics in that it defined itself as political, but it was not a discourse of power in the sense of shaping decisions that would directly influence major events or the course of social life for many individuals. Rather, the decisions the participants in her associations elaborated together, through their discourse, were decisions about how to influence other discourses, i.e. through sending a letter to the editor of a newspaper, sending a telegram to a court of justice, publishing a leaflet, arranging a demonstration, and so on.

Carlota had no access to and no interest in such discourses of influence. She was interested in academic discourses in that she remembered her own student years with pleasure and tried to keep up a bit in her field. She also received reports of university life through José Arturo, but this was sporadic and partial, since he felt that his mother knew nothing about engineering and therefore could not be interested in what happened in his classes or in what he talked about with his co-students. Carlota's female friends were in similar situations, so if any of the academic discourse entered their conversations, it would be in small pieces, sporadically and without causing any strong feelings, and these pieces carried little authority, because they were, and were seen to be, only tenuously connected to their authoritative sources.

The same was true of another kind of discourse, or rather a special category of discourses, that housewives did not usually enter at all. I refer to discourses about decisions that directly influence events that in their turn will directly or indirectly influence the personal lives of large number of persons. And it was the type of discourse that was the everyday professional role of their husbands to take active part in: the discourses of decision-making in business management, administration and government, major technological decisions, and so on.

Enrique spent his day in meetings, telephone conversations and reading and writing texts that shaped decisions about the production of expensive industrial equipment. He did not himself influence any individual's day to day life, but the way he participated in this discourse influenced to some degree decisions about investments and types of production and thus, in a further step, it influenced the material space in which people would work, what that work would concretely consist of and how much they would get paid for it, and in an even further step it had some effect on exchange rates, employment rates in the country, and so on. Arturo similarly spent his days in meetings, telephone conversations and reading and writing texts that had similar effects, even though his decisions were about distribution, not production, and his position was situated somewhat lower in the chain of command. But the two chains of command were of similar type in companies of similar type, big state-wide companies with transnational ownership.

I had little direct access to this type of discourses. Their existence, however, was an obvious fact and much of what they were about was publicly known.[50] What is interesting here is their social shape. In what situations and in what relations was this type of discourse activated and what happened then?

It seemed that the men kept this discourse largely confined, both in time and space, to their work. I heard very little "shop talk" during the fieldwork. One reason for that may well have been that the men did not talk shop when women were present. They might take for granted that their wives were not interested and had nothing to contribute to such conversations. And the women, as a matter of fact, did not try to pry open that discourse;

they did not usually read the business news in the press, for instance. Those who were interested might comment with their husbands in private, but it would have been a breach of norms if they had commented on their husband's professional activities with their women friends and even worse in mixed company.[51]

So gender influences the distribution of shop talk.

But an additional reason for its absence from leisure contexts might be found in the view my informants had of work in general, and of the barrier between work and leisure in particular. The word "work" (*trabajo*) had a very negative sound. They might have actually loved their professions, especially its creative aspects, gotten much of their self-confidence and pride from them, and even enjoyed the material comfort of the office and the more or less agreeable company of colleagues; but they did not like the idea of work. In general, in Spanish, the word by itself conjures up images of being forced, of having to do disagreeable things, of becoming tired, of being ordered around, of not being autonomous but included in a hierarchy. Leisure is the space for individuality, idiosyncrasy, autonomy and fun! Fun especially comes in the shape of being with freely chosen others. This was what people found at the club, for example. To speak of one's work there was therefore not appropriate. The demarcation between work and leisure should be kept clear. It was symbolized for instance in that men dressed differently at the club than they did at work. Several men at Club Aguafría insisted to me that it was very important for them not to talk about work at the club. I interpret this as an overdetermined fact, having to do both with the wish to maintain a clear barrier between work and leisure and the awareness of situations of competitiveness and hierarchy that could arise at the club, in groups of friends, if the discourse of important decisions were to enter there, since the club members had different interests and varying degrees of power and influence.

For whatever reasons, there was little shop talk. And the effect of this on gender was that the gender division of labor was symbolically underlined and materially reinforced – women had little access to discourses of decision-making. Carlota participated not at all in that sphere and had little knowledge of it except for what Arturo might choose to tell her about it while they had dinner on weekdays, and she would probably be interested only if the information offered had something to do with Arturo personally.[52] Enrique told María more about his working life, since she was more interested. She said they talked a lot about the general economic situation of the country and also of the company where Enrique worked and the decisions he had to make. But they had little time in their everyday life even to talk of more immediate matters, the many facets of family life and the many daily decisions to be made about that. One can say then that María had some indirect knowledge of but no direct participation in this type of discourse, and that this was more than what most women had.[53]

María had partial access to discourses about power, as I have shown: the moral discourse of a Catholic university, the university discourses in general and the political

61

discourse of social movements. This afforded her a better grasp than Carlota had over what was going on in Spanish society outside her own family, even though the two women received about the same amount of information from mass media. But the discourses about power María had active access to were not discourses of daily influential decision-making.

Carlota actually did have some access to that, through her friendship with María José, and she participated directly in it when she worked in María José's office. Because of this, Carlota had strong opinions on such matters as taxation of small businesses and legislation on employment. She had also had some personal experience of what it is like to sit in an office and solve problems via letters and telephone calls. She listened with interest to María José's tales of sales contracts and public relations. But María José's business was very small (only one employee besides herself) and Carlota herself had no impression of having been connected to the economic processes in the city, much less to important decision-making.

Both Carlota and María lamented that they had too little time to read novels and they hardly ever went to theaters, concerts or cinemas. In other words, they had little contact with aesthetic-artistic symbolic expressions (except through television). They regretted this and blamed it on lack of time and on living too far from downtown. That is, they recognized the existence of this discourse and the desirability of participating in it.

All the discourses mentioned here were important for the middle class as a whole, but they were differentially distributed according to a number of factors. Gender was one factor among others but probably the most decisive one, largely due to its importance for the social division of labor. However, that other basic principle of social organization, age, also influenced the map of discourses. I cannot go into that in detail here, but the fact must be mentioned. María and Carlota were of similar age and similarly situated in relationship to discourses of other age groups. They had some, but limited, access to the discourses of youth through their children, and María also through classmates and young activists in her associations. They had some access to the discourse of an older generation through their parents. But they considered both of these worlds of opinions and interests too different from their own to take much interest in them. The barriers of age were at least as effective as those of gender and culturally much more licit. Gender sorted more subtly, and any pointing out of its effects was bound to encounter emic resistance.[54]

In middle class Madrid, then, gender was one of the factors, a main one, that organized the social map of discourses, and the distribution of discourses influenced the gender order. There will be many examples of this throughout the book, and the significance of it will be analyzed in the final chapters. But it should be apparent already at this point that there was asymmetry in the gender order. Women and men did different things, and therefore saw and heard different things, and thus accumulated different habituses and different resources. Nobody denied this. But it was a fact that was differently interpreted. For some, the differences were only in kind, so that the gender order seemed complementary and balanced as to power. For others, the differences were of such a degree and of such types that the gender order must be considered hierarchical.

Chapter 4. Modes of management of meaning[55]

The experience of cultural complexification

The situation in Spain after the changes of the 1970s and 1980s can be summed up as follows: the country had changed from many small-scale societies, very different among themselves but each one well entrenched, to one big and perhaps not well coordinated, society. There had been great complexification and that process continued to fuel itself. It is the effect of this on the gender order that is the topic of this study, or to be exact, how the effects were handled culturally. To this end, we must arm ourselves with some concepts.

People react differently to change and complexification. This is not surprising. If I myself, whoever I am, do not have ready-made answers, but have to improvise, I can expect that others have to do likewise and that we come up with non-identical answers. The next step is then to compare notes with each other. Is my interpretation truer, more practical, morally better, more successful or more satisfying than yours? What can you tell me to help me understand what is happening to me? Is the same thing happening to you? What shall we think of it? How shall we sort and label it? How do I know whether I can trust your interpretations?

This is the stuff of cultural negotiation everywhere, but it takes on a sense of acute importance when change accelerates, and it takes on a massive weight when change is so massive that very few persons can isolate themselves in some more or less stable corner of society. If change is not only wide and deep but also fast, the interpretations and negotiations around it cannot be left to experts. There is no time for intellectuals to study and publish, nor for the mediators, such as school teachers and priests and journalists, to read and assimilate and offer confident interpretations to the laymen. While the experts do their job, each person has to work out something of her own. Therefore, later, when the experts begin to catch up, there is more work for them – more stories to be collected and greater variations in ideas to be interpreted and coordinated. So things continue to be lively, for good and for bad, for quite some time.

A strong sense of doxa (Bourdieu) or common sense (Geertz, Hannerz)[56] used to be common in Spain. Work was what it "always" had been, with similar social organization and similar tools for generations; and the neighbors were known as whole persons, including family histories; in many parts of Spain they were in fact known by family nicknames that had also been inherited for generations. Excepting the cities, where only a small portion of the population lived, and excepting the upper classes, an even smaller number, Spain was a country of doxic worlds where things were taken for granted to a great degree.[57] Certainly there had been historical upheavals, such as the many civil wars during the last two centuries, and cultural upheavals, such as rural rebellions[58] or waves of early industrialization and urbanization and accompanying political and religious debates.[59] These events had naturally left traces. But since the economic level continued to be very low for a majority, since so many made their living from an agriculture close to subsistence in level and organization, since tools and social organization of work changed little, since formal schooling was very limited, and since recent generations lived in a dictatorship interested in erasing all traces of ideas that did not coincide with its own, the awareness of social and cultural variation was low. What there was, was mostly in the shape of vague stories of some granduncle or former neighbor who had done strange things and very often had to suffer for it. These vague memories were furthermore shot through with conflicting interpretations and a sense of danger and threat.[60]

The idea of permanent differences between villages found expression in numerous rituals to mark village borders (see e.g. Lisón 1977, Prat et al 1991, Sánchez Pérez 1990).

Exactly how doxic the villages were is not important here; what is relevant is that they were very much more doxic than the urban contexts, and that both villages and cities have since become less doxic. During the Franco regime, expansions of meaning were kept at bay on purpose for forty years; the social interests that would defend status quo had a rather firm grasp over most of the machineries of meaning (media etc.) beyond immediate life worlds. Cultural stability was seen as a means (among others) of maintaining political calm and social stability. The dominant mode of management of meaning was therefore hostile to debate as such, not just to certain opinions.

From this contradictory but ever so quite doxic world, Spaniards moved quickly into a complex society with a correspondingly complex cultural map in a matter of a decade or two. The cities started growing in the late 1950s; the 1960s saw deep economic transformations that brought with them thorough changes in social structure, above all urbanization and a powerful and growing middle class of a new type; the 1970s was the decade of political debates and the dismantling of the dictatorship; and the 1980s saw the consolidation of new political structures, legislation along general European lines, a wider social spread of secondary schooling, primary education for almost everybody and a fuller development of the complex division of labor of an industrialized country.

The net effect for everyday life in the cities was that people with different backgrounds and different opinions and different social roles, and who were not used to such diversity, had to learn to interpret each other well enough to be able to live and work together. New patterns of shared ideas were emerging. But Madrid in the 1990s could not produce doxa. On the contrary, it was a city where a number of factors combined to destroy any surviving pieces of doxa. Both new and old factors.

Cities are usually hostile to doxa. One factor is sheer size. Madrid now housed over four million persons. Of these a very small portion were urbanites of longer standing than second generation, and only about half were born there, the younger half mostly (CAM

65

1989). Most of them had roots in rural villages, either personally or through their parents. People talked of "my village" (*mi pueblo)* as a self-evident reference and usually without specifying where it was or how large. The important thing was to have a "my-village" to refer to, and most people did.

These my-villages were scattered all over Spain. The second largest contingent of immigrants, after that from surrounding Castile, came from Andalusia. About one fourth of Madrilenians could be said to have Andalusian background,[61] that is over one million, which would make Madrid a bigger Andalusian city than Seville. But Madrid was neither Castilian nor Andalusian, it was characterized by ethnic variety above all.[62] This is the second anti-doxa factor.

Naturally some Madrilenians had been urbanites for generations (although it was rare to meet a person whose four grandparents were all born in the city), and there was an urban tradition: barrio festivities, local anecdotes, a popular entertainment genre (*la zarzuela*, sometimes called the Spanish operetta), some ethnohistoric literature of a popular kind, and so on. But urban traditions are by their very nature not very doxic.

Politically, there was also a special tradition, but it was definitely an anti-doxa one, a tradition of conflict. Madrid was at least partially an industrialized city already toward the end of the nineteenth century and it was the center of the socialist labor movement (whereas the coastal areas tended more towards anarchism). There is a labor history full of strikes and battles from then on.

Events in Madrid were usually influenced by the fact that the city was also the capital of the Spanish state and housed a bureaucratic elite as well as landed aristocracy. Socially, then, there has always been a division of labor, and there have been class conflicts with strong loyalties on each side, but where some people always had trouble defining their own position. Not fertile ground for doxa.

Literacy is another anti-doxa factor. The popular classes of Madrid were largely illiterate up to the civil war, and in practice until much later, but the rate of illiteracy has never been as high as in rural areas. Madrid has aspired to be the cultural center of Spain as well as the political one. By the 1990s, the range along the dimension of education was not as wide as it used to be, since illiteracy had been almost eradicated in younger generations and university education had mushroomed, but as late as the early 1970s new half literates were produced, since there were not enough schools for everybody.[63] Even so, as a whole Madrid was by then a literate society, depending for its everyday functioning on such things as traffic signs and printed advertising, and citizens were expected to be literate enough to be able to function in society.[64]

Habitat (rural versus urban), regional origin, language, class, division of labor, political loyalties, education – these are some of the dimensions that create differences, and in Madrid all of these social differences came together in actual lives and real situations to multiply each other's complexities. In such a city, doxa cannot survive. Or, one might think that if there was any kind of doxa it would be some sort of relativism:

what goes without saying is that nothing goes without saying. Certainly this was what many Madrilenians felt. Yet, for all of this, there was an overall tendency, still in the 1990s, to think and act as if the world was much more doxic than it was, and this caused problems, intellectual, emotional and practical everyday problems.[65]

Hannerz describes the complex cultures of our times as full of "gaps, overlaps, contradictions and unequal intensities in cultural management" (1992:127). Common sense, he says, is cultural business as usual, and therefore not very applicable in such fluid situations. Evidently the picture I have sketched for Madrid is one example of an extremely fluid situation. There were no unchallenged routines in any walks of life. Of course learning was just as embedded in living as it is in more stable contexts. Most people act more than they reflect. But reflection could not be avoided and few people felt they could wholly trust what they learnt through living. Appearances had proven false, and inherited knowledge inapplicable, too often. One must be skeptic, observant, ready to change one's mind.

In such a situation, some people react by looking around for defenses against what is happening. They try to erect barriers against the uncomfortable challenges to what they are used to taking for granted. They may for example try to construct social contexts that fit old ideas, in order to prove that they are still valid, and in order to live according to them without having to question or even mention them. Club Aguafría was one such context. It was founded by conservative interests, and it had a clear ideology of stable family life, which would presumably be furthered by constant interaction among people with similar lifestyles and opinions coming together as families to do "sound"[66] things like sports and social dinners.

Even such a place could not be immune to the pervasive changes Spain had lived through. Club members sometimes got divorced, members' young adult children began to protest against the different treatment of women and men in club statutes,[67] some newly admitted members turned out to be of a kind not initially intended as desirable members (i.e. not very conservative), some old and trustworthy members might do strange things, such as vote to permit bikinis or introduce an anthropologist, not all speakers invited for social occasions said safe things only... But for all of this, uncomfortable phenomena could be kept at bay most of the time, so that the club atmosphere could be "sound," at least to a much greater degree than most other social contexts. When doxa reigns, one speaks not about its meanings so much as in terms of them, as Hannerz points out. That kind of cognitive security had been unattainable in Madrid for some time, but at the club it was a semi-conscious goal, and the feeling among members that most of them more or less shared was that such a goal provided a sense of security in itself. Outside the club, Madrid was a steaming bubbling pot of cultural negotiation, but inside the club, whatever members thought inside their heads, they acted in terms of a type of common sense they all recognized.[68]

In most social contexts in Madrid in 1991 the pervasive experience was that one could not be sure when one's own brand of common sense applied. It might or it might not. There were certain visual, linguistic and contextual signs to go by, as we will see, but these signs had a tendency to change, too, rather quickly. And apart from the lack of security in specific contexts, there was the more generalized feeling of insecurity in not knowing exactly with whom (what categories of people) or with how many one shared one's common sense. One could not make a trustworthy map of cultural distribution, i.e. a reliable inventory of other existing perspectives, something which is, as Hannerz points out (1992:126 ff), an important part of each perspective in a complex context. The logical result in Madrid was a general sense of distrust, expressed in common phrases such as: "There are no values anymore." "People say one thing and do another." "There is more hypocrisy than ever." "Don't trust anyone – everyone is always pretending a lot!" "Young people today have no ideals." And some old sayings about sociocultural skepticism, such as "appearances are fools" and "believe the worst and you will be right," took on new meanings and were frequently voiced.

Hannerz sums up what happens to common sense in complex societies in a way that fits the Spanish experience well, if only we add that for Spaniards it was a recent and intense experience: "In the conditions of a complex society, any variety of common sense may become a little less stable, more fragile and embattled, more aware of its limits (...). The recurrent confrontations with alternatives which contradict it can result in uncertainty or ambivalence, or in an orthodox mode, in an emphatic reassertion of those truths one feels should be self-evident. They may also foster sensitivity and reflectiveness, and cultural creativity." (1992:132)

In other words, people have to act on the fact that common sense, the guide for action, must itself be acted upon. Meaning is not just meaning, it must be managed. It is indeed logical if some people rebel and try to deny this or at least protect themselves from such uncomfortable changes, but it is also logical if others delight in the new opportunities. And of course there can be all sorts of mixes and in-between attitudes, and one individual can house several. The most basic tendency, however, will be towards innovation; such are the dynamics created by the sheer increase in the mass of knowledge and the complexification of its distribution. Even tradition has to be reinvented, if you want to have it; to just keep it the way it was is definitely impossible. Cultural innovation may then be institutionalized, and so will the opposition against it; newspapers, churches, schools and universities, and so on, will sprout ideological markers that are not so much about political left or right as for or against cultural change. And this is what happened in Spain.

La movida madrileña

As an illustration, let us take a quick look at the phenomenon known as *la movida madrileña* ("the Madrilenian commotion" in approximate translation), much talked about throughout the 1980s but supposedly occurring mainly during its first half.

What was it? No one seems to have ever given any description acceptable by all. Perhaps the best definition is actually that it was undefinable. It was an explosion of creativity of some kind, and different people tend to describe it as concerned mainly with what they themselves were involved in or found interesting. I have heard it defined in terms of only a dozen artists and fashion designers; I have also heard it defined as a very generalized atmosphere that found expression all over the city in poetry readings, shaggy barrio rock groups, an ever more diversified night life, floods of underground publications, a period of intellectual and artistic sparkle and also social inventiveness, intense interaction between all kinds of new "alternative" categories of people. Neither extreme seems real. I have also seen comments to the effect that the movida did not exist at all: that it was a figment in the imagination of a bored bourgeoisie, or that it was wishful thinking by a handful of unsuccessful artists. It has been said that it was something the state and city administrations invented in order to qualify Madrid for the title of cultural capital of Europe without having to spend any money on supporting artists or creating institutions. It has also been described as mainly the world of drugs and prostitution in the Malasaña quarter (e.g. in a novel by Juan Madrid, 1993), i.e. as disorder and social disintegration.

The movida is hard to define, probably, because it was a collectively invented label that seemed useful for many different purposes, and so it grew several incompatible referents. But even if no piece of reality can be accurately described with the term, the term is interesting as a phenomenon in itself. Why, if the movida was impossible to describe and perhaps did not exist, was everyone so interested in talking about it? Even if the conspiracy theories were correct and the term was invented by political or commercial interests, why did it catch on to such a degree?

My suggestion is that the term did have a referent, but of an elusive kind. It was something people were thinking about, and therefore needed a word for, but which was not really describable in terms of people or places or objects. We could call it the spirit of the times.

This was the time when the most intense period of social changes was coming to a close. The economic boom of the early 1970s had given material results that by now had consolidated, and what further economic change there was seemed to be downhill. The political transition had been a tenuous and long-lasting enterprise but seemed now to be reasonably stable and safe, if not completely finished. The people who had moved to the cities had become used to them, few rural immigrants were coming (since there were no jobs), and the children of the immigrants had grown up in the cities and become urban teenagers and young adults. They were the ones who formed suburban rock groups and filled the universities to bursting. This was a time of great cultural and social complexity, still growing and fueling itself, but a complexity that was no longer just a stunning dumbfounding obstacle to be grappled with as best one could, in order to survive – as it was so insistently portrayed in film and TV comedies throughout the 1970s.[69] It had become familiar, and one could now take stock of it and interpret it.

These were the times, in sum, when the great collective experience of profound change was no longer just confusing and exciting. The results could begin to be lived with. It was like the moment after a move, when the furniture and kitchenware are in place and one can sit down, have a cup of coffee and start thinking about where to hang the pictures and how one is going to feel about living in the new place. New ideas had had time to crystallize, new categories of people had had time to find each other and establish dialogues. It was no longer a time to be confused and silent, but it was not yet a time of new varieties of stable common sense, not yet a fully furnished home. There was cultural disconnectedness, as there must be in a complex society; this was no longer experienced mostly as a threat but neither, yet, as a mere fact of life.

To my mind, the best expression of these times and of the movida madrileña, are the early films by Pedro Almodóvar.[70] These films are portraits of violent clashes between perspectives – between or within individuals – and they are done in an appropriate style of desperate humor, deadpan stark contrasts, wild rhythms and angles. The events in the films are wholly unlikely, yet wholly recognizable in their component parts and in the way the absurdities of life force the protagonists to invent appropriate phrases and faces for any kind of inappropriate situation. No individual Madrilenian life has probably come anywhere near the number and degree of absurdities contained in an early Almodóvar film, but Madrilenians recognized their own experiences of dumbfoundedness and harsh training in instant adaptation to whatever lurks around the next corner. In contrast to the typical 1970s comedy protagonist, who feels lost and confused and tries to prove a worldliness, a "modernity", which is patently false, the typical Almodóvar protagonist behaves as if common sense were stable, swims through chaos with graceful assuredness and manages to find old sayings and common sense attitudes that fit with situations that burst all limits of the expectable.[71] Nothing is confusing to her/him, because life is full of unexpected disorder, which is just what is to be expected.

What Almodóvar's protagonists do and say was familiar to the Madrilenian audience, and in this mirror they could laugh at how ludicrously inadequate, yet somehow comfortingly workable, such a style of reaction toward the new events was. To create his images of cultural chaos, Almodóvar sometimes juxtaposes types of people who in traditional thinking are opposites and adversaries (e.g. the housewife and the prostitute as friends and neighbors, or a nun and a whore coming together on the basis of two shared appetites: lesbianism and drugs; or the wife of a violent policeman understanding well (unlike her husband) the sexual minorities that surround her in her apparently normal apartment building, since she herself is a masochist). Sometimes he creates new characters that seem to signal new possible freedoms (for instance a taxi driver who has made his car into an orgy of personal decoration, yet does not live up to the arrogant macho stereotype of Madrilenian taxi-drivers but is tender-hearted and service-minded; or a twelve-year old drug dealer who is the sanest person in his family and its only hope for salvation). And above all he paints a rich gallery of sexual possibilities where everything that feels good is good and all stereotypes about what goes with what are systematically overturned.

Almodóvar is unique in many ways, but he captured the spirit of the times, and he did it in a very traditional Mediterranean way, by using gender and sexuality as key metaphors.

La movida madrileña, I think, is a label with a very abstract referent, something like the spirit of the 1980s that Almodóvar portrayed: the exhilarating and scary possibilities of a cultural kaleidoscope, when people have learnt how to turn it but are not yet sure of what will happen when they do.

Cautious and expansive modes of management of meaning

After the historical experiences of the 1960s and the 1970s, the attitude toward change had become fundamental for Spaniards. It directed and shaped many of their other interpretations of reality. Individuals and groups could certainly slide around on a continuum of more or less positive or negative opinions on change, and their attitudes could also change over time or according to situation. But to get an approximate picture of the stakes involved, let us set up two polarized ideal types to start with. I will call them the expansive mode of management of meaning and the cautious mode of management of meaning.[22] How meaning is managed in practice is illustrated in the empirical chapters, and will show how people adapted their modes according to context but yet tended to stay within the general mode that fit their habitus best. Each mode had flexible outlines, but there were limits beyond which the individual would become distinctly uncomfortable.

In other words, there could be all sorts of mixed modes, and individuals could subscribe more or less consistently to them and adopt different ones temporarily according to situations and purposes. The modes are abstractions, not corresponding to any specific categories of individuals or situations.

Cultural negotiations around change in middle class Madrid took the shape of debates on issues like sexuality, social justice, rationality, family life and gender. What I suggest here is that no matter how important these issues were in themselves, they also expressed a deeper division that had to do with attitudes towards cultural diversity, complexity flux and the changes that had brought it all about.

Here is a sketch of the basic features of the two modes:

The cautious mode of management of meaning

People who want to live in an unquestioned world, a highly doxic one, must consider social organization as something given by nature, not changeable by fickle humans. They must believe that if there is cultural diversity and social complexity, it is because people are different by nature and have naturally ordered tasks. They would thus tend to ascribe people to roles and ascribe characteristics to individuals by way of recognized "natural" categories.

In Spain, the social categories recognized in such thinking are old and very general in Mediterranean societies, fixed categories of above all gender, age and social prestige. The cautious managers of meaning find it natural and inevitable, for example, that children and adults should live in different worlds, and that children should therefore not be expected to understand parents' reasons but should just obey them. They find it natural, biologically given and also socially necessary and good that women and men be mysteries to each other and that husband and wife therefore can meet only in given roles with clearly assigned authority patterns, while both sexes tend to find their friends within their own. Classes or races can also be interpreted as given by nature. Individual differences within any of these ascriptive categories are accepted and even considered a good thing (according to the disposition for self-affirmation) as long as they stay within the defined limits of the category. However, to break those limits is not just wrong, it is unnatural.

The categories are seen as timeless, and in Madrid, among cautious managers with high education, this was expressed for instance in admiration for classical Greek culture and in a preoccupation with the idea of civilization. The taste in art and home decoration likewise sought fixed norms. Everywhere, there must be hierarchies of better and worse, was the idea. If in a given case it was difficult to discern any hierarchy, this caused discomfort. The feeling was one of lack: there was no "correct" criterion (yet), or one had not been able to find it. One must therefore search for one criterion (and not, as in an expansive mode, try to create and experiment with several possible criteria). (Chapter 7 offers an illustration.)

In such thinking, "values" are as eternal as social categories. One should not have opinions about them. If something can be doubted and discussed, it is not a value, not a "true" one. Opinions are an evil, divisive thing. If "true" values are applied to an issue, the "correct" belief will result. Within each ascriptive category, everyone has so much in common with all others that they should agree on values. An individual who does not is seen as provocative, seeking to disrupt the peace, and not, for instance, as creative or innovative. Since values are not debatable, the motive for debaters can only be a perverse wish to infect innocent people with doubts and hatred. If such individuals are not stopped from gaining adepts, chaos will ensue, it is felt. Religion is the best bulwark against chaos, since it guarantees the correctness of the values.

So the cautious managers of meaning can be authoritarian and ruthless. To them, dissenting voices are monsters, and monsters must be cut down. But they can also be very tolerant; they are confident that if the disturber of the peace is just a "sound" person deep down (which they assume to be the case if they know her parents or general background), sooner or later her "nature" will automatically lead her back to the one and only right path.

But since chaos is so threatening to a world view that rests largely on clear categorizations, ascription is a necessity. Only ascription assures a clear indisputable assignment of each individual to a place in society. The favorite argument against any liberalizing proposal becomes: "That is impossible! What would happen if everyone started doing anything they liked..."

It is as if there were nothing at all between absolute categories and absolute chaos.

The expansive mode of management of meaning

Those who would have labeled themselves "progressives" around 1980, and for whom there seemed to be no handy name around 1990, had a very different attitude toward change and toward social order.

They approved of change, and therefore saw ascription as an obstacle. To ascribe people to set categories and roles can only work in an unchanging society, where the categories and roles to be filled can remain the same long enough to be filled with new individuals once in a while. In a situation of change, people must be able to move in and out of roles, and many roles must disappear and new ones be created. Even when roles stay more or less the same, ascription to them may become irrational in a changing society. For example, perhaps in the past only a gentleman's son was in fact equipped to lead a great business firm (due for example to inherited contacts or unchanging technology), but in a changing context he will be less efficient than whoever got the best grades in business school. This is so even if "we" agree on what counts as a gentleman, which "we" in fact usually do not.

So the discourse of merit and rationality seemed to fit better in Madrid, the expansionists thought. The widespread discourse of "self-realization" also pointed away from ascription, of course, since it was all about the search for a place in life where as much as possible of one's individuality could be expressed, irrespective of ascribed identities such as age or gender. The discourse of "freedom" worked in a similar manner.

And the central value words for large sectors of the Madrilenian middle class, and especially the culturally dominant sectors of it, were precisely these: self-realization, justice, freedom, merit, rationality.[7] Their discourse was in fact a 20th century version of the Enlightenment, and this discourse dominated at state universities, in the largest newspapers (e.g. El País), the serious cultural magazines, the debating programs on television and radio, etc.[74]

With such a world view, ascription becomes repulsive. It is seen as irrational, because it does not assign people to roles according to their individual talents, which means they cannot contribute to society as well as they might. It is seen as unfree because it forces individuals to do certain things because of how they are categorized, no matter their wishes and talents, and unjust because ascription is based on things that cannot be changed voluntarily. Where ascription reigns, self-realization becomes impossible, merit becomes irrelevant, freedom and justice become empty words or have to be carefully redefined. No wonder the dictatorship favored rigid social categories, people of this conviction concluded, forgetting that many "ordinary village people" also did.

Instead of ascription, achievement is the best organizing principle, according to the expansivist managers of meaning. It does not lead to chaos, quite the contrary. And perhaps a bit of chaos once in a while may not be all that negative, should it occur. It should not be allowed to cause irrationality, but if it produces innovation it is good. All structures tend to congeal, so to avoid irrationality they have to be turned upside down and inside out once in a while. "Rebellion" was included among the progressive value words as were "flexibility" and "imagination". The more radical even talked about "subversive" acts and opinions as something desirable. Positive ideas of "choice" and "pleasure" were less revolutionary but still too subversive for a cautious world view.

In the expansivist world, none of the characteristics usually used for ascription should be allowed to organize either private or public matters. Merit is the only legitimate criterion for employment or political responsibility. Interests, opinions and tempers should determine choice of friends even across gender and age lines. Neither gender nor class nor race are considered to determine personality; to think so would be "prejudice", i.e. irrational and unfair, wrong in every sense, according to the expansivists.

Inevitably, emotions and opinions clash, and with an expansive mode of managing meanings, more things happen more unpredictably. Reality cannot easily be interpreted. In the 1990s, experience was not always the best guide for anyone in Spain, and less so for the expansive-minded born in the 1940s and 1950s, since they considered that their own experience had been shaped by a reality they did not approve of and since they believed their education had been "backward" and therefore had to be "overcome" with the aid of sheer thinking and determination. There was thus a strong tension between the constraints of reality, such as it appeared to common sense, and the need to go beyond it with the help of ideas. For the expansivist, to give in to the comfort of common sense was never quite legitimate, whatever the issue. Common sense was always suspect, even when there seemed to be no alternative.

There will be examples from observed situations in the empirical chapters. We will meet both cautious and expansive managers of meaning and their handling of clashes.

Two modes in one society

The two modes are ideal types, I insist. But at a sufficient level of abstraction, they could be recognized in Madrilenian reality. According to a person's basic attitudes towards change, there would be a tendency to evaluate social and cultural complexity in different ways. The foremost meaning to be managed was the meaning of change, and once change is interpreted and evaluated, a lot of other attitudes follow.[75]

The cautious mode ran into immediate difficulties. To be fully workable, it would require a stable situation where common sense could reign, and that was not what was at hand. Madrilenians who managed meaning cautiously did not usually deny change, but they certainly felt that it should not be allowed to get out of hand. It must be controlled, limited, channeled. The Club Aguafría discourse, for example, contained many "musts" and many references to the ill effects of all "extremes", and many topics were considered best not talked about at all.[76] Since reality and mode of managing meaning diverged, reality had to be kept on a leash.

If change is considered good, on the other hand, and individuals are thought to be different among themselves and encouraged to search for ways to express those differences, then such caution is negative. It slows down, hinders, mutes, oppresses. Change may be confusing, but the confusion can only be resolved by an open-minded search for new combinations. And social diversity is one helpful instrument in these efforts. People learn from each other. That is, they learn as long as they do not hide too much from each other, as they do when they are cautious. Instead they should express themselves, not just for their own pleasure but in order to give information to others. These ideas defined the expansive mode of cultural management in Madrid, which was usually and consequently also expressive.[77]

As we can see, the two modes were incompatible and mutually harmful.

Now, as concepts they are ideal types or abstractions. I am not talking about the "two Spains" of political and literary myth.[78] The contrast described may be more than a little related, historically, to old structural divisions in the social body, but I think it more fruitful to see it as one of several dilemmas produced by the recent social changes and for which people had to find answers, however provisional. Just which structural categories tended towards which mode of cultural management, and why, is less interesting than the fact that there were different modes, perhaps a whole series between the two polar ones, and that they clashed with each other in certain ways.

The two modes also had something in common. Subscribers to both tended to be adamant that they were the only knowledgeable and sincere ones. In other words, both modes declined to take the other seriously. In this light, the expansive mode was more self-contradictory than the cautious one.

But there may be more rhetoric than conviction for both in this attitude. There was at least one piece of data that indicated curiosity about the contents of other people's worldviews: the popularity of debating programs on radio and TV.[79]

The empirical chapters offer examples of various kinds of lives, situations and opinions. I have chosen them to illustrate the complexity behind my analysis. Any generalization must be made with due consideration of the multiple attitudes toward change and complexity and the different modes of managing meaning.[80]

Introduction to Part II: Hedges

Madrilenians tended to socialize with people similar to themselves, so the places for sociability can usually be described in the same way as the clusters of opinions in chapter 4. The people, the things they do, the places they go to, the things they talk about and the way they talk about them all vary more or less in parallel.

Part II is about Club Aguafría and represents one extreme of the Madrilenian diversity of life styles and opinions. Its members were conservative and used a cautious mode of management of meaning. Their caution made them hedge on controversial issues much of the time. The club was closed off from the outside world by high hedges, which to my mind symbolized their defensive attitude.

Chapter 5 explains what the social clubs meant in Madrilenian life in general and presents two contrasting types of female Club Aguafría members and their discourses. In chapter 6 there is a description of the club as material, social and symbolic space. Chapter 7 offers a description of a symbolically important activity at the club. the women's efforts to "cultivate" themselves. This was where the most purely conservative gender discourse reigned, and it was here that even conservative women drew the line as to what they would accept in men's opinions of women. Finally, in chapter 8, the significance of the club as a context for cultural negotiation is related to the larger city.

Club Aguafría was both special and representative. In many Madrilenian contexts, this type of opinions and lifestyles was used as the "traditional" point of reference. Hopefully, the description of Club Aguafría will offer the reader a point of reference from which to measure the distances to other standpoints described in the rest of the book.

It is important to remember, however, that Club Aguafría does not represent anything like a "baseline culture" or a pristine "ethnographic present" of Madrilenian life as it used to be before "all the change" began. Just as much as all the other variations we will meet, Club Aguafría was one possible adaptation to what was happening. It was not traditional, it was just defined as such.

Chapter 5. Club Aguafría as a context for cultural work

While in Madrid to prepare this project, I sat one evening talking to some old friends. They knew about my previous project in Benituria, and I said that I was now planning to do something similar in middle class surroundings. I explained what sort of middle class I was thinking of and added, "The class you yourselves belong to." Then I asked what they thought their neighbors would think if I moved into the area and began to try to make friends, doing interviews, etc. They said they could not answer that. They did not know the neighbors well enough to predict how they might react. "And just like we don't, no one here knows the neighbors. You would have a hard time, not because anyone would oppose your study, but because it would be difficult to establish the contacts you need." They continued pondering my needs, and said that middle class people do not live the sort of barrio life I had described for Benituria. "They are mobile! They move all over Madrid... The only place where you go regularly and have a group of people where everyone knows everyone would be the club... Yes! The Club! Of course!"

This was how I decided to do fieldwork in a social club.

What sort of thing were they, then, the social clubs that so many middle class Madrilenians belonged to?

Many or most of them were defined as sports clubs, but sports did not center the attention of the members. There was always a swimming pool or two, several tennis courts, and often a few other sports facilities. But there was also always a bar, or several, a restaurant, and a few rooms in which you would find magazines, a TV set and sets for chess and similar games, but where the main activity was just talking. Some clubs were elegant, like country clubs in the United States, and one important sign of distinction was golf; a club with a golf course is always an expensive one. But there are also clubs for middle-middle and even lower-middle class. There were clubs that catered mostly to the residential areas where they were situated, while others attracted members from a wider area, perhaps due to some special facility or some ideological factor.

The social club was the nearest middle class equivalent to working class barrio life. It was a place where you could count on meeting people you knew without calling them ahead of time, where you could sit for hours talking without having to go through the trouble of inviting people to your home. Unlike barrio bars, the clubs were not gender segregated, at least not evidently so (but cf next chapter).

Membership was usually by family and family life was important. A common motivation for joining Club Aguafría (as well as two other clubs I knew well) was "for the children", "to have somewhere to go on Sundays where we can all go together", "to be able to be outdoors during the weekend without having to spend hours in traffic jams", "to have a place where even your teenagers will want to come, so that you can know where they are".

Club Aguafría was a reasonably representative social club for the middle-to-upper middle class. It was more conservative than most, because of a historical link with a religious organization, but it was not socially exclusive, nor were the installations very luxurious. To join, one had to be introduced by two members and buy a "share", which at the time of my fieldwork cost around 500.000 pesetas, which was also the approximate medium monthly salary of members.[81] The monthly fee was only 10.000 pesetas The club had been founded in the mid 1960s in an area that was then a new residential area of some prestige but relatively low prices, because it was considered far away from downtown Madrid and had rather bad communications. It had plenty of green space and open views over the surrounding countryside. Since then communications had improved, the prestige of the area had increased and the prices even more, ever more buildings had crowded in, including some office buildings, so that there were no longer very many open public spaces, but there were still gardens with private swimming-pools around most apartment buildings The club could buy no land to expand, but on the other hand it boasted a relatively good accessibility in comparison with other clubs of similar standing.

The club had about 600 member families. There would be more if they had more space, because there was a waiting list, the club leadership told me, but as it was they felt that to have more members would mean too much crowding. There were a very few member families that consisted of one person only, and there were a few young couples, but a large majority were couples with children. The average was probably around four children per family, but there were some with eight or ten. The size of a family did not make any difference for the fees. There were a few separated individuals, but this was not usually talked about, and the common thing to do in case of separation was to sell the share and leave.

The club leadership insisted to me that it was a club for "ordinary" families. The fees were not excessive for the middle-to-upper middle class, but naturally they were much higher than the Madrilenian overall average could afford. What the club leadership meant, apart from not even thinking of working class people, was that it was their policy to make the club a place for ordinary family activities: games, sports, fun, friendship. Not, that is, a place for showing off fashion, meeting the famous or the rich, or establishing business contacts. The members I talked to said the same thing, but unlike the club leadership they also usually underlined prestige as a motivation for joining. A few would say with pride that it was an "elite club". More common were phrases like, "Well, I could have joined a club closer to where I live, but this is a nice one, and you know that you meet a certain kind of people here, not just anybody. A sort of guarantee, let's call it that."

What did the members do at the club? Why did they go there? Details are presented in chapters 6-8, but first two basic considerations must be explained. I call them *philia* and *aparentar*.

Philia is my name for a disposition[82] which makes sociability a key symbol for a good life. I dare say that it is a prominent disposition all around the Mediterranean area. It makes people feel that being around other people, especially in verbal interaction, is one of the most important and most fun things one can do in life, and that anything that hinders such activity is bad. Naturally the strength and the expressions of the disposition vary according to region, class, etc. In Spain it is usually called friendship, but it is not the same thing as the intimate relationship called friendship in Northern Europe. It has little to do with intimacy, secrets, trust (although naturally such relationships exist, too) and more to do with having a lot of people around, having a good time in company.

In villages and working class areas of towns and cities, men find this "atmosphere" (ambiente), as it is also called, mainly in bars. Women have to find excuses related to their daily tasks, but they do find them, they meet and talk while sewing, shopping, watching the children play.[83] Even so, to be a housewife is incompatible because so much of daily work has to be carried out without having anyone to talk to.

It was not as easy for the new middle class to find forms for this sociability.

That great male institution, the bar sociability, is something middle class men had lost. Or almost lost. Some of them (like Rafael in appendix A) had chosen a bar where they were regular customers and knew the other regular customers, just like working class men. But it was unusual. Most middle class areas did not have the type of bars working class barrios did, with newspapers, game boards and television sets. Instead they had "pubs", which were more elegant places, or "*cafeterias*", coffee houses, which served sweets and were more used by women than men. Neither pubs nor coffee houses invited socializing between people who did not already know one another. A common pattern was for men to have appetizers at a bar near their work place, usually with colleagues from work. At such bars there was little socializing between groups, and women might also use them.

If the men, in moving "up", had lost the bar, women had lost the socializing around household tasks that working class women had. Some of them did little household work, because they had maids. Most of them were careful to maintain a certain aloofness from neighbors, thinking that too friendly a relationship with someone who lives very close might become uncomfortable in case of a conflict. They lived in buildings that did not make it easy for neighbors to get to know each other: walls were thicker than in working class dwellings (although seldom completely sound-proof), one did not meet in the staircase because there were elevators, errands were handled by a door watchman, and so on. And since material well-being was so important for prestige, no middle class woman would dream of asking a neighbor to loan her an egg or a vacuum cleaner. Nor would she dream of taking her sewing and a chair to sit on the sidewalk, the way village women did.

It was not even acceptable to take sewing into the garden, if there was a garden around the building, nor could one just go down and sit in the garden without any excuse. Shopping offered some opportunity, but not much, because it was mostly done in supermarkets, and people did not talk to each other while waiting in line to cash out. Mothers did not pick up children from school, since most of them went to private schools by bus. Mothers of small children met in playgrounds and parks, too, perhaps more than working class mothers did, since they had more playgrounds and parks to go to, and more time to do it. If there was a garden around their own building, they would feel freer to talk to the other mothers in the certainty that they were of similar economic standing. But there was always more caution in addressing strangers than for working class women. Some of the young women sitting with small children might even be maids and should not be addressed, and nowadays it was difficult to tell who they were, since uniforms for maids were becoming rare.

An added difficulty for both women and men is that the disposition for philia includes a feeling that sociability should be spontaneous, not arranged. A good atmosphere is something that is born, it cannot be made on purpose. To meet in each others' homes sounded like a fashionable idea to most middle class Madrilenians, but in fact they did not do it very often, because it took too much planning, and also because while sitting in a home, no uninvited people can suddenly drop by. One has to spend the whole evening in the same company, something which can give a feeling of being cooped-up, forced. But to meet in public places also requires planning in a big city, because of distances, amount of people around and social inequality. And even while sitting in a group at a sidewalk café, the sheer size of Madrid makes it improbable that somebody one knows will chance to walk by. Perhaps people did not consciously wish for that, but if it happened, it was always extra pleasure according to the disposition for philia.

The clubs were a solution. At a club one can always count on finding someone to talk to without having to arrange anything ahead of time. At the club one knows which sort of people one will meet, so one can talk to anyone, without awkwardness, even without previous introduction. One can sit down with a group while simultaneously staying in contact with other groups nearby, one can circulate, one can move into another room or another activity for a while and then come back, conversation partners arrive and leave every so often... Things happen. That is "atmosphere," ambiente.

But status influences sociability. Middle classes may be insecure everywhere, according to common sociological wisdom, but a middle class that had existed for only a short time, in a country where class differences had been and still were strong and crucial, and in a country where so much had changed recently, the middle class must be especially insecure. But this was something people were loath to admit. They had to pretend a lot of things, above all that they had much more money than they did, but they must also pretend a psychological security that they definitely did not have. Their role models were vague, which in itself added to insecurity. They had to improvise a lot, as they might admit. But for many, the vague role model they seemed to try to imitate was that of the elegantly nonchalant, thoroughly secure, traditional upper class Spaniard.

Life at Club Aguafría was very relaxed to the extent that people obtained what they went there for, long-lasting group relationships with conversation as the central activity. But life at the club was also very tense in that one had to pretend a lot at all times. This was called *aparentar* (keep up appearances, pretend, show off), and was lamented by club members themselves. Among the first things people I met told me about the club was this: "Here at the club there is a lot of aparentar, you'll notice soon." And I did. The description was correct. And later on many told me in confidence something like this: "As for me, I think your work seems very interesting, you can count on me, I'll try to help you. But I don't think it will work out. You must understand, people will think... they will believe that you are trying to find out how much money they earn. Or other things... Everyone is always pretending such a lot, so then a person like you, wanting to know things, is very uncomfortable..." Of course they were talking about themselves.

So prestige was one important reason for aparentar, and prestige meant mainly to pretend to be richer than one was, and to hide such possible shameful things as a humble background or family events that did not measure up to the ideal image of the happy nuclear family. Two other reasons for aparentar were cautious mode of management of meaning and the cultural construction of tradition (cf chapter 8).

In spite of all the limitations, however, the conversations at the club had as their main real purpose, and sole visible purpose, the pleasure of being with friends. Conversation with friends is authentic pleasure in a verbal Mediterranean culture. It is an art. It is like listening to music. (Cf appendix C.) It is a disposition for something emotional, in that it weaves together and embroiders relationships. It is also a rational pleasure, the pleasure of exercising abstract thought. It is like writing a book or attending a seminar for intellectuals. This is true also for very non-intellectual persons. In all corners of daily life, for all walks of Spanish life (with minor regional variations), friendly conversation is a pleasure for its own sake, whatever other benefits it might bring as byproducts, and it is a well-rounded pleasure, with emotional, rational and aesthetic factors.

These factors should ideally be nicely interwoven. Any predominance of one at the cost of the others makes the conversation less fulfilling. This can be shown if someone forgets her duty to balance them. For example, if a person gets carried away with the actual content of the argument to the point of forgetting the social factor, the others are bound to make efforts to restore it, usually by some well chosen joke that undermines the serious argument and re-establishes the importance of social relationships. Similarly, if someone emphasizes intellectual or emotional factors to the point of forgetting the aesthetic aspect, she or he will be accused of being clumsy and in all probability there will soon be some well-turned comment, a joke or a song or some expressive body language, that gets all the attention, however poor in social or intellectual content. (We will see examples of this, especially in chapters 13, 19 and appendix A.) A conversation should have a rhythm and a harmony and a succession of changing themes and surprising turns, otherwise it becomes a bore. And boredom is the specter to be held at bay at all costs. Pleasure is the opposite of boredom, as sociability is the opposite of loneliness, according to these dispositions.

If conversation is pleasure, due to deep dispositions, it is also a necessity, due to present circumstances of social change. Cultural changes have to be negotiated. Let us look at two examples, ethnographic sketches of representative sociability at Club Aguafría, one in winter, one in summer.

A winter Sunday afternon – the conservative women

Arriving at the club, as usual on foot, I met Isabel coming downhill in her car. She stopped to greet me through the window. She was not leaving, she was just looking for parking space. "See you up there," she said.

But instead of walking all the way up to the main club house, I decided to take a look inside the Cabin. Outside it, on the still sunny and warm terrace, a group of small boys were playing something like football among the tables and chairs. One elderly woman was keeping an eye on them and also at a group of little girls playing with the swings by the building corner.

Inside, I greeted Sofía who sat at a table with four or five other middle aged ladies and one small girl. There were two tables occupied by couples and some children, and four or five tables with only men, smoking a lot, playing cards and domino. A fire was crackling in the fire place. A few women were seated on the overstuffed couches in the opposite corner from the entrance. The bar was empty. Even the waiter was nowhere to be seen, and the women at Sofía's table were complaining about that, they wanted their afternoon snack.

Isabel came in behind me, grumbling about the dense smoke. "The others will be up in the main building," she said, slightly irritated at having to tell me that. Then she saw Sofía. "Just a moment," she said and walked up to her table. Sofía got up and the two of them sat down at another table, Isabel got out some money and Sofía got out a dainty notebook. They were probably collecting money for some wedding gift again. Many of the children of their friends were getting married this year.

I waited by the table with the other ladies. They were busy unwrapping and re-wrapping a series of, to my taste, very ugly little figures made of plaster. There were two small rose and gold colored angels, for example, and several of the other figures had a vague air of something you might find in a baroque church. Sofía explained that a club member made them to sell. At that moment another woman came up to the table and started handling the figures with authority. Before I had time to make any mistakes, Sofía, who I think could read my thoughts at that moment (we had had occasion to agree that neither of us were impressed with the artistic level of the paintings at the club exhibitions) hurriedly told me that this woman was the artist herself. "And look here, this holy water font, isn't it a beauty?" I did not have to answer, because the artist leaned over to one woman who showed interest in buying: "For a Christmas gift, for example, it is just the right thing. Don't you think so?" she said to us all and the women nodded agreement, whether out of politeness or enthusiasm was impossible to tell.

Isabel had now finished her business, so we left. At the door we met her husband Leonardo in search of a group of men to play cards with. "The men seem to prefer the Cabin," I said. "Yes, and the women prefer the main salon, where there is less smoke," said Isabel resolutely, admitting no further comments about that.

We saw no one from our group in the main salon. We sat down together, ordering some coffee with milk. Isabel insisted to the waiter, as she regularly did, that the coffee be really hot this time, "and not like yesterday, when I had to send it back. Don't let it sit on the counter while you do something else, it does get cold then, you see, at this time of the year. And mind you, the milk must be hot, too." The waiter kept a poker face and said, "Of course, señora, you are right." Isabel sighed to me, "It's a disgrace that one should have to explain these things over and over again. It is so self-evident, don't you think? But no. Unless you make sure and insist, they serve you sloppily."

At that moment Victoria, an elderly lady, sat down with us. She had had lunch with her family at the club that day, so she had some fresh opinions on the new restaurant keeper. "It's about the same as before. For a first course there was a fish soup, and those who had that said it was all right, and I had a salad with rice and maize and some other vegetables, not bad but not very interesting either. And then for the main course there was Riojan style trout, which could pass but was not very filling, or else simple beefsteak but very small servings. The men complained they did not get enough no matter what they chose. Now, there is one piece of good news, they have a dessert table, all sorts of fruit, even kiwi, and several cakes, and ice-cream of course and flan and all the usual stuff. That is nice, at least it gives you a happy feeling if you finish the meal right." Victoria smiled sweetly.

Gloria arrived and immediately declared she had no opinion on the new restaurant keeper. She wore a tired face that seemed to tell us she did not want to have any opinion on anything today, so we let her be. No one asked any questions. Irene arrived and introduced a friend of hers, Maruja. They started commenting on the imminent wedding of Maruja's daughter. She was studying in the United States and had met an American man. The women prepared to commiserate with Maruja about her bad luck in having her daughter marrying so far away, but Maruja pooh-poohed the idea, saying that it would not make much difference, they talked a lot on the telephone anyway, perhaps just as much as they would if she lived in Madrid, and Maruja planned to go and see her often. All the women then hurriedly agreed that these days going to America is no big thing, and there were jokes about the traffic in Madrid: "It takes longer to get to the airport than from there to New York!"

Maruja explained that her daughter would finish her studies in spite of getting married. "She has two years to go. But her fiancé has finished his studies and he has a good position already. That is no problem over there. Precisely the other day he called us to tell us he had got a job, «so now I can support your daughter«." Maruja gave a small laugh. "But my husband said, no, I will pay for her studies." She made a funny face to signify that the fiancé had felt relief. We all laughed.

Now Inés arrived with her unmarried sister Luisa, who lived with Inés and her family. There were no more seats at our table, in front of the fireplace, but Irene gave up hers, saying she was going to play cards anyway. Maruja said it was time for her to go to mass. These comings and goings interrupted the conversation for a while, and to fill the pause several women complemented Isabel on her new fuchsia-colored blouse. She answered simply, "Yes, this color is becoming." Someone else had new earrings and was also complemented. I took the opportunity to complain about the fact that I seem to have developed an allergy and can no longer wear earrings for pierced ears. "Not even gold ones," I said – the kind of "riches-dropping" they themselves did constantly. Several of the ladies offered advice, for example to paint the pins with nail polish. Others were consoling, saying that clips are coming into fashion.

After a while almost all the women in our group left to play cards. Gloria and Luisa stayed, they did not play. Luisa, fingering her pearl necklace, said she was not very interested. Gloria said with a bored expression that neither was she, and besides she found it too much of a trouble to learn, she had tried, "but I was not good at it, I guess I did not pay sufficient attention." Lidia arrived and greeted us and asked for the others with evident worry. Gloria laughed, "Yes, they have started the game, but rush over, they are in the bar, they will make room for you!"

Gloria and Luisa said the card playing was a rather new thing at the club. Not for the men, of course. "But the women only began to play last year," Gloria said. No, said Luisa politely, "they started about three years ago, but little by little." Gloria was sad. "That is why the atmosphere is coming apart. We talk a lot less now, they always want to play. It used to be a great pleasure to come to the club, there was always someone to talk to. And now that the children are grown up..." She pointed to a group of women at another table. "Now they are almost the only ones who have a regular tertulia,[84] like we used to have, every Sunday, without exception."

When a couple of other women came over to keep Gloria and Luisa company, I walked over to the card tables. Lidia and Inés were playing as one couple, Isabel and Mariela as the other, canasta was the game. Sofía appeared. She stood behind Mariela's chair, giving her advice. Inés was annoyed and after a while she could not keep quiet: "Please, Sofía, let Mariela play, she is the one who is playing, don't tell her anything." Sofía left with an unfathomable smile. Inés felt like excusing herself: "I couldn't help it, I just couldn't stand it." Mariela: "You did the right thing, she was making me very nervous." To me: "You know, I have not been playing for very long, and she just reminds me of all the mistakes I used to make, so I make them again." The other women commented unfavorably on Sofía's tendency to meddle where she was not wanted. "Look, now she has sat down to play over there! Did you see that, at Consuelo's table? Ana got up to give her her seat. Yes, I was on the verge of doing the same thing, telling her, you play instead of me, if you are so very interested..."

There were only women playing in the little room behind the bar in the main building. The men played in the Cabin, and the bridge tournaments for couples were held in another, larger, salon. When one couple had reached eight thousand points, as agreed beforehand, my friends ended their game and went back into the salon.

The conversation was now rather languid. They were waiting for their husbands to finish their games. It was not very late, only around eight thirty, but there were comments that the men were taking their time. Isabel told about how she had gone down to the Cabin one day to look for her husband. The others looked surprised, so Isabel felt she had to explain. "Yes, he had to go to mass, and when he starts playing he forgets everything, so I had to remind him," she said, even though she had started telling the anecdote to fit the apparent consensus that sometimes the men make the women wait without any good reason. The other women did not back her up with examples of their own, so it was obvious that her action was an exception and was not quite approved of. But neither did they disapprove verbally.

After a while the men dropped in. At first only José Luis, Gloria's husband, by himself, and then one other man who had come directly from work just to pick up his wife. These two men sat down with the women, joking a little, but not taking any real part in the conversation. Like the women, they were waiting. José Luis was the only man in this group who took part in women's conversations sometimes, but only if no other men were present. Then the other husbands arrived in a group, standing around making wise-cracks about what they supposed was the gossipy character of the women's sociability. One or two of them stood behind their wives' chairs without saying anything. The women gathered up their coats and said good night to each other.

Like the others, I said good night and kissed cheeks and started to look for my coat. (The club had a room for hanging coats, but no one used it, the coats were just thrown across backs of chairs and sofas.) No family considerations forced me to leave; I did not really need any excuse, but just to say something, I said I felt it was time for dinner. But as the main group headed for the hall, it became evident that Mariela had to stay, her husband had not appeared. She too had stood up and thrown her fur-coat over her shoulders. She said she would go down to the Cabin and wait there. I realized that this was a good chance for me to get a glimpse of the men's world, so I said I was not in such a hurry after all, I would keep her company. She looked happy and relieved and sat down again. "Weren't we going to the Cabin?" I said, sheepishly. Mariela smiled. "I was, but since you are so kind to stay and sit with me, we won't have to!"

So we stayed in the main salon. And even though I did not get that glimpse of the male world, the evening was fruitful, for Mariela was so thankful that she repaid me in the currency she knew I coveted: she told me things about her life. Without my having to ask, she talked about many things, even the kind of things that were hardly ever mentioned at the club. And she said so. "Now, what I just said I don't want you to comment with the others. It is funny isn't it, that we are such old friends, but there are certain things we just do not tell each other." This was probably, in part, a way to make me feel good, a way of declaring friendship between us. But it was also true. It concurred with my observations, and some of the other women had also used moments of privacy to tell me things which they did not want the others to know. And they were always the same kind of things: honest complaints that they did not always have money for everything, some doubts about the future of their children, perhaps because they had not really obtained such brilliant grades after all, tales about daily life in their home. Not exactly short-comings, but things that did not shine and glitter.

Mariela confessed for example that she did not always feel like coming to the club every week. She worked all week (she was a kindergarten teacher) and she needed the weekends for housework and she was often tired, she would like to stay at home and watch TV. But she had to go, at least once a week, because her husband wanted to go. "And it is natural, he does not want to be locked up in the house." Then she admitted that even for her the club sometimes served as a handy excuse in order not to have to "complicate my life with relatives all the time." For example, she had a brother and a sister-in-law who had seven children, "and they love my cooking! Sure, having to cook for nine persons every day, my sister-in-law prefers to have me do it every once in a while!"

Another example: Lidia had talked about Paris earlier in the evening. Mariela had said nothing. Now she said that it was an old dream of hers to go to Paris. She had never been there, "but some day I will go." I wondered to myself whether perhaps she had not even been abroad, but that was the kind of thing I dared not ask, it might have been too much even for this temporary atmosphere of confession.

Mariela also talked about how her efforts to lose weight always failed, she admitted that she liked such an old fashioned thing as embroidering and that her husband Sebastián also had some "vulgar" hobby, she stressed that not everyone at the club had made as good careers as they tried to make people believe, and some of the ones who really did have elevated positions did not brag about it at all...

After all of these confessions, perhaps she felt that I ought to offer something similar, so she asked me about how old people live in Sweden. She had read somewhere that they were mostly confined to old people's homes or even lived alone, could that be true, did the Swedes not love their parents?

When Sebastián finally appeared, after about an hour, Mariela was quick to ask him to order something for me from the bar. I protested. She insisted: "You said you were hungry! Ha, don't you believe I did not hear it! I know you are hungry and because you stayed with me you will have dinner very late – Sebastián, order some sausages or something, please!" Apparently, ever since I pronounced that little excuse about time for dinner, she had thought that I was hungry, but she had not ordered anything herself. I don't think this was because she did not feel it appropriate for her to address the waiter herself (some of the women were slightly shy about that, but most were not, and Mariela was after all a professional woman); it was probably rather that she wanted to make sure I would not insist on paying. She really wanted to treat me, and the best way to do that was to make a man order – in her world, a man always pays, no woman can argue with that.

So we had beer, sausages and croquettes. It was past ten thirty when we left. They gave me a ride to the metro station.

A summer afternoon – another kind of women

In summer the indoors facilities were practically closed. The bar and the restaurant moved to the terrace, some of the indoors furniture was taken away for cleaning or mending, the curtains were never opened. There was a sleepy air of abandonment over the salons.

Outdoor life was much more relaxed. One saw more of the family life that in winter was mostly just talked about. It was like a dry norm blossoming to life.

Of course, family life is never as idyllic as the club members constantly made it out to be. But on the terrace at lunch time on a not too hot day in July, it was the beautiful side of it that was visible. Groups of people laughed and talked around the bar tables under the sun shades. People kissed each other on the cheek as they arrived or left. Groups of men stood by the bar with beer before lunch and brandy after lunch. The children ran about with balls, pool toys and ice cream cones. Extended family groups were seated around the restaurant tables underneath the pergola and horizontal sunblinds. There was human life, lots of it, human happiness poured into the family form. What was not as visible were the barriers between the groups. The people did not laugh and kiss and chat with everyone, only inside their own groups. But the others formed the appropriate background, the necessary atmosphere. The happiness would have had much less meaning if it had been hidden away in some private space, like a garden party, or played out among total strangers, like a beach.

The small children acted up, fell and cried, fought and cried, and generally acted like small children of all social classes. They used much the same language, too. "Don't be a beast!" "Grandma has arrived, can't you see, idiot!" "Dad, look what I can do!" "Mom, can I have another ice-cream? Then, why can he? And all the cousins, they had two for dessert already, and you promised..."

The teenagers talked much like other Madrilenian teenagers did, too. One young man told a friend that his group was leaving. The friend said he preferred to stay for a while longer. "OK, so you stay. You do what you feel like, man." Pronounced in quite a friendly manner. (Literally: Like whatever comes out of your balls. *Lo que te salga de los cojones.*) But then, how will I get home? "You gotta be street wise, man, find your own solution!" said the first young man, now more sharply. (Literally: Search for survival, man. *Búscate la vida, tío!*) Each single comment from a male teenager's mouth was shot through with the fad word "tío", literally uncle, in Madrid slang a general fill-in word with the approximate meaning of "man". The female teenagers used the same word almost as much when talking to boys and sometimes when talking to girls, but then in the female form, *tía*.

There was a father taking care of a baby on the terrace. That was not a common thing, but this young man did not seem to be aware of doing anything out of the ordinary. He was trying to rock a little girl to sleep in his arms, she was about one year old, she had a pacifier in her mouth and tears in her eyes; he rocked her, walked her, looked tenderly at her, talked softly to her... He was not playing a role for the benefit of the public nor was he trying to hide from the public. He was simply doing what ought to be done. But I was not the only one to notice the fact that it was a man doing it.

Around most of the tables, the families were now approaching dessert time, and there were lots of discussions, about what to have, about finishing your meat first, about wanting to run off and play... The mothers mopped up spilled coke, mediated in sibling rivalries, explained why certain desserts were not right... The fathers were mostly irritated or distant, playing the role of boss of the table, in charge of all direct communication with the waiters. The adults ordered different varieties of coffee and complained if the waiters got it wrong. If it had not been for the textile tablecloths, the brand name wine and the reserved deportment of the waiters, it could have been any family restaurant in a working class district.

At some of the tables, card games were already beginning. Mostly the players were either all of the same sex or else they were couples, but today I saw something new: at one table sat three men and one woman.

But most of the women sat with other women after lunch. At the table next to mine, a group of women were talking about some rural place one of them had been to recently. The others commented: "Oh no, uhuh, if someone invited me to spend three months at a place with no running water I would not even go, not me, not for a week even..." From other tables were heard comments on the usual themes: children's studies, shopping for clothes, recipes, school worries, relatives and their family problems, parents and their illnesses.

At one table sat five men in suits, but they had taken their jackets off. All five had white shirts and light grey suits. They were ordering brandy and anisette (male drinks in all classes) with the coffee. I thought they were business men on a business lunch, but

89

with their coffee they settled down to a game of cards. They talked a lot, shouting at the waiter from a distance, joking loudly. No table with all women ever occupied that much acoustic space.

After lunch, I changed and went into the pool area. Groups of women sat under trees, talking very little, resting and digesting the lunch. Since it was mid-week, most of the men who had come for lunch had gone back to the office. The few men left sat by themselves, reading a newspaper or just looking towards the horizon, the bleak dry Castilian landscape outside the club hedges which drew sharp lines between the green inside and the greyish yellow outside. The only couple I saw together was Sofía and her husband Alfonso. She was combing his hair. She often did, and the other women laughed about it, embarrassed. It was as if this tender attention and physical contact was immoral but immoral in such a subtle way that it could not be stopped, and therefore it was uncomfortable. And slightly ridiculous. Groups of teenagers lay on their towels in circles, heads together, chatting, teasing, joking, once in a while throwing someone into the pool. Otherwise the pool was empty, since digestion time was strictly observed. Younger children ran about.

I found Lupe in her usual corner, a sociable area near the pool where there was often rather free movement between the groups. Today she had a girl of about ten with her. Lupe herself had three children, all over twenty. She explained that this girl was her friend and neighbor Maite's daughter. Her name was Carmen. Suddenly the woman beneath the sunshade next to us reacted: "Carmen! Sure, why, I'm sorry I forgot! Congratulations!" She got up and kissed the girl on both cheeks. The girl looked embarrassed. Lupe laughed. "Oh, I am sorry too, so sorry, I completely forgot it was your saint's day today!"

Soon afterwards Maite arrived, and Lupe rebuked her jokingly for forgetting her daughter's saint's day. Maite laughed and said they never celebrate saint's days much in her family. A couple of other women on towels nearby joined the discussion and started to compare saint's day celebrations in their different regions of origin. The conclusion was soon reached that no matter where they came from, whether regions where saint's days are important or regions where they are hardly noticed, for these women they were a thing of the past. Sure, one kisses the person if and when one remembers, and perhaps small children get to invite their playmates for a snack, but that is about all.

Maite had brought some post cards she had received from one of her daughters and read them aloud. The teenage daughter was traveling around Europe by train, and Maite explained about a new kind of ticket for youngsters, really cheap, they can travel as much as they want to for one month, all over Europe. It was called Interraíl. I said that it was very popular in Sweden. None of the others had heard of it before.

Someone asked Maite if she was not worried about the girl. Sure, said Maite, but one has to let them go nowadays anyway, you can't stop them. The others nodded. "And she got very good grades in school, and we gave her brother an expensive skiing trip for

Easter while she had to stay home then to study, so now we had to give her something. But we did ask her to call home, collect, every other day, and so far she has, plus sent the post cards. Right now she is in Hungary. She is a very good girl, absolutely reliable, I have no reason to think she would do anything she knows she shouldn't." The others said of course, they did not question that (they had to make sure Maite did not take their question as an expression of doubts about Maite's moral standing), but one never knows, things can happen that are not her fault... Maite said that she was traveling with an older male cousin and two of his friends, apart from one girl friend. She said this in order to assure us that the girls were well protected, and she therefore a good mother in spite of her permissiveness, but the other women looked skeptical, as if they thought the risk was rather worse, then. The word sex was never mentioned, but that was evidently what the discussion was all about.

It was clearly a good moment to change the subject. Two women turned to the always popular one of traveling. One said that sure, Hungary, very interesting, but on the other hand she had heard that all the countries of Eastern Europe were in such bad shape that it was uncomfortable to travel there. The other one said that she and her husband were planning to travel around Galicia in August. "Even though we have been there already, of course. But we feel we want to see it again, to really get to know it. To travel more slowly, more at your own pace, to really enjoy it. You know, the first time there, the important thing is to see the cathedral..." The other woman filled in: "Yes, the first time you go wherever, you have no initiative." She said the first time she had been in Germany, "in each city we just got into buses and they took us places and I did not get much out of it." The first one: "Right, that is what we did too, you take one of those tours in order to know where you are, to get an idea, but then..." Both of them talked about how it is necessary to go abroad to educate yourself "but what we do wrong is when we go abroad without first getting to know our own country as one should."

The self-deprecating surface of these remarks clothed but did not hide the fact that they went to prove that they had all traveled a lot. That was what they wanted to demonstrate. At another level, the conversation was an instance of the cultural exploration of the techniques of traveling that in fact most people were just learning.

Somehow the travel talk led to a discussion about the youngsters of today. The strange atmosphere caused by the opinions on Maite's daughter's traveling had not been exorcised sufficiently; some repair of good feeling was needed. Sure, you have to give young people some freedom, the women said, but they go to extremes, they turn day and night inside out, they go out in the evening and stay out till early in the morning, then they sleep all day, and you can't say anything to them, because they will just protest that all the others do the same thing. And, true, they study very hard, and they have to, competition is hard, much worse than in our times, so certainly they need some relaxation. But when we were their age, we had fun with a lot less. And they don't really seem to have fun. They laugh less than we did, they have fewer friends, they don't seem to dream about anything.

One point they especially stressed was that youngsters today seem not to be romantic at all. "You see that they have a girlfriend or a boyfriend, but it is not the same thing, they do not feel the excitement we felt. I ask my son, but don't you dream about the future, and he says no, so I say that in that case it is not love, but he says it is... He says their love is different from ours."

Now the talk turned to change in general, as always happened when a conversation veered in an appropriate direction. There were all sorts of different opinions on what the change had meant, for better and for worse, and how young people had been affected. Lupe concluded on a note that all accepted: "Anyway, we cannot tell them anything and in part it is our own fault. The young people of today have seen their elders adapting in such lousy ways to so many things that have changed too fast, that they don't want that, they want other things. They can't see us as models."

Obviously, these women saw themselves as exceptional for their generation, however. They went on to criticize middle aged people in general and especially the "average" club members. They found them lazy and unintelligent. Lupe said, "They come to the club to forget. They just want to sit and not think at all! Why do you think they play such a lot of bridge?" I said that bridge requires some mental effort. "No, but what I mean is they just want to sit here, together, without having to talk." I protested that people were talking all the time, and this led us on to a discussion about friendship. All the women in this group said that they were good friends, but that most of the others were not, they were all very superficial. "They talk, but very superficially, about nothing really. And that is not real friendship. In a sense, there is no real friendship at the club. Saying hello because you see the same faces year after year, that is not friendship, not really. That is like not seeing reality."

In my terms, this was one instance in an ongoing negotiation about several cultural issues: the women distanced themselves from more conservative club members; they criticized traditional forms of sociability and groped for new definitions of friendship, and they tried to ground their arguments in the key criterion of Reason.

As usual in this kind of context at the club, the talk turned to the Opus Dei[85] members, and the judgments were uncharitable: they were unsociable outside their own closed circles, old-fashioned in their thinking, secretive, manipulative... There were anecdotes of Opus doings outside the club, too. But then Maite started to talk about her own voluntary church work. She wanted to make it clear that religion was important to her, and that her criticism of Opus Dei was not to be construed as anti-religious.

She had five children. I asked if that was due to religious beliefs. She laughed and said that the first few were, but after that... Carmen was the youngest one, so now Maite had started to work. "Real work, for a salary." She had found a job easily enough through some friends; at first she had helped out at their office without pay. It worked out fine at home, her husband agreed with her working, so he cooked during weekends, she cooked Monday through Friday. And they had paid help for cleaning, and the kids were pretty good at making their own beds and picking up things.

But it was difficult for her to work at first, for other reasons. She had never worked, not even before getting married. "And I thought it was all different. I was so naive, I thought it was more like church work, like wanting to contribute, like... like being with friends." Big laughter. "And then I saw that what people did was rather defending each one his little piece of ground."

At one point, Maite said that there were not many progressives at the club. I asked her what she meant, and explained that when I did my study in Valencia, everyone used the word "progressive" constantly, but that now I hardly ever heard it. The women were surprised. They had never really thought about the word. But they were rather clear about what it meant. It was a positive word to them. "It means that you don't stop cold in the tracks." "It means that you want to learn new things." "And that you are not closed to people and ideas, but open and receptive." "The opposite of Opus people," giggled Lupe.

We talked about how all the changes had forced people to improvise a lot. They said that it was certainly true that it was tiring in the long run not to have anything stable to lean on, to trust, to go by. "That may be why things are beginning to go backwards now." They did not seem to be very worried, but it was clear that they had negative feelings about this possibility. And not a little scorn. Just like the progressives in Benituria, these women felt very sure of being on the right side. It was the intelligent side, they thought, and probably the winning side, in spite of temporary backsliding.

In other words, the term progressive had the same referent and did the same cultural work as in the Valencian working class ten years earlier, even though it was much less frequently heard. It meant a positive stance towards change, and it served to draw a line between people who approved of change and those who did not. And just like in Benituria, substantial examples of change were not considered necessary. The implicit substantial referents were probably not the same, however, as the discussion of Maite's daughter's traveling goes to show. If any working class progressives had been present, they would have felt only contempt for the need to safeguard a young girl's virginity For them, the progressive stance would have been to approve explicitly of the girl's opportunity to learn and to enjoy herself. They might have felt there was danger involved, but they would not have said so. Middle class progressives, in less conservative contexts than Club Aguafría, would have reacted in the same way.[86]

As the sun started to go down behind the dressing room building, mothers called on their children and moved towards the outdoor or indoor showers. I saw some of the women of my usual group coming out, already dressed and on their way towards the afternoon snack and sociability session on the terrace. They motioned invitingly to me. And questioningly – it was not well accepted to sit in groups different from one's own usual one. Maite said she had to leave to go shopping with Carmen, she wanted to buy her a gift after all, and then she had to make dinner, some relatives were coming from out of town. Lupe said she would wait for her husband, he had said he would drop by the club after work and have a quick swim and pick her up.

Chapter 6. Space, Clothes and Activities

Let me now describe what was communicated about gender and related issues (especially family, children and body) in non-verbal ways at Club Aguafría. The most important symbolic codes were: clothes, the use of space and the type of activities. Naturally club members talked about these things, too, but that is exemplified in other chapters. We will see that all in all, gender was one of the main themes of club life, albeit always flexible and interweaving with other themes and principles of organization. The other two major themes of club life were socializing and class distinction. The first was recognized, verbalized, positive, but an ideal one knew one did not live up to as much as one would like; the second was enveloped in polite euphemisms, yet symbolically and emotionally quite strongly underlined.

To understand what the club meant, one must also situate it in the larger surrounding space. Let us do that by making an imagined trip from downtown Madrid to the club.

To arrive in another world

Many anthropological monographs begin with a description of the anthropologist's arrival to the field. The bus that climbs the winding mountain road, the ship that arrives to the island... It is a tempting device. But to place Club Aguafría, the relevant contrast is not with the surrounding physical landscape, or even the surrounding area called Aguafría, but with the social landscape of the whole city.

Let us imagine then, that we are in Madrid, somewhere downtown. Perhaps we have been taking a walk through the quaint quarters of old Madrid, where sturdy aristocratic buildings are grouped around narrow winding streets full of gaudy night life. Or perhaps we have been visiting friends in a peripheral working class area, where eight-story buildings stand in straight lines along streets bustling with traffic of all imaginable kinds, where children play on the sidewalks where also all the cars that could find no room on the streets are parked, where hardly a blade of grass can be found but balconies brim over with geraniums, and where all sorts of heavy odors float out from bars, restaurants, car body shops, hair dressers', vegetable stalls, bodegas... Then, perhaps we have taken another walk through the central bohemian quarters with its injection needles and dogs, poets and prostitutes, school children and housewives and philosophers and alcoholics... And if it is a summer day, we have probably rested at a side walk café on Gran Vía where watching the people walking by is more fun than going to a movie.

Now, we take the metro. We submerge ourselves in an underground world, with winding, dimly lit tunnels where humidity filters through the roofs, sometimes dripping and forming puddles on the floor, with beggars and musicians and hordes of illegal vendors wherever the tunnels open up to form underground cross-roads. We are lucky not to have to ride in one of the old rickety noisy trains, which are finally being taken out of service, but even the new trains are crowded and noisy. Our bodies are now hot and sweaty, feel dirty and tired.

We get out at the final station of this line. More tunnels, more crowded underground cross-roads, stairs to walk up or down, some escalators too, a bar and a newspaper stall... Finally fresh air and daylight. We are in a huge round open space where several major streets converge and the traffic rushes around to sort itself out towards other streets.

We find our bus stop, marked only by a metal sign on a post. We look longingly at the construction of small roofs going on at some of the other bus stops. Soon perhaps this bus stop, too, will have a roof to protect travelers from rain in the winter and the implacable Castilian sun in the summer. As it is now, there is not even a scrawny tree to give shade, except way off near a building, where some younger travelers, trusting their speedy legs, dare to await the bus, which, it is well known, will not await tardy customers. A woman in Romany clothing walks up. Several of the persons waiting in line take small sideways steps away from her and hold on to their purses. She stares at the maneuvers and hisses scornfully. We are steeped in the smoke from a churros stall nearby (churros are popular donut-like snacks fried in barrels of oil), and all around the big open area are dozens of stalls selling cheap earrings, leather belts, flowery blouses and shirts...

The bus is late again. It is supposed to leave every fifteen minutes, but there is no set schedule. The driver has to ward off criticism from the passengers as they climb aboard. He mutters and shrugs, it is not his fault, another driver is ill, you tell the company to employ more drivers, it is not as if there weren't hundreds of qualified drivers looking for jobs...

Since we are among the first in line, we get to sit down. Lucky thing, because the trip takes another half hour. Lucky, too, that the bus has air conditioning. We ride through wide streets teeming with traffic, then through streets with more elegant apartment houses along the sides, the social standing marked by narrow strips of grass in front of the entrances. We see a recently built shopping center where well-dressed women and well-behaved teenagers walk about in groups. Traffic is still heavy, until we pass under a freeway into Aguafría. Here the majority of the apartment buildings are set back in lush gardens, surrounded by metal fences and hedges. The sidewalks are almost empty, we see only some middle aged ladies on their way to church and a couple of young Philippine girls in tell-tale pastel-colored housecoats, the usual maid's uniform. Young people dash about on motorcycles.

We step off the bus into the afternoon heat, but to our surprise it is not as hot as before. The greenery all around sends out a welcome freshness.

As we walk through the entrance gate to the club, we realize that we are already marked. We do not belong. Our clothes cling to our sweaty tired bodies and we are on foot. Through the gate come air-conditioned cars with people looking as if they have just stepped out of the shower.

The street inside the gate is lined with parked cars and with trees and flowery shrubs. To one side are the tennis courts. No more traffic noise, just the soft tick-tack of tennis balls and the sleepy whizz from the irrigation. And some birds chirping. There are human voices, to be sure, but they sound muted and discrete, too. The people look as if they belong to another race: they look taller, blonder and healthier than people outside. They are taller and healthier, because they have good food and good doctors, but the blondness is mostly a matter of fashion and hairdressers. Some of the beautiful body shapes are false impressions, too, created by well-fitting garments, but since it is summer, some too-large bosoms and too-underdeveloped biceps are in view.

We pass the courteous watchfulness of the doorman, and the arrival story ends.

Club space

Madrilenians are category conscious in general. The areas of the city are defined by social status, and the space inside dwellings is demarcated by function. To this, conservative sectors of the middle and upper class add a striving for distinction from lower classes and a stress on "respect", meaning approximately symbolic hierarchy. They categorize people according to age and prestige at all times, and they feel an ideological distaste for disorder, i.e. there is a preference for clear categories as against improvisations or mixtures in any sort of context.

So it is natural that they should categorize club space, too, and that the important criteria should be the same ones as in social life in general: function, age and gender. Class was a decisive criterion for belonging to the club, but once inside it was not relevant, since it was taken for granted that all club members were of acceptable social standing. Approximate economic level may have influenced membership in the smaller groups, that was difficult for me to find out since it was a very sensitive issue, but whether or not it was one possible factor in group formation, it was clear that other factors were more important.

All the classifications were tinted with symbolic expressions of a cautious attitude towards the human body, especially sexuality. This was quite conscious and sometimes used to legitimate segregation (age: "I don't want the children around in case someone should happen to use certain words..."; function: "It is a good thing the hedges have grown so well; before, one could see the people around the pool from the parking lot ")

The arrangement of space was quite clear-cut. There was respect for all kinds of separations. One could even say that the generally cautious mode of management of meaning at the club had one of its clearest expressions in a cautious use of space. Many of the norms were spelled out in a set of written rules, the *Reglamento de régimen interior,* the breaking of which incurred formal sanctions, and there were also informal sanctions in the form of gossip and heavy social disapprobation of anyone who broke the rules, written or not. Many of them were quite specific about behavior in the various areas.[87]

Children were exempted from most of the rules. They must put on shoes and preferably some other piece of extra clothing when they moved outside the pool area, and they were never seen naked, but they moved freely between all the areas and behaved in a rather self-assured manner.

Club members socialized mainly in small-to-medium sized groups. Most had a group they belonged to, and there was little overlap or fuzziness at the frontiers between the groups. Most of the groups had their favorite corners of the various areas, but there was no monopolization of any facilities.

The sorting of ages was flexible, but only young people went to the disco parties, only small children and their parents participated in the children's parties that were arranged for Carnival and other occasions, only adults attended auctions of antiquities or art exhibitions, and so on.

The main areas of the club were as follows:

There was one main pool area surrounded by lawns where one could sun-bathe, a secondary area where one could rest in the shade of trees, and a third area around the children's pool. The whole pool area was surrounded by a high fence.

There were two ways to reach it. The normal one was to go by way of the building which housed the gymnasium, the showers and the areas for changing clothes. The showers and dressing areas were separated by gender, and only very small boys accompanied their mothers into the female side. Clothes-check-girls on one side and shallow pools to clean one's feet in on the other marked the limits of this liminal area, out of which one could only walk barefoot on one side or completely dressed on the other.

The other way to reach the pool area was by way of the so-called terrace. This was an area with tables, a bar, flagstone floors, flower beds, sunshades over the tables and high hedges separating it from the non-pool areas. It was possible to come into this area from the street or from the main building, as well as from the pool area, and this had to be so, since both swimmers and people who came to the club for other purposes might want a drink or a meal, and the indoors bar and restaurant were closed in summer. Therefore it was in theory also possible to walk from the street across the terrace directly to the pool. But that was not done. If one came to the terrace in street clothing, one left for the street. If one came to the terrace from the pool area, one was dressed in pool clothing and could therefore not go into the street at all.

Because the terrace was the only area where people in street clothes mingled with people in pool clothes, it was a liminal area in a much stronger sense than the dressing-building with its mere frontier-guarding role. More about that shortly.

Talking about the "generations" at the club (the founders, who were just becoming grandparents, the middle-aged adults and the young couples who were just becoming parents), one woman said, "Haven't you noticed the differences according to floors?" She was comparing the three pool areas to a building. "It is not as clear as it used to be, but you can still see it. The grandmothers like to sit up on the hill under the trees; then here around the pool are the normal people, like us, central ages in the central area; and down by the children's pool is where mostly the Opus Dei people used to sit, since they have so many children."[88]

The largest outdoor area was dedicated to ball sports: six tennis courts, two paddle tennis courts, one pelota court and one area for children's ball play.

The pool was not used for swimming very much. Children and youngsters did swim some but mostly just played. Many adults used it only in the same way they used the outdoor showers – to cool off every so often in order to withstand the rigors of sunbathing. Tennis, on the other hand, was a true predilection for many club members. The tennis courts were almost continually occupied, year round.

In view of the family ideology, the lack of facilities for children was strange, but could be explained partially with reference to the age structure of the club. It had been founded in the 1960s, and mostly young families had joined then, so there had been many children all during the 1970s, and there had been an indoors play room for them then, and the building called the Cabin had been mostly occupied by women with small children, while the men smoked and played cards in the main building. For a while the club had even employed two young women to watch over and play with the children. ("They wore uniforms and everything," said someone with pride.) But during the 1980s most of the children had become teenagers, and the indoors play room had been converted first into a ping-pong-room, later into a party room with music facilities. Since this second generation was now having children of their own, there was some talk of opening a new play room.

But the age structure and club history could not be the whole explanation, since there were club members of all in-between ages, too, and since some of the people who began having children in the early 1970s were still having more in the late 1980s. The ideological emphasis on family life was not matched by special facilities for children; children were rather liminal or free beings who played everywhere.

There were three main buildings. One was the dressing building with the gym. Another was the Cabin, a cottage-like structure with a somewhat rustic air. It consisted mainly of one large room with overstuffed couches and chairs, and coffee tables and folding card tables casually arranged around a huge free-standing fireplace, and a bar in one corner.

The main building was much larger. Like the Cabin, it had a terrace facing south. Indoors, it housed the offices, toilets, a coat room, a spacious entrance hall with a watchman's counter, the restaurant with its kitchen, a "library", a TV-room, a billiard room, the youngsters' party room, the main "salon" and several smaller "salons".

All the rooms called "salons" were furnished with several sitting groups, heavy lamps and big potted plants, and two of them had fireplaces. Carpets were a recent improvement. (Carpets are not a common item of Spanish furnishings in general, so they are powerful markers of distinction.) All the salons, in any combination, could be rented by individual members for private celebrations. But that was unusual. The everyday activity in the salons was to sit in groups talking, but one could also bring anything one wanted from the bar – drinks, coffee, snacks, fast food.

The bar was open all day. The restaurant was open from 2 to 4 PM for lunch and from 9 PM to midnight for dinner. The dining room was quite large. On weekdays it gave a forlorn impression, but during weekends it was necessary to book tables in advance.

The walls of the so-called library were covered with bookcases with glass doors, but only one of them held a few books; most of them donated by members I was told. In the others were prizes the club had won in bridge or tennis tournaments. There were newspapers, a few magazines and several catalogues from gift shops. A dignified silence always prevailed in the library. Sometimes there were youngsters studying, alone or in twos or threes. Usually it was empty.

The TV room was almost as quiet as the library except when there were popular programs, such as the South American soap operas at lunch time, which mainly women watched, or the news, which mainly men watched. There was thus always a tendency to gender segregation, but it was total only when important soccer games were transmitted; then the room was crowded with men only, of all ages, even the doormen peeping in from the hall.

One could grade the indoors spaces on a noise scale, from the well-respected silence of the library, via the murmur of polite conversation in the salons, the livelier conversations where cards were played (except during bridge classes and tournaments), the joking and laughing by the bar counters, and finally the din of family life in the dining-room at meal times. The only shouts heard were when important socccer goals were scored, then the TV room would explode and the enthusiasm or grief could be gauged throughout the building.

Quarrels were made invisible. If voices started to rise, someone would stop it before it went too far.

There was a gender difference in the use of acoustic space as well as in body movement. Just like in other Madrilenian contexts, the men strode with longer steps than the women, gestured more widely, called the waiters or shouted greetings or each other's names across longer distances, and so on. But at the club, this gender difference was not very pronounced. The men drew a fine line between approved male expressivity and what they would have considered vulgarity. The women were as subdued as "elegance" required, and that included some deference to men in the usual European and Mediterranean ways, and it included a definition of femininity as low visibility. But this tendency was balanced, sometimes cancelled, by the general Spanish disposition for self-affirmation (cf Thurén 1988), so that a woman upset, a woman enthused or a woman surprised, could temporarily use as much space as any man for both body and voice.

My activities were compatible with the club style of interaction, as long as I adhered to all the norms myself. Even when I carried out the mini-survey on women's employment (cf chapter 16) and systematically approached people to whom I had not been introduced, this was gracefully accepted. There was only one piece of club space that I was asked to treat in a special way. The administrator asked me not to approach unknown people in the dining-room. "You know what meal-time means in Spain. It's the time to relax, to be with the family, people don't want interruptions then. Later, when they are having coffee, that's another matter..."

I agree with him that meal-time is holy for Spaniards of all categories. And it was true that the family was the sorting principle in the dining-room. Except for business lunches on weekdays and occasional group dining, people did not have their meals in the company of friends but with their families, on Sundays usually extended families. Only after dessert and coffee would they get up and move around and sort themselves in different ways. What usually happened then was that the friendship principle took over, and then gender, age and mode of management of meaning also became relevant criteria for whom one sat down with.

On Sundays, year-round, families with small children would arrive and leave together. Teenagers arrived and left with their parents or by themselves or in groups. On weekdays during the summer, women would arrive early with the younger children, and their husbands and older children when office and school hours permitted. On weekday afternoons in winter time, the club was rather empty, and the people who were there had usually made arrangements by telephone first.

In some groups, couples socialized together; in other groups women and men separated on arrival. The Cabin was dominated by groups of men only, playing cards. The main salon in the main building was dominated by groups of women only, talking. Usually only men stood by the bar counters, especially in the indoors bars. Women ordered whatever they wanted and then sat down. The indoors bars were liminal areas, too. A person could have a beer there after a game of tennis without having to shower and change clothes first. I never saw a woman do this, however. For men, the bar was also the place to go if they did not find any of their friends, so there were sometimes solitary men there. Women without company were seldom seen anywhere. If they could not find their friends, they might sit down alone in a salon, but they would be uncomfortable, and they might prefer to join their husband in the bar or even by a table with card-playing men while they hoped for some female friends to show up.

Summing up, we can say that the different spaces of the Club were quite well defined by function and noise level. Gender and age were always relevant principles of categorization, but they were flexibly applied. The permanent groups of friends were based on shared interests and opinions, and husband and wife always belonged to the same group, while children and teenagers formed their own groups.

Of the various principles for organizing space and interaction, gender, age and function were conscious and verbalized, while opinions and mode of management of meaning were not. Age and function organized as much as or more than gender, and in contrast to gender they were considered legitimate principles one could and would refer to. Nevertheless, gender was the only principle that was always present and always carried a symbolic load. People were never unaware of the gender composition of a group or the dominance of one gender or the other in an area, and there was no playing with gender symbols, no ambiguities permitted.

Clothing and bodies

The human body was the key symbol for all the categorizations and for the gender regime of the club as a whole.

There is an old tradition of suspicion of the body in the Mediterranean area. In Christian countries it has been reinforced by Christian norms and expressed as Christian feelings. I am thinking of the complex treatment of sexuality, but also of little everyday things like women covering their hair and arms in church, nuns' cover-all dresses and the pupils' drab uniforms in religious schools.

The norms vary in time and space, of course, and also according to personal inclinations. In Spain in the 1990s, conservative Catholics still felt strongly about "propriety" in dress, by which were meant that one should dress so that the shapes of the body were blurred, and female shapes must be hidden more carefully than male ones. (Cf Yolanda's explanation from the Opus Dei point of view in chapter 17.) But this norm was not always easy to translate into practice. At Club Aguafría, the dress code was influenced by three equally important criteria: "propriety", "elegance" and "modern leisure." Simplifying, we can say, that propriety tended to cover up and elegance tended to underline and uncover the body, while modern leisure did either according to function, which meant that it sometimes went much farther towards nakedness than elegance would (e.g. bikinis), while at other times it covered up much more than propriety would require, but did so in a way that went counter to both propriety and elegance (e.g. bulky jogging dresses).

The contradictions were resolved in various ways according to groups and also in different ways by women and men. Women had to be much more cautious, men could be more leisurely. The management of the body was especially crucial in summer around the swimming pool, where anti-body feelings clashed with the modern requirement of exposing the body to the sun (and possibly to the water). The problem was solved by very careful management of space and by small symbolic markers to tone down the nakedness.

We have already seen the cautious management of space around the pool area. It was separated from the rest of the club premises by fences and hedges. The normal and correct way to pass in and out of the pool area was by way of the dressing room, where each individual body was transformed to fit the rules for the other side of the fence. This building was thus a liminal area where different-looking bodies must be carefully separated. The frontiers between the building itself and the worlds on either side were also marked, most clearly by the shallow foot-pools towards the pool side. They were built in such a way that it was impossible to bypass them. If one wanted to take shoes into the pool area, one had to take them off and wade barefoot through the foot-pool. Another foot-pool (somewhat easier to bypass) separated the pool area from the terrace.

It is significant that the written club rules included many specific rules on dress for the different areas, and that there were especially many about the pool area. It is also significant that the dress rules were well respected (while for instance the prohibition of eating food in the pool area was freely violated and this did not cause much comment, and I doubt if anyone took seriously the prohibition of tobacco and alcohol for minors).

In the pool area, everyone wore bathing suits, since it was mandatory, but middle aged women would sometimes drape a piece of material around their waist or wear a big unbuttoned blouse over the bathing suit. Only very young women, or women with exceptionally good figures, wore bikinis. Small girls, too, wore suits covering their nipples. Teenage girls would often throw a t-shirt over their shoulders or tie a towel around their waist. There was also a clear difference between lying down and moving around. As soon as a woman got up to walk somewhere, she would ascertain that the bathing suit had not slipped out of place anywhere, and she would often add some of the little extra pieces of clothing.

The men also preferred to use more material than average Spanish men did on a public beach. I saw no men in "slip"-type swimming trunks for example; they all used the boxer shorts model, sometimes knee length. This was true for small boys, too. Just like the women, the men were careful to put on sandals and a shirt to go to the terrace, and they might put on a shirt when moving around.

Another way to disguise the nakedness was to wear jewelry. Most of the women wore gold chains around their necks, and ear-rings and finger-rings and sometimes bracelets at all times in the pool area, even when they went into the water.

One reason middle aged women did not swim very much may even have been that wetness underlines the nakedness of the body. Another was that many of them did not know how to. If they did swim, they hardly ever wet their hair. The fact that the women did not move around very much in the pool area also had to do with body self-consciousness. Young people of both sexes ran about a lot, and the adults commented on that, saying that "youngsters like to show themselves off." To move about without much clothing on, then, was to show one's body. That might be permissible for youngsters, but it was doubtful to what extent, and for middle aged women it was risky, for reasons of decency as well as for reasons of prestige, since their bodies were no longer as beautiful as they should be in order to offset the moralistic principle with that of beauty or modernity.

The feeling for propriety was considered correct and morally good, but also somewhat old-fashioned. It must not be overdone. And just what was overdoing it was different for different groups. I am sure it was no coincidence that I was told innumerable times the story about how bikinis were permitted at the club. It was a story of a clash between two dress codes. It went like this: Up until a few years ago, bikinis were forbidden at the club. But they had been fashionable on the beaches for many years, and the topless fashion was already arriving in Spain, too. So a group of young girls decided to start wearing their bikinis at the club to see what would happen. They were warned by the administrator and then by the board, so they had to stop. But then a sympathizing middle-aged woman invented a trick, which the younger rebels soon imitated: she made a bathing-suit for herself that looked very much like a bikini but was technically one-piece, because she sewed on a string of material uniting the upper and lower parts in front. This precipitated a dramatic vote at the next general assembly, which the pro-bikini people won by a narrow margin.

The terrace was just as liminal as the dressing-building in that it separated the pool area from the rest of the premises. It was less liminal in that it did not allow for the nakedness of showers and backstage manipulations like combing hair and making up faces, but it was more liminal in that it allowed mingling of people in street clothes and people in pool clothes. To make this possible, the people in pool clothes had to put on some extra pieces of clothing and wear shoes, and the people coming in from the street usually signaled some relaxation in dress, for instance taking off jackets and ties and adopting relaxed body postures.

At lunch time, the women wore their bathing suits but covered them with long loose blouses and/or big pieces of material draped around the body and tied above the bosom. Children up to about ten could wear their swim suits only, but often their mothers insisted on putting at least a shirt on the boys and a short skirt or shorts on the girls. On hot days this was a source of conflict between mothers and children. Men wore their swim suits and unbuttoned shirts.

Around eight o'clock, the people who had spent the day by the pool got dressed. The usual dress for an evening on the terrace (beer, snacks, card games, perhaps dinner) was shirts and sports slacks for the men; the women emerged from the dressing building well combed, perfumed and with make-up on, wearing good quality cotton shifts with bare shoulders, preferably with a matching short-sleeved short jacket to put on after dark, or perhaps a straight cotton skirt and a light colored short-sleeved blouse. Once dressed, they seemed to move more gracefully and talk more.

After dusk, the mixed-type dress that was acceptable at the terrace as a liminal area during the day disappeared. The excuse for the relative nakedness had been the requirements of sun and water, so when the sun went down and the pool closed, the body had to be presented according to the principles of propriety and elegance only. The nakedness that "modern leisure" required was marked off in both time and space.

Winter dress was much less problematic, since there was no question of nakedness. But for the women there was still an issue of propriety versus elegance. In most of the groups propriety won. Madrid had become a fashion city in the late 1980s, and in downtown nightlife there was plenty of imaginative dressing. But at the club, there was little daring.

The usual club dress for women for a winter afternoon was skirt and blouse. The skirt should not be too narrow but straight, not wide and loose, although pleats were acceptable. The blouse should be cotton or silk and freshly ironed. Whereas the skirt was almost always in one color only, and a rather dark one, the blouse could have some pattern and could be any color. A strict pant suit was also acceptable in most groups. The shoes were usually pumps with medium size heels. Almost all the women had fur coats, and usually they wore colorful silk scarves which they did not always take off with the coat but left over the shoulders for a while or sat and played with. Or, if a woman had a skirt which tended to creep upwards as she sat, she would drape the scarf over her knees, to cover them but at the same time to show off the beauty of the scarf. The hair-dos were impeccable, usually short and permanented. Not a grey hair in sight on anyone below sixty. A woman who wore her hair long had to have exceptionally beautiful hair. Long hair was sensitive because it expressed the dilemma of propriety versus elegance, and it did so in the dangerous language of sensuality, but hair had long been a reasonably allowable symbol of sensuality in Spain.

The men were slightly more casual. They too would always be very well ironed, showered and perfumed, but they avoided the kind of suits they all wore at work. They generally preferred casual slacks, white or pastel-colored shirts (sometimes striped but never any other patterns), and in winter they would usually wear a sweater in "masculine" colors, such as brown, beige, dark blue, dark green or dark wine-colored.

Compared to their everyday apparel, the women dressed up for the club and the men dressed down. This makes sense, because for both genders it was a way of marking off club life as leisure. Most of the women were housewives and did not have to dress up at home, where nobody could see them, and domestic chores require practical clothing. Almost all the men worked in offices where they had to dress in strict suits. The men came to the club to see friends, as opposed to colleagues or clients, so they did not have to show off as much as at the office; the women came to the club to see friends, as opposed to being alone, so they wanted to show off more.

The different groups at the club had different dress codes. They all subscribed to the general preference for propriety over elegance or originality, but some emphasized leisure more than others, and some individuals were more interested in fashion. Some club women were knowledgeable about fashion because they had boutiques of their own or worked in boutiques. They would sometimes test the limits of propriety, but suggestively sensual dress was never seen. Women's summer dresses were made of thin, cool materials but never of the kind that clings to the skin. The men never wore imaginative shirts, they never wore their shirts sexily half open, they never wore scarves or other colorful details, they never wore attention-catching belts, and their slacks never hugged their behinds.

All middle class Madrilenians adhered to a code of propriety, to some degree, but it was not usually interpreted as strictly as it was at Club Aguafría. In the rest of Madrid there were two other principles that contradicted propriety in dress, apart from elegance and leisure. One was originality. Dressing was one arena on which the disposition for self-affirmation could be played out and find many expressions. The other one was what we can call the code of progressivity, i.e. a way of dressing that signaled an expansive mode of management of meaning and left-leaning political opinions. This meant tight blue jeans for both men and women most of the time, colorful shirts for men at least during leisure, and in general not very sensual dressing but less emphasis on the clearly anti-sensual. Big ear-rings were important for women according to this code, too, but they should not be gold, they could or even should be bought from street vendors or in artisan boutiques. Strong colors and unusual materials could be used by both women and men. This dress code communicated an opposition to the idea that the body must be hidden or down-played, and this in turn communicated opposition to the whole set of opinions and "traditions" associated with "proper" middle class life. The absence of this dress code at Club Aguafría could be interpreted as one more mark of status. One more kind of symbolic hedge.

If one is of the opinion that the body is something dangerous or ugly that should be hidden, and if one participates in a constant game of prestige, it becomes important to hide the body with expensive clothes in such a way that one is assured of prestige points for quality and decency. Extra points for elegance would be welcome, but one would rather forgo them than risk possible minus points for too much daring, "bad taste".

For people who participate in the same constant game for prestige, but who have changed their basic idea about the body, it becomes important to emphasize the body, instead. That was probably the reason for the extremely small bikinis seen on Spanish women on some beaches, and it was clearly the reason for the great interest in fashion among many middle class women. For the working class, fashion was too expensive, and the work both women and men did require practical clothing, so both women and men used a practicality criterion above all. But they hid their bodies, too, because they usually shared the Christian definition of the body as something to be hidden.

The new Madrilenian middle class, as a whole, was an improvising set of people. They had lived through basic changes in all aspects of life, so they knew that categories are not forever. One must change some things, while other things change themselves whether one likes it or not, so one has to adapt. New categories must be developed, and one needs to experiment. The fact of gender as a cultural categorization becomes visible, and it becomes at least semi-permissible to play around a bit with it (cf chapter 4 on Pedro Almodóvar's films). Even the basic idea of strict categorization is no longer self-evident. Flexibility might be an alternative.

But at Club Aguafría, most people did not want to doubt. They wanted to guard against change and reinforce the threatened categorizations. Experimentation was out of bounds. Or, if tried, drama would ensue, as in the bikini story.

Activities

As we have seen, the most important activity at the club was socializing, and the most important aspect of socializing was talking. One could even say that all other activities, rules, areas and rhythms were adapted to that main purpose. For many members, other activities served mostly as excuses for arranging satisfactory situations for socializing.

However, the activities had symbolic significance, too. The club leadership expressed a wish to "modernize" the club, and used this as the main argument for building the gymnasium, for reforming some ball courts and for introducing bridge tournaments. Some club members were happy that bridge had become so popular, since they felt this increased club prestige, and they were also the ones who would sometimes express a certain contempt for the many (and almost all male) members who insisted on continuing with the "popular" games of mus[82] and domino.

Year-round activities

Tennis was foremost among the organized activities. The club organized lessons for beginners, there were constant club tournaments between members and city-wide tournaments against other clubs. The climate of Madrid permits outdoor tennis year round, except for an occasional very cold winter day and except for midday hours in summer. Mus and domino were played year round, too, as well as bridge, canasta and other "salon games", as they were called.

Other year-round but less regular activities were:

- Dinners. Perhaps with an invited lecturer, or to celebrate something and/or give awards to the winners of some tournament.
- Special festivities, e.g. Carnival, New Year's Eve or an Andalusian evening at the time of the great spring feast in Seville.
- Private celebrations.
- Art exhibitions. For the opening, the artist would offer drinks and snacks to all visitors, and there would be quite a crowd circulating, looking, commenting, and then sitting down in their usual groups to talk until dinner time, when everyone would go home as usual.

- Commercial arrangements. For example, a fashion show. But the general club policy was to be restrictive with anything that might be interpreted as giving special privileges to anyone, member or outsider.

- The restaurant was open in all seasons, of course. Its prices were modest. Sunday lunch at the club was a focused year-round activity; more people came in summer, but for the club regulars, it was in winter that Sunday was the high point of the week, when "everyone" would be there.

Summer activities

Most of the activities were seasonal. The summer season counted from the time the pool opened, May 15, until it closed, September 15. In Madrid, the weather usually permits swimming later than that, but after vacations people did not feel like prolonging summer activities. August was somewhat slow, too, because it was the vacation month and club members traveled a lot, but those who stayed in Madrid came regularly to the club "to breathe". In June and July the club was crowded all week and even more during weekends. Some members came only in summer. There were special summer activities like swimming contests and pool games, mostly for children.

The permanent socializing groups were the same as in winter, but they were more blurred. It was easier to move from one group to another around the pool. There was always the excuse of going into the pool or to the terrace for an ice-cream, and on the way you could stop to greet and chat with anyone you happened to meet. There were also many temporary and ill-defined groups, since there were many who did not belong to any of the permanent year-round groups, and their presence made it easier for everyone to transcend the usual divisions. Many more youngsters than in winter would come, too, and their horseplay would add liveliness to the atmosphere.

Lunches were eaten in family groups, or just mothers and children if the fathers could not make it. The hour of general socializing was at dusk. The main activities were talking and card games as usual. Around ten, some would prepare to leave, to go home for dinner, but in summer in Madrid it is delicious to sit outdoors at that time of day, feeling the temperature soften. So some groups of friends or families would have dinner there; others ordered sandwiches and snacks with their afternoon drinks so that later they did not feel like any "real" dinner. They would just sit, "cool-bathing" (*tomar el fresco*, literally "take the cool").

Winter activities

The main activity in winter was socializing and talking. On sunny Saturdays and Sundays, the terrace of the main building would be crowded with families having lunch there; on cold days they would have lunch indoors; and on such days it might be almost as necessary as in the summer to book a table at least a few hours ahead of time.

On weekdays, on the other hand, the club would be almost empty during the day, except if there were special events. Most people would come only if they participated in some special activity, such as classes or tournaments. Towards five o'clock, the time for after lunch coffee, a few groups of women friends from the most regular groups might arrive. A few more would come around eight, with their husbands. On Fridays, Saturdays and Sundays the regulars counted on finding their friends just like in summer. They would sit around the fireplaces, talking, playing cards. Tennis and bridge players would come and go as their schedules required, leaving and rejoining the larger groups to which they belonged.

There had been gymnastics classes a couple of years earlier, just when that started to become fashionable among middle class women. But few had attended, and those few had soon given up. They said that it was uncomfortable, since there was no real gymnasium. They had to do it in the main salon, the floor was hard and cold, and it was too cold to go down to the dressing building to shower afterwards. I am sure these explanations were sincere, but I am quite sure that it was also uncomfortable for the women to more or less undress and to move in strange postures in a place where non-participants of either sex might look in, and where they were usually so careful to conserve propriety. During 1991 a gym was built and a physical education teacher was hired on a part time basis for the following season. It was taken for granted that the classes would be for women, but some body building apparatus for men was being purchased.

The so-called cultural activities were popular. The club organized city walks, lectures and visits to museums (cf chapter 7) as well as some excursions. The popularity was noticeable in the number of participants as well as in the prestige it gave to be able to tell others that one took part.

Familism and children

The club defined itself as a family club. It strove for "a very healthy atmosphere" for adults, children and youngsters alike. It wanted to promote family togetherness. It wanted to provide a place to relax without such drawbacks as the wrong kinds of people or morally doubtful activities. Politics and professional contact-making were banned, tolerance and playfulness were the keys. The dominant discourse had it that everyone knew everyone, or could get to know everyone if they wanted to. There should be no clique-building and no hierarchies. Everyone addressed each other by the first name and the informal pronoun of address, tú.[20]

Naturally, dominant ideology seldom coincides totally with practice. But the overlap at the club was rather large. And the reasons people gave for being members coincided nicely with club ideology: to give the children a roomy place to play during weekends, to get out of the house and meet people without spending a lot of money, to do sports to keep in shape, to widen their circle of acquaintances, to have a place to meet their friends under relaxed conditions.

But not everyone knew everyone. One of the most common complaints (especially from relatively new members) was that the club atmosphere was "closed", i.e. that it was difficult to get to know people. "People function in groups," they said. Another constant complaint was that the atmosphere was not at all relaxed but centered on the need to aparentar.

Nor was the atmosphere as family centered as members and board liked to affirm. Certainly there were plenty of children around, but there were few special facilities for them. They mostly ran about freely, and they would certainly be admonished if necessary by anyone who happened to be near. But their presence was never very emphasized and perhaps not really desirable. They would play on their own, and when they came up to the parents' tables on various errands, the parents would usually show a slight irritation. They would comply with the children's wishes if they were about ice-cream, handkerchief, water or bandaids, but it was uncommon for a parent to get up and go and see what had happened if a child complained of abuse from another child or from club personnel, and I hardly ever saw a parent play with their children except in the pools.

In other words, it was clear that the adults came to the club to be with their adult friends, and the children came along and were expected to take care of themselves. And so they did, just fine most of the time. But of course it happened that some child stood by a parent's chair whining, without letting itself be persuaded to "go and play" ("¡Vete a jugar!" was the standard parent command, hardly ever elaborated with any specific suggestions). This was experienced as awkward, almost shameful, by the adults. It was difficult to combine the upkeep of perfect social façades with children's requirements. A whining child was a symbol of weakness, failure, and it was an inconvenience for the most important activity, that of adult conversation.

The children were not emphasized, then, as growing individuals. But they were emphasized as links in the construction of families. The conversations almost always contained plans for future weddings and comments on recent ones, and newborn children were always greeted with great enthusiasm the first few times they were shown off at the club. Everyone who had any connection at all to the parents would come up to look at them and comment on them, not so much their looks, size and health, although that too, as the fact that the family in question had increased, that so-and-so had become a father, so-and-so had become a grandmother for the third time, so-and-so had become an aunt for the first time, and so on.

This great emphasis on the family as an institution and as a source of emotional satisfaction, in combination with the ideological emphasis on couple relationships and socializing in permanent groups, had several consequences for gender at the Club. For example, it made it almost impossible for a separating couple to remain members. It made it unlikely that separated, divorced or unmarried individuals would apply for membership. It made it necessary for professional women to demonstrate that they were good mothers and wives, in spite of their other interests. It made it necessary for mothers of near-adult children to show pride in their accomplishments and especially demonstrate strong emotional commitment to their steps towards family building of their own, and play down deviations from the normal paths. It made it difficult to discuss that which is discussed more than almost anything else in general Madrilenian conversation: the changing gender roles in Spanish reality, and the many urgent and painful issues related to that.

The subtext of the conservative Spanish discourse on the family was that gender roles should not and could not be changed; that would be against nature and everyone would suffer. As a whole, Club Aguafría could be read as an ideological text translated into social practice that went to prove that the Family was alive and well. In this sense, Club Aguafría was extremely gender conservative.

Still, there were degrees, as we saw in the previous chapter and as will be discussed in chapter 8. And in the next chapter we will see what the most extreme form of gender conservatism looked like.

Chapter 7. Cultural Fridays – Civilization and Misogyny

The new middle class based its position on merits. The men had studied to obtain special knowledge and sell it in exchange for good salaries. Some of the women had studied, too, but far from all, and those who had studied had usually not kept up to date after becoming housewives. Add to all of this the fact that one of the concepts with which social inequality was legitimated was "education", and it becomes obvious why the middle-class women found it highly desirable to improve their standing and image when it came to learning.

Of course this was not what they said. They felt that "culture" was interesting and elegant and that their "education" (whether understood as formal studies or as innate class qualities or just good behavior in general) qualified them for understanding and enjoying it. So they looked for it. But few found their way to any sophisticated forms of art and even fewer to active practice. I did not even meet very many who played the piano, but music, painting, gardening and ceramics were among the most common forms of practice among women who had any interest in art at all.

"Culture" was more consumed than practiced. The most common form while I was in Madrid was for a group of women to gather once a week to visit monuments, churches or museums together, usually with some guide or teacher. In this way the absorption of knowledge was rendered socially visible and also, because of its sociability, more enjoyable than lonely endeavors like reading. This type of activity was arranged by many kinds of organizations.

Most members of Club Aguafría whom I asked about club activities mentioned "city walks" and "visits to museums" among the things that were most popular "especially with the ladies". They always hinted at a large etcetera, but the only real example I was given was that of one group during the previous winter season. Possibly this activity was relatively new, but club members liked to think of it as firmly established.

I want to describe this activity here, first because it was a representative activity for middle class women in general, second because it was a prestige activity at Club Aguafría, and third because it was intimately connected to both the economic base of the new middle class (educational merits) and to the asymmetrical division of labor (and merits) between women and men.

One further reason is that the discourse that dominated during the Club Aguafría "cultural Fridays" (as they were called) was a rather extreme example of the conservative version of the club discourse. We will also see that although the male teacher and the female participants agreed on most aspects of this discourse, the women protested when its misogyny was expressed too literally. In other words, the description will show where the line was drawn between the discourse accepted as conservatively normal and what was unacceptable as too reactionary". (What was unacceptable in the opposite direction, that of "too progressive", was what much of the cultural negotiation was otherwise about at the club, as we saw in the example of Maite's daughter's traveling, in chapter 5.)

During my year at Club Aguafría, three series of cultural events were arranged, all with the same leader, a university art professor. Let us call him Vicente. He became very popular among the women, in spite of his authoritarian style and ferocious misogyny. The participants were in awe about his "solid knowledge" and "brilliant expositions".

Series I: Old Madrid

The first series consisted of walks in the old parts of Madrid. Each week the group visited products of a certain time period, mostly churches but also convents, bridges, authors' homes, palaces, parks. Some forty persons, all women, paid the "tuition fee" but only about twenty took part regularly. Vicente stopped at street corners to point to façades and statues, went into churches and had the women sit on benches while he talked about paintings and sculptures and the tombs of famous men, and sometimes stopped in a park or on an open square to give some general background. The information was generously interspersed with anecdotes and more sparsely with sarcastic references to leftist ideologies, radical youth and the present Spanish government. The women liked the anecdotes, even when they were a bit risqué, but they disliked and never commented on the political references. As far as I could tell this was not because they disagreed, but rather because they did not understand, since they were not interested in politics, or perhaps they just felt that such comments were in bad taste.

This series took place in November and December. The weather was usually humid, grey and cold, between five and ten degrees centigrade. The ladies wore fur coats almost without exception, but no one ever covered her head and most wore silk stockings and high heeled pumps. The walks never lasted for more than an hour, but there were always complaints: that it was too cold to be outdoors, why did we have to stand still for so long, the teacher took us only to places where we could not sit down... One day I covered my head with a wool scarf and drew lots of laughs; it was taken for granted that I did it as a joke. To these women, a scarf-covered woman looked like a peasant. For some of them, but not all, it was unfeminine to wear slacks. To wear boots on the coldest days was acceptable, but only just.

The walks started at twelve and finished around one. For the next hour or more we stood or sat in little bars, having wine or beer and tapas[21]. The teacher took it upon himself to show us "traditional" bars, local corner bars with local steady clienteles but special because they were in the old parts of town and because they had old-fashioned furnishings and perhaps some old-fashioned tapa specialty. The women found the facilities and the customers of those bars almost as exotic as foreigners would, but they enjoyed the tapa foods with expertise: they knew how to cook something similar, they had an old recipe from their village, their mother had always said, their husband preferred.... Some of them wrote down addresses. Once somebody suggested that we ought to arrange similar walks by night, along with the husbands, to visit "these bars that belong to our culture but that you never go to otherwise". The suggestion was met with apparent enthusiasm but was never brought up again.

The walks certainly took us through parts of Madrid where this type of middle class person did not often set foot. One day we walked through a rundown area close to my home, and I was surprised and amused when I realized that I felt scared along with the others; later I understood that this was not only due to mass suggestion. Having lived in downtown Madrid for some years, I had learned how to pass more or less unnoticed among prostitutes, pick-pockets and drug dealers, but in the company of twenty fur coats and kilos of jewelry my sense of danger was realistic.

Some of the comments Vicente made to have us laugh were of the usual joking-conservative variety of discourse on sexuality.[22] For example:

– As we entered the church at Quiñones Street, he explained that the well-known equivocal expression "I saw you at Quiñones" comes from the fact that there was a house of prostitution next to the church. "You know, there is usually a brothel next to each church!"

– We were admitted into a chapel belonging to a convent of secluded nuns. "It is strange, isn't it, that there are still places like this, in the middle of this modern noisy Madrid of ours, these little nuns (*monjitas*) completely hidden away... In this convent they do not even have any heating, so I am sure they keep cool (*estarán fresquitas*), the poor little ones (*las pobrecitas*)!" The insistence on talking about the nuns in the diminutive had the effect of associating them with asexual little girls, but also reminded us of their bodily individuality. Vicente reinforced this with lots of anecdotes about sexual relationships of nuns with priests, monks and kings.

In spite of the ladies' generally good opinion of Vicente, and even though they were quite accustomed to listen to male sarcasms about the shortcomings of females, they were irritated with Vicente's evident misogyny. Sometimes it fused with his authoritarianism. Examples:

– Walking through the narrow streets of central Madrid it was not always possible to keep a big group together. Whenever a part of the group was held up by a red light or a car parked across the sidewalk, he grumbled about "lazy women".

– Once in a park, one woman climbed a stone rim to hear better and he made her step down again. "I am the teacher! You women always try to be important!"

– In the beginning the women were eager and interrupted him often with questions, but he effectively put a stop to that by answering things like: "If I tell it all here in the street, there will be nothing left to tell you once we are inside!" or "Do you want to tell it all or will you leave it to me to organize the lecture?"

114

Once in a while the women answered back. "Now, that was too much! We are not idiots!" Once Vicente excused himself, saying that it was not easy to tell a lot of things in a short time, in a digestible form and with all the traffic noise in the background. But usually the women said nothing, and usually Vicente put them in their place if they did.

On one occasion, telling a story about some woman who died young, he added, without any apparent reason, that seeing how difficult women are, it would be better if they would all be so kind as to do that. In the next church he said something about how priests were a difficult lot. Paquita said, with sharp sarcasm: "I thought women were the difficult lot!" Vicente answered quickly, "They are, but priests are even worse." Paquita laughed, both angry and amused, "Well, I am glad to hear that at least!" For a few seconds there was mutiny in the air but then the women settled down to their usual style of graceful bantering, pretending – even believing? – it was all just good fun.

Later in the bar, however, one said straight to his face, albeit with a charming flirtatious smile, that he was a misogynist. He answered more calmly now, and also with a flirtatious smile, that of course, he had to suffer so many women, about seven hundred university students plus several big groups of housewives. "And almost every day, mind you!" Several women in chorus: "And what about us! We have to suffer our husbands! Every single day!" Suddenly Consuelo asked Vicente what he thought, really, seriously now, about the modern Spanish woman. He turned serious and fiddled nervously with his cigarette, reflected for a few seconds and then said that he thought the Spanish woman was a treasure, in foreign countries there was no one like her, she knew how to cook as well as sew... Consuelo laughed with bitter irony: "Yes, listen to that! She cooks and sews!" But Vicente would not be interrupted: ".. And she knows how to raise children as well as how to work."

Matilde whispered to me: "I think he is a misogynist, racist, anti-clerical, anti-communist – and neither is he a rightist!" We giggled over her politico-grammatical creativity. Another woman overheard and added: "Right, the generally embittered kind."

On another occasion when Vicente said something about bad women, Celia protested: "The problem with us is rather that we are too good." "Too submissive," added I (it was difficult to keep quiet). Other women agreed and repeated: "Right, too submissive you said it." That day Vicente did not come along to the tavern. The women criticized his style. "He gives us little anecdotes instead of real information." "He thinks we are idiots." "Or else he thinks we are not really interested – but just because we are housewives, it does not mean that we are not seriously interested!" "He probably does not consider it worthwhile to prepare the lectures carefully just for us."

But in spite of these mini-rebellions, most of the participants were very satisfied. Several took notes, some of them said they would take their children along on the same walks later. One lady said she wanted to bring a recorder so that she could send the tapes to her daughter who was studying abroad.

When Vicente was present, the conversations in the taverns were usually about what we had seen or else just flirtatious banter. But when he left, the women reverted to their usual housewife shop talk: children, parents, illnesses, housework, festivities with relatives. There were also comments about how they had arranged things to be able to spend the morning out of the house. "People think housewives don't do anything, but if you don't organize everything carefully you don't get any free time at all, and if you don't do the things you have to do, you yourself suffer the consequences."

As to religion, it was taken for granted throughout the cultural events that all participants were believing and practicing Catholics. But nothing was taken for granted about their knowledge of religious art, Church history, etc. As to popular expressions of faith, it was taken for granted that it was something they should not know anything about. One day we visited the Church of La Paloma, the Dove. The Virgin of the Dove, a painting in this church, is venerated by the people of Madrid. In a popular sense, she is the patron saint of Madrid, even though the official patron is the Virgin Almudena. One woman told me that she had come here with each one of her children soon after they had been born to present them to this Virgin. This was practically the only time in any Club Aguafría context that anyone told me about adhering to popular religious customs.

After the last walk, all of us (except Vicente) went to the club and had a Christmas lunch together. The administrator came in with his arms full of dark red roses and walked around the tables, handing one to each woman personally, each rose wrapped in plastic and decorated with a pink silk ribbon. On each one hung a little card where the club wished the ladies a Merry Christmas and expressed hopes that we had learned "unusual" things about Madrid.

Series II and III: Old Civilizations

The second and third series were more ambitious than the first. Perhaps some participants had let Vicente or the club leadership know their wishes, or perhaps Vicente himself understood that they wanted "a higher level" as they themselves expressed it. There had been some loose talk in the taverns of continuing with further series, and the theme of "old civilizations" had been mentioned.

The second series started in late January and some twenty-five women took part. Most of them had also participated in the first series. After Easter, there was a third series with practically the same participants.

During these two series, we met every other week at the club for a regular lecture, and every other week we visited a museum to look at objects from the civilization the lecture had been about. The civilizations were: Ancient Egypt, Mesopotamia, Ancient Greece, Islam, Old Mexico and Perú.

Vicente's worldview came out very clearly in his lectures and, as I said, it can be understood as an unusually succinct conservative version of the club discourse. Some examples:

– In the first lecture he stated, as a general background fact, that all societies have classes. "That is why marxism has failed so scandalously, because it postulated a society without classes, and that is impossible."

– Another general fact, according to Vicente, is that there are heroic periods and periods of degeneration.

– "The difference between savages and civilized peoples is something obvious." The savages are, he said, nomads and polytheists, while civilized peoples are always sedentary, organized in states and usually monotheists.

– Talking about Egyptian religion, Vicente said very respectfully: "Now, I don't want you to be offended, please, and I am a Christian, certainly, but even so I have to tell you that Osiris is very much like Chr_st. Please, don't interpret this as blasphemy." The similarity lay, he said, in that Osiris was born at Christmas time, he preached love and he was murdered at the age of thirty. He stressed these coincidences as if to point out a significant mystery.

– Talking about the Bible, he said several times, also in a cautiously respectful voice in order not to offend anyone's religious sensibility, that one has to read it with a certain critical attitude, "because the Bible was written by Jews, so they tell things their way."

– One oft-repeated theme was that one has to counter the "black legend". "Now with the fifth centennial, everyone is talking about it again, that the Spaniards are bad. But that is one-sided talk, one has to tell the good things, too." Examples of good things: "The Spaniards did not traffic with slaves " "We may have stolen the gold from the Indians, but then the English pirates stole it from us." "We gave the horse to America." "We gave the potato to Europe and with that we ended hunger in Europe."

– Vicente mentioned several times that the Spaniards were impressed by the American civilizations they conquered. "So much gold, so much organization, so much order. And that is what is needed for a society to be civilized, order. And not like what we have in Spain today..."

– Vicente hinted constantly at racial differences, even though he did not use the word "blood", as the women did. He said for example that there were one hundred and seventy countries in the world, but only about ten that created culture, always the same ones, millennium after millennium: Italy, Greece, Egypt, Spain, France... "When do you ever hear anything about great cultures in Ghana or Burma!?" "Now, this to some people is racism, but it is not racism, you can interpret it in any way you wish, but those are the facts."

The lectures were usually very authoritarian in style, in spite of their apparently jocose character. Vicente laid down truths and answers, hardly ever questions, at most "mysteries". And the women had learnt not to interrupt him. At the end of each lecture, questions were allowed, and the ladies then usually asked things having to do with religious matters. They wanted exact names of mythological figures, they wanted to make sure they had got the dates right, and they were worried by any little detail they imagined might contradict Christian truths. This was the only point over which the women sometimes disagreed with Vicente, now that he had learnt not to be openly mysogynist. For the rest, their attitude was that of respectful learning, with learning understood as pinpointing facts.

Matilde once asked if Vicente thought there was any one civilization that was "the best one". He exclaimed: "Greece! Without a doubt! Because the Greeks were marvelous, they made beautiful objects, they have never been equaled. And because the Greek civilization was the only one that developed science and philosophy." Celia looked doubtful and said something about the Chinese. Vicente: "Yes, well, a little bit, Confucius and Lao Tse, but that was about all. And the Chinese did not develop any science at all, and it is thanks to science that the West has been able to dominate the world." He said this as a self-evidently positive fact. And added (this took place during the Persian Gulf war): "The fact that Schwarzkopf is able to defeat Sadam Hussein goes back to Plato and Aristotle."

Vicente often made comparisons between ancient Greece and present day Spain. He said that the ancient Greeks had firm values and that it would not be such a bad idea for us to return to those values. When we visited the Archaeological Museum to look at Greek objects, he told the anecdote about the Greek woman who told her son to be brave in the war, "and she said that thing about, either you come back holding your shield – that is: with honor – or else lying on it. That means dead! Those were the times! And not like now, when the mothers complain... you saw them on television yesterday I suppose, weeping (Vicente imitated female sniffles) that their sons are taken off to war, boohoo, they take him to the Gulf, bring him back to me... And the guys are only sent to rear guard duty! Rear guard!"

Vicente's attitude was of triumphant sarcasm, certain of the usual consensus around his values. But this time he was wrong. Without realizing it, he had offended Motherhood, that one female value that the women felt totally legitimated to defend. Consuelo said sternly, "Now, look, my son has left today to begin his military service, and I am more there with him than here." Another woman backed her up, "The thing is that you don't have any children." Vicente was offended, "I do! I have two daughters!" But a chorus of women interrupted him, "Daughters, yes, sure, daughters... They don't do military service!" They also said that he was not a mother, just a father, so he could not understand maternal suffering. Vicente had to give in, but he would not recognize it. "Now, now, ladies, don't fight each other..."

Race was a theme that cropped up often, not just in the positive way (some peoples are civilized, not all), but also negatively (some peoples are savages and there is nothing one can do for them). For example, at the Ethnological Museum, the theme was

"American civilizations", but Vicente did not seem especially inspired. Mostly the women walked around on their own in small groups, and their attention was mostly caught by exotic details. "Poor people, what a way to live." "Look at that funny dress! I would never dress like that!" Even Vicente himself mostly said things like "Look, what a horrible house."

One woman said, "Eegh, they are so ugly, all of them! How come they are so ugly?" Someone said that the photographs she was looking at were from the Philippines. "Oh, so they are Philippines. Yes, that explains it, I had noticed it with the Philippine maids serving in Madrid. Haven't you seen how terribly ugly they are, all of them?" The woman who said this was one whom I considered to be a bit of a friend, so I had to protest. "How can you say a thing like that!" But she misunderstood me. "No! You are thinking of Isabel Preysler[22], that is what we all do, but she is an exception, really, just you stop and look and you will see, they are really horrible, poor things..."

The racist theme was expressed more subtly by a woman whose daughter had spent a year studying in Sweden on an exchange program. She had enjoyed it, except that it had been very cold, so the mother had been worried about her health, and it had been difficult for her to make friends, and she had had to change family, because where she was first sent, everything went wrong. "They had family problems, and that was very difficult for my daughter, she tried to stay neutral but it was impossible. Now, I mean really big problems, you see. Really. They had adopted two children from Nicaragua, and those poor things could not adapt to Sweden, which is very logical, so they kept escaping from home and getting into trouble." I asked at what age they had arrived, if they remembered anything from life in Nicaragua. She understood what I was driving at. "No, not a thing, they were babies, only months old, when they came to Sweden. But there is always something, don't you think? They are not Swedes, after all, they have other customs..." I said that my opinion was that customs are learnt, not inherited. "Yes, certainly they are learnt, I think so, too. But I think there is also always something else... in the genes, too. Don't you think so? Something... just as we inherit the color of the eyes or the shape of the nose, those will certainly not be the only things, there are other things that come from the parents..."

After the visits to the museums, we went to taverns as usual. After the lectures at the club, we ordered drinks and tapas from the club bar and sat in the main salon. The conversations were perhaps livelier than normal club conversations there, but they completely lacked the giddy vacational air they had at the downtown taverns. The usual group formations also stood out more clearly, whereas in the taverns everyone talked to everyone and some new friendships were actually formed.

Chapter 8. Managing meanings at Club Aguafría

Middle class Madrilenians had different sets of ideas because of their different personal histories and because the city presented them with different experiences. This meant that there was a lot of cultural work to be done if any kind of common sense was to be established. All the conversations described in chapter 5 are examples of cultural negotiation around sensitive matters.

Could Club Agufría be conceptualized as a subculture?

Ideas can be seen as sets of clusters. That is one way of analyzing a discourse landscape to define categories and borders and the relations between them. If these clusters coincide more or less with categories of persons, they are sometimes called sub-cultures. One can ask questions for example about how many sets of ideas are present in a given geographical or social area or how the contents of them can be described. What does the discourse world look like? It is never an even field.

But the concept "sub-culture" presupposes that the various kinds of differences sort themselves into well-ordered sets that together form a whole, and that is not always the case. Club Aguafría was not a "common corner in society" as E.C. Hughes phrased it (Hannerz 1992:62), not a place where a distinct sub-culture could grow in the rich soil of social similarity and interaction with a constant set of others. On the other hand, it can be described as an "interpretation center" (C.W. Mills, quoted in Hannerz 1992:62), where a number of individuals gathered with a purpose.

The members of Club Aguafría could not pretend to isolate themselves totally from the rest of society nor to build a sub-society. That would be impossible in Madrid today for anyone and especially for people of middle class professions. But they made an effort to isolate themselves to some degree, in their leisure time, in order to surround themselves with people who thought and acted in similar ways. In this way, there was less to doubt and negotiate, so interactions became more comfortable. This was a rather conscious goal at the club. Less conscious was the resulting tendency to negotiate meanings in order to increase the areas of possible consensus, i.e. to interpret together all the new situations and combinations that modern Madrilenian life presented to people as more or less existential problems. If such a venture could be successful it might even offer an opportunity to escape from the need to constantly negotiate new meanings and instead to be able to negotiate increases in certainty, building growing redundancies, growing areas of thinking that could be taken for granted, handled as if they were doxa, even though everyone knew that they could not be. The highly doxic world the club members longed for had been irremediably lost, but it was possible to construct miniature models of it, and they might not be altogether unworkable. Something like aquariums for fish whose sea has disappeared.

On the individual level, too, modern Madrilenian life created problems. Not only was there a lack of harmony among the ideas of different persons, but individuals were also affected by a lack of coherence inside their own sets of ideas.[24] Different terms have been proposed for individual slices of culture.[25] Let us use Bourdieu's term habitus, in order to include not only conscious ideas but deep reflexes, feelings, automatisms in the body. By definition, a habitus is always internally dynamic, and different habituses continually influence each other when they come into contact (inside one person's head or when several persons interact). Now, in Madrid in the 1990s, each Madrilenian's habitus had been shaped by so many different contexts and loose bits and pieces of ideas, that its internal dynamism was uncomfortably strong. People had to try to calm it down to be able to live with it; people had to search for key metaphors or ordering principles that could accommodate most of what surrounded them in everyday life within some new order that would at least seem to make sense.

So there was both external and internal stormy weather. In chapter 4, we saw that an expansive mode of managing meaning can handle such a situation with less self-contradiction than a cautious one, yet the social conjuncture also produced the cautious mode. The middle class was especially torn in different directions, since they owed their position to the complex division of labor (a fact that would promote an expansive tendency) and since at least some of them saw an expansive mode as dangerously subversive of social order (an attitude that would promote a cautious tendency).

All conversations at Club Aguafría were quite cautious, but of the two groups of women in chapter 5, the first was much more cautious than the second, who felt more of a need to negotiate caution (called "close-mindedness" by them) as such.

Hannerz phrases the division of labor and its role in the distribution of culture as a series of collective problems: "Can specialists be trusted? Can a coherent understanding of the world be reached, and a way of dealing with it be found, through a summation of the varieties of expertise?" (1992:54) Most members of Club Aguafría would like to answer yes to these questions, being specialists themselves and proud of it and earning good money because of it, but most other Madrilenians, including many of the middle class, would answer no, without much of a doubt, and the club members themselves knew, from their own internal contradictions, that the negative answer was closer to lived reality. People in general, experts or not, had different opinions; things that used to be beyond doubt, seen as "objective facts", could now be understood in various ways.

Hannerz continues: "How are complex cultures affected by the interrelations of coexisting modes of cultural management, differing not least in their stance toward the production and integration of meaning?" (1992:54)

Club Aguafría was a place where people were trying to work out an answer, in conflictive negotiation with general trends in other directions. Club members would have liked to obliterate the difference between expert knowledge and general sharing. They certainly wanted their own expertise to be safeguarded as expertise, since their living depended on it, but they were not worried about that. (And correctly so. Modern society cannot do without experts.) But they tried to believe there was Truth to be found, and that Education would ferret it out, and that all people with common sense would realize that this was the Truth as soon as they were taught correctly. In their ideal world, then, experts (that is they themselves) define reality and others agree, without conflict, the only problem being one of efficient communication from the top down.

The striving for such an ideal world could explain the attitudes we saw in chapter 7, both Vicente's authoritarianism and the women's acceptance of it and efforts to absorb his teachings.

In the Madrilenian world as a whole, however, such an ideal was a flagrant case of wishful thinking. We can see the club as a valiant effort to contradict everything that was happening. And that implies a further contradiction: in doing this, the club itself increased the complexity of the city scene as a whole.

The club can be described, then, as a kind of intentional, partial sub-culture. A context which should ideally be as inclusive as possible of the members lives. They went there for leisure, and the idea was that they should go there often. They found many of their friends there, perhaps most or even all.[26] Some of their cultural needs were met there and they tried to see to it that all relevant questions about which it was necessary to have an opinion should be interpreted and answered at the club. Now, one problem was that this cultural work had to be carried out as if it were not going on at all. For people to whom a maintenance of an appearance of reigning doxa is an important part of their world view, difference in itself is negative, and debate and conflict even more so. Things should be self-evident. So cultural meanings must be negotiated, but this should be invisible.

Middle class Madrilenians of the 1990s worked out most of their cultural negotiations at a rather impersonal level and in very varied contexts: university, places of work (small companies, big companies, transnational companies, state and municipal bureaucracies, own businesses, and all of these dedicated to very different kinds of work), newspapers, radio and TV, clubs and associations, the lively night life with its myriad specialties, and so on.

But in a verbal and sociable baseline culture, as Spain as a whole was and is, people's dispositions tell them that meanings should be managed in face-to-face-relationships. So people tended to organize part of their daily life so as to create contexts where this would become more likely. Groups of friends tended to see a lot of each other and be quite stable through time, for instance. Something similar was true for associations, which tended to become groups of friends, too.

In this sense, then, the general phenomenon of social clubs was just one expression of a multi-formed collective effort to replace lost social worlds with new contexts and situations where meanings could be worked out face-to-face and consensus worked through over and over until it would take on doxa-like qualities. Club Aguafría was special because it was unusually conservative, but in all other respects it was quite representative for this phenomenon.

Most members of Club Aguafría had been members for a long time, and the groupings within it tended to be very stable. Few individuals circulated between groups even temporarily.[27] There was an ideology of "everyone-knows-everyone" that seemed to contradict the fact that the groups were rather closed. But the contradiction is resolved if we consider that the overall goal of club life was to create a social world where meanings could become stable. The smaller groups with their permanent membership offered the best immediate context for that effort from day to day, but the surrounding larger context was a suitable background, more or less common-sensical for all, where the various smaller groups came together and measured their differences and similarities without finding any differences that caused irremediable cleavages. The club background as a whole stabilized and legitimated the ideas worked out in the smaller groups.

Conflicts could not be allowed to come out into the open. They existed, but they were hidden away or denied, and if anyone should behave too openly in a non-conforming manner, she or he would become an outcast. A disposition for doxic thinking requires non-debate; therefore conflicts must be repressed if they are not to become unmanageable.

In spite of the apparent success of club life in creating a stable and outwardly harmonious context for management of meaning, however, this social world was partial. Members lived in different parts of Madrid,[28] they had different types of jobs, they had networks of relatives and sometimes friends outside the club, and so on. The social and cultural complexity that they would deny was actually always present.

The solution was to be careful. The style of interaction as well as the mode of management of meaning became cautious. The key word aparentar [29] certainly had a lot to do with prestige, but it also had quite a bit to do with the need for caution in cultural negotiations the existence of which were denied. Members had to adapt to what was interpreted as the club consensus. At least while at the club. Even if one suspected that the consensus was superficial and fragile, and even if one felt that the club world did not live up to the goal of ensuring a doxic world.

Club life could not be a totalizing context for negotiation of meanings, because it was not inclusive of all areas of members' daily lives; it was situated in the midst of a surrounding society in which the members took an active part. And the need for cautious behavior was in itself a third factor which further limited the effectiveness of the negotiation that went on at the club: since hardly anyone hardly ever stuck her neck out very far, one seldom learned anything important. So one was left largely to oneself to work out solutions to dilemmas, and one might come to fear that one's solutions were too idiosyncratic, not presentable, since one could not risk trying them out in company. So one had to be careful, not "open", and in this way each member contributed to further caution and lack of open debate. A vicious circle reproduced a tense and superficial cultural code, not much to go by in everyday life, and ill-suited to other dispositions in the club members' habitus, but stable as far as it went.

This was not a conscious process. But it is a likely explanation of one fact that mystified me and that seemed to mystify many club members themselves: The fact that a context created purposefully and consciously to be a place for friends to meet, and where this did in fact happen, had come to be a rather cold place, where almost all participants complained that they could not be open and sincere but had to be on their guard at all times, and where this furthermore was not a cultural style people were comfortable with. It contradicted the great informational needs of a complex society and of individuals recently arrived to complexity. It also contradicted the disposition for relaxed sociability, philia.

At this time, Madrid as a whole sported the common features of big city attitudes: skepticism, cynicism, street wisdom. In the eyes of most people, nothing was holy. Anything could be debated, anything could be doubted. But the doxic disposition had also survived and what it produced at this time was a tendency to deny variety, a wish for firmer "values", a nostalgia for older social settings (whether actually experienced or not) in which people were able to judge one another on the basis of personal knowledge, and therefore trust one another, and therefore enjoy each other's company. Or so one would like to believe. The clash between the big city and the doxic disposition was violent and undecided for some people, while others managed to create a coherent compromise in their own mind.

Certain sectors of the middle class, then, wished to maintain doxa. To do anything at all with doxa on purpose is self-contradictory, since as soon as you start thinking about something, it is no longer doxa. It enters the universe of discourse, that which can be debated. To think about or talk about that which is doxic creates the need to verbalize clearly that which ought not to be verbalized.

This paradox can be resolved with the aid of a discourse of "tradition": Idea X is good because it belongs to tradition, and because it does, it cannot be doubted, not debated (if you subscribe to the cautious mode of management of meaning). It can be glorified, described, celebrated, underlined, defended and so on as tradition, and thus talked about without self-contradiction, but it cannot be debated as orthodoxy can.

This was what happened at Club Aguafría much of the time. (The best example of this is in chapter 16.) And I believe it was a third reason for the great need for aparentar (along with prestige and caution). If it is necessary to refer to tradition in order to legitimate a life style, and if that tradition is continually contradicted by reality, both in your own life and in the surrounding wider society, then tradition has to be invented. It is not self-evident, but one has to pretend one believes in it as if it were. And that in itself is no small feat of pretense. It may become necessary to hide family scandals, minor career mishaps, unusual opinions and so on, not just in order to safeguard one's prestige and not just because others do so, but also in order to keep one's image in line with what tradition prescribes. The three needs overlapped and influenced each other at Club Aguafría, but they were different in that the competition for prestige had mostly to do with an image of individual success, the caution mostly with an image of individual morality, and the adaptation to a set of "traditional" norms mostly with an image of an ideally stable society.

In this cultural climate, to defend "tradition" and to make constant efforts at a polished image of prestige and morality had a political meaning. Club Aguafría was a conservative place, both because of how meaning was managed there and in the usual political sense. These two senses are not identical but neither are they independent of each other. Inside the universe of discourse, different ideas can be combined in various ways, according to conjuncture, and an idea X can be seen as more or less conservative. But to want to keep something out of the universe of discourse altogether is always a conservative interest. Whoever opposes that is less conservative, whatever her opinions on any specific issue.

Perhaps this is what it used to mean to be a "progressive" (*progresista*) in Spain. There were progressives all over the political scale and with different types of life style. What they had in common, in spite of all the variation, was an opposition to "tradition" – even though some of them, themselves, could well be described in terms of certain very Spanish traditions (for instance anarchism or Krausista liberalism[100]). Perhaps the term progressive had gone out of style because it was too inclusive to fit the 1990s universe of discourse, where more detailed differentiations had to be made. But as long as there were strong ideological forces trying to keep the universe of discourse small and well delimited, making efforts to keep certain "holy" or "natural" themes out of it, so long would there be a need for a term that covered all other stances, all those who accepted debate. That is why Lupe and her friends could feel "progressive" in relation to the club, even though they were conservative in relation to Madrid as a whole.[101]

As a matter of fact, the kind of people who used to describe themselves as progressives had a vocabulary in common around their opposition to "tradition". For example, they often used the verb "denounce" (*denunciar*), not in the strict legal sense of "take to court" nor even necessarily in the political sense of "oppose and attack" but in the wide sense of "reveal and criticize". In other words, widen the universe of discourse. They also talked a lot about "taboos" (*tabúes*) and this concept had nothing to do with religious taboos. It often referred to prohibitions related to sexuality (scanty clothing, flirty behavior on the part of women, mentioning of bodily functions...), but this was not the central focus of its meanings. What "taboo" meant, in the progressive discourse, was rather approximately the same as doxa: some idea that was so much taken for granted that people would get upset and lack arguments if someone tried to suggest that it could be otherwise. One young woman said for example, "I can't move to a place of my own. I would like to and I could afford it, and my parents don't need my salary. But for them it's taboo. According to them, young people just don't move out before getting married." She did not mean that her parents would consider it religiously wrong or even morally suspicious if she moved. That might or might not have been the case; she just meant that to them it was unheard of, it was something outside of what they could conceive of. It was not an alternative that they could be for or against; it was not inside the universe of discourse for them.

The "progressive" stance, then, was to "denounce" "taboos"; in other words, to widen the universe of discourse. Other relevant emic terms were "openness" (*apertura, ser abierto*) and "rationality" (*racionalidad*). These two concepts were opposites of that which the progressives were against and which they described in terms of emotional resistance to change, closing your eyes or your mind on purpose; in progressive thinking, that would mean remaining stupid and losing the opportunity to think rationally and make better choices for your family, your company, your country or whatever.

The "progressive" vocabulary could be heard at Club Aguafría, but not often, and when it was heard, it was usually surrounded by paradoxically cautious hedges: "as the expression goes", "as people say", etc. That is, marking a distance. And the dominating emotional resistance to change at the club was seldom described, unless one actually wanted to describe certain groups at the club negatively. (As for instance Maite and Lupe did, cf again chapter 5.)

In other words, to be "progressive" was to adopt an expansive mode of management of meaning. In Spain in the 1990s, this was not necessarily but usually combined with leftist political opinions. On the other hand, to be conservative in the usual political sense of defending market mechanisms and opposing measures in the direction of social equality, was not necessarily to adopt a cautious mode of management of meaning. For a conservative politician that mode would even be contradictory and inefficient, since he would need to enter debates. But the dominating mode of management of meaning during the Franco regime was decidedly cautious, so whoever felt sympathy with that regime tended to prefer the cautious mode, even in the 1990s (and later). The result was that among cautious managers of meaning one found mostly political conservatives, including the ones who were usually called "the nostalgics" (i.e. nostalgic for the Franco regime), but not many politicians, and among expansive managers of meaning one could find both conservatives and progressives.

No Madrilenian could ignore the existence of the expansivist vocabularies nor their political sub-text. In conservative contexts, such as Club Aguafría, however, one tried as far as possible to speak and act as if they did not exist. The political opinions at the club varied widely, according to club members themselves, but they were never openly discussed.[102] Political events could be commented, but only in such a way that conservative opinions were clearly read into the comments, and read only between the lines, not openly stated. My impression was that most club members stood to the right of center and that a not very small minority stood far to the right, including some "nostalgics". I also met club members who supported radical peripheral nationalism (like the Catalan or Basque ones, termed "terrorists" in rightist vocabulary), read critical or populist newspapers and probably voted socialist. But they were a minority, and they knew it, and as long as they wanted to continue to take part in the social life of Club Aguafría, they kept such opinions out of sight, i.e. they adopted situationally a cautious mode of management of meaning that contradicted their opinions and feelings.

Anti-doxic factors and stances cannot be opposed with arguments, because then doxa would shrink to mere orthodoxy. Club Aguafría was one kind of solution for people who wanted to live with unquestioned ideas.

Introduction to Part III: Expanding

Let us now move out from the hedges of Club Aguafría to obtain a wider view of Madrilenian life.

Since urban daily life consists in meeting different people for different purposes, an urban anthropologist must do the same. But since I wanted to describe variations, I also had to move around on the ideological continuum, and that was something most Madrilenians did not do. They did it so little, in fact, that they sometimes managed to believe that their own lifestyle was the only normal one and that all the variations (that they could not help but notice) were minority quirks.

The situations described in part III have been selected to represent diverse arenas for cultural negotiation. They exemplify the contexts middle class Madrilenians could choose from to socialize, and in what ways these contexts served as fora for debate. They also represent diverse points along the ideological continuum and diverse modes of management of meaning.

Big city life and changing times taken together mean that contexts are not just there, they have to be created. They can be created to be permanent or they can be temporary or one-time-affairs; they can be as informal as a group of friends, or they can be as formal as a club with statutes and collective property. In quantity, and therefore in accumulated cultural consequences, the informal contexts count for more than the formal ones. Friends meeting when they feel like it to talk about whatever comes up. But in the 1990s, that was not enough for many Madrilenians, so they created plenty of formal and semi-formal fora.

I have excluded the most formal ones from presentation, because only a minority took part in them, and because information about them could be obtained in other ways. Representative ones would be for example the associations that took up so much of Marías' time (chapter 3), organizations that tried to influence collective life (feminists, human rights, ecologists, pacifists, neighborhood associations, political parties...). The people who took part in them were found near the opposite end of the ideological continuum from Club Aguafría, and chapter 13 presents that type of persons in an informal situation. Church activities were another kind of formal fora, and very influential ones, but again, we have met the type of people who participated in them already, at Club Aguafría, and Church positions on key gender issues were well known, and summarized here in chapter 17. The parent-teacher associations at both state and private schools brought together all kinds of persons in order to solve practical problems, so they bristled with debate. And all of these activities were reflected in the media, of course. The outlines of these more formal debates around the topics of work and sexuality will be found in parts IV and V.

In chapter 9, the forum described was in one sense very formal. It was a class. One had to pay to participate, and the activity had a clear purpose, that of improving the participants' physical fitness. But what is interesting for our purposes is that this context was used by the participants for debate and sociability, too. Most of them came along to a bar after class, and the conversations there were like most conversations in Madrid, friendly-but-not-intimate, moving haphazardly from one topic to another, and personal examples from the participants' lives were used to illuminate points, to strengthen arguments, to ponder paradoxes. This social activity was so important that many of the participants continued in the same class year after year, even sometimes after having moved to another area. Any type of activity could be used as an excuse to establish fora for cultural negotiation, and there was a strong tendency to make them long-lasting.

The gym class was held in Aguafría, the residential area where Club Aguafría was situated. It was a conservative area as a whole, and the mode of management of meaning was moderately cautious, but it was much more expansive than the one that reigned at the club.

The Book Club (chapter 10) had also originated in Aguafría, but over the years people had moved and new members had joined, so the connection to Aguafría was tenuous. It was now a Madrilenian, not Aguafrian, club. It was informal in that it had no statutes or dues and no permanent meeting place, and the participants certainly felt that the meetings were relaxed in style and that the main purpose was their own enjoyment. But some traditions and a few shared ideas about courtesy and propriety gave structure to the meetings. The mode of management of meaning was in some ways more cautious than in the gym class, but the express goal was to "have no taboos," by which was meant that no topics should be excluded from debate and no opinions should be unacceptable. An expansive mode of management of meaning was thus a goal even if it was not altogether practiced.

For Madrilenians, the ideal context for both sociability and debate was a more or less permanent but not too intimate group. One owed a permanent commitment to it, but one should not have to tell more than one wanted to, one should not have to invite people home, there should be a neutral place where one could come and go as one pleased. Clubs filled that function, like bars did in the working class. But some people felt a need for something slightly more serious. More emotional commitment, better understanding of each other. Still, the goal was not an exclusive relationship between two persons who signal their friendship by telling intimate things to each other, as is common in Northern Europe. There was more emphasis on "having fun," which was doxically defined as being in a group, and on a feeling of "security", knowing there was a number of persons on whom one could count in case of need. And such groups, too, could serve as fora where one could think about and discuss aspects of everyday life as well as weightier issues. Chapter 11 describes such a group.

Finally chapters 12 and 13 are examples of the most common type of get-together, friends meeting in each other's homes or in a restaurant or bar. Chapter 12 describes an informal dinner with a rather cautious mode of management of meaning. It was experienced by the participants themselves, however, as "open-minded". As always, gender issues came up spontaneously in the conversation. The discussion in chapter 13 was prompted by me, but the context was a very relaxed get-together of a group of friends who saw each other regularly and enjoyed debating anything, the more controversial the better. What was "daring" for the people of chapter 12 was "normal" or even "reactionary" for those of chapter 13.

Chapter 9. A Workout Session and a Chat in the Bar

The gym class I attended throughout the field period was held in a small gymnasium behind the parish church of Aguafría. The church was nicely set on what looked like another large house lot, with a narrow piece of lawn in front. Behind the church was a yard with smaller buildings around it. One was a home-like structure, one was the parish daycare center with a small playground set apart, and the third one housed offices and classrooms and in the basement the gymnasium. All sorts of classes were held in this building: guitar, flute, ballet, workout, and above all so called "recuperations", i.e. classes in normal school subjects to help students with their homework, to catch up when they had fallen behind or to pass the September exams if they had failed in June.

Pilar, our teacher, held classes there, but she had nothing to do with the parish, she said, she just rented the facilities. The class I participated in was one hour twice a week beginning at six thirty in the afternoon. Some fifteen women participated, most of them between thirty and fifty years old, some younger, including the daughters of two of them. The class held just before ours consisted of young girls with high ambitions whose agility caused us such awe that we had to joke with them constantly. Whenever there were not too many of us, Pilar let the girls stay and practice in a corner during our class and once in a while she would glance over at them and correct them.

I will describe a class in springtime. As usual, I arrived some ten minutes early but for once I was not the first one there. Rosa had left her job early and sat on the brick wall in the yard, waiting. She was a big friendly woman who worked as a translator for a transnational company. She had no children. Apart from myself she was the only one in the class who did not live in Aguafría; she had moved recently, but not very far away, and she wanted to continue in Pilar's class which she had attended for several years. Like the other women, presumably, she came as much for the sociability as for the physical education. We chatted, and little by little the others arrived. Once in a while we looked in through the basement windows to see if the other class was nearing its end, but when only five minutes were left before our time, we trouped in. Pilar accepted this sign and told the young girls to do their stretching while we undressed.

There was no dressing room. The women from Aguafría arrived already dressed for class with just a jacket on top, or now in early spring perhaps only a big sweater or wide blouse. The atmosphere in this group was quite relaxed, in part certainly because a gym class does not allow for so many pretensions and taboos as club life, but in part also because the women were not among the richest in Aguafría. Those who could afford it, one might assume, would prefer the sports hall across the street, where there were showers and other facilities. But it was expensive. All the participants in my class loved Pilar's style and said so, and I am sure they were sincere, because Pilar was an enthusiastic teacher, but I doubt that that was the only reason they chose her classes in the ugly, crowded and insufficiently ventilated basement, which was cold in winter and hot in summer.

We took off our street clothes in a corner of the room, leaving them on hangers on the wall. Pilar came over to the little table in the same corner to take note of who had paid for the month. She gave no receipts. Then we spread out over the floor to our usual positions and Pilar turned the cassette-player on and got the class going.

The class program was more or less the same each time, with small variations. The stress was on appearance, especially exercises to flatten tummies and firm up buttocks and thighs. But Pilar managed to avoid monotony, using her personality generously and riskily to make us laugh. For one kind of leg-lifting, for example, she instructed us to take a position half lying on the floor, leaning on one elbow. "Very saucy," she said to make us understand the angle of the hips, and then again "very saucy, very pert!" to tell us we had found it. During the warm-up she could suddenly turn around and scowl and scream, "My, my, what an ocean of droopy tummies!" When one woman whom she considered in better shape than average did not do what Pilar thought she was capable of doing, Pilar would pretend to threaten her with her fists. Once when she thought all of us were lazier than usual she went over to the hangers, found a belt and started lashing it like a circus whip in the air, striding around the room as if she had boots on. When we groaned that we could take no more stomach exercises, she would grin and make her voice hoarse and suggestive: "Just think of the beach this summer! Bikinis!" When she taught us a new exercise for the inside of the thighs, which consisted in lying on our backs with a big ball between our flexed knees, pressing inwards on the ball, she explained "You'll have to find those indecent muscles! Just think of your husbands!" That comment was one that made the women flinch, it was on the very edge of the acceptable, but they did not protest.

After class, five or six of us always went across the street to a bar to have a beer. Each time one woman paid for everyone. There were no established turns, but somebody always offered to pay. Usually without tipping. And usually we did not sit down but stood by the counter, since that was cheaper. The bar was an expensive one, but there were no cheaper ones nearby. Aguafría is a "select" area, but many women residents did not have a lot of money to spend on themselves.

I never quite got over my surprise that Madrilenian middle class women, always so fussy and particular about their appearance, would go into a bar after a gym class without showering first. But there were no showers in the parish building, and apparently the chance for a beer and a chat counted for more than the appearance. In spite of everything. In this context.

One day Martina said she could not join us, she had to go home and have a shower and change right away. She said this with a significant smile as she lifted a corner of her t-shirt, revealing a tight wrapping of plastic all around her middle body. So inside the bar, we continued to talk about this method for losing weight. Some had tried it, most thought it useless. And very uncomfortable. Rosa said she used Biomanán, the diet crackers, every summer. "As soon as the heat comes, I don't feel like eating anyway." Several others agreed, they also ate Biomanán in summer, and it was effective, but in winter it was difficult. Most of them were slightly but not very overweight (like most Madrilenians), but they compared themselves to the beauty ideal in fashion, which was the same as in other European countries: extremely slender.

Pilar came back. She had dashed home to check on the workers who were installing a sunblind on her terrace. She lived in Aguafría, in a big apartment in a good building. Obviously her husband earned much more money than she did.

We talked about Pilar's children. All three of them had had hepatitis this winter, one after the other. "I cried one whole night last week when the girl came down with it, too," said Pilar with a strained grimace "I have been working so hard, so hard, to avoid contagion. Washing all their clothes separately and everything. And of course cleaning the bathroom all the time, all the time." Someone asked, more surprised than critical, if her apartment had only one bathroom. "No, three, but it did not help," said Pilar.

There were hypotheses about what could have caused it. It all started just after Christmas, so someone said that oysters are always dangerous. To eat oysters for Christmas was fashionable. No, said Pilar, "we didn't have oysters, but all seafood is risky, it could have been the clams or the crabs." Then advice was offered, about artichoke concentrate, homemade marmalade recipes, etc. Pilar shrugged, she had spent the whole winter cooking marmalades.

Perhaps to change the subject, Pilar asked how my work was going. I mentioned my constant observation that women of our age said that women ought to dedicate themselves to the family but that they were proud of their daughters who studied and worked. Marga, Sara's daughter, who was just a little over twenty, said that she for her part was not sure whether she wanted to have children or not. All the others stared at her in surprise. She explained, calmly: "I would love to have them, I am crazy about children. But I would not want to have them only to give them over to another person to care for them. If I have to do that, I would rather not have them. And I am working now and that is what I want to do, I like it. And mind you, I have not even been able to get a job in my profession. I finished social work last year and with good grades, but I am working in an office, just normal office work. But I like that too. And I have hopes, I think I will find a job as a social worker some time. That is what I want to do. Now, if I decide to have children, then I would stay at home with them. It all depends. What I might do is to have them when I am thirty or more." I asked if the obstacles she saw for combining children and work were mostly practical or mostly emotional. "Just practical. I am crazy about children! But a lot of conditions would have to be met. I would have to have a good job with good flexible working hours, for example only mornings so that I could spend the afternoons with them, and I would have to earn enough so that I could have a girl to help me at home, and I would have to have a husband who saw things the same way..."

Some of the women sighed and said she might as well decide not to have them, then. Those conditions were impossible. Their faces expressed a bit of general resignation but also, and more, of the contempt of the experienced for the unrealistic ambitions of the young. Rosa said, "What an awful thought! Of course you should have children, their grandmothers will take care of them!"

Sara, Marga's mother, shook her head, laughing uncertainly. She had had four children and stayed at home with them, but she had recently, over fifty years old, found a job in an office, and she had confessed to me that her whole life had taken on a brighter hue and that she wished she had gone to work much earlier. Obviously, she did not want her daughter to repeat the same mistakes, but neither would she be willing to quit her job again in order to take care of grandchildren.

To help Sara out, Elisa said that nowadays many grandmothers work, too, so they can't help. Marga explained that she had said that she did not want to turn her children over to anyone, not even to her own mother. If she had them, it would be because she wanted to be with them herself.

As a counterargument, Elisa gave her own example. She had three children. She had stayed at home for the first eight or nine years of her marriage, but after that she had been working and she was convinced that all women ought to work and that all those who do not would actually like to. "You are not a worse mother because you work, because you feel better about being with your children when you are with them if you have not been forced to spend all day with them. And I have always arranged things so that I could spend time with them after work." Capable women can do both, was her message: be mothers and earn money.

Sara sighed, "Fine. Excellent, good for you, but certainly you know that it is a question of money. Not everyone can do it. And if you come home from work and have to start cooking and ironing..." Elisa said "of course," but made a face as if she had never considered such a possibility. Evidently, she had always had maids. She was not one to brag about money, but her house, her clothes and her manners communicated a probable upper class origin, higher at any rate than the others. Pilar mediated, saying that sure you feel doubts, her second son had been wholly raised by employed girls, and sometimes she had asked herself if maybe that was what had caused his strange personality.

Elisa continued talking about her work and how much she loved it. Her job was to prepare fashion collections. She talked about having to have an intuition for what people will like a year from now, about selecting models and materials. But it was not her own company. Sara asked how she got the job. Elisa explained that her mother had had a fashion house of her own, so Elisa had worked for her before she got married. "Even so, don't you doubt it, it was hard for me to get started anyway, after having stayed at home for so many years. And because my husband did not want me to work. And because I did not know what it was like to work for strangers."

Sara smiled sweetly but said that she knew more than Elisa about how hard it could be to adapt to working late in life. She did not want any confrontation, nor did Elisa look offended, but there was a short pause, as if the other women expected Sara to continue, giving examples from her experience, but she chose not to.

Pilar resolved the impasse teasing Elisa about her leotards with black lace edges. "Didn't you notice how all the men in the bar stared when we came in!" "Let them stare," muttered Elisa, "people in this country have no idea about fashion. In other countries this is exactly what they are wearing right now, in France for example, lots of lingerie look. And I like it, but we don't sell it, you have to make collections in order to sell after all, and here no one wants to wear these things. Because they say you look like a strumpet."

This group of women had a much more relaxed attitude to these things than what was common in Aguafría. Nobody but Elisa would wear visible black lace, certainly, but at least they were able to mention the matter and laugh about it. In the gym class, the body was not taboo in the usual way – as it cannot very well be among women who see each other sweating in leotards. Once, as we were leaving the parish yard, one woman saw that the shoulder pad of another had slipped out of place. "Your anatomy is coming apart!" she laughed, reaching out to correct it for her. The other woman slapped her hand, but in a friendly way, and corrected it herself without embarrassment. If this had happened at Club Aguafría, she would have been terribly embarrassed, but the scene would in all probability not have happened in the same way at all. There, only an intimate friend would have dared to point out the faulty appearance and only with great discretion.

Even flirting could be an allowable if somewhat risqué theme for conversation after gym class. This April afternoon, Pilar told us that she was going to go the *feria* of Seville, the great spring feast of that city. She reveled in our attention as she told us about some friends who invited her and her husband every year, and how they "knew everyone" in Seville, which meant they had a great time and were invited to all the right places. The feria is known in Spain as a very aristocratic feast, where you have to belong to the right circles in order to gain access to the right festivities, the so called *casetas*. But Pilar also stressed the fun. She told about how people dance all night drinking lots of *manzanilla* (the typical Sevillian white wine, similar to sherry but lighter), "but you never see anyone drunk, because they mix it with water; oh yes, they prepare special editions for the feria, because if they did not, oh my... And around three in the morning you have a big meal, because otherwise nobody would have the stamina for it all. And on Monday they go to work. I mean, they go to the office, but they don't work much until Wednesday." The women enjoyed this tale of acceptable norm-breaking.

Since Pilar talked a lot about dancing, one of the women dared to ask her if there was any flirting. Pilar's eyes sparkled. 'Oh yes, lots!" The others' interest flared: how, what, how much, married women too? "Yes, a man might ask you to dance, but only if they have seen you dancing for at least an hour, so that they know that you do dance, otherwise they won't. You just start dancing and then they will draw closer..." Pilar showed with gestures. And she told us how once a very beautiful man, very beautiful, behaved in a fresh way with her, "but he was so beautiful, well dressed and well groomed and everything, and the hair combed back like this, very straight... And he began to dance close to us, in that moment there were six or eight women friends all together, and all of a sudden there he was, and then little by little he situated himself and danced all around me..."

This was one of the very few times in Aguafría I heard a woman talk of men in a physical way. Perhaps the only time.

Later the man had asked Pilar to come for a ride on horseback with him the next day (the riding promenade that is part of the feria), but her husband had heard it and shouted at him. And later he had been angry with Pilar, even though she said it was just a joke. But he had said that she had looked at the other man and given the impression that she really would be capable of going off with him.

Suddenly Pilar realized she had been carried away by her own tale. She needed to repair her image a bit. "Now, of course this could only happen at the feria. I would never dream of flirting like that here in Madrid. The feria has a very special atmosphere, everything is just like a joke. And flirt seriously? No, I would never do that." But the other women continued to chat eagerly about flirting. Someone said that nowadays the feria comes to Madrid, too, they prepare an area of the Retiro park. Another woman said she had been there, but that it was not the same, "it is more like... well, more vulgar." Pilar agreed, "Yes, in Seville, if you are invited to a caseta you have to be totally elegant, from head to foot." With this comment, she definitely drew the curtain on the slightly licentious talk she herself had initiated. Her words indicated that vulgarity consisted in unfashionable dress and low economic status. That was the most common way of using the word in Aguafría, and a much less sensitive one than the meaning the other woman had probably intended: sensuality, play with the limits of decency. In both senses, of course, the word was used to underline class differences. The vulgus, the ordinary people, did discipline their bodies less and did not/could not dress by middle class standards, and in the eyes of Aguafrians this signaled faulty character.

After about an hour, we paid and left the bar. The women walked off in different directions, but Pilar had her car parked near the bus stop, so she kept me company until the bus came. She found a theme for conversation that fitted the situation and created a feeling of identification between us: she told me how much she loved her profession and how she made efforts to keep up to date in it.

The gym class was not a very expansive context. Several of the participants lived in the area of Aguafría, they lived materially comfortable middle class lives, and although none of them was a member of Club Aguafría, the discourse kept mostly within cautious limits in a way similar to the Club atmosphere. But because there were only women present, it was possible to talk in a relatively relaxed way about women's bodies and clothing and even, albeit more restrainedly, about sexuality. The participants used the classes and the after-class bar sociability as occasions to compare notes on things that worried them, in other words, as fora for cultural negotiation. At this occasion one topic was sexuality, with light touches (lace, flirting), and another the burning question of how to combine a profession with motherhood. Both without coming anywhere near radical issues, like actual infidelity or doubting the values of motherhood.

Let us now move on to contexts with more expansive modes of management of meaning and where the atmosphere of cultural negotiation was more evident.

Chapter 10. A Book Club Meeting

The Book Club was a club without any membership lists, without dues or statutes of any kind, but that had nevertheless existed for many years. A number of women met once a month to discuss some novel they had agreed to read. They did it because it was a kind of "cultural" activity that as such gave prestige and increased their "education", and because most of them were housewives and liked to get out of the house, and also because they had a disposition for philia that made social occasions very important for them, and because they were more or less interested in literature. All of these reasons except the last one were common reasons for women's activities. The exact forms for the get-togethers were less important than the fun and the security of having a place to go on a regular basis. Naturally, like all arenas for cultural negotiations, this one too was frequently used to compare notes on controversial issues. In comparison to Club Aguafría, and even to the gym class, the mode of management of meaning was less cautious. The participants expressed a conscious goal of "having no taboos", i. e. to let an expansivist mode reign. But that goal was not quite reached.

A few words about the participants: They had all met through some connection with Aguafría. If they did not live there now, they had lived there, or they had some relative or close friend living there. But the club was not defined as of that area. The women's age varied, the oldest were around sixty and the youngest not yet thirty. Most of them were housewives, but not all. Those who were not had professions that permitted them flexible hours – a boutique of their own, an economist working from her home, a part time biologist... Politically and religiously they were average, but their level of academic achievement was higher than average. Since some of them had little schooling, this also meant that the total range was wider than usual. This was tacitly and indirectly recognized in the fact that no one ever commented on anyone else's knowledge. No one corrected anyone's interpretation, nor did they react negatively to the academic language that some used and I am sure some others did not understand. Nothing was too much, nothing was too little. This was possible because the important thing was not to reach any consensus or to learn anything really new. Such a goal would have endangered the "good atmosphere". The important thing was to show an interest in literature. And, of course, enjoying the company.

Let me describe a typical meeting. It was a hot day in May. This month's hostess was Teresa. The time was eleven in the morning as usual. Some twenty women gathered in her living room. This was a few more than average, perhaps because an author would come this time, but it was not a famous author and as it turned out most of the women had not especially liked the novel we had read by her. Everyone greeted everyone, or at least that was the idea; since we were so many, perhaps a few cheeks were not kissed by absolutely all lips.

Those who arrived early did greet each other conscientiously. They sat on Teresa's three couches and conversed, but as more and more women arrived, there were not enough seats, so the women stood around in groups, talking, raising their voices as the general noise level soared, but maintaining composure in body language. Two of the women were foreigners with husbands in international careers. When Teresa thought that a majority had arrived, she invited us to step up to the table she had prepared with tea and coffee in thermoses, pitchers with juice, plates with cookies and sandwiches and three cakes. The women served themselves, some sat down, but most stood balancing their cups and plates, chatting. How is your new baby, where are you going for your vacations, did you like the book, it is already getting hot...

The atmosphere was like a cocktail party in that the conversation was lively but fragmented and neutral, but the competition for prestige was muted and mostly expressed in clothes. The women were well dressed: skirts and blouses most of them, but fashionable and good quality ones, and in spite of the heat several women had brought some sort of matching cotton jacket. There was some competition with the food that was served, of course, but not much, because the variations were minor. A well furnished home offered prestige, too, but years passed before the club returned to the same house, so if some woman did not want to open up her house for inspection, it was easy to avoid. The homes I visited through the Book Club were similar to most others that I saw. Some were furnished with light-colored furniture and modern art reproductions; most tended toward a conservative style with heavy furniture in dark wood and realistic paintings in heavy frames. All homes were always perfectly dustless. In the living room there was always a coffee table with one or several couches plus a few armchairs. All homes also had a formal dining table, usually with high-backed chairs around it or along the walls, either in one part of the living room or in a separate dining-room.

There was no hint of competition in verbal brilliancy of the kind that dominates other types of Madrilenian intellectual encounters. Nor did I notice much of the ferocious social control that was always present at Club Aguafría. Whenever I said anything about that club, these women would sneer or shudder. They saw Club Aguafría as a bastion of "closed mentality". By this they meant more or less conservative political standpoints plus a cautious mode of management of meaning.

It was close to twelve o'clock when we sat down. Teresa had by then arranged chairs in a circle, as many as would fit on her shady terrace where one could at least imagine a slight breeze, and the rest inside the room but close to the open doors. María Angustias had gone to fetch the author, María X., by car. She was now introduced and given coffee and sweets and a chair. She had short straight black hair, no makeup, a flowery blouse, blue jeans and sandals.

139

"Shall we start?" asked María Angustias, taking on her usual role as moderator. She rang a little brass bell and the women stopped chatting. The author was welcomed and a few women began asking her questions right away, but soon María Angustias interrupted them and suggested that we follow the usual system, talking by turns once around the circle, and after that anyone could talk as much as they wanted to, as long as it was only one at a time. "If not, I ring the bell," she explained to María.

The idea was to comment the book we had all read, in this case María's recent novel. Usually the women were very honest in every way: one of them might admire a book and the next speaker might say she thought it a book for idiots; one might make a long florid speech, sometimes even using written notes, and the next one might say she did not feel like saying much because she did not think she had understood it. There were always two or three who said they had not had time to read the book, and they needed no further excuses, no comments were made. Tolerance was not only a verbalized group value, it was actually practiced.

Now, with the author present, the first few comments were courteous and flattering. But after a while the atmosphere relaxed and warmed up. Several dared to say they had disliked the novel, but they said so with polite smiles and always giving some sort of argument for their opinion, even though the argument was sometimes very personal, such as having been reminded in an uncomfortable way of their own mother.

With varying terminology, many of the women coincided in finding María's novel cold, distant, somewhat abstract, too technical. María defended herself, saying she had tried to write in the style of a film script, since she had been told "by people who know about these things" that that was the right thing to do today. Other women preferred to comment on the persons in the novel; they talked about who had a warm personality, how they had identified with someone's feeling of loneliness, how someone else's fear of death was very understandable given the circumstances, how they had hoped the love story would work out... María laughed heartily, "You talk about them as if they were real!" Little by little, her good humor and humble manners gained the women's appreciation.

As usual the themes of religion and politics were avoided, even though the novel touched on them. The only vaguely religious comment came from Leonor, one of the oldest women in the group, around sixty. Talking about fear of death, she smiled sweetly and said she was not afraid. "I say my prayers every night, because I am a Catholic. But then I forget about it! You can't think about it all the time, that it might happen tomorrow..."

The novel was largely about loneliness, and almost all the women said something about that. They said that people seem to feel lonely nowadays, especially young people, they don't have any values to go by anymore, in almost all the books we have read lately there is something about loneliness, not all change is for the better...

In Madrid, such comments (especially about lack of values) were often used to stand in for an openly conservative discourse. At Club Aguafría, at least, the intention was usually to lead up to the conclusion that recent political changes have been bad, that the family is being undermined and that we would be better off if women would stay at home and schools would teach Catholic values as they used to. Some of the women in the Book Club certainly meant to convey such ideas. But not all.

This came out with unusual and risky clarity talking about May-68. One person in the novel said that those ideas really did not reach Spain until a year later, in 1969. Now, in the meeting, one woman said glumly that in her opinion they never arrived. Another explained that you would only notice them in the university world.

María then tried to elaborate: what May-68 really was about was an attempt to join the students' struggle with the workers' struggle.

Such language was too strong for the Book Club. Leonor said, always with her sweet smile, that such disruptions never leave anything better than it was before, and she asked María directly if she could name a single example of anything durable that had come out of it. María shrugged, sadly. Leonor triumphed: "But I happen to know a couple of persons who participated directly and what has happened to them afterwards is disastrous!"

But María did not give up. She insisted with force and dignity that she was proud to have learned how to see society in a critical light, and that she would never stop practicing that attitude, the desire to improve society, because our society is not the best imaginable one, and if it were, it would still be our obligation to keep on trying to improve it. Her words created no awkward silence, as I feared, but neither did they cause any further debate.

The emotional climax of the debate came when María confessed that she had picked the name of a hated school mate for the evil woman in the novel. "But in spite of everything I feel bad about having killed her in the novel," she said. The women shrieked with laughter: "Aha! Your unconscious betrays you! You got your revenge, right?!"

At one point María asked what we had thought of the sex scenes in the book. I wondered to myself if she knew she was treading on tabooed ground or not, if she did it on purpose or not. Sex was the third subject, along with religion and politics, that was never mentioned in the book club discussions, no matter how much sex there was in the book of the month. María asked if we had found the sex scenes "too strong". The women said no, but without great conviction. "Sometimes the context requires it..." said one. María then explained that some colleagues had told her that those scenes were lacking in expressivity and that that had worried her. "Perhaps they ought to have been more temperamental, more carnal somehow..." The women then all exclaimed a forceful no, not at all, they thought it was quite enough as it was.

After María left, many women commented favorably on her personality, but the things they mentioned had little to do with her opinions or her writing. They had been especially surprised when she said she was forty years old and had two children and was married;

they had thought she was just a young inexperienced woman. They laughed about how she had talked about "women's problems" such as sagging breasts as you grow older. "Of course they sag," she had said," but why operate? If they are mine as they are, they are mine, and if you operate them, then perhaps something else will start sagging!" In Aguafría, aesthetic surgery was a common topic for conversation, and many women did have operations. There was much more talk than surgery, but María's opposition must have sounded surprising to them, yet they did not say so. They also accepted without much comment the fact that she had said that she was married for the second time and that her children were "one from each marriage".

It was now after one o'clock. Fina hurriedly said that she was reading a very interesting book by Julián Marías, the Catholic philosopher, and she suggested we all read that one for the next meeting.[103] Even though this was the first time ever that a book that was not a novel was suggested, the women did not discuss the proposal much, they just all got out little notebooks to take down author, title and the name of a book store where it could be found. This was the usual process: whoever suggested something first usually got her way without much discussion.

The hostess was decided in the same way. Angela said, "We have to meet at my house next time, you have never been to my house and I have been a member now for two years." Her address and phone number were also written down in all the little notebooks and a date was agreed upon with a little bit more but not much more discussion.

As usual, about half of the women had left before one thirty because they had to go home and prepare lunch for their families. But as usual, the other half stayed on until around two o'clock. By that time the hostess was usually nervous, she herself had to think of lunch. But Teresa was not, her husband would not be home for lunch and her children had lunch in school. The last six women left as a group when it was almost two thirty but stood chatting for a while longer on the sidewalk before going in different directions. As usual, too, everyone felt satisfied with the "cultural" morning and commented on the good atmosphere. I said that I had wanted to be more critical of the book, but since the others were not, I thought perhaps courtesy did not allow it. They assured me I was wrong and urged me "to speak your mind sincerely next time".

Only one woman had a car. She offered a ride to two women going in her direction. One woman hailed a taxi, and the two remaining ones walked to the bus stop.

Widening the circles from the extremely cautious and conservative atmosphere of Club Aguafria, this chapter describes a context in which the women participated in order to discuss. They wanted to feel free to talk about any subject in any way they wished. The reading of novels gave them pleasure but also some prestige, at least in their own eyes. Their mode of management of meaning was therefore meant to open up horizons. To be expansive, in my terms. But there was little questioning of central tenets of cautious modes, and in this example meeting, María's opinions were somewhat uncomfortable. A "good atmosphere" was thought to be one in which everybody would feel relaxed, and that required upholding of major parts of both orthodoxy and doxa. An expansive mode of management of meaning was a goal, but it was practiced with remaining caution. This type of context would fall near the middle of a continuum of expansion/caution, as things stood in middle class Madrid at the time of my fieldwork.

Chapter 11. A Friendship Group

Catholic communities

Some parishes organize an activity that builds both on the Christian idea of community and on the Spanish disposition for philia. Persons who want to be active Christians form permanent groups and meet regularly, usually under the leadership of a priest. They are sometimes called base communities (*comunidades de base*). They may celebrate Mass together, they may meet to discuss how to live a good Christian life or they may just meet to chat and have dinner together. Similar groups exist in other contexts than parishes; I knew for example of one group founded by a Jesuit employed at a private girls' school. He formed a group consisting of parents of girls at the school. When I heard of it, the group had met once a month for eight years, and none of the daughters were in the school any longer. The idea for such a group is to be permanent, and they certainly seem to be stable for very long time periods.

These groups attract people from all social classes, but my impression is that they are especially common in the middle class. They can play a similar role as a tennis club or a gym class or a book club, giving its members a stable reference group of peers.

However, the process of secularization in Spain is especially pronounced in the urban middle class. Logically then, some practicing Catholics stop practicing and perhaps even stop believing. What happens to a Catholic friendship group if that happens to its members? It might break up, of course. But the disposition for philia and the predilection for stable groups may override the loss of faith. I was introduced to one such group.

Nosotros

Let us call it Nosotros (=we). That was not its real name, but it had a name and it was similarly simple and sentimental. The group had existed for thirteen years. During this time some members had left, a few new ones had joined and some had left for a while and then rejoined. But most had been active members for the whole time. It had started as a regular parish group, but there had been conflicts with the parish, so it had become independent at an early stage. At that time, all the members were still practicing Catholics, but because of the conflict, many stopped going to Mass or started searching for other ways of practicing. Then, little by little, they withdrew from Catholic practice altogether and their faith was eroded by the general process of secularization. In 1991 none of them went to Mass regularly, a minority considered themselves Catholics, a few said they believed in some sort of divinity but were not sure they were Christians, and most felt agnostic or atheist. Some were interested in astrology and Oriental religions.

144

They met twice a month. As they explained it to me, their purpose was above all to continue to deepen and strengthen their friendship, but they also wanted to have a good time. A key phrase was, "we want to have a project in common with other people." They had plans for buying some sort cf rural property together, where they could spend weekends and vacations once in a while (most of them also liked to travel during vacations), and where they hoped to spend their old age together. The plans were realistic and far advanced. This may not be representative, but the type of group definitely is, and its evolution over time may well be.

I was invited to join the group on the condition that I did not "just observe" but "participate in the same way as all of us".[104] I wondered if this was possible, since I was divorced. I knew that these groups usually consist of married couples. Yes, I was told, this group, too, had consisted of only married couples to begin with, but that was a thing of the past. There were a few new members who were single, and several original member couples had separated. Usually the women had stayed in the group and the men had not, after separation, so there were now more women than men, but there were all possible combinations: men who had stayed but not their wives, separated couples who had continued coming, one never-married mother, and one man who had brought his new woman. There was also one unmarried man, a priest, but he had no leadership role in the group. He had been introduced like all new members through friends who thought he would fit in. The total membership was around forty persons. The majority were married couples, still.

Since all of the original members had belonged to the same parish, many of the members lived in the same area of Madrid, a middle class area of slightly less prestige than Aguafría. But many of them had since moved to other parts of the city, and new members might live anywhere. In 1991, most of the members were between forty and fifty years old, and most of their children were teenagers or young adults. Many of them knew each other's children, but the children were never present at the meetings. The youngest member was thirty-four and the oldest fifty-nine.

The regular meetings had a clear structure. I will describe one such meeting. The group also met once in a while to plan their rural investment, they sometimes went to the theater or went out for dinner together (the whole group or parts of it), and they organized a potluck Christmas dinner each year. They had recently also begun to meet once in a while separated by gender. "If the men want to go to a football game together, we women go to a movie or something," one woman explained, but later I learnt that there had been a lot of talk about the changing "roles" (i.e. the gender order) in the group, and that they were planning to "work" with that theme at some later time.

At the meeting I will describe, the first one I attended, there were twenty-two persons present.

One evening with the group

I arrived by car together with two couples I already knew. During the drive, the two men kept joking about the mysterious "rites of initiation" I would have to undergo. This was normal light-hearted sexually tinted joking, the wives did not object, but one of them felt the need to tell me that they were just joking. The meeting was held in the home of one couple that had a spacious individual house. As we entered and I was introduced to one person after the other, they all hugged me and kissed me on both cheeks. That is normal greeting behavior between friends in Madrid, but between people of different gender who have never met before it communicates emphasis on friendship. There was an atmosphere of expectation – they were all curious about the new member, and they made no effort to hide that, and I was curious about them, which they well understood and joked about.

One man was dressed in a strict business suit, because he had come directly from work. All the other men wore sports clothes, many jogging dress. Some of the women also wore jogging dress, but most wore loose slacks and sweaters. Most of them also wore the ever-present symbols of femininity, ear-rings and gold chains.

While we were waiting for everyone to arrive, people moved around chatting in groups. Some paid money to a woman who sorted it in envelopes. I asked if they were some sort of dues. Oh no, there were no dues, they were just paying for some special food products one of the couples had brought from their village. "We often do that. If someone travels somewhere, they take up orders in case someone wants something from that place."

Three women showed me around the house. Parts of it bore clear signs that it was the regular meeting place of the group. On the wall of one bathroom, there was a big piece of cloth covered with little pockets. Over each pocket was a name and in each a pair of soft slippers. Everyone exchanged their shoes for these slippers before entering the big room that had been especially arranged for the meetings. It was sparsely furnished with just a few chairs and couches along the walls, a bench with a music set and several small lamps. The floor was carpeted and strewn with cushions of varying sizes. There were a few art objects, and on the wall there was a set of decorated tiles that spelled the name "Nosotros ".

We had arrived at the set time, eight thirty. By nine o'clock someone said we ought to start even though not all had arrived yet. Everyone went into the meeting room and found places on the couches or on the floor. Those who chose the floor stretched out on their backs, the others found comfortable sitting postures. The meetings always began with half an hour of relaxation with soft low-volume music. The lights were turned off, but there was a soft light from the record-player and some light from the hall. No one spoke, people hardly even moved. Such discipline is highly unusual in Madrilenian social life. They had picked up the idea some three years earlier, after some members had attended courses of meditation and corporal expression. In general, I was told later, they had experimented quite a lot with the forms and contents of the meetings.

When the lamps were lit again, people stretched, sat up, yawned, coughed. Then the talking resumed, everyone had to greet the two couples who had arrived during the relaxation, sneaking in quietly. But then someone clapped his hands and said, "Let's start working!"

The "work" was the central activity at the regular meetings. This had developed from the early discussions on Christian ethics and practice, I am sure, but the members explained it as an activity that helped them to get to know each other and to keep mentally alert. "Most of us have jobs that require a lot of thinking, but technical thinking, instrumental thinking. I have a need for more personal thinking," said one man.

I had been told that the group had spent quite some time "working" with their "personal trees". Those who wanted to – not everyone did – could draw a tree representing their life, and this was then discussed collectively, one whole session for each tree. But this had become boring after a while, they said, so a committee of three men had met to think up some new kind of activity. The spokesman for this committee now gave his report.

To work with "values" was what the group had given the committee as a starting point. The "method" the committee had now come up with was this: First we would each name the values we thought most important in our lives, we could go around the room once or twice, but without commenting on each other's suggestions. This was just to choose one value. We could choose several, since the plan was to work with values for a period of time, but we would choose just one to start with tonight. Then we would disperse into three work groups (called white, blue and green – the names of the members of each group were on big sheets of papers hung on a wall, and I noticed that members of couples were always in different groups). In each group, each one would tell about concrete personal experiences with that value from three points of view: One experience that had shown the positive side of that value, one that had shown its absence or its negative aspect and finally how one felt about that value now. Then we would reunite in the big room to comment together.

The method was accepted without much discussion – also uncommon in Madrilenian social life.

The values suggested in the first round were: simplicity, friendship, love, coherence (intellectual or emotional), to feel good about yourself, harmony. (They struck me as exactly what one might have expected.) A few more were suggested but met with derisive comments, so they were retired from consideration. Most of the men said one word only; the women tended to express their values in full phrases, and they usually mentioned several, tentatively, waited for comments and then decided on one. A few persons just said "I pass" and that was accepted without comment. One man, whose turn came late, laughed and said he had planned to suggest friendship, "but listening to this, I feel more like working with patience! Patience to endure all of you!" Apart from this, there was little joking, also an unusual feature in a Madrilenian gathering. There was a second round to vote for one of the three most-often mentioned values. The result was even between "love" and "friendship", but after some discussion it was agreed that they were similar values, and that they had discussed love much more through the years, so that now friendship was a more promising topic.

There were seven persons in my group. Four of us sat on cushions on the floor, three in chairs. Bernardo was elected spokesman and got out a piece of paper to take notes. Pili arrived later and joined us.

Agustín began. He said friendship had meant a lot to him ever since he came to Madrid to study when he was very young and felt very lonely. One day recently, back in his home village, he had met an unknown man who gave him a big hug. Agustín had been taken aback, at first, but then realized it was a childhood friend. And he said he felt then that that big hug, without any preceding words, was a great proof of friendship, so he felt deep affection for the man in spite of not having seen him for so many years. The negative thing was the absence of friendship in the city.

Bernardo: "The most beautiful proof of friendship in my life – and this is something you have heard lots of times, I have talked about it a lot – is when my mother had that accident, and when we got back from the hospital, two men from the group, neighbors, were waiting for us and came into the apartment with us and sat for a while, not saying much, just to be there. As to the difficult or negative, I don't know what to say."

Gabriela told a similar story. Her father was dying of cancer and she had taken him along on a weekend trip with the group, "and you were just exquisite, all of you, and my father kept saying that he felt he could die in peace knowing I had such friends." For a negative example she said there was one person in the group with whom she had had a conflict, and they had never been able to reestablish good communication after that, and that made her feel uneasy and hurt.

When it was my turn, I told of a good experience of special communication with two friends. The negative aspect for me is that, living in two countries, I find it very difficult to keep good friendship alive. A friend of mine had complained that real friendship with me was impossible, because nobody could count on me, since I was always on the verge of leaving. Friends have to be generous and give of themselves to each other, she said, and I could not. And I felt sad because I felt she was right. The group consoled me saying that hers was a very ungenerous comment.

Luis said that good friendship is what they had had earlier, when everyone in the group lived in the same area of Madrid. Then he felt safe and in good company always, not now. As to negative experiences, life is too full of them to tell about it. He said this in a sullen fashion. There was a not-so-veiled accusation of treason against the members who had moved. Somebody said later that Luis had a village mentality and wanted the city to be like a village, especially for people to stay in their places, not just spatially.

Rodrigo, the priest, told a long story from his work in a poor neighborhood in the 1970s. It was about a young girl who had fallen in love with him and how they were able to turn this problem into a true friendship. The negative example was also about illicit attraction, but this woman "did not respect me; that thing did not change into friendship but rather something like sexual harassment."

Pili remembered the time when she had just separated from her husband and had to fix the kitchen floor, and the furniture was too heavy for her to move, so a couple of men from the group came to help her get it out, and after the floor repair was done, one day when she came home from work, all the furniture was back in place! Friendship for her meant "total solidarity, to give oneself wholly to others, beautiful generosity." She gave a second example, of a neighbor who had offered to lend her money so that she could get a lawyer when her separation procedure was going badly. Her negative experience was of not feeling accepted sometimes in the group, especially immediately after her separation.

Ana said she was a selective person, she preferred to have just a small group of friends. That is very beautiful and very necessary in life. But she was also reserved. She never opened up totally to other people. For that reason she could give no negative examples; she had no negative experiences because she never expected much.

On the third point, one's present feelings about the value, nobody gave concrete examples, but there were many abstract speeches about what ought to be.

When everyone had made their personal statement, there was not much time for discussion, but we did ask ourselves whether the essence of friendship was only practical generosity, which is what the examples given seemed to indicate. It was my negative example that especially brought this up; if I had not said what I said, I believe the descriptions of material help would have gone uncontested, as they did in the other groups. But stated abstractly, the discussants felt it was definitely wrong, there must be something more to friendship than help, something "more spiritual".

When the whole group gathered again, the three spokesmen reported in detail, which took a lot of time. Bernardo read aloud from his short notes and filled in from memory. Carmen's notes were a lyrical story about what had happened in her group, where they had preferred not to give personal concrete examples but instead talked about their wishes and longings. The others commented that that group had been the most intelligent one, they had said very beautiful things. Especially Román had spoken very sincerely about his psychoanalysis, where he had realized that love, simplicity and friendship are really one and the same thing, a marvelous diamond. The third spokesman was Alberto, but he had taken no notes, "I hadn't realized I would have to do it like this." He tried to report what each one in his group had said, but it took a long time, because all protested and interrupted him and gave their own versions. When he came to Enrique, he looked at him and said, "Well, what?" Enrique looked uncomprehending, "What what?" Alberto: "Can I tell it or not?" Several voices: "Come on, for heaven's sake! What seven can hear, we can all hear!" Alberto: "OK, but stop me if you think I go too far." Enrique just shrugged. Alberto said that Enrique had confessed having his wife as his best friend, and that the negative thing was that they did not always manage to be best friends. No one except Alberto seemed to think that this was a sensitive thing to say.[105]

There was some discussion on method. The group work had taken too much time, many felt. But the majority thought that the small groups permitted more people to say more things. "We can try it for a few times, at least, and see what happens." All agreed that the discussion on friendship had been superficial, there was much more to be said. "We will have to dedicate more meetings to it."

The date for the next meeting was set, and suddenly people got up with impatience. "Now! Finally! Let's get going! Time for food!" etc. The hall was immediately crowded, as everyone took their slippers off and put on shoes, and there were lines in front of the bathrooms. Little by little we gathered again in the "*bodega*" (literally: wine cellar) in the basement. The floor there was concrete, and there was no heating, and it was a cold winter night, but after a short while the room became comfortably warm with body heat. There was a bar, one big wooden table plus a ping-pong table, benches fixed to two walls, and a few loose chairs. On the walls were shelves for wine bottles and ceramic-ware and a few practical things, like napkins and sets of forks.

The food parcels were unpacked. This was mostly the women's job. But most of the men helped. As their wives opened salad boxes, they poured on oil and vinegar. As their wives unpacked sausages, they got out knives to slice them. As the women arranged the loaves of bread in a common basket and olives and nuts on plates, the men placed napkins and forks on the table. The original idea had been for each person to bring a sandwich so that the meetings would not have to be interrupted by dinner time. But sandwiches were no longer popular. Most had brought something that could be shared by all. This particular evening there were omelets, peanuts, salads, ham and sausages, olives, many kinds of cheese and a special kind of canned green peppers from someone's village. Wine was served in plastic glasses, something I had never before seen in a middle class context. Everybody laughed at my surprised face and explained how through the years they had found a model that meant as little work as possible. "No pretensions! The important thing is to have fun together!" The host couple bought the wine, the napkins and the plastic glasses, as well as coffee and herb tea, as needed, and the cost was shared by all.

Since there were not enough seats for everyone, people stood or walked about while eating. After a while a couple of women went upstairs to prepare coffee and herb tea and came back down with big thermoses. One couple had only wine and peanuts. They explained that they had small children, so they had preferred to have an early dinner with them before coming.

The conversation consisted mostly of tales from everyday life. And lots of joking, of course. I heard nothing more about the topic of the day, friendship, and hardly any comments about the "work" session as such. This impression was confirmed at later meetings: "work" was clearly separated from "dinner", in style and topics. The atmosphere had changed radically from discipline to relaxation, from earnestness to teasing, from abstraction to concreteness.

Suddenly Román stood up and demanded silence by clinking a fork against a bottle. "Listen! I am going to tell you a story! You have to listen to me, eh! Listen, shut up! (Little by little the voices died down.) I am going to tell you a story and you have to listen to me, because otherwise... otherwise I did not like the olives! So there! Well, once upon a time there was a family man with two children. The oldest boy was in the last year of high school, right? And the girl was in eighth grade, the last year of primary schooling, as you know. So then, obviously, they both wanted to participate in their class trips..."[106] At this point he whisked a big sheaf of lottery tickets out of his pocket, and the expectant audience broke into booing, but he still managed to shout over the din that they cost 200 pesetas each. There was more booing and laughter, but most bought a ticket or two.

As people started saying good night, around one o'clock, several persons asked me what I thought of the group. I said fine, but that I was a little surprised, I had thought I would have to introduce myself in some way, tell them who I was or at least something about my study. This made them adopt a friendly protective attitude, laughing, proudly saying that the group was very open, they had no ceremonies, we will get to know each other, don't you worry about it... They rejoiced in having this beautiful thing to offer.

Everyone helped to clean off the tables, pack the leftovers and carry things upstairs, but the host couple had to insist, joking rather aggressively about it, to make a few persons stay for half an hour extra to wash dishes and clean the floor.

The priest gave me a ride home. He told me about his middle class background, but his father had been in the service of the republic in the thirties, so he lost his job after the civil war, and the family was poor while Rodrigo grew up. That was the reason, he said, for his commitment to the working class. I had already realized he was one of the so called "red priests" who worked in poor neighborhoods during the Franco regime, using Church privileges in the service of political opposition.

What is friendship?

This first meeting certainly gave me an impression of a friendly group of people, with a strong commitment to the group. But several members later told me, without other group members present, that they had misgivings about the group. For one it was not intellectual enough, for another there were some persons in the group whom he or she would have preferred not to have to ever see again, for yet another it was not what it used to be. Yet they continued in the group. And they found it difficult to give me good reasons. "I don't know, it has meant so much in the past..." "I guess I would feel like a

151

traitor if I quit..." "Well, I guess I feel that even if it is not perfect, it is the best there is. This world of ours just does not give me any better offers."

It was not my impression that this was a general feeling; on the contrary, I believe that for the majority the group was a warm harbor, indeed. The misgivings are interesting, however, because they prove that to have misgivings was usually not enough to make people leave the group. There was something else that was stronger and that something else was impossible to verbalize. At a later occasion, I met a woman who had left the group because she did not like the "methods" they had been using lately, but she had decided to come back anyway, to participate in the socializing, not in the "work".

My interpretation is that it was a combination of the disposition for philia, the impossibility to satisfy that disposition in traditional ways in a big city, the fact that the group did satisfy it with its regular meetings and space for relaxed socializing along with fringe benefits like permanence and at least some satisfaction of intellectual needs and the general need, in changing times, to have a forum for negotiating new cultural meanings. The mode of management of meaning in the group was decidedly expansivist (the goals were: no "taboos" as to topics to be discussed, honesty about controversial ideas, no aparentar, etc.), and some of the non-verbal symbols and actions were, too (taking off shoes, lying down in gender-mixed company, sitting on the floor, loose-fitting clothes, the relaxed gender roles, practicality as the main criterion for the serving of food). Interestingly enough, however, the conversations during dinner often took on a somewhat cautious air. They were relaxed in style, but the management of meaning became less free than during "work". Probably, some of the group members were not really comfortable with an expansive mode of management of meaning and adhered to a more cautious mode in their life outside the group.

The meeting described was interesting also because of the topic. The generalizations that can be made from what was said fit my general conclusions about how middle class Madrilenians construe "friendship". The examples given of positive experiences were practically all about material generosity. Some had to do with money, most had to do with practical help in moments of need, like moving heavy furniture. This must not be misunderstood as crass materialism or calculating selfishness. The material generosity was appreciated as such, of course, but it was appreciated above all as a sign – the one really trustworthy sign – of commitment to the relationship, which in turn made people feel secure.

A few persons mentioned "communication" as an important goal to strive for. But communication was not the protagonist of any concrete example of positive experiences (except my own, but it inspired no comments). Lack of communication, on the other hand, was mentioned in several of the negative examples: not being able to overcome a previous conflict, not feeling well understood in the group, etc. There seemed to be little appreciation of deep and honest communication as a goal in itself; it was rather treated as a necessary prerequisite for other good things, like permanence and generosity, to happen. It was not a goal as such, but its absence hurt and awakened fears.

The examples of material generosity were usually described as occasions where what had been given had been given "selflessly", without any thought of reciprocity. In spite of the philosophical education of several of the participants, nobody mentioned Aristotle's classical problem: how can friendship be purified of its instrumental content? For the group members, it was important that a friendly relationship not be instrumental in the sense of there being expectations of returns, but it was clear that material acts were the main proof of friendship. And all the examples were told from the viewpoint of the receiver. Nobody told any experience of the beauty of giving. Nor was this absence pointed out in the general discussion. (But the beauty of giving was a main theme in the poems that two women brought to the next meeting.)

The reactions to my intervention are interesting. I complained about the impossibility of keeping up a continued deep communication with my friends, and this feeling was understood but it did not inspire further comments. The complaint from a friend of mine that my absences made it impossible for me to be a true friend was understood exactly in the way my (Madrilenian) friend had meant it: an absent person can obviously not do what friends are for, give help if needed. Now, the situation made the others see this from my point of view, and they then thought that the ungenerous one had been my friend. One must not demand constant availability. But it should be offered and given. When one can.

The possibility of friendship between persons of different gender was not discussed openly, and no woman gave any example of friendship with individual men, but a couple of the men gave examples of friendship with women and seemed to underline this as something extraordinary. Enrique had given the friendship with his wife as the important positive experience, and when this was reported, two other men filled in with similar feelings. The women said nothing on this issue.

Apart from generosity, the fundamental feature of friendship was what I consider to be the central focus of the disposition for philia: good companionship. Not to have to be alone. To feel surrounded by people. To have fun. To be unconditionally accepted, in bad moods as well as good.[107] A few comments were actually about how to differentiate "good companions" from "true friends", but the theme was dropped for lack of interest. The two concepts are semi-doxically fused.[108] And the negative example par excellence was to have to feel lonely, not because of deception or treason, but because one simply does not know a sufficient number of others. Agustín's experience of coming alone to a big city to study is paradigmatic, as is Bernardo's tale of how group members came to sit with him at a difficult moment in life. One can compare this to the traditional custom of "accompaniment" for instance after a death. Friends, relatives and neighbors do not only attend the wake and the funeral, but they are supposed to come regularly for a period of several weeks, just to sit, to be there, for a few hours each afternoon with the bereft family. Spanish philia is the need for the presence of other human beings, independently of the content of the interaction. Philia can be fulfilled even when there is practically no interaction at all beyond the mere physical presence of others. This is sometimes one aspect of bar life, for instance when a lonely person prefers to read the newspaper at the bar, even if he does not count on meeting any acquaintances there. Witness also the predilection of students for studying together, even when just reading, not necessarily writing, discussing or checking.

The problem of autonomy did not come up. Not even in Carmen's group, where the terms of the discussion had been quite psychoanalytic. The word "respect" was pronounced a few times,[109] but it did not bring with it any pondering of the dilemma of companionship versus independence. Nor was there any mention of the common phrase, that was almost inevitable in similar contexts in Benituria: "One chooses one's friends, but one cannot choose one's relatives." The question of choice has much to do with autonomy, and it is a focused theme in philia in many ways. One should remember that autonomy, integrity and independence are important values for middle class Madrilenians, emphasized in all sorts of contexts and often to the point of sounding coldly selfish to a foreign ear. There is also a style of interaction that can be called self-affirmation that centers on the demonstration of one's independence.[110] "I do what I feel like" or "I don't have to give explanations to anybody" are common phrases in everyday interaction. Now, in a context of thinking abstractly about friendship, people did not feel any qualms about the possible limitations of autonomy or integrity it can imply. The two collide in practice but not in theory. Only one person, Ana, declared herself "independent" and "selective" and said that this meant that she preferred not to have many friends and not to be very open about her true feelings. Her opinion was passed over in silence by the others. It did not fit in. But even she expressed no real worry about her autonomy. What she said was rather that she had plenty of it.

Naturally, the members of a group like Nosotros might be more sociable than average, or they would not have joined such a group to start with, and the experience of belonging to it for many years must certainly have had an effect on individual personalities. However, their construction of friendship coincided nicely with my general observations. They may have been more than average emphatic and more articulated on the issue, but the scaffolding of the idea building was the same as in other groups.

As to mode of management of meaning, it was obviously expansive and quite consciously so. One could even say that the group "work" centered on exploring ways of expanding the "mentality" the members felt they had grown up with and were trying to change.

Chapter 12. Dinner in the Garden

In our review of representative contexts for cultural negotiations, we now come to the simple and informal one of just getting together. It was the most common arena, but the most difficult one to describe, since it could take innumerable forms.

Close friends call each other often, and especially women had long conversations over the telephone. But face-to-face meetings were preferred, and seen as necessary to keep a relationship going. The most common form for women to meet was to go shopping together and then have lunch in a restaurant or just an appetizer or coffee at some bar or cafeteria.[111] Just like men, women with employment found it convenient to meet their friends over lunch at a restaurant. Couples would usually gather in medium-sized groups, three or four couples, to go out in the evening. They usually met at a bar, which gave everyone a time margin, since it was difficult to be punctual in Madrid; then they would go to a movie, theater or concert, or perhaps to some place where one could have drinks while listening to some special kind of music, or they might just have dinner, in that case preferably at a restaurant that someone in the group knows to have some interesting specialty. Whatever their choice for the main entertainment, the evening would finish with drinks[112] at yet another bar, now of the pub or cocktail lounge type. Such an evening out usually lasted until two or three in the morning.

The Madrilenian middle class also considered it a good idea to meet in each other's homes, even if this was less common. The general pattern was similar: appetizers (both drinks and tidbits to eat) were served at arrival, in the living room, dinner was cooked by the hostess (not the maid, even if there was one) and served in the dining room, then coffee and liqueurs or other drinks in the living room. Again, it was not polite to leave too early. Arrival time was somewhere between eight and ten and one would stay til two or later, depending on how well one knew the hosts.

To get together with one's friends used to be an activity very much segregated according to gender and usually something that took part outside the home. That was still so for the working class (cf chapter 21 and Thurén 1988). But in the middle class there was much ideological emphasis on 'the couple", so, logically, social life was also usually based on couples.

Let us take a look at a dinner party that will serve as a representative case. Except that the hostess was a separated woman. But this fact may have been one reason for her arranging dinner parties in her home, because like all separated women she complained that many of her friends would no longer invite her to their parties and outings. On the other hand, it was more difficult for a separated woman to take such initiatives. It was not so much that people did not accept the break-up of marriage. It was a controversial issue, true, but no longer to the point that separated people are ostracized. It is rather that middle class sociability was seen as something for couples. (Cf also chapter 16 about men's paying.) This was just as much of a problem for the widowed or never-married as for the separated or divorced.

María José was an energetic woman, around fifty-five years old. Her self-image was of unconventional attitudes. I saw her as a woman who had lived a very conservative upper middle class life without questioning it very much, but with certain bohemian touches that served as emotional support for her when her marriage broke up. I had met her through acquaintances from Club Aguafría, but she was not a member. She lived in a detached house in another area, similar to Aguafría. Her parents had been big landowners (but not aristocracy), who had lost most of their land and rural connections during the economic restructuring of the 1950s and had not been able to reestablish themselves as industrial capitalists. This is one of the normal types of background in the upper middle class, even though less common than having risen from lower middle class. Her brothers had studied, but they were not especially well off. She herself had married a man with some money and a business of his own besides his engineering degree. Her separation had gone well, from her point of view, so she had no economic worries. Two of her children were already married; the youngest daughter, Conchita, was living at home, studying at university and planning to get married soon. María José had explained to me that she was making a conscious effort to enlarge and consolidate her social life, since she could foresee that she would soon be living alone. She was afraid of being lonely, but she was not one to suffer her fate passively. She made plans and arrangements. She did not say, but I thought, that she also had hopes of finding a new male companion. Not a husband, however – she was a Catholic and would not consider divorce.

The dinner

María José called me one day in early summer to say she was preparing a dinner party. She had invited three couples, friends of hers of long standing. The occasion was that one of the couples was visiting Madrid. "We have known each other since before I got married, but now they live in a town near Barcelona, so we don't see each other very often." The man was a friend of María José's husband from engineering school. Another couple were lawyers, both of them, and had helped María José with her separation procedures. The third man was some sort of a mining expert. "We will have dinner in the garden, because I think we will feel better there, it will be cooler, but instead of spending time in the kitchen myself I will order something from a Chinese restaurant, I want it to be very simple and relaxed."

It was. The guests arrived between nine and ten in the evening. The women wore simple but well designed dresses and little but tasteful jewelry. The men wore slacks and striped shirts, two of which had American-style short sleeves.

Juan Antonio, the mining expert, was very interested in anthropology and had read Marvin Harris, so the conversation started from there. His wife, Mary Luz, was a housewife, but she said that this year she had been very busy doing a course on restoration of old furniture. "One class a week only, but a lot of work in between classes. It has taken all my time, really, it has been very interesting."

We had sangría, patés and cheese while we waited for the others. They arrived with a box of chocolates and a tray of some salty things which María José added to the table of appetizers. Her maid simultaneously prepared another table off to one side, where she placed the Chinese food, served in the boxes in which it had come from the restaurant. We served ourselves, buffet style. We had sangría throughout, ice-cream for dessert, and both plates and glasses were of the fake glasslike material called Duralex which was standard at cheap restaurants in Madrid. María José seemed to have gone out of her way to underline the simplicity of the occasion. Few if any of my other informants would have dared such an under-communication of status.

She had obviously talked to the others about me, they were all very curious about my work. But there was no aggression in the air. Miren, the woman lawyer, indicated that she had timidly feminist views. Her husband, Pablo, complained that she dominated in their house. He said they even received letters addressed to "Mrs Miren Fernández and husband." Everyone laughed and teased him about it, but lightly. "And you feel bad about that, right?" "Come on, that has only happened once!" Pablo admitted that but insisted: "It has happened."

Conchita had come out from her studying to have dinner with us before she was to go out with her boyfriend. Pablo said that once when he had called María José, Conchita had answered the telephone, and she could not remember any Pablo, so he had explained, "your mother's lawyer" and she had exclaimed, "Oh, Miren's husband!" Everyone laughed, but Conchita tried to smooth it over: "Well of course, it is only logical, because I hear my mother talking about her friend Miren and her husband Pablo..." The laughter increased, since she seemed to confirm what Pablo was saying, even though in fact it would have been very strange for María José not to mention the name of her female friend first.

For a while we talked about how the men were childhood friends. Jesús, Pablo and María José's husband had all been classmates in grade school. Juan Antonio told of how he was the younger brother of Jaime, another member of the group, so they made him carry all their school bags and walk a few steps ahead of them, calling him their slave.

María José told about how she had been the first one to get married, and how all of them used to visit her home, and how Pablo had been especially tiresome, always the last one to leave... Miren said she hated the group in the beginning, all they did was to remember old things as if on purpose to make her feel left out of it. There was especially one man she could not stand; luckily he had later disappeared from the group or the thought of having to see a lot of him might have given her second thoughts about marrying Pablo. But Pablo had made things very clear to her: "You bet friendship is important! He told me that either I accepted his friends or else he would not marry me!"

María José then talked about how one of her daughters had recently gotten married, and how she had decided to invite the two as yet unmarried girls for a cruise, "before they too left me." She told many anecdotes from the trip, and the others listened attentively, asking questions that showed that they themselves had never been on any cruise, and unlike at Club Aguafría, the lack of (this kind of) travel experience did not seem to be any source of shame for them.

The interest centered on the co-passengers. María José said they had been placed at a table with an English family, "because you had to write down what languages you spoke, so we said English, but then we could not understand them at all, so we sort of regretted that."[113] There had been people of many nationalities, all ages, and, most interestingly for her, several separated persons, both men and women, and some of them like herself traveling with their children, but younger ones. "That was when I realized that separated fathers have to spend part of their vacations with their children, and men don't know what to do with children, so they take them on a cruise!" There were few young people and not many complete families, but many couples of all ages, some on their honeymoon, some elderly... She would like to go on more cruises, "but then I'll try to find one with more Spaniards, because then you have more fun." Between the lines, we could understand, then, that the social aspect of the cruise had not been satisfactory, due to linguistic and cultural barriers.

During the party, María José's separation was a very much present fact, mostly implicitly, but María José herself found many occasions to refer to it and at one point someone joked about this. I remarked that it was a recent thing, so naturally... but María José countered that it was four years ago, a very long time already, she thought. Jesús joked that separations seemed to run in families, and it turned out that there were several separated women in María José's family. I said that if you have seen a separation in your own family, it might seem less scary, so you are more ready to take the step if it becomes necessary. That comment was much appreciated, and there were several further remarks about how a separation can become necessary, how it might really be the only solution, and even a good solution sometimes... María José received these remarks like some kind of consolation or courtesy towards her.

Suddenly she said she would like to know what women look for in men. "And vice versa," I suggested. "Yes, and vice versa," repeated María José politely, but then she insisted that she could not really understand what women want men for. It can hardly be physical attraction after a certain age, she said, and if you do not need his economic support either, then what could it be? "I think it is company, just some good permanent company," she said finally, answering herself, and evidently talking about herself.

Then she mused that after her separation she felt she had become a little bit like a man. The others protested energetically, as courtesy seemed to require. "What are you saying, come on!" They laughed to make it look like a joke, but they seemed to fear it was not quite a joke. "I mean," said María José, "I make my own decisions, now I even prepare my own income tax declaration... a lot of things I never used to do and now I do them very well..." She was surprised at herself. She went on to say that she had lost femininity, because to be feminine is to depend on someone, and she had lost that. It was a loss, she insisted, but she looked pleased when the others said it was rather a gain, she had proven her intelligence and capacity to learn and act. Smilingly, charmingly she managed to make the three men assure her that she was very feminine anyway. I spoiled her performance a bit when I said that I could not see dependency as something positive. "No, but I am not thinking of dependency like that of a slave, but rather not to be too self-sufficient and end up lonely," said María José.

The men asked many questions about Sweden. (The women did not seem interested, or perhaps they were just not as well informed as the men.) This was when their more conservative attitudes came out. They seemed to want me to confirm that "even" Sweden was "returning" now to "normal" capitalist ways. One said he had heard that it was not a very religious country, but that religion was to become a required subject in the schools again. I said it had always been, but that it was not a subject to teach one religion and its values but rather something like the history of all religions. I had to explain that difference a couple of times; it was difficult for them to grasp. To them, religious teaching was doxically the inculcation of certain values.

There was also talk of how even Sweden and the United States, after Reagan, were returning to "family values". We discussed the theme of divorce for a minute or two, but it created no sparks, they all accepted it, at least for others if not for themselves, and they did not agree with my memories of how controversial the debate about the divorce law had been ten years earlier. But then Miren said that for her the theme of abortion was more controversial, and the discussion blossomed.

Miren's position was: "The law on abortion is not necessary, I think, since there are now so many efficient contraceptive methods, and young people are so well informed..." Perhaps not so well informed, look at statistics, said I. Oh yes, protested the others, they are very well informed, very well... But no one would give any example, so I mentioned the one of sex education in schools. "We all know that it exists and is required now, but we also all know that there are many teachers who refuse to teach it, because they feel shame or whatever..." This comment was not appreciated, there was a short silence. So I continued, "And contraceptives are not one hundred percent safe." Miren said she did not think abortions were necessary anyway. The feminists were saying horrible things like the other day in a television debate one feminist had said she would like to have the freedom to get pregnant in order to abort... How horrible! everyone exclaimed.

But if the theme of divorce was not controversial enough, this one was too controversial, especially when they understood that I accepted abortions. So the conversation turned instead to the problem of what to tell the children about sex and contraception. María José: "If my daughter is fourteen or fifteen and she is going camping with her school, I am not going to tell her, look, just in case you go to bed with someone, there is this... I am not going to tell her that, because I don't want her to do it." Of course not, said the others. "But if they have the information already, then you have to say something, so then what do you do?" whined María José. And the phrases that were usually heard in this type of semi-cautious context were pronounced: I won't say that I approve of it, but today... Some experience... perhaps... but what I absolutely won't stand for is this pattern of today with one, tomorrow with another...

Suddenly Pablo exclaimed, for no obvious reason, that all in all, one had to remember that total equality is impossible, because a woman can never be as efficient as a man at work. He gave the usual arguments: that women think of their family and their home more than a man, so they cannot concentrate on their work, and they have to stay home with sick children and so on. Of course he thought it was correct to give women the best conditions possible, but a woman employee can never be profitable, at least not if she gets a man's salary, that is just the way it is and there is nothing to do about it. Pablo's attitude was too aggressive for the others to accept in good grace, but their counter-arguments were lame, because the content of what he said struck them as self-evident.

Juan Antonio and Mary Luz left early, saying they had to get up early in the morning to go to a wedding. María José showed the rest of us around the house, since I had not seen it. We all complimented her on the beautiful garden. She said she enjoyed gardening so much she was thinking of firing the part-time gardener. When Conchita got married, she would probably fire the maid, too. "Aren't you afraid of living alone in this big house?" I asked and got immediate support from Miren who said she could never do it. María José took pleasure in offering us examples of her enjoyment: how she had breakfast in different corners of the garden according to the season, how she had seen the trees grow, since she had lived in the same house for almost thirty years... She could never contemplate living in an apartment! She said she was a "country girl" who wanted to stay close to the ground. "City people don't even know in what phase the moon is most of the time, and I always do!"

Jesús and Charo gave me a ride home. I asked about their social life in Catalonia. They said they belonged to all three clubs in town, because they felt they had to, for business reasons, but they hardly ever went. They did not like the Catalans and longed for an opportunity to move back to Madrid.

Comments

This dinner party was special in many obvious ways. But it was representative in other ways, especially in how the conversation became really lively only when controversial issues came up, but threatened to die down completely if the issue was too controversial.

In my terms, the guests enjoyed the occasion for socializing and used it quite efficiently for negotiating some cultural meanings that were important to them, especially the one of the sex life of the younger generation, and for María José especially the need to define herself as a feminine woman and "normal" female friend, in spite of her separated status. She negotiated the cultural construction of femininity. She wanted it to stay close to ideas of seductiveness and essential difference from masculinity, ideas she felt were old and comfortable and beautiful, but she could not deny her own experiences, nor the fact that she enjoyed her new feeling of competence and independence. She was also doing impression management using a new criterion: the thing with which she could impress the others was not charming incompetence but intelligence and the capacity to learn new things and adapt to a new situation. There was much ambiguity in her feelings and in her comments and in the reactions of the others. Definitions slid around and they were handled with apparent caution and elegance, but there was no absolute avoidance of sensitive things, like femininity, sexuality in old age and even the most sensitive of all, the power relationships between women and men.

The context was clearly middle class, but the economic level was somewhat higher than that of most Club Aguafría members. This was probably one reason for María José's stress on simplicity. She herself said that the guests were old friends for whom she felt no need to go through special efforts, and that was probably true, but it would not have been sufficient reason by itself for a more insecure woman.

The reason I committed a mistake, indicating an unacceptable opinion on abortion, was that the mode of management of meaning was difficult to define. It tended towards expansive, and especially María José was struggling with herself, having been forced by circumstances to question important certainties and now also pushing herself further along the road towards an open-minded attitude. She had previously tried hard to give me the impression that she was quite progressive. Miren and Pablo were talkative, intelligent persons and started out joking in a lighthearted way about such a sensitive issue as gender power. Juan Antonio admired Marvin Harris, who is usually considered a leftist in Spain. I misread all these signs. Not that I thought I was in radical company, and I had not really believed the others would approve of abortions – but I had believed they were ready to scrutinize all possible positions. That was not so.

The mode of management of meaning oscillated and vacillated, but at no point was it either clearly expansive or clearly cautious.

The discussion of young people's sex life had started out taking for granted that it should not be allowed expression and ended up admitting, very cautiously, "some experience... today..." The discussion on women's position went in the opposite direction, starting from a good-humored acceptance of Miren's professional status, even of the fact that she competed with her own husband, and a discussion of femininity that seemed to take for granted only that nothing should be taken for granted, but ending with a strong normative outburst (from Pablo) which was not really contested by anyone.

The conversation was most relaxed when the men reminisced about their childhood friendship. In that context, even Miren's cutting remarks were just good fun.

Miren was the person with the most progressive attitude as to gestures and style of interaction. She made her presence felt in a straightforward way and did not hesitate to interrupt the men. She was of course used to interacting with men and behaving in a self-assured manner at work. María José, who had always been a housewife, behaved in a much more "feminine" way, deferring to the men when they pronounced definite opinions, but manipulating them into complimenting her or saying other things she wanted them to say. But María José was perhaps the only one who had taken a really critical look at her own life. Charo and Mary Luz said little. They were housewives and probably felt like a silenced minority in the company of three men, two professional women and one separated woman.

The men talked mostly to each other, and like most middle class men they showed some irritation when the women demanded their direct attention, but unlike most of the men at Club Aguafría, they asked the women questions and listened to their answers. The situation of a dinner party with no male host was not obviously uncomfortable, and no one commented on it, but perhaps it was somewhat awkward for the men. They had to treat María José both as a hostess (give her compliments) and a host (turn to her as the central point of reference). If this felt strange for them, they handled it gracefully.

Evidently, all the guests accepted María José's separation. They accepted her dinner invitation, they were old friends, they seemed to have broken off relations with her ex-husband, i.e. they had taken her side in the conflict. When she spoke about her separation, they were attentive and supportive. But accepting María José's separation was not the same thing as accepting separations in general. This could hardly be stated openly in her house, and that may have been why nobody wanted to discuss divorce, but it was a clear subtext in the comments that followed my improvised explanation of why separations can seem to run in families. In these comments, separations were treated as terrible misfortunes, and the message was that in spite of everything, a separation might be a solution. But only in exceptional cases.

María José's wondering what a woman wants from a man sounded like a risky topic at first. But she defused it immediately, excluding any consideration of "physical attraction". No one protested when she stated that such a thing is out of the question after a certain age. It is possible that she had wanted someone to protest, complimenting her on her attractiveness in spite of her age. But it is also possible that they all took for granted that sexual activity is for young people only. In any case, she seemed honestly puzzled by her question, and her answer (good company) satisfied everyone's idea of an interesting but non-risky conclusion.

Chapter 13. Nature and Change

The arena for cultural negotiation to be described in this chapter was a friendship group, but not an institutionalized one like Nosotros. The occasion was an informal get-together in which some old friends had some food and discussed pretty much what they felt like, like in the previous chapter, but in this case they did so on my initiative. In other words, it was a group discussion, but the participants knew each other very well, and they were the kind of people who enjoyed debating for debating's own sake.

Like in the group discussion in appendix A, the participants were four couples, middle aged, of similar economic level and similar professions, but different from the other group in that they considered themselves "progressives". What that word meant to them was a mixture of Enlightenment ideas summed up as being in favor of "change" in a general way. Some of them voted communist, the rest socialist, none confessed any religious beliefs, most of them had been active in parent-teacher associations, neighborhood associations and similar. They considered themselves "atypical" but did not feel like outsiders in their society, just "more evolved" than the majority. They can be contrasted with the group in appendix A, but neither group was extreme on the Madrilenian continuum of opinions and modes of management of meaning.

I will offer a detailed report of almost the whole discussion, since it constitutes a good example of expansive management of meanings. The participants felt positive about debate and were eager to take on any argument that came up. They did not hesitate to pronounce controversial statements, quite the opposite, they enjoyed confrontation and even exaggerations. They did not search for consensus. And to them, their "progressive" opinions included precisely a positive attitude towards criticism. The evening was fun, they agreed, because it was an occasion to scrutinize new ideas, applying merciless reason even to things once considered sacred.

The host couple was Cristóbal, 51 years old, an engineer employed in a state service company, and Cristina, 33, formerly an office worker, now a housewife, trying to get pregnant but also going to various courses in the hope of establishing some small business of her own. They had no children together, but it was Cristóbal's second marriage and he had two children from his first marriage. Both were of middle class background, the kind of older middle class (civil service) that had little money but high educational pretensions.

Antonio, 49, formerly an employee of an export company, had recently started a business of his own, exporting the same things to the same foreign countries. He had been successful and earned "an awful lot of money," according to the others. His wife Manolita, 47, was a housewife but carefully pointed out that she was not a "maría" – the despective word for a tradition-bound woman – but got out of the house often to participate in associations and cultural activities. They were both of rural extraction.

Emilia, 45, had worked as an elementary school teacher for a few years before she got married. After fifteen years as a housewife, she decided to go back to work, but since she could find no teaching position, she had ended up as an assistant in a marketing firm and was now very much interested in that work. Her father was a policeman; she had grown up in a medium-sized village. Her husband Ignacio, 46, an economist, had worked for a big transnational company for all of his professional life. He was now head of a sales department. As a child he lived in a village near Madrid, where his father had a small factory. It had to close down in the 1960's, when the market for its traditional products disappeared, so his family had known both good and bad times.

Nati, 52, was also an elementary school teacher who had worked for a few years before she got married. Then she had stayed at home for many years and had just recently gone back to work. Her husband Pedro, 54, was an engineer, employed in a transnational company manufacturing industrial machinery.

Cristóbal and Cristina had lived together for several years before they recently got married. The other three couples were married for the first and only time and had not lived together before marriage. They all had two or three children, all the children lived at home except for Cristóbal's and all studied at university.[114] Emilia and Ignacio lived in a one-family home, the others in apartments.

They had all been friends for a long time. They got together about once a month, usually to have Saturday night dinner together, either in a restaurant or in each other's homes. They had lived in the same area for many years and knew each other through networks in that area. I knew two of the couples quite well, too, from my own period of Madrilenian middle class living. This may have been part of the reason for the very relaxed atmosphere.

When beer and wine had been served and we had started helping ourselves to the selection of appetizers (tapas) Cristina and Cristóbal served on the living room coffee table, around which we were seated informally on chairs and couches, I placed the tape-recorder in the center of the table and gave my usual explanations.[115] Emilia asked if my study was about middle aged people. I said I interviewed all ages. This caused some joking, and then Emilia said that she thought people between 40 and 50 would be the most interesting, because this generation had very special experiences. She said this with the authority of her professional experience (the marketing firm where she worked did group discussions as one of its techniques!), but the others agreed emphatically.

Change and women's socialization

Emilia: "Especially one of the themes you said we could talk about, our children, well, because in our generation there is a situation that the younger ones do not have, because we have been educated with a number of values that are no good for us now to transmit to our children. We are an in-between generation, for whom the values of our society now have nothing to do with the earlier ones, and we are like a bridge in between. That is, we have been educated, they told us what was good and bad, but we cannot tell our children the same things."

This was an unusually clear statement of a feeling often expressed by people of this age.

The others gave various examples of things that have changed; then Emilia continued in her lecturing style: "Except in some cases, like Nati's mother who was a teacher, too, and mine too, who, well..... but not really... but the normal thing when we were little girls was that, we were told that a woman's job was to get married, and that was what we heard at home and everywhere, it was what society valued. Even families of a certain economic level did not even consider sending the girls to university. They sent them to nuns' schools where they learnt to embroider and some French. (Nati: "Or the teacher's college!") Or teaching, yes.[116] Like you and me. But... And then there were the lower levels, where maybe the daughter had to serve as a maid or work in a factory and so on. But as soon as the father had some land, the girl stayed at home helping her mommy. Because a woman's career was marriage, right?"

After some supporting comments and more examples from the others, Emilia went on: "So then, what happens nowadays? Well, now the whole society and the mass media bombard us, telling us a woman has to work outside the home. And women of our generation have a hard time, not just professionally, because they cannot get a job, because they have no skills, but there is also a contradiction in values. That is to say, now society treats a woman who stays at home... like... an even despectively."

The conversation turned to the common insulting words for housewife (maría, maripili, maruja, tía María, etc), and there was a short discussion about what they connoted exactly.[117] It was suggested that a maría was a woman with conservative attitudes, or a woman of low social extraction, or a woman with no intellectual capacity, or a woman who simplifies issues and will not accept any innovations or complications in her life, a woman who offers no interesting conversation, at least not about anything beyond cooking and childcare.

Out of courtesy it was pointed out that Manolita was not like that at all, and Manolita agreed, but she also said that people do treat you with less respect than if you have a job, and also that her many activities had a touch of therapy for her, to get out of the house. And Emilia drove home her point of how unfair this is, when women have been taught that this is what makes a good woman, to learn to sew, to cook very well... Manolita

165

filled in, "to learn everything you have to know, certainly." "What a woman has to know" is the traditional phrase for housewifely tasks.

Cristóbal pointed out the added injustice that a woman who works outside has to work inside the home, too, and Nati said that they call it to be "liberated" but in her case it was the opposite. "A woman who works, like I do, for example, is not liberated. On the contrary. She has two jobs. They say she is now independent of her husband, but no, it has nothing to do with her husband! You have to do it all! That's what!" The other women discussed abstractly for a while what they would like "liberation" to mean. Nati went on with her concrete tack: "Whatever you like. But you leave home at nine in the morning, for example, like I do, and yes, true, you can get out of the house, you dress nicely, you leave for your job. But afterwards you come home and you have another job there. So! Even if your companion[118] helps you, or if he does not help you,[119] you have another job. So you are not at all liberated, you are doubly... so really... I am sorry, but!"

Pedro felt attacked and said something about the kids being too lazy to help. Nati argued emphatically that the children should be taught to help, as she had heard they were in the United States, but that the way things have been in Spain it is impossible, the kids are used to mommy doing everything and besides they have heavy loads at university... The discussion centered for a while on how difficult it is to give the children an education different from the one you yourself has received.

Nati described her typical day: "I get up at seven to wash dishes and make beds and leave the house more or less decent, I go to work, I come back, Pedro usually buys the food, I call him from work to tell him what to buy... and so on... and at eleven at night, or twelve, before going to bed, I am still ironing, and... (suddenly emphatically self-ironic) and happy about it! Yes, that's another thing, on top of everything I am happy about it!" The women laughed and the men said that that was because she had been taught that those were her duties. Nati: "Sure, and so Pedro says, why do you make such an effort? Get a maid or something.... and I say, yes, I should... I do have some help, twice a week, not a lot, but... the thing is I am happy to do it, too!"

Choice and liberation

Manolita pointed out that Nati was happy because she had had a choice. Her situation was not an imposition on her. Everyone agreed that that was an important factor.[120] Nati said she was much happier now than before she got a job. Pedro said that was true, she was easier to get along with. Manolita said that evidently Nati felt more "realized," and Nati agreed.

Nati: "And then there is another thing, and that concerns you too, even though you don't work. And that is that it seems like... if you don't do it yourself, it does not get done the way it should." She was referring to the housewifely sense of ultimate responsibility and pride. Manolita understood that but thought such feelings were old-fashioned: "No, not me, oh no, not me, not any more, I have liberated myself from that! I have evolved more than you have!"

Meanwhile Emilia had been insisting that the next step to take was to liberate oneself from the pressure to find a job, because a woman can be liberated without it.[121] Someone pointed out that she herself worked and was happy to do so.

Emilia: "I wanted to talk in general, but if I have to talk about my particular case, I'll tell you that sure I feel much more realized in my job, I love it, I have been very very lucky to find it, to enter a world I knew nothing about, and to learn little by little, I feel fantastic about it, and I have good working hours, and... and the atmosphere in a marketing firm is very different from a company where you make products or... it is an atmosphere like among intellectuals, and the relationships are not hierarchical like... like a boss and his status..."

I asked if she had been yearning to go to work while she was a housewife. "Sure For a long time. Actually when I got that job it was nothing like what I do now, it was an absolutely stupid job, to clip questionnaires together, or to do telephone interviews. Everything else has come little by little, but when I started, it was a kind of work that does not realize anyone, not in the least, but I took it because I wanted to get out of the house. I am... I did not like being a housewife. Besides I am not a good housewife." She explained how she had none of the feelings Nati and Manolita had been talking about, and she said that as soon as she earned enough, she had found a maid and let her do everything. "I do nothing at all at home!" she said, with pride and a giggle, knowing she was being provocative. This made Nati give a long explanation of how she did not really like housework either, it was just that she did not like to see things dirty, and if you have a maid, you have to be at home to supervise her, otherwise... "Or you pay her for five hours and she works for two, that has happened to me." The best solution was to get all family members to cooperate, she thought. It seemed to be such an obvious and easy thing, yet it was so difficult to make it work.[122]

Men's housework

The women dominated the discussion totally, until I said I thought the men must have something to say on this topic, too, at least something about how they had felt when after many years all of a sudden they no longer had a housewife at their service. Had they felt a pressure to do household tasks?

Ignacio: "No, no, no, quite the opposite. In my case, I mean. In my case, I think Emilia has been emotionally more stable ever since she went to work, so then I think the whole family has gained a lot in that sense. As to cooperation, well, I have always tried to help and... and, well, sure there are a number of things in the house that are her responsibility, and they still are, right? And even though she says she does nothing, that is not true, she does, because she is responsible enough to do it – aren't you? I mean to see to it that someone does it. And there are certain things she does herself. But for example, if on a given day it is a question of cooking, well it might be me or it might be her doing it." Emilia said Ignacio did more cooking than she did. Ignacio said he did most of the shopping, too. Surprised, I asked how he had learned. He explained that he had lived on his own while studying, away from his mother for many years, so he had learned how to shop and everything, it had not been difficult at all. "But apart from that, I think, too, that it is a function that ought to be shared, like so many others. Not that there cannot be a division of duties in the home. There is. But I do certain things, and she others, but we can switch, and besides we relate to each other about it, and so on. So, all in all, it has been a rather positive process..."

I asked if there was no longer any problem for a man to go to the fruit store, to the fish store...[123] Manolita said that there certainly was. Cristóbal protested, he went to those stores, and to the market, too, and there was no problem. All of a sudden all the men were talking eagerly, telling their various experiences and anecdotes, with many jokes about misunderstandings. For instance about the women's norms of turn-taking. A man has to learn by watching them, but sometimes the women break their own rules when they see a man in a food store. Suddenly, Pedro said he thought there were just as many men as women in the market nowadays. The others protested. Nati repeated that she had to tell him what to buy, and Pedro protested angrily that he had gone shopping ever since they got married. Or even before that, since childhood. Nati insisted and Pedro answered back, and the others started laughing, telling them to go outside and discuss it and come back in and tell us the result. The conversation shifted towards the kinds of stores or markets they did their shopping in. One man said he even shopped for food in the village where they spent their summer vacations.[124]

Antonio, who had said nothing, now spoke up. "Well, I guess I am the one who helps least at home (the men laughed), for the obvious reason that (one man: that you are a deserter!) that Manolita does not work outside, so then she has more time to... but anyway (several voices were trying to interrupt him), wait! But anyway, if there is shopping to do, especially big things and so on, then I always..." Manolita pointed out that he took no initiatives for shopping, and Antonio agreed. Manolita said he was not educationally prepared for shopping and even less for ironing or loading the washer... Much laughter. Antonio admitted good-naturedly that he had no idea how the washer worked. I said that of all household tasks, the one that the men in my previous study in Valencia hated most to be asked to do was to hang laundry to dry. All the men agreed and gave comic examples: "Imagine me with some wet little panties in my hand, shaking them out..." Nati said that in her building, the kitchen terraces were covered (with brick lacework), so no one would see him, but Pedro still did not hang laundry.

There was more talk of how Pedro hated to see the children so lazy, and that unfortunately he had always worked so much that he had not had any chance to influence their education. Antonio said he thought the problem of lazy kids was a very general one.

168

Cristina said that since her mother had been alone with three children, they had been taught to work very hard at home, her brother too, so for her it was not strange at all to see Cristóbal start the washer or cook a delicious plate of clams. "People may think I am a worthless woman, a whore, a nobody, a slut, that I am awfully selfish, I know, I have noticed that. But it was no surprise for me to see Cristóbal vacuum or wash the dishes, I have seen my brother do things like that all my life!" Someone said she must have noticed that what was normal for her was not normal in other families, and she said of course she noticed, but that she still thought that what her family did was the normal thing and what others did was abnormal.

I said that we do not live on islands. My two sons, when they were children, had even said once in a while in so many words that they would not wash the dishes because that was for women only. Cristina laughed and said that her brother could never say a thing like that, "we were three against one, we would have killed him! But in your case it was the other way around, three men and one woman!" Lots of laughter.

Degrees of normative consensus

Ignacio said that one important change is that nowadays everyone is always thinking about how to share the tasks. "And before it used not to be like that, quite the contrary, it used to be that the children and the husband had to be perfectly waited upon by the mother (women's voices: of course!), so she would take out clothes for you to wear, clean your shoes, and so on (the women went on confirming and underlining what he was saying). So this is a whole concept that has changed completely in a matter of thirty years."

Pedro asked if he could tell an anecdote: "My son did his military service last year, and one weekend he went with a friend to his home in Ciudad Real. And it was a lower class family. So then, well, they slept in that house, and in the morning they had breakfast, and then my son got up and gathered up the plates to wash them. And: 'Where are you going! What an idea! You can't do that! '" Everyone was saying, yes, yes, and laughing in recognition. "And my kid told me about it, sort of surprised, too; in other words, for him, that point of view, he said, my, what a... I don't mean to say that he washes the dishes at home, or that he does not, but there he did. He did it because it seemed natural to him, right? He was the guest, so he wanted to give a hand, contribute... but the friend's mother was terribly offended!"

I said that he could not be completely ignorant of that attitude, it is all around us. Nati and Pedro said that in their house it was not, and then they got involved in yet another argument about how recalcitrant the kids were. The others said that certainly the youngsters of today know women who not only do not ask men for help but are actually offended if a man offers to help. The grandmothers, for example, usually. But they all stressed that, in Emilia's words, "our kids have a completely different idea. They may help or not, in practice, but they know that the normal thing is to help, that is the norm." I insisted, that "most of the Spanish women of the generation of our mothers were just like that woman Pedro's son met, they defended their territory."

Emilia: "Oh yes. My mother, for example, she was so surprised when Ignacio started coming into our home,[125] and later after we were married, too, we would finish a meal and he would get up and clean off the table, and... I remember that she would always say to me, aren't you ashamed? (background laughter) Aren't you ashamed of yourself, your husband cleaning the table and you sitting there... just calmly sitting there... My mother admired my husband an awful lot, Ignacio was a discovery for her. Here is this gentleman out of the blue who knows how to do everything. Because Ignacio has always done a lot even before I went to work. Now he does more things, but before, for example during weekends, to vacuum, to iron his shirts, he has always done things like that... And my mother was completely surprised, and I remember her telling her neighbors about it, with great pride. (Ignacio murmured something.) Didn't she? My daughter's husband knows how to do everything, he even changes diapers... Because when our daughter was born, we were in the hospital and we decided... my mother always thought that she would be the one to be with me in the hospital when I was to give birth, but then Ignacio told her, look, we prefer for you to stay at home, this is our thing and we prefer to be by ourselves, the two of us, we will call you afterwards, and so on.[126] And when my mother came to visit, she felt terrible about it, because she thought that the one who ought to be there with me was her, and for Ignacio to come to visit. But since she had to accept it, she did. But when the girl – I could not move, I had stitches, and the girl needed a change of diapers, Ignacio got up to change her, and I remember how she walked towards him, sort of like saying, but how are you going to touch the diapers...? For her it was a surprise, but Ignacio did not let her."

There were examples of how mothers used to travel far in order to be with their daughters when they gave birth, or else the daughters went back to give birth in the home village to be with their mother. Cristina said that in spite of everything Cristóbal's oldest brother, over 60 years old now, had learnt how to change diapers on his mother, who was incapacitated, and bathe her and everything. Emilia: "Well, things have improved, we have managed to change a few things."

Antonio then told the story of his parents. "They are over seventy, approaching eighty, and they grew up in a small village, in Andalusia, where the male chauvinism is so deeply rooted. Well, my father helps my mother to set the table, to clean the table..." Many voices expressing great surprise. Someone asked if he had always done it and Antonio said no, of course not, he had started when quite old, and then the others were less surprised. I asked if Antonio had asked them about it.

Antonio: "No, they would just say it started little by little... I think they have learnt from their children! He learnt from us, because when we were kids we had to help to clear the table, each one had to take his or her plate and take it to the kitchen, so then he probably felt a little odd, sort of like: here everyone takes his plate except... so little by little he has started doing things until now he does everything."

I asked if it was because his mother had health problems. Manolita had another explanation. "No, but my mother-in-law is the typical woman who is not a housewife. She is a housewife, because she is a woman, and to be a housewife is something that has fallen on top of her like a bitter fate. She is a terrible housekeeper, a disaster. (...) And my father-in-law is exactly the opposite. So then this fact... when my mother-in-law cooks, the kitchen is not a kitchen, it is all hell broke loose. Therefore, the only way for him to have some order is for him to do it himself. Now of course, as long as he was working he did not notice, nor did he care, poor man, but as soon as he retired, naturally... it has been a necessity for him." Antonio thought it had been out of conviction, too.

Manolita's comment could be interpreted as one instance of the so common complaints about mothers-in-law, but her tone of voice was empathic, and Antonio did not seem to be disturbed by this public criticism of his mother; Manolita's intention seemed rather to be to prove that there are women who are not born with housewifely talents.

There was some talk of how change is always possible, and how even some deep-rooted things can change all of a sudden.

Women and careers

Nati: "But generally, the women I know, the normal thing is for them to... to be like I say. I know even of persons, women I mean, even women who have had high positions, and they have had to choose, and this is the truth, too, I am telling you, that they have had to go home because the child has a sore throat and a fever, she has to do it all, so she has had to quit that high position of director general or whatever, where she had to travel and leave the family on its own. That, in Spain – I am telling you the truth, because I know it, you see – that is very difficult. (...)"

Someone said that another problem for women in high positions is that a husband usually does not accept her being highly placed, at least not if she earns more money than he does.

Cristina told about a role play they had done in one of her courses, a course for unemployed women, organized by the Institute of Women, to give them more self-confidence. "The theme they gave us was this: you are a high executive in a company, you have had to work very hard to reach this position, and study too, and with your husband and your children and everything, you have had a very hard time but you have reached this position, and now you are at the top of your career and they offer you the possibility to go even further, you are to... well, a lot more, a whole lot more... like your dream come true. But you have to go to another city. And there is no option, either your husband quits his job and the whole family moves with you, or else you can't go. And look, the discussion was just terrible! The husband won!"

There was some misunderstanding and Cristina had to explain again that it was not just a question of debating the issue. "We played it like a play, using any arguments we could think of, but there had to be a decision, and the most terrible thing was that he won! She could not go!" Cristina was outraged and to underline it even more strongly she told about another role play on the theme of rape. "This woman has a lover, but she wants to go back to her husband, and then she meets this lunatic who rapes her... and in the game, it turned out the woman was a whore and had not been raped at all, just because she had a lover! Isn't it funny! We are so unfair! We are such beasts! And then after the games we had to give ourselves marks, and the husband won every time. The husband was the victim! The same thing in the game of the high position. They said about her husband: oh, the poor guy!" Manolita: "Well, that is our generation." Cristina: "There were girls of my age and even younger, and also older, of your age, there were women of all ages. And he won!"

Nati said she thought the man's job is always more important, anyway. There was a surprised silence, and then quick jokes to cover it up. It was not acceptable for a woman in this group to have such an opinion. But it turned out Nati had been sarcastic. She explained how Pedro just leaves when he has to go on a business trip. "He just packs his suitcase and leaves, hey presto, there you are, and he calls me from wherever. Fine. But during the three or four days he is away, I have the whole responsibility for everything, and if I have a teachers' meeting or a dinner with friends... (...) If I had to make business trips, what would happen?"

Now the discussion heated up quite a bit and fragmented into several for a good while. Emilia explained in detail how the law on maternity leave had changed and that now the parents could choose which one of them would stay at home with the newborn child. Someone mentioned a neighbor of theirs, a certain Felipe. "It was in the press, too. This law went into effect just a few months before they had their child, so when his wife had the baby, he was the only father who opted to take paternity leave. Well, it was because his wife has a business of her own, and she would not stay at home, so then, fine..."

Emilia: "Fine, but he just wanted to get some extra money!"

Cristina: "Not at all!" A very heated argument ensued between the two of them, mixed with lots of laughter. Emilia felt that Felipe's paternity leave was a sham, for the money, and that his intention was not to take care of the baby. Cristina: "I don't care, Emilia. If my husband has a business of his own, and I stay at home, because we have a law or my company has an agreement with the union that I have a year's maternity leave, nobody is going to call me a pig for taking it..." Emilia thought that would be different, because in the case of Felipe it was he who had the salary and she the business. Cristina said that he had the same right to a leave to take care of his baby as a woman would have, and yet he had been so badly criticized at the company where he worked, she knew some people there who knew about it, he had to quit his job. "He can't go back now! The gossip killed him! Not just the company, but the workmates!"

Emilia, realizing she herself had argued in a direction opposite her usual opinions: "Which goes to prove that society is slower, it comes along behind the laws, even though we are always saying that the laws lag behind..."

Nature and education

This provoked comments about the Swedish parental leave,[127] so I explained how Swedish fathers, too, use up very little of the total parental leave time. The men immediately said they thought that was normal. There were eager comments about the biological meaning of motherhood, and about how a father acting like a mother acts against nature.[128] This was the point at which the group consensus around "progressivity" split up along gender lines into radical female demands and male defense of status quo.

The women tried to say that breastfeeding is one thing, but both parents can give a bottle. Ignacio said that when women work, they are deprived of the opportunity to fulfill certain duties that their nature gives them. Not just breastfeeding. There must be a deep relationship with the child...

Cristina: "That goes for the father too!" The men: No, no, no! Cristina: "To be tender to a baby, to hold it without feeding it, anyone can do that. And they should!" Ignacio: "I do not agree." Nati said that in her experience it is always the women who stay home with sick children, even though the teacher's collective bargaining only gives them the right to two days, so they risk their jobs, but the women do it. Ignacio, eagerly: "Yes, yes, yes, the women!" Nati said she did not mean to say that it was biological, "but even so, when my Margarita had to have an ear operation, and she was already fourteen, who asked for time off from work? I did, and I had to find a substitute on my own and I had to pay her out of my own salary, to be able to do that, but I did."

One man said we now live in a society of rights.[129] Cristina exploded again: "I do not agree with you! The rights are not the same for men and for women. Nor being a person..." The men also got angry and shouted about the mother's role being much more fundamental than the father's. Manolita said softly she thought it was just a matter of education. The other women asked the men if they meant to say education had nothing to do with it but only biology, and so on. The word "nature!" with audible exclamation marks, was heard again and again in the fray, usually by male voices, and the word "education!" usually by female voices. There were comparisons with other animals. But these men (unlike the ones in appendix A) did not deny their own responsibility for small children. They said fathers too had a responsibility, but that the role of the mother was much more important and much more natural. They also used the somewhat more progressive-sounding (because education-related) argument that women's psychology is better adapted to childcare, and here they did come close to denying their own capacity for empathy. The women fumed that that was a good argument for men who want to be lazy.

Pedro's key argument is a good example: "All you have to do is to look at the children. Whom do they turn to? Who can make them obey? The mother, always! Who is the parent who most probably will fail to fulfill their needs? The father, always. In other words, a mother who... a mother who does not take good care of her children is something – something that makes you sick! In other words, a bad mother is something much worse than a bad father. Undoubtedly." (The women protested about education and habits.) "No, not habits, not at all! It is the biological role, that is what it is." One woman said in an exaggeratedly calm voice, marking a definite chasm: "I do not agree." Another said, "Neither do I" in the same tone of voice. Gender war seemed to be declared.

Cristóbal then broke the masculine front, but ambiguously so. "I think it is educational, derived from the biological situation. So then it is both; in other words, at first there was the biological importance of the mother for the children. And that in the long run gives an educational tendency, too. Even though now both could play the same role, but because of the past, our biological past..."

Pedro and Ignacio insisted, it was biology and only biology. Ignacio said that perhaps when a child gets a little older, say three years...

Cristina told the story of a friend of hers who had a small store and could take no maternity leave, so her husband who was unemployed had taken care of the baby, and very good care, and he was the happiest father on earth and more of a mother than any mother...

Pedro: "I think (...) that lady would have preferred a hundred times to take care of her child herself. Due to whatever circumstances she could not do it, just like there may be mothers who are separated from their children due to illness and the child is given to an aunt or grandmother. Or the mother dies (...). But those are exceptions. So! I think that by nature the majority of women, I can't give percentages, but evidently what they desire is, if they have a child, to take care of it. Personally, they themselves." (As he spoke, the women were shouting: "Of course!" angrily all the time, and trying to make Pedro understand that that was not the question at all, but whether he himself could imagine taking the responsibility for a baby.) "Not to give it to the husband nor to their own mother..."

Fathering

Suddenly Ignacio suggested a novel idea: "I have felt envy or something like it many times, because I could not carry my children inside myself. And my wife could." There were long and varied comments on this, and the atmosphere relaxed and changed from confrontation to reflection. Emilia said Ignacio had worked a lot with the children, bathing them and so on, because he wanted to, not as a duty, but because he envied her. "And because he felt that need that you say only women feel. In his case, he felt it. He preferred for me not to bathe them, because he had to work, so he could only be a father for a few hours, so at least he almost always gave them their bath."

Antonio, who had been very quiet, now said that the psychology of a man and of a woman are conditioned by their culture... Pedro, shouting again: "Yes, but of a culture as old as memory! So!" Then he insisted again about universal features of motherhood in all species of animals and all cultures and I could not keep quiet. "I am not supposed to talk here, but I can't keep quiet any longer!" There was much friendly laughter as I delivered a short lecture on basic anthropology, emphasizing variation.

Manolita remembered a TV program about the couvade: "The woman was giving birth, she dropped that baby just like that, in a moment, and then she walked over to the husband's bed, and the man lay there with his baby, while she went back to her tasks. To chop wood! Hell! And they are human beings!" (Laughter.) Emilia said the birds take turns, 50 % each to care for the eggs. Ignacio said birds are very different from mammals. Pedro again talked about breastfeeding and basic ties. Neither men nor women changed their arguments very much after my mini-lecture. Cristina mentioned the custom of letting another, paid, woman breastfeed a child. Pedro said that was cultural, yes. Cristina triumphed: "Well now! In that case there is no rejection! Just because it is another woman. But it is not the mother! Then the men accepted it, then she was not a bad mother if she did not care for her baby, as long as the husband did not have to do it." Pedro was clearly against the ropes but tried to say that it was a solution if the mother had no breastmilk. Cristina and Manolita emphasized the issue of class and money and said that if a wet nurse can replace the mother, then so can a father with a bottle.

Pedro repeated that in emergencies one can give a baby to anyone, the grandmother, an aunt, the father... but it is bad for the child. You rob it of a newborn's natural experiences. Antonio said something about how modern society is creating artificial conditions for everyone.

I suggested we switch to some other theme, since this one seemed to be exhausted. This was accepted with relief.

Strong women

Pedro said: "I want to suggest something. I have to say one thing. It is a thesis that I defend. Woman is much more resistant than man. That is the first point. I mean, she is stronger." Questioned, he said he meant by nature. A man has more physical strength but a woman is more resistant. Antonio said he did not agree. Pedro tried the anthropological tack, saying he knew that in many cultures the heaviest tasks fell on women, not just housework but agricultural tasks. "With this I want to say that, not that it is justifiable or anything like that, but that there is also a certain predisposition for a woman to take on heavier duties than a man."

This was followed by a short surprised silence. Then Manolita exploded: "So, we are the donkey on which you load everything!" Lots of laughter and many arguments, all the women saying, what a comfortable philosophy for men, that was some expression of men's bad conscience, etc. But the atmosphere was relaxed. The idea was just too far out.

Nati turned the mood to serious discussion again. "Now, seriously, the truth is that a woman, whatever her work, an executive or director general or whatever... she has to... I am sure of this, they said it in a TV debate the other day, any woman, whatever her job, is the only one who has to wear an apron at home. You know, in class I am the señorita.[130] Because they call us, the teachers, señoritas. Señorita this, señorita that... And when I get home, I change clothes and put on the apron, because I have to."

Antonio: "And then she is the maid!" Laughter and comments. The men said that for some specific social circumstance to change, a lot of things have to change, implying that it could not be done promptly. The women argued that that meant that they could be changed, after all.

Pedro said that there were matriarchal societies, where the women ruled. Not many, but some, and in Spain there were residues. For instance the Basques, said someone immediately.[131] There were comments to the effect that Basque women make decisions concerning money and everything, but one woman said that this was mostly among the fishing population, where the men were often absent. Someone mentioned Galicia and the same arguments were offered.[132]

Cristina: "But even so, the men don't do a thing around the house."

Pedro: "Of course they don't do a thing. (...) Because the woman rules!" He explained that if a woman has the authority, she could subject the man and make him do the heavy work. So if she does not do that, even though she could, it must be because women are better fitted to do the work of childcare. By nature or by culture. "So then, why is that so? I think it is because a woman is more capable of efforts..."

The women exploded in laughter and irony. The discussion worked itself back and forth over the same arguments of nature versus culture for a good while.

Change and confusion

Emilia: "Ten years ago it even seemed natural that it must always be the man – just to change the topic a bit – who took the initiative to establish a relationship with a woman, or the sexual initiative. And is that reason enough to think it is biological? I refuse to believe that! Besides, society is proving now that it is not true." The other women seconded this argument. Pedro protested again. Emilia said that it used to be argued that the sexual initiative belonged to men by biology and now this has obviously been proven

176

false, so the same thing might happen with other things called biological now, like motherhood.

Straight-faced, Pedro said, "I want to say something very reactionary!" and there was an explosion of laughter, whistling, screaming. "Now! Again?! Really reactionary this time?" Pedro: "I think that this change, that has been so fast in culture, because of the evolution and the technological advances, these last fifty or sixty years, is causing also some erroneous behavior." (Sarcastic laughter from the women.) "Really, the thing is that we think everything that is done now is good, and that all progress is good. Well, we'll see." The women turned serious and said that obviously not all change is for the better.

I said this was one issue that interested me, too. The general idea has been that change is equal to progress; that idea has been automatically accepted for a number of years. What did they think of that?

Evolution

Antonio took it on himself to establish the terms of the new topic: "One thing is obvious, and it is that nature needs many years for evolution to take place. (...) We are changing at a speed that is way above, very much beyond the normal evolution in nature." (Affirmative murmurs.) "That means that this evolution goes a little bit against nature. And somehow this has the effect that people adopt attitudes that afterwards we cannot accept. And this creates important social problems."

There was uncertain silence, as so often happens in Madrilenian discussions when someone establishes a baseline that is neither surprising nor controversial, yet not quite self-evident enough to serve as a jumping-off point for new arguments or examples. I asked Antonio if he meant that we have to change our nature in order to accept social change. Knowing the political outlook of this group, it could be surmised that they would not agree to such a formulation.

Antonio: "No, it is just that the mind, the human mind, eh, is not prepared to evolve as rapidly as we are evolving." He said that he did not want to define which changes are good or bad; he just meant that changes are being produced at such a speed that many minds are not able to follow. I asked again what this had to do with biological evolution. Nati said he probably meant cultural evolution.

Antonio: "No, I was referring to biological evolution and the evolution of the universe as a whole. It is very slow. And we are biological beings, we have a mind that has to evolve. And our mind is evolving much faster than it logically should."

The others now turned to the invention of agriculture and the coming of capitalism and other examples to place "recent" evolution at different points in time and make Antonio see that the horizon of a couple of decades that he was talking about had little to do with biological evolution. But Pedro said that the settling of the nomadic hunters had been much slower than the social changes we are seeing now. "And in this country we do see this, just think of family relationships, or political relationships... Here, there have been so radical and so deep and so wide changes, so, well, I can't even begin to... In a very short time, the things we have had to assimilate!" (Dramatic pause) "Well, evidently it is very difficult. So I mean that for there to be a really deep democratic sense in all parameters..." (Sarcastic supportive laughter from all the others, probably thinking of the many "undemocratic ticks" that people of their kind see everywhere and talk about and criticize.) "Come on! Nobody will believe that! Just scratch us a little bit on the surface and the authoritarianism comes out, that is what we have been taught." (More laughter, many comments.) "Anyway, culturally..."

Emilia said that was what we had said earlier, about how we have been educated and what we want to transmit.

Ignacio: "I think we have to distinguish carefully between biological evolution and intellectual evolution, just to call it something. And I think that the speed of man's intellectual evolution is much greater and much faster and much more pronounced than the biological evolution."

The discussion fragmented into several for a short while. Pedro then tried a new biological argument, saying that women are not as aggressive as men. The women protested strongly but did not agree among themselves if aggression was determined biologically or socially... There were jokes about premenstrual tension and about modern wars.

Emilia shrugged: "Except that a man can lift heavier burdens and a woman, having a smaller hand, is better at making electronic components..." Antonio said some women exercise hard and become as muscular as any man. The others protested that that had nothing to do with the argument. Emilia said such a woman was unnatural. Pedro continued his anthropological line, saying women could not hunt because they were neither strong nor fast enough, and Cristina said they could nevertheless carry forty children on their back... Again the discussion fragmented into several parallel ones, most of which were about different sports and why they were or were not separated by gender. Someone said something about hairdressers: why are there more male than female hairdressers?

Manolita: "But that does not mean anything because they are usually effeminate." Antonio asked what that had to do with it. Manolita: "Because they are structurally very similar to women." Some voices protested but the majority seemed to agree. Pedro reflected that the differences between the sexes were certainly a matter of degree, but suddenly he exploded again: "But for heaven's sake! Where do the cultural differences come from, those who have been inherited for so long? There must be some reason ... Or do you think God came up to Adam and Eve and told them, you do this, and you...? Or what?!" This earned Pedro an important point, because it made his position seem progressive in comparison to fundamentalist religion.

178

Many excited voices. The discussion kept coming back to the same point. There was a problem that had not been solved.

Cristina, very aggressively: "Of course! Something comes from nature! But Pedro, do you let your hair grow long, do you go?..." (she made ape sounds and ape gestures with her arms scratching her sides) "And do you grab your woman and go, 'macho, macho'? That is out of fashion, man! You walk around playing the macho man now, and people will say, what's the matter with Pedro? Because society has changed now!"

Pedro, conciliatory: "Well, I am going to have to start doing just that." General laughter.

What do we want?

I proposed we quit discussing nature versus culture, "because the truth is nobody knows. But it seemed to me a while ago that we were actually talking about, sort of between lines, not just what is but what we would like. Weren't we?" Agreement. "What do we want? To what extent do men and women want to be different?" I explained that most recent changes in Spain and in Europe in general had been in the direction of more similarity between the sexes. Not just equality in the sense of justice, but equality in the sense of similarity. "We talk about men in the kitchen and women in the labor market. But how much similarity do we really want?"

There were a couple of false starts. There seemed to be a feeling that this new angle was interesting, but so new that it was difficult to say anything about it. Ignacio said that yes, he thought that what the feminists want is exactly that, similarity, and that is an important error, a great loss. There can be justice without similarity. "What a woman should do is to have some basic freedoms that permit her to develop herself, in any way she wants to, and that is enriching, certainly, it would enrich society much more than if it is like now, an opposition. Even though the road of opposition may be quicker." Too much similarity would be a social loss, agreed Antonio.

More false starts and tentative questions.

Emilia said she did not really think feminists want to be like men. "They want equal rights. But as a first step... in this society women have been so marginalized, in so many ways so unfairly marginalized, that the first step towards being able to develop as a person is to try to obtain those minimal rights. And perhaps often they exaggerate, there are feminist groups that exaggerate. and make it seem as if they want to be like men. But I don't think that is what we want."

Pedro muttered that they do too want to be like men. Nati said she would like to know what has happened in societies that are more advanced than Spain, like the United States or Sweden. Emilia seconded: Have the women there completed that first step? Ignacio said something about the consequences of technology. New protests and tentative comparisons with "advanced" countries.

179

Ignacio: "Well, what I wanted to say is that technological progress is not the same thing as social and human progress. So for example American society has had a human progress that has had to turn back in many ways. I mean, in a feminist sense, the feminist groups and all that stuff they had in the United States, well, that has all moved backwards instead of forwards. (...) Besides, the American family is not as humanly advanced as the family in Europe. From what I know now, their behavior seems to me to be much more regressive, to judge from what Iñaki (his son, who had studied for a year in the US) tells me about how that family behaved, much more regressive and much more hypocritical and much less personal..."

Nati: "So then it is cultural, because you are not going to say..."

Ignacio: "... I am not going to say they are more humanly evolved than we are, they may be more evolved in other ways, but humanly I think they are not. I think they are very Indian!"

Since this comment made everybody shut up for a second, wondering whether Ignacio was serious or not (a truly racist comment would not be acceptable in this group), and since the new theme did not appear to lead to any interesting discussion, I suggested we try to specify what it is we want. Ignacio said that was not possible. "We would have to explain cases. I said freedom in the sense that she should have the same possibilities a man would have. That she should not be limited, socially or as a citizen. Like in Sweden, the same legal and social conditions a man has. So that if she wants to, she will be able to develop the way she wants to."

Antonio: "Develop as a woman."

Ignacio: "And not imitating men. That is what I understand, what I would like for it to be like."

There was a discussion on the symbolic markers of gender in dress and adornment. The women pointed out that what would have been considered "homosexual" twenty years ago was now normal grooming for men. Pedro agreed that this was a cultural change but wondered if it might not have biological explanations, too. He hinted at sexual attraction, and Cristina aggressively responded that in that case he ought to walk around with his genitals visible and puffing up his chest to impress women. Pedro said that certainly there are societies where men dress up, but what he meant was that there was no human society where the difference between the sexes was not clearly marked. Asked what he wanted, he said that men and women ought to have the same rights and the same opportunities to develop as human beings, but the division of labor cannot be eliminated, that would go against the development of the human race. Everything would become much more boring. And specialization is a sign of progress, after all.

Emilia said she thought it was an error for feminists to try to be like men, and for young women to dress like men, in blue jeans for example. That just opened the door to the kind of reactionary thinking Pedro was expressing, she said. It would be much better if men imitated women, caring more for their looks, for example. Antonio tried to agree, saying that European women have lost their femininity, but Emilia immediately turned around and asked what the heck he meant, should we stay behind curtains, doing embroidery, or what! Antonio assured her he only meant that women ought to accept their roles as women, remembering that they should try to be attractive to the opposite sex, the way it has always been.

Nati now pronounced a manifesto: "I want to be a person. Since I was born a woman, I want to be a female person, but I want to be independent. I don't want anyone to trample on me, and at work, at my place of work, women and men are the same. I want to be equal, but I don't want to be a man! I want to be free, think whatever I feel like thinking..."

There were comments on the difficulties for women in the labor market, but Nati went on with great energy and conviction: "And then at home, too, I want to be a person. I don't mind if some day I feel like it and I go into the kitchen, and make, let's say, a dinner for seven people, I don't mind! What I do not want is for that to be my obligation just because of being a woman, that I will have to do everything and everything will have to depend on me. (...) Because I am a hard worker and I don't mind working. But I don't want anyone to set limits for me as a person." She went on, repeating and underlining, for a good while.

This is a good point to interrupt the transcription, even though the discussion continued for another half hour. It went back over many of the same arguments again; there was some special attention to the difficulties for women of getting and keeping executive positions; pros and cons of special labor legislation for women were mentioned; people reminisced about the first women to go to university and how fast an exception had become the rule; and talking about how women and men still choose different types of studies, the discussion returned again to the issue of nature versus culture.

Comments

The next day, I commented the tertulia[133] with several of the participants, separately, over the phone, and all of them said that they thought it had been a lot of fun. They also pointed out that there are certain things that people do not say when their spouse is present. There was more consensus in appearance than in fact, that was at least what the women thought. "The men say the right things, but they don't always mean it." But in the case of Nati and Pedro, the comments went in the opposite direction: I was not to believe they had serious marital problems, they were just in a tense period because the family had not yet adjusted to Nati's working, and Nati was not as radical and Pedro not as reactionary as they had seemed, they were just saying exaggerated things for each other to hear.

This was a group that enjoyed debating for its own sake and they were all interested in the issues that came up and debated them as intellectual problems. They gave personal examples, certainly, but that is the Madrilenian conversational style. In comparison to the tertulia described in appendix A (which covered largely the same topics), this group was more progressive in that their consensus was found further to the left on the political scale and endorsed change in general as improvement. Their mode of management of meaning was also different. The general attitude was to place anything that might come up under the harsh light of reason. There was no feeling that certain topics should be exempted from that light nor any fear that any given opinion might sound too subversive. Quite the contrary, in this tertulia, to come up with surprising and dangerous ideas rendered extra debating points.

Except when it came to the issue of motherhood, that is. It upset the men, while the women continued in a critical mode. This should have made the men defensive and aware of a contradiction, and some of them seemed to feel something like that once in a while, but as a whole they did not. They had to make an effort, at times, not to fall into cautious habits, for instance saying "that is not normal!"

The gender patterns of interaction in the two tertulias were different. In the one in appendix A, the men dominated totally at first, and then the women took over little by little. In this one, the women dominated totally at first and the men entered only when I invited them to, but after that there was approximate balance. One may assume that in the other group, the men were used to dominating, in part because their norms did not consider that wrong, in part because the group had originated around the men, and in part also because all the men had jobs in which they were used to dominating the interaction, whereas their wives did not. But the issues debated awakened stronger feelings in the women, so they slowly fought for and gained center stage. In Cristóbal's and Cristina's home, the issue was at first defined as something for women, but as soon as it was made clear that it should be considered important for men, too (I said so and the women agreed), the men accepted this, and thereafter women and men interacted on equal terms.

In both tertulias, the issues of men's housework and nature versus culture became the most burning ones.

The importance of the theme of change was clear throughout the discussion, both on and between the lines. One good example was Emilia's comment that some things do improve. Her phrasing and tone of voice were grudging, and her intention was to say that yes, some things have improved but there is still a lot left to complain about. For expansive-minded people, to be complacent about change could easily sound lukewarm on progressivity. It was reactionary to think change was bad, but it is not progressive to think that change had been so good that no more was needed. However, faced with the example of a man, and a not very young one to boot, who took physical care of an infirm mother, she chose to interpret this as change, and good change. The ladies of Club Aguafría, if they had been told the same example, might well have approved on grounds of family values, or else they might have disapproved, heaping blame on some woman who they thought should have taken on the task instead of a man, but in either case they would not have thought it an example of change as readily as Emilia did.

The gist of the arguments in this group (at least of the women) was that no tasks should be assigned on the basis of gender. When Manolita spoke of "learning everything a woman has to know", it was automatically understood as an ironic phrase.[134]

There was consensus, then, on anti-ascription in general. There was stress on "being a person" by which was meant having the opportunity to choose what to do with one's own life.

Asked what sort of gender order they would like, the participants found little to say. They tried, but they were more used to criticizing the present. Asked to cut loose from present reality and engage in wishful thinking, they either stayed at the abstract level of value words (justice, freedom) or else drifted back to well-rehearsed battles against present circumstances.

For both women and men in this group, to change the present gender order was highly desirable. For the women this was of immediate personal urgency; for the men it was part of their general progressive outlook, but on the issue of gender they were careful to set limits and note doubts. For example, the comments on evolution and the need to adapt slowly to new things would not have been acceptable in the context of a discussion on "democracy" or "capitalism".

Both women and men had given plenty of thought to the division of labor, and it was not even necessary for them to waste words on the fact that the division of tasks influences such things as social power, marital relationships and individuals' possibilities to be "persons". They differed on many details, but their commitment to change as something good had a logic of its own, a dynamic logic that had evidently brought them all a long way from the values they had been taught by their parents, and a logic that therefore tended to carry them on in the same direction on new issues. Whenever a "progressive" direction of change was defined, they knew what to think. It was only when undefined issues came up, for example that of equality-as-justice versus equality-as-similarity, that they hedged. In general however, the women appeared to have thought more about these issues, so in that sense they really were "women's issues", and in general the women were more emphatic in their arguments, feeling more personally involved and more secure in their opinions, whereas the men ran into some contradictions between their belief in change and their feelings that some things ought not to change, at least not too fast.

Introduction to Part IV: WORK

The chapters in parts II and III were each about situations of cultural negotiation, describing anything people talked about. The situations were chosen to represent different types of arenas and different modes of management of meaning. However, certain themes and arguments recurred in all types of situations, and usually had to do with work and sexuality.

Some women took it for granted that women have the same wishes, needs and capacities as men to do salaried work. And some of these women, like Esperanza (chapter 15), were surprised when they came up against specific obstacles for women. Others, especially feminists, took the obstacles as proof of the general injustice of the gender order and struggled to eliminate them. A moderate version of such a discourse could be seen as the new hegemonic discourse about women and work, i.e. the discourse that dominated mass media, state universities, school textbooks, etc. Yet others, like the conservative women at Club Aguafría, found this kind of thinking outrageous and dangerous. For them, a woman's place was in the home. If by nature or culture, or if for practical or moral reasons, the arguments varied, but their feeling was that the matter should not even be discussed, it should just stay the way it had "always" been, because otherwise everyone would suffer. Finally many, perhaps a majority, vacillated and did not know what criteria to use to make up their minds.

As to the new hegemonic discourse on sexuality, the situation was similar: there was a "traditional" discourse that was the officially accepted one during Franco times, and a new radical one that turned the older discourse on its head and found many of its arguments outside Spain. And then there was a compromise which looked timid in comparison with the radical propositions but stayed closer to actual practice than either of the two more militant discourses. More on this in part V, but I mention it here because of the parallells to the discourses on work.

In chapter 16, there are examples of various positions on work and of how they clashed with each other in a debate. Since the participants came from Club Aguafría, the social emphasis was on the conservative discourse, yet that discourse was not taken for granted but on the contrary presented in a defensive manner, while the joking and progressive ones were more relaxed – except for the most progressive discourse, represented by a lone feminist who hardly got any hearing at all. The situation is an illustration of and almost a metaphor for the whole Madrilenian field of discourses on gender.

In chapter 15 we meet a woman, Esperanza, who felt certain that she was right to insist on gender equality. It was both morally and rationally correct for her, and she meant equality both in the sense of justice and in the sense of similarity. However, her life had placed her in circumstances where she was so isolated from other people who thought like her that she felt she was "from another planet."

These two chapters must be read against each other. They are about people who think in very different ways. Yet they refer implicitly to each other, or rather to distorted images of each other. And the speakers could well be neighbors, work mates or members of the same clubs. The strength of their feelings must be seen in that light.

Before these examples, chapter 14 offers an overview of the various themes that were frequently connected to any discourse on work, and it offers some data on the reality behind the talk. There is also an example of a serious, reflective but conservatively Catholic position.

Chapter 13 would fit as well in this part as in part III. Appendix A would fit well here, too, and for the same reasons. The participants in both these tertulias discussed the gender order in general, neither I nor they themselves saw the discussion as especially centered on work, but the division of tasks between women and men became in fact the nucleus of very many of the arguments.

The participants in Cristóbal's and Cristina's tertulia (chapter 13) were the kind of people with whom Esperanza would have been comfortable. Unlike her, they were lucky to move in social circles where their points of view were the ones taken for granted. The participants in Matilde's tertulia (appendix A), in spite of the situational radicalism of some of their arguments, would have found them and Esperanza much too radical for their taste. They would have been more comfortable with the conservatism of the Club Aguafría type of discourse although not in complete agreement.

Chapter 14. Talking About Work

The gender issue that seemed to divide people most clearly of all concerned women's economic activities. This was related to the old view of life as divided into two spheres, public and private, and the cultural interpretation of this in parallel with gender, so that men were associated with what was seen as public and women with what was seen as private.[135]

However, it was not a clear-cut relation. True, most women did not have employment outside the home, there were few women in politics, and so on. But for middle class Madrilenian women it was not very controversial to participate in other activities than work outside the home (as long as their services to the family were not affected). It was not at all controversial for women to further their learning, for example; on the contrary it was seen as very desirable by all, whether it involved by taking gardening courses, doing yoga, going to university or visiting museums. Political activities were controversial for some people, but they were not usually seen as related to gender. In radical circles, it was taken for granted that the wife had as much of a right to political activity as the husband (and the discussion would instead center on the redistribution of tasks to make it possible). In conservative circles the idea would be (almost) as far-fetched for men as for women, since politics were considered either as an evil or else as something for professionals.

The controversy around women's participation in the public sphere centered around the concept of "work". This was expressed as a problem of quality of life in the home. The fact that a woman having a personal income may affect the power balance between husband and wife and between the genders in society at large was seldom mentioned. If it was, it was phrased as an increase in women's autonomy inside the couple: a woman with an income can "defend" herself in case her husband should do something unacceptable. This makes her more of a "person", and to be a "person" depends on a number of other things also connected to having a job, such as being able to buy gifts for relatives, invite friends for a meal or a drink, move around in the city with self-confidence, having colleagues, having a professional identity, etc.

The strongest logical contradictions arose around this same issue. For older women, who had been housewives all their lives, the very existence of these discussions was experienced as an attack on their dignity. To defend themselves, they insisted, all women should do what they themselves had done. They did not phrase that as being a non-person, obviously; instead they talked of innate femininity, pride in family, love, and above all of an implicit necessity. The life of a housewife was a dignified life only if it was a non-choice, an ascribed role. And many thought this should be taken for granted; to have to argue for it was an indignity in itself. But they took it for granted that their daughters should study and work. Awareness of this contradiction was repressed. Such women avoided talking about their own lives and their daughters in the same context, and if they were forced to, for example by an anthropologist, they were disturbed.

For younger women, the contradiction became a practical one. They did not want to choose between family and career. They wanted both. But to combine them under present ideological and material circumstances was objectively very difficult. They knew that, but they repressed the knowledge and said only that there must be, there will be some solution. The refusal to discuss such a difficult issue is very understandable, but there was no way around it. The choice was indeed impossible and the issue was central to an individual's identity as it was conceptualized. As long as it was not renegotiated and reconceptualized somehow, there could be no good solutions.

For some women, then, it was preferable not to discuss the issue of work at all. But it was hard for them to avoid it, for one thing because material circumstances forced it on their attention, and for another because for other women it was the issue above all others.

But before we look closer at the discourses, we need a few facts about women's employment and about domestic activities.

Women in the labor market

In Spain, women entered the labor market in relatively large numbers during the sixties and especially the seventies. Relatively large, that is by comparison to earlier situations, but not in comparison to the rest of Europe. In 1991, a large percentage of adult women were still housewives. Those who worked for pay often did so under uncertain terms, such as short term contracts, illegal work for piece rates in their own homes, etc. Demography was not on their side; the population of Spain grew with five million between 1958 and 1972, and with another five in the next fourteen-year period. [136] This was the baby boom in Spain, somewhat later than in the rest of the Western world. This big generation flooded the labor market during the eighties. For that and other reasons, unemployment figures remained very high for over a decade, stubbornly refusing to go below 20%. Add to this the ideological emphasis on the family as an economic unit and the fact that men's salaries were higher than women's, and you can see why it was "logical" and "functional" for women to stay at home and in charge of all housework and thus help husbands, brothers, fathers and sons to earn more money for the family than the women themselves could. Add also the personalistic tendencies that made contacts the most important resource in the labor market, and the fact that men moved outside family and kin circles much more than women and therefore had much more of this resource than women, and it will become clear that Spanish women could hardly expect to conquer the labor market to the same extent as their European and North American sisters had done and even less to reach elite positions within a reasonable lapse. Nevertheless, such was the ambition of young women in the 1990s.

187

The rate of feminine labor activity in Madrid in 1989 was 31,6 %. Of these "active" women, 19,6 % were registered as unemployed. (As compared to 9,9% of the men in Madrid and 25,4 % of the women of all of Spain.) Almost half of the women who worked full time had a university education. 82% of women with such studies had a job. Separated and divorced women had almost the same activity rates as men.[137]

The types of activity were clearly defined by gender. Domestic servants and cleaning personnel together represented almost 24% of the salaried female workers in the private sector of the economy, according to official figures. The proportion was probably much greater if we add the black labor market, which used to be calculated as about one third of the Spanish economy.

Women's unemployment was larger than men's in all age groups, and on the average more than twice that of men (23% versus just over 10%).

"Real" female unemployment was higher than the male one to an even higher degree than what the statistics show, since many more unemployed women than unemployed men refrained from registering. They became housewives instead. However, this tendency was probably less important among women with high education, and that might explain why women with high education had higher unemployment figures than women without. (For men, it was the other way around.) The higher figure would then be closer to the true female unemployment (Sallé and Casas 1987).

Middle class women had more access to work outside the home than working class women. More of them had higher education (but far from all, cf chapter 4), and they all had better contacts with key persons in the labor market, through the men in their families, than working class women did, and there was less unemployment in many (not all) of the middle class occupations. They had maids or asistentas to some (fast diminishing) extent, as well as money for products and services that facilitate domestic tasks (school buses, canned and frozen food, taxis, dry cleaning...).

But there was less legitimacy for their working. What they could earn made little difference for family comfort. There was more loss of quality of life, especially when the jobs they desired were exacting ones. And when they were housewives, they spent less time in the kitchen and more time doing creative things for family fun and well-being than was the case in working class families, where the housewives must make up for tight budgets with practical work (especially cooking and mending). A woman's income was almost inevitably lower than her husband's, and the difference between their two incomes was much greater than in the working class. If a woman should happen to earn a higher salary than her husband, her marriage would be in jeopardy, according to the folk wisdom expressed in both middle and working class contexts. A middle class wife also has an important role in upholding family prestige. (There is a list of examples in chapter 16.) She should accompany her husband to business dinners, keep her home always fit for visitors, etc. These duties of distinction and safeguarding of the merit resource base are difficult to fulfill for women with jobs.

So the issue was momentous. It was anything but a question of personal whims. But that was how it was frequently conceptualized. "She wants to work..." "She had that whim." Or when her husband has opposed it, "She is not a strong personality, so she gave in..."

Searching for solutions, some women looked forwards, others back. The innovative attitude was to try to imagine new forms for child care, family togetherness, division of tasks, and so on, preferably in such a way that the wife would have time for a job of her own. The more "traditional" (but really also new) attitude was to try to redefine the situation of a housewife, referring to new exacting tasks of motherhood or domestic creativity, but always upholding the family as a non-negotiable value that should not be tampered with.[138] [139]

Domestic tasks: Complaints and some help

In comparison with the women in Benituria, the middle class women talked less about their household work; they seemed to take it more in stride. There were fewer complaints about heavy loads, no doubt because the loads were actually lighter. But when one remembers that they never compared themselves to working class women, and as a rule knew little of their life and were not interested, the lack of complaints makes less sense.

The logical thing would be to compare themselves to their husbands, who did very little household work, and whose extra-domestic work required little if any physical effort, whereas housework does, even if you have plenty of electric appliances. But only quite radical women made this comparison. Many women criticized "men" in the abstract for not "helping" at home but made exceptions and excuses for their own husbands. Most of them pointed to the many hours their husbands worked. They said the husband had to get up early five or six days a week, whereas they themselves could sleep a little later. At least, that is, if they did not have school-age children, or pre-schoolers, or a large family, or elderly relatives living with them. They said the husbands got back home very late, when they themselves had finished their day's work. Actually most men had time off around lunch and could rest on their non-working days, whereas the housewives never had any totally free days, but only a few women mentioned this. The main difference they mentioned was that the husbands had to follow a time schedule, whereas they themselves were "owners of their time". They could leave tasks of sewing, mending or cleaning for another day and go to play cards with friends, for example, they said. Now, of course, the tasks were not done by anyone else; they had to be done later. And other tasks were impossible to postpone. And a housewife's day as a whole has to be organized according to the schedules of husbands and children. And we have to remember that we are talking of husbands with high level positions. I never heard any woman comment or even wonder about the freedom of an engineer or an executive to arrange his daily schedule to his own taste.

Nevertheless, the participation of men in household tasks was an urgent and sensitive topic in the middle class, just as much as in the working class. It was just differently phrased and the opinions more polarized.

In Benituria most men felt it was their privilege as men to receive full service in the home: food, clean clothes, well kept children, a clean nice home. Their role was to contribute the money, their wives' role was to make that money stretch as far as possible. In other words, theirs was a clear image of gender complementarity. But a minority of the men and half or more of the women felt this was old-fashioned, no longer workable, perhaps morally wrong. They felt that the work load should be "fairly" divided between husband and wife, so that both worked the same amount of hours and both were able to contribute similar things.

In the middle class, it was more generally accepted that a family is a shared project in which men are as interested as women. The men took it for granted that they should have opinions on how to educate their children, for example. Now, to what extent that interest translated into practical work with household tasks was a matter that was not at all as much discussed as in Benituria. According to surveys (Durán 1987, Inner 1988), Spanish men do very little but think it is too much. In so far as there were still servants, even if only part time, the issue was not as burning for either women or men. In so far as the men had exacting jobs that required them to come home very late or travel often, there could be no discussion, because it was impossible for them to share the tasks. In so far as the women worked, the issue became much thornier than in the working class, because then the woman's job was likely to be exacting and absorbing, too, but on the other hand a maid then became both a necessity and a possibility.

One hitch, however, was that servants were becoming scarce. I calculated that less than one percent of my informants had live-in maids, *muchachas*, which would coincide approximately with national statistics. It was much more common to have hourly help, *asistentas*, ranging from a few hours a week to five-six hours every day. But even hourly help was becoming difficult to find or keep. For many middle class women the most recent experience was not one of moving towards a leisure class life style but on the contrary of having to work more than before. And domestic work is manual, often even physically tiresome, so in this sense the women's work was similar to the despised kind of working class tasks, while their husbands all sat behind desks, dressed in suits, working with paper and telephones and often with the help of secretaries. Women with maids could hardly avoid recognizing that they and the maids performed similar tasks.[140]

There was another contradiction around domestic help. In one sense it was definitely part of a desired life style. It was elegant. It was not elegant for a woman to have to clean the bathroom, nor for her husband to have a wife who consequently could not sport the exquisitely shaped and painted nails that most middle class women valued highly. On the other hand, however, many men felt uneasy at the thought of an outsider intruding in the sanctity of the home. The help usually came while the men were at work, but even so some men explicitly forbade their wives to employ domestic help, using the argument of intrusion as the main or only one.

So, for these reasons – the manual character of domestic work, the increasing amount of it, which decreased wives' quality of life while that of other family members increased, and because they might perceive a devaluation of their own efforts in the attitudes of their husbands – women could come to criticize their "traditional" gender role.

Most did not. But those who did, complained more than working class women did, and they had access to more elaborate arguments.

Domestic tasks increased in intensity in Spain in similar ways as has been documented for other European societies. There were more appliances, but also higher standards – for instance, there were more clothes to be washed, and they must be washed more often, and the variety of materials and colors required specialized knowledge and lots of sorting; more dishes were used and must be first rinsed, then perhaps washed or at least placed in the dishwasher and later taken out and placed in the cupboards. the education of the children required reading, consultation with experts, and so on; children's school work required mothers to help with homework and vigilance of their study hours. The importance of high education prolonged the maternal duties until the children were close to thirty years old (cf chapter 2) and the importance of education as property made the mothers' efforts to ensure the children's good results crucial for the reproduction of middle class life. There was also more work in connection with invitations to the home of friends or husband's professional connections, although this aspect was not (yet?) very burdensome, since in Madrid the new middle class (so far?) definitely preferred to dine out.

Shopping for food took a lot of time in Madrid. Most of the shopping was done by women, including shopping for children's and husbands' clothes and major household items like furniture. As to food, housewives with no work outside the home usually shopped for fresh products every day. This was true for all classes and all residential arrangements except perhaps for families who lived in distant urbanizations and had to go by car to buy anything at all. Such families did their shopping on Saturdays, and weekly shopping was becoming more and more of a family affair, much like in the United States. Some big supermarkets had begun to stay open on Sundays, too. Married women with extra-domestic work usually did some daily shopping for bread and fresh vegetables and the rest on weekends. In any case, food was culturally emphasized. Most husbands would complain if their wives used too many ready-made food products or if the vegetables were not fresh, and in most families there were special inherited recipes from the home villages that took a lot of time and effort to prepare.[141]

A woman's domestic duties did not stop at the front door or in the market. As we saw in chapter 2, the family – actually the women – continued to supply most basic welfare in Spain. This was true for all classes. Women had to accompany relatives while they were in hospital, take care of the ill and the elderly in the home, etc. This also meant that the domestic load varied greatly with family size and health and over the life cycle. This made it difficult for women to plan their careers. And that in turn offered employers the argument that female employees were not trustworthy. The chain of interlocking factors is well known from other European countries; in Spain it was just more tightly forged. It was also a more recent phenomenon and therefore less clearly understood, so that arguments of personal blame and naturalization were very effective in discourse.

Seasons

Domestic work also varied according to the time of the year. There were certain times of the year that made women complain of overload.

One was vacation time. The most common type of vacation was to go for a month to a beach or a mountain area to stay in a "second residence" of one's own or with relatives. This meant rest and leisure for all family members except the wife. Instead she often had a heavier load than at home – more guests, a smaller kitchen and a less well equipped dwelling in general. If an older generation was present, there were also tensions around both cooking and cleaning; the older women tended to be more exacting and disapprove of "modern" ways of cutting corners such as paper napkins, disposable diapers or canned tomatoes. This was a problem for all women, whether they had extradomestic work or not.

Another time for complaints was September. In families with school age children, September was the time to buy school clothes and school books, possibly make arrangements for a change of school, visit the school and talk to the teachers, and so on. None of this could be left to grandmothers or paid help, and the shopping was time-consuming.

But the worst complaints I heard came around Christmas time. At least that was true of the middle aged women; perhaps the younger ones had more fun preparing a good time for the small children. Many of the middle aged women said that Christmas was not much fun anymore, because the children did not appreciate their efforts, and they themselves were sick and tired of it all.

Christmas was one time of the year when family life was on display, and it was usually a family occasion, so for the wife it meant lots of cooking and cleaning and planning, perhaps also arranging for out-of-town relatives to visit for a week or two. It was hard to deny the beloved ones this special time, but it required a lot of heavy work. For professional women it was impossible to come anywhere close to the expectations; for housewives it could turn into something like an examination of their most valued skills, and for all it was difficult to combine the heavy extra load with the expectations of relaxation and fun. The combined influence of increased standard of living and foreign customs had also complicated the celebrations and made the season longer.

As Christmas drew near, all conversations among women were permeated with comments on what they planned to do. Some reveled in explaining complicated recipes and complaining – actually bragging – of how many guests they would have and how they would arrange the sleeping quarters. Others spoke more about how they had "liberated" themselves from the requirements. And the most common attitude was somewhere in between: It's not as much fun as it used to be, the children do not appreciate it any longer, and my mother-in-law is so tiresome; I hate to cook so much, this year I will try to plan better... besides, is it really important?

In all of this there was almost no mention at all of husbands' participation, not even criticism of lack of participation. The men were like the children and the invited guests: the effort was for them and they were to judge the results.

Image and choice

During the 20th century, Spanish society evolved from patrimonial forms towards salaries, i.e. one's position was determined less by what one owned and more by what one did. This was one more reason why women of higher classes felt defensive. Their exaggerated aparentar and their constant talk of expensive objects and activities makes sense in this light. Especially women who were over forty in the 1990s, who had in all probability not themselves obtained much formal education, and who therefore could not define themselves by what they did, had to insist more on the importance of what they had.[142]

It used to be very prestigious to be able to say that you were a good housewife. It was necessary for a good image of self, in front of self and others. For many, this was still so around 1990. But it was now also possible for women to say that they were not good housewives, that they did not like household tasks because they were not good at them.[143] This may have to do with the change in the definition of the housewife role. It used to be an obligatory role for all women. One had to prove one was good at it, or else one was no good as a woman, since there was not much else.

Now, staying at home was seen as a choice. In actuality, of course, it was not a free choice but determined largely by circumstances beyond individual women's control, but it was defined as a choice. So housewives must make their "choice" appear rational or at least likely as a choice. They would underline the pleasurable aspects – they feel self–realized, they said; they love their children, they enjoy having the freedom to organize their time, and so on. And the women who were not housewives could then feel free to explain why they did not choose to be – they were better at something else or liked other tasks better.

Themes around work

A discourse can be described as a certain pattern of topics, placed in certain relations to each other like points in an irregular net. Around the topic of work, there were a number of other topics. Some of them were connected to the work topic only for persons of certain persuasions, others were seen by most people to be so connected. But the common net patterns were well known to everybody and used as references in discussions.

There were two topics concerning the division of labor that came up frequently in Madrilenian conversations. One was the division of household tasks among family members, especially the distribution according to gender (but also the participation of children, and the decrease of the workload with technological change, cf chapter 13). The other one was the extra-domestic work of married women. It is possible that my presence caused some of this, but that in itself goes to prove my point, because whenever a person expresses interest in women's issues, it is presumed that she is especially interested in the issue of women's work. (And perhaps sexuality.) I did not have to ask about it for it to come up, it did not come up only in arranged situations but in all sorts of natural conversations, and it came up in both mixed and women-only situations. It is also a topic I heard discussed in middle class Madrid contexts throughout the 1970s. When I wanted to organize a debate at Club Aguafría, the board suggested precisely "married women's work outside the home" as an appropriate topic (chapter 16).

In the media, work was not discussed as much or with as much joking and imagination as sexuality was, but it was discussed for instance in the TV debating programs or in talk shows and interviews, and it was referred to by entertainers (e.g. jokes about husbands forced to iron their shirts...) and participants in game shows (e.g. arguments about how in our family women have always had employment, it is the most natural thing in the world...)

What did people say about it, then? There were a number of themes that recurred in similar ways in most contexts. Most of them were general themes but with special relevance for the issue of work.

CHANGE. The talk of change was everywhere. Few persons doubted that there had been deep social change and that it had been somewhat uncomfortable for all. The main attitude was that it had been good, after all, but where the more radical discourse was about change as a promise of improvement, a more cautious one was to see most of it as good, and quite inescapable, but add that it should be carefully weighed and judged before it was accepted.

For the most conservative, certain kinds of change were especially threatening, as we have seen. The loss of "values" referred to a general feeling, but it was often exemplified with selfish career women as well as sexual looseness. More specifically, the change in family patterns was seen as a threat to the family, not as a renovation of it. The increasing competitivity and consequent hard work and little leisure for the younger generation made conservatives upset ("life is losing its aesthetic and leisurely qualities") but this also seemed to confirm their interpretation of society ("life is a struggle," "young people can't just play around.").

The worry about competitiveness and lack of leisure was more widely shared. There was a widespread fear, also beyond conservative circles, that society was becoming less "human", less comfortable, more complex, more opaque. And much of this worry centered on the changing roles of women, especially women's desire to work outside the home. If they do, they obviously cannot fulfill the role of "humanizing" life in the same way they have "always" done.

So "working women" were seen as both a threat and a scapegoat on which to blame any social ills. And "too much work", for everyone, was a very general accusation against modern society. "Too much work" cannot be a good thing, by definition. Cf below on pleasure.

BIOLOGY AND GENDER. When the changing roles of women were discussed, most men and some women who wanted to argue for status quo in the gender system would refer to innate differences between women and men. And they were almost exclusively exemplified with the division of labor. Most of the arguments were positive, saying that women were good at domestic tasks, but it was perfectly possible to argue in the negative, saying that women were not well suited for the way the labor market worked or that men were not well suited for family duties.

Some went as far as to describe men as irresponsible with their families and even with small children. Irresponsibility and callousness with children were not otherwise characteristics to be taken lightly in middle class Madrid; quite the contrary, both women and men tried to present themselves as responsible and sensitive (for instance in contrast to the lower classes, to youngsters or to people of other countries), and in other contexts men used the argument of irresponsibility to deny women access to the world outside the home. But when the discussion required it, men often chose an unflattering self-image rather than face the threat of change in the division of tasks.

For women and men who wanted to deny the importance of biology, it seemed necessary to take the same examples and turn them upside down: women are good at everything, men are good at everything, it is just a question of learning and habits. In either case the main examples always had to do with the tasks that were seen as paradigmatically male and female.

CLASS. The class issue was sensitive. People talked about it and recognized differences, even underlined them in order to present themselves as exceptionally successful. But apart from radical circles, the word class was scrupulously avoided. It smacked of socialist discourse (sometimes rephrased as "envy"), on the one hand, and on the other perhaps of a type of prejudice that was not quite comme-il-faut, namely the idea that "class" means "different kinds of people", possibly with genetic differences.

The social differences that were too evident for anyone to deny were referred to indirectly, with cautious euphemisms about "certain kinds of people", "the circles you move in", etc. and above all "education". It was usually understood that the members of the new middle class had what they had because they had earned it. So class was conceptualized as a question of work, capacity and moral worth. But the difference between professional men and housewives as to the work they do was seldom pointed out in this context. That would have undermined the unity of class and the unity of the Family.

EDUCATION. The word education was a potent and polysemic symbol. It stood not only for studying, but also for good manners. And in the expansive mode of management of meaning, it was emphatically used in the sense of socialization, as the opposite of nature or biology, especially when it came to gender differences. In other words, the tension between ascription and achievement was usually phrased as biology versus education.

Education was also closely tied to work. Social mobility was usually phrased as a question of access to university education. People did mention inherited money, chance and changing criteria for prestige, too, but first and foremost education. And education was usually conceptualized as a sacrifice in time and money for both students and their parents, and very hard and ungratifying efforts on part of the students. One did not seek it for pleasure or out of a desire for knowledge but in order to get a good job. So education was related to work in two ways: it was a prerequisite to obtain the kind of job one wanted and it consisted of hard work.

Now, when the issue of women's work came up, the conservative argument changed to stress education as an extra, as an option, as an adornment, as a source for pleasure. Or possibly as something that was good to have in case of an emergency. The less conservative argued that women should study in order to get jobs "exactly the same as men". It was difficult to argue for education as pleasure without sounding conservative, especially as to women. And education as a resource for critical discernment or empowerment was talked about only by the most progressive. For others, it became education as refinement, i.e. blending into adornment again.

CHOICE. This was a key word for all Madrilenians except the most conservative, and women could use it with good effect to protest their situation. Its use to argue for women's right to go to work is exemplified especially clearly by Mary Cruz in appendix A. The counter-argument usually had to do with responsibility or with women's nature. The absence of choice could not be presented as positive in itself, except in the very conservative discourse which saw women's role as something that should not even be reflected upon, but even in that discourse choice was never explicitly opposed. In all discourses, the foremost example of choice in women's lives was that of whether to work outside the home or not.

STRENGTH AND GENDER. The strong belief in personal merit had different consequences for women and men, and this was exemplified in the tertulias. For instance, in Fernando's view of what women have to do in order to make careers. (Appendix A.) Strength was always a positive word, whether used about women or about men. There were few references to physical strength (except in the discussions about biological determination of gender characteristics). What was meant was moral rectitude, psychological resilience, determination, verbal skill, and so on. Strength also, but almost always implicitly, referred to access to social resources (capital, prestige, useful networks).

A common anti-feminist argument used this in the following way: a) It was pointed out that feminists complained that women were disadvantaged in society. b) "disadvantage" was then construed implicitly to mean "weakness"; c) and the argument went on to prove that women were really very "strong", i.e. intelligent, strong-willed, good mothers, good at manipulating their husbands, etc; d) and the conclusion was that the feminists were wrong and the gender order should not be changed, because women did a very good job and were valuable in their present roles, and they were not disadvantaged in them. The argument sometimes continued: e) to say that women were weak was not only wrong but insulting, so the feminists were doubly wrong.

MEN AND HOUSEWORK. This seemed to be the most controversial issue for most men in this study. In group discussions they found it hard to argue against women in the labor market. On this point they usually tried to stay within a progressive discourse; even conservative men said that women have a right to work "if they want to". This was necessary because of the cultural emphasis on personal autonomy and choice. But as soon as someone pointed out (and some woman usually would) that if women work outside the home, men have to "help" with household tasks, the men protested strongly. At this point they found any argument useful, even arguments outside their normal discourses, even arguments that meant that they ascribed to men characteristics they usually interpreted as strongly negative, e.g. irresponsibility.[144]

SHOPPING. When the issue of household tasks came up, shopping was always mentioned along with cleaning, childcare and cooking. It was a major task, cf above. There were different opinions about the gender definition of it. Some said that as many men as women shop for food nowadays, others that hardly any men do. The truth was somewhere in between. The norm that men should not enter food stores was probably stronger in the working than in the middle class, and the progressive sector of the middle class had a positive norm that men should now learn to shop (cf chapter 13), but in fact more men were seen in the stores of Benituria than in those of Aguafría. In working class families, many wives did in fact work outside the home, and they did not have maids to help them, some of them even worked as maids themselves, so the husbands had to do more housework, in spite of the norms. But they did so under protest and with strong tensions in the couple relationship as one consequence. In the middle class, either the wife stayed at home, and then the husband did not have to do any shopping for food at all, and very little of any kind of shopping, or else the wife had a job, and then she probably did some shopping for food herself, possibly the husband did too, a paid household help might buy the daily inevitables like milk and bread, and the whole family probably did the bulk shopping on weekends, the husband going along and helping, but the wife doing the planning and taking most of the decisions. This male participation was referred to as "help", usually positively although with varying interpretations.

PLEASURE. It was perfectly licit in most Madrilenian middle class sectors to refer to pleasure as a goal in life. "The good life", "to know how to enjoy life" and similar phrases were effective arguments, even norm-like in quality. Consequently they could be used to justify any choice. When it came to work, they could be used to explain why a woman would want to work ("she wants to", "it is fun") or why she did not ("I would have no time to enjoy life"). Of the two, the latter argument was the one with most cultural resonance, since "work" has traditionally been construed as something hard, uncomfortable, necessary but bad, almost anti-pleasure. The women of Club Aguafría preferably justified their leisurely life with other arguments (morals, the defense of the family and so on), not pleasure, but they, too, liked to underline that they were happy with their place in life not just as a fulfilment of duty but as pleasure, enjoyment. For many women, such talk was necessary to stress their choice, if they were housewives, but for the most conservative it was not perceived as a choice to be a housewife, yet they too referred to pleasure.

ASYMMETRICAL ARGUMENTATION. The women participants in the tertulias usually agreed easily on what a woman's needs and duties and responses to problems are, whereas the men seemed to know little and disagreed among themselves on women's needs and emotions. The men tended to concentrate on women's duties and take them to be about family obligations. Men's needs, duties and responses came up only when the mode of management of meaning was decidedly expansive, since such a focus falls outside traditional discourses, according to which men are the unmarked gender whose characteristics are only discussed as "human" ones.

This meant, among other things, that even though "work" (if unspecified) was taken as something for men, men's actual duties and activities, men's reactions to work, men's needs, and so on, were seldom discussed. Except, of course, to underline what the women had to do – carefully described – in order for men to comply with their – undescribed – responsibilities.

WOMEN'S DOUBLE BIND. The division of labor created a double bind for women.

A double bind, according to Bateson (1973) consists of four elements: if you do one thing, you are punished; if you do the opposite you are also punished; there is no third alternative possible; and you cannot just opt out of the situation because something makes it important for you to act in it.

The fourth factor is clearly present: the gender order is an all-inclusive aspect of social life. Nobody can opt out.[145] No matter how you behave, your behavior will be at least in part seen in light of your gender. In Madrid two contrasting models for feminine behavior could be distinguished; both were seen as necessary and both were negatively sanctioned. The women must be feminine, i. e. submissive, soft, responsible, loving, uncomplaining. If they were not, they were punished sexually (no marriage at all, perhaps no love life at all, or for the married the risk that the husband may leave) and economically (low salaries for unmarried women, no income at all or only a low income after much legal trouble for divorced women). But the women must also be strong, assertive, i.e. unfeminine. If not, they were punished economically (no personal income) and in daily life (heavy workload, no chance to "realize themselves", criticism for not being "modern" enough, etc).

Was there a third alternative? Yes, in the sense that there was much talk of the "superwoman", the woman who manages to be a perfect mother and housewife and at the same time an efficient participant in the labor market and able to switch behavior and personality as she switches roles.

But the superwoman was not a true practical alternative for most Madrilenian women. Certain material conditions were absent (accessible childcare and care for the sick and the elderly, certain features of labor legislation, etc.). Furthermore, the superwoman was usually seen more as a threat than as an alternative. She works herself to death, her life is no life, people said. (*"¡Eso no es vida!"*) Some North American and European women had fallen into the trap, said my informants. Madrilenian middle class women talked a lot about superwomen, using the English word, and usually in a negative way. Whether feminists or traditionalists, they thought it important to enjoy life, to have leisure, to see one's friends, to safeguard one's mental and physical health. So then there was no real third alternative for them. Many younger women, however, were marching straight into the superwoman trap.

So how can this double bind be transcended? That ought to be the main topic on the agenda, one might think, but it was not. It was too difficult an order. It was too difficult to even begin to conceptualize the point of departure of such a discussion. The feminists tried, but their discourses were little known, and what was known about them was considered too far out. As it had to be, seeing the requirement of transcending such a double bind. The feminists knew this and expressed the difficulty, and the hope against hope, saying that the feminist revolution would be the most profound one of all. It seemed clear that a lot of issues and concepts will have to be redefined for the gender debate to break out of its present closed circle, a lot of things that were at that time not seen as directly related to gender.

Covering the retreat

What follows is an example of a defense of traditional ideas about women and work and the contradictions such defenses ran into in the 1990s. It shows how Madrilenians could not talk about women's work without implicating their whole world view. That was so on all points of the continuum, and that was the main reason why the issue of women's duties, domestic or extra-domestic, was so hard to deal with. For people whose opinions centered on "family values", women's work outside the home was ideologically undesirable and threatening for basic world views. Even so, even women from such families, took tentative steps towards the labor market.

One sunny winter day at Club Aguafría, I began talking to a family sitting next to me at the terrace having lunch.[146] Four small children ran around between their table and mine and almost turned over my wine bottle. Their mother said she was sorry. I introduced myself, and after we had talked for a while, I moved over to their table. I did not have to ask many questions – they themselves started talking about changing times and dissolving morals. They had normally conservative ideas. What was interesting were the small but significant differences between the family members and the way they phrased them. The clearest difference was between the grandmother, around sixty, and the mother of the children who was just over thirty. The man of similar age turned out not to be her husband but her brother, and that probably meant that both of them spoke more honestly and less tensely about the issues that came up than if they had been a couple. It was also interesting because they had been educated in the same family and shared basic values, yet there were differences between them.

Let us call them the Mother, the Sister and the Brother. (The Sister's husband was at work; the Brother did not explain where his wife and children were, but he did have a wife and children.)

The main differences were those one would expect. The Mother was the most "traditional" of the three, and she used every opportunity to say that young people nowadays "rebel" too much. The Sister's favorite theme was that nowadays, if a married woman works outside the home – she did, but only temporarily – the husband has to "learn more things" and "help more".

The Mother said she had always been a housewife. That was not a choice, that was just the way it was. "Women lived in slavery," she said. I said I thought that in those times women did not see it as slavery. "Of course not," said the Mother with great authority. "You did it for love, of course. But that was the way it was and a woman could not do anything else outside the home." She used the word slavery several times, but apparently without critical intent. Perhaps she meant only non-choice, and that was something she found positive.

Her complaint was instead that young women today do not take such a life as a matter of course. Sure, she said, it is not necessarily bad for a married woman to work, but only on the condition that she does not use her job as an excuse to exploit her husband. I asked what she meant by exploiting, and she explained that many a young married woman nowadays makes her husband work a lot in the home, and she does not pamper him at all, and with the excuse that she too works, she puts a broom in his hands, and that is not right, she forgets that he comes home tired and needs his time to rest. When she herself was a little girl, she was taught to be very considerate with father: Daddy is coming, children, hush, hush, Daddy is tired...

I said, "Now, let's see. What you are saying is that a woman ought to pamper her husband and see to it that he gets the rest he needs..." The Mother nodded emphatically, and I saw a spark of rebellious expectation in the eyes of the Sister, who sat intent on what I would say. "Even if both of them work..." But at this point the Sister made too obvious a face and the Mother realized where I was taking her and rectified, "No, no, I am talking about a case where he works and she does not." The Sister asked, "Then, what of the case when the woman works, too? Eh?!" and the Mother winked at me, "See? See how the young people rebel? That is what I am saying!"

The Brother now joined the Sister to argue that men have to change, too; you just cannot leave a woman alone with the whole responsibility. The Brother was a physician, working in a big hospital, and he said that he noticed it in his work, that he fell into the old traps, he could not avoid it, he had irregular hours, and there were expectations, 'and before you know it you have no leisure time left and you hardly ever see your children, and that is not what I want." He had had to learn to be more generous, he said. He had been selfish, because most of his colleagues were, and sure enough, you are very tired when you get home...

This discourse sounded reasonably progressive in a way, but there were also clear overtones of a traditional Catholic discourse of "generosity" versus "selfishness", where the opposition is doxically between individual and family needs, and where the family is considered the morally worthier choice. For Catholic women, this is a deeply accepted norm. For Catholic men, it creates a contradiction between religious teachings and cultural norms stressing male independence. Those for whom religion wins the contest tended towards the discourse the Brother was using.

There were differences between Sister and Brother, however. They both placed the family above the individual, but the Sister insisted that fathers have to learn more about being fathers, whereas the Brother insisted that nothing can replace a mother. That does not mean that a father is not important, too, he said, and spoke proudly of his own relationship to his children. But there was a clear although implicit "but" in every phrase. Or at least that is how the Sister interpreted him, to judge by her insistent opposition to everything he said.

Since all three kept repeating that a mother is unique and that motherhood is such a great and important thing, I asked if they thought this was necessarily so, and if so, if it was by nature or due to education. The Sister jumped at the opportunity to say that it was obviously due to education. "We are taught that that is how it is." The Mother hesitated and hedged but ended up saying that a woman has something a man can never have. The Brother and the Sister agreed that men and women are rather similar by nature, and that most of the differences are due to education. But in the end the Brother insisted that "we are 90% the same, but then there are those other 10%, more or less, that are the way they are, and the woman has something a man does not have, so for the children she is much more important. Like in our case, our father died when I was seven, and that was difficult, of course, evidently, in many ways, but I think it would have been much worse if it had been the other way around. If our mother had died, we would have had much less integration, much less togetherness, much less family harmony."

All three thought that things had changed profoundly in Spain during recent decades and that it was difficult to adapt. They were not bitter or fearful. But after a while it became clear that they felt they were involved in a decent retreat.

The Mother said that change is fine, in itself, but what we have now is excessive. (*Desmadrado* was her word, a colloquial word meaning that something runs wild, like a river overflowing its banks.) Her example was that children see "a lot of things" in school. "There are always classmates who do everything, everything. Like a girl who goes out with her girlfriends and so on, perhaps starting at ten years of age, because her mother does not want to take the trouble to look after her, and (imitating a little girl's peevish voice): I don't have to go to mass! and things like that..."

As the Mother spoke of "supposedly liberated women", the Brother suddenly affirmed that the most machista women are the same ones who say they are feminists. "What do you mean?" I asked. All three exclaimed, "But that is evidently so, you must have noticed!" No, I was sorry, could they give me examples? The Brother said, "Yes, I see it at work, in the hospital, there are many women working there, and I hear them talking among themselves. They go, my husband did this or that, he helps me a lot, the other day he cleaned the kitchen for me, and he bought me this or that... And so on and so forth. And they obtain all those things by going to the hairdresser or something like that. I mean, there is a lot of talk about woman as object, but what they do themselves is to convert man into an object." And all three said that this is that old famous left hand[147] at work.

What they wanted to communicate was that they were against such unfair weapons and against the framing of the relationship between men and women as a battle. They would have been surprised if I had told them many feminists would agree. To them, feminism meant unfair advantages for women. Why this would simultaneously be machista, I did not understand. Possibly they mixed several discourses, calling the traditional manipulation machista because it is associated with a gender order that is criticized by feminism.

They could not very well say that women should be submissive to the point of not defending themselves against abuse (although just possibly that was what the Mother meant when she used the term "slavery" so ambiguously). But neither did they want to appear to defend any kind of transgression of norms, and the norms they defended were strict. And they were norms that explicitly commanded women to be submissive up to some uncertain point. To clarify that point and to verbalize norms about what women should do beyond it would seem logically necessary for such a discourse, but seen from the inside of it, it was both unnecessary and dangerous.

This can be compared to the discourses on sexuality. We will see that there were three kinds: one that was strictly conservative and outrightly forbidding; one that was jokingly conservative and did not question the categories of the prohibitive discourse but made transgression into a major motive; and a third one that endeavored to change the rules of the game. All three types had to do with attitudes toward authority, and the differences between them were similar whether they dealt with sexuality, religion, state power, loyalty to an employer etc. A critical discourse always tries to expand the universe of discourse. It tries to discover new categories to be analyzed and possibly changed. In the case of patterns of authority inside the family, the Madrilenian version in the 1990s tended to delegitimize any authority based on ascribed characteristics. The joking conservative discourse, on the other hand, took these patterns for granted, but it took constant mockery of them equally for granted. In such a discourse, manipulation and seduction come to be almost the same thing, and they are fun and semi-licit. They are necessary to grease the social machinery. According to the strictly conservative discourse, however, manipulation is subversive and seduction is immoral. Authority should reign uncontested and unhindered. Rebellion is gravel in the social machinery.

So this family subscribed to the strictly conservative discourse, in spite of their initial cautious use of a progressive vocabulary. They did not accept seduction any more than rebellion. They were hard at work creating a discourse that would defend authoritarian values with a non-abrasive vocabulary.

Since they did not have any special purpose in talking to me, did not know anything about me beyond my brief presentation of the study, and no one else was listening, one can assume they honestly believed in the values they expressed. They may even have been so immersed in a social world where those values were unquestioned that they were truly ignorant about some of the criticisms directed against it. For example, I happened to say something about those absent fathers who plan their lives to have many children they have no time for... It seemed to me I was just repeating what the Brother had just said. But the Sister gave me an honestly surprised glance and said that it was not a question of planning, children just come. So I asked if they thought family planning wrong. This issue was by this time not very controversial; most people, even most practicing Catholics, did plan their families in some way, to some extent, even though some did not like to talk about it.[148] It was an issue that divided only the very conservative from the extremely conservative. But this family reacted as if they did not even know what it was. The Sister gave me a hesitant glance: "Well, the thing is... I think it is a matter of... they just come... you get the children that God wants to give you. Isn't that so?" Her tone was pleading.

She had four children, with one-year intervals. So did her brother. But her youngest was close to four, his somewhat older. They had obviously not continued to have one child every year. They must have taken some decision.

It was clear that their main worry was the education of children. I said I supposed they would want to teach their children the values they believed in, and that that would be difficult. That was the right thing to say. "Of course it is difficult!" they exclaimed. The Mother gave more examples of the bad things all children have to see in school nowadays. I said it depends on which schools (that was the normally accepted phrase at the club, and it usually meant that one must send one's children to private religious schools because state schools are not trustworthy). But the Brother and Sister said no, all schools are the same in this sense, and no matter how hard you try to choose one that seems good, there are things you cannot escape anywhere today... And then there is the television, and what they hear in the street and from the movies, and even what the teachers say... They painted a picture of cultural war, with their values under siege.

I asked how they handled the children's TV watching, and the Sister said that was a very important question, and it was a good example of what one had to do nowadays to be a good mother. She proudly explained that she was careful to read the program each week and find out if the Friday and Saturday afternoon movies were permissible or not,[142] and if they were not, she would see to it that she had a video movie prepared to show on that hour instead. "Because you can't just forbid," she explained, "that won't work, all you get then is rebellion." And during the week she selected their programs, too. "Usually the children's programs on Antena 3, cartoons. I think they are the most inoffensive ones there are. And the kids know that that is the program they are going to watch and that is that, there is no discussion. Nobody gets to watch anything else." She gave a little ironic laugh. "And that is why I say that being a mother is limiting, too. Because I don't get to see all the things I would like to see, either!"

The Sister thought that working outside the home was important for a woman. "But the family comes first. And that is why a woman can never compete with a man professionally. I have lost many professional opportunities, because I have had to say no, because of my family obligations." That is why fathers have to learn "to be more fathers," she added. But the mother is more important for the children. And that is why a woman has to be a mother above all, she concluded.

Her Brother nodded with approval but pronounced her slightly blind to men's needs. The Mother both nodded and frowned, hesitating whether to accept this modernized version of her values, and finding her daughter's talk of women's professionality unnecessary. But understandable, perhaps, in today's dangerous world. The Sister's position, in other words, was the most rebellious one of the three. But basically they agreed, in prescribed family harmony.

Work in focus

As we have seen, the issue of women's work outside the home was acutely controversial. It contained crucial contradictions that must be resolved for women to carry on with their lives, no matter what choices they made. Men were uncomfortably affected, too, albeit more indirectly.

Cautious modes of management of meaning ran into great difficulties (cf also chapter 17), since the very mention of these contradictions felt risky in such contexts. In more expansive discourses, the discomfort often expressed itself as aggressive joking.

The difficulties were based on collective arrangements such as the structure of the labor market, school and office hours, availability (or rather lack) of care solutions for children and the elderly, and so on. But in everyday discourse, they were almost always expressed as dependent on individual characteristics, such as will power, ingenuity and capacity for effort. This made it extra difficult to talk about the contradictions. They must be resolved, and it took personal effort to resolve them for each individual, but there was little help to be found in collective analysis. The process of cultural negotiation was thwarted in this area.

The historic moment can be described as one of unsteady change from a gender order based on complementarity and ascription to one based on similarity and achievement. Such moments tend to place many individuals in unforeseen dilemmas and traps. (Cf e.g. Collier 1997.)

The fact that work outside the home was a material prerequisite for personal autonomy in middle class Madrid[154] was not focused in the discourses of any type. This absence could prove to be dangerous for many women as individuals and also for the project of long term changes in the gender order.

Chapter 15. The Reluctant Housewife

Esperanza's story illustrates the situation of women who have not adapted to or resigned themselves to the so called "traditional" model of a woman's life but have not found a clear model for anything else either. She felt like an anomaly. Her story also illustrates the common situation of class change that had not been emically conceptualized and therefore was experienced as confusing. Her father could be classified as lower middle class but was of working class origin and had more of a working class ethos. Her own situation, in terms of her husband's profession and income level, was upper middle class and rising. She herself was a housewife who would like to have a job but did not think she could get one, and this appraisal was realistic. She was 32 years old at the time of the interview and had two children, a daughter of six and a son of two.

Esperanza and I had met several times in a semi-formal context, when she offered to give me her life story. She understood well what I wanted, perhaps too well to be an ideal informant, but this was true of many middle class Madrilenians. And she understood that her role was to be personal and sincere, not brilliant and well-informed (imagined requirements other potential life story tellers were often afraid of not living up to).

Markers used in this chapter:

E=Esperanza speaks.

– =I speak.

(…) = something has been left out, usually repetitions or unimportant details.

I have included some details of the interaction around the interview to give the reader an idea of the rhythm and atmosphere of the situation. Parentheses are used to describe non-audible parts of the conversation, mainly gestures.

Esperanza's story

Esperanza lived in a fashionable new area of high rise apartment buildings surrounded by parks. The buildings contained no stores or schools, there was nothing but apartments and garages and small playgrounds in the area. The bus stop was distant, so Esperanza offered to pick me up by car. She drove around the area to show it to me. Most of the buildings were between three and five years old but the prices had already more than doubled.

Each apartment had a corresponding garage, but even so the street was crowded with parked cars. Esperanza laughed, "Sure, those are the wives' cars, just like mine, see? That is why they are so small. The big family cars are the ones they park in the garage, and also the ones the husbands drive to work. So the garage is empty all day and the street is crowded."

Esperanza was just as sarcastic about the generous green areas. "Sure, gardens and pools and what have you, but communications are bad, so you have to have at least two cars, and the mothers have to drive the kids around all the time." I saw a couple of private guards, and Esperanza explained that each building had one, some of them with dogs, but that it was not very necessary, the area was not hard hit by crime.

Inside her apartment, she showed it all to me, bathrooms, bedrooms and all, without the usual reticence. She told me the price and I agreed with her that the size and quality of the apartment did not justify it. "We pay for the location."

As we sat down in the living room to begin the interview, I said, as I always did. that she could just begin anywhere she wanted and tell me about her life more or less in chronological order, commenting on anything she found important. I wanted her to choose where to place the emphasis and on what themes to elaborate and what things could be more or less abbreviated.

E: Well, I was born in Madrid in 1958. We lived in a middle class apartment building. My father is a *perito*.[151] For many years he had two jobs, until only eight or nine years ago. Our situation was without any luxury but without problems. Nor did we have a lot of expenses nor any special hobbies. My mother did not work outside the home. she dedicated herself to us.[152]

Esperanza went on to tell about how much her grandmother, who lived with them, had meant to her, and how her younger brother was very different from herself. She thought she had been the black sheep of the family, the rebel who always protested, always asked "why do I have to do that?" And how angry she was when her mother answered "because you are a woman."[153]

E: So I worked out my rebellion very early. If they said for example I had to be home at ten, I would come home at ten thirty... I don't mean to say I was disobedient, really, but why me and not my brother? That kind of education... My parents would never admit that it was discriminatory, but you can see clearly that it was, right?

She did not think her parents had been unduly strict, but they controlled her more than they controlled her brother. She said she had been quite docile as a little girl, and that her rebellion started in earnest when she went to university, at seventeen.

E: I began to study to be an industrial engineer, because I loved math. But without really knowing what to expect. As to counselling – nothing. The course they call preparatory in school, at least when I did it, contained absolutely no counselling at all. Perhaps they said something when they saw your grades; they would say: let's see, yes, hmm, perhaps science is your thing... but nothing. Not at all. I did not know anything about the content of the studies. I knew we would study math, physics, chemistry, calculus, drawing, algebra, and I knew little more than that, really. Perhaps we were told, you know, industrial engineering always gives you a good job... In that sense, we can say that perhaps there was a sort of seed of rebellion in me, but it was not yet very defined. Later I studied journalism, and when people hear that, they get all confused, right (laughter)? Because... engineering and journalism, one thing has nothing to do with the other. But after reading and... well, just a lot of thinking, then I realized that journalism was my thing.

After a long discussion about the contrast between journalism and sciences, I said that perhaps we ought to stick to some sort of chronology. What about school...

E: Yes, school, I have gone to a whole lot of schools, but it was because my parents changed them. (...) Yes, private schools. Yes, for quality I suppose. Actually up until sixth grade I was in a religious school (...). But they were more or less liberal.[154] From then on, or perhaps from fifth grade... I had never been much of a practitioner, not even a believer, but let us say that I did go to mass...

I asked if her parents were believers or practitioners.[155]

E: Not in the least. My father not at all. Not my mother either, she used not to go to mass or anything. But now she has fallen into some kind of mysticism, she signs up for trips to all the places where they say virgins appear. She is sort of like illuminated, she does very strange things.

– So you went to mass even though your parents did not?

E: Well, that was later, when I was older. But well, yes, because I went to that school... and because I was in the scouts. In my scout group we had a leader who gave talks, and we went to mass and all that, although actually... You know how scouting works, don't you? (– More or less.) We had a group of children of ten or eleven. Let's say I went mostly because my friends went: come on, let's go. But later Mary Carmen and I – Mary Carmen was my best friend then – we discovered that it was a stupid thing to go to mass, it was just all about whether so-and-so had gone or not and whether that lady had some hat... Of course we considered all of that stupid, so we stopped going. Even so, if for example her mother asked, when we got back, she would ask, have you been to mass? Yes, yes, we have been... and then perhaps... But later we said that we were not going to go any more and that was that. Why am I telling you this? It is not especially relevant.

– You were talking about school.

E: Oh, yes. Yes. I did sixth grade in a religious school, and then the preparatory course in a state secondary school[156] and after that to university, to engineering school. And that is when I came into contact with politics. Inevitably, in view of the times.

– Yes, let's see, you were born in 1958, so this would have been...

In 1975! we exclaimed simultaneously and laughed, remembering the significance of that year, when Franco died and Madrid was a continuous swirl of demonstrations, secret meetings, rumors... After a few comments about this and some clarification about her schooling, she continued.

E: Yes, yes. You can imagine what the university was like then, and the engineering school, too. And we can say I sort of dived into it (...)... and, oh well, that year it was all demonstrations and the grey ones[157] riding into the school on horseback, and us escaping, running... and even though I was sort of... I began to realize that political parties existed and all that sort of thing, but I was not very politicized...

– Hadn't you been interested at all, earlier?

E: Well, man, interested, yes... but we did not know anything. Everything was hidden from us, I did not even know what a political party was, practically. I used to read the newspaper, more or less, but you know, with the censorship we had, and the parties were illegal, and in school we had the national spirit class,[158] that was what they taught us about politics, so we did not know anything, really.

We discussed this for a while. In some families, knowledge and opinions from before the civil war had survived as an oral tradition, but many parents kept silent because they wanted to safeguard their children from the disillusionment they themselves had suffered and also from possible political persecution.

E: And another thing was that my father had a very cautious temper. Be careful, you should not talk about those things... and so on, you know? (...)

Esperanza told anecdotes of meetings, contacts with foreign groups, forbidden reading and how her father found out. He did not disapprove of her activities as such, but he was afraid for her sake. He did not want her to risk her studies or risk being arrested and mistreated by the police, which was a common experience in those days.

E: And I had a few problems, but... it was nothing important. What I want to say is that it was all very interesting, because from then on I have kept up an interest in politics, leftist politics of course, and although I am not a member of any party, my vote has always been to the left (...). All of which you may find a bit shocking, seeing... (a gesture all around, signaling her expensive apartment and its prestigious surroundings), my present situation, right? For some people this is... But, well, not for me, not really, because I have other friends who... (laughter) It is very common (her voice gained strength) and you must have found a lot of it, I am sure. Right?

I said yes, I had the idea that this new middle class was very polarized politically, many very conservative and many very leftist, so as a matter of fact I was not at all surprised.

E: I have observed it very vividly right here, in this building. Before we moved in, I thought it would be a new area, new people, I would be very integrated because there were sure to be people of a progressive kind... (...) Yes, that is what I thought! I am very naive, as you can tell. Because then we moved in, and who are they? They go to mass every Sunday... the children... well, I got married in church and we have had the children baptized, but... (I interrupted: Did you?) Yes. One contradiction after another, as you see. Because my husband is of the opinion that it is easier to go about things in the normal ways than to have to give lots of explanations.[159]

– So it is not because of some belief of yours or his?

E: No! So, what a situation, right? (I said something about Franco times and inescapable considerations...) Of course. But all of that still has not been lost in the families... In other words, if I had not married in church... actually I did have a dialectical, well, a small controversy with my mother-in-law...

Esperanza explained in detail their reasoning around the baptism and their church marriage. I got the impression that she would have preferred to take the opinions of others less into account, but she was careful not to make me think that she criticized her husband's points of view. She did not comment at all on why his views prevailed over hers, and she left open the possibility that she herself had been unsure of what she really wanted or dared to do.

E: But at least, I plan to give them total freedom if they want to take the first communion... naturally I am not going to encourage it, not in the least, and the girl is taking ethics in school.[160] The school she goes to has traditionally been a secularistic one. Now they do teach religion, but anyway, she wants to take ethics and not religion. When they get to the age of the first communion, a lot of children get together and do it and then they change back to ethics (laughter), for the sake of the presents, that special day and so forth.[161] And well, in that sense then, I try not to... I am not going to lead them to it, but if they want to do it, I'll let them.

Esperanza realized she had slipped off the track again, and we went back to discussing the type of neighbors she had. Of course there were all kinds, she said, and she tried to be fair and objective, but she was quite ill at ease in the neighborhood. "I have to learn to be more careful with what I say," she repeated several times. And she gave examples that she considered shocking of the reactionary attitudes she had encountered.

E: What I notice is that there is a certain carefulness around your private life, and some people are very fussy with their image. As for me, for example, when I take the children down to play, I am often dressed in blue jeans, very often, or I just wear any old clothes I feel like... and then you notice that some persons even look at you a little like... like perhaps you haven't painted your fingernails. And I don't always paint my nails, because... because I just don't, that's all! Or maybe I haven't got a whole lot of makeup on. Things like that. And well, I don't know, they... not all of them, but... some.... and some are tremendously class-ist! If they see you talking to the maids... For instance, I go down and there they are, my friends' maids, and I come down with mine... well, right now I don't have a maid, because she quit, but before... or perhaps I came down with her to look for the kids, and they see you talking to them, it is as if they were saying, but what is she doing there, talking to the maids, how horrible (scandalized imitating voice). You have to stay clear of the maids and naturally make sure they know that you are the Señora and she is the maid. So then, if they see you talking to them...

- Do they boycott you, then?

E: Not exactly boycott. (...) There are a number of us who usually coincide down there with the children, and our conversation is usually about the children, housework, and little else. And whenever we have perhaps strayed a little bit away from that, to opinions and so on, then later I feel that it has not always been positive, because then you notice, how shall I say, a certain tendency to categorization. (...) So, really, I don't feel very enthusiastic about sitting there by the playground chatting with them. On the other hand, sometimes it is sort of relaxing. As I told you, I quit my job when the boy was born, but it was not like giving up a satisfying job... It was a job that was not satisfying for me at all, and that I had had since, let's see... you see, ever since I was seventeen, since I started at university, I have worked. I have spent twelve years in this same company, office work, a type of work that... well, let's say that I could see that they would never recognize what I really wanted to do. (...) So there was no professional future and I was not integrated (...), it was a matter of my education not being the same as that of my colleagues. So in some way, even if you don't talk about it they could see that my kind of life wasn't like theirs, either. So then, automatically, they dislike you. In any case my earnings were far from important for my family. (...) So, I am going to take a break to see if I can find some way of channeling my profession. I am a dreamer, I know, because it is very difficult to find a job as a journalist, but I never lose hope. I would even work without pay for some magazine. People don't usually understand that. And then there is something else, my husband... (here she lowered her voice to a whisper, saying something about his high salary). It is very complicated. So I quit that job, or rather I am on maternity leave,[162] but it was not satisfying at all. So, what I was going to say is that sometimes when I go down to the playground, I look forwards to it, can you believe it? (...) Or else I talk with the maid. Which, with all due respect and everything, is not the kind of conversation that can become interesting. From a human point of view, then you talk... sometimes I even try to give her advice or something, like, look, you have to get that certificate of primary schooling, or... But anyway, it is never an intellectually interesting conversation. Or like with friends. Or with the children. Whom I love, I have a great time with them, but in the end I feel like a prisoner. All in all. (Lowering her voice again, sadly.) You have heard this story thousands of times, I suppose.

– Yes. And I have lived it. (We both laughed.)

E: The other day... sometimes I get depressed, I do. (She gave a rather abstract and normative little speech on living in a couple relationship, on love, on mutual promises, etc.) So in this society, in Spain today, you would think the men are married, too. But if he has to leave, he goes out the door just like that, and here I am, I take care of the children, I take care of the home. And once in a while, just to go and listen to some lecture, I have to make a thousand complicated arrangements! A thousand arrangements! So then, is that fair? (strong voice) I rebel an awful lot. Sometimes I feel really bad, really bad. (We laughed, probably at the face she made.) At other times I tell myself, you have to take it, it is just your own contradictions, this is your life for the moment, and so on. But no. Really... there are times when it frightens me, that I feel so bad. (Her voice died away in a whisper again, saying something about a mortal trap.)

– Now, Esperanza, I can't answer you personally the way I would like to, because this is an interview, but somehow you are asking me to analyze...

E: No, no, I am just letting out steam; I am utilizing you!

We laughed again and I told her a little of similar periods in my own life. Then we made yet another effort to return to chronology. I asked her why she interrupted her engineering studies.

E: It wasn't what I had thought, because of the contents and... well, I didn't know how to study. I had always been a good student, getting good grades without much effort. But in engineering school that was no longer enough. It was necessary to know how to study. You had to study for many hours, and I did study for many hours, but... no, I think I did not study systematically, and also I was so much into this political thing and so on, it took a lot of time... On top of that I was sort of influenced by my parents. My father always said, don't worry, if you want to study you study, whatever it costs... but there was always a certain ambiguity. Concerning this theme. You see, he started to work when he was fourteen, he worked and studied (...). So his life has not exactly... it has been hard, you see, because he studied and worked at the same time. So then I was very much influenced by this concept. That first year, besides being in engineering school – which is sufficient by itself (laughter), you shouldn't do anything else because it is very hard... but I also went to a language school and I took courses in typing and shorthand. (– Why?) Why? Well, because of this ambiguity that I noted. My mother would go: look, see what your cousin is doing, and so-and-so is already earning a salary... So there is a dynamism so that in the end you just say...

– But you said your salary wasn't really needed in your house?

E: No. No. But neither... neither did they see university studies as important, not as important as one should. I think that perhaps, for them it was like, even though they said we should study, if we worked it was like seeing that we were now ready and able to carry on our lives into adulthood. And then on top of everything else I started to teach private classes... I earned a lot of money... well, a lot of money for me, I was a student, I always needed money, sure, because I smoked, too... and etcetera, etcetera. And I never like to put pressure on my parents for money. Not like my brother, who, whenever there was something he considered he needed, he asked for it, but I have always been more like... I don't know, like a responsible girl who does not want to worry her parents. So if the books I needed could be found in the library, I did not buy them, I read them in the library... things like that. So that is why I tell you...

– Did you notice any difference between you and your brother, in that perhaps your parents thought his studies were more important?

E: No, no, in that sense I think they treated us the same. That ambivalence I talk about, that was the same for both of us.

Esperanza stayed in engineering school for three years. At nineteen she started working for a big company with set career levels. She described how she entered *oposiciones*, the competitions for jobs, and usually won the number one, which meant she got first choice for a position within the new level she had qualified for. She rose quickly. But the administrative work did not inspire her, and her bosses felt that she did not put all her energy into her work. She also had problems with some work mates.

E: That was a really fascist section, but fascist; I don't mean it now just in the sense of invective, no, I mean it in the full derogatory sense that it usually has. Because I remember, for example, when the 23 F[163]... I felt awful and terribly worried, and they were just rubbing their hands that next day, looking at me when I came to work: now you'll see what you are in for, all of you reds... more than one will be shot... Just like that!

– And this shows that those people, too, had you categorized automatically, because I imagine you did not talk much about politics at work...

E: No, but it was not necessary (laughter). (...) And my relations with the company have also been a little bit of being labeled... on the other hand, they have appreciated my work, because I know I do good work. (...) But anyway, it is a job that means nothing to me.

We spent some time going through the details of her work and the organization of the company. And her studies.

E: I continued studying English, I had always done that. Then I got married and wanted to do more things. My workday ended at six in the afternoon, but I needed to do something more. Because my husband did not get home until late, and there were only the two of us, and I did not like my work, so there was an emptiness. What did I do? Ah, yes, I took lessons in painting and drawing (giggle), I also did a lot of reading, some drama, which I really loved, I loved it, it relaxed me a lot. And then I began to study journalism and finished that.[164]

– Meanwhile you were working and you were married and you also had your first child...

E: Yes, the girl, sure.

– Tell me how that was possible!

E: Yes, but I have paid a high price for it, to be sure. It has cost me a lot, because I have been terribly stressed, I don't think I have recovered yet. (...) Let's see, I got married in 1981. Then the girl was born in. . 1984? Yes, in 1984, that was the year I started the second year of journalism, and still working full time. (...) Now (giggle), when I look back at it, I say, I must have been crazy, absolutely crazy, because this has meant a tremendous wear and tear. And emotionally as well, naturally. Listen: From the moment the girl was born, I had planned to ask for maternity leave[165] to be able to study and, well, have more time for the baby. But precisely then they started to talk about a restructuration of the company. I turned in my petition for leave, signed and everything, when one girl who is a lawyer there, called me, as a personal favor, and said she would not advise me to take that leave, that there would be problems for me to return... And my friends all said the same thing, there was pressure on me... So I changed my mind and went on working. And studying and with the baby. What I did was to ask for a reduced work day, 50%, so I only had to work four hours a day. But in the end... you are out of the house all morning anyway, there is a lot of tension, I had to punch a clock and everything. I hired a person to be with the girl. That year I had signed up for morning courses at the university, because I had planned to quit work, so in the end I hardly went to class at all, I managed with notes that classmates took for me... and the next year I went to evening classes, the fourth and fifth courses I studied at night. Yes, I have worked and studied...

– Did you finish in five years?

E: Yes, but it was horrible. Horrible, because it has had a price... (...) I felt tremendously guilty with my daughter sometimes. And then at times neither could I concentrate on my studies the way I would have liked to. I wanted very much to dive into it, take part in debates, in all the things that were organized – and I couldn't. There were classes every day, but I could only go three times a week, or two, and if the girl was ill or something, none![166]

I asked why she did it, if it was because of her frustration with her job.

E: In part. And in part because of the frustration I felt about my studies. (– The interrupted ones in engineering?) No, not at all, I was no longer interested in engineering at all. But I was interested in journalism, and I liked it a lot. So I started to study journalism when I was – what age? Twenty-five, and the girl was born when I was twenty-six, so... I finished when I was about thirty, right? I could have finished earlier if I had had the time, because if you really want to work in something like this... at thirty you may feel young inside yourself, but when you go looking for a job, then you are thirty already and that is too old... And I don't... I mean, I would like to find a job, but my economic situation permits me to... I mean, if I really needed it, I could find a job right away, but I want to find one I like.

She gave some examples of jobs she had applied for and varying hypotheses of why she did not get them.

E: Well, and in the end I am thirty-two years old now, soon thirty-three, I would like to work in my profession, there are certain themes that interest me very much... women, education, health and so on. A lot of things – but to find a job and one that relates to these things, that is very difficult.

I said she could return to her former company, perhaps, when her *excedencia* time was up.

E: But I don't want to return there! I have the excedencia, and it is a kind of security. But I feel I have wasted too much time there. (...) In the end, what have I got? A little job that is worthless. It is secure and everything, yes, and I have to return, but I would prefer not to return.

She had had one experience of working as a journalist. It was only a short contract, and the pay was ridiculous, but she enjoyed it immensely, and she was proud to have found it through entirely open channels, no personal contacts. This experience also gave her a few but valuable contacts with a magazine, where she had since collaborated without pay once in a while. Above all, the experience had given her new hopes and a feeling of having learned something about the practical world of journalism.

– Is that your whole professional experience?

E (laughing): Yes, that is the whole of it!

– Now then, tell me something about your marriage. How did you meet?

E: In engineering school. (...) Yes, he studied the same thing. When I entered the first year, he was in third. And I met him, well, in the same way I met a lot of people... there were very few of us girls, so as you can imagine there was a certain interest in us. We had to hear, lots of times, the other women and myself, that we were there to look for a husband. So just imagine, later, when I started going out with him, people said: this one made it already! and so forth. But anyway, later that was only an anecdote, because I would like to believe they said so only in jest, otherwise... So I met him, and later what we did was, he taught me to play mus.[167] And then, well... I am going to say this in student lingo: we cut classes and went to play mus. And then, with my tight schedule and everything, we did everything except studying... (...) I met him when I was seventeen, we started to go out when I was nineteen. I got married at twenty-three. So we were engaged for four years.

– Did your parents know about it?[168]

E: Oh yes! (laughter) We may be very radical about some things, but about others we comply with the norms. Yes, our parents knew about it.

She began to say something about not being liked by his parents, but at that moment her six-year-old daughter came into the room to tell her mother that a friend of hers at school had called. When the girl left, I asked how come she did not call her "mother" but a short form of her name, "Espe". Esperanza said that this was not something they had done on purpose, the girl had just picked it up from what other people called her. Neither had she insisted that she wanted her to call her "mother". But once in a while the girl did, and Esperanza liked that. I told her that some Swedes have the children call the parents by their personal names. Esperanza found that a rather "cold" idea.

E: And also, just imagine everyone's looks! Say I am in the park and she calls me Espe, then automatically you are the maid, not the mother! (We laughed.) No, thank you!

Esperanza underlined again that she was a rebel, but as to her engagement she would have liked to be much more of a rebel. I interpreted this as a veiled form of saying they stuck to accepted sexual morals. This was hard to ask directly about, so I opted for a more radical question, one which was easier to answer in the negative without losing a progressive image: Had they lived together before getting married? Esperanza laughed.

E: No. But I would have loved to do it! One of the absences I have in my life is not having lived my own life, purely my own, for a while. I mean, I ought to have left my parents' home to go and live with some girlfriends or perhaps alone or perhaps with him...

– You went from your parents' home directly to married life.

E: Yes. And, well... in other countries, to live with other people is much more normal. It means that people emancipate themselves, that they have their own life, and then later... then they decide whether to share it with someone or not...

– But that is not the way it is here. (She tried to interrupt me, but I did not let her.) Look, I have insisted that my children do precisely that, and they wanted to, too, and some of our radical friends have done the same thing, but a lot of people, even quite progressive ones, think it is a little bit like throwing them out from home.

Esperanza (sadly): Of course, of course. That is not accepted at all here.

– Or maybe not like throwing them out, but what people ask me is: "How come you don't want to be with them?" As if I was lazy, not wanting to give them service.

E: Yes, the thing is... that interpretation is doubtful sometimes... because I try for my daughter to be independent, even at a cost to myself. Because often it is less bother to have a dependent child, a child that stays close to you instead of going off far away, a child that does not climb trees or ride the swings, then you don't have to worry, and so on. And people criticize me, for example: How can you sit there so calm when the girl is climbing up there? As if it were a question of my nerves! No, no, I am terribly worried and nervous much of the time, staring at the swings, will she fall, will she fall, will something happen or not... But I don't want to limit her movement and so on, right? (...) But I don't know how... so at times... I don't know... I don't know, I hardly dare say it out aloud (little laughter)... but I feel very misunderstood. Very misunderstood. That is the role of the upper middle class. Because I just don't fit into the patterns of this class, although I do fit with a few things.

She talked about how to find some context with people like herself. Not a political party, she did not believe in any of them any longer. Perhaps a feminist group, but she was not sure. Feminism has such a bad reputation, people identify it with lesbianism and hysterical frustrated women, she said and gave a few examples of what had happened when she had uttered timidly feminist opinions at social occasions. What she wanted was some sort of context for debate.

E: What I can't find is people who just like to talk about these things. There are some people here, nearby, who perhaps experience the same thing, and so on, but in the end... they end up accepting that there is nothing to be done about it. (low sad voice) Like I will end up thinking; that you can't do anything about it...

We speculated together about the possibility that some of her neighbors might be just like her, but that they did not know it, any of them, since they were all careful not to show their opinions too clearly.

E: People don't open up much. I don't either, sure, true, but there are some things that really make me explode. (...) Sometimes I feel like... maybe I am the strange one, I am not living on the right planet, nor in the right time period. Sometimes I have this feeling of rootlessness, very strong, very... uncomfortable.

I tried to be hopeful, saying that things will get better after they have had time to settle down a bit.

E: Sure, things take time. (We both laughed at this banality.) Anyway, speaking of this new class of high status, I have observed something else: I notice, I mean, I have friends, from work or through my husband, who are actually in the same economic situation we are. But perhaps they come originally from another class, so they have always been high class, and we have been middle class. So then, we have the same type of income, or my husband may even earn somewhat more than another man. But, but you notice that... that they have absorbed things with their mother's milk all through life... on the other hand, perhaps they can't tell... a symphony from Ravel's Bolero! Because they don't have a reflection in culture nor in other things, right? But even so, they have something, like they are different, right, like an image...

– Sure of themselves?

E: Yes, or an image of being sure, an image of... difference... they are different. Even in taste, aesthetics, they have absorbed it from childhood, and you are starting to learn now, as you go along. (...)

– Listen, Esperanza, let's finish. Just the question of your marriage, now. When did you get married, you were twenty-three and he...

E: He was twenty-five.

– And you did not have the first child until...

E: Because I was on the pill. And I am now, too. So then, I have had them when...

– Well, I won't even ask if you have any problems with... I mean, since you don't have any religious beliefs.[169]

E: Oh, you mean with taking the pill? No, the only problem with it is that I have high cholesterol (giggle). But about these things we could say a lot, but well, in this area I undermine myself and I have no right to, because here the responsibility of birth control and conception and post-conception and all of that, it all falls on us, the women. Really, the men don't think that they...[170]

– Yes, but listen (I was getting impatient with her readiness to comment on anything, even though this was what I wanted her to do), your husband's career, how does that come into your life? Had he started to work already when you got married, or did you wait until...

E: He... we waited. (...) And well, as soon as he started to work we bought an apartment, well, with a bit of savings I had, and a bank loan we applied for and a little that our parents helped us with...

She talked about that first apartment, how it was much cheaper and smaller than the present one, and how it had not been too difficult to pay for, but that they had been scared when they bought it, taking a big risk as they saw it then. From the context I concluded that they bought the apartment as soon as it was economically possible, in order to get married then.[171] Esperanza let this theme lead back to her husband's career, and then somehow her associations led her to speak about the mismanagement of the state budget. I wanted her to talk about her own life, so I asked if they had a family budget.

E: You mean if we prepare a budget for household expenses? Not in the least! (big laughter) Or, well, let's say that we have an overall... not really a budget, but for example we pay 200.000 pesetas a month for the apartment.

She specified that this included payments on the loan, building maintenance, gardening and cleaning, gas, electricity and heating.

E: Then there is the school fee... this is my fault, I guess; I have insisted in an exaggerated way, but I did not want my daughter to go to a religious school.

She talked about how religious schools are cheaper at the same level of quality because they are subsidized by the Church, and how state education was out of the question because the quality was so low.

E: So the school fees for the girl amount to 50.000 pesetas a month. Which is a lot. (She gave the name of the school.) It is... it used to be the school of the progressives, one of the progressive elite schools in Madrid.

At this point I turned off the tape recorder, somewhat abruptly. We could have debated any number of issues for hours, but the interview had already been long, and the daughter had looked in a couple of times asking for her afternoon snack.

Comments

Esperanza's story illustrates three important themes.

First, the theme of work and gender. There was a clear contradiction in Esperanza's life between what her education had led her to expect and her present circumstances. Her parents wanted her to study, and she did study, for two professions both of which usually give its practitioners the means of survival as well as personal satisfaction. But she got married and had children. That was also included among her expectations, as a normal part of life and as the only form for happiness. But given the gender order in which she lived, it meant that she did not have much of a chance to practice her profession. True, there was general unemployment among journalists in Madrid for both men and women, and she would have had a better start if she had not wasted time studying engineering and holding on to a not very qualified job. But it was above all the fact of being married and a mother of two that placed her near the bottom of any employer's list of preferences. (If she had been a man, some knowledge of engineering might even have been considered an extra advantage in the curriculum.) She was objectively a housewife, subjectively something else. Neither of the two horns of her dilemma were idiosyncratic; on the contrary her problem was very common, as she herself knew and said.

Second, the change of class was an added complication. In this, too, she was representative, although she did not seem to be aware of that. The fact of starting from a low point and reaching a higher point could logically be construed as a success story. Not so for the Madrilenian middle class. Esperanza might be proud of herself and of her husband deep down, but the image of rising from rags to riches did not give her personal security, quite the contrary, and even less could she use it for social or professional advantage. She could not construe it as: "I have great merit; look at the distance I have covered thanks to my/our efforts." Instead, she felt inferior. She had not absorbed upper class security with the mother's milk. But neither did she accept inferiority as the correct angle. Nor had the new middle class created a clear representation of itself as a new phenomenon. The result was alienation and confusion.

Third, the combined effects of general cultural change, economic development and individual change of class, plus some plain bad luck, had meant that Esperanza had no access to a context for cultural negotiation of meaning. And she felt this lack acutely. The fact that she had a high education and access to media debates did not remedy the lack. It rather increased her feeling of missing out on something. There was cultural negotiation going on around her, but it was of a kind that did not serve her purposes. It only served to confirm her feeling of being an outsider. It was not just a question of different opinons. She felt she was different in some deep way. In my terms, this was an instance of clashes between different modes of management of meaning. Esperanza liked to question and debate things. Her attitude towards change was that of openness, learning. The people she met in her daily life abhorred this, they preferred caution and careful management of images.

Esperanza's story is an example of how easily people in Madrid at this time – people of all classes and circumstances – came to feel lost, outside the mainstream of events. This was a general experience, due to macro-events. It was of course interpreted differently according to habitus and experiences. Her story is also a good example of how gender complicated that experience and exacerbated the objective frustrations, and it illustrates how this could be so even for women lucky enough to have a good marriage, healthy children and a very comfortable economic situation. And it shows how "work" is a key to understand all of this, from both emic and etic points of view.

Chapter 16. Housewives on the Defensive

When I was first given access to Club Aguafría, I asked the president if I could introduce myself publicly somehow. It seemed right to let all members know about my presence and to give interested people more information on the project. The president and the board agreed, but months passed before it was decided how the occasion would be arranged. The club – or at least this board, recently elected – had ambitions to organize activities of a "serious" kind. During the previous season they had had "cultural evenings" which combined lectures, discussions and dinners, but they had not attracted any large audiences. They lamented that but said they just had to face it: the club members were not especially interested in intellectual activities. But perhaps I would be more of an attraction, since some people knew me personally.

I understood that it was my own responsibility to advertise the event. So during a few weeks I mentioned the plans at every opportunity I got and asked people what they thought. Of course people are interested, most said, but the club is a place to relax. A few expressed it more clearly: It is out of place to discuss serious matters at the club, because one does not want to risk being labeled. Politically labeled, presumably. Some women also said that this was a typical matter that women decide: If the men are interested, they may attend or not, but they go to many other places, too, so they do not usually feel a great need to go to the club to discuss. The women might. And if a woman decides she wants to go, she will convince her husband that he has to go, too, because she does not want to go alone. "So just try to convince some women and you will get double the number!"

There was certainly some truth to all of this. A further factor might be, as the president said, that people were not really interested in "serious" matters. They said they were, but that was part of their constant aparentar.

Still, we decided to try. The president thought I ought to present the project in the shape of a debate on a topic that would arouse some passion. But not too much, of course. It turned out he and another board member had already decided to suggest a topic: The issue of whether a married woman should work outside the home or not.

I accepted this suggestion gratefully. It was interesting that an almost all-male board should have thought of it. I imagined that they had made an effort to think of something related to my project, and this was one "women's issue" that was of some interest to men, too. Or logically ought to be. But as we talked on, I realized that the board members had just tried to think up an issue that was interesting enough to attract a decent audience, yet not so controversial as to be risky. I found it curious that the board members would consider precisely this issue just right. My impression was that it was very controversial.

From women's point of view, the issue might be too sensitive for the serious-but-light evening the board had in mind. And so it turned out.

What about the club women themselves? Anecdotes from a mini-survey

Before the debate, I wanted to have an approximate idea of the club women themselves – did they work outside the home or were they housewives?[172] So I decided to ask around.

The questions were: Do you (or: your wife) work outside the home or not? If so, what kind of work is it? What is your husband's (or: your) profession? Since many women volunteered information on two other points, I later added them as questions: Have you (your wife) always worked? Have you (your wife) never worked?

During a couple of weeks I walked around, asking these questions. This was a good way to widen my circles, too, I thought. Sure enough, people responded amiably, I was asked to sit down, my questions were answered and commented upon and often the occasion turned into a general conversation. There were almost always voluntary comments on how housework was arranged in each case, how many children they had, what level of studies they had attained, where they had grown up and other relevant information to make me understand why they had arranged their lives in the way they had.

Some men avoided telling me their profession. "Oh, it's hard to explain, it has to do with the construction business..." The women never did that. They usually reported their husband's profession (if he was not present) in a factual way. Of their own profession, they sometimes spoke in the same factual way, sometimes they reported with great pride that they worked, sometimes with equal pride that they were housewives, sometimes with shame that they were housewives, sometimes telling long stories of how they had switched from one to the other and why. The women never joked about it.

Some men signaled a joking, half defensive, half aggressive, distance to the "women's issue": "No, if my wife worked, I would not work!" or "I have to work, because my wife will not support me." Others answered seriously and then usually expressing respect for women's workload. "I would not like to change places with my wife, she works more than I do." "A woman's responsibilities are very great." "Of course women ought to work, too, even if they do not need the money." If they thought women should work outside the home, the reason given was seldom the progressive standard expression "to realize themselves" but the meaning was similar, in a lighter vein. The women should work "to have fun", "to feel better", "to get some distraction", etc. One man corrected my formulation: "It is not a question of whether a woman «should« work but of whether she «can«," he said with a sympathetic face. But neither he nor any other man said anything about the possibility of men taking over some of "women's" responsibilities. Neither did most women, but some did. For both men and women the practical difficulties, the load of household and family duties, were the great obstacle.

221

My interest in the matter was often interpreted as an interest in women with jobs. On a couple of occasions, a tableful of women said none of them had a job, but then they would look around and see someone who did, and they would ask her to come over, saying: "Look, this is Mary Carmen, she has a job..." Because of this, the result of my survey may be lightly skewed in favor of women with jobs. The reaction is interesting in itself, however – it is the fact of having a job that is seen as interesting, or at least as what can be of interest to a social scientist.

Some of the conversations grew into mini-interviews. Puri, for example, was a professional woman just over thirty who was happy to talk about her situation. She had two children, six and eight years old, and a live-in maid. "Without a live-in maid you can't work. I have tried, it just does not work out, at least not with the kind of job I have." She worked for a medium-sized transnational insurance company and had to travel a lot. "Besides, you can't find Spanish girls, you have to employ Philippine or Portuguese or Polish ones." I asked if the problem with that was that they had different ideas about how to treat the children. Other women had told me that, but Puri looked shocked, as if I had suggested she was prejudiced. "No, not that, I may have been lucky with that, except with one who just did not like children. But anyway. The problem is that the children spend more time with a stranger than with their mother. And there are many things you have to do yourself anyway. And if they are sick and you have to take them to the doctor, now, what can you do, because your husband... (soft laughter)... you know! Don't even ask him!"

Without my bringing it up, she went on to talk about the problem of prejudiced employers. "It was funny, for the job I have now, they interviewed me three times, each time at a higher level, and the last interview was with the general manager of the whole company, and in the last two interviews they said the same thing, they told me, look, we think very highly of you, we would like to employ you, but you have one drawback – you are a woman!" I laughed and she nodded: "Yes, as clear as that!" She was proud to have got the job against such formidable odds. And she saw herself as a completely professional woman. But the problem with the children hurt. It was not mainly the lack of time for domestic tasks, but the lack of time to be with them. "They have even asked me, crying, Mom, please, no more maids!"

My questions served, too, as an excuse for some people to air their favorite complaint about the club, its "closedness". As always, there were also complaints and jokes and anecdotes about aparentar. It was now possible, said a few, to aparentar by bragging about a woman's professional achievements. For some, this was an "advance," for others it was a most ridiculous form of aparentar.

One group of people in their twenties reacted in unusual ways. One man laughed about my topic, as most young men tended to do, and said he had nothing to tell me, "because I have never been a woman." Much laughter. But the other men were willing to discuss. And the one woman in the group was, very much so. She said she found it absolutely fascinating that a person like me would do a thing like this (my project) at the club, and the idea of the debate was even more unheard of. I asked why she was so surprised. "Because, obviously you must have noticed, this club is not the right place for that kind of thing. And then you are going to present certain ideas, right?" I said no, but she did not listen. "And they won't accept it, and they won't understand..." She shook her head in sadness, while the men laughed and someone said she was a raving feminist. Her husband explained that she had a hard time getting used to the club, and she retorted that neither did her friends accept him. They had only been married for a few months.

Just as these young people supposed, many older people automatically found my questions – which I took great care to phrase neutrally – suspicious of feminism. Sofía gave a representative answer for conservative women over fifty. She said that "this thing with women's liberation" had never interested her at all. "What interests me is to get breakfast served in bed!" Then she laughed and said that she really had a very comfortable life; unfortunately nobody served her breakfast in bed, actually, but she was used to a certain comfort and could never imagine exchanging it for the discomfort of having to go to an office. "When I was young, these things were seen in a different way, and for me, now, I still think in that way." As I prepared to go and put my question to another group, Sofía smiled polymorphously, "Let's see if they are as frivolous as I am!" She meant to make me understand that she guessed my evaluation of her, and that she did not agree, but she also seemed to express some genuine ambivalence about herself.

Sofía was representative, but not average. The same can be said about the women who said they did work outside the home. Many of them were convinced they were a majority (which they were not, cf below), and many said something like, "Oh here, at this club (or "in the middle class") you are going to find that everyone has a job nowadays."

The closest thing to an average club answer was something like the following woman, who, however, thought she was unusual: "I am kind of a special case, because I have started to work recently, after my children left home. I am a nurse, but I worked for only a short time before I got married. And then with the children... I think the children need their mother at home, oh yes I do, definitely. But when they are older, that is another thing. So I had to stay at home, because I have five children, and I have been very happy and very glad to have them and proud of them, oh yes. Perhaps it is different for women who only get one or two..." She was proud of herself all around: for having had many children, for having cared well for them, for being tolerant with women who make other choices, and for having gone back to work at a mature age. The last point, however, was the one she emphasized the least.

Altogether then, people collaborated amiably with the survey. The fact that many volunteered further opinions and facts seemed to indicate that the matter was not so controversial after all.

But the debate would prove something else. It let passions loose and confronted opinions from the whole scale. The difference in context explains the difference in reactions: At the debate there were people with widely differing opinions talking to each other, which was uncomfortable and did not fit the cautious mode of management of meaning, whereas during the survey, I usually found people sitting with their own groups, i.e. in situations where they felt secure and free to speak their mind. And in which they were usually under the impression, too, that their own opinions and their own life styles were "normal", both in the sense of correct and in the sense of representing a majority. The fact that so many could be so ignorant about the contrasts in ideas and practices among club members goes to confirm the common impression that people did indeed "function in groups" and that there were few bridges between the groups.

Before turning to the debate itself, let us look at the survey results.

Survey results

Number of persons for whom I obtained data: 224. (114 women and 110 men. 214 were married, i.e. 107 couples. Three were young unmarried men. One was a middle aged unmarried woman, one was an elderly widow, and five young unmarried women.)

I do not have the exact ages of the respondents, but the proportions were approximately the same as for the club membership as a whole, excepting persons under twenty-five whom I did not interview unless I made a mistake guessing their age, and excepting persons over sixty-five, in the same way. To include retired persons was not very interesting for the purposes of the survey, and among women over sixty-five professional work was extremely rare anyway; and as to the young club members, they were students practically without exception.

The men's professions: engineers (26), lawyers or judges (20), economists (15), physicians (6). Eighteen men had their own businesses, but I estimate that about half of them were also engineers or economists. Seven men described themselves as "administrators" or civil servants or said they did administrative work without specifying. There were two bank employees and two journalists. And one agronomist, one military officer, one architect, one psychiatrist, one salesman (i.e. who described himself as such – several of the engineers and economists also did sales-related work), one "contractor", one airline pilot, one sports teacher, one personnel director, one dental technician.

Number of women who worked outside the home: 34. Five more studied: three law, one architecture, one business administration. And five said they helped their husband in his business, usually with office work or as receptionists; they were all unsalaried, "of course".

Number of "housewives", i.e. women who were not employed nor studied nor did any other professional work at the moment: 69. (The middle aged unmarried woman did not want to describe herself as a housewife, but neither did she work. She lived with her sister and her family.)

Women's professions (except housewife): Office work or civil servants (8), own business (6 – most of them fashion boutiques), elementary school teacher (4), other teachers (4), selling something in the home (3), nurse (2), lawyer (2). The others were one of each: Psychiatrist, chemical engineer, economist, pharmacist, computer programmer, executive secretary.

Number of women who had never worked outside the home, not even before marriage: 29 who said so explicitly – of these four had studied to be an elementary school teacher and a few more had studied for other professions, such as lawyer, doctor or social worker, plus nineteen more who hinted at it or evaded the question. Probable number: over 40, i.e. a higher proportion than those who had jobs at the moment. The most common level of studies among these women was high school or equivalent.[173]

Number of women who had always worked outside the home (except for short periods of maternity leave): seven for certain, plus another seven probably. Most of these were below thirty, but two were over sixty.

The young students are not included in these numbers. The women students all said that "of course" they planned to work. They also planned to get married and have children, "of course."

Of the three unmarried men, one said his fiancée planned to work. "She is studying for a master's degree, and that is in order to work, evidently. But when we get married, we'll see. I hope to have children! And it may work out for her to work, anyway, but if it does not, we'll see..." The two men without fiancées joked about it, saying that they planned to find wives who could earn plenty of money.

The proportion of women working outside the home at the time of the survey turned out to be around 30%, which coincided with the percentage for Spain as a whole.[174] But only about 10% could be described as professional women in the sense that they had not spent long periods as housewives. And most of these were young.

The most common pattern for the older women was that they had not worked before they got married, and they had of course not worked while raising their children, but some of them had helped their husbands in their businesses. When the children had grown up, most of the women preferred not to work outside the home, but some wanted to. Those who tried to find employment were usually frustrated. The option with the greatest probability of success was to open some small business of one's own.

Other patterns could be distinguished. Most of the women who worked underlined that they found this natural and necessary and that they were happy and proud to be working. They would never quit unless forced to, and they did not think they could be forced to. They said this even though a majority of them had been housewives for many years. Many of the housewives similarly emphasized that their situation was their own choice and that they were happy with it. Some of them added normative comments: "Children need their mother!" "I have never worked nor have I wanted to. Put that down: Nor have I wanted to!" "I am a housewife, as a woman should be!" and so on.

However, quite a few housewives made just as great efforts to make sure I understood and wrote down that they were sad not to be able to work, that they had tried, that they would have liked very much to earn money of their own or to have been able to complete their studies. Two or three had found a job late in life, after much trouble, only to be laid off when the company closed down. Two or three had taken the unusual (but statistically increasing) step of registering with the state unemployment agency, INEM.

Another pattern was that of a woman just over thirty with a university degree (four or five in the survey) who had worked before she got married and afterwards, too, and even after having one or two children, but who had given up recently because she could not find domestic help or because the work load or the sense of letting the children down was just too much. These were the unhappiest lot, but most of them (not all) said they hoped to be able to go back to work in a couple of years.

There was also a pattern of sporadic working, or of moving in and out of the labor market according to ages and health of children, geographical moves, etc. A few women gave long lists: helped in father's business, studied to be a teacher, got married and quit, helped in husband's business, sold children's clothing at home, studied some more, worked in a friend's office without a salary in order to learn, did voluntary social work for the parish...

The older women were more varied than the younger. All the different patterns could be found among women over forty. Among those below thirty, almost all had university degrees and employment related to that degree.

"It depends" – thoughts about what working means

One phrase preceded a large proportion of the comments the club members volunteered: "It depends." If one wants to work and if one can work, and in that case with what, it all depends on many things. The factors most often cited were (in informants' words):

– "It depends on your age." "Not in our generation. Now, the young people are altogether different."

– "It depends on how many children you have." "Yes, and on how old they are!" "Yes, and if they are healthy!"

– "It depends on whether a woman has studied or not. Women with university degrees usually want to work."

– "No, it is much more a question of personality, what you feel like."

The women who had quit work because they had small children naturally talked of problems with daycare facilities. But strangely enough, hardly any woman who was not in that situation herself, or had a daughter who was, took up the issue. This could be because of normative pressures to be a good mother, and the construction of good motherhood as requiring total concentration on the children. Younger women insisted that they questioned such ideas, but no one volunteered any positive arguments for daycare facilities. In middle class Madrid outside the club it was not uncommon to hear arguments to the effect that daycare facilities are good because they stimulate small children's imagination and develop their social skills. But the club women who used such facilities tended rather to explain why they "had to" use them; they felt a need for excuses. One pattern was, in fact, that the first child was cared for at home because the mother was still studying, or because a grandmother could help, and later, when there were two or more children, a maid was a solution that was not much more expensive than a good daycare home. The daycare home was a last choice.

The strong normative pressures to be a good mother came to include all housework, because household tasks in general and the specific duties of childcare were lumped together. The "it depends" that came into play then was the salary a woman could earn. If she earns enough to pay a good maid, she can (perhaps) go to work, otherwise not But such comments tended to include long lists of the many tasks that no maid can do for you: cook Christmas dinner, go out for dinner with the husband's business friends, supervise the children's homework, take the children to the doctor, buy clothes for them, arrange birthday parties for them, invent games for them during vacations, make fancy dresses for them for Carnival, talk to their teachers, find out about summer camps and scholarships for them, get passports for them when they start to travel, go downtown to pay the husband's parking fines or buy tickets for the skiing trip, file a complaint with the Telephone company when it charges an erroneous amount, renew the furniture, remember grandfather's saint's day, visit grandmother in the hospital...

These lists showed that middle class women had important social responsibilities beyond practical domestic tasks. One reason why it was difficult for them to have careers of their own was that they were in charge of upholding family prestige and a middle class life style. But this was never said in so many words. If they had verbalized it, they would have fallen into two ideological traps. It would have made their choice look like self-sacrifice, which was unfashionable. And it would have made the prestige game too visible for comfort. The emphasis on innate femininity and generous dedication to the wonders of raising children, on the other hand, were completely licit reasons for the club women. They even gave them extra prestige points.

The conclusion was too obvious to be made explicit: even if a woman earns a good salary and finds a good maid, her working outside the home is bad for her family. Unless very special circumstances are at hand, such as: if all the children are grown and situated, if they do not need practical help from their mother with their own children, if the husband is in good health and his career is stable and does not require the family to move, if all other close relatives are also in good health, and if the woman earns a good salary. The truth is of course that women who have been housewives most of their lives can seldom earn good salaries. They have a hard time getting any job at all. And by the time the children are grown, the older generation may need their help. When old people can no longer manage their daily lives, their daughters or daughters-in-law are the ones that take over their household work. Later the old people move in with their children. There are few old people's homes, and the idea of placing one's parents in one is monstrous to most Madrilenians, of all classes and persuasions. For the middle class, however, one (temporary) solution is for the siblings to chip in and pay the salary of a maid for the parents.

Many women of forty or older said that they had not realized when they were younger how dangerous it is for a woman to depend economically on her husband. They usually laughed about this and said something about how ignorant they were, but they also often underlined that it was not as dangerous in those days as now. Family life was "more stable" and "happier" then. In any case, they said, young women today do well in "defending themselves", i.e. in earning money of their own.

What was hardly ever mentioned in this context was the fact that legislation had changed. When these women were young, divorce did not exist (annulment and separation did). And they did not then have the legal right to open a bank account or get a job if their husbands did not give them permission. I find it strange that they did not talk about the legal aspect, seeing that, first, it had been much discussed in mass media; second, so many of the men and some of the women were lawyers; and third, they did cast about for ways of explaining their former attitudes. Perhaps it was a politically sensitive thing to make allusions to Francoist legislation. Unlike most social contexts in Spain today, Club Aguafría was a place where one could not take for granted that one's interlocutors rejected Francoism.

In spite of the many objective constraints and conditionings, most of which the women recognized, the working-or-not issue was mainly phrased as a matter of individual desire. "If a woman wants to work..." Thus, any negative consequences were automatically blamed on the individual woman.

The debate

In the main salon, chairs had been arranged in a half-circle facing a table with a microphone. Some twenty-five persons attended. Of these, perhaps half were women I knew. There were only four men. Two sat beside their wives, one sat far away from his wife, on a chair that stood off to one side, as if he did not really mean to be there, one left before the debate was over. A fifth man sat beside his wife for a short while and then left for the bar.

This man said later that he would have liked to stay, but he was afraid that his presence would influence his wife, so that she would not feel free to speak her mind, and since it was a debate for women... I said it was not for women but about women. He smiled politely and said yes. When I told this to some of the women in my group, later, they laughed without mercy. "As if he would be able to stop her from talking! Come on! The truth is she had made him come into the salon, and he was ashamed of that in front of the other men. And he preferred to be with them in the bar."

Most of the men in the group had come to the club with their wives, but they stayed in the bar. For their wives, this was natural, but two of them later commented that they thought the men had been really curious and would have liked to participate but dared not. The men's laughter from the bar was heard through the closed doors throughout the debate, like a symbolic underlining of the cultural strength of gender segregation.

I spoke for about twenty minutes about anthropology and about my project. Then the debate began and lasted for a little over an hour. Around ten o'clock the arguments had started repeating themselves, but a few participants were still full of ammunition, so I suggested that those who wanted to could stay for dinner, so we could go on discussing in the dining-room.

During my presentation, some of those who knew me well, including one man, asked questions about methods and ethics. They did it to help me create a lively atmosphere and also to give me a chance to explain what they knew some people at the club were too suspicious about to ask. Most of the women, however, looked bored during this part.

But as soon as I mentioned "studies about women" everyone took it for granted that I was talking of feminism. One woman (with short hair, jeans and in other ways more radical-looking than most club women) did her best to make me explain the universal oppression of women, and when I refused and instead relativized, she angrily accused me of being a hypocrite. The men, for their part, already showed signs of preparing their defenses against the attacks they expected. I had to insist that I was talking research, not politics, and that even though I naturally had my own opinions, I was there to learn. I was seconded by one person, a blond, smiling woman sitting in a corner. A friend of hers said little but also helped with nods and smiles and some personal examples that showed that she understood what I meant. But the rest of the audience either looked skeptical or made exclamations to the effect that of course you are a feminist, stop pretending!

In order not to disappoint the feminist too badly, I let her give a couple of mini-speeches, but then I handed out copies of a summary of the results of the survey and steered over the debate to that: Look, this is what the women of the club actually do, what do you think about that?

Isabel began by saying[175] that she felt alluded to where I said that women who work for their husbands are unclassifiable. She did not feel unclassifiable in the least! "I work! True, I work for my husband, but what is wrong with that? I am still a professional woman, I worked in an office before I was married, and I do the same kind of work now.

True, I do not get a salary, but that is just because I find it absolutely ridiculous to take money out of an account in order to pay a salary to myself and then pay that money back into the same account!" I said, "Please, Isabel, I did not mean 'unclassifiable'as an insult!" Isabel said she understood that, but she had adopted an angry face that she kept for the rest of the evening. I explained that I meant that we could discuss, among other things, what constitutes "work" and what not, and that her arguments were very interesting in that sense. For example: Is it necessary to have a salary in order to say that you have a job?

Alicia pointed out that there are many other kinds of activities that are also not paid but could still be seen as work. She had worked a lot for the parents' association at her children's school, for example. "It was a lot of work if you count the hours and if you look at the effort I made and the responsibility I had, but I was not paid. I even had to pay for things with my own money, like envelopes and stamps." Alicia's attitude was calm and neutral, but her intention was to defend the "dignity of the housewife".

Someone said that voluntary work was very good for women, and that women had always done it, but someone else thought it was just as bad as having a "real" job, because it took time away from your main responsibility, the children and the household. This was of course the main bone of contention and the debate exploded. Most of the women in my group were adamant: a woman's duty is first and foremost to those who need her most, and anything else is selfishness. But other women in the same group said that a woman nowadays has to "defend" herself. They said so cautiously, but they were immediately shouted down with strong normative and moralistic arguments.

A woman from another group tried to mediate, saying that of course women have to be mothers first, but they can do other things too, and actually, if they do not, nowadays their own children will not respect them. "You sacrifice yourself and no one will thank you for it!" The other group said that they did not think they had sacrificed themselves, they had enjoyed doing it for their children's sake. The woman retorted: "How can you enjoy it if those for whom you do it say they wish you had not done it? Believe me, today's youngsters are ashamed of ignorant homebody mothers!" Predictably, the other women said they did not feel they were ignorant in the least. Someone said that it is working women who do not have the time to cultivate themselves. But someone else also said that a lot of non-working women are frivolous, just interested in having a good time.

The debate thus gave perfectly distinct information: the topic was controversial, and it was so because the idea of women's work outside the home presented a dilemma that was unsolvable given the present cultural parameters and material conditions. The complete continuum of opinions was represented. The battle lines were sharply drawn.

The most emotional arguments and the least willingness to listen to other opinions were on the side of the housewives who wanted to be housewives. They were clearly on the defensive. I had not attacked them, but they considered the mere existence of a woman like me a personal affront and the arrangement of a debate on this topic as a grave sign of how housewives were misunderstood nowadays and how their dignity was eroded.

And they were right in a way. Their standpoint, their whole lifestyle, was under real attack, not from me, but from all sorts of mass media messages, from the new legislation (for example on divorce), from the opinions of people around them, including many club members, and, most painful of all, from their own daughters. Some women of their age and opinion reacted by trying to "learn". That was the argument used by the working women of their group. The housewives, however, entrenched themselves to defend what they considered too valuable to permit any discussion about.

They were also wrong. The new hegemonic discourse on women's work was very much about women's dignity and autonomy, about their possibilities of opting out of a bad marriage, about their possibilities of raising their children even if the husband should die or abandon them or become ill or unemployed. But these women heard no such hopeful messages about new possibilities. They did not consider the lot of women who for whatever reason do not have the option of staying at home with the children, nor had they felt any personal professional temptations (or if they had, they had thoroughly repressed them). They read the new messages as being about "forcing" women out of their "natural" place, the family, and making it difficult for them to comply with their traditional and necessary duties of making everyone comfortable and happy. The thought of working in an office did not awaken associations to self-realization, widening social circles or new honors; they associated it instead with "indignities" like having to leave one's children or elderly parents in the care of strangers, having to take orders from strangers, probably males, and having one's personal worth judged by criteria that had nothing to do with "feminine mystery". To them, there was only one dignified option. and that was the dual gender organization of economic responsibilities. Any talk of women earning money had the effect, as they saw it, of undermining the orthodox division of responsibilities. And that was dangerous.

They did not say, and probably did not think, that they themselves were in danger, since it was too late for them to enter the labor market, but that was objectively so. Their "dignity" (in the sense of economic, cultural and emotional security) did in fact depend upon a gender organization that exempted them from earning money. But since that aspect of gender had been associated with many other things (girls studying less than boys, women unable to handle bank accounts, the idea of men being more rational, etc.) that all now agree have to be "transcended" and "left behind" if "development" (in its ideological vague sense) is to run its course (and they did believe in "development"), they could not defend the old gender order with rational arguments. They could only fight a battle of retreat, trying against all evidence to present their option as the only option. Since it was a losing battle, it was difficult to keep emotions under control. To show strong emotions about the issue was also part of the argument (according to the cultural construction of emotion as persuasive; cf appendix C, p 11).

At the opposite extreme was the feminist and her wish to give the debate an expansivist frame. She gave up when she did not receive my open support, and well before the debate was over she left. I am sure she felt she could not convince anyone and that she did not hear anything interesting. From this debate, she could learn nothing new about what arguments to use herself, and she was not interested in listening to the other side. I felt terrible about letting her down, but if I had supported her, I would have lost the opportunity to learn about the opposite arguments. The defensive housewives might well have walked out of the room, such was their state of mind.

In between was a majority of women who thought that it might not be all that selfish for a woman to want to have an income of her own in this changing world. One never knows, they said. A job can give her some economic security. It can also give her some personal satisfaction, and this might not necessarily hurt her children. But of course she must pay a price in the form of a double work load, now that it is so difficult to find a maid. The arguments of these women were tentative and timid in content, but more expansive than cautious in their mode of management of meaning. They wanted to try out ideas, analyze arguments.

Near the end of the debate, I asked the audience what they thought about the idea that both husband and wife work outside the home the same number of hours and also inside the home to the same extent and with the same tasks. All the women in the room cried out in unison: "Impossible! That is utopic! That will never work!"

Finally, here was something they could all agree on, albeit for different reasons. Some said it was biologically impossible implying that that was a good thing, since it made any talk of changing gender roles ludicrous. Others said that it might be possible, and probably desirable, but it was still impossible with the kind of men that exist now, i.e. biologically possible, but still culturally impossible. The men smiled, uncomfortable or sarcastic or perhaps relieved.

Soon after ten o'clock I declared the debate finished, and most of the people except my group left. Five women offered to be interviewed for the project. A couple of women gave me their cards and wished me good luck. One woman whispered that I could count on her, anything she could do to help with the project, but she did not want anyone else to know.

We joined the men in the bar and were told that the plan to have dinner in the dining-room had been thwarted: the dining-room was completely occupied by another meeting. My group quickly agreed on a nearby Andalusian restaurant instead.[176]

Dinner and jokes

Eighteen persons got into half a dozen cars and drove to the restaurant. Between eleven and one o'clock we drank a lot of white Andalusian wine and ate a selection of delicious Andalusian seafood. The atmosphere changed completely. The serious and angry faces

232

from the debate disappeared before we even got into the cars, and the usual conversational caution wore off quickly, too, as soon as wine was served.

Two women continued talking to me about the dilemma of working or not. María Angeles was a nurse. She said she felt very "identified" with her job and had no problems with housework. Her husband did not "help" but the children did, and she had an asistenta, and her working hours were pretty good. She did not in the least seem to feel that these opinions made her exceptional in the group. Dolores also wanted to see herself as a professional woman, but she had not worked for over twenty years and this frustrated her very much. She said she had made a decision when she got married to dedicate herself to her family. She thought then, like the other women of the group now, that that was what a woman had to do. Later she had regretted it deeply, but there was nothing she could do about it. She felt she had made a commitment and that it was wrong to change it.

While we talked, the others had started making the usual sexual jokes. Suddenly Carlos, María Angeles' husband, stood up and shouted, with a clear address to our corner of the table and the clear intention to make us change the subject: "Yes, yes, perhaps you women work a lot, that may be true, OK... BUT WHEN IT REALLY COUNTS, DO YOU DO WHAT YOU SHOULD!?" The sexual allusion was obvious, all the women started to protest in jest, and all the men started saying things like "oh, what a headache!" in mock female voices... As usual, the message about sexual activity was that it is something men want and women try to avoid. And the meta-message was that a dinner with friends is an occasion to laugh a lot, but not for any serious discussion. Another meta-message was that men set the general rules.

When it was almost time to go home, Irene remembered something and shouted on top of her voice: "Today is the International Women's Day!" She laughed sarcastically, and everyone else started to laugh too, and to correct her: "No, wrong, it is the international day of WORKING women." A man filled in: "No, no, all women work an awful lot!" in a tone signifying the opposite. Irene laughed some more but protested: "That's not true, we all do work a lot." Then she looked at me and brought home her main point: "Whatever the feminists say, all women work a lot!" I looked at Dolores, María Angeles and Alicia, whom I thought would have a better idea of what feminism was, or who would at least feel a need to defend their own ideas, but they laughed just as much as everyone else.

Meanwhile Carlos had picked up the bill and figured out how much we had to pay. "2.500 pesetas per beard," he said. "Beard" is a normal joking synonym for person, like "head" in English, and does not necessarily refer to men only. All the men got out 5.000-peseta-bills, to pay for themselves and their wives. I got out 2.500 pesetas. That created the usual protests – a woman cannot pay when there are men around. "I said beard!" cried Carlos, refusing to take my money. One of my closest friends in the group, Alejandro, got out 7.500 pesetas, to pay for me, himself and his wife. I protested, saying they always invited me and I never got to invite them, so in that case I was rather the one who should pay 7.500... I started to get out more money and there was a whisper around the table as Alejandro stood up, laughing and joking but ready to stop me physically from putting money on the table.

The incident was peaking. I knew I broke a norm – a woman should not argue with a man about money – but I could not help breaking norms, no matter what I did, because there is another, very strong, norm that all persons with the means to do so should invite as often as they get invited, and there is also a norm or disposition according to which a person should insist almost to the point of scuffles. These norms combine well as long as everyone is part of a couple, but they break down around working and/or separated women. (Cf chapter 12.)

Carlos quickly and intelligently defused the situation announcing a new calculation: Each couple was to pay 5.500 pesetas, and that way they would invite me between all of them, as a way of thanking me for the "lecture", and the difference for tips! It was now both possible and necessary for me to put my money away. And thank them all.

The incident was unusually dramatic, but it was representative for what happened many times during fieldwork, and it goes to show to what an extent a working woman was an anomaly in the social life of "traditionalists," and much more so if she had no male partner who could handle the friendly scuffling with other men on her behalf. In all-female contexts, these women would mock fight each other over bills with as much skill and insistence as the men, but when men were present, they took no part at all.

Introduction to part V: Sexuality

Sexuality was the other big topic that cropped up in conversations related to gender. However, its presence was largely indirect. It was a focus of cultural interest but also of moralistic restraint, emotional discomfort and normative limitations. It was definitely a "thing" that was constantly construed in discourse, even though the key words were heavily burdened down by complex rules for their use and meanings. Because it was both emphasized and repressed, it was difficult to handle but must be handled.[177]

Sexuality is not the same thing as gender. They encompass each other. Gender is a principle of categorization that has consequences for the cultural construction of sexuality, and the cultural construction of sexuality has consequences for both the cultural construction of the gender categories and the social organization of the activities of those categories.

In the Mediterranean area, sexuality and gender are usually tightly coordinated, to the point of being confused in people's minds. The old ideas on honor and shame hardly survive in Spain today, but they have shaped ideas on gender and sexuality in many ways, especially in the sense of equating the two.

Because sexuality and gender were confused, and because both were in central focus in many areas of cultural negotiation, sexuality was much talked about. But because of the European tradition of repression-cum-salaciousness (cf e.g. Foucault 1984/1976) that talk was seldom open and direct. On the other hand, because the talk of sexuality was not usually open and direct, to be open and direct about it was a key symbol of radicality.

In the early 1990s, opinions on sexuality in Madrid ran the complete gamut, from outright hatred of the body to extreme opposition to this view, an opposition that included ideas about sexuality as the greatest good in life and fervent belief in anything that could promote this good: open marriages, sexual education, no closing of bathroom doors (cf Thurén 1994), freedom of choice of sexual "option", sexy clothes, nudist beaches, etc. In Spain in general, churches were less conspicuous than discotheques, sex shops, and newspaper ads for prostitutes. The whole phenomenon has been called the *desmadre sexual,* approximately meaning sexual anarchy, a phrase used by both proponents and opponents.[178]

The "liberal" or "progressive" view of sexuality was quite similar to its equivalents in other European countries as to contents. It was different from them, nevertheless, in one important way: it was a position defined as opposition. It would be an impossible position, of course, if it did not fit with individual experiences in daily life, and as the process continues it will become ever more firmly rooted in habitus. But after forty years of a dictatorship which rested ideologically on a conservative Church for which sexuality was mainly a treacherous threat to spirituality, the liberal position was based more on a need for "ideological coherence" than on actual new experiences.

The emic view was of a scale of "openness" with mainly two possible positions: "very closed" or "very open". An outside observer could distinguish a number of positions, but it was not easy to order them on a scale of open/closed, since emic criteria were several and did not place the positions in parallel ways, in spite of the emic impression of precisely that. A further complication was change, of course – what was radical ten years earlier was now timid. Finally, even if we simplify and sort the possible positions in two or three clusters, these clusters would not be easily comparable, since the rules for what could be said and the conversational stakes in the conversational games played were different in each cluster. This can only be described by presenting examples. But for the examples to be informative, some description of positions must be given first.[179]

What I will call the conservative position was a cluster of ideas about sexuality held by persons who generally considered themselves "conservative" or "traditional" and who managed meanings in general and especially meanings related to change with caution. Conservative opinions on other matters, especially religion and politics, often coincided with conservative positions on sexuality.

The reverse was not true – radical politics did not necessarily imply radical positions on sexuality. However, there was some tendency for a general clustering at the opposite pole as well.

In between was a cluster of opinions on sexuality that were widely acceptable and not associated with any other general cluster of opinions. This cluster will be called hegemonic here, since it dominated mass media, education and legislation,[180] and since any deviation from it called for an explanation in most social contexts.

The conservative position will be described in chapter 17, the hegemonic in chapter 18.

The presentation is partly based on material from media. Neither the ideology nor the practice of middle class Madrilenians can be understood without relating them to mass media and other indirect sources of discourse, since these played a large role in their everyday lives. True, it was a very verbal culture. But the individuals were literate, and a majority watched television and listened to the radio regularly. So their ideas originated largely outside face-to-face contexts. They negotiated their significance for their everyday life in conversations, so of course many ideas originated there, too, but indirect sources that abound in everyday life weigh more heavily when it comes to topics that are difficult to talk about, like sexuality.

Part V is meant to show that gender in middle class Madrid cannot be understood without understanding how sexuality was construed, how sex and gender and sexuality were confused, and how culturally central and socially divisive these issues were. Two chapters describe the outlines of the two main opposed discourses and the third, chapter 19, exemplifies how these and other positions could be referred to in conversation and what other issues could be used to argue for a given position on sexuality, or vice versa, how opinions on sexuality could be called in to shore up arguments about other things.

Chapter 17. The absent presence: Conservative positions

The battlelines around sexuality in the 1990s were largely defined by Catholic thinking. Historically, the Church has defined the official discourse on sexuality in Spain. This chapter will therefore offer examples of discourse from the Church, from a religious lay organization and from an influential Catholic writer. The last two occupy the "most closed" and "most open" positions, respectively, within the conservative sector of the continuum (if such it is). Inside the church hierarchy, different positions are possible, but I will describe those that can be deduced from authoritative texts, such as those authored by the Bishops' Conference.

The Church during the "Transition"

The transition from dictatorship to democracy, approximately from 1975 to 1982, was a difficult period for the Catholic Church in Spain. Those were years of fundamental political debates: Should state power come from the people or not, i.e. should Spain become a democracy of the Western European type or not? Should it continue to be a centralized state or some sort of federation? How should "reconciliation" between all Spaniards come about, that long overdue real end of the civil war that was impossible during the Franco regime? How should the first elections be organized to avoid bloodshed? Could the result of the first elections be considered a mandate for the writing of a new constitution or not, and how should the constitution be conceptualized?

The Church had its own special worries. In general: How would these basic changes affect its position? More specifically: Would the special concordat between Spain and the Vatican be respected? Would the king retain the old regime's power to name the bishops? What would happen to Church patrimony and state subsidies if the state was declared non-confessional? Would the Church retain its old privileged influence over education at all levels? Since a total separation of Church and State was considered undesirable, how could it be avoided? What exactly was it in the new circumstances that produced a trend towards secularization and how could it be arrested? Would a democratic state mean even stronger trends away from Catholicism?

Most of the bishops and other Church representatives had a lot to say on all of these matters throughout the transition period. And logically enough there were divisions inside the Church that paralleled those of the whole country. But somehow, by 1980 most priests and bishops had accepted democratic principles, the separation between Church and State,[181] and the fact that canon law would not automatically be civil law.

In spite of the momentousness of these issues, however, the really great controversy, the really dangerous battle, was the one over divorce.[182] It raged from the early days of the transition until the new law took effect in 1981. And the arguments in this battle are very interesting for our purposes here. The word sexuality hardly appeared in them. Apparently they were about spiritual and material protection of abandoned women and children. Yet, underneath it all the real problem was the unmentionable one of sexuality.[183]

One representative Church statement:[184] "Divorce is not a remedy for the harm that one tries to head off but rather it becomes an open door towards the generation of evil. (...) Any marriage is, by natural law, intrinsically indissoluble, that is, it cannot be dissolved by mutual and private agreement between the spouses. (...) The indissolubility of marriage is not an imposition of society nor does it grow exclusively from an added religious precept, it is rather the very essence of conjugal reality. (...) It is true that the judicial order should not be confused with the moral order. However, a political power that is indifferent to moral values lacks reasons to oppose the injustice and anarchy that might disturb the well-being of the political community or to ensure respect for human rights in the life of society." (Bishops' Conference, 1981, quoted in Aradillas 1986:218)

In other words, the bishops de-legitimized the legislators saying that the divorce law, as projected, was a threat to the stability of the state. And their judgment was not just religious, nor partisan, they said, but based on natural law and objective facts. Strong words, indeed, especially coming from the highest representatives of an organization that some, probably large, part of the population believed knows what is good.[185]

What was it that was so dangerous about the law, then? The bishops' text contains references to "the weaker spouse" and the children, who should not be abandoned. But there is no mention of the possibility of protecting the weaker partners with laws of alimony and child support.[186] Nor is there any mention of the fact that many separations in Spain are initiated by the so-called weaker party, because the so-called stronger party does not support the children, does not comply with other conjugal duties or mistreats the spouse.[187] Nor has it been a Church argument that legalization of the many de facto families in which the parents wished to but could not get married anew would protect children and strengthen the Family (i.e. as defined by the Church).

Divorce does create social difficulties, in this the bishops were right. But this is not the crux of their argument. Instead, what they really underlined with repetitions, examples and strong references to higher authorities, was what they called "conjugal reality". That this referred to sexuality can be shown in many ways. For instance, there was a common euphemism for sexual relations, "making use of the marriage." More clearly, the bishops banned divorce even in cases where there were no children and where the spouses agreed on the divorce and its economic conditions. Furthermore, religious law permits separation, which has all the effects a divorce has except to permit a new marriage. That is, weak spouses can be abandoned, children can be exposed to injustices, and so on – the only thing not sanctioned is for once married persons to have sexual

239

relations with anyone else than the first spouse. In that sense, and in that sense only, marriage is indissoluble in the eyes of the Church.

Some bishops concluded that non-Catholic religious marriages, civil marriages, and even common-law marriages, were just as indissoluble as Catholic marriages.[188] And bishops who expressed such thoughts did not mean to say only that this was so in their interpretation or according to Catholic dogma – they implied that their law was universally valid.[189]

Now, there were differences within the Church itself. Some bishops actually tried to explain that religious interpretation is one thing, civil law another. In the early days of the discussion (1979-80) this message was hard to understand for many Catholics. On the level of letters to the editor and bar discussions, there were many angry outcries to the effect that the divorce law was undemocratic (the favorite argument of the period whatever the issue discussed), because it was a limitation of freedom, the freedom namely to remain married if your spouse wished a divorce. Such a spouse's freedom was not considered, since his or her wish apparently placed him/her outside the moral universe.

From the other side of the debate, the moral authority of the Church was constantly questioned. The corruption of the ecclesiastical courts was described in detail in the press, it was pointed out that the Church had never protested publicly against torture or capital punishment, etcetera. The Minister of Justice tried to explain, in 1980: "I think it is fine for the Church to say that Catholics ought not to divorce, but the State has to write legislation for everyone. I think that as a whole this society is in favor of a divorce law." (Quoted in Aradillas 1986: 206.) From the viewpoint of traditional Catholicism, this argument was completely beside the point.[190]

The so-called progressives sometimes even debated the issue of sexual morals head on. And when they did, their references were a world apart from the bishops'. They talked of personal freedom to search for happiness. They talked of sexuality as a physical and psychological need, and a need for everyone, not only for married persons. They talked of sexuality as a way of relating deeply to other persons, as a way of keeping couples together, and as a way of exploring one's own body and its expressive possibilities. They even talked of sexual "options", meaning the freedom to search for pleasure according to one's own taste, including homosexuality. The feminists even went from "claiming the right to orgasm" to "sexual anarchy – why bother about orgasms" in bewilderingly few years. What was always opposed, even in less radical circles, was the idea that the body is bad.

So on one side of this polarization, sexuality was positively illuminated and spoken about relatively frankly. The other side preferred not to mention it directly, but its discourse was coherent and insistent. It was about an unnamed but pervasive threat to order.[191] In its silences, it placed sexuality on the cultural center stage with even greater emphasis than the "progressive" discourse.[192]

In other words, both sides placed sexuality center stage, but they did so with different words and with such different criteria of relevance and morality that they talked past each other. And they met in debate mostly on pages of letters to the editor in the newspapers – most other contexts for discussion were separate. What was Good at University was Bad in Church. What was self-evident at the discotheque was a most urgent and difficult worry at the religious school parent-teacher-association meeting.

By 1990, things had calmed down. The Church continued to take polemic stands on issues related to sexuality, but during the 1980s other issues had become more important for it, especially the crucial one of control over schooling. The hegemonic discourse to be described in the next chapter was now more or less accepted, perhaps in a mood of resignation, by some factions inside the Church itself. For those who tended towards hatred of the body, however, there was still support to be had from religious quarters.

El Camino – one extreme of body-hatred

"Treat your body with charity, but no more charity than that which you employ with a treacherous enemy."(226) "He was right who said that body and soul are two enemies that cannot separate and two friends that cannot meet."(195) "Free me, Jesus, from that filthy crust of sensual rottenness that covers my heart, so that I can hear and easily follow the call of the Holy Ghost in my soul."(130) "Marriage is for the troops, and not for Christ's staff." (28) "When you come to a firm decision to live a clean life, chastity will not be a burden for you: it will be a triumphal crown." (123) (The numbers refer to maxims. My translation.)

These words were written in 1939 by Jose María Escrivá de Balaguer, founder of Opus Dei, the organization that was to become the first "Secular Institute" in the Catholic Church, and that was to attain an important influence over politics and economics in Franco's Spain from the 1950's on. His book of maxims, *El Camino* (The Road), was treated as the fundamental text within the organization. "The greatest best-seller of our times," was what it was called by a woman who tried to convince me of the excellence of the organization and its ideas.

The importance of the anti-body theme in this book comes out clearly in the short Introduction. It consists of only five paragraphs, of which the longest reads: "Your main enemy is you yourself, because your flesh is weak and worldly and you have to be strong and heavenly. The center of gravity of your body is the world; your center of gravity has to be heaven. Your heart belongs wholly to God and you should dedicate its love completely to Him."

There is also a clear theme of gender hierarchy. The book has nothing to say to women directly, but this very absence indirectly tells them they are less godly than men. For example, the Introduction addresses the reader as "he" and speaks of "faultless gentlemen". In maxim no. 22 the ideal person is portrayed as one who learns to become an angel by being first a strong, virile man. In many maxims, the lack of virility is listed along with other grave faults, such as selfishness, cruelty and above all, of course, lust.[193]

In the public mind, the Opus Dei is better known for other things than for its hatred of the body. It is, for example, known for its secretiveness (members seldom admit being members) and for its elitism (persons with physical handicaps or without university education cannot attain full membership). It is also sometimes said to have a work ethic closer to Calvinism than to Catholicism.[194] The fact that there are degrees in its membership, and that one must live a chaste life to reach the highest degrees, is well known, of course, but there is more emphasis (both from members and non-members) on the fact that according to the Opus Dei the "world" is not bad. What that means is that one does not have to enter a convent in order to live a Christian life of perfection. One can be a follower of Christ by working in the "world" and doing one's best – and for many that includes marriage. And, of course, in that case, all the children God wants to send. A suspicious attitude towards the body can be deduced from the oft-commented fact that Opus Dei members dress conservatively, with care to hide any body forms that could excite lust. But suspicion is one thing, the hatred expressed on almost every page of El Camino is something else.

At least I was surprised by this hatred, in spite of everything I had heard about the Opus Dei. And even more surprising was it that the woman – let us call her Yolanda – who insisted on lending El Camino to me considered herself a feminist! So I accepted her invitation to visit her in the Opus Dei residence where she lived and worked to discuss with her.[195]

Yolanda and her residence – body-hatred in practice

The entrance door was small and half hidden behind a tree. A receptionist let me in through a second locked door of beautifully wrought iron and asked me to wait in a hall that looked like a medieval castle in a film: dark grey flag-stone floor, high white walls, sparse furniture in dark wood. The small windows did not let in much light, nor did much come from the candle-shaped iron bracket lamps that were lit even though it was not yet dark outside. There was a smell of bleach.

Yolanda arrived: low heels, straight skirt, blouse buttoned all the way up, woollen cardigan. She showed me through the building, a maze of halls, tiny gardens, sitting-rooms of various sizes, study rooms, a dining hall, a library, a lecture hall and a chapel. There was a swimming pool and a tennis court in the yard. Yolanda said that some eighty women lived in the residence, about half in rooms for three, the others mostly for two, and just a few single rooms for the staff.

Naturally only women lived in the residence. Most of them were university students, but those who wanted to could stay on after finishing their studies, Yolanda said. The kitchen personnel were students, too, "in a sense. We teach them cooking and general hostelry skills. It works like a trade school, we want to have that too." She winked: ' And besides, in that way it is cheaper for us!" She showed me the cleaning apparel and explained how they all took turns washing and scrubbing. "Even students have to know what a married woman should know, right?"

There were young women concentrating on their books in all the study rooms. "We try to create a studious atmosphere, very studious." But the library was locked, "and even so a hundred or so books disappear every year." Again the disarming smile.

The furniture was generally stern, but no two rooms were exactly alike, and the variation, the little doilies and flower vases and many framed photographs created something of a homelike atmosphere. I asked who the people in the pictures were, and Yolanda told me about "a man who is like a father for all of us and lives in Rome", about "a girl who died of cancer and who was so sweet, she will probably be canonized, we loved her very much", about the first woman who "signed up – let's call it that! – for the Work"[196]... Yolanda added, "We are really like a family you see – but a very big family!"[197]

Yolanda herself had lived for a total of seventeen years in Opus Dei residences. I asked if she had made any vows, but she denied the existence of vows. "It is just a private commitment. No ceremonies, nothing official at all. But let's say they know they can count on me."

After arranging a tray of tea and biscuits in the kitchen and taking it to one of the sitting-rooms, Yolanda initiated our discussion expressing her opinion about the present Pope, who, she said, is doing a lot for women.[198] She especially appreciated his declaration that women are not supposed to be submissive to men, "the submission should be mutual." She also complimented me cordially on my two great Catholic countrywomen, Saint Birgitta and Queen Cristina. Then she asked me what I thought of El Camino.

I explained the revulsion I felt for the basic ideas in the book: hierarchy, obedience, chastity. Yolanda said she understood my feelings and that many expressions in the book sound strange today; they must be understood in the context of the times when they were written. For example, obedience is not meant to be a violence to one's own spirit, quite the contrary, it is meant to be voluntary, an exercise to promote spirituality, in order to reach greater freedom. "Because the whole Work is based on freedom above all, a lot of freedom," was one of Yolanda's two key arguments. The other one: "One has to distinguish between what is essential and what is accidental." I asked why the 1939 text was then still considered basic for the Work. Yolanda said that read in the right spirit, it teaches you self-discipline, dedication and so on: positive things, love, not hatred.

Since we found it difficult to understand each other on this abstract plane, we decided to talk about concrete examples. I chose the hatred of the body as the first theme.

Yolanda said she agreed with me "a little" on this point. This is an old tradition, older than Christianity, and deeply entrenched, so there is cultural logic in that it should have found an expression in Christianity, too. I said that this explains but does not excuse the fact that Christianity has continued and reinforced the anti-body tradition. Yolanda did not think so, she thought that there are no really Christian ideas that are anti-body. What you see are just earlier ideas that Christianity has fought unsuccessfully.

To exemplify, she quoted the Founder (Escrivá de Balaguer) to prove that as time passed, he no longer expressed himself as he had in 1939. He had once said, for example, that if art is good, it has something divine about it; he had seen the Capitolian Venus and it did not inspire any temptation in him at all, he just gave thanks to God for making woman so beautiful.

It seemed that this theme was not yet concrete enough, so we moved on to the example of the dress code.

I asked if it was true, as I had heard, that Opus Dei forbids women to wear slacks. Yolanda laughed and asked me to look around. I then saw that a few women in the groups trooping through the hall wore slacks, some even blue jeans. Yet there was an air of carefulness and chastity about them all.

Yolanda explained: One is free to dress as one thinks is right, of course. Lots of freedom! One should just dress as fits each occasion. One should not, for example, overdo the wearing of slacks.

I asked what was meant by "overdoing". Yolanda said there were no exact rules, but at home or for sports or housework slacks are fine. It also depends on which slacks. And which skirts and which blouses, too. In public, a woman should dress "decently", which is, she said "an idea that I think is shared by anyone with common sense." I said I was sorry but I did not accept that. What exactly did she mean by "decent"?

Finally Yolanda got down to concrete descriptions. A woman should never dress so that her body is emphasized. If she does, she treats herself as merchandise. And that is wrong, a woman must be a person. She must defend her female dignity. And that of other women. She has to dress in such a way that whoever looks at her does not think of her body but of what she says and does. This is what is essential. How exactly that kind of dress looks is accidental.

For each line of argument, Yolanda introduced concepts that were doxic to her, in spite of her philosophical education, and I questioned them relentlessly, like a pedantic college student. This was possible because she herself had suggested the discussion, and she took my criticism in good stride. What was meant by "modesty", "female dignity", "beauty"...? I said that I honestly thought there was a hatred of the body underneath it all, otherwise there would be nothing undignified about showing that a person has a female body. Yolanda then graciously admitted defeat, laughing, and I had to laugh along with her. She was making a tremendous effort to adapt the Opus Dei discourse to what she thought would be acceptable to me, but there was a point beyond which she could not go.

The concept of essentialism came up over and over again. For Yolanda it meant approximately the opposite of relativism. For me, it meant attributing a quality of naturalness and inevitability to human products. It seemed to me the main difference between us was that she considered masculinity and femininity as God-given essences, while I take them to be mainly cultural constructions. She honestly thought that men and women have the same capacities and potentialities, that God has given them both a double duty, to multiply and to build culture, both should do both. The present division of labor is unfair and does not comply with biblical commands. But: men and women must do their similar work in different ways, respecting the eternal differences between them.

So we switched to the theme of feminism. Yolanda saw herself as involved in a serious struggle inside the Work and inside the Church, a defense of the idea that the feminine is different but equal. She called her position feminist. In this struggle she had some allies, for example the papal attitude, but mostly enemies. She explained that the Church has been dominated by men for so many centuries that it has absorbed myriad male prejudices that have nothing to do with Christianity. I said that certainly there is a Christian version of feminism, but that I could not understand how she could combine this view with her sincere admiration for the Founder and his book. But by now Yolanda was no longer discussing with an opponent; she addressed me as an ally in the feminist struggle, and even though I could not admit that our struggles were the same, I felt I had to accept her offer of good feelings along with another cup of tea.

Yolanda sketched her background. "I have always had a positive view of Woman in general and above all I have never been able to believe in the inferiority of women, because in my home... now, I mean, I love my father a lot, lots of affection and all of that, but there is one thing that has always been clear in my mind and it is that my mother... well, it is just that she was the strong one."

When I left, it had started to rain. A group of residents were just about to leave, to go to a movie, and Yolanda asked them to accompany me to the metro station. They acquiesced, crowding around me with solicitous umbrellas. During the ten-minute walk I asked questions and they answered: They studied economics, languages, engineering... Most of them had "official" boyfriends and planned to get married... One said she had recently decided to give up the thought of marriage and stay on in the residence while she worked for a doctorate in law, but she had not yet decided whether to become an Opus Dei member. "So far it is just a place for me to live, where I feel comfortable. And safe!" she laughed with a mysterious wink as we arrived at the metro entrance.

Marías – the intellectual Catholic version

The Opus Dei anti-body attitude is extreme. Most Madrilenians I met felt contempt towards it. For example, any woman's too doughty appearance could be criticized calling it "opusino", Opusean.

But there were other versions in Christian anti-body tradition. One that was usually accepted as liberal and intellectually refined is that of the philosopher Julián Marías. In the Book Club, his name was often mentioned with reverence. It was said that he was a great defender of women, "without falling into any of the extremes", by which was meant approximately Opus Dei on one side and feminism on the other. Marías, born in 1909, published several books on women, and at one Book Club meeting we discussed one of them: "*La mujer en el Siglo XX*" (Woman in the Twentieth Century) published in 1980.

This book discusses women's situation in a changing world. Marías refers mainly to Spain but offers examples also from other countries, so he seems to intend for his arguments to be universally valid.

He considers himself a great admirer of women: He is generous with exclamations about women's generosity, beauty and intelligence. But he quotes no woman's opinions. The book is unabashedly a discussion about women – or rather Woman – from a male point of view.

The twentieth century has brought certain improvements for Woman, such as running water and access to education, says Marías, but the nineteenth century was happier, for all, because women were more sure of their femininity. There were clear norms, which makes for harmony. He does not accept the image of Victorian times as puritanical. As proof of its vital sexual atmosphere he adduces can-can, vaudeville shows, Renoir and Toulouse-Lautrec, i.e. (in my terms) a sexuality defined as male access, especially visual, to women's bodies, especially women who had to earn their living giving such access. Nothing is said of women's access to pleasure; instead Marías implicitly criticizes later trends (cf below). The difference, he says, is that in those times "it was done with good manners." (34)[199] Marías bemoans the disappearance of domestic service, which made satisfactory family life easier to attain, and he thinks this loss has to do with the efforts to convert the relationship into a labor contract. Instead it should be, and was, a relationship of teaching, participation in good family life, urbanization, a powerful motor of social change for women. "How many little maids have I not taught to read and write when I was a boy!" (43) The possibilities for maids to construct a harmonious family life of their own is not discussed.

I believe these examples are enough to give the reader an idea of Marías'general outlook. It has a clear class bias. As to gender, he does not believe in its existence. The difference between women and men is eternal, essential, given. At the same time, he is paradoxically (and typically for this kind of discourse) afraid that women today run the risk of losing their femininity, and this would mean that they would also lose their humanity. Because, he says, there are only two versions of humanity, there is no neutral humanity, there is no humanity as such, there is only masculine humanity and feminine humanity, so if women stop being women, they will not even be persons. One even suspects a veiled threat here: women have hitherto been very sure of their capacity to capture men's interest, says Marías, but he is not sure this will continue to be so (112).

Marías' ideas about sexuality are more complex, but very much related to his view of sex/gender.

At one obvious level, his discourse is the usual Catholic one: sexuality is not good in itself; it is bad and dangerous if it is "mechanical" and purely physical. Chastity can be very beautiful, a value in itself for both sexes. For sexuality to be good, it must be "humanized" with love.

On the other hand he talks of sexuality as a great force in human life, as a motor of all our vital desires. He does not use the word lust (it would have to be a negative word in his vocabulary), but he speaks of "drama" and "longing" as something positive. He thinks chastity is a good thing for young people, but mainly because he thinks it augments "expectations" and "fears", and that in turn will enhance the beauty of sexual life when one finally gets married. Another advantage with chastity for young people is that it results in respect for "the important fact that women's purely sexual impulses awaken rather late."(38) But he forgets to relate this to another fact of sexual organization common in societies that emphasize chastity, and which has been normatively stressed in Spain until recently, namely that women get married much younger than men.

The main condition for sexuality for Marías is the contrast between the sexes. If the sexes are not strongly contrasted, attraction, sexuality and probably even love will disappear. There must also be mystery. "You cannot speak explicitly about sex, because then it evaporates, dissipates, volatilizes." (110) Norms are just as necessary. He laments the fact that all sexual norms are nowadays called "taboos" and considered as something to be "overcome".

Sexuality is everywhere. For Marías, non-sexual encounters can occur only between people of the same sex. "Men among themselves and women among themselves are interested in each other when they plan to do something, and their interest is conditioned by the common enterprise. A man and a woman are interested directly in each other." (114)

For all this, Marías thinks the most important thing that has happened to women recently is the disassociation between sexuality and reproduction, and he takes pains to convince the reader that this is not a biological fact. It is a historical fact that has caused the present crisis in the relationships between the sexes, and he is mostly sceptic about the consequences. But, he insists, simplification will take us nowhere.

One good example of how far he is ready to go is his apparently bold discussion of premarital sexual relations. He recognizes that they do happen, nowadays, that they are even common, that they are even the basis for a great many marriages. But he does not question the negativity of such developments. "Once such a relationship has come about, there is a great probability that the woman will tend to marry that man; and since the sexual relations are usually superficial, hazardous and not very deeply personal, the "conditioning" that they bring about is usually in the end just as lacking in personal choice and intimacy as the family arrangements in the times when marriages were made for 'convenience'." (85)

If sexuality has to be "humanized" by love, we have to ask what is meant by love. Marías thinks it has little to do with "feelings, passions, emotions, etc." (222) It is not a matter of "psychic life but of biographic life". "The person in love thinks about a thousand things and themes, goes through different moods; his psychic life turns to other realities than the loved woman; but he is no longer alone, ever: he projects himself mysteriously with that inseparable person, in her presence or her absence. The man and the woman in love need each other mutually to be each one that one *who he or she is* – the I that each one must be as man and woman. *My project includes the woman with whom I am in love.* And the impression of "eternity" that the feeling of being in love provokes is justified, because he who loves, even if only recently, *is now loving from his whole reality since ever*, and he feels that it has to be also forever. If I *consist* of the love for a woman, it is contradictory not to love her, since the man in love is the one who loves a certain woman." (222; emphases in the original) Love is also a vocation, a destiny and happiness. It is happiness, Marías underlines, not only if the love is happy.

In other words, for Marías love is a command and a discipline: no matter what you actually feel, once you decide to relate yourself to a certain person in terms of the word love, this must be the basis for your life from then on. The "humanization" of sexual relations, then, consists not in tenderness or togetherness, as the word might suggest in other discourses, but in permanence. We are back with the bishops.

The difference lies in that Marías recognizes that love has a sexual expression and that this is not to be avoided but searched for and perfected. "Sexuality is a capital ingredient of heterosexual love, but it does not consist in it, it is no more than *one* of the forms of projection of one person towards another. Together with all the others, it is one of the elements in love's *argument*. When sexuality is loving, it is not a biological or psychological mechanism; it is made up of imagination, memory, projection; it has a history and a personal meaning. *It is the form in which the love between two persons happens dramatically, in the real form that the empirical structure imposes on human life, that life whose manner of existence is corporality*." (223-224; emphases in the original) In other words, if Marías' conditions of love – permanence and discipline – are met, the body is good. After all.

The Book Club – inarticulate opposition

The discussion of Marías' book in the Book Club began in a tentative and cautious manner. Two of the dominant women of the group were great admirers of Marías, and their arguments were so emphatic that the other women did not dare to say much at first.

But little by little an opposition took shape. Someone quoted Marías to say that women are only efficient when dependent, and she hesitatingly asked us if that was what he really meant to say. Another woman exclaimed: "Yes! See?! We are always dependent! If we keep quiet, fine, but if we ask for something, bad." This was followed by a gale of laughter and then the chase seemed to be on. Several women liked the idea of female essence but not Marías' opinion that women are now on the verge of losing it. One woman said: "If he were to come to this meeting here today, he would be very gallant and courteous with everyone, but he would not treat us as equals. A woman can do everything, as long as she is not equal to men, that is what he ends up saying."

Another woman pointed out the place where Marías says that women cannot be friends in the same sense as men can, because between two women there is always a certain rivalry, they must make sure which one wins. Again laughter and many comments to the effect that that is how men are, not women at all, quite the contrary, and Marías can say a thing like that only because he has no idea of what women's lives are like. Several women said that men don't have to know anything about women, whereas women understand men, because they have to learn that in order to survive. One woman said that it is not true, as Marías takes pains to prove, that the Church has always defended Woman – what about the debates about whether women have souls or not!

An almost feminist atmosphere invaded the usually so cautious group. Marías served as a revulsive. The two dominant women had to backtrack and say that they had written "no! no!" here and there in the margins, and what they liked about Marías were really other things, but...

One of them made a last effort, saying that total equality is impossible, anyway. The others did not accept that idea (as they actually had at previous book club meetings). "That depends on what rules you set up!" The first woman tried again, talking about the beauty of the idea "I am I and my circumstances".[200] One woman answered: "Well, but he thinks it is terrible for women to work, because there is nobody at home when the children come home from school. But he forgets the circumstances! He talks only about the middle class. Working class women have always worked, because they had to." The others filled in: yes, and in those cases there are women at home anyway, grandmother, or an aunt or a helpful neighbor or...

In other words, this discussion was a lot more heated and much more daring than was usually the case in the book club. Even the word "class" could be used, for once. But the word sexuality was not mentioned nor was the theme discussed indirectly. That was much too sensitive, even during such a sudden rupture of the usual group norms for conversation. I commented this afterwards with one of the members. She said the club had a basically very open atmosphere, they had really managed to respect all sorts of opinions. I said yes, I had noticed that – except for certain themes. For example, talking about Marías, they all seemed to take for granted that everyone in the group was a believing and practicing Catholic. She laughed: "Sure! There are certain themes that are taboo. For example, religion, we don't usually talk about that. But we are not all Catholics, at least I don't think so, at least I am certainly not." I then broached the subject: "And another taboo is sexuality." She nodded. "Yes, true. We have hardly ever talked about that, and just imagine, it has been years, and just think of the novels we read, many things come up, there would be lots of appropriate occasions... but no."

So, even in this single-gender forum for debate, among women who had known each other for years, and even during an unusual outbreak of taboo-breaking in the argument, sexuality could not be discussed. Not even in the context of a book that gave it positive and religious connotations.

Main themes

In spite of the great silences, sexuality was present enough in conservative Mediterranean discourses for the key themes to stand out.

The main themes were essentialism, dualism and complementarity, love and anti-rationality. There was also a lack of awareness of conflict inside the family and a lack of awareness of social circumstances. Since we are talking of educated persons, "lack of awareness" is perhaps not the correct term. In the case of philosophers and politico-religious actors, one is tempted to talk about purposeful legitimation of status quo.

Sexuality was also so tightly connected to gender in the conservative discourses, that it is difficult to disentangle the two, and an attempt to do so might distort the core idea, which was the entanglement itself. So let us sum up the key themes in analytic terms.

Essentialism

In essentialist thinking certain things are as they are because they have to be that way. It is "nature", "God's will" or the only practical solution. One does not usually try to describe the contents of basic concepts. The important phenomena, those which are seen as "values", are absolutized, they are even written with capital letters much of the time: Woman, Mankind, Love, Nature... Doubts as well as analysis indicate a lack of solidarity with the values in question. Implicitly then, this is a worldview that exacts belief and submission and ends up being anti-intellectual.

The Spanish conservative essentialism in the view of gender has it that there are two sexes. They are not genders at all, but sexes, i.e. once and for all (and probably by God) given entities with non-changeable characteristics. What exactly those characteristics are and how they should be valued can sometimes be discussed (as Yolanda did, for example), but it cannot be doubted that there are two opposite and ever-lasting sets. In some versions of the discourse, their complementarity is emphasized, in others the hierarchy between them.

Modernization of essentialism: Yolanda said – and Marías would agree – that it is too crude to say that men and women are meant for different tasks. Their reformulation was: Men and women can and should do the same things, but in their naturally separate ways.

Whether traditional or modernized, gender essentialism flows into sexuality essentialism in such a way that the two determine each other. For men, women represent sexuality and the body. Women's own views are not discussed. The organization of sexuality is seen to be the same as the organization of reproduction, and that in turn is seen to determine the division of tasks.

Dualism

Dualism is a common general form for thought, applicable to most themes (up-down, right-wrong, black-white, etc.). Since this general form exists and is powerful, it gives strong support to essentialist thinking on gender.

According to conservative discourses on sexuality, there are two sexes, and since this is "evidently" good and at the same time the only thing possible, clear contrasts between them are good. One cannot admit the existence of any in-between categories, and the blurring of borders is a great threat to Order. Women and men are essentially different and complementary and mutually exclusive. Sexuality is both proof and reinforcement of this. Therefore, any sexuality that does not reinforce the dualism is bad. This goes for homosexuality, of course, but it also goes for any experimenting with new ways of obtaining pleasure, it even goes for experiments in other fields of activity that would seem to question traditional forms for sexuality. Therefore, the constant preoccupation with whether women's studying, women's earning money, new dress fashions, etc. might perhaps be dangerous to "sexuality", i.e. to the one kind of sexuality considered good.[201]

In spite of the dualism and the negation in theory of any possibilities of degrees, the conservative discourses contain a considerable amount of worry about degrees. There is much talk about more or less feminine women and much discussion of how to defend women's "dignity", which usually means fixed gender characteristics.

Logically, if femininity is shaky, then masculinity also becomes shaky. But there was little talk about that. Apparently, in the conservative discourse, men are not subject to the same temptations and loss of "dignity" as women are. But some awareness of the threat to masculinity would certainly go a long way towards explaining the preoccupation with gender characteristics in the discourse of people who say that they cannot be doubted.

Love

Love becomes a necessary theme to make this discourse humane. If the sexes are sexes, not genders, and if men are active, strong and intelligent, and women are the only ones given to suffering, sacrifice and the care of children, there must be something that binds men to women. If not, the world would truly become a cold and dangerous place. Just as the conservatives say, women would be defenseless and men would be cut off from human warmth. So this something cannot be conditioned by personal whims. It must be placed beyond risk. Therefore, Love is obligatory, a question of purposeful permanent commitment. But this functional argument for Love is never made explicit. It would be self-contradictory. Love must seem beautiful and natural, not disciplined and instrumental.

Sexuality is sometimes – e. g. by Marías – recognized as a positive force that strengthens Love. But it is more often portrayed as a threat to Love, since sexual attraction waxes and wanes and finds varying objects; Love must be permanent.

The conservative discourse negates women's sexual desire so thoroughly that in the 1990s it had not even begun to really worry about the effects of women now becoming aware of their desires, approving of them with less fear than formerly and also, sometimes, having economic and social possibilities to act upon them. This would seem in all logic to have to be the great conservative worry, but it was not, not expressly at least.

Instead it was mostly men's sexuality that was discussed and feared. And this is logical in another sense. Men's sexuality is strong and capricious in this construction, and men do have sociocultural power to act upon it, but their acting upon it can undermine the couple, the family, the whole society, especially if it can no longer be channeled into traditional double morals. Therefore men's sexuality must be repressed, because otherwise men will abandon their families.[202] Until recently, the main method of repression had been to forbid explicit references to sexuality, so as not to remind anyone of its existence, [203] i.e. censorship of media, not accepting sexual education in the schools, preferably not even giving the children any information at home, but on the other hand taking the measures necessary to desexualize public life, i.e. closing parks at night, carefully regulating dress codes, forbidding kissing in public, regulating carefully the spaces that nowadays require visible bodies (especially swimming pools), and so on. That is how it was in Spain during the Franco regime, and these everyday regulations were then a prominent aspect of the Church discourse.[204]

In this light, a discourse like Marías' does become revolutionary, since he talks openly about and enhances the goodness of sexuality. So it is understandable that his admirers in the book club were shocked to find themselves on the conservative side in the discussion – they saw themselves as very open-minded.

Mystery

The whole conservative discourse on sexuality looks quite coherent. It has its dark corners and thorny contradictions, but they are so old and so constantly silenced that they are usually invisible even for the opponents of the discourse. Nevertheless, logical analysis is dangerous to it. One suspects some awareness of this in the constant references to "mystery", "emotion", "unquestioning acceptance" and so on as positive values. Anti-rationality is also a value in itself.

Marías uses the word "beauty" for things that are the way he thinks they should be. Beauty should not be analyzed, just accepted. The bishops speak of religious mystery as the greatest good. During the Franco regime, various ideologues wrote about the supposed Spanish national character as strong, emotional, brave, dedicated and so on and opposed all these positive values to the negative ones of intellectual calculation and self-interest, which they imputed to other European nations.[205]

This may seem strange, since there was at the same time a very strong emphasis on self-discipline and social order. But the solution to the apparent paradox is that the self-discipline was to be always in the service of social order, not of selfish interests, and social order was not a rational construct but a given. One's *entrega* (uncritical surrender to a cause or to a person, another key concept of the regime as well as of discourses on women) should involve all one's feelings, one's whole being. One should live, just live life as given, with emotional dedication to the given, and one should take care to distance oneself from any "cold" or "ugly" standing back to look at and analyze it.

In the circumstances of the 1990s, when events have made individual and collective self-analysis inevitable, this discourse was in trouble. The so-called progressive discourses had had great success, and "rationality" had become a major value word. Even the conservative party Partido Popular now subscribed to it. Only extreme rightist organizations still used the emotional language.

However, the conservative discourses on sexuality (and on Woman), still stressed values such as Love, Vital Force and Mystery. Some voices in the debate recommended "safeguarding" of at least this parcel of life from rational analysis. But such arguments were losing force.

From the conservative point of view, sexuality is the greatest force but cannot be talked about directly, so the important political battles are fought over such things as abortion, divorce and married priests, i.e. things that threaten the view of sexuality as occurring only inside the family and the family as permanent. Those two conditions cannot be met if sexuality is construed as a positive expression of individual, perhaps even temporary, desires.

When conservative discourse refuses to talk about sexuality openly but declares battle on related issues constantly, those who would oppose it become convinced that sexuality is precisely what one must talk about. And one must talk about it rationally, explicitly. And in positive terms, yes, but those positive terms have to be about individual choice and bodily pleasures. They cannot be about great mystical forces. Nor, really, about love. Which is a problem, since progressive discourses also emphasize love. But they construe love as individual feeling, choice and communication, in opposition to self-discipline and duty.

Let us now take a closer look at the evolution of the so-called progressive discourses; they had been establishing themselves for a couple of decades and were becoming hegemonic around the time of my fieldwork.

Chapter 18. Increasingly present: the new hegemonic discourse on sexuality

There are, of course, discourses on sexuality that contradict the conservative ones. There is first a joking type that only contradicts them in appearance. There are also true challenges. Among these, I will concentrate on the moderate type that was the most effective challenge, not because of any intellectual qualities but because of its wide acceptance. It could in fact be called the hegemonic discourse on sexuality in Spain around 1990.

Joking about it

The conservative discourses described in chapter 17 were hegemonic during Franco times in Spain. By hegemonic I mean, here, that they dominated all public contexts. In a sense they were more than hegemonic and more than orthodox; they were close to exclusive in the press and other mass media, in Church discourses, in legislation and education. Oppositional discourses of all kinds were banned from such contexts with some efficiency. In semi-public fora of a non-oppositional type, such as business dinners or parent-teacher-association meetings in schools, the conservative type of discourse dominated in the sense that it was taken for granted as the only kind one could use without excuses.

However, it was often lightened up by joking. Depending on the contexts, the jokes could be more or less daring. The sexual joking might appear to be a counter-discourse, but in fact it only apparently contradicted the anti-pleasure aspect of the hegemonic conservative discourse, and it never contradicted its gender philosophy of masculine precedence, female seductiveness and nature-given features of both genders.[206]

To understand this, one must remember that the troublesome relationship to sexuality in Spanish society has never included total repression. The concept of sin has never been taken very seriously by any but a few. Most jokes are about sexuality, as are practically all common swear words. This does not mean that sexuality is not a most awesome and most forbidden area to tread in its conservative version. There is no real contradiction in this. The "obsession", as Spaniards themselves call it,[207] produces both awkward silences and florid expressions. Camilo José Cela is as logical a product as Opus Dei.[208]

This goes for both women and men, but one must remember that in traditional thinking women are the ones charged with upholding a minimum of balance in this shakily overwrought cultural edifice. It is when women refuse that responsibility and instead ask for some obsessional freedom of their own that there is real danger for cultural chaos. Feminists recognize this and some of them see it as their most powerful lever for change. The traditional machistas, who usually interpret sexuality as a game of domination, can also recognize it occasionally.

For example, Enrique de Obregón, an amateur historian, finishes his pseudo-serious history of Spanish sexuality, with these words: "Has nothing changed then in a hundred, in five hundred, in a thousand years? Yes, something has changed. Woman is neither slave nor object any longer, and that is a lot. A very big lot. Precisely those who demand most sexual permissivity are almost always men who do not fully appreciate the sexual revolution that women are realizing, day by day."[209] Then he hurries to calm his ideological friends. "Let no one fear. The victory of sex will not be the defeat of the couple. Quite to the contrary, it is its culmination." (1990:207-208)

The tone of this book is set in the Introduction: "Sexuality was, and still is, a source of multiple pleasures and not a few troubles. (...) Of course there have also been, and still are, killjoys who tried to fence in nature (...) but all proved incapable of hindering the evidently uncontainable flow of sex. To this flow, all peoples of the Earth contributed, and still contribute, as is natural, only some more than others. And we Spaniards like to think we are among those who contributed rather more." (1990:7)

The book brims over with examples of baroque licentiousness through the centuries. The text on the back of the cover gives a good idea of what is considered fun and daring in this discourse: "The most memorable battles were the most hilarious[210] ones, and they were fought in the beds of palaces and whorehouses. In this book the reader will find the names of: The most libertine kings and princes. The most licentious queens and ladies. The most famous bastards. The most depraved bishops. The most obliging courtesans. The most reckless homosexuals. And the secrets of: The right of the first night. The whorehouses of all of Spain. The sexual conquest of America. The laws that governed fornication. The eroticism of witches and sorcerers." (1990: back cover)

In other words, there is a lot about transgression of social norms but no questioning of cultural categories. The actors and the types of acts are the same as in the serious conservative discourse. Sinfulness has simply been turned on its head, it is now daring conquest and witty cheating. This version of sexuality would not be much fun without the concept of transgression of awesome norms.[211] There is very little on imaginative exploration of the body, for example. Adultery, impotency, whores and illegitimate children fill the pages, but there is not a single description of a sensual caress. If the reader has never heard of female orgasm, he will not learn from this book that it exists. Women are usually described as "obliging", "willing" or "generous". And when they are described as being out for something of their own, it is usually money. It is altogether logical, then, that the sexual woman par excellence is the whore. On the other hand, that a prostitute might do it for money only is never hinted at. That would leave the client in an unflattering light, of course. This whole discourse makes sense only from a male perspective. And "modern" ideas have made few inroads on it. Cervantes would feel at home in de Obregón's book if he were to come back to life, but Masters and Johnson might not.

The argument of fun is effective, in literature as well as in conversation. A person who tries to give the conservative moralistic argument straight has to carry great authority. Perhaps only priests can do it without appearing ridiculous. Fun is always a strong argument, and it crops up often in my data. In part this also has to do with the general characteristics of friendly conversation (cf appendix C), but when the topic has to do with sexuality, a coquettish, joking attitude is even more appropriate than in other thematic contexts.

Progressive-minded people joked about sexuality, too, of course. But their jokes were more critical in intent (the anti-clericalism was not so much about licentious priests as about sexually ignorant priests, for example). And they were probably not as frequent. When repression lessens, the need for letting out steam also lessens.

There was thus a traditional licentious discourse with clear norms about what men can say, what women can say, when a man takes the initiative for this kind of joking, when a woman should laugh, etc. and how it must all be done in order not to be misunderstood as a true sexual invitation. In such contexts, a progressive person who refuses to play according to those rules is seen as just as much of a killjoy as the stern moralist. For conservatives it may seem pointless to differentiate between the two. For the progressives, it was the conservative sense of humor which was faulty, but they usually preferred joking to moralism, even when it was actually further from a critical stance.[212] In general, I found the joking style of talking about sexuality mostly conservative.

Subversive and acceptable oppositions

Apart from the ubiquitous games of sexual joking, there were during my fieldwork two parts to the opposition to the conservative discourse:

First, there was a new hegemony, i.e. a set of opinions which were widely accepted, and to which the conservative discourse now had to address itself. Second, there was a new subversivity. In Franco times, the oppositional discourse, considered subversive then, stood approximately where the new hegemonic discourse stood around 1990. But since the hegemonic center of gravity had moved along the continuum of substantive opinions about what is true, what is good and what is acceptable, the subversive one must also move.

Here, I will not pay much attention to the subversive variety. It existed, it worked as vanguards usually do, producing new ideas that were sometimes taken up in the hegemonic discourse, and producing all sorts of arguments that were sometimes contested but usually just ignored.[213]

What then can be called the new hegemonic discourse?

I am thinking of the kind of discourse that could be pronounced at a parent-teacher-meeting in a grade school without scandal, even if not all present agreed. I am thinking of the kind of discourse young grade school teachers offered their students in natural science class. I am thinking of the kind of things conservative informants sometimes grudgingly accepted in conversation but hardly in emotion or in practice, but which progressive informants liked to think one could "nowadays" take for granted.

The best place to find good examples of this discourse was television. Spaniards watched television a lot,[214] and during Franco times it was television that was most carefully censored precisely because its messages had such a wide reach. In the 1990s there were now several privately owned channels, and their treatment of sexuality vacillated between progressive-minded debate on controversial issues and the traditional licentious joking discourse in the shape of stand-up comedians and generous numbers of lightly clad "hostesses" in the most unlikely programs. The state channels were still the most widely watched, however. Other media often debated their program policy. This meant that what was not widely acceptable hardly reached the screen; and vice versa, what was said on television tended to become accepted after a while. The average television discourse coincided rather nicely with the average of my informants' discourses (but not at all with that of Club Aguafría).

A discourse must also be widely acceptable to find its way into magazines with large circulations and government social programs, so these, too, are good sources for examples of the new hegemonic discourse. The subversive or very radical discourses did not appear in such places.

What can be said on TV must be accepted

Let me give a few examples of treatment of sexual themes in the state television about which there had not been, to my knowledge, any outcry in other media and which my informants accepted without much comment (except at Club Aguafría).

First, contraceptives. In the 1970s and 1980s, it was unthinkable to mention them on television. Up to 1979 they were even illegal. Towards the end of the 1980s, very discrete advertisements began to appear. One slogan, for example, was "So that one plus one will not make three." A calm voice pronounced the phrase against a background of soft music and a picture of a beautiful sunset. There was no picture of the product nor any explanation of what it was for.

In 1991, there was a government-sponsored campaign to stop the surging numbers of teenage pregnancies and HIV-infection. Its main slogan was the witty "*Póntelo, pónselo*" = Put it on yourself, put it on him.[215] This led to much joking in all media and in conversations and graffiti. And it was soon reflected in advertisements. As Christmas approached, the seasonal ads for drinks played on it. A drink called Ponche announced itself as "Pónchelo," and one brand of anisette showed a winking woman with a bottle in

257

her hand saying "Pónselo claro" (literally: "Tell him clearly." But it could also mean: "Serve it to him straight.")

Another good example is menstruation. In Spain, menstruation has been seen as a sexual fact and it has been very much tabooed in conversation.[216] It used to be almost as unthinkable to advertise menstrual pads on television as it was to advertise contraceptives. By 1990 such ads were commonplace and there were also some for tampons. The first ads for pads employed euphemistic expressions such as "for those special days" or "women's secrets". No longer. In 1991 there were plenty of pictures of pads, some of them demonstrating their capacity of absorption (with colorless liquids). In some of the ads, not just mature women but young girls appeared, and to play with the sexual overtones of menstruation was no longer taboo. In one ad a beautiful young woman showed the handy packet containing a folded pad, then she winked and stuffed it into the back pocket of her jeans and mounted a bicycle, and there was a close-up shot of her buttocks as she pedaled away. The idea between lines was that with the right pad, a girl was free to do sporty activities even on those special days.

Still, I was surprised when I saw an ad for tampons featuring very young girls. This was daring, as the style of the ad itself indicated, but I never heard it commented upon by anyone. A prettily sweaty teenage girl comes into her room, takes off a few pieces of sporty clothing and disappears into an off-screen bathroom. A friend of hers comes in and sits on the bed. This second girl looks a bit moody and asks her friend if she has a pad to lend her. "No," says the sporty girl's voice from the shower, "but I have Tampax". Out from the bathroom comes a package of tampons flying through the air. The second girl handles the package, without opening it, with surprise and some fear. She asks if her friend really uses tampons. "Of course I do," says the voice. "And nothing happens?" "No. Nothing happens, you just try it and see!" "Are you sure nothing happens?" "No, nothing at all!" says the first girl, coming out of the shower in clean clothes, fresh as an apple.

The whole spot bristles with cleanliness, purity. But it breaks with at least three important taboos. The first one is to talk about menstruation at all, although that had been weakened. The second one is to show a girl who practices sports and takes a shower while probably menstruating. Women born approximately before 1960 in Spain usually think that exercise and bathing during menstruation is dangerous. And the third taboo is so strong that the hint is extremely light, yet I am sure most spectators understood it – it refers to the hymen. A young girl can use a tampon without breaking her hymen. "Nothing at all happens!"[217]

By the 1990s, pornographic films were shown on state channels (but always after midnight). And one program of magazine-type, shown at an hour when most but not all children would be in bed, included an item of "elegant" (i.e. not too risqué) strip tease each week, along with debates, interviews, singers and musicians.

The clearest example, a full demonstration of the new hegemonic discourse on sexuality, was a program that ran once a week for several months in 1990, called "Let us talk about sex." The anchor was Dr. Elena Ochoa, a beautiful, blond but chaste-looking woman. With the aid of a team of sexologists, psychologists, lawyers, etc. she offered basic sexual information and answered viewers' questions. The program was carefully designed to give a clinical impression: there was no joking, the formulas of courtesy ("good evening, Doctor Ochoa") were endlessly repeated, there were surveys, computers, invited experts with serious faces and constant references to research and more experts. Some of my informants, for instance a group of feminists, laughed about it and called it hypocrite and conservative. It was definitely not subversive. But all sorts of controversial themes were covered: homosexuality, fetishism, female orgasm, transvestitism, etc. The viewers who called in asked about their own problems, such as frigidity, premature ejaculation, marital discord about frequency of intercourse and the efficacy of all sorts of popular contraceptive devices.

As a result of this program, Dr. Ochoa became popular and appeared on many other shows. For example, she was once invited to a debate with the conservative congressman Alberto Ruiz Gallardón. The theme for the debate was "sex without love" – a rather subversive theme in itself (cf chapter 17). The program anchor started the debate by saying that right now, around nine o'clock in the evening, there are some people who have not yet met the person with whom they will be in bed within a couple of hours – what do you think of that? Ruiz Gallardón said that he just had to begin by telling everyone something personal, because he was so happy and emotional about it – he had just had a son! This gave him the opportunity to talk about his four wonderful children, his extraordinary wife and his happy marriage. After that, it was not easy for Ochoa to explain that love is a relative concept, it all depends on what you mean by sex without love, because in a sense sex is love, etc. She ended up accusing Ruiz Gallardón of talking only about stereotyped love and marriage, but he countered elegantly, saying that some stereotypes are very valid. The anchor person then presented the result of a survey that was carried out while the program was being aired. With a 2.5% of possible error, some 77% of the women and 56% of the men said no to sex without love, and 13% of the women and 32% of the men said yes.

Some time later, Ochoa participated in a debating program of the usual kind, together with six or seven others, writers, psychologists and one marketing man, all between forty and fifty years old, approximately. The issue was the sexual practices of youth "nowadays". A burning topic for the middle aged, as we have seen. But these debaters did not worry about how to stop it, as Club Aguafría members tended to do. They wondered rather whether it was good enough, or if today's youth are missing out on something.

There was much talk of lack of appetites. Sex requires time, said several participants, but today people are burdened by stress, monotony, hurrying always. They don't feel well, so they cannot express well-being.

Someone said that one must not think people think less of sex, or do less, just because they talk less about it. Today, there is less frustration, it is easier to resolve the matter, so there is less need to talk about it.

But, said a woman writer, in the discotheques today there is none of that flirtatious atmosphere, that sex-is-in-the-air feeling that there used to be. The youngsters meet, talk, drink... but then they go home, each to their own place. Yes, said one debater, "obviously! There is AIDS today!" No, said the marketing man, that is not the reason; it is just that when young people today go out, they do not think it necessary, as we did, to look for sex at all costs. Saturday night is more about drinking a lot... The others laughed: Sure! That is why! If you drink a lot, you can't do anything!

In the end consensus was established around the following points: Young people today are knowledgeable and very tolerant. Above fifteen or sixteen, there are hardly any virgins of either sex. And that is good. They learn from each other, which is a lot healthier than learning from older people, the way it used to be. The reason they do not talk much about sex, is probably that they do not feel as frustrated as "we" used to, or else because they have transcended even that "phase" and feel free to choose whether to do or not to do. A few years ago, if a woman was young and rebellious, sex was a requirement, you had to go to bed with whomever suggested it to you, because otherwise you were a reactionary.

Ochoa was the only debater who tried to say that those experiences were not all that common and that for "most people" there were "still a lot of taboos". The others seemed to interpret these comments as a defense of conservative values and responded with sarcasms. I would say that empirically, referring to average urban Spaniards, Ochoa was more right than the others. But in this kind of TV program, "is" was almost always confused with "ought to be". The point was not to represent reality but to negotiate new interpretations of it. The debaters were also concerned with showing off their own expansive thinking and plentiful experiences.

The lack of desire was commented on some more; all seemed to be worried about it. But then, said some, the old model did not exactly whet appetites either. Perhaps the men were always full of lust, but that was just because of their frustration. And as to married women, nothing at all. Marriage was horrible for women because of all the ignorance and all the prejudices. "How many have not preferred to wash the dishes directly after lunch in order not to have to take a nap with her husband!"

From these examples and from my conversational material, I draw the conclusion that sexuality could be talked about without adopting either a joking or a moralistic attitude, and that this could be done in a medium like television without causing scandal. Even highly controversial sexual issues, such as sex without love, could be debated in the same manner as the latest political scandal. Opinions differed, but the generally accepted frame of reference for judging the validity of opinions was science, rationality and individual well-being – not religion or traditional morals. Religion was hardly mentioned, and phrases like "a healthy society" smacked too much of Franco times to be acceptable to most people.

Nevertheless, there was plenty of evidence of moral confusion and worry about the collective consequences of individual actions.

The new ideal woman has lovers! Magazines, government, teenagers and condoms

In her study of magazines for women, Gallego (1990) describes the "image of the new woman" that these magazines began to sell successfully in the 1980s. In contrast to earlier ideal images of saintly motherhood, practical domestic knowledge, etc. this new ideal image stressed success in the labor market (typical headline: "Work like a man, dress like a woman."), a capacity to participate in cultural events, and of course also good motherhood and careful grooming of looks ("Pregnant, yes, but not fat.")

However: "The aspect that is most characteristic of the discourse on "the new image of women" is the inclusion of a theme that has been taboo until recently: sexuality. If until now the "ideal" woman was presented as something like an asexual being – sexuality as condemnation – the new image of women that is now being vindicated is above all that of sexual liberation. From 'being passive' she has gone on to have a frenetic sexual life. (…) The new image of women offers a very exacting erotic criterion, and it frequently praises infidelity or charge of lovers." (Gallego 1990:91) Typical headlines: "Am I as good a lover as he dreams of?", "The ten errors that kill love", "Do you love him the way he desires?" (All headlines from Gallego 1990:92).[218]

One measure of the hegemonic status of the liberal-moderate discourses was their acceptance by government agencies. Sexual education was taught in schools, for example. (Or rather, it was supposed to be taught, and this seemed to actually happen in most schools, but many teachers found it too uncomfortable and excused themselves from it and some parents protested.) Another example: the Women's Institute[219] organized a Working Conference on Sexuality in 1985 with the express purpose of "implicating all three levels of the Administration in the preparation of a global working project on sexuality." (Instituto de la Mujer, 1986:5) The resulting publication included sample reports of activities from different parts of the country, such as pedagogical experiments, adult courses, etc. and a concluding chapter with a sketch for a political program. This chapter begins with a reference to "the politico-ideological suspicion that this theme and its novelty raise." (1986:93) The program emphasized campaigns on contraceptives, campaigns to "sensitize" the population about the need for sexual education, and programs for special courses for teachers, health professionals and other groups. There would be special pilot projects for "high risk categories", defined as adolescents and persons over thirty-five years of age. That adolescents were considered high risk obviously had to do with the many unwanted teenage pregnancies. Why persons over thirty-five years of age (in 1985, that meant persons born before 1950) were at risk was not explained, but one can surmise that they were thought to be the ones who grew up with least information and most efficient official silencing of the topic.

The campaign for condoms in 1990 was evidently one of the practical results of this program. It was controversial, and at Club Aguafría it was condemned just about wholesale. But according to the survey that the Women's Institute carried out in December 1990, the population as a whole was in favor of the campaign.[220]

A nationwide survey on "the value system" in 1981 included the item "happy sexual relations" among thirteen suggestions for what makes a marriage happy. The respondents placed it fifth, after fidelity, mutual respect, understanding and tolerance, and children. 57% of the total thought a happy sexual relationship was important.[221]

Now, surveys such as these and the ones on television or in the publications of the Women's Institute reported averages, of course. The Spanish population was too divided for averages to be very informative. And the middle class was polarized on most ideological issues and especially on sexuality. The most extreme discourses, that of body hatred and that of "sexual anarchy", both had their strongholds in the middle class. It was probably the urban middle class, too, especially its well-educated segments, that had accepted most readily the new hegemonic discourse. And it was of course mainly members of the middle class that produced its most wide-reaching versions, through TV programs, school textbooks, doctors' recommendations, and so on.

Hegemonic discourse – characteristic features

What were the characteristic features, then, of the new hegemonic discourses on sexuality?

There was, first, an absence of express opposition to the main features of the conservative discourses (as described in the previous chapter). Those features were negated in intention and consequence, but much of the time there seemed to be no need to explicate the details. A head-on confrontation, like that between Ochoa and Ruiz Gallardón, must rather inevitably end up in mutual accusations of facile stereotyping. This was so, because it was not only the substantive opinions that differed (whether you are for or against abortion, for instance), but the criteria for what can be analyzed and how it should be discussed. The solution was for each discourse to debate its own issues and ignore those of the others. And when those other discourses could not be ignored, they were labeled rather than debated.

Second, there were a few key themes that tended to coincide with themes that were also centrally focused in the progressive discourses about other things than sexuality. Third, there were some features that all the discourses on sexuality more or less shared.

Let us start with the treatment of the conservative themes. The dualism of the conservative discourses was neither present nor absent in the hegemonic discourse. The contrasts between male and female were not constantly underlined as necessary for

262

sexual desire to exist or for sexual functions to be good. On the other hand, the idea that women and men are two distinct categories, not at all overlapping, was still there and continued to be quite doxic for most people. It was energetically contested by the most radical discourses, but their messages did not reach the whole population.

There was also the essentialist definition of sexuality as an innate drive that does not change its essence according to circumstances but at most finds different outlets or creates frustration if repressed. This view may actually have been strengthened by the insistence on sexuality as a legitimate desire, as a "need" even, in the hegemonic discourse. On the other hand, essentialist thinking as a whole was being driven back by the general experience of a people that had seen all manner of "truths" crumble. The hegemonic discourses on sexuality did not accept the radical suggestions of sexual anarchy and relativism, but they did include more timid proposals along the lines of Dr. Ochoa: that anything that feels good is good, so you should not worry about whether it is "normal" or not. The message was not (as in radical discourse) that sexuality is whatever you make of it, but rather that whatever feelings "it" produces are good, because "it" is good. "It" exists and is what it is, so it should be accepted.

If there was essentialist thinking in the hegemonic discourse, it was mostly unawares, however. The cultural emphasis was no longer on normative truth ("what must be because it is"), but instead on empirical science ("we must learn more"). And what is learnt should be made available to all. "Education!" was the key word above all others.

The conservative theme of "humanization" is only necessary if sexuality is seen as something beastly, and if human beings are seen as very different from other animals. In the hegemonic discourses, both these propositions were seen as too out of date to merit discussion. "Love" was taken to be good, and it was certainly emphasized, and sexuality without love was suspect, but sexuality was not so bad that it must be compensated by a lot of good. Human sexuality is human, it does not have to be humanized. Similarly, permanence in a relationship was generally considered a good thing, but not necessary.

The emphasis on transgression in the joking variant of the conservative discourses was no longer very relevant. If there are no cultural "taboos" and if normative obstacles to the active search for pleasure are in themselves negative things, they must not be transgressed in jest, but combated in earnest.

And this was one reason why subscribers to conservative positions so often found the hegemonic discourse puritanical (because they did not joke about sex in the usual manner), while the subscribers to the latter found the former repressive (because they did not question the "taboos"). In other words, both parties accused each other of the same sin: anti-pleasure. The conclusion must be that physical pleasure was, in spite of everything, a shared value. Asceticism is an old and tenacious strain in Spanish culture, but its traditional expressions, especially sexual abstinence, had little legitimacy now except inside the Opus Dei, while its modern expressions, such as weight-watching, sports and exercise received much lip-service but little practice.[222]

Where the conservative discourses emphasized "mystery", with a corresponding devaluation of systematic human thinking, the hegemonic discourses insisted on education, information and science, on enlightenment in every sense of the word. The battle was pitched on the familiar European ground: thinking versus feeling. However, the conservative discourses placed a limit on feeling, insisting on Order, and the hegemonic discourses placed a limit on the rule of the head, insisting on the free use of the rest of the body, too.

So far about opposition to the conservative themes. The key themes of the hegemonic discourses were in a sense a number of variants on the theme of rationality. There was the criticism of "taboos". There was the emphasis on "education" both in the sense of spreading information and in the sense of social constructionism, anti-essentialism. There was also the theme of frustration, a sort of popular hydraulic theory of sexuality as an innate force that will always find some outlet – so it is more rational, was the implication, to allow it its "natural" outlet. This was mainly used as an argument against repression, however, and its relationship to essentialist thinking was not discussed.

Another major theme was the emphasis on change. New attitudes were seen as good unless the opposite was clearly demonstrated, and it was not clear how such a demonstration could be persuasive, since praise of old things was ipso facto suspect.[223]

These two key themes (rationality as the ultimate criterion for what is good and correct, and change understood as improvement) coincided with the key values of "progressive" thinking in general. From the PSOE party towards the left among political parties, in popular movements of all kinds, in intellectual circles in both middle class and working class contexts, one could find the same superordinate values.[224]

The key themes did not always combine easily. Contradictions resulted. One relevant example is the attitude toward pornography. There had not been any important debate on pornography in Spain since the conservative opposition was broken in the mid 1970s. Feminists usually opposed it, using the same arguments as in other Western countries, but these were not well understood and little attention was paid to them. In an ideological climate of "anti-taboo", any argument for limiting that which was formerly prohibited was suspect of wanting to reintroduce "taboos," and this was especially so in the field of sexuality. Therefore, for most (non-conservative) people, pornography was an instance of "liberated sexuality", and not, as in feminist discourse, an instance of "the limitation of sexuality to the traditional and male perspective."

Finally, the conservative and the hegemonic discourses on sexuality shared some ideas that seemed to be quite doxic (in that they were silently taken for granted) even though they were questioned by the subversive discourses. Not surprisingly, these ideas were just special expressions of general ones that were deeply rooted in the gender order.

The ideas on sexuality associated with the conservative discourses have been excellently summarized in a minor study of sexual argot:[225] "The conclusions (…) are very close to the traditional thinking of European speakers of Spanish: female sexuality seems not to exist, women's behavior is a function of men's pleasure, intercourse is understood as aggression and it is always the male who is in charge." (Calero in Bernís 1991:385)

These ideas were ever-present, and usually not verbalized. Nevertheless, they were not quite doxic; they were usually not accepted as true, even by subscribers to conservative discourses, if they were directly asked. The hegemonic discourse had influenced them to the point that they had to give lip-service, at least, to the idea that women, too, have sexual desires and can and should attain pleasure from intercourse, that for this to happen some "foreplay" is recommendable and that a woman who takes sexual initiatives is not necessarily unfeminine. However, in the conservative discourses such ideas had to be carefully specified, since they were close to the edge of the acceptable.

As we saw, Marías' effort was precisely this: to uphold the key ideas of the conservative discourse while apparently accepting the now uncontestable key ideas of the hegemonic discourse. The result was just right for middle class women of conservative disposition with an intellectual need to feel modern, e.g. the leading women in the book club. But for just slightly less conservative women, e.g. the other book club members, it took little reflection to make them discern gender hierarchy in such thinking, and that was unacceptable to them in spite of their cautious attitude to the sexual theme.

If the conservative discourses by now marked a small but careful distance to those previously doxic ideas, the hegemonic discourses naturally marked a clearer and wider distance. Even so, they still participated in them in subtle ways. Dr. Ochoa was adamant that women too have the capacity for and the right to sexual pleasure. But in spite of the evident "taboo"-breaking of her program on so many issues, she chose not to take up the even greater taboo of gender hierarchy. Men's wish for domination and what a woman should do if her right to pleasure is not accepted or understood by her husband were passed over in silence. The general effort was to present sexual activity as pleasurable, but this was perhaps overdone – a common criticism against the program, from both conservative and radical angles, was that it made sex "bloodless" and "too safe". If the aggressive component is taken out and little sensuality put in, this is perhaps an inevitable result.

In any case, the doxic idea that "sex is war" had hardly been debated in the hegemonic discourses, and to the extent that it had been taken up in subversive discourses, it had been either in the form of defense of sado-masochism in the name of the general anti-taboo thinking ("Why should war be bad?"), or else as a radical-feminist total rejection of heterosexuality as too dangerous and/or too unsatisfactory for women ("It is too war-like!"). And the idea that in the war of sex, man is the aggressor and woman the more or less compliant victim could not be debated in any but the most subversive discourses, since an opposition to it would easily be construed as too normative and therefore anti-pleasure. Criticism of gender hierarchy might have been implicit in the hegemonic insistence on women's right to pleasure, "too", and also in the general progressive discourse on "equality" and "justice", but it was not explicitly debated as a prerequisite for a sexuality without domination.

Perhaps for this reason there was a lingering sensitivity around the sexuality of young girls that was also shared by all the discourses. The conservative ones preached virginity and chastity for all but most especially for young girls (and construed this as "protection" of the girls), whereas the hegemonic discourses rejected chastity as unnatural. But they, too, hesitated to reject it altogether when it came to very young girls. The association of youthful femininity with chastity was deep. The TV ad for tampons is a good example. It was in a sense daring, mixing youth, purity, menstruation, sports and showers and hinting at virginity. But precisely its treatment of virginity conceded a good deal to the conservative discourses: it was not mentioned, only hinted at, with a caution that a conservative would interpret as tactfulness, and it was presented as something the girls were naturally concerned to conserve. If sexuality is aggression, a young girl expressing sexual desire is easily seen as a monster. If sexuality is dangerous for women, at least until they learn to defend themselves, young girls in sexual contexts appear naïve and exposed.

Young Madrilenians, even those of quite radical opinions, tended to call promiscuous girls "whores". Boys did it more than girls, but girls did it too, and for the girls there was a distinct dilemma between the "modern" requirement not to be "too narrow-minded" and the opposite requirement, that had not disappeared, to make sure one did not get a reputation as "too easy".[226]

In spite of their new daring, the media did not present any images of sexual pleasure for women. Pornography for men, strip tease of women, and lightly clad women hostesses on TV were the foremost examples of "open-mindedness". The women's magazines, even when daring, invited women to be sexually active for men ("Do you love him the way he desires?"). The one major point treated from women's point of view, and brought up often, was that the new openness, especially sexual education, had freed women from the old curse of having to suffer sexuality in marriage. The improvement, then, had been from the negative to the neutral, but not to the positive. This was of course true of Western culture as a whole.

Left, right or person?

Such then was the new hegemonic discourse on sexuality, uneasily perched between the conservative and the subversive discourses. It was uneasy, that is, because so much in it was vague and undefined and because there were such loud voices suggesting strongly contrasting views in both directions. It was not uneasy in the sense of being narrow in acceptance. The point of gravity on the continuum of attitudes toward sexuality had really moved. Not as far as the proponents of sexual anarchy would like, but it was now the conservative type of discourse which was on the defensive. (Just like it was on the theme of women's work, cf chapter 16.) Club Aguafría was one place where it still dominated, but even there it was under mild and discrete but constant attack by, for example, such discussions as the one about Maite's daughter's traveling with male friends (cf chapter 5) or by the fact that some members now remained members even after a matrimonial separation. (In conservative thinking, separation was a sexually tinged event, because the suspicion was that it must be due to excessive acting out of illicit desires by one or both spouses.)

I have called the different types of discourses conservative, hegemonic and radical or subversive. I use these words in part because they correspond approximately to emic usage (although emic usage was much more dualistic), in part because they fit the fact of objective change. I do not use them in the ordinary sense of right and left on a scale of political opinions. But they do coincide partially with such a scale.

Or they had coincided, at least in the public mind. This, too, might have been changing. I find it symptomatic that the widely read newsmagazine Cambio 16 ran a cover article in 1993 under the title: "Sex – left or right?"[227] It included a number of short comments from famous "writers, thinkers and politicians who asked themselves the classic question: Is sex rightist or leftist?"

The general answer was that "there is no ideology when it comes to sex." One might think the question would not be interesting, in that case, but in Spain it was, because it had indeed been a classic one. And there were discernable differences even in this minuscule sample of nine. In the magazine, a conservative writer answered in the typical conservative-joking style that rightist people probably "do it better" because for leftists it is just a matter of hygiene, while for rightists it means they might go to hell, "so naturally they give it everything they've got." Like de Obregón, he also thought that Spanish men are exceptional lovers and that that consists in doing it a lot. A university professor of political science said that sexuality ought not to be a matter of ideology, but it is, and most societies tend to limit people's sexual imagination. That was an acceptable example of hegemonic discourse with just a touch of subversivity. A more hegemonic statement was that of a well-known leftist sociologist, who said that rightists are more restrained and leftists more permissive, but he added cautiously that he did not want to judge which might be better. A woman writer took a more subversive stance, declaring, "Sex is neither leftist nor rightist. I think that right now it is also a weapon for domination, even in the Western world. At this moment, the apparent sexual liberty has turned into another means of controlling the population."

The headline above these comments was: "Here rules the Person." That is a clearly hegemonic statement in that it referred to the ideal of the individual's right to control her or his life. The individual was construed as a participant in society without status distinctions, and her or his right to think and act were construed as opposed to any attempt to impose on everybody moral views not shared by everybody. That was the kernel of the new hegemonic discourse on sexuality, because it was the kernel of the

267

expansive mode of managing meaning in general: The Church can no longer have the last word on what is right and wrong, so we must all invent our own criteria.

Chapter 19. Sex, coffee and cultural negotiation

In face-to-face situations among middle class Madrilenians, sexuality was an absent presence much of the time, a lurking trap the conversation might suddenly fall into, and if it did, the way out was usually through a joke. It was more absent the more carefully set up the context. E.g. in the book club it was hardly ever mentioned, even when one might think – and some of the participants themselves thought – there were good reasons. The ladies at Club Aguafría mentioned it very seldom and never in relationship to themselves or their families. But at dinner parties and other more relaxed get-togethers sexuality did come up once in a while in conversation, although usually in the form of jokes, hints and allusions.

The sexual joking was in fact one of the factors that made it difficult to discuss sexuality seriously. The joking hemmed it in, set it off, kept it branded as "special". And this special character had a genderized aspect. It was for men to joke and for women to laugh and to make sure the jokes did not go "too far". This made the topic even less likely in women-only contexts.

If sexuality was discussed, it was usually discussed as a thing to be negotiated and defined. One had to define oneself in relationship to cultural change, and that was difficult to do without referring to sexuality. But for many it was also difficult to accept that sexuality was among the things that must be negotiated.

Club Aguafría members were outraged by the government campaign for condoms. A couple of common phrases were: "It is fine to try to give the young a minimum of information, but one must not make propaganda." "It is not a question of condemning them to hell for ever, but neither should they be allowed just to jump into bed, frivolously, today with one person, tomorrow with another." "It is not that one should control the young, but because they are young, they cannot be expected to be responsible at all times, so they need to be protected."

In other words, they did not want to be identified with any absolute moralistic or authoritarian stances, but they expressed as clearly as possible their basic distaste for sexual activities. And the control of youngsters was phrased as help, education, love and protection. The idea of protection implies that sexuality is intrinsically dangerous, but it was the protection, not the danger, that stood out in the discourse.

Sometimes it was admitted that there were two good reasons behind the government campaign: the danger of AIDS and the high figures of teenage pregnancies.[228] Condoms help on both counts, was the government message. And in radical and middle of the road middle class circles this was accepted. But in conservative circles, whenever someone ventured to argue in this vein, someone else was bound to say "yes but": Yes, information but not propaganda; or yes, as a last resource, but better to teach the youngsters moral values and the importance of love. I.e. the less sex the better, and talking about sex is risky, because it reminds people of things they had better not think about. Between the lines was the vague idea that: if you don't talk about it, it does not exist. Apart from the special symbolic load of the theme of sexuality, it was also an instance of the general Mediterranean (cf appendix C) cultural construction of words as something very close to deeds.

In view of all of this, it is understandable that sexuality should not crop up very often in my group discussions. Not even in group discussions with young people. The topic was too sensitive, perhaps not for them among themselves, but definitely in the presence of a curious adult taping the conversation. But once in a while it did come up, in spite of everything. In one group discussion most of the time was taken up by topics seen as sex-related: marriage, divorce, the morals of youngsters... The women present represented a rather broad spectrum of conservative and middle of the road opinions, and they knew each other well enough not to be shy. Let me therefore describe this occasion. It illustrates well the major part of the range of opinions about sexuality in non-radical middle class Madrid: what can be said and how, what issues were seen as important, what were the majority opinions, which opinions could be tried out but must be retracted in the face of opposition. In other words, it was a clear example of cultural negotiation around sex.

In Rosa María's home

Alicia had introduced me to Rosa María. They were both housewives most of the time, but they had a part time business organizing trips for youngsters. Rosa María lived in a residential area on the outskirts of Madrid. She offered to organize a tertulia in her home, with some of her friends and neighbors. Alicia took along her cousin Teresa, who had lived in Brazil for twenty years but was in Madrid for a visit. Eight women took part in the group discussion. Except for Teresa, Alicia and myself, all the others knew each other as neighbors. All the women were married, all had children (two or three, except two who had five each). The ages were between thirty-five and fifty-three. All considered themselves housewives in the sense that they were responsible for their homes. Alicia and Rosa María were the only business women, and only one had a salaried job, as a secretary.

As usual, I had told the hostess she should not prepare a fancy party, and I had offered to bring some cookies, which the hostess had told me I must absolutely not do, she would be offended if I did, so as usual I had brought a big box of chocolate instead, and as usual the hostess had laid an elegant coffee-table and served some sweets with the coffee. The women, also as usual, protested they did not want any sweets, because they would get fat, and as usual they ended up devouring the chocolate.

We met at the usual after lunch coffee hour, around 5 PM. I ran out of tape just after seven o'clock, when Rosa María's husband came home. But he disappeared into another room and we continued talking until almost 9 PM. The atmosphere was very relaxed and cordial, in spite of the sensitive topics – or perhaps because of them.

The house was an average middle class home: five bedrooms and a small garden made it a little bit extra, and the area was a good one, but there were only two bathrooms, and the livingroom was average in style and comfort.

Perhaps the discussion became unusually frank and interesting in part because I chanced to introduce it in a way that made me more conservative (=safe) in the eyes of the women than I usually managed to appear, and it was also a reference to something that really worried them. As part of the initial suggestions for discussion topics I said: "Someone told me the other day that what we were taught when we were young is not of any use for us now to transmit to our children..."

The women were already interrupting to agree: Yes, right, that is precisely what I am always saying... Nothing at all...

I continued: "Someone said that, and it stuck in my mind, like a tremendous thing, right? We can comment on that if you like, or about the children, or the importance of couple living or... (the interruptions continued all the time, showing that interest had been awakened, so I was about to decide to launch the discussion on the first theme) Or, we could do it a bit more fun, like for instance if we could be eighteen years old again..."

Now came the decisive interruption:[229] "You mean, knowing what we know now? Uuuuhhh! Wow!"

Other voices filled in, for and against the idea. Alicia said she thought we would commit new stupidities. Most were somewhat skeptical, but Loli was adamant that she would definitely like to try again. So I asked her if there were any special things she would do differently. Her friends laughed and said that she would not get married!

Loli: "Well, I don't know... above all go through life without a lot of prejudices, try to arrange for more happiness. Yes, yes. I don't know... No, yes, I would get married, but much later. That much is obvious." Her face showed that her marriage was unhappy, and that she knew that her friends knew it, but that she was not going to say so.

Several women agreed, they too would marry later in life. No one gave any examples of what was bad about early marriage, but one ventured a risky statement: "Now, knowing what it is like, I would not get married."

Her intention was serious, but the others opted for laughing. She insisted, explaining that she would have liked to be an independent woman. Of course she would have liked to have children, but an independent woman can have them and not worry about the daily problems so much. "And as to men, if you really want to, you can have fun with someone for a while and that is all. If you really want that. (Another voice: "I would try to do as little as possible of that.") I would try to be less tied down by the family, the customs, the husband, the neighbors... "

Throughout her explanation, the other women filled in daring comments of their own, and all were laughing hard. Then Alicia decided to restore normative order. She said that as you get older you learn not to feel tied down by unimportant details. This made everyone say something about how they had become more independent with time. I returned to my question: "Well, do you think you can use your own lives as examples, whether good or bad, when you have to tell your children they can't go out dancing until six in the morning or that they have to study more, or..."

"It has nothing to do with it! The life we have lived, it is what Alicia is saying, it is no good for us at all, what we have done does not serve either as good or as bad examples, because all situations have changed an awful lot. We had to be home at ten in the evening. And people said, everyone said... even the foreigners, because you know, I used to know a lot of foreigners, too, Swedes and everything, and they all said, well, what is it that happens in Spain at ten o'clock in the evening, since all the girls have to go home then?"

Everyone laughed and started telling their various stories. Alicia: "And my children, if I try to tell them about that, they count me out automatically, they double over laughing and say, but Mom, your times were different. And that is it, period."

The women laughed again and said that times are really different, too, so what can you answer?! One giggled that her children insist that her times were long ago, which made her cross.

But one woman thought she had to go against the general opinion. Her parents were not strict: "Well, I had to be home at ten thirty, but if I called over the telephone and said, listen, I won't be home for dinner, then it did not matter in the least. They understood."

"Well, you were an exception."

Alicia (eagerly): "Well, no, no, listen, it was the same for me. My mother was an only child, so they controlled her very much, so then she did not want to control us too much. I have never felt tied down or frustrated for lack of freedom, and I mean it."

Loli: "No one felt frustrated, because in those times it was the same thing for everybody."

Alicia: "That's right! I had to be home at ten, but if some day I was late and I called, no problem; I just told them where I was and with whom and why..."

There was general agreement that not all parents were strict and that you were not frustrated. Besides, they said, there was no point in staying out after ten, because since everyone went home at that hour, there was nothing to do.

Rosa María: "There was no fun, right. The problem we have now is precisely that. My daughter says the fun starts at eleven or twelve or one o'clock. That is the problem. You can tell your daughter, look, you are not going, because... And another thing, apart from having some moral criterion or whatever, or just the custom of not letting them come home late, it is a fact that Madrid is a very unsafe city."

All the woomen took up this common topic and talked of robberies, drunken driving and above all drugs. But you can't convince the youngsters that there is danger, they just think you exaggerate, they said. Rosa María thought perhaps the youngsters could be allowed to stay out until one, but not until two or three.

Alicia (whose children were older than Rosa María's): "It depends on the age, Rosa María. You'll see, as they grow, you will have to change. Because your daughter will tell you: Mom, if I have to leave at one, I am going to have to leave with the babies of seventeen. When she is twenty-two... "

Many voices interrupted her to offer examples of how the problem looked in other families. But Alicia returned to the fact that one cannot stop the youngsters. "Because they are happy! Because for them, the city at night is a dream! And I find it very understandable, eh, I have always loved to have fun."

All of the women agreed, they too had loved to have fun when they were young, and one has to understand that nowadays the fun is later. It seemed as if they were about to agree that today's youth do nothing that they did not do themselves. And the implicit reference was to the simple fun of being with friends. But suddenly one woman decided that this was not the whole truth.

María: "I don't know about the rest of you, but I can't take myself as a good example for my children, because I am sure that when I was young there were many things I did not do just because I could not."

The others did not want to let go of their rosy view. They said that sure, naturally she had cheated as much as she could. Everyone cheats, they said. Everyone has invented an excuse now and then. But then they turned serious again, they recognized that young people sometimes want to do things they should not do, and that there really are great dangers. And the greatest of them all was that young girls might become pregnant. Someone said that this danger has not disappeared, and someone else said that on the contrary it has increased.

Alicia: "My mother had the same fear, of course, she was so scared that I would become pregnant, and I ask myself now, why was she so afraid? Why, when we did not dare! We did not even let the guys go beyond holding hands! We did not let them do anything, because we believed that if they kissed you, you could become pregnant."[233]

The women joked about how ignorant and stupid they had been when young. Someone said their poor mothers were even more ignorant, that is why they were so scared. Loli: "And going by our own experiences, we always suspect the worst (significant giggle). Yes! We are suspicious. My daughter tells me, oh Mom, for heaven's sake, everyone is going, so and so is going with so and so, and they are all going camping together. And I say: Ah yes, but you are not going! And that is what I tell her! (with authoritative voice) And she says I don't trust her."

Someone said that we should believe the worst, because when you do, you are usually correct (common saying). The others protested, saying that you can't generalize like that, not all youngsters are untrustworthy. Alicia: "But Loli, in my times it was already beginning to change a little... or, I don't know, maybe because my mother did not like to control us too much or whatever, or maybe because I always cheated and tried to get as much as possible... Anyway, I did go camping. Now of course, I went with my brother and his friends. And I had a boyfriend, and I have lived in Madrid alone with my boyfriend, and I went on weekend trips with him. And I did not go to bed with him until we got married!"[231]

María Angustias then told the story of how her older sister Fina had had many boyfriends and used her younger sister, María Angustias, as a shield to be able to go walking with them in the park, and how their parents would punish them physically when they were discovered. This led Rosa María to brag about her talent to discover when someone tries to fool her, and as an example reminisced about something that had happened on one of the excursions she and Alicia had organized.

Rosa María (with pride): "I have that sixth sense, oh yes, it is so clear I do. And it is true too. When Alicia and I travel with the kids, she says to me, listen, do you know what I think, I think that so-and-so and so-and-so and so-and-so are pulling our leg. And I say: me too! Look, do you remember the brothers (she gave their last name, and someone reminded her that the tape recorder was on, but Rosa María went on with her story, already so full of laughter she could not be stopped). No, but it is an experience worth telling! Yeah, those two guys who were a bit dumb in the head. So they went, Rosa María, let the girls... You are always saying no all the time. Let the girls go out with us tonight, you are too suspicious, always thinking the worst, and we don't do anything, really we don't do anything. (One woman said that in that case they might as well go out during the day time.) So I said fine. And it so happened that we were staying right next to the beach, in a little low building, and they did not know where we were staying. And we took a walk there – and the things we saw! (She laughed harder and harder, becoming quite excited about the image of sexual activity she was conjuring up.) So I said, look at how they are not doing anything! Those two did not do anything, to be sure, they were being idiotic as usual, drinking gin and singing patriotic songs! But right next to them there were a couple of guys working over all the girls there, one by one. (Her voice broke into falsetto.) In front of our very noses!"

Alicia kept her calm. She said they had not been out walking, they had been standing at the window and the beach was some distance away. But true, they had seen things. Rosa María was by now so carried away by her story that she forgot that she was going to tell about how she would not let herself be fooled. She mentioned more names, forgetting that there might be someone in the room who knew the parents, and she was screaming with laughter, losing self-control. "Right there! On the beach! We could see them all working over all the girls right there! So I said, what a place to stay, if we had known what a view we would have..."

Alicia: "But listen, Rosa María, you don't have to leave Madrid to see things like that. Just driving along the M-30 (major freeway), for example going home sometimes if I take the exit of (name of a park) – it makes me sick!"

Alicia's voice was suddenly stern. A few other women stopped laughing with Rosa María and switched to telling their own stories of places in Madrid where you can see terrible things, like youngsters "doing everything" even at seven o'clock in the afternoon... In other words, they tried to balance Rosa María's discourse of traditional licentiousness (sex as the greatest fun precisely because it is the greatest prohibition) with the discourse of traditional norms (sex is forbidden). But there was no stopping Rosa María: "But those are people you don't know! But when you see them with their first and last names right in front of your very nose..."

The conversation split up in several for a while; then order was slowly restored. Someone said that with so much freedom and so many experiences, young people nowadays are sometimes disappointed. The future loses its glow.

Alicia: "Look, I think it is neither better nor worse than what it used to be, it depends on how things have turned out for you. As to me, I have certainly had a good time. I married at twenty-two. And at twenty-seven, I had four children (dramatic pause). But thanks to having had a lot of fun in my youth, I said, thanks to that I can sit here now, happy and content to take care of my children... I had them because I wanted to, too, eh, because I did not try to stop them from coming in any way, because I was sure I wanted to have children. Or well, perhaps not so close together, but anyway. But whatever little it was we tried, it failed, too." (Laughter)

In other words, Alicia once more took it upon herself to ensure normative order, redefining "fun" as something innocent, since everyone understood she did not mean to say that she had had sexual adventures in her youth, but at the same time presenting herself as anti-repressive, speaking out for the advantages of having some freedom. Rosa María explained to those who did not know Alicia that she had had five children and a sickly mother-in-law living with her. Alicia said that had it not been because she had felt so free and happy in her youth, she might well have been the kind of woman who would have abandoned her children and husband to go off to see the world. That was a risky statement, indeed, but she could afford it after having established her great moral worth as a mother of five and dutiful daughter-in-law, and also having said she had not gone to bed with her boyfriend before marriage even though they might have had the opportunity.

Rosa María continued in the background saying that Alicia had really been a saint. But Alicia's cousin Teresa may have thought that she was presenting herself as too frivolous. For whatever reason, Teresa now took it upon herself to declare the full validity of traditional norms. She spoke slowly, clearly, with great emphasis, with great authority:

"I think when we were young, if we were lucky enough to live in a home where they were not too old-fashioned, we had a very easy life. And a very happy life. So then we

275

felt no need to stay out until six in the morning. Nor did you feel any need to go off with your boyfriend nor to be out in the streets at night, because during the day you had enough fun for both night and day. And the next day you could go for more. (Voices saying yes, of course, etc.) You had norms. And children need norms very much."

She told some negative examples of normlessness in Brazil. Someone said that that was different. Teresa countered aggressively that the family is basic everywhere, and a child knows whether you repress him fairly or not. But you have to show him that there is authority, a principle of authority.

The others had been silent for a while, and now they started to recover and tried to interrupt her. But Teresa would not let herself be interrupted. Perhaps her many years abroad had made her forget how a Madrilenian conversation is woven together, or perhaps she had an authoritarian personality. The women were trying to say that they agreed with her, totally, completely, and so on, but they said this in ways that indicated that they wanted to add their various buts.

Teresa: "And when you do not impose a principle of authority, the child drifts off, and he asks for it. And they exaggerate their behavior, in order for you to get your authority out. When I was a girl and my mother kept saying from early morning on that she was going to thrash me, and she did not thrash me until late at night, I often felt like telling her: why don't you beat me right now! (Many voices saying yes, but...) So then, there were no problems like the ones we have today, with girls losing their criteria by taking the pill, so that they won't get pregnant, playing the game, getting lost on the way, getting frustrated. (Many voices: That is just what I was saying. Yes, but... Listen...) They are unhappy, because in each relationship they leave a piece of themselves. (Someone said that so does a man.) Not a man. A man is an animal. A woman feels. So the woman loses, from one relationship to the next. There comes a moment when a woman feels that she herself has belonged to several men without any future."

Teresa reached the end of her speech and the other women started discussing, all at the same time. Their usual conversational skills jumped back after having been knocked out for a minute or two, and there was now a forceful eruption of strong emotions and varied opinions. My interpretation is that their reaction was one of stupefaction, because Teresa's discourse was not strange at all, it was rather much too familiar. What she said was like a portrait, or almost a caricature, of the middle class conservative discourse during Franco times. It was the kind of discourse these women had grown up with, a discourse that had still been dominant when they got married and started their own families. But it was a discourse that was no longer heard in Madrid in such a crude version. And it was logical for Teresa to use it – she too had grown up with it, but then she had moved abroad and missed the period of cultural change and political transition. So she had not learned that authority could now be a dirty word unless properly circumscribed and justified, and that one was no longer supposed to punish children corporally. The women were shocked at hearing such an unmitigated version of their old discourse. The skeleton in the closet was suddenly visible.

María tried to protest that freedom is not just for men. Teresa seized on this to emphasize her message again. "A man gets in and out of a bed without leaving anything. And a woman leaves a feeling. Except if she is some indiscriminate whore." The protests now broke out immediately: "It is exactly the same thing..." "Men are animals..." "No, but they do not have the same sensitivity..." "They are less concerned..." "They feel less..." "No, because the same thing can happen..." "I don't agree with any of you..." "Men experience sexuality in a different way..." "A normal woman does not..." "No, Pili, I am convinced, too..." "I think men make love with romantic felings, too..." "I get so mad..." "It is not fair..." "Right, it is a social injustice... "No, not social, natural...

Alicia: "It is like the injustice that we have to bear the children. It is nature's injustice."

Loli: "But just because we have the children, we can't accept a different norm from men."

Teresa: "Well! I am going to ask you something. Suppose that you are a little girl and you find out by some chance that your father has a lover. You feel very bad, of course, it hurts, you feel bad. But suppose that they tell you it is your mother who has a lover. You feel awful."

Alicia again felt like reestablishing a lost balance, but this time away from Teresa's exaggerated normativity: "Well, and what if he is rich?" She laughed. Teresa (unperturbed): "Because you have your mother on a different pedestal." Loli (with some desperation): "But that is because of an error in our education!!!" Teresa: "No, because woman has a different nature."

Again, many voices suggesting arguments in all directions. Loli tried to say that if your mother is unhappy with your father and if she is lucky enough to find some little satisfaction... Rosa María tried to laugh off the controversy, joking that she would applaud any woman who dared to have a lover. Someone took her seriously and said that very few women have lovers: if they fall in love with someone they leave with him, they do not stay with their husband. Women cannot stomach sporadic relationships. Someone else said that she felt sorry for men, because it must be more "enriching" to be in love than just go to bed with someone.

Suddenly Pilar had had enough and screamed: "I don't feel like it, Rosa María! I just don't feel like it! If you accept it for men, then you have to accept if for women, too."

There had been some misunderstanding here. It is no wonder misunderstandings occurred, for one thing because so many spoke at the same time, and for another because they tended to speak very abstractly and indirectly. Anyway, Rosa María good-naturedly said that she did not mean to say that it was good for anyone. Pilar repeated that she refused, she just refused. Teresa took over again.

"Now, what is a happy life? The life of a person who gets married and gets along – I am not going to say that there are roses without thorns, but a normal marriage, that is what we all want to have in our life. A normal family. (Voices repeating: Normal, yes, normal.) Right? Now, if we go beyond those parameters and your mother married a man who gave her a terrible life, and suddenly she found another life, but – in general a woman does not have a lover at the same time as a husband (voices affirming once more this important fact). But why is that? Because a woman invests feelings."

But Pilar wanted to make her opposition to sexuality without love even clearer. For her it was not just a norm, it was what she felt: "But Rosa María, I think that a woman, what she is always looking for is a different feeling than what a man looks for. You can't tell me that I can have a man just to go to bed with him. Because I don't feel like it. On the contrary, what I am looking for is a person who can understand me. (Someone: "And what if you find a wonderful lover?" Ironic laughter.) And if he is a wonderful lover and afterwards I feel more lonely than ever, after five minutes he has abandoned me. I want something more than that!"

This was now a rather daring exchange, coming close to saying that intercourse can be pleasurable in itself, even though Pilar thought that such pleasure would not satisfy her by itself. Someone dared to suggest that one could perhaps go to bed with a good friend. The others protested, repeating that woman's nature is different. Alicia relativized: "But today there are women like that. You know that." Several voices: "Sure there are. But that is not what is typical."

More heated discussion, all voices simultaneously. As it calmed down again, an oppositional voice was stating that stability should mean mutual understanding or it is worth nothing. Someone else pointed out, as self-evident, that men can have that sort of emotional stability with one woman and a sexual relationship with another, and others replied that even if that does happen, it should not.

This was the type of argument where in a less conservative context someone would have been sure to say that things as they are are unfair to women, and these women came close to saying it, and perhaps they thought it. But they did not say it. Instead they implied that such a man is immoral. Rosa María said that for women such things do not happen. Loli: "Look, Rosa María, I am sure that if you educate a boy and a girl in the same way, they will behave similarly in life."

There were some protests. Loli anticipated them and continued: "As to morality, I do not agree with those tendencies you are saying, all of you." (Lots of attempted interruptions.) "The way you educate women while small and all of that, sure, but then in their private life, their life apart from their children, I think they have... they could have exactly the same as what men have."

Loli had broken the consensus about the innate gender differences in sexual response. There was a short confused silence. Then someone exclaimed: "Not exactly the same, oh no!" And a great din broke out. Someone attacked Loli with arguments about the

278

maternal instinct, and she did her best to accept its existence and combine it with her defense of women's right to pleasure.

Alicia: "Look, I don't agree with this, because... look! "(It took her several false starts to get the floor.) "I have four, I mean the four oldest, because the fifth one is still just a teenager, that is different. My boy is the third child, between three girls. And when he was little he played with dolls, he played house, he played shopping (little laughs in the background, voices saying of course, sure...) And all of that, of course. Because on top of three sisters he had a mother and a grandmother. His father left at eight in the morning and came home at eight in the evening..."

Someone laughed: "And just think, the way Andrés looks now!" Meaning: very masculine. Alicia: "Now, yes, but you know why? As a reaction and as opposition. Can't you see that he will never do what a girl tells him to do, now? (Voice: "Of course not. ') Because it went so far that if I said, Andrés, what kind of sandwich do you want? he would go, the same as Anabel (her oldest daughter). And when he started at the mixed daycare center, he had only girls for friends there. He was afraid of the boys, for him they were something strong and not normal; the girls were very soft, very calm, he was used to playing with them, he was not a rough boy, he did not kick, he did not punch, he did not fight. And the boys fought. The first blow that took off in there, Andrés always found it landing on his nose. So it came to a point where I feared for him. (Short dramatic pause. Everyone understood that she meant she feared not only for his male gender identity but for his heterosexual identity and that this was a serious fear indeed.) And I think it was because of the education he was getting. I had to send him to karate class, I had to switch him to a school for boys only, and in the summers he had to go and stay with relatives already when he was very little. Because I said: This boy is in danger! He is not going to turn out right!"

The women agreed. Only one dissenting voice was heard, saying that a boy's education is not necessarily better, women should not give up what they have had, women's education has been much more all round. Alicia hurried to say yes, of course, she had not meant to imply anything else. But the dissenter evidently had said what she did in order to get back to the topic of sexual pleasure.

"I think it is much more all round if a woman in love, if she is really truly in love, goes off with a man (short hesitation) – to the cot! (Laughter, voices protesting in jest: "Sure, woman, yes, yes...") No, but I don't mean to say that they are married nor that it is an adventure – no! I am talking of love (with emphasis, dramatically lowering her voice). When a person is in love with a person, I find it more all round for her to go with that person and have that relationship (several voices tried to interrupt and protest), than for a normal person to go to bed with someone without giving it any importance."

Alicia: "Well, but you feel like that and you experience that because that is what you have been taught since you were little."

"Well, and maybe because I have felt it like that, too."

279

Perhaps Alicia had misunderstood her. In any case, she wanted to continue with the theme of the influence of education.

Alicia: "If not, you... because if otherwise... (Suddenly lowering her voice with scandal and drama.) If not, why do all the daughters of whores end up as whores? (Voices: "Sure, they do, yes.") Because that is what they see in their mothers. Because that is what they learn, that they go off with one and then with another and so on and that that is no problem for them."

"But what I want to say is that if we talk about how women and men are different, and you say that a woman has to be the same as a man, I say no, not me! I think I would not like to just disassociate that and say, listen, now I feel like that, like going off with someone. That would horrify me, and since it horrifies me, I think: the stomach men have to have in order to say, today my body feels like it, so I am going off with a woman I don't know! (Someone said something about frivolity.) No, it is not the frivolity of it, but never mind, it is saying: come on, I feel like going with a person... If it is like a friend? Fine, fine. But perhaps for me, that... Really! And even though I am the kind of person who have had better friends among men than among women, you know! But there are friends of mine with whom I would never go to bed even if they had thrown themselves all over me like I don't know what... And even so, we were very good friends. And even so, the other thing... it is different."

Several women carried this thought in different directions: one to say that women always suffer more than men; another to say that friendship between women and men is rare; a third, Rosa María, taking up the main point, that of gender essence.

Rosa María: "The guys are different! For a boy, it is a different thing. He can go to bed with a girl and that is just fine for him."

Pilar: "Rosa María, come on, don't tell me that they did not instill in you when you were young that it was mortal sin (RM: "Yes.") and that you could not even get married, because for the man whom you married you had to arrive as a virgin (RM: "Sure, sure.") and all of those... – all that nonsense! (Laughter. Voices saying yes, others saying no, others saying yes, but...) You had all of that deep inside your head. A woman does not have to become a whore just because... none of our daughters, if by the time they are twenty-four they have had two or three experiences in their life. (Protests and affirmative exclamations.) And that does not mean they will end up on a street corner."

María Angustias said she agreed, but on the condition that those experiences had been when the woman was in love. Someone else said, yes, fine, but there is always a risk if they start too early. Several others repeated this idea in various formulations. In other words, they now debated sexual activity as if it were a potent drug: Can it be admitted if it gives you pleasure, or is the danger of addiction and consequent social disaster too great? The previous issue, whether women have the capacity for sexual pleasure without love or not, seemed to have been settled affirmatively, even though most of the arguments had been against.

Maruja introduced a new factor: age. Not just youth versus maturity, now, but age in the light of chances of marriage. "If my daughter is thirty years old and she comes and says to me: I am unmarried, and I am going to live with so-and-so. (Several voices, anticipating the argument: "In that case fine, just fine, let her do what she wants to do.") Then I say to her: Fine, you are old enough, and you have to... if that is your decision. But if she says the same thing when she is eighteen, then she breaks my heart. (Voices: "Naturally! Me too!") And what is happening today is that the eighteen-year-olds are already saying those things."

The women meant two things: that a non-virgin has a diminished chance of finding a new fiancé, so a young girl should not risk her virginity, and that a thirty-year-old has little chance to get married anyway, because of age, so she has little to lose. And perhaps they also meant that a thirty-year-old is less vulnerable, less in need of protection from the negative sides of sexuality.

At this point voices were raised for changing the topic. But Pepa said that in that case she just had to tell us something first. "A friend of my son at university, he said that there were girls who were virgins and they said they were not, because they were ashamed! (Scandalized outcries) Yes, and it was a survey, you know, at the university. When the girls came out from the building, these people were there, asking them if they were virgins and so on, and there were some who were virgins but said they were not."

Alicia: "That happens when you have no criteria to defend your values."

Pilar: "They felt that, now here, in front of this other girl, I don't want to be any less of a woman than you, because..."

Various voices agreed: "At our age we don't care, we say what we feel." "Young people are afraid of what their friends will say." "They will laugh at them." "Yes, they will think you are some little mousy thing that has never done anything wrong." "If you are afraid to say you are a virgin, you are afraid, too, to say you have to be home at ten, or anything." The women admitted that things had been turned upside down and that what was now shameful was being a virgin, but some of them made it clear that they saw this as proof of the moral weakness of today's youth, not just a change of customs.

Maruja told a long story of some young relative of hers who had had a long-lasting relationship with a young man. Maruja had thought the young girl exaggerated the young man's trustworthiness, and she was right, he was not true to the girl. So they broke up and the girl was desperate. "So just imagine if she had gone to bed with him! She would have died!"

In other words, she was saying that one reason not to allow early sexual relationships may be that it is morally wrong, but there is also the practical fact that such relationships do not last. The implication was that permanence is necessary for sexual relations to be allowed. The other women took the clue to tell other stories that illustrated other practical reasons for abstaining. Some of the examples: young women suffer when relationships end; both boys and girls have a right to innocent pleasures in youth, before they take on the heavy burden of permanent relationships; once you commit such a serious mistake as having a sexual relationship that must end, you are likely to commit other mistakes, too; your whole life is destroyed when a serious relationship is destroyed, the disappointment is unbearable...

In all of these comments, there was not a single mention of lust, but lust was what was understood as the great risk factor. In spite of all the caution and indirectness, the discourse was not really prudish, but it made sense only if one took for granted that sexual activity is not pleasurable in itself. When the women talked of pleasure, they usually meant the fun one can have when one is not burdened with the responsibility of a sexual relationship.

Then one woman felt it necessary to recover the reference to present day circumstances: "I am not saying a woman cannot get married again, because today society will accept that. And there are men who do not mind and will marry her even if she has already had a child. But her possibilities will be only half."

The topic was running out of steam, and I was thinking of changing it, when someone asked me with more suspicion than politeness what I thought. I had been too silent for comfort. I explained, cautiously, that I did not think women and men were very different from each other by nature, nor by divine will. "I think it is society that shapes us differently. I agree with you that with the society we have in Spain, above all the one we have had, women have certainly been educated and turned into something very different from men. So what I wonder is... the thing you were talking about, about how the ideal is to have a good family, a good couple where husband and wife get along. I wonder to what extent that is possible? Two people who have been educated so differently, can they really get along?"

The women exploded in exclamations about what a difficult issue I was presenting. Alicia said love was the answer. Loli said: "Love and a lot of patience (*paciencia*), patience on the part of the woman who has been educated for that." Alicia thought that comment needed correction: "On the part of the woman and on the part of the man!"

This started a discussion about how much each one contributes to the harmony in a couple relationship. At first it was about emotions, understanding and patience, but soon it veered towards practical matters.

Alicia, suddenly critical: "He excuses himself saying he brings the food, he gives you money to live well and have a good home, and with that he washes his hands."

One woman, with great emphasis: "We are talking about us! But I want to tell you one thing: what you are all saying is true, for us, but my hope is that it will be different in the future. I am trying to raise my children for it to be different." I asked what she wanted the future to be like for her children. "I would... look, what I wanted to say is this: I think that here in Spain so far people never got divorced because a woman, for a series of reasons, would always bear with (*aguantaba*) everything. She had to take it all, and there is a sort of blackmail in it, too, in that a woman can't want a divorce, because the women of the transition[232], eh, there are some that are not independent."

This was a radical discourse for this group, but perhaps because the topic was less sensitive than the previous one of sexuality, the protests were lame. She continued: "Economically, or that she did not have a university degree or not a good job. Then she had to stay with her husband. Because he is the source of..." "Of everything!" said several voices. "Right. And she has to take it. So this is sort of a lost case. (Sad silence.) Almost lost for women of these forty years in Spain."[233] There were some timid suggestions of alternative "solutions", like having a rich father. "So here the husband has become used to being a real despot. A Spanish husband has been a despot. He has thrown his shirt on the floor, knowing that a woman had to pick it up, he throws a piece of paper on the floor and, really, well, he feels very important, because he goes to work, and the woman stays at home, and that goes for a majority of men, eh."

I asked if that was what she did not want for her children.

"Exactly. That is what I believe has been happening up to now. We all agree on that. Now, I think it should not be like that. And I think that we ourselves, it is on us it depends if it is not to continue like that, we are women, and just like I am saying that men have some things and some advantages, we have the advantage, for now, that the children... or the advantage or the responsibility of educating the new people." There were voices saying yes, but in a calm reflective manner, neither protests nor enthusiastic seconding. These thoughts seemed to be difficult to handle but not terribly controversial. "Since we are of the transition, we can't work outside the home, so for now and today we have the children in our hands. And some women are doing a very bad job."

Alicia: "The majority. Because we continue to educate the children in the same way..." "The machista way!" said someone. Pilar said it was monstrous. Alicia repeated her argument. A cautious consensus seemed about to be established. Even Teresa said it was a good thing for a young woman to study for a profession in order to have an option in case her matrimonial plans should misfire. But she insisted that the first option should be a "normal marriage". Other voices however were getting enthusiastic about the thought of having a job and being able to throw your husband out in case it became necessary.

Alicia told us about her daughter Anabel, whose boyfriend had six sisters, plus a mother and a grandmother. Anabel thought that as long as there were so many women in the house, her boyfriend did not have to help at all, and Alicia thought that Anabel was making a big mistake. "Because she is a modern girl who plans to work, and they are going to want to share everything, the household tasks, the children and everything, so they are going to end up fighting, because he is used to being waited upon. Like his father. Because he just says two words and all those women hurry to do it. She will find herself in that situation."

After some more discussion about the need to be responsible and not break up a marriage "too soon" and the need to "make love grow" rather than making demands, the topic of education resurfaced.

Loli: "We educate our daughters the same way as our sons. Equality. You want your daughter to go to university and to be totally independent, economically. So that, if she has bad luck and her husband mistreats her, she will be able to say: so far and no more! So that she will be able to defend herself. Do you understand? Or if he does not love her or she does not love him. In case of whatever might come up. Because what I think is indisputable is that it ought to be forbidden by law for someone, when you are twenty, or eighteen, or twenty-two, for a priest or a court to say that there you are, you are going to stay with that man by your side until death do us part! (Voices seconding.) Because you will change, and so will he."

This was where Loli had started the discussion several hours earlier. In spite of all the normative talk, the discussion had led to a point where she could now generalize from her own unhappy experiences and pronounce a new moral rule.

The topic was not explored further, because someone was asking Teresa about life in Brazil, and the conversation centered on that for quite a while. The discussion continued for two more hours, in a very warm and relaxed atmosphere where a couple of the women dared to confess marital problems, one shed tears over a child dead in an accident, one woman had to leave on an errand but came back because the discussion was so interesting, one woman told us honestly about her non-prestigious part-time work in the police department, including anecdotes about her chauvinist male workmates, and so on. It felt as if the difficult topic of sexuality had created an atmosphere of unusual sincerity. We had run great social risks talking about it, so now more risks could be taken.

Furthermore the negotiation had been successful in that the consensus had moved to a new balance point which felt acceptable to all. At least for the moment.

Comments

This tertulia ended in a feeling of unusual warmth. But it was quite representative as to interactional style, the situational roles and the women's impression management.

The difficulty of the topic of sexuality lies not only in its being morally and politically charged. I am sure that for many of the women there was the added fear of revealing unmentionable ignorance. These women had had very little sexual education in their youth, and what there was they usually got from priests and boyfriends, each with their own axes to grind and limited knowledge of female anatomy. Since it was now shameful to admit too much ignorance on this topic, the only type of confession one heard was about what a person used not to know. But young women loved to tell anecdotes to demonstrate their mothers' warped ideas, so even if we charge a good deal of that to young people's wish to prove their own knowledgeability, in contrast to that of the older generation, one can presume that many middle aged women really had not had much opportunity to complete their sexual education later in life.

On the issue of the sexual activities of youth, there was also some honest ignorance but more impression management. There was uncertainty in this group, as in many other contexts, of whether the thing to do was to pretend that young people do not really do very much more than the previous generation (in that way the speaker would earn points for believing in the goodness and innocence of humanity and for her own impeccable moral standing) or to pretend that one was well informed of the many tremendous things that happen nowadays (thus earning points for being up-to-date and free of prejudices). This is one angle on the issue of sexuality on which there was no consensus in general, so people had to adapt their discourse situationally, but even when the prevailing tendency of the situation at hand had been sounded out, one was not safe, because it was such an unstable point that it might turn around in the middle of the conversation.

The clearest consensus, in this group as in most, was that there had been a lot of important change. The women felt that their own lives could not serve as examples for the younger generation, since their experiences had become irrelevant. But there was no consensus on whether this should be accepted or deplored. And among those who felt one ought to insist on old, albeit modernized, norms, there was still no consensus on workable methods.

The women in this gathering leaned towards conservative opinions in general, and it was not a strongly polarized group, but some of them expressed social criticism with a progressive flavor. They delivered their opinions with the usual aplomb, but there was great uncertainty in the air about just how radical one could appear without causing a serious breach of good feeling, and this uncertainty was not resolved during the tertulia.

The mode of management of meaning was quite expansive. This was one reason for the warm atmosphere that grew during the tertulia. The combination of rather conservative opinions and a rather expansive way of handling them was not very common. But possible.[234]

There was a good deal of ambivalence on almost all of the substantive issues discussed. There was especially strong ambivalence around the general definition of the moral quality of sexual activities as such. Are they good or bad, are they dangerous, if so for whom, or perhaps for all?

There was ambivalence on the issue of pleasure. It was discussed if sexual activity, whether good or bad, might give pleasure in itself, or would it be pleasurable only if combined with love. Some of the women had definite opinions, but no collective consensus was reached and my impression was that most of the women were unsure of their own view of this issue.

Few middle class Madrilenians in the 1990s would go as far as to say that women are not capable of feeling sexual pleasure even when they are in love. In this group, at least, it was apparently taken for granted that such pleasure does exist. But some of the comments can be interpreted to indicate that some of the women doubted even this. Perhaps some had no personal experience of sexual pleasure.

And whatever women require to feel whatever kind of pleasure they can attain, is their pleasure similar to that of men or not? Again, an issue not clearly spelled out but of evident concern for the women. They were not sure of what the truth was, and they were not sure of what they wanted the truth to be.

The greatest ambivalence of all was felt around the issue of sexual activities (whether pleasurable or not) as dangerous for order in general. Moral order and social order were seen as synonymous in this light, and the desirability of order was taken for granted on the surface of the discussion. Judging from their other utterances, some of the women could have been expected to express the more progressive opinion that strong order can slow down change, and is therefore not always good. But they did not. We can presume that they might have in another context. Especially the fact that the majority of the women opposed Teresa's stance only in a lukewarm fashion probably made the more progressive-minded feel that the situation had to be kept within the perimeters of a more or less conservative discourse, in spite of the tentative subversivity of the treatment of sexuality.

The negotiated sexuality

What we need to understand about Madrilenian middle class sexuality around 1990 in order to understand the Madrilenian middle class gender order, is that:
- first, sexuality was a central issue for debate;
- but, second, what sexuality is, was usually not an issue for debate, on the contrary, it was doxically taken to be about bodily desires towards other human beings, and about the sometime result of those desires, intercourse. In other words, sexuality was seen as a given, not as cultural construction;
- but, third, it was in fact energetically being constructed in the ongoing debates, in this tertulia as well as in all of society, and the participants acted as if they found it very necessary to participate in this construction, otherwise their "given" would be threatened.
- And this feeling was in fact realistic, even if illogical in light of the view of sexuality as a given, because, fourth, there were several and widely varying positions possible on what is good and bad about sexuality and how it should be managed;
- and because, fifth, these positions were mutually antagonistic;
- and, sixth, culturally central and emphasized in such a way that it was impossible to bypass the issue.
- And, most important for our purposes here: seventh, this minefield could not be avoided in a discussion of gender in Spain. Most Madrilenians construed gender as based on sexual dualism and they construed sexuality as dependent on there being clearly differentiated gender categories. Homosexuality was seldom mentioned, and if it was, the

definition of it depended also on the existence of only two and clearly different.ated gender categories. Not all but many furthermore construed the division of labor and the distribution of power and the distribution of personal characteristics according to gender as essential ingredients of sexuality.

Part VI: Anthropological words

Chapter 20. Summing up: Processes and Power

The empirical chapters have offered examples that I find reasonably representative, and I hope they have given the reader sufficient ethnographic insights "to think with" while reading my conclusions. The three final chapters present generalizations that can be made from the ethnography. I have arrived at my conclusions through careful scrutiny of the arguments used by my informants, especially in the taped group discussions but also in other situations.

Here, in chapter 20, we will take a new look at the arenas described, where cultural negotiations take place. The major topics found in the negotiations will also be summed up and brought to a higher level of abstraction, permitting a better understanding of what was at stake. I will point to the connections between the arenas, the contents, the dispositions for certain interactional styles and the outcomes of the negotiations in order to explicate the significance of this empirical study for the main theoretical issue of feminist anthropology: how can power relationships between the genders be described?

The Madrilenian gender order in the early 1990s was a composite and moving product of discourse, historical conjuncture and class. It was a specific situation, in which women were indeed becoming "persons" according to their own definitions of that word.

Where was it negotiated? Forms and arenas

Looking at forms and arenas for negotiation, we have seen that gender organized the rules of participation in and access to them, in such a way that men's viewpoints had a better chance of being heard and being taken seriously.

This was being contested in various ways. Women entered male arenas, new female arenas were created, the gender specification of some (male or female) arenas was under doubt. Most new arenas created were mixed. Few arenas were exclusively male any longer. The feeling of change in these things was so strong that my work was often questioned by Spaniards, especially by the progressive-minded. For them, gender as a principle for spatial organization was no longer a relevant object of study because it was disappearing.

But we must not confuse the general direction of trends with actually achieved results. Let us review my observations in middle class Madrid: What major arenas were there for cultural negotiations? To what extent and how were they gender-marked (even if not exclusive)? What new arenas were being created? Where could people of either gender negotiate any theme that was important to them? Where could the gender order itself be negotiated?

Gender negotiation went on in almost all situations in Madrid. Quite a lot was taken for granted in socially segregated contexts, like Club Aguafría or friendship groups or private parties, since people chose such contexts on the basis of similarity in opinions on basic issues and similarity in mode of management of meaning. But where the mode of management of meaning was expansive, even protected contexts could bristle suddenly with unexpected contestations (e.g. as in chapter 13). And most contexts were not neatly segregated according to opinions on gender.

The mass media were fora for debate in which only a very small minority could participate actively. Universities might be thought to be the ideal context for critical debate, but in Spain they functioned and were seen mainly as professional schools, where the overriding goal of students was to pass the exams and get grades good enough to obtain a good job, or any job at all.

The major part of the cultural negotiation took place in contexts of sociability. Since sociability was a key criterion for a good life according to the habitus of most Madrilenians, sociability got done. There were innumerable forms for it. And since talking had high entertainment value, sociability consisted to a very high degree of talk. When it did not, this was commented on and seen as negative.[235]

Naturally, different arenas lent themselves to different kinds of talk. But even relaxed occasions, like a dinner party in the garden, usually had a tint of debate. This was so because people did not usually hesitate to bring up topics on which there were different opinions, since the interactional style was very tolerant of differences of opinions (cf appendix C). This was the case even among the cautious-minded, as long as the differences of opinions were kept within what was recognized as acceptable, well-known parameters. Such parameters were changing, however, so safe topics were becoming scarce.

But the spontaneously occurring debates were not enough for the most expansive-minded. Special arenas were created, like the Nosotros group, the Book Club, and the many political and cultural associations. Lectures followed by discussion were popular.[236] And the group discussions I arranged were welcomed and used for personal purposes. There was much creativity, both in the search for new arenas and in the effort to create more permanent groupings. The popularity of social clubs can be seen in this light, too, even though other factors meant that caution usually reigned to some degree in them.

289

A special case was the feminist effort to create new arenas for women only. The feminist movement in Madrid opened bars, organized women's festivities, arranged lectures, art shows and film festivals, ran a film discussion club, and so on; all of these arenas were for women only. Very few middle class women were organized feminists, but very many of the feminists were middle class.[237] I have not included any examples of internal feminist discussions in this book, however, because the movement was at the moment quite marginal. What was said in its fora reached few ears other than those physically present. There were plenty of references to "feminism" in general gender debates, but they were usually far off the mark. People outside the movement knew little about what positions existed inside it, and it was not easy to find out unless you joined, because the media coverage was close to zero.[238]

Arenas compared according to class

The arenas varied according to class.[239] The most important difference was the degree of gender segregation.

In Benituria, predominantly working-class, almost all spontaneous sociability was gender segregated. Women met and talked to each other above all while waiting in line in the food stores and while waiting to pick up their children outside the schools. Women living in the same building sometimes had intense friendships, helping each other with housework and having coffee together. There were some, not many, small friendship groups getting together to chat on a more regular basis. More common was for mothers of small children to form temporary, but very appreciated, relationships with other mothers when they sat in parks or playgrounds with the children.

A major determinant for women's sociability was that it was not quite legitimate. All of the common contexts were working contexts. The women found excuses for and ways of talking to each other while they were doing something else. This went for the often intense relations between adult daughters and their mothers, as well; they saw a lot of each other, but the context was usually cooperation in household activities.

Men had an unquestioned right to socialize without any excuse. The absence of excuse was even underlined in discourse; it was considered important for a man to be able to say "I don't have to give explanations to anyone!" There was also a well-established institution for male sociability: the bars. Not all men used them regularly, but most did, and no women used them in the same way. An ironic but common word for a group of male friends seeing each other regularly in a bar was "the parishioners" (*los parroquianos*), a word that conveys the sense of belonging, commitment and semi-institutionalization of their sociability.

Then there were clubs and associations. They could be sorted along a continuum of progressivity, where the two main criteria were orientation on the political left-right-scale and degree of gender segregation, and these two tended to coincide. The mixed-gender contexts were above all the neighborhood association, the leftist political parties and the parent-teacher associations at the schools. Both women and men belonged to and were active in voluntary church activities and the organization of the city festivity, *Fallas*, but inside these organizations the activities were divided according to gender. The one non-formal context for mixed-gender sociability was kin, especially Sunday lunches with parents/in-laws and summer stays with them in home villages. Socializing as couples was a phenomenon one knew about, talked about and perhaps tried to emulate, but it was culturally uncomfortable and not very common.

The middle class situation was different. First, gender segregation was not very legitimate. Even the conservative ladies of Club Aguafría would have protested if I had pointed out to them how segregated their social life was in fact. Second, there was much more emphasis on the Couple. It took precedence over mother-child relationships inside the family much more so than in the working class; there was more talk about it, more negotiation about what it implied, etc. This found expression in social life, so that much of it was based on couples. So much, in fact, that widowed or separated men and women found it hard to participate. In spite of all of this, the couples tended to separate during the interaction itself, as we saw. Either they just arrived together, and then found separate spaces, as happened at Club Aguafría and at some dinner parties, or else they would sit together but talk mostly to persons of their own gender.

Organized activities were never formally gender segregated in the middle class.[240] In practice, however, many activities were segregated. The "cultural Fridays" at the club were attended by women only, and meant for women only, since they were held at a time when men work. But this was not formally recognized.[241] The same was true for the Book Club. Clubs and associations that met in the evening were usually considered more "serious" and were never totally gender segregated in practice, but men often dominated them. The idea the Nosotros group had recently had, to try out some separate activities for women and men, was seen as something new and interesting, perhaps as a first step towards deeper reflection on gender ideas; it was not seen as any reverting to old patterns. But it was at least in part a concession to the fact that women and men sometimes had different visions for group activities and a recognition of the fact that they had some difficulty understanding each other even when talking about the same things.

Middle class women had a recognized right to leisure that working class women did not have. And some of them had the means (time, money and freedom of movement) to use it, too. But others did not, and this turned into a contradiction for them, a visible and culturally uncomfortable one. Some women complained that they had to spend hours, even days, organizing all sorts of details of housework in order to be able to get out of the house to go to a lecture or see friends. In spite of the good economic position of all families I met, many of the women were careful with their money when they were out on their own – they tended to choose cheaper restaurants, for example, and tipped little, and to share the bill was much more legitimate than it was among men. There were stories about husbands who controlled their wives' movements, making scenes if the wife was not at home when he came home from work or if she did not answer the phone when he called. These stories were always told in confidence, because such behavior from husbands was not legitimate, so it was difficult to know how common it was, but it did exist, and this shows that the legitimacy of women's freedom of movement was not well rooted in dispositions.

Middle class men usually felt too distinguished to go to the corner bar – if there was any corner bar at all in the areas where they lived. The social clubs constituted the substitute for bar life for many men. Others had no substitute, except to the extent that their office functioned as one.

Very few middle class men practiced sports and even fewer took part in such traditional upper class male activities as hunting. Most of their social life was gender mixed: leisure based on the couple and working hours in gender mixed offices. The men had less need for uni-gender contexts than the women, however. They dominated professional life both numerically and hierarchically. Leisure was segregated in practice to some extent, and for the rest, the men dominated there, too (cf below on interactional style).

The women did go shopping, like working class women, and they did sit with their children in parks. But since they did not usually know who the other women around them were, it was not easy to start talking to them. Besides, they did more and more of their shopping in supermarkets. Some women did not even have the excuse of going out with the children, either because a maid did it, or because there was a fenced garden around their building where even small children could be left alone while playing.

So all in all, middle class women and men had fewer opportunities to get to know people or even talk casually to strangers. Both women and men had few daily opportunities to socialize in uni-gender contexts. Both women and men tended to participate in formal sociability (associations, etc.) much more than working class men or women did, but those who did were still a minority compared to the whole class. Couple sociability and kin get-togethers were the most important informal contexts for middle class people of both genders. The social clubs were the major contexts for the kind of sociability that fitted well with the preference for having a circle of friends that remained permanent for many years and whom one could see without having to plan for it. Spontaneous but regular was the ideal, and that was possible, to some degree, at the social clubs. That was why they were important arenas for negotiating cultural change, but other factors, especially the middle class need for aparentar, limited their use for this purpose.

So there was a felt need for new kinds of contexts. And they were being created. What overall consequences they will have for the gender order was not yet clear. But the following generalizations can be made: Old uni-gender contexts were disappearing. Some of the new contexts were uni-gender in practice, almost none in theory. Most of them were mixed gender. Some of them were modeled on parish discussion groups, but they were often explicitly considered an alternative to Church contexts, permitting freer debate. Both women and men searched for new contexts and both found them. Housewives had more time but less freedom of movement than men or employed women. Gender themes were frequently on the informal agenda of all arenas where cultural negotiation went on.

How was it negotiated? Dispositions

The style of interaction is also relevant for a full understanding of what happens in the construction of meaning.

All dispositions that influence social interaction influence the outcome of any negotiation of meaning. For example, the speed of cultural change in Spain had to do with fast social change, but it also had to do with the fact that people negotiated meanings intensely, talking a lot, and that most individuals participated in many different arenas. Thus a lot happened quickly.

Appendix C describes the basic norms for conversation in Madrid. Chapter 4 outlines two modes of management of meaning that can also be seen as dispositions, for greater caution or for greater risk-taking in negotiating meaning.

Some dispositions for interaction were closely connected to gender and therefore influenced especially the changing construction of gender.

According to a very deep and strong disposition, women deferred to men. Men spoke more. Neither men nor women tended to notice this, because it was so natural to them, i.e. doxic. And if it was pointed out, people would deny it, since it went against the present hegemonic discourse on equality and justice, and since women were far from silent and not always openly submissive. But it was a deep disposition related to the definitions of femininity and the strong naturalization of it, in Madrid as in most European contexts.[242] Women would argue forcefully, for example, but they argued on what the men defined as the topic for discussion. Women would interrupt a lot, both each other and men, but the men interrupted more and let themselves be interrupted less. A woman practically always answered if a man addressed a question or an argument directly to her; men did not always answer when women did the same. Women softened their arguments with smiles and jokes if they threatened to become too controversial; men felt no such need. The deference was there and it had consequences.

Since men dominated mixed gender contexts, uni-gender contexts offered women more of a chance to negotiate, and they therefore tended to speak more when there were no men around.[243] Consequently, men did not obtain good knowledge of what women really thought. Since women and men did not negotiate well together, and did not seek very much interaction across the gender line, the differences in opinions and dispositions that the socialization and the division of tasks created were not overcome; women and men continued to live in different cultural worlds to a great (even though diminishing) extent.

And since the uni-gender contexts were decreasing in quantity and cultural legitimacy, women were losing more than men of one vital resource: access to arenas for discussing the things that concerned them. Men were losing their uni-gender contexts, too, but they had more opportunities to set the agenda for the mixed contexts.

Due to the way society as a whole was organized, different things changed in each gender world, and these changes were not well ironed out in common debate. Therefore the ongoing social changes increased some differences between the two worlds and created some new ones, even though the general direction of change was away from segregation and ascription. One result was that women and men preferred to socialize in uni-gender groups, and this was so even for many who would deny it because it contradicted their feeling that gender segregation was unfair and becoming inoperable.

Because women and men had approximately the same opportunities for uni-gender sociability, and men dominated the negotiation in mixed-gender contexts, men's total input into the negotiation was greater than that of women.

And as long as the disposition for male dominance/female deference in interaction survives, this will continue even if women gain access in large numbers to important public arenas (uni-gender or mixed). When they do, their dispositions will probably change, but that will happen more slowly.[244]

The fact that women did not speak as freely in the company of men as men in the company of women, afforded women more information on men than vice versa. But it increased the visible dominance of male interpretations of reality.

This complex picture increases manifold the general complexity of the process of negotiation around gender. In Madrid in the 1990s as well as in many other contexts in the so called Western world, opinions on gender separated the genders more than any other kind of opinion did and separated the genders more than it separated other categories.

What was being constructed? Themes

The thematic areas of work and sexuality were those that the Madrilenians obviously talked about and knew that they talked about. But through these, other larger or deeper issues were being worked out. If we look for the themes used as general referents to organize discussions and back up arguments, we find that the two most salient ones were "changing femininity" and "achievement". Both were related to the general social change away from ascription. So was a third general theme, "genderization" in the sense of foregrounding of gender among personal characteristics, achieved or ascribed.

As a matter of fact, work and sexuality can be understood as concretizations of these three more abstract themes. Femininity, achievement and genderization are not emic

294

labels. They are my terms for what the talk of work and sexuality was about at a higher level of abstraction.

Femininity is a basic ingredient of any gender order at any time or place. Even where more than two genders are recognized, they always include male and female, so features that mark something as male or female must have some specification even though the amount of specification (scope) varies as well as the cultural emphasis (force) on it.[245]

For the Madrilenian middle class, femininity used to be seen as a natural and eternal category; it was defined as a type of behavior and also a mysterious essence that enveloped any female human being and could be easily recognized by all. It could be present in different degrees, and it could be evaluated positively or negatively according to context, but all female human beings, even very young ones, had it in some degree, and its overall presence was doxically good, because it was thought to be inevitable, part of the order of things that had to be for life itself to be. Femininity could be recognized outside the human realm, too. Female animals were said to have it when they were maternal or coquettish. Even inanimate objects could sometimes be described as feminine (certain types of music or painting, certain materials, etc.), but at this point the usage became metaphorical.

In the 1990s, much of what was considered intrinsic to femininity was contested by many women. Those who considered themselves progressive opposed especially seductive and submissive behavior and the images of weakness and capriciousness. They said that such behavior or imagery was undignified, and placed women at a disadvantage in all contexts. They also opposed the division of tasks and resources in general. If femininity used to be something which could be summed up in the ideas of submission, repression of sexuality, self-sacrifice for the sake of others, and the idea of submission had now become unacceptable, then the idea of femininity must change.[246] But it was difficult to see how it could be changed, since it was naturalized, and since the alternatives proposed – autonomy, equality, etcetera – were rather unattainable in practice, given present social arrangements. So there was an impasse: femininity could not stay the same but it was almost impossible to change.

Does it exist at all? Such a question was too radical to be asked, except perhaps by feminists, and only some of them. But parts of what used to be considered essential femininity were contested by very many women, including many who were quite conservative in other ways. They said that they wanted to "become persons," and they strove for a degree of autonomy even when they did not question other social arrangements.

What was meant by "person" was hardly ever made explicit, because it was taken for granted. It must be read between lines. To be a person seemed to refer first and foremost to individual autonomy: to be able to make your own decisions in everyday matters, not to have to give in to the will of others or to have to manipulate others in order to get what you want. For some it also meant autonomy in a wider sense, to be able to influence not only your own immediate life but factors that influence your life and perhaps those of others. And for very many it also meant psychological strength, will-power, not letting yourself be easily outvoted or persuaded. Concrete examples might be: to decide when and if to have a child, to decide what sorts of sexual pleasure you want, to be able to join an association if you so choose, to be able to choose your friends and activities, (not only in the sense of not being constrained, but also in the sense of having the opportunity to choose, to have something to choose from), to have the means of making up your own mind on social and political issues, to be able to sign contracts in your own name, etc.

To be a person was often, but not always, associated with having a personal income. ("Now that I work, I don't have to ask anyone if I want to buy a gift for my parents.") And some women used the classical phrase of masculine pride, "I don't have to give explanations to anyone," i.e. I go where I want to go, no one can control me and no one has any right to know more about me than what I choose to tell them.

People who do not earn money in their own name would indeed have a harder time to get such a stance accepted by others, by their own family especially. I take that to be an objective fact, and many Spanish women said so. This means that the most feminine type of woman, according to the "traditional" discourse, the housewife, would find it hard to be a "person". For some, a housewife was a non-person almost by definition. For others, a housewife can be a person if only she tries to be a new kind of housewife. If she is assertive, if she has a strong personality, if she does not sacrifice her own wishes constantly, if she strives to free herself from the "ignorance"[247] associated with housewives, then she is "becoming a person" in spite of not earning money of her own. In either case, the opposite of "to be a person" was to try to live up to the old feminine ideal of living for others.

Logically then, if sacrificing yourself was the foremost feminine virtue, then "to be a person" was to move away from femininity. But that was not how it was expressed.

The cautious managers of meaning would still express their "becoming persons" as something done in a feminine style. They would agree with Julián Marías (1990; cf also ch.17 here) that all human beings are either feminine or masculine, that there is no neutral, ungendered version possible. For others, the idea of "becoming a person" was opposed to the idea of femininity, because women used to be defined as the marked gender, while the normal person was masculine. There was a logico-cultural contradiction between "person" and "woman".

Some middle class Madrilenians, usually but not only women and progressive ones, recognized, verbalized and criticized this contradiction. They wanted "person" to be compatible with "woman", they said, and they desired the end of "traditional" separations of "feminine" and "masculine" persons, without necessarily denying the importance of gender. It was not clear whether such thinking might show a way out of the impasse. New social arrangements would be required for testing in practice to become possible. It had become possible for some individuals. They were no longer very few, but they were not yet a sufficient number to make a thorough renegotiation of the whole gender order feasible.

But neither could things stay the same. Since femininity could no longer be easily described, since there was little agreement on what it was or used to be or should become, since women evidently varied among themselves and very few seemed to fit the "traditional" ideal, the idea of femininity no longer served very well as an argument for ascribing women to certain positions or ascribing certain positions to women only. This increased women's possibilities to choose for themselves, thus further undermining ascription.

Since femininity had been very strongly associated with woman-in-the-house, the present situation of change was conceived of as woman-getting-out-of-the-house. The changing femininity and the resulting new roles and goals for women were discussed above all in terms of economic activity, and only to some small degree in terms of other public activities such as politics or cultural associations. If there were more talk of other public activities, women's choices might perhaps be further facilitated, but the emphasis on work cleared part of the general ground, at least, legitimating women's movement out-of-the-house.

The public sphere was emphasized in the critical discourses, the private in the traditionalist ones. This made for facile simplifications on both sides.

In the cautious discourses, the private sphere was mostly talked about in terms of love, motherhood and care, and these were seen as values at risk, something that could be lost, whereas women's autonomy was tacitly written off as impossible.

In the critical discourses, the values of care and family solidarity were more often discussed as obstacles for desired changes. They were not discussed as examples of substantial change (as they were in Benituria). The substance of childcare was changing, since there was objectively less worry about procuring enough food, about protecting against cold and infection, much less heavy manual work such as washing clothes by hand and carrying babies, now that there were washers and strollers. On the other hand there was much more emphasis on psychological tasks like giving affection, creating strong autonomous individuals, etc. and on social tasks like helping with school work. The substance was also changing: fewer risks to health; more choices as to timing and number of pregnancies, fewer children closer together meant less time dedicated to motherhood over a lifetime; but higher ambitions and greater possibilities for the children in a more complex world meant new duties and perhaps more anxiety of a new kind etc. But this was largely culturally invisible.

Perhaps that was so because the importance accorded childcare and motherhood was not changing very much. They were construed as central to a woman's life and happiness, central to family life and central to society in general, and they continued to be key metaphors for femininity. These important values must be guarded, the problem was how to maintain them while changing them so that they won't hinder women from becoming persons, was the common opinion.

Genderization. Femininity is related to genderization, i.e. the cultural weight assigned to the categorization of anything (people, tasks, places, toys, etc.) in terms of gender. Femininity refers to certain characteristics of the category known as women. Genderization refers to the importance given to a person's gender characteristics, whether male or female or whichever they are thought to be. In Spain, there was great genderization of people, both in scope and force. I.e. a person's gender was relevant in most situations, and the fact of genderization was culturally visible and strongly sanctioned. However, women were still, in the 1990s, more genderized than men. Their gender was relevant in more situations than men's. Their gender was seen as the one in need of reconstruction, or as the one necessitating special sanctions in order to safeguard order or naturalness. Conflicts in the gender order were called "women's issues".

This was not to say that differences within the gender categories were denied, on the contrary, they were frequently underlined in the negotiations around gender, albeit with different purposes. Progressives tended to signal other structural categorizations as overriding (especially class and regional "nationalities"). The common progressive position was that gender should not count. Conservatives tended to stress individual idiosyncrasies and psychological causes for them, while strongly naturalizing and ideologically emphasizing gender essence. Similarities across gender lines on the basis of other categorizations, for example class, were also recognized by some, but this was less talked about. For cautious-minded middle class Madrilenians, talk of class was always risky, and their belief in gender essence required gender to be the classification that overrided all others.

The discussions on genderization almost always ended up being discussions about nature versus nurture, or, in the Madrilenian terms, nature versus education. One side argued that genderization (of whatever the discussion was about: labor market, domestic tasks, personality traits...) might well be cultural and changeable, but some important part of that which was genderized was so because it must be, it was not gender but sex, so it was foolish and dangerous to try to change it.

"Nature" in these discussions meant both, "regulating order" (as in "it is natural for women to be more responsive to children's needs") and "not-culture" (as in "women are closer to nature than men"). The term could be used in both these senses in order to justify the subordination of women. However, the latter sense was less often used. The Western tradition of opposing nature to culture was certainly very much alive in Madrid, and women were often seen as closer to nature and men as closer to "culture" (society, civilization, learning, technology...). But the most common type of argument in contexts of gender debate was the other one, the reference to nature as something that regulates things and must be allowed to do so, and consequently anything "unnatural" is bad.

The reference to nature in the sense of regulating order was used to defend status quo. It was used to argue that, even though women are perhaps capable of any kind of social task, it is not convenient for the general good that they choose freely. In such arguments it was "natural" for women to take care of small children and to be sensitive to the needs of others. It was not usually made explicit, but it was always implicit and sometimes verbalized, that men were not naturally capable of such things, and that therefore everyone would suffer if men had to take over caring tasks. So, in the name of justice and equal burdens, men have to do other things, that women should not do, or women will be overworked, and, again, everyone will suffer, because women will not then be able to do well what they have to do no matter what.

This argument of nature was seen by many as inescapable, and indeed even very progressive women found it hard to contest. Conservative women used it about themselves, and they experienced counterarguments as attacks on their innermost self, since they identified their social worth with this special capacity. Some women refused to accept the argument, most tried to contest it while simultaneously subscribing to it in part. That women and men were different by nature, in some sense, was quite doxic in Spain in general.

That this places women at a disadvantage was also generally accepted as true. What it means in terms of what women can do, should do, will want to do, etc. was very much debated. Between "natural difference" and "justice" was a grey area, in which most of the examples used in the debates were located. They were generally accepted as examples of what really happens, "most of the time" (because they were usually about things that almost everyone has personal experience of), but the conclusions to be drawn from them were controversial.

One such example, the most common one in the debates, was the question of a small child who awakens in the middle of the night and cries. It was generally accepted that the mother will hear this long before the father's sleep is disturbed, and it was also generally accepted that even if the father also wakes up, it is the mother who will get out of bed to attend to the child. The conservative position was that this is due to natural gender differences. Women's "maternal instinct" or "greater sensitivity" is what makes the mother wake up first and also what makes it more imperative and more satisfactory for her to act on what she hears. The progressive position was that this was certainly so, in practice, yes, but it was due to education. If boys were socialized to be responsive to the needs of other human beings, men's hearing and capacity to change a diaper would be exactly the same as women's. At this point in the argument, someone defending the conservative position would usually say that certainly boys and girls should all be socialized to develop their intuitions and so forth, and certainly a father can attend to a baby in the absence of a mother, but it is a natural fact that women give birth, therefore it is probably also a natural fact that they have other innate characteristics that make them more suitable to take care of small children, so we must be careful, we must not tamper too much with these things, we must adjust the social organization of labor to nature or else something really bad may happen, will probably happen. From this point on, the progressives could be as ingenious as they pleased, but they would not be able to budge this argument. The answer was always "Yes, that may all be very well, in the name of justice and so on, but we cannot, must not, dare not, tamper with nature."

The status of "nature" in the discourse, then, was very strong and a legitimate reference. But if "nature" determines what genderized individuals can do and want to do, society ought to be organized around ascription. That was far from the case in Spain, especially not for the middle class whose status, values and everyday life depended on the opposite of ascription: achievement.

Achievement or merit was the basis for the social position of the new middle class. Since it was construed as something that arises out of individual competence, it could not be denied to women who proved competent, and since many women did prove competent, the prestige of merit accrued to them in the same way as to men. The logical consequence was to include them in the move away from ascription, so that just as a certain family background or useful connections were no longer thought sufficient grounds for employing or promoting a person, neither could male sex be. Since this logic was not easy to convert into practice, however (unless male resistance disappeared, the labor market was restructured and family life reorganized), arguments had to be found for excepting women, not from the prestige of merit, and not from the recognition of individual capacity, but from the social positions that accrued to men on the basis of such merit. This led to conceptual complications, the issue became socially infected, and the arguments invented increased the internal contradictions of the gender order.

Achievement as a principle for social organization also implies an emphasis on the differentiated individual. For Madrilenians of whatever opinions or mode of management of meaning, there was no doubt that individuals should be idiosyncratic and autonomous. There was even a general opinion that individuality was more important than gender, so that gender characteristics should not be allowed to stand in the foreground. Variation and "strong personality" were positively stressed, and they were equally appreciated for women and men. There was a logical contradiction between this and the idea of gender as given by nature and very decisive in its psychological consequences, but this contradiction seldom seemed to bother Madrilenians. If pressed, people would explain that there was always some part of a person's capacities that was due to education and another part that was due to nature. It is a question of which is which and of proportions.

In everyday spontaneous conversations, achievement was discussed as related to these things: professional merits, formal education, and strong personality. Freedom was seen as the opposite of ascription. Formal gender segregation was therefore not acceptable to anyone.[248] The division of tasks must be legitimized with something else, such as naturalness and voluntary inclinations. Legitimations were certainly found, but the lack of cultural legitimacy for formal gender segregation meant that women's mobility was not easily circumscribed.

Conservatives experienced a contradiction between their belief in merit and their belief in natural gender. They tended to emphasize achievement in other contexts, but when it came to gender, they tended to prefer arguments that ascribed certain tasks according to gender independently of individual variations. The more progressive were quite determined that achievement should be the order of the day. The conflict for them was mainly one between women and men, where women were ready to go all the way and delegitimize all ascription, calling all observable gender characteristics "due to education", whereas men hedged around "motherhood" (including in that most domestic tasks), which at least some of them, even among the most radical, would like to retain as innately specific to women.

Certain themes were not discussed, even though they would seem to be relevant for the negotiations that were going on. I am thinking especially of masculinity and religion.

Manhood, masculinity and men's roles were discussed only by the most radical, and then only from the angle of new roles for men, especially in family life. The roles that had traditionally been assigned to men, such as professional roles and family breadwinner, were discussed as new roles for women, but not as old roles for men. One could imagine possible debates, for instance, about what the old roles had meant in shaping men's personalities, or what the predominance of men at most workplaces had meant for the definition of various professions or for the labor market as a whole or for how men conceptualized their family life. But I heard little if anything along those lines.

Masculinity as such was hardly discussed at all. It was implicitly taken to be what it used to be, the opposite of femininity, and no further reflection was found necessary. Even when men complained that femininity was not what it used to be, they could retain an implicit (and illogical) view of masculinity as the opposite of femininity, yet unchanging. Not even feminists discussed masculinity very much except as resistance to feminist vindications.[249]

Religion was seldom mentioned in gender debate. Variation in belief and practice was simply recognized as an empirical fact. It was not interpreted as very conflictive in personal life, and it was seldom connected to debates on social issues. One could interpret this silence as a sign that the question was too risky to talk about at all. But that can hardly be so in view of the tradition of vociferous anti-clericalism in many quarters and in view of the intense controversies around Church positions not very long ago, for instance on contraception and abortion. But in everyday situations there was a kind of protective shield between personal belief and the Church.

The Catholic Church as an institution was certainly mentioned, especially by the progressive-minded, as the foremost example of resistance to change. But this happened much less than fifteen or even just ten years earlier. The most common themes, if religion was debated, were rather the contradictions people experienced between their former religious feelings and their present perception of what was "true" or "rational". This happened mostly in progressive circles.

In conservative ones, religion was not questioned but not very much emphasized either. Someone might say "we have to go to mass today, because we won't have time tomorrow" in order to excuse themselves for leaving early on a Saturday afternoon, and some people at Club Aguafría seemed to manage to mention going to mass in many different contexts. But these were social uses of the reference to religion, as excuses or for prestige. The contents of Church teachings were seldom mentioned, nor were religious experiences or feelings. They probably were in situations defined as religious, such as catechism, pilgrimages or base community discussions. And an Opus Dei member, like Yolanda (chapter 17) would ground her arguments in both Church teachings and religious feelings. But in the great majority of everyday communicative contexts, religion was conspicuous by being largely absent.

In view of the role religion has played in Spain, and the political and educational role the Church still had, this was quite a surprising finding. And seeing how important gender issues have been for Catholic teachings, it is a finding that is most relevant for the description of the present gender order.

It seems that for the progressive-minded, the Church was mostly an obstacle for change, in the gender order as well as elsewhere in the social edifice, so it was discussed as such. But its importance was receding in the discussions because it was receding in social life. For the conservatively inclined, it was hard to deny this decrease in the protagonism of the Church, but it was a painful fact that one preferred not to remember. It was preferable – and culturally possible – to speak as if one took for granted that everyone was a practicing Catholic, yet not really talk very much about it. As to religious feelings beneath whatever was one's visible practice, they were too intimate to discuss publicly, especially if one was not very sure of what they were.

In other words, the absence of references to Church and religion did not mean that Church and religion did not influence individual opinions. But it did mean that Church and religion did not enter the collective reconstructions of meaning very much. Whatever the feelings of individuals about it, it was a matter that was being marginalized from public debate.

Negotiating power without mentioning it

Most interdisciplinary feminist studies have treated three substantive themes: the division of tasks (work), the issues concerning hierarchy, autonomy, decision-making, resources, etc. (power) and the area of all sorts of emotions, especially sexuality (cathexis) (Connell 1987). The two outstanding topics of the gender debate in middle class Madrid, work and sexuality, corresponded approximately to two of these.

However, the third substantive theme was missing, and it was the one that feminism has especially focused on, that of power. The great feminist question has been: Why have women had less power than men in general, in Western societies? Less power has usually been understood as less personal autonomy, less power of decision over their own bodies, and fewer opportunities to influence social life. Madrilenian feminism asked such questions, of course, but in all other contexts of negotiation about gender, the power theme was largely absent.

It was not passively absent, however. In many situations people tried actively to keep it out of the negotiation. In the group discussions, for example, when I read my list of suggestions for things to talk about, they were well accepted if some participants began by giving examples taken from the areas of work or sexuality, but if someone chanced to say something about power, the atmosphere would become tense.

My interpretation is that what was happening to the middle class gender order in the Madrid was not just a rearrangement of tasks, not just a blossoming of new symbols and meanings, but a substantial realignment of power between women and men. This was the heart of the change, and the most difficult aspect to talk about. Any change of the balance of power between major categories in a society is bound to be painful and controversial, and more so if the categories were conceptualized as complementary and thus supposedly not in any power relationship to each other at all, or in a perfectly balanced one.

I am not saying women were obtaining more power. That could be so, or they might be losing. What is clear is that both gender categories were losing some of their former advantages and gaining some new ones.

The overall situation in 1991 was moving and unstable. That was another thing to make the topic touchy. It is hard to arrive at an opinion when reality is blurred. When the topic did come up in group discussions or spontaneous conversations, and no one managed to distract the attention from it, the discussion would become confrontational and confused (cf. for example chapter 13). Examples would be brought up to show that men have all the power, that women have all the power, that there is complementarity and equity, or that everything is changing in one direction or in the opposite one; the examples were never convincing to anyone holding a different opinion. "Power" was hardly ever defined, but there was much sliding around between different meanings, especially between factual power and legitimate authority and between psychological strength in intimate relationships and social strength in institutionalized relationships, and it was never recognized that much of the confusion was caused by this slippery usage. Few other topics caused the same consternation.

Power was not usually a substantial theme. But that was so because power was the major issue being negotiated through the other themes..

Discourse maps. Themes and arenas together

We have seen that space was genderized for the Madrilenian middle class in the sense that women tended to be at certain places more often than men, and vice versa. Since certain kinds of cultural negotiations were confined to, or mostly found at, certain places, this means that women and men did not have the same probability to enter some of them. In chapter 3, the combination of a description of discourse with a description of genderized space allowed us to catch sight of an important fact in the balance of power between women and men.

We saw that Carlota and María had a measure of choice as to what discourses to participate in; there were also some they could not avoid; and finally there was one, and a very important one, from which they were almost wholly excluded. Men, too, had a measure of choice and men, too, could not avoid some discourses; but very few middle class men were excluded from the discourse of consequential decision-making. Instead they were excluded from some all-female types of discourses. But the two exclusions carried very different weight as to consequences for power.

In middle class Madrid, then, gender organized the social map of discourses, and the distribution of discourses influenced the gender order. Even if it had been true that the cultural category of gender were irrelevant inside the major types of discourses – e.g. if it had been the case that no reference was ever made to gender characteristics in discourses of power, or if nobody ever noticed the gender of the other participants in a conversation – gender would continue to sort who participated in which discourse and therefore also, indirectly, and because gender socialization was different, what the discourses looked like.

That is, the division of labor according to gender distributed individuals differently in relation to various discourses, so that there were more male participants in some and more female participants in others. And vice versa, the social distribution of discourses influenced the gender order. More men than women had access to key discourses and this limited women's opportunities in many ways. They learned less than men about some things. Men learned less than women about other things. So there were misunderstandings. And women learned less about things a person ought to know in order to participate effectively in collective decision-making outside the family. And the collective decision-making as well as certain kinds of crucial cultural negotiation were more influenced by male ideas and habituses than by female ones.

The social distribution of discourses was also one thing that in itself shaped both women's and men's habituses. And because it contributed to making women and men different from each other, it reinforced the cultural construction of gender as natural and strongly dualistic, with clear contrasts between the categories and a clear demarcation line between them. What this amounted to was a feedback loop that reinforced the genderization of space and power even if the people involved were to decide that they did not want this to happen. There were other such loops, and they probably reinforced each other, too.[250]

This chapter is an empirical summary of fieldwork data. The next chapter is also a summary but focusing more on concepts and a wider historical and geographical comparison.

Chapter 21. Summing up: Models

What about the historical context of all the talk about change? What was the gender order "before" like? What is the relationship between the discourse on gender change and material changes? To think about such issues requires concepts and models. Anthropological analysis usually means first an approximation, a coming close, in order to understand, and second a distantiation in order to generalize. In other words, first lots of details, second abstractions to obtain theoretical understanding.

Spanish modern

Modernization can be many things, but when speaking of Europe one thinks usually of the following processes: the emergence of capitalism, industrialization, urbanization, secularization, the demographic revolution, the Enlightenment ideas about human rationality and the move from status based on ascription towards status based on achievement.

All of these are related. Focusing on them in different order or with different emphasis, one can tell different stories about each one and about their connections to each other. They have also occurred in different order and at different speed in different parts of Europe. But they were all about search for new knowledge, new ways of thinking, and new material power.

Obviously modernization in Spain did not begin in 1975. It was a long process, there as elsewhere. And in spite of the somewhat peculiar history of Spain, the general outlines of the process have been similar to the rest of Europe. What has been specific to Spain is that it has been a weak, hesitant, stop-go process, with an unstable material basis. But during the 1970s it consolidated. Small village living, illiteracy, subsistence economy and pre-modern technology ceased to be the reality of all but a small portion of the population. In a short period of time most of the processes usually associated with modernization in a capitalist state accelerated and spread their effects: secularization, decreased power based on descent, inheritance and land holding, increased power of movable capital, growth of a new middle class, a move from status and ascription toward merit and achievement as basic principles for the organization of socially necessary labor, urbanization, greater social and geographic movement, and so on.

These material changes logically caused a cultural modernization, too. Large areas of doxa moved into the universe of discourse and came under the light of debate. Words were applied to what had been wordless areas of life. This had happened much earlier, centuries earlier, to small privileged sectors of the population. Now it happened to everyone. The fact that such an important experience crossed class barriers also affected the interpretations of those barriers, on both sides of them.[251]

In such a conjuncture of history, some people react with enthusiasm for the new vistas opening up. An equally logical reaction is fear and ambivalence.

All Spaniards have had to reinterpret their place in society, in the world, in relationship to others and to their own selves. Around 1990 the process was in a phase of cultural liminality and therefore of cultural creativity. But nothing new is completely new. There is no zero point in social life. Nor do old things totally determine the new things. There is a dialectical continuity. This was reflected in all the conversations reported here. In one sense, much of the discussion was about which things were old, "traditional", and what criteria to use, old or new ones, to evaluate new phenomena. The one thing around which there was consensus was the fact of change. To a lesser but still large extent, there was also consensus that change in the sense of modernization had been good.

And there was consensus that the gender order (usually called "the roles" or "women's situation") was one of the things that had changed most profoundly, even though those who evaluated this as negative tended to deemphasize the change as well as consider it temporary, and even though those who wanted the most radical changes tended to think that what had happened was far from sufficient. There was nevertheless wide agreement that the changes had been in the direction of more "equality". Whatever opinon one had about the desirability of that.

"Change" as a topic

Change was constantly discussed in Madrid, as we have seen. But it was usually seen as something produced automatically by time. Causes for specific changes were seldom mentioned. Causes for resistance to change were lamented by the progressive-minded (especially religion and lack of education, sometimes seen as related). The tradition-minded could discuss pros and cons of change, but this was risky; they might be labeled as "not up-to-date" even by their like-minded. The progressives tended to suspect that any discussion of pros and cons was an effort to legitimize the rolling back of change. And "back" for them meant back to social hierarchy and rigidity, limits to cultural creativity and probably slippage towards dictatorship. A popular theme was instead that of how "evolved" or not someone was. But it was not as popular as it was in the working class in Valencia a few years earlier. The significant labeling now was not so much about how far and how fast people had managed to "evolve" as about what more or less stable positions they had arrived at.

Because causes for specific changes were not much discussed, and because change had come to be seen as one big amorphous automatism, it was both easy and difficult to use general social change as an argument for change in the gender order. It was easy in that the ubiquity of change made naturalization of gender conditions ("the roles") less plausible. One could legitimate further changes in the general direction of progressive values with reference to what had already happened, arguing that it was all one big process that could not be interrupted. It was difficult in that the counter-argument became: If all the changes we have seen have not changed the gender order more than what is the case, it must be because the gender order cannot be changed. It is natural, it must stay as it is. Or rather as it was. The actual changes in it are unnatural side effects of other changes and will disappear once things calm down.

How to influence change actively in desired directions was hardly ever discussed except by politically active people.

The emphasis on change in the gender order produced stereotyped ideas of what it used to be like. This was talked about. The stereotypes of the past were generally accepted as true. We have seen that they painted a picture of family togetherness (whether as "harmony" or as "repression"), womanhood as motherhood, femininity as seductiveness or submissiveness, etc. The main attitudes to these "old things" were three. To some, they were old-fashioned and therefore irrelevant, so one need pay no attention to them. To others, they were old-fashioned but dangerous, because they threatened society with back-sliding, so one must be on guard against them, struggle against them. To others again, they were the only natural ways, the only ones with divine sanction, the only ones that made people happy, and now they were being undermined, so one must defend them.

Faust or Gretchen or what-else-is-there

For Spanish men, the process of modernization opened up exciting new possibilities to act. They were individuated in a new way. There was a sort of Renaissance and a sort of Enlightenment at the same time as economic development offered new material opportunities to act on such emancipatory ideas. No wonder there had been an explosion of creativity in all areas of life. (Cf for instance chapter 4 on the Madrilenian commotion.)

But individuation is dangerous, as the drama of Faust shows. According to feminist re-readings of Faust, modern men needed the gender polarization, which was historically reinforced during the modernization process.[252] Without it, the process of modernization would have been too cruel and modern human beings too homeless. When a person moves out from the home, away from the security of kin solidarity and from the certainty of religion, it is great help to have someone stay behind, keeping the hearth warm.

Whatever we may think of this analysis as history, it was exactly what most Madrilenian men said. They defended gender polarization with desperation, even sometimes against the grain of their own convictions, and to the price of denigrating their own gender.[253] They thought they could not give in to women's demand for equality. They experienced such demands as selfish and foolish and unreasonable, because if women got what they wanted, everyone would be unhappy. They seemed to really, honestly believe this. They also felt some guilt and therefore great discomfort with the whole issue.

Almost all of my female informants had close, warm and duty-laden relationships, and they did not want to lose them. Therefore, it was difficult and dangerous for them to face the requirements of the new times. They could not be totally individuated.

The ladies of Club Aguafría argued for their female role with reference to the need for counterbalancing the ruthlessness of the male world. If women do not accept responsibility for caring for people, everyone will suffer, they said. Their daughters argued for their right to participate in the project of modernity as individuals. Their arguments were based to some extent on such ideas as equality between women and men or having the knowledge and the will to act, but also on the value relativism of postmodernism, clothing it in a discourse that fit well with their class values of competition and pleasure. "I too want to earn money. Why not when everyone else does!" "One never knows these days, anything can happen, I have to defend myself." "I, too, want to be able to go out for a drink with my friends and have fun." But, contradictorily, they combined this with reassurances about their female sense of responsibility. "Now, naturally, if I have to choose between the family and the profession, I choose the family. The most wonderful thing in life is to have children, and if you have children, you have to take care of them."

They refused to recognize the dilemma, because they wanted to be both Gretchen and Faust. They did not want to think that these two roles excluded each other.

Nor did the younger women at Club Aguafría seem to feel any need to challenge existing norms, even though they did not reproduce the life-style of their mothers. They invented new "traditions", especially in the form of social darwinist legitimations of a privileged life in the upper middle class, and they tried to combine them with old ideas into an ideological cocktail acceptable to the conservative sectors of that class. Their role model was perhaps neither Gretchen nor Faust, nor the obedient virginal Mary nor the rebellious artist Madonna. It was rather something like Margaret Thatcher. They had an image of the successful woman as one who knows how to compete with men, in the male world, on the same conditions as men, without asking for "special privileges" (like quotas or time off for child care), someone who can be as tough as the guys but still believe in conservative values. They also defended their right to be seductive and they appreciated flirtatious men. They saw that as proof that it really was possible to combine the best of both worlds.

They were emphatically not feminists. But they used the advantages that feminism has gained for women. Many young Madrilenian middle class women were extremely unaware of women's history. Some of them did not know, for example, that when they themselves were born, their mothers did not yet have the right to sign a contract without their husbands' permission. Those who did know did not reflect much about it. They now

309

lived in a state where gender equality was guaranteed by the Constitution, that they did know, and that seemed to be enough for them. They did not voice much worry about the extent to which the Constitution was carried out in practice.

Outside Club Aguafría, many young Madrilenian women did feel the burden of a forced choice. They had to choose between being Gretchen-like women like their mothers (i.e. sacrifice their life projects in order to support other people), or pseudo-Fausts (individuals with capacity and will-power in spite of being women). The choice was an impossible one in the terms it was presented since they made "woman" and "person" incompatible. However, the experience of fast and deep change had made practical circumstances seem alterable. Such women would therefore fight for women's right to participate, and through this struggle they were altering the definitions of the terms. "A real woman" was no longer synonymous with "a good mother", for instance, and the word "sacrifice" had gone completely out of style.

In a sense modern womanhood in Madrid was an out-of-phase modern manhood. Like the men, women were being individuated, they stepped out of the family, away from ascribed permanent roles, and became victims of feelings of guilt, fear and self-doubt and the ambivalent longing for an idealized past. But also filled with pride and excitement and perhaps an exaggerated appreciation of individual strength and autonomy. The phrase "women must become persons" was the everyday expression for the process of individuation for women in Spain, while the ambivalence found expression in a longing for "values" and a projection of "feminism" as the cause of present difficulties.

European women's modernization cannot be the same as men's because it occurs at a different historical moment, circumstances are different, and the fact that they have been observers of men's modernity for a couple of centuries influences their own interpretations.

Even if it were true (and it was not) that women and men lived under similar formal conditions, these conditions would not translate into the same practical circumstances. Social arrangements cannot mean the same when one enters them from different directions and carrying different kinds of luggages. In Madrid, this was culturally visible even when not clearly conceptualized.

So, what is "tradition"?

The defense of old things was very often expressed as adherence to "tradition". Now, tradition can be many things. The women of Club Aguafría, for example, saw themselves, and were seen by others as, traditional. They were in the following senses:

- they wanted to be good wives and mothers above all (even if they had a job outside the home);

- they saw marriage as a career and as a lifelong holy duty (and it must be life-long or it is not a secure enough material base; they feared divorce and widowhood and for good reasons)

- they saw their husbands' interests as their own and refused to contemplate the possibility that there might be different interests inside a family.

Many other ideas on gender could be called traditional, because they were equally old. The Club Aguafría ideas were traditional in the sense that they were not new but also in the sense that they were called traditional during the Franco regime, and they were so hegemonic then that anything that opposed them was seen as new or idiosyncratic, i.e. not traditional.

Using that definition of the word, however, the Club Aguafría women were not traditional in the following senses:

- they found, like their husbands, consumption more important than saving;
- they accepted (in practice if not in discourse) the intense night life of youth;
- they considered their daughters' professional ambitions legitimate;
- they emphasized the couple relationship as the most important aspect of the family (even though they also emphasized their relationship to the children);
- they did not usually live near their parents or other relatives, so they took little part in the sociability and daily exchange of practical help between related women that has been so important for Spanish women of all classes.

All Madrilenians talked about "old mentality", "traditional families" and so on. But such an old entity did not correspond to reality. It was an entity in discourse, a label for what was perceived as "not-new". There was agreement on its major characteristics in comparison to present circumstances (less freedom of movement for women, more control of sexuality, stronger stress on family solidarity, etc.), but agreement was far from total around the substantial expressions of these characteristics, and they could usually not be specified in time and place.

It was a mistake to believe that everything called old was old or everything called new was new. But it would be an even worse mistake to believe that such labeling in discourse was meaningless. The map was being redesigned, the cultural negotiations moved old and new features around and painted them in varied colors.

My suggestion is that the discourse entity usually called "old roles" or "traditional women" referred to a set of features of a gender order that may never have existed in its pure form anywhere but which is recognizable across time and space as a specific kind. It is an ideal type, and its features can be found around the Mediterranean area now and in the past, in different versions and combinations but recognizably different from what was now happening in Spain. Therefore any instantiation of these features was felt to be "old", whether or not it was. Anything that looked opposed to these features was seen as "new", whether or not it was.

I would say that the Mediterranean gender order, at this level of abstraction, has the following four fundamental features:[254]

a) Gender is a central organizing principle, on which many other features of social organization are made to depend. I.e. the gender order has great scope, reaches into most corners of social life. (Gender is an organizing principle of social life everywhere, but it can organize many or few things. In the Mediterranean area, it usually organizes many.)

b) Two genders are recognized, women and men, and they are conceived to be mutually exclusive and strongly contrasted. I.e. the gender order is strongly dualistic, and the dualism is symbolized in many ways. (More than two genders can be recognized. And where there are only two, they can be seen as more or less similar.)

c) The two genders are placed in a hierarchy, in which women are sometimes conceived to be superior in some limited ways, sometimes not, but men are considered superior in overall capacity and trustworthiness, and therefore accorded all legitimate authority.[255] I.e. the gender order is asymmetrical in symbolic power; this usually leads to asymmetry in economic and social resources as well.[256]

d) The things that are organized by gender (distribution of tasks, resources, etc. and the symbols around it all) are strongly sanctioned. Breaking norms often has dire consequences, and in case of impracticability (for example, if the only woman in a family is ill, there is impracticability around all women's duties in that home independently of the number and health of male family members), one searches far and wide for other ways of getting "women's chores" done (bringing grandmother, asking women in the neighborhood, buying ready-made food...) before doing anything that blurs the gender dualism. I.e. the gender order has great force. (This is not universal. In many of the societies anthropologists have described, the gender order can be situationally adapted without much ado and the attitude towards the sanctions is practical and flexible.)[257]

Furthermore, sexuality is used as the central metaphor for this whole order. Since gender is used as a metaphor for many other things, so is sexuality. Since gender organizes many things, sexuality is seen as relevant for many things. Wherever gender is, sexuality is. Gender and sexuality are even conceptually confused with each other, so that a man washing dishes becomes suspect of impotence, a man with long hair of homosexuality, and a woman working as a taxi driver of profligacy. And changes in the gender order are feared because they are seen as putting biological reproduction at risk and placing pleasure under siege.[258]

This is so because gender, sexuality, the separation of private and public spheres and the division of tasks have all been intimately connected. Greatly simplified, the thinking goes like this: The home is the sanctuary of innocence and shame, and the street is where exciting and dangerous things can happen. Sexuality is the foremost example of excitement. And since the home is for women and the street is for men, sexuality is for men only. Men have sexuality, they can act on it. Depending on time and place, women can be considered to have very much sexuality, too, and therefore have to be enclosed in order not to disrupt social order, or they can be considered to have very little of it and therefore easily accept not getting very much and getting only what their husbands give them. But in either case men are the ones who are free to act, search, learn, explore, wish for pleasure and demand satisfactions. Women are not supposed to do any of that, whether they are supposed to be pining away for it or be happier without it. Women represent sexuality for men, but only men can do something with their sexuality. This is symbolized in the importance given to the penis.[259] Women are in the home, with the children, and men are in the street, with the penis.

With such thinking, it becomes difficult, indeed, to see sexuality as pure pleasure. It becomes too important. It is what one desires most and also the most dangerous thing. The result is that it must be surrounded with strong norms, but that those norms will inevitably be broken. The whole set of connected ideas can be seen as a dangerous game. One way to defuse it is to blame the participants seen as powerless – women.[260] Women always do wrong, but by prohibiting the access of women to essential spaces, that wrong is enclosed, prevented from having wide repercussions. Another way, which also fits well with that other constellation of ideas that sees mind and body as separate, is to blame not the women themselves but their bodies. Female bodies are seen as the locus of sexuality. They are therefore very attractive and very dangerous. They must be hidden, preferably even from the women themselves (enclosed, carefully clothed, limited in movements, etc.). In either case, the dualism is reinforced.[261]

Thus it becomes logical for Mediterranean feminists to fight just as much or more for sexual liberation ("conquer the night" as one Spanish slogan has it, read pornography, criticize Church morals, have lovers, dress sexily, explore their own bodies, and so on) as for economic autonomy.

Looked at from this high level of generalization, the Mediterranean gender order is a set of features that reinforce each other so that the whole edifice becomes very stable. It has in fact resisted commerce and wars with people with different ideas, changing demographic circumstances, changing subsistence bases, technical inventions, modes of production and forms of government. Always, of course, adapting and changing its details. But the main features are recognizable throughout most of the area through centuries.

This is not to say that it is unchangeable, nor of course that it is caused by any mysterious Mediterranean essence. It is a historical product, as such it is variable in time and space, and even the fundamental features are liable to change at some point in time. Perhaps that point in time in Spain arrived in the late 20th century. Circumstances were certainly new in a new way.

The things that were called "progressive" or "new" or "modern" in relation to gender issues in Madrid around 1990, were, as a matter of fact, always things that contradicted this model. In that sense the model serves as a picture of what one was moving away from, and also as a reminder of what one was up against if one wanted to change it actively.

The model also serves to explain why the emphases in the discourses on gender and change fall where they do. Many of them point to the contradictions that have usually been produced in Mediterranean gender orders, especially that old staple of Mediterranean anthropology, conflicts around how to define the family: marriage, relationships between in-laws and inheritance. In urban Spain at the time of this study, it focused on the functions of the family (security or personal satisfaction) and its inner frontiers (individual autonomy versus family solidarity).

There are clear contrasts between the features of the Mediterranean model and the requirements of modernization. Faust will not be confined to an ascribed role, even less to an inferior one in a predetermined hierarchy. Whether man or woman, Faust wants to try different tasks and question rigid categorizations and sanctions.

Most of the old-new contradictions were summed up in the conceptual opposition between "woman" and "person" in the Madrilenian discourses.

Expressed by me now, in words that I never heard in Madrid, but in a way that I think explicates the implicit subtext of phrases like "women must become persons": A "woman" is a functional part of a family first, individual second, while for a "person" it is the other way around. A "woman" is complementary to a "man", and the question of hierarchy is doxic, whereas a "person" accepts complementarity only if hierarchy is guaranteed not to follow, and even then only as a matter of "choice", not as ascription on the basis of naturalized characteristics. A "person" is active, can achieve things, and refuses to be categorized by others. A "woman" must look and behave so that her gender and her sexuality are always clearly contrasted to those of a "man", whereas a "person" is a collection of characteristics of many kinds, chosen, achieved, ascribed or innate, of which none should be selected at the expense of others in order to ascribe her permanently to any social category. A "woman" is one comprehensive role, a "person" is an individual who can have many roles in shifting combinations. A "woman" is like all other women in some basic way, never mind real variations, whereas a "person" is differentiated, never mind real similarities. A "woman" is first of all a gendered human being, a "person" can be gendered or not, depending on the situation.

Faust is a symbol of individuation. In the Madrilenian middle class, women were struggling for individuation. Or against it. They could no longer just stay inside given roles.

A "person" was not the same as a "man", since it was said that women should become persons. But, as it was usually expressed, women too should become persons. Men already were, was the idea. For some this was an uncomfortable implication. Both conservatives and feminists sometimes felt that "personhood" was too similar to "manhood" to be desirable for women. But for most, the opposition between "woman" and "person" was something to be transcended. It may be an absolute opposition on the conceptual level, but the feeling was that real women do not have to become "men" in order to stop being "women". And this was expressed with the aid of that third term, "person".[262]

In this light it becomes possible to understand why everyone I met during fieldwork, from Yolanda to the feminists, from Club Aguafría housewives to the Nosotros progressives, insisted that women must become persons. What substantial changes they visualized varied greatly. But the idiom of personhood served all their different discourses, because it pointed to the key experience of modernization (individuation as a result of social change and complexification) and the problems that experience poses for the basic features of a Mediterranean-type gender order.

A re-negotiated model of the gender order

If we look at the cultural negotiations in middle class Madrid from the angle of the four fundamental features of old Mediterranean gender orders, it was the one of hierarchy and power that was really being renegotiated, even though this was seldom verbalized. The issue of scope was being debated; there was agreement that the scope should be diminished, i.e. that fewer things should be organized by gender. But exactly where the reach should be curtailed and in which way were issues for continued debate.

All of this affected the fundamental feature, that of force. How important is gender, how terrible is it when gender norms are broken, what should the sanctions be, how can it all be symbolized? These questions lay slightly beyond the reach of the universe of discourse, but they were connected to sexuality, which lay within, so they were discussed in terms of sexuality. There was consensus that gender was important, and this was often expressed with references to the goodness of heterosexuality, and the logical implication was that sanctions should be strong. But faced with examples of strong sanctions, people of all persuasions drew back and referred instead to individual freedom to do what one wants with one's life. This was probably because even if there was consensus that gender was important, there was no consensus on how. The complexification of social life had produced too much variation. Faced with concrete examples, therefore, it was difficult to have any definite opinion, and conflicting legitimations were referred to, especially "family values" versus "being a person".

The dualism of the gender order and the desirability of strong symbolic contrasts between the categories, was not much debated. The symbols were changing, and this was often experienced as loss of contrast. Some men now had long hair or wore ear-rings, for example, and this was as uncomfortable for the tradition-minded as women's wearing slacks was twenty years earlier, and the progressives tended to use such examples to argue that the symbolization of gender contrast was diminishing. But most women and almost all men still dressed in a way that underlined the contrast.[263] Men took up symbolic room in a way that underlined masculinity as dominance: louder voices, taking of initiatives in mixed groups, speaking for their wives in debates and with waiters, etc. Ambiguous symbols caused remarks about "I want to be able to see which kind it is", and even debates on non-symbolic gender issues occasioned jokes about how "in springtime you know which kind you are" as if any questioning of the present symbolization of the gender categories were a questioning of all dualist sexuality. As a whole, the dualism was upheld with both old and new symbols, even though simultaneously some of the old symbols were defined as symbols of something else, e.g. progressivity, and others were about to go out of fashion altogether.

The emerging middle class Madrilenian gender order, then, was taking on the following features, in comparison with the Mediterranean model:

The hierarchy was de-legitimized, but all substantial opinions on it were strongly contested, there was no consensus. This was so sensitive an issue that it was seldom debated head-on. Instead it was confused with the other features or debated by means of them.

The dualism was debated in terms of sexuality. The symbols of gender contrasts and dualism were widely accepted and seen as safeguards of heterosexuality. Individuals who played with these symbols were few and considered very radical; at the same time, their existence was often mentioned as "proof" that gender symbols were no longer firm. Radical experiments sometimes moved into the area of accepted symbolizations after a while.

There was confusion around hierarchy and dualism. An undermining of strong dualism was seen as an automatic undermining of hierarchy, also, by both opponents and proponents, but this was not clearly verbalized. A negotiation around the relationship between hierarchy and dualism lay as yet outside the universe of discourse.

So did the issue of the force of the gender order. The force was seen as strong in an inevitable, natural, given way. And connected to the force of sexuality. Even the most energetic critics of the present order, the feminists, took for granted that the gender order was a very important social structure, a central part of individual experience and something that must perforce awaken emotional storms if threatened or modified.

The scope was, however, debated. The key themes here were two: "work/woman-out-of-the-house/achievement" and "sexuality/femininity". A common position was that women were as capable as men (achievement), therefore they can work and should work in order to be persons. This undermines the old formula women:private::men:public. All movement of one gender into social spaces formerly defined as pertaining to the opposite gender decreases scope. Since the new forms of sexuality proposed require freedom of movement, and freedom of choice, they too imply decreased scope. Many social and physical spaces were in fact being degenderized.[264]

But, the proponents of less scope would insist, this would not cause the threat to heterosexuality that some people feared. Nor would it make life harsh, leaving children, old and ill persons without care. Women can do new things, and their old tasks will still get done. The only condition is that men take on their share of them. Translated into my terms, the argument was: gender should continue to organize some things, especially heterosexuality and probably personalities. But it should not organize the division of tasks nor public space; and the most basic division of all, public-private, should not be parallel to male-female. If the scope of gender is curtailed in the public sphere, it must be curtailed in the private sphere, too. For instance, both men and women should cook, both should have knowledge and control of family economy, etc.

For conservatives, this proposition was truly dangerous, threatening both social stability and cultural security, so it must be opposed, but it was very difficult to oppose, since it was legitimized with freedom of choice and movement, "justice" and "equality". Thus the constant self-contradictory disclaimers, like, "one must keep up to date, and I am no nostalgic, but..." and on the other hand, "I am no feminist, but..." And we get the constant references to the one really stable referent of the opposite kind, nature. And we get the small and localized but emotionally explosive defensive stands like the Club Aguafría debate on women's work. Scope was where the real conflict was clearly played out.

The cautious-minded <u>resistance</u> to the general trends of change in the gender order can also be summed up with the help of the features of the model. The conservative discourse leaned on the following points.:

Since the gender hierarchy was being undermined, there was <u>stress on hierarchy</u>. It was difficult in the 1990s to argue that hierarchy is a natural feature of social life (as was common to argue during the Franco regime), and it was even more difficult to argue for a gender hierarchy based on ascription of gender roles, since ascription was not quite legitimate even for the most conservative. But achievement was very legitimate and culturally stressed. So one could argue for hierarchy on that basis. One would then reach the conclusion that if there are few women in top positions, or in the labor market as a whole, it is because they are not able to do these jobs as well as men. They are good at other things, like caring for the family, one can admit, but they are not as good as men at things like making decisions or treating people in an impersonal way. The hierarchy will then be seen as produced by innate characteristics, not discrimination, and therefore legitimate.[265]

The <u>dualism</u> was not very contested. But there was some resistance due to a feeling that it was being attacked even when it was not, since for the conservatives hierarchy followed almost inevitably from the dualism. There was also a general feeling of disgust at the play with some symbols of dualism (men with earrings, etc.) and at what was seen as sexual "frivolity". And the two overlapped. So there was careful management of all gender symbols, especially the body-related ones: dress and undress, movement, appearance. For instance, the Club Aguafría dress rules and rules about how to move between the different areas of the club, or the careful dressing both there and elsewhere, and in the extreme case the Opus Dei emphasis on hiding the body.

Since nobody really contested the <u>force</u> of the gender system, there was no need for resistance on this point.

There was strong stress among conservatives on the <u>safeguarding of scope</u>. This was culturally complicated, however, for the same reasons as the defense of hierarchy. Conservatives defended gender marked territories (bar life, kitchens, labor market...). Gender segregation occurred in social interaction, even though most situations were mixed. Such things happened as if by chance and were defended as such. They were difficult to defend as things to be consciously striven for in this discourse, since they were supposed to be produced by nature. But the housewife role was strongly defended with all sorts of arguments. And the near-doxic idea of nature as an ultimate referent and as a ruling principle made the defense of gender essences legitimate. With reference to nature, even the not-so-conservative who felt they must make a last-line-stand on some gender issues (for instance progressive men) could argue that some things were impossible or dangerous to degenderize.

Because of the centrality of sexuality in the Mediterranean gender model, the struggle to change it was largely couched in sexual terms (freedom of movement, the body as pleasure, etc.). And due to this, the defense of status quo also centered on sexuality. But since sexuality was an absent presence in the conservative discourses, the defensive stance took on self-contradictory features. Sometimes the emotions found outlets in aggressive sexual joking. The most pervasive result was avoidance of the subject, "tabooing", even while discussing such inevitable and related topics as divorce, abortion or modern films, but the avoidance became very strained around such also inevitable topics as sexual education or contraceptives.

Many features of Madrilenian social life reinforced the changes in the gender order in a direction away from the Mediterranean model.[266] But other factors, and very strong ones, shored it up. They were so strong in fact, that even though they were openly defended only by a minority, an uneasy impasse around gender issues remained prominent in daily social life.

Individuation at a fast pace

The purpose of this study, when I started out, was mainly descriptive. A good detailed description is valuable in itself, ethnography is always knowledge. Another piece of human possibilities made known.

The context of fieldwork was middle class Madrid; the wider context was 20th century industrial and capitalist Europe, and the historical background was a Mediterranean economy based on wheat, olives and sheep and centuries of authoritarian government. Around 1990 Spain stood at a crossroads that was especially noticeable in a centrally situated and lively class context like middle class Madrid. The cultural habits of the population continued placing gender relationships, especially sexuality, center stage as symbols of change and danger, safety and and security, pleasure and chaos. And it was all talked about in the general Mediterranean style: social encounters, loud voices, much emotion, but also creative verbalisation of unclear new phenomena. And much reflection.

So I wrote a description. But I found that as my work proceeded, an image emerged of the relationship between the historical moment and the need for cultural change. People talked about their interpretations of what had happened in their personal lives and in the general surroundings in their lifetime. The image was one of collective cultural tension and struggle inside the individuals. They had lived through dramatic times of Spanish history, the final years of a dictatorship that did not give up peacefully; yet violence was more or less contained and material changes supported the change.[267] These collective experiences had left an imprint on individual thinking. And on what was talked about and how it was evaluated.

In other words, an ethnographic study of discourse can reveal dynamics of change along with resistance and inertia.

This is a feminist study and there can be no doubt about my own opinions. I hope for a not too slow process of change in the gender order in the direction of equality and justice. I believe firmly that no society can be good to live in for any of its citizens as long as certain categories are hindered from developing their human potential.

But it is an ethnograhic study. Not a political treaty. I propose no solution nor do I predict anything about the future; I just report on what was happening at a given time and place. I have offered information on ongoing sociocultural processes that constitute a point of departure for further debate about where we (however defined) want to move and how that might come about.

Chapter 22. Women, Men and Persons

So, what is the grand sum of it all?

The Madrilenian situation was emically defined as one of great change in which it took courage and effort to live. It was not as exacting as it had been a few years earlier; things were settling down, people thought, but it was still evident that not everyone had the courage and strength required. Some people were caught in "reactionary ideologies", never managed to "free" themselves from "old mentalities", or, expressed according to the opposite pole of the continuum of opinions, let themselves be "manipulated" or "fooled" by transient new things without value, perhaps even dangerous. When it came to describing oneself, most people said they were "trying to learn" or had "come a long way", and they contrasted themselves both to their parents and to their children. "Nothing in our life can teach our children anything, it is just not relevant for them."

Gender was seen as a fundamental factor in the general situation of change. So it was important for everybody to have opinions on all gender-related issues.

A gender order can be seen as a complex provisional result of all social and cultural processes that in any way affect women and men (and possible other genders) in different ways. It can also be seen as an entity which influences those other processes. It can be summed up in various ways. The grand sums that used to be labeled as "male domination" or "oppression of women" were rather crude. Even if it is true that such a grand sum would show, in most societies, that men have more privileges than women or that women suffer more injustices (emically or etically defined), and even if this is a tremendous social fact, it is also true that such grand sums do not help us understand why it is so. Simplifications blind us to crucial dynamic aspects of the gender orders, such as contradictions.

What feminist anthropology can do is to describe the intricacies of different gender orders. It can detail complex configurations of tensions, conflicts and contradictions, and it can show how a certain apparent grand sum does not necessarily coincide with the ongoing processes of reproduction of the gender order. What is seen, what is and what is becoming are three different things.

A strategic study object within this general field is social and cultural reproduction, usually imperfect, i.e. the processes of change. This is especially so in historical contexts where other crucial things change and one can therefore presume that the gender order must also change.

One must usually narrow down that study object even further. At least this is true if we want to include big cities in our science. And since big cities constitute an increasingly common human habitat, we must study them if our long term goal is to understand human society in general. In this book, the object of study has been the verbal negotiations around a changing urban gender order.

The Madrilenian middle class had to redefine gender for itself. The basically complementary structure of the division of responsibilities and the correspondingly dual cultural construction of the gender order as being about two well-delineated, symbolically opposed categories of human beings with very different personalities no longer fit the social or economic circumstances. They also entered into contradiction with the culturally emphasized ideas of equality, justice and freedom and with the principle of achievement as a basis for social status.

The feminist questions to such a situation are: Do women win or lose in this process? Do they consciously try to defend old privileges, or do they consciously try to adapt to the new opportunities, or do they try to do both? Or are they not conscious of change at all? How do men react to the situation in general and to what the women do? What are the real opportunities for women, what can they gain? And where are the risks?

The anthropological questions to such a situation are: How is the situation emically defined? What processes of change are culturally visible? Are there important things going on that people do not seem to be aware of or do not find important? How do different processes of change influence each other? How can the gender order be described?

The ambition of this study has been to offer an anthropological description with data that are needed in order to answer the feminist questions.

In Madrid, the changes in the gender order that were seen to need renegotiation were related to sexuality and work. Legislation and economic structures had changed in such ways that marriages were no longer guaranteed to last a lifetime. Ideas about sexuality and the individual in relation to society made this look either like a great loss of security and "values", a loss that must be combated at all costs, or else like a great gain in knowledge and freedom that must be defended and adapted to. In other words, sexuality could be about pleasure, not just about biological reproduction, and that meant that a lot of other things had to change, such as the conception of the body, the authority of the Catholic Church, and the definition of marriage. If this meant that "the family" could no longer function as the basic context for economic security, but was rather an arrangement for personal satisfaction, then other means for collective security would have to be constructed, and within the family, room must be made for individual goals and daily activities that point to those goals. To the extent that women used to see their activities as a sacrificing of themselves on the altar of family happiness, then at least they, too, obtained some share of the resulting happiness and security. Now there was no guarantee for that. Now the sacrifice was greater. So, for some, the legitimation must be stronger, while others concluded that such a sacrifice must not be practiced. So the ideological polarization increased.

Behind the negotiations around sexuality and work were negotiations around the old European dilemma of the individual versus greater collectivities, such as family or state, and the issue of the legitimacy of the search for individual satisfaction. Is Faust to be let loose or not? In the emic Madrilenian terms: What is a person? Can women be persons, too?

For women to be "persons" as implicitly defined, the scope of genderization would have to decrease a lot more than it had and its force probably must as well. The dualism of the gender order, which was not much questioned directly, would have to be made less stringent.

Above all, the issue of power must be faced. The concept of "person" foregrounded autonomy. Gender hierarchy thus became an obstacle. It was already delegitimized in discourse if not in practice. If men or women wanted to retain their old advantages, new means must be found. If women wanted to contest men's advantages, this was a good opportunity. In any case, the gender order must be related to other hierarchies and their legitimations in some sort of workable arrangement.

But the processes were complex enough to defy conscious manipulation. The changes in love relationships, in the access to individual incomes, in the composition of political bodies, and so on, would have manifold and contradictory effects, and the outcome would be new power relationships. The grand sum of them all might continue to be hierarchical or might become less hierarchical or even perhaps something approaching egalitarian, and that is important in itself, certainly. But more than the grand sum, what is interesting to describe is the complex nature of the processes that made reproduction of the gender order far from automatic.

Pros and cons

In the Madrilenian middle class situation in the early 1990s there were a number of factors around discourse that facilitated increased autonomy for women and changes in the gender order in the direction of fewer gender-specific constraints. There were also factors that worked in the opposite directions.

Let us sum up these factors, calling them for simplicity's sake possibilities and obstacles (from a feminist point of view). But it is not possible to separate them into two neat lists. Most factors that have been illuminated in this study can be seen to have two faces: they open up for new possibilities and simultaneously constrain the processes of change in the gender order.

– The cultural emphasis on talk as entertainment, and the generally good access to situations where talking was done, where talking was often even the main activity, furthered cultural change. In any direction, obviously. (In a less complex social environment it might just have reinforced things as they were.)

– This was even more so, since talk often took the form of debate. This had to do with the cultural construction of a good time as something that includes a lot of animated talk about things that arouse passion, and the cultural tolerance for differences of opinion and minimal need to work for consensus and harmony in conversation (cf Appendix C, and Fant 1989). This in itself made for complexification of ideas, and it facilitated and legitimated cultural negotiation. It was therefore a factor that created change, in itself, and that made it difficult to maintain "taboos", i.e. areas or topics exempted from negotiation.

– But in spite of the love of talk and debate, not everyone found it legitimate to talk about everything. Certain topics were "taboo" in certain circles, and whatever was considered related to tabooed topics was never easily treated and analyzed, so such ideas tended to be reproduced without much change, except in so far as change was forced by other events in society, but clashes often tended to make precisely these topics even more sensitive. The fact that tabooing itself was not very legitimate in Madrid made people who felt a need for certain taboos act in defensive ways, further protecting their ideas from inspection. One strategy was to surround oneself with like-minded.

– The fact of fast and deep social change and the corresponding need for cultural work, plus the great complexification of society, had intensified the wish for verbal interaction. But it had also caused psychological difficulties and cultural confusion, and this in turn caused defensive tendencies, such as social exclusiveness, tabooing of topics, nostalgia for cultural certainty, etc. Since these two tendencies clashed, the effects were unevenly distributed. There was a certain overlap between cautious modes of management of meaning and conservative opinions, on one hand, and on the other between expansive modes of management of meaning and progressive opinions, but the parallel was not total. There was one continuum of opinions and evaluations of what was happening (from enthusiasm to rejection), and another continuum of preferred ways of dealing in conversations with those opinions and those events (from expansive to cautious). The partial overlap between cautious modes of management of meaning and conservative opinions had to do with the fact that a cautious mode safeguards larger portions of life from scrutiny. So conservatives would prefer a cautious mode, generally, and cautious managers of meaning would tend to become conservative.

– The low predictability of where a given social context was located on the two continua made for certain general tendencies toward caution, even among the expansive– minded, as long as a situation was not well defined.

– The delegitimation of most things associated with the Franco regime worked in the direction of facilitation and legitimation of debate and of progressive evaluations of events, even though the dictatorship was receding into history and the after-effects were no longer as prominent as they had been ten or fifteen years earlier. In a cultural conjuncture where anything that could be called constraint, undemocratic or unjust was illegitimate, anything that could be called change, freedom, equality or justice was easily defended.[268] Thus, hierarchy had been delegitimized in general, and the scope of the gender order was under heavy siege because of the delegitimation of ascription.

– The fact that women were doing many new things, plus the fact that this was culturally visible and a key topic of conversation, possibilitated imperfect reproduction, i.e. change, of the gender order. Gender was on the cultural agenda, and there was much empirical material, examples from everyone's daily experience, with which to construct arguments.

– Women's earning an income of their own, and the way sexuality was constructed and acted out and experienced were two especially delicate topics and not always legitimate. When they came up, what could be said and how much, depended very much on the persons present, especially on their mode of management of meaning. But the fact that these two aspects of social life, that have usually been seen by feminist studies as central in the gender order, were very much on the cultural agenda, was in itself hopeful. It made a high degree of reproduction of the gender order unlikely. The very fact that they were so sensitive in the Madrilenian situation seemed to be related to their close connection with power. This was seldom verbalized, and it was not very visible, culturally, but the connection seemed to be vaguely experienced, and the topics appeared pressing for everybody, for this very reason.

– Many aspects of the gender order, and many ideas which supported status quo indirectly, were not yet on the cultural agenda. Some were not even possible to introduce because they were doxic, invisible, taken-for-granted. But enough key ideas of the gender order were under debate for a further widening of the universe of discourse to be predictable.

Gender, discourse, and class

One variable that certainly caused variations between women in Spain was class. Some of the differences between the women of Benituria and the women of Madrid may also have to do with the historical differences between the Valencian and the Madrilenian regions – economic, socio-structural and cultural differences. Finally, the fact that I was in Benituria in 1983 and in Madrid eight years later certainly makes a difference. Even so, the two studies can be compared to show some significant class differences as to gender and discourse.

In comparison to the situation in Benituria, the situation in Madrid was as follows:[269]

– The love of talk was similar, but the types of arenas were different.

– Beniturian arenas were more informal and improvised, and to a large extent limited to the barrio itself. Madrilenian arenas were more organized and spread out all over the city. Yet Beniturian men and women had more opportunities to talk to strangers, whereas Madrilenian women and men were more careful to choose with whom they spoke.

– Madrilenian men had much greater access to socially consequential discourses, both actively and passively, than any of the other three categories.

– The variations in opinions and modes of management of meanings were similar, but both continua were much more polarized in Madrid.[270]

– The Madrilenian women spoke more in mixed gender contexts than the Beniturian women, because it was much more legitimate for them.

– In both studies, men spoke more than women in mixed-gender contexts.

– Middle class men seemed more irritated at women's counter-interpretations, when they caught glimpses of them, than working class men did, probably because it was much more legitimate in the working class for men's and women's worlds to be separate and different.

– Middle class women had more freedom of movement, both in theory and in practice, than working class women, but they had fewer opportunities to socialize in uni-gender contexts, so they had less of a chance to arrive at collective solutions to their gender-specific dilemmas.

– Middle class men also had fewer opportunities to socialize in uni-gender contexts in their free time than working class men did, and their work places were probably in general more gender-mixed, but they had more time and more resources to move between more varied contexts, both while working and for leisure, and in most of the contexts in which they moved, men and male-style interaction dominated.

– In spite of all the limitations to the pattern of couple sociability in the middle class, it did exist to a much greater degree than in the working class, and it did mean more communication across the gender line.

The tendency for middle class gender worlds to draw closer to each other at a faster speed than in the working class could therefore be presumed to continue, but not beyond a certain point. That is, dualism would probably decrease but continue to have the support of factual contrasts between the genders. In combination with middle class women's insistence on having professions and being recognized as "persons", this tendency towards greater similarity would probably also mean a tendency towards greater equality, although it also carried with it certain new obstacles for women, especially for their possibilities of constructing counter-hegemonic discourses. The ideological polarization might help, however, forcing everyone to define their positions. But this would depend on what happened in other parts of social life, of course, especially in the political order.

The danger of frustrations in intimate relationships (couples, families) due to the tensions in the gender order was great in all class contexts. The emphasis on being a "person" and the substantial meanings this concept was given (economic independence, power of decision over own life, participation in public life) were approximately the same. That meant more frustration for working class women, because they had fewer opportunities to study and obtain the kind of jobs that would compensate them for the price they would have to pay (a heavy workload) in order to obtain an income of their own under present general conditions, and most of them did not contemplate other forms for participating in the world outside the family. Younger middle class women, however, were acutely caught in the dilemma between family and career, because they were socialized not to see it as a choice at all. They wanted both and believed they could have both. And since they had the material and educational resources, there was no obvious excuse for failure, and there was little cultural work going on around how to interpret the structural obstacles. They were in for rude awakenings, like Esperanza (chapter 15). Some of them might be able to conceptualize it as a social problem and perhaps try to do something about it, but to judge from present discourses, most of them would see it as a question of personalities (their own or of people around them), so one could predict more personal strife than structural change. In chapter 14 we also saw that family responsibilities of middle class women (of all ages) were heavy, but this was partly invisible in discourse, at least if there was domestic service. And the (partial but important) loss of a housewife's efforts to assure family prestige, children's psychological and scholarly success, etc. could not be compensated for by the salary a woman could earn if she chose to work outside the home (cf Carlota, chapter 3).

The Madrilenian middle class gender order in the early 1990s

In spite of all the differences, a few things were common for the gender orders of the middle class in Madrid and the working class in Valencia. Situated in the same country, significant structural determinations were the same: legislation, school system, economic cycles, etc. Mass media were largely the same ones and the salient points in the cultural negotiations around gender were the same. Both were big cities with correspondingly complex social organization and processes of cultural complexification, and these in turn had specific consequences for gender, as we have seen. Both cities had had substantial immigration from other parts of the country, so that the traditional cultural heritage had become diluted. Both had varied labor markets, similar rates of unemployment and similar rates of female economic activity.

In neither city was gender segregation very strict in practice, nor was it culturally legitimate, but in both places it did exist in practice. In neither place did women suffer obvious restrictions on mobility in public, but in both there were a series of practical circumstances that made women's presence much less likely than men's in certain places, and these places were usually of value for both women and men (the sociability of bars, places of consequential economic and political decisions, the importance of being able to earn an income), and thus it is possible to say that there was a degree of gender segregation and that it had more negative consequences for women than for men. More specifically, in both cities, the labor market was gender segregated in the same probabilistic, non-absolute way, and the consequences of this were more evidently negative for women, and more so when combined with the high unemployment rates.

These circumstances affected women of both middle and working class, not in exactly the same ways, but clearly in different ways from men and in such ways that one can say that gender crosscut class. Both social dimensions were both objective and subjective, both produced noticeable differences in experiences and opportunity.

And because the differences in experiences and opportunity were real, gender came to be conceptualized as central and dualistic, and it remained hard to see the sociocultural constructions that upheld the gender order as a whole. It was easier and more common to interpret them as "nature".

The crosscutting of gender and class left conservative middle class women in a contradictory position. They might appear conservative since they said they wanted to conserve a previous state of affairs. They were seen as and called conservative by the hegemonic Spanish discourses. And in this book I have called them conservative for lack of a better label. But conservative in this case is not the same as dominant or hegemonic. These women were rather involved in a struggle of resistance against a new kind of hegemonic discourse that had had great material effects – in the organization of the labor market, in legislation, in the reconceptualization of sexuality.

It is undeniable that the Madrilenian middle class as a whole was hegemonic, and it was hardly revolutionary. It had much power in the shaping of the future of Spain. Many younger women participated in that power. But the conservative middle aged women excluded themselves or were excluded from participation in social affairs outside the family. And precisely the conservative women were the ones who refused to recognize the existence of differences of interest within the class or within the family. They defended class interests, so they were part of the dominant structure. They defended the united front of the family, which locked them in the role of "women".

Their defense of class interests cannot be written off as false consciousness, at most as a lack of insight due to their lack of access to key spaces. Their perspective was incomplete, but not wholly wrong. They did participate in some class privileges. But they did so as women. And they were precisely the ones who insisted most forcefully that they wanted to be "women". Yet, they were losing old securities and privileges that belonged to them as "women" and not gaining or not wanting to use the new privileges pertaining to "persons".

Women, men and persons

In Spain around 1990 there had been many profound processes of change at work for about three decades and they all influenced each other so that it was difficult for anything at all to stay the same. On the other hand the old truth holds that there is nothing new without roots in the old. But an effort of analysis is necessary to distinguish what is old in

327

the new. It may not be the obvious things, those that people call "tradition". It may be rather the way people conceptualize change and continuity, or it may be the way people talk about it, or it may be the way people decide what makes a good argument.

In urban contexts, the complexification of the social world is probably what changes the experience of everyday living most profoundly. But in Madrid, it was a type of change that had not received an emic label. It was impossible to name, difficult to discuss. At most, it was pointed to in phrases like "you can't trust anyone these days", "there are no values anymore" or "there are a lot of strange people around."

The changes in the urban gender orders are intimately interwoven with economic, political and ideological changes and with the social complexification.

Few Spaniards of the late 20th century experienced themselves as agents of change; they tended to conceptualize change as something automatically produced by time. They did act and they did have opinions, and their image of self was far from passive. The ideal personality (for both genders) was strong, active and autonomous. In the middle class there was more of a feeling of taking part in macro events than there was in the working class, but this went much more for men than for women, and it did not include changes in the gender order. Gender was essentialized. Either status quo was naturalized and defended as morally right and socially and biologically necessary, or else change in the gender order was naturalized as an automatic result of other changes. In either case, the question "what do we want it to be like?" was difficult to handle.

At the same time, gender was an important topic for debate. Whatever opinions people embraced, they were concerned with defending them, and the emotional temperature of debates on gender issues tended to run high. The subtext often seemed to be either: unless we insist that femininity is given by nature and unchangeable, it may not stay the same; or: unless we insist that society is moving towards greater freedom and justice, and that that includes women, too, inevitably, this desired movement may not come to pass.

Neither view was far off the mark, in fact. In any society, things happen that individuals do not control, and there are macro processes most people can do little with but adapt to. But talking is also doing. What is said influences social organization. The main way people take part in the process of change in the gender order is by discussing it. Middle class Madrid was a sociable and verbal cultural context. Gender changes stood out in daily experience and were considered and experienced by all as decisive for quality of life and personal happiness. So people discussed gender issues, shaped new opinions on them and then – somehow, indirectly, in the long run – modified their way of acting on them, too.

This study has shown what the discussions on gender issues looked like. It asked: Where do they take place, who takes part, which issues are discussed and which are forgotten, tabooed or invisible? And what consequences do these facts of the organization of discourse on gender have for the social organization of gender?

This focus has illuminated a series of contradictory tendencies. It has shown that the changes are deep and the resistance strong. It has shown that most informants suffered from a feeling of contradiction inside their own thinking and perhaps between their thinking and their doing. They often called this "incoherence" and criticized each other for it. The study has shown a field of ideas and a social distribution of opinions and fora for debate that made it impossible for people to ignore the outlines of ideas very different from their own, but it was very possible to live as if those other ideas did not have to be taken seriously. Yet it has also shown that the changes were so deep and so intimately interwoven with other social changes that it would seem dangerous for middle class Madrilenians not to recognize the complexity and potential explosivity of the situation.

Hardly anyone did, however. There was first of all a simplifying tendency to interpret the field of opinions as two opposed camps, instead of the fluid, many-stranded and situationally flexible albeit polarized continuum I have portrayed.

Then there was strong mutual disqualification. Accepting for a moment the two-camp image, we can say that the progressives tended to write off traditionalist thinking as old-fashioned, on its way out of its own accord, perhaps still irritatingly strong but without any real rational or moral merit and without any chance to survive in the long run. The traditionalists tended to write off progressive thinking as a passing fad or as subversive irrational thinking of small minorities which may upset normality but not overturn it, all in all something rather disgusting that one wants to have as little to do with as possible. Both sides saw the other as self-evidently wrong. The thinking of the other side was warped and the motives and personal worth of its proponents suspect, they implied. This dualist and aggressive simplification of social issues was a factor in itself. It was a dangerous cultural basis for further simplification and aggression in case of social crisis, and it put obstacles in the way of serious efforts of self-analysis.

That is not to say that there is no self-analysis going on. Quite the contrary. The changing times had certainly forced people to think. Not only did they have opinions on what was happening, they also had ways of managing meaning in order to form and defend their opinions. I have called two opposite such ways the cautious and the expansive modes of management of meaning. They are ideal types, I insist, but they clarify our view of the ongoing debates. We have seen that it was decisive for the outcome of each verbal encounter which mode dominated it. We have seen that most people tended to prefer one or the other. The modes sat deep in their dispositions But which mode dominated a situation could change with the topic or according to the success of different arguments or according to what the participants perceived was at stake.

What was going on was too complex for facile conclusions. But the selected situations, presented in as detailed a fashion as space allows, should give the reader an understanding of what the debate on the gender order in middle class Madrid was about and how it was carried out in the early 1990s. And the focus on discourse and complexification, plus some of the concepts suggested, are intended as a contribution to the methods of description and analysis of the gender orders of the world.

For most readers of this book, middle class Madrid will probably not look like an exotic tribe. But anthropology, if it is to be critical, must not limit itself to study distant circumstances; it must cover all human experiences. I have reported on a sociocultural reality that must be described along with all others, independently of how similar or how different it is from what is usually called "Western" or "European".

It is also high time for critical anthropology to stop studying only "down". Influential social categories should be carefully scrutinized, particularly at moments of salient change and when they are internally divided. For all of these reasons, the middle class Madrilenian gender order is a strategic object for critical anthropology.

In my opinion, this study will continue to be interesting in the future; local circumstances will have changed, but critical anthropology should still find this report useful for comparative and theoretical purposes.

I do not presume to know what people thought. I have reported on what they said. And I have placed what they said in three kinds of context: social (who says it, where, with what effects), textual (what ideas go with what others, what chains of arguments are common) and logico-cultural (how do these sets of utterances relate to each other and to social reality, what is recognized as normal discourse, what contradictions are produced and what tensions do the debates point to).

This gender order in evident change was not at all cut loose from continuity. For good and for bad, continuity was there, present and inescapable, both as a hypostatized "tradition" that was more real in debate than in experience but no less influential for that, and as invisible taken-for-granted things, doxa and dispositions, that determined what could be discussed and what not and how people felt about it all.

Finally, the ethnography shows that these aspects of the gender order were the way they were precisely because they were situated in an urban society undergoing continued complexification. When social arrangements are broken up and rearranged, ascribed roles must change and sometimes ascription itself will become suspect. If "woman" has been a culturally central ascribed role, real women may come to feel uncomfortable with that role and with the very label for it. They may prefer to be "persons". At the same time, they may want to retain other features associated with their half of a dualist gender order. In such a situation, there will be a wide choice of opinions and a great need to work them out in cultural negotiation to give them shape and to persuade others of one's own interpretations. And the negotiation will itself make the universe of discourse grow, place more things under the light of debate and further undermine ascription. "Women" will become "persons", whether they like it or not, and whether men like it or not. And that will set the stage for a new act in the drama of gender.

Appendix A: Work and anger

This appendix offers added empirical description of how Madrilenian conversations worked and exemplifies especially the discussion about the division of labor in the tertulias I arranged. In this particular one, this topic took up most of the time and became unusually heated, but the way it was discussed was representative – all the common arguments were there, and the contrast between women's and men's opinions was quite typical. It was also representative as to type of participants, overall rhythm, style of interaction, and so on.

The mode of management of meaning was largely cautious (especially on such themes as class and politics) but the participants did not want to see themselves as conservatives, so they adopted an expansionist attitude towards debate in general. That was probably why they accepted having the tertulia at all, and why the men acceded to discuss 'women's things". Above all, the tertulia is representative in the emotional importance it gave to the theme of work and how it forced these normally rather cautious women into quite a critical attitude, while forcing their husbands into an argument of biological necessity, with which they were not quite comfortable.

It is interesting to compare this group discussion with the one in chapter 13. In both of them, women and men ended up confronting each other, the differences between their ideas were parallel, and they argued with similar references to other ideas. Most especially the men defended the idea of innate gender characteristics, and used this idea to defend status quo in the division of tasks, while the women thought gender was mainly produced by education and used complaints about their personal circumstances to argue for cultural and social change. And in both, this caused some tension for the couples. These similarities are striking in view of the differences: the participants in this tertulia were much more conservative than those of chapter 13, and their political references and their opinions on other issues were very different. Even their way of handling marital tension showed clear contrasts.

Matilde called me one day to say she was planning to invite a few friends for Sunday lunch, so it would be a good occasion to have a tertulia. Matilde was one of the few Club Aguafría members who treated me as a real friend. She was an intellectually agile person, eager to learn about new phenomena. I was a new type for her. Her personal mode of management of meaning was expansionist, but she was surrounded by caution and accepted that as a natural state of things.

She was middle aged and had been married for some twenty-five years. Her eldest son was already working as an economist, her next eldest was studying abroad, the teenage daughter was finishing her secondary studies and getting ready to go abroad, too. The youngest son was only twelve. Except for the one who was abroad, they all lived at home.

In her youth, Matilde had worked for a short while in an office, but she quit to get married and had never had an employment after that. She had no professional preparation and no special dreams about a career, but she was clearly dissatisfied with her housewife life. As she was an energetic person, she needed little time for housework, even without much asistenta help, and she was constantly casting about for things to do: she helped with parish work, since she was quite interested in both religion and social work; she participated in cultural activities for housewives; she liked to read novels; and she cultivated an assortment of friends of unusual kinds. (As a matter of fact, I felt like a specimen in her collection.)

Her husband Víctor did not especially approve of her activities. Neither did he actively disapprove. He let her be.

Their social life centered on a group of couples in which the four men were the original friends. They had studied engineering together, graduating in 1966. By that time all four of them were engaged, and the women became friends, too. None of the couples lived in Aguafría. One lived in a good area downtown, the other three in outlying upper middle class areas. Matilde and Víctor were the only ones who had a one-family house. They had moved in quite recently.

The area was brand new. One could tell because there were hardly any trees, the gardens gave a bare impression, and the big billboards announcing the sale of the houses were still in place. I had to walk one kilometer from the bus stop, and the nearest stores were even farther away. Matilde and Víctor showed us around the house with pride, asking us to imagine all the furnishings they had not yet had time to buy. They joked about the great cost of it all, but they mentioned no exact prices and did not complain in earnest. The house had two stories plus an attic and a roof terrace with a beautiful view of an expanse of grassland and beyond it the skyline of Madrid.

After lunch, Matilde arranged us around the fireplace and brought coffee and a cake on a small tray. She served it in the traditional time-consuming way, asking each person about preferences and complying with them before she handed each cup and plate over. Sometimes a husband might serve the liqueurs meanwhile, but in this case Matilde served them, too. The bottles were then left on the table so that those who wanted more could serve themselves.

The other guests were: Fernando and his wife Mary Cruz, José and his wife Alejandra, Rafael and his wife Lourdes. The men wore light-colored slacks and white shirts with a knit sweater on top. Alejandra was the only woman in slacks. All of the women wore earrings and something around the neck and also several arm bands around each wrist. Their hairdos and makeup were perfect. Fernando had a matching sports coat, too, but as he sat next to the fire, he took it off. Rafael had an American type crew cut hair. The other three men all had what I would like to call "Madrilenian short", i.e. the male haircut that was acceptable in a bank or an office in Madrid: not long, but not tightly cropped and perhaps some curls around the ears or to one side of the forehead.

During lunch, all the couples had told me how many children they had and what they were doing. All of them had their one, two or three eldest at university, all of them at private universities, studying engineering, economics, law or business administration.

All eight were around fifty years of age. Only one was born in Madrid, the others came from various regions. All four women had been housewives ever since they got married, except Mary Cruz who had worked for a short while long ago. To ask about social background was too sensitive, but I knew that Víctor came from a farming family in a rather poor region and Matilde from the older type of upper middle class, and there were some clues that the others came mostly from the lower middle class of the older type (small businesses or farms).

After the coffee was served, Matilde asked me to explain about my project. She had forewarned the guests, as I had asked her to do, but I gave the usual background explanations, while Matilde made room for the taperecorder on the table. As usual, at all tertulias, this was an awkward moment which everyone present cooperated to overcome, joking about the taperecorder and what uses I might make of their possible indiscretions. But, also as usual, after a few tentative comments about different topics, some issue came up that all felt like debating, and as soon as we got started on that, the conversation flowed easily.

The only thing unusual for this tertulia was that the women forgot their good manners after a while and argued quite forcefully for a position that was not quite feminist, and that they themselves would definitely not call feminist, but that they saw as opposed to the male view of things and also opposed to the "traditional" discourse they otherwise subscribed to, and they felt forced to defend this position even at the cost of sacrificing social harmony, because of their feelings of frustration and injustice. It was not unusual for women to speak in this way when by themselves, but it was unusual for them to do so with men present.

There was a clear progression during the tertulia. The men talked more than the women did throughout, but much more so in the beginning than towards the end. And while in the beginning it was the men who defined the issues and declared what was supposed to be the consensus on the issues, the women gradually took over the initiative. They kept their voices cordial and their smiles charming, but their comments became biting and the men turned defensive. Two men maintained their interest in the conversation, throughout, while Víctor yawned openly towards the end, and José was rather quiet all afternoon. Rafael and Fernando competed in a friendly but intense way for control over the conversation.

The transcription is divided into chapters with theme-headings, to make it easier to read, but it is verbatim except where otherwise indicated.

CHANGE AND COMPETITION

Fernando began by saying that the most important fact in any study of Spain today is that there is a very strong contrast between generations, because of the change the country has gone through. The young generation of today has nothing in common with our generation, they are totally different from us. I said that this was precisely one of my themes. Alejandra said that young people today have a much harder time, and Fernando elaborated on this, saying that we have copied the American system, everything is terribly competitive now. Everyone agreed in principle, but there were also comments to the effect that young people today have a good time, they have much more fun, there are not so many taboos, they are not as afraid of so many things as we were.

The comments on competitiveness referred to studies and work, the ones on fun to sexuality and leisure in general.

I asked the men if they had not felt, while studying, that they had to get good grades in order to find good jobs.

Fernando: "The idea of competition was not in your mind. I mean, that job, you had it almost by right, just because you had been able to study and graduate."

Víctor underlined the truth of this, and José added that there was little television and not the kind of programs we get now, so full of competition. Matilde reminded us all that engineers used to be scarce, that is why there was no competition, and an engineer had a high status that lasted a lifetime, she said.

Rafael interrupted, saying he did not agree. Several voices exclaimed enthusiastically: Yes, yes, like in a television debate, tell us your disagreements! In other words, this was the point at which the initial strained remarks out of courtesy towards me shifted to another gear, that of real discussion, real entertainment.

Rafael said that certainly there were plenty of job opportunities when they graduated, and he himself had had many offers and for a while worked simultaneously in three different companies, all supposedly full time jobs. But on the other hand, he thought he was a special case. His parents had no money. "When I graduated, I had to go to work the very next day. But many of our classmates, you know it, took their good time to find a job, sometimes a year or more. And that is not so now; I know since my son is in his fourth year of engineering[27] and I can see that at least in certain specialties it is the other way around: already in the fourth year the companies come to interview them and so on, and they have no problem finding a job. At least not in Madrid."

Someone said that he was talking about engineers, meaning that they were the privileged ones. "Sure, I compare what I know something about. And comparing our times and their times, things are better now. For the time being. But on the other hand, there are factors working in the opposite direction. One very serious problem for young people is the problem of housing (he lowered his voice dramatically). It is an almost unsolvable problem for young people today. In our times, we did not have it. In other words, there are things that are better, and, as to work, there is more of it, I think."

334

The men told their different personal experiences from different periods, and the women kept reminding them that it all depends on what professions you are talking about and that engineering is very special. Two of the men had executive positions and described their view from the other side of the job interview table. Rafael said for example:

"Things are going much better now than for example just five years ago. In 1985 there was a problem. We had a project in Saudi Arabia then, so we needed engineers to go there, and we advertised in the press, and hundreds came to apply! Hundreds! Not now. You place an ad in the newspaper now and if you get five or six to answer it... But that was just because there was a deep crisis then, and now there is no crisis. But perhaps in another three or four years there will be one again. The first person to get laid off in a crisis is the engineer. Because he is the one who spends the money..."

Voices: "And the one who earns most money!" "And the one who spends it on consumption, too!"

Fernando: "No, he is the one who invests, because he decides about investments, he makes the projects, he is the first one to...(interruptions) No, the simple truth is that there is a crisis every eleven years, that was what they taught us in school. Perhaps the cycles are shorter now, but just take a look at the economic history of Spain and you'll see a crisis every eight or nine years, something like that. (Laughter in the background.) Right, seven years of fat cows and seven of lean ones!"

CLASS

When the men had discussed this hypothesis for a while, Mary Cruz timidly raised her voice: "But... persons of a certain level... but.... even in our times, the young guys who could not study, they could find jobs in lots of places. Now, a young boy like that, if he does not have at least some preparation he can't get in, even as an errand boy! (Giggles) Well, because there are no errand boys any more, so... But I mean, there are no opportunities, and that it depends, too, on what circles you move in."

Everyone nodded to this vague reminder of social class.

Rafael: "Before, it used to be the classic thing, when we were young... I mean, we are young now as well (laughter), but let us say when we were younger, what used to happen was the classical thing that the father, when the young man rebelled and did not want to study, his father said, look son, in that case I will get you a job. Now he can't say that!"

This brought lots of laughter and comments on how people used to be forced to work from very early ages. The attention returned to the great differences between "then" and "now", and the theme of unemployment was forgotten.

The men reminisced about a class reunion they had had twenty years after graduation. They had invited a famous teacher to give a lecture on generational differences, and he had said that the new young generation has no ideals. They study because their parents want them to.

This made everyone uncomfortable and there were lame efforts of protest. That the young people of today have no ideals was an extremely common phrase, and in conservative circles it was an indirect statement to the effect that democratization had brought social and moral instability. In this group, noone wanted to give such a conservative impression, but neither was it easy for them to say the opposite. There were also differences within the group. Mary Cruz said she knew lots of young people who had more ideals than they had had. "Did we have any ideals?" she asked provocatively. The others said of course we did, what do you mean, now please, Mary Cruz...

Alejandra said that both generations had ideals, but of different kinds. The ideals have to be different because society is so different. There is more consumerism, and so on. The discussion centered for a short while on whether one has to be a realist or whether one has to try to change things. Rafael decided to put matters straight:

"The thing is that Spain used to be a very stratified society. You could not go from... one situation to another. And that was why so many studied difficult things and entered official competitions for jobs. Because if you managed to obtain a permanent job as a state lawyer or notary or solicitor, or if you managed to graduate in engineering, then you placed yourself in a situation where you could lean back and take it easy and just continue that way. And that is not so any longer. Now, there is much social mobility in Spain."

There were protests. Rafael clarified: "Well, maybe there is less than in the United States, for example, because they have a lot of social mobility, right? But I think there is mobility in Spain. As much as or more than in England. Because England is a very stratified society. I think there is much more mobility here. First of all because everyone has access to university studies, there are lots of universities, there are even... (some interruptions) Yes, before it was more like... But what I mean is that in Spain it is much more of a merit... In comparison to many other countries, Sweden among them I think, and definitely the United States, where there is a mentality, that, just because an individual studies and manages to graduate from university, that does not automatically mean a grand standard of living. You can have a high living standard without graduating. And here, in the Spanish mind, there is something very deep, I mean in our generation, not in the new ones, I don't know about them... that if you want to reach a comfortable economic level, you have to study. Or at least you have to have money in the family. And that has changed. It is changing."

This was commented on for a while, in all directions. It is changing, it is not changing. Inherited money or status is more important, studying is more important. The young people depend more on studying than we did; status is more important now than it used to be. The theme was clearly interesting to all, both the men and the women. There were jokes about the importance of marrying right, too: women had to consider a man's worth in terms of grades and specialty, and men could aspire to obtain "patrimony through matrimony".

WOMEN STUDYING

I pointed out that studying used to mean different things for men and for women. "I don't know what it was like for you, but it used not to be taken for granted that a woman should study. And if she did, it was not taken for granted that she would use her studies to get a job."

Lourdes: "No, a woman would study just in order to study. Because later she would get married and stay home with the children." Several more comments in the same vein. Fernando said that a lot of young girls have that same mentality even today. "My daughter says that. She studies economics and several of her classmates say they plan to hang their degree on the wall for decoration. They are family girls, they want their degree just to have it." Several women protested this implicit criticism of women's motivations. Lourdes said studying helps a person to be more of a person. Everyone agreed to that.

Mary Cruz: "But at least now they have an option, whether to hang it on the wall or use it. We hung it on the wall because we wanted to, too, because if you did not want to, you did not have to hang it, but things sort of pushed you towards hanging it. That is the truth." The other women agreed: If you studied, that was considered nice, but if you wanted a job, that was different, then obstacles were placed in your path. I asked if they had studied. Mary Cruz said she did not finish, but she did do three years of philosophy. Alejandra said she had studied to be a secretary. Neither of them had ever had a job, they said. Lourdes said nothing. Matilde had studied some English and French plus secretarial skills and had a job as a secretary for a year or two before she got married.

Víctor: "Seeing how much effort it costs today to graduate, especially in engineering or economics for example, I wonder if a woman who does not plan to go out and work in her profession later, is it really worth it for her? Well, if she has an intellectual level that permits her to whip through it without much trouble, sure... but... I mean, there are many who complain about the sacrifices you have to make to graduate..."

Many comments to the same effect. Studying is very hard, everyone fails once in a while, most students have to repeat exams all the time, so they have to give up weekends and vacations, at times they can't even go out with their fiancés, young people today are really very disciplined, they have to be...

CAREER OR FAMILY

Lourdes suddenly said, defensively: "Now, there comes a moment when you have to choose between a career and a family, and there are many girls who would rather have a family. That is what I think!"

Matilde, alert: "Why?!" There was tension in the air, the discussion was nearing a controversial point and Lourdes had just indicated that she leaned towards a position they all recognized, that of "traditional" defense of the woman as a mother above all. Lourdes' remark also showed that she thought the discussion so far had run the risk of undermining such a position, something which was not evident to me, rather the opposite, and the others looked surprised, too, but now they would have to declare their standpoints.

José: "Today, the majority of the young girls today, I don't know if they have made up their minds if they want to dedicate themselves to their family or not."

Many comments of all kinds: It is a big decision... Whatever you do, it will be uncomfortable...

They all seemed to take for granted that a young woman has to choose between family and career. So I told about how I had asked young girls at the Club what they planned to do, and how they seemed to take for granted they would not have to choose. They wanted to combine a career and a family, and they seemed not to realize it might be difficult in practice.

Mary Cruz: "No, what I think about those girls is that they are going to have a much more difficult life than we have had, really. Because I know some young women from the choir I sing in, they are married and they go on working, and well, they have time to come to choir practice once a week, actually they don't have the time but they find the time... But what I see is that these girls are exhausted. Exhausted! And evidently they can't have children."

Fernando: "Sure, they have to choose. They eliminate things."

Mary Cruz: "Actually, the first one who is going to have a child, she is going to have it now, any time, after having been married for six or seven years. And of course she wants to go on working, and she has reached a certain level, she is head of her department and so on. This baby she is going to have now – and she is going to keep right on working! (Dramatic silence, then the other women protested that that would not be possible.) What she has now is a serious problem. Either she leaves it with her mother or she leaves it with someone else, anyone, or she has to quit work. Another woman I know, Marisa, well, she has no children yet, they have not been married for very long, but well, nobody of their age talks about having children, and I can understand that. If they get up at seven in the morning, they go to work, they don't come back until seven or eight at night... what will they do when they have a baby? Their babies will be born, I don't know when... (More background comments, both men and women were upset thinking that such a good and necessary thing as having babies seemed to be on its way out.) And above all, what I think is that the day they have a baby, the baby and the job, it won't work, because until we make it clear that a baby is also something for the father, and not just for the mother, well, then what happens is that the woman becomes either sick or neurotic."

Fernando: "What she has to do is to make it an issue for labor legislation."

Mary Cruz, sharply: "Oh no! It is just a matter of educating the men."

Now the discussion had taken a turn noone except Mary Cruz had foreseen.

José: "Well, but company legislation helps, because if your husband says, look, I have to go home and take care of the baby..." His tone indicated that that was to make himself ridiculous. Several voices spoke agitatedly at the same time. Mary Cruz had to fight to regain the floor. "No, but... What I mean is... Listen! But why is it that a woman can do it? She has to say it, at the office, but a man can't?"

Fernando, paternally: "But that is what I am saying, that is why legislation has to change." The agitation grew and for several minutes it was impossible to distinguish anything on the tape. Finally I restored order, saying that legislation is actually changing; it used to be that neither mother nor father had the legal right to stay at home with a sick child, but now both do. The discussion centered for a while on what legal changes have come into effect and which ones might be on their way.

Alejandra: "But the problem is, there is a series of problems, and I imagine that when a company has to select a new engineer, well, logically if they have to choose between a woman and a man, the woman will give them a lot more problems than a man."

Mary Cruz: "Sure." Someone disagreed. "You say no? You don't think so?!" Several voices tried to make new distinctions between "before" and "now" and between types of companies and types of professions. The voice of Víctor dominated for a while, and Matilde exclaimed: "You are one of those who think in that way!" She meant to criticize her husband because he would not employ a woman.

Víctor, angrily: "Now look here, this is the way it is, let me tell you. According to the latest statistics, the countries with the lowest birth rates in Europe are Italy and Spain. That means that the deep change in Spain during the last ten or fifteen years, that we have changed from being the country that... with the maximum birth rate, to being that of the lowest. Why? Because this whole problem that Mary Cruz explained has come up, and on top of that, the legislation has not helped. Right?" One man said yes. "So then, what does a woman do? Evidently, she cuts out the child. In other words, she cuts the production of children."

Many voices again tried to interpret this in all imaginable directions. For some, what Víctor had said was proof that things were getting out of hand, so that some changes ought to be rolled back, and that is what Víctor himself seemed to mean; for others it was proof of the opposite, that women were victims of circumstances, and that circumstances must therefore be modified. But no position was clearcut.

Lourdes: "But what about the couple, how does that work? When you have to choose..." The discussion continued with many simultaneous voices. There were comments about couple problems and their relationship to labor problems; comments about how a woman always thinks of her child first, no matter what; comments about how companies discriminate against women; and protests that at my company there is certainly no discrimination, quite the contrary, the women have so many privileges... Alejandra continued talking about how having a baby and taking care of it takes so much time and energy. Fernando finally managed to gain the floor for himself:

"You must realize, Alejandra, one thing, that taking into account the fact that a woman now has only one or two children, and that in a professional lifetime of thirty years, you are talking about five or six months. And the truth is that that has very little significance."

DISCRIMINATION AND MERITS

Víctor (who had lived abroad): "I have seen a lot more discrimination in the United States than in Spain."

Rafael: "As to a woman's work (one woman started to protest) – wait! Wait until you hear what I am going to say! I am going to say that... I am not going to say that you are right, but you'll see that you are right, in your womanly way." (Several women laughed in the way women laugh when a man complements their sex and they want to show they appreciate that and identify themselves as real women.) "Fernando may be right. I have worked for most of my life with an oil company. In my company there are about, let's say two hundred university graduates. Two women. (Dramatic silence.) So if we look at the facts... " Many voices interrupted and Rafael was not able to regain the floor in spite of shouting the key word "facts" several times.

Then Fernando asked if he meant literally only two women, in the whole company, and Rafael confirmed this. One woman asked if he meant of their age, or if there might be more young women. Rafael insisted: "Two women university graduates in the whole of (name of company), Limited!" Fernando: "Because women are lazy!" One woman: "Not at all, come on, no, no, no!" Rafael: "You can talk later. Maybe you don't care about the company. I am stating the facts. Two women."

At this point the reader may find the positions confusing. What Rafael was so emphatically stating as a fact can be interpreted as discrimination against women, but that is not what he meant. What was not necessary to say, for these merit-conscious people, was that for them it was evident that a person reaches his or her goals if he or she is really a capable person. The fact that there were only two women in that big company therefore meant that women do not have what it takes. The women tried to protest but found it hard to argue "against the fact". Alejandra tried to justify discrimination with a vague reference to the earlier dicussion about women having family responsibilities which make them less valuable as employees.

Rafael: "I want to ask you one thing, Fernando. You who have passed the official competition for the Ministry of Industry[272], how many women industrial engineers are there in there? I bet there are many more! Because they tend to prefer public employment, because... because... I don't know why!" He seemed to imply that women were not good enough for the harsher competition in private companies.

Matilde said that the reason was that in a ministry you work only in the morning, so you have the afternoon free for household tasks, but Fernando and Rafael went on talking to each other about how in their companies there was no discrimination at all, the procedures were fair, so if there were few women, it was because of their lower merits.

Alejandra: "Naturally, I can understand that, and if I were the company I would certainly understand, too, that women create problems, but on the other hand..." Many voices interrupted. One woman shouted "I would employ as many women as I could!" and all the women laughed heartily at this.

Fernando: "Well, to tell you the truth, my criterion is that I have always employed as many women as I could for office positions. But for street work (he meant selling), I take none! (A short surprised silence followed by whys.) Well, because if the child gets sick she can't go to Barcelona, she can't go to Cádiz... (Women's voices: Of course!) She can't go anywhere! And a man goes."

I decided to do a little provocation of my own: "True, that is what happens – as long as it is the woman who stays at home if the child gets sick." Matilde, triumphantly: "That's what I was saying!" Mary Cruz, equally emphatic: "As long as the mentality does not change..." There was laughter, perhaps to defuse the tension. But Mary Cruz built it up again: "A child has two parents, not just a mother, so..."

Rafael shouted my name several times until he got exclusive attention from everyone. "Marie, here is my opinion. In Spain there is much more equality for a woman in the labor market than there is in the United States. In the United States – and my personal experience is that I have analized it through my work, I have gone through perhaps a thousand CV's. And there, when the people come for an interview, the women, having more merits than the men, ask for approximately half the salary, for office positions." Laughter, several partial discussions. Someone said that salaries in Spain are good, too. Rafael managed to regain the floor to explain that he meant to say that in Spain women and men are paid exactly the same salaries for the same jobs. There was a short but lively discussion about whether this was true only for university graduates or for everyone, and Rafael said that at least it was true for office personnel. "Here and now." Two other men gave their personal experiences of always paying their employees the same, regardless of sex. One woman said uncertainly that she had heard that this was not so in Spain, but she did not have up to date facts...

Rafael: "In Spain, yes, in this I agree with Fernando, in that if a woman obtains a certain position, and she has a certain salary assigned to her, and she gets in, then she is paid the same. The thing is, she does not get in! (Giggle.) I told you, there are two in my company. And they are in technical jobs, too, sure, in positions where they are not indispensable, just in case... That is just the way it is." He leaned back, satisfied to have proved that things have to be the way they are.

There was a short discussion about the proportion of women who study engineering. In their class there had been only one. There were humorous remarks about whether this was too many or not. There was agreement that there were many women in all engineering schools now, but disagreement as to when they had started entering in large numbers. Matilde said that anyway it was clear that women came later than men.

DIVISION OF TASKS AND DIVORCE

Matilde: "In any case, if I am allowed to introduce this in this conversation, it is a fact that today it is harder for a woman... It is harder to combine her family life with work, in that... in that before (voices: yes, yes, before...) Yes, it used to be that if a girl worked, she normally had the support of the grandmother, and the support of a live-in maid, and these things don't exist any longer."

Mary Cruz: "Sure, that is if you consider it conceivable to leave the child with someone else, but I think that to have a child in order to leave it in the hands of a maid... I think... I think that is pathological! (All the women declared their various opinions on this.) In other words, if you have a child, which is one of the most important things in life, then to leave it in the hands of a maid..."

Fernando: "Right, that is why you could not go to work. But I think that people now think in a different way."

Rafael: "Yes, but of course, but... What I wanted to say a while back was that there is one variable that has changed women's attitude altogether, or in part, in this time lapse. And that is the theme of the stability of marriages. It may surprise you, but just try to remember, twenty years ago, to talk about a separated woman, to talk about a divorced woman in Madrid, twenty years ago that was extraordinary! It was something really strange..." Voices saying true, twenty years ago, and ten years ago, too...

Rafael continued: "Today a young woman gets married and says to herself, but how could I quit work? Pepita on the third floor, her husband left her and the poor woman did not have... And she is starving to death! (Voices: Sure, that can happen, yes, it does...) Sure it happens, and all the time! And that circumstance is decisive, I tell you. (Voices: Yes, one has to think about it...) If one has to think about it! Sure one does! Listen, I love you a lot, but if you leave, as I can see happens to other people and before it used not to happen... that is an important factor to make you go on working. (Women's voices saying sure, yes.) As to me... come on, the secretaries especially... in my company (a man's voice: What a company you have! Laughter.) – look, if a woman builds a good career, perhaps she has lots of motivation and so on... but there are... there are many details in there, that... I can see how they feel... If they were totally sure about this issue, and if they did not need a little bit of money, because we are talking about only the little bit they get, then they would stop working, because their work is not very motivating either. (Voices: Obviously, of course...) And many of these gals are there... (someone tried to interrupt him, so he raised his voice) They sit there from early morning, just to make some photocopies, things like that... and in the afternoon to take care of their families. And very often I see her, like, crying on the telephone, because they are worried about their families... it is horrible. And why are they there? In part because of what I said, my husband might leave any day or whatever might happen... and that has changed a lot, that used to be a totally abnormal thing." He felt empathy, but his gestures made it clear that he meant that things used to be better the old way that caused less stress.

Again the discussion broke up into many for a while. The theme was painful but not too difficult to talk about. There were many examples of situations among their acquaintances.

Rafael: "And I think that when a man leaves home in the morning to go to work, snap! He disconnects the home until he comes back. The woman, when she goes to work, keeps thinking the whole time, what is happening with this, what is happening with that, so she is neither here nor there, nor. ."

Fernando: "Yes, listen, I see the same thing. They keep calling home (voices saying: of course), and again, one hour later, back on the phone, listen, take this out of the freezer, I forgot..." Lourdes gave an example of a woman doctor, which she found especially horrible. "With her profession, she has to be there with her five senses focusing on the patient she has in her hands, and she is worried because she left her son with a fever and nobody at home, and so forth... It just does not work, she can't, she has to quit one thing or the other."

NATURE

Víctor to me, paternally: "That is what I was saying, Marie, that this is one thing that is biological or ancestral. You carry this in your genetic memory or in the genes. If you compare with the animal world, you'll see the female with her young and the male... "

There was laughter. Víctor's change of gear signaled another way of discussing the theme. The men spent a few minutes offering saucy remarks about how biology steers our lives and why this is a good thing. I had to give an answer, so I said that male birds often take care of their young as much as female birds do, and you can't compare with animals, because there is always some animal to prove any point you want to make. More laughter; then the women insisted we should compare with human beings only.

Fernando: "No, excuse me, we have to compare with mammals, because we humans are very far from the birds! Millions and millions of years away! (Women's voices trying to interrupt.) Wait! But as to the mammals..." (Men's voices insisted that it is biological, sure it is, it has to be...) I had to give another mini-lecture on how mammals also have different habits apart from the live birth and the suckling, and on how human beings differ among themselves according to culture. The men tried to interrupt the whole time, but the women were eagerly expecting to learn good arguments from me, so I did not let myself be interrupted.[273] I also said that among human societies, an arrangement like the one we have here and now, where the whole responsibility for children falls on their mother alone is rather unusual. Even in Spain it used not to be so clear cut, Matilde had reminded us of the role of grandmothers, and there are also siblings... there are fifty thousand ways to arrange childcare ..

Rafael: "But the general rule is that the mother, or the female, is responsible for the young..."

Matilde: "As long as she suckles them!"

Rafael: "Oh no! The thing is just that the period until the animals are emancipated varies according to the species. But until the day they leave, it is the mother..."

Fernando, with his usual aplomb: "Look, in all of our families there is probably some ancestor who walked out the door and left his wife there, stuck with lots of kids and all surprised (a couple of the men laughed heartily at this), but probably the reason is just this very one, that he cared not a shit about the kids, and besides –" (He must have made some suggestive gestures, because everyone laughed suddenly.)

Víctor: "The most famous doctor we have had in Spain, Marañón, said clearly that the difference between a man and a woman (Fernando went on talking, about how men are mixed, not pure types...), because even in his times people were saying that there had to be equality between men and women, and he said that biologically a man is made for work and a woman is made for bearing children. As clear as that." Matilde: "How very comfortable for him!!! Now, for his wife..." Víctor raised his voice, and there was a long argument between the two of them. Víctor's position was that a society in which women want to work outside the home is an unnatural one, and Matilde's position was that Marañón was a man, so he did not understand. In the end, Matilde shouted: " As to the housewife, who can tell her that her job is very beautiful, and who pays her for it??!!"

Víctor: "Her husband pays her, that's who!"

MEN AND HOUSEHOLD WORK

Matilde: "No, I think that one thing is clear, that today this whole social part is focused on women, for example, let's see... the Institute of Woman. So then... What I mean is, here we have not said a thing about men. What a coincidence that we have not talked about men! Why? Because in actual fact life has changed so much, and we are forced to take a kind of decisions – (a man tried in vain to interrupt her) So then, about the men... it is flabbergasting, we have been... What they can't say is that... criticize women like that, and one just must contemplate what a woman has to face in her home, that she has to have the children, and, listen! that is life!" Many voices tried to interrupt her, with arguments, numbers and examples from other countries.

Rafael: "No, no, I am not criticizing... (repetitions) what I want to establish as a fact is that from now on women are going to work. And what Marie is saying is true, you ask any young girl, or my daughter who is studying economics now, or anyone, and in general they will say, sure I want to work. Later, listen, circumstances will... in a couple of.. if she gets married, which she will... but her present idea is no longer what it used to be. Before it used to be that she got married and..."

Matilde interrupted: "Listen to this! Your daughter, if she finds a husband who will help her at least minimally, she will work. And everything will work out just fine, if only the husband accepts that that woman has to work, and that she has to (women's voices supporting Matilde, saying that this was the essential point) have help with the children and everything, because otherwise it will not work out. (Other women echoed her:

Otherwise it will not work out!) And that is the point, because a woman's working also contributes security for her husband."

The men agreed to the last point, but Matilde looked around belligerantly, knowing that she had provoked them. Several partial discussions broke out, each person telling humorous tales about what would happen in their home if there was to be a change in the division of tasks.

The many different discussions continued until Alejandra slowly made herself heard by all: "What I wanted to say to Marie, since she comes from a country where they are so far ahead they are already coming back (common expression), because they are years ahead of us, and this is relevant... She must know about this, because I have heard that for example the ideals that we have had, and now the young people don't, it has to do with... I have heard it said that that is so... That marriage is more stable that way, and then you have certain values, that, I don't know..."

I explained, as I often had to do, that the differences between Sweden and Spain are not as big as people think, and they are diminishing; certainly Sweden has had legislation about maternity rights and so on for many years. "But there are no abismal differences. The thing is that all of this has existed in Sweden for a much longer time, so for example there are hardly any housewives anymore in Sweden. Almost all women work outside. (Attempted interruptions about how this cannot work.) But how do they work? Part time! (Voices: Yes, of course! Otherwise...) Because it is still the women who are in charge of housework, mostly."

Lots of laughter and comments. All the men said they too wanted to work part time! Matilde doubled over with laughter at my desperate attempts to stop the flood of sarcasm from the men. They took it all in jest and said they too were tired, they too loved to spend time on the couch... Matilde: "They got you there, Marie!" Then she turned serious and addressed her husband: "You just want to work less and play tennis more!" Lots of laughter, now at Victor's expense. Fernando said he too wanted to play more tennis, "but with my son by my side, mind you!" The women asked what he would do if the son had a fever, or if he would also wash the dishes... "No, I would just use paper plates!"

CHOICE

There were more questions about Sweden and I explained about schooling, daycare, working hours, commercial hours, and so on. Maternity leave and permission to stay home with sick children attracted special attention.

Matilde said: "I bet a father never stays home with a sick child!" She was convinced she knew the answer and went on: "Because I think that when you have acquired a set of privileges over centuries, then you will never let go of them voluntarily, never!" Many voices tried to interrupt her and Rafael won: "What I wonder is why women dislike so much staying at home!?" All the men went, "Right, right! Answer that one!" in challenging tones, and the women shouted different protests: "It is not that, it is if you don't get any help, if you don't have any money of your own, if it is not your own choice..."

Rafael: "The only reason you are uncomfortable in that situation is if there is something else, your work or something, that makes you..."

Mary Cruz: "Not at all. My starting point is that I have loved to take care of my children. Now and always and as long as it is a choice. I mean, you decide, I want to stay in my home, with my children. That is your choice... then you are happy. Now, if you don't want to stay at home by yourself in your house but want to work outside, too, and in some way, like sort of, well, having another kind of personal development, and it turns out you can't because everything combines to stand in your way, that is what makes me mad, I think that is what makes most women mad, that it is not really a choice, they just tell you you have to do it, like it or not."

The men said that if women had a choice, they would choose to take care of their children, so what was the difference? Childcare is wonderful!

Matilde: "So why aren't you men happy with childcare!?" Laughter and giggling. The men tried to protest. Matilde went on teasing them until Rafael suddenly said: "But I would. I would stay at home, I really would."

Fernando: "I am not saying I would not. What happens is that you have to work anyway. I am saying the same thing as you. The companies have to understand this. It might be her or him. And as long as this is not accepted by the employers..."

MOTHERS AND FATHERS

Matilde turned to me: "But now, one thing, you, the way you... let us say, starting from what you have learnt so far from this study: why do men feel such a dislike of feminine tasks? In general." I said I did not know and perhaps that was the very reason I dedicated my life to gender studies. And I declared that I definitely did not think it biological. The men tried to interrupt me the whole time. I insisted, that the ideas about women and men are deep, they are not just about tasks but about what sort of human beings we think we are, etc. One man heaved a deep sigh. Fernando said he did not know of any occidental society where the division of tasks was not the same as in Spain. Other voices talked about Muslim societies, they are different, but the idea about women and men is basically the same, anyway. Again there were sexual innuendos: when springtime comes you know which kind you are... the juices tell you what you have to do...

Mostly it was men's voices saying these things. The women laughed politely but also tried to make me go on explaining, giving them more arguments they could use. It was tempting, but I decided to be a good neutral ethnographer and ask new questions instead. "Fernando, what exactly do you mean now by maternal instincts?" He took it as an indirect attack and braced himself.

Fernando: "If you have to... If the woman ties the child to herself during the suckling period... I mean, then there is a difference already. That means that during a few years (the women corrected him: just a few months), or a few months or just one or two, that makes no difference, that period is there, and..." Everybody now stated their opinions on the importance of the suckling period. Some said it was inconsequential, others that it was this period that explained why mothers understand what a child needs and fathers don't, others insisted that the difference in understanding was there before the suckling, even a mother with no breast milk knows... Mothers are more lenient with the children, said one man, and the women said they thought the opposite. There were constant references to biology.

Matilde: "But why does it have to be biological? Isn't it rather a question of being around the kid, of getting to know him well... Sure, that is always so, that what you don't know well, you don't like. And why don't you know him? Because you spend most of your time out of the house, and you don't feel like... There is this lack of interest, to say, this child is wet, or look at his face... If the child needs to say something, who does he say it to? To Mommy who is at home, and the mother knows that this child you have to treat like this, and that one a little bit more like that, and the father knows very little, that is the truth."

Fernando said his father spent a lot of time at home, he had the time to learn, and still he did not have a good relationship with his children, and Mary Cruz confirmed this. Two women said that it was not just the quantity of time but the quality. Fernando said that was exactly what he meant. Mary Cruz said that some mothers have a bad relationship with their children, too. Once again the discussion fragmented for a while, until Matilde asked me to impose order. I used the occasion to ask the women if they had never thought of going to work after they married. Mary Cruz then remembered that she had actually worked for a couple of years, but she quit. I asked why.

Mary Cruz: "It was, like... like what I said about the women in the choir... Sure, because it was: go to work, come back... I felt that if you have a job, you want to do a good job, right? So, as for the job, I was really happy with it. I got out at five in the afternoon, I went home, then you have to do everything you did not do during the day, because it is not just all the things, like going to meetings at the children's schools and I don't know what, this one has his first communion and that one needs help with her homework... I went to bed sick. Sick, do you hear! And the next day, start work sick... No! That was not what I wanted."

Fernando: "It was also a matter of your not having patience. It is the same thing as with marriage. A woman loves her children much more. So she has a lot more patience with her children, right?"

Mary Cruz giggled: "Sure, it wasn't exactly a job to go crazy about... and neither did they pay me very much!" Fernando insisted that anyway she had more patience with the children than with her job. Mary Cruz got mad and said that what she had to take for that low salary was more than what any man would have been able to take.

Fernando: "Now, what would a man have done in your situation? Well, look, the kids would have been awfully dirty... " The discussion was fragmenting again and parts of what Fernando said were lost in the noise, but he was giving one example after the other of careless housekeeping and neglect of children. "What does a man do when he sees that the baby has a diaper that has been wet for hours? Well, he just thinks that with a bit of talcum powder it will be all right, whereas a woman..."

THE IDEAL LIFE

Matilde, sarcastic and impatient: "Fernando, what marvelous publicity you are making for yourself! (Short pause) No, but, I wanted to say, what Marie was asking before, about our ideal life, if we could choose... I mean... I want to ask: your own ideal life, is that the one you have had?"

One woman said that in her case, not at all. Mary Cruz said that if she could choose now, with the experience she had now, she would have taken things a lot easier. "If I had just gone about it more calmly, I could have gone on working and I could have taken good care of my children, too. I would have found some person with some education, not just anyone, someone who could be with the kids for a few hours, instead of me spending every minute of the day with them... so then... I would have done it in a more serene way... At the time." The other women eagerly supported her comments, saying that if they could start over again, knowing what they know now, they would never spend all their time caring for children, ten years at home, doing the same thing all the time, never...

The women seemed to forget about their previous doubts and closed ranks against the men's concerted attack on their rights to choose.

Lourdes had been silent for a long time and now admitted, hesitantly, that she had worked before she got married, but just because she liked it. She was not paid. But she liked it.

Matilde murmured: "So, out of four of us, three would change their life... in other words, we think our model has not been the best one imaginable..." I asked: "Would you change your life?" Matilde, very serious: "Yes, I would." Víctor: "Sure she would – she would even like to change her husband!" General laughter, but Matilde and Víctor shot angry glances at each other.

Mary Cruz: "But listen, Matilde, that is very different, because you don't have the same mentality now that you had when you were twenty, neither do I." Matilde nodded: "Of course not." Mary Cruz: "So then, this is tremendous, this thing we are saying, it could never be..." Matilde: "No, I am just saying that if it really was that we could choose..." Mary Cruz: "Now!" Matilde: "Yes, now." Mary Cruz: "And go back. Well... Naturally, with the experience you have of the errors you have committed and the things you have not done well, then you would try not to repeat them, so you would do it differently..."

I asked what the main errors had been for her.

Mary Cruz: "Well, as I said, to be so obsessed all day long... because in this country they teach you a lot of things... but you have a baby, they put it there and tell you, there you are! Take care of him! And you discover that you know absolutely nothing about children, so then for me it meant so much anguish..." I asked if she would still choose to have children. Mary Cruz was offended: "Oh yes, my children, yes! Of course!" I asked about her studies. "I would have finished them. Yes, I would have finished them. I think."

Fernando: "In my next incarnation, I will not marry a Basque woman!" This was too strong – Mary Cruz was Basque. Someone laughed, but someone else exclaimed a shocked: "Well now!" Matilde, the good hostess, tried to change the subject: "Marie, you have to ask the men the same thing too!" But Mary Cruz wanted to repair her marriage: "Oh no Fernando, you know the way I think, I am not saying that I am unhappy. Right now I am very satisfied with my life, but I have been through bad periods. And I am not blaming anyone for it, probably I am the one to blame. (Protests, many comments.) No, really, because I take things too seriously..." Many voices tried to calm her down, she was too serious now: You know what things are like, please Mary Cruz, that is the way life has been organized, we all have our difficulties...

Matilde: "And that was what I wanted to lead up to... that the women of our generation, we are not satisfied with our... (protests) No, I just want to say that things could improve... (more protests) I think that young girls today do not think our ways were better (the background voices agreed with her on that point). And I think theirs is better. True, it is more difficult. It is difficult." Someone said you have to combine so many things. "Exactly, that is what I meant. If society does not change, it will evidently be extremely difficult. But – it will change. I think things are going much better. So... (male voices protesting) Why does a woman, just because she happens to bear the children, eh? a lady who already... does it have to be that function and nothing more? Why? Yes, you condemn her, for many years, to do all of that, she alone, and after that you can't expect her to join the professional world!"

The men protested and the women returned to the problem of the young women who think they can combine family and profession. They talked about the support and help needed, but how the young women will see to it that they get that help, because they are convinced, they are going to do it anyway. But it will be very difficult. "It's crazy," said one woman.

CROSS-CULTURAL COMPARISONS

Víctor wanted to return to the argument of biological necessity. He reminded everyone that I had said that Sweden was not so different from Spain, and he said that when in spite of plenty of cultural difference people do the same things, "when there is something so general in the human race, there must be some biological base." The discussion went back to take a second look at this argument.

Víctor told of an article he had read that said that women in Japan had to have the bath ready for their husbands when they came home from work. He said that sounded horrible to us. But the same article said that 92% of Japanese women wanted to get married. That, to him, was proof that women want to have children, no matter what, so it must be biological.

Lourdes: "To bring up the children and to prepare the hot bath for the husband is not the same thing!" The women all laughed. The men protested.

Matilde, in pretend earnestness: "Perhaps it really is some biological force, now that I think of it, something very big, because if it was up to the men, humanity might come to an end." The women giggled. "Sure, because we women want to have children in spite of everything." Laughter and strong protests from the men.

Rafael: "Now we must let our friend of Mohammed speak." He pointed to Fernando, who said he had traveled a lot to Saudi Arabia on business... "But the models of behavior, if that is what you mean (to the women), it is in your own interest that none of it gets imported here." He gave a mini-lecture on segregation and said that the Arabs treat their women like animals.

Matilde asked me if there were any societies where women dominated. I said I did not think so, but that men do not dominate as much or in the same ways everywhere. And that in some places women have a series of advantages... Rafael teased me: "Is that where you want to go and live?" To return the teasing, I said yes, and the women laughed and said they too wanted to go there. Then they asked what those societies were like, and I gave a description of something like the !Kung of Kalahari, as an example, without mentioning names. Víctor asked suspiciously where those societies were located. "In Africa probably?" On different continents, I said, but usually in places with little stratification in general. The women looked disappointed, and Víctor said that examples from such backward places meant nothing to us, and he looked triumphant, as if I had proved his point instead of my own.

WHAT ABOUT MEN?

I asked the men if they did not think the present gender system disadvantaged them, too, not just the women. They exclaimed, immediately and unanimously: "Of course!" I gave examples from the discussion we had just had, about bad relationships with the children, about not being able to be with them very much, about the heavy responsibility to earn money... "Or like someone said, that the children love their mother more, because they know her better. Is that not a pain in your heart?"

The men said "Of course!" again. Then they started specifying: It depends, on the age, and on your point of view, and if the children turn to the mother that is just another proof of the biological tie...

José: "I, as a father, for everything to... for everything to be in its place, the civil society has to make sure to legislate and... education and relationships and so on... so that everyone can develop naturally. That would be the ideal thing. So everything that we are discussing, it is all a consequence of society not being ruled by sufficient mechanisms to make us all happy."

Matilde said that such mechanisms are created if there is a felt need, and as long as there is a problem for one gender, and the other does nothing about it... and besides, who makes the laws? Who makes the decisions? José tried to answer, but Matilde was quicker. "So the crucial question becomes then, just like Marie said, to what extent are you men happy with things as they are? Do you think they are just and equitable?"

Rafael said he thought they could be improved. José said so did he. Víctor and Fernando said nothing. Rafael:" True enough, men in general do not say that this system is perfect. That much is obvious. I think I would like to spend more time with the kids." There were jokes about Rafael's youngest son, with whom it seemed he actually spent a lot of time. Rafael glowed warmly, explaining how this young son accompanied him everywhere from Saturday to Monday morning, even to the corner bar. Lourdes said it was not such a big deal. Rafael said he would still like to have even more time for his son. "What I say often, I have said it to her, too (nod towards Lourdes), is that the older children... you see, I have four more, who are older, this last one is the grandson, that is what I call him... My older children hardly ever tell me anything. I have to ask her about them, and sometimes... yes, true, I feel envy. That could be improved, I would like for them to feel close[274] to me. They seem to think I am some sort of bad guy. I don't think I am such a bad guy... but they confide totally in her, they tell her everything. So then..."

Alejandra asked if he never asked himself the reason for this. Another man protested that the question was unfair, and the discussion broke up in fragments for a while. Rafael said that it is not true that men are hard and brave. Fernando said he disagreed totally. Rafael confirmed his position. Fernando asked him if he really wanted to spend more time with the kids. Rafael repeated: Yes, oh yes, more time and more closeness. Fernando wondered if he was thinking of taking them to the park or to play tennis. Rafael said of course.

Fernando then brought his point home, like after a cross examination in court: 'But actually reality is very different from that! The harsh truth is that you will find two centimeters of dust all over your house. And you will find that you will have to do it every single day, that you have to change diapers and you have to wash them too, and I don't know how many things... so then..." I said that I had not asked them if they wanted to be in charge of the household, but Fernando continued: "You would not worry about that, because men do not worry about such things, because they don't have a critical sense about dust. That is, you pass your finger here and look at it, a little dusty, bah, a bit more or a bit less... Whereas a woman falls to pieces! And another thing, you see a baby with a wet diaper, so what!" (He repeated what he had said a while earlier about men's callousness to babies' discomfort, now with theatrical gestures that made everyone laugh a lot.) And a woman falls to pieces over that, too."

Rafael: "And? So what?" Fernando: "So then they will bawl you out something terrible, that's what! Then what would happen? Since she would see that her scolding leaves you immune, more or less, well, no, instead of waiting for two hours, maybe you would change the diaper after one hour, but the woman would not be able to stand that either, she would end up taking over that role again." Víctor said of course. Fernando finished by saying that a man will not accept doing what a woman requires. Rafael agreed in principle and the two of them spoke lengthily about biological differences, again, and about how women have a greater love for children.

But in the end Rafael insisted: "Well, but Marie asked me for my opinion, and I have said what I would like, in all sincerity, and that is truly this, that I would like to spend more time with my kids. Why? Well, because I have noticed that my older children, well, we get along fine and everything, it's not that, but there is no closeness. Nothing at all. I have to find out things about them through my wife. That is the way it is."

Fernando, with a conciliatory gesture: "OK, OK."

Rafael: "And it hurts. So. I would like to spend more time. You talk about dusting and so on... I don't know. I am just saying that I would like to spend more time."

Alejandra: "But I asked you a question. What do you think is the reason for this, that your children do not turn to the father but instead always to the mother... why do you think they do not approach you first?" Rafael hesitated and said something about too personal a question, but then he decided to answer. "I actually think that – and in this I have to admit Marie is a little bit right – that society and the forms of organization we have had so far have made men take on artificially a certain role, and women another. Some things are for men, everyone agrees... like the decisions in the home, what used to be called head of family until recently... Nowadays they ask you who is the head of the family! (Laughter.) But until recently it was assumed that it was the father. So you felt you had to comply with that role. Just like who-was-it said, they gave her a child and she just had to accept to care for it. Because someone had to bring him up. So therefore the father's role has often been, well, eh... sort of very hard, like wanting to impose order there. What does that mean? It means that when you impose order, you sometimes impose order a bit drastically. And then what happens to the one who imposes order – that he is the bad guy!" (Laughter)

At this point the tape had to be turned for the second time. I asked if they were tired. Perhaps we should stop recording? But they just continued the discussion.

AUTHORITY

Matilde said that there used to be such an authoritarian image of the father but no longer. Alejandra exclaimed defiantly: "I believe in authority!" Matilde went on to say that women's complaint today is rather that the father is never at home, and when he is he does not take on the role of "the big bad wolf" as he used to. "In other words, women have to take on that role. And the kids continue feeling close to the mother nevertheless.

352

In other words, I don't think that it is the authoritarian role that robs a father of his kids' trust or love. It is being there! Understanding their problems!"

Mary Cruz: "That's it. The dialogue! The dialogue!"

Matilde: "... the dialogue, the being around..."

The two women spoke at the same time for a while. Fernando interrupted: "Our case is the opposite one, because I am not the authority figure, quite the contrary. (Giggles in the background.) And I agree with you. It is the authority which creates distance." Rafael said it was the same thing at work.

Alejandra: "But there is a kind of authority that you can have even with love and understanding, it is not merely a question of brandishing a stick in your hand. And that other kind of authority is valid. I think it is." This normative comment made everyone state in various ways that they, too, believed in the good kind of authority.

Mary Cruz: "But talking about work, are you men happy with the work you do? That life of slavery, working from morning til night? Because I complain, but... but it seems to me that your life is an insane life. If I were a man I would not like to..."

The other three women filled in, saying men have no time for anything, but perhaps they are afraid to admit they don't like it. One man said he would prefer to have a business of his own. Someone else came back to the idea of part time. The discussion fragmented into eight monologues, as each person explained what she or he would do with the extra free time. The tension disappeared completely and there was much laughter over the imaginative suggestions. Leisure was easier to talk about than work!

LOURDES' ANGER

But suddenly the tension came back, as Lourdes addressed her husband harshly, saying he never did anything worthwile during weekends, anyway.

Everyone laughed, but the laughter was strained. Matilde once again took on the hostess role of smoothing over. Rafael himself tried to make a joke out of it, describing vividly how lazy the others also were on Sundays. But then he decided he had to defend himself in earnest and turned to Lourdes: "Now look, Lourdes, now look... What do I do when I come home for lunch, you tell us all! Who clears the... come on, there are seven of us, too, and all of it, all of it.. (Lourdes muttered: "Yes, the plates.") True, right? Absolutely all of it..." There were more jokes, but Rafael got angrier and kept repeating that he cleared the table, all of it, and also helped with other things, as much as he could, in what little time he had.

Lourdes kept up her attack with plenty of personal examples of his sloppiness. Rafael changed to a pleading tone, turning to me: "Look, Marie, I agree that the thing could be improved and it is true that I would like to spend more time with my kids." Alejandra mediated, telling Lourdes she should accept what Rafael said, since he was sincere. Then Rafael accepted Fernando's invitations to go back to joking, and the two of them talked for a while about how they would love to work part time and play lots of tennis. They would not be bored... Matilde wondered if they meant they would use their extra time to help their wives so that they would have a chance to go out together. Rafael said that was exactly what he meant.

Lourdes: "No, but listen, when something comes up and I have to go some place, or whatever... he says (she lowered her voice to imitate a man's voice full of importance): Today I have given up everything for your sake, you know... (The other women laughed in recognition.) In other words, he rubs it in so much that in the end I just say, OK, never mind, I'll go alone. (The women giggled.) Because one thing I won't do is thank him for the company, on top of everything! Not me!" (Laughter.)

Alejandra: "He sends you the bill, right?" (common expression)

Rafael did not know whether to be angry or hurt and tried a few more arguments of each kind. As an example he told about his Saturday games of domino in the corner bar.

"Well, so it was one of those long weekends and I thought this bar, the owner is a friend of mine, that it would be closed, so I sat there reading the newspaper next to her. I was not bothering you, was I, Lourdes? So one of the kids starts laughing. He says, listen Daddy, aren't you going to your game today? I say no, because the bar is closed. So she goes, no it isn't, this morning I walked past and it was open. So what I am saying is that it was she who threw me out of the house!"

Lourdes: "Sure I did, because you turn unbearable." General laughter and comments. Matilde asked if anyone wanted more coffee. Rafael said I must not believe men are happy with the system. Matilde asked if anyone wanted more cake. At that point I turned the tape-recorder off, but then everyone was disappointed and wanted to continue. I said the arguments kept repeating themselves. "Just ask us new questions!" they said.

NEW QUESTIONS

So I did, and the discussion continued in lively style, but the arguments turned lamer, so from here on I have abbreviated more.

We talked first about complementarity versus similarity. I explained quickly that what we had always had was specialization, each sex did different things and collaborated with each other. Another possibility would be to do the same things, half of each. "Then we would be equal, not just in the sense of justice but we would be more similar, we might understand each other better. How about that?"

Mary Cruz: "I am all for that!"

I said I was not sure myself, there were perhaps advantages with complementarity, too. Lourdes said she would try anything new, because what we have, we know already. The discussion fragmented for a while.

José said he had the impression that young women of today are a lot more industrious than young men. "The situation is that sons find the labor market open and ready for them. They have their working niche perfectly defined, ready-made and prepared. And a woman does not, a woman has to make it for herself. And that is sort of the ideal." Then there was more discussion about part time.

Rafael: "At least it's more human, isn't it?"

Lourdes: "Youngsters today have only one child. Or two. But they have grandmothers to babysit for them." She gave a few examples.

Alejandra: "I think it is distressing when you have to, when they are only five months old, you have to take a child to a daycare center, I can't stand it, it makes me cry. (One woman said "me, too"; the others were protesting.) Only five months old!"

Two men commented that that was probably where the grandmothers came in, to fill in the gap until the child was older... Alejandra said she would be prepared to help her daughters if they wanted to work. "Because I know it's going to be very difficult for them."

"None of that!" Mary Cruz exclaimed and emphasized that you have to have a choice. "What is unacceptable is that they just tell you, you stay put there, like it or not. It is unfair if your sex determines your whole life."

Fernando then introduced a new idea: A couple could agree for the husband to stay at home with the children. That way the women would not be discriminated against at work. Strong protests. The consensus was that that would be impossible.

José said the determining factor would be the level of income. Mary Cruz: "Obviously, but since she is a woman she will earn much less money, so we are back with what you said in the beginning, that they should pay men and women the same, and I am sure that if the husband stays at home and the wife goes to work there will be less money in that house (some sexual joke in the background) than if it is the husband who works outside."

Rafael said that a woman might have another advantage, if she was a state employee; then at least she would have security. The other men went back to insisting that sex did not influence pay in their companies. Matilde said a woman would have to prove she was a thousand times better at her work than a man in order to get the same salary.

Fernando described how in his company there were some women employees that were really very valuable. He would like to promote them. But he could not because they always left the office at the established hour "and that is no way to have a career."

Matilde: "Why? Because they have children and because their husbands probably will not..."

Fernando: "They have to come to an agreement with their husbands! That is not my problem. But I offer them the opportunity in exactly the same way." He tells them they can have a position that would be just right for them, but they must be flexible. "You can change. If you do, you will get a higher salary, and perhaps, well... you might reach a certain level... But they don't pay any attention!"

The women went on saying a woman has no choice and the men went on saying they do. Only Rafael said the choice may not be a real one, because a person is tired after work, and a tired man can lie down, but a woman cannot, therefore she will choose to work fewer hours.

Fernando insisted that the woman ought to tell her husband that she would accept the position no matter what. An ironic woman's voice: Great! Fernando: "And the husband will say, oh, well, you must decide what to do, because I am not going to babysit. In other words, he refuses. And that is another thing... but she has the possibility."

Comments to the effect that her only choice then is to do something drastic, like get a divorce.

Fernando: "Right, but – why won't they get a divorce? Because he knows she will take care of the kids. But then she has to say, no, no, no, wait a minute, you are mistaken. I am going to take that job, and I am going to come home late, and no, I am going to have a long workday, so therefore I am not going to wash a single plate, that is your problem and you have to solve it. (Laughter, protests.) So then that guy, naturally, seeing that the situation is so clearcut, well, he has only two choices, either he backs down and says, true, something must be done, and he won't read the newspaper when he gets home from work. Or else he gathers up his things and says, well baby, if that is the way you want it, there you are! You made your bed, you lie in it! (Common expression.) He leaves. (Protests, laughter.) But she has the possibility of accepting that job. It is just as hard on him as on her. But it does not happen, and the reason is that the woman, ancestrally, biologically, loves her child more, so therefore she does not accept. That is the reason."

Mary Cruz: "Biologically or out of pure selfishness, I'd say. I mean, it might be, too, that we call selfishness biology." Short silence, surprised laughter. Voices: Sure.

Rafael had now thought up some new arguments in his fight with Lourdes and tried them out. I suggested again that it was time to finish the discussion, and this time one woman said that soon the traffic jam will start, so I interpreted this as a signal and turned the recorder off for good.

Rafael and Lourdes offered to give me a ride. Rafael talked all the way to downtown Madrid, right through a thick traffic jam, while Lourdes said very little.

Next day I called Matilde to ask if she thought the tertulia had caused marital problems. I was worried. But she laughed it off. "In that case I think I said just as bad things to Víctor, and it does not matter, he knows me, he accepts me the way I am. Rafael and Lourdes get along, they have their ups and downs, don't we all? With or without your tertulias!" Her comments were too smooth to convince me, but at least she exonerated me of any responsibility.

Comments

This tertulia exemplified many things. The talk of change permeated the conversation and defined several of the issues. The mode of management of meaning was reasonably expansionist, even though the opinions would not qualify as progressive by most

Madrilenian standards. I suspect Alejandra and José kept as quiet as they did because they would have preferred a more cautious style.

The issue of whether male and female behavior is determined by nature or culture was experienced as central by all, but it was the men who kept coming back to it again and again to insist that the women's complaints could not be taken seriously. To avoid questioning the present division of tasks, they did not hesitate to denigrate themselves; they went as far as saying that men are irresponsible and insensitive by nature.

The word "class" was scrupulously avoided.

The women found it hard to verbalize their complaints. They loved their children, they did not want to be unfeminine, and being feminine was largely defined for them and by them as loving housework and childcare. Yet something did not quite fit. When they managed to verbalize this hard-to-catch problem, it was in the form of some argument about choice. Of being a person, of not being forced into a role, and so on.

Religion was conspicuous by its absence. The participants were all practicing Catholics. The Catholic Church has a lot to say about the issues discussed. Yet at no point during the tertulia did anyone make any religious statement or refer to any Church position.

The strong general belief in personal merit had different consequences for women and men, and this was exemplified at several points in the tertulia. For instance in Fernando's view of what women have to do in order to be successful in the labor market. He did not think they were discriminated against. If they were not successful, it was their own fault, he said in effect. He found no excuses valid. They have to be strong; weakness is a fault and causes its own punishment. Merit counts, nothing else. What he thought women lacked was ruthlessness, and he criticized them for it. Yet, he believed in biologically determined differences of character. There is a contradiction here, which could only be solved in two ways as long as we stay within Fernando's worldview: either the labor market has to be reformed so that women can earn merit despite their biological handicap, or else men must accept full economic responsibility for women. Fernando contemplated neither.

The men did not like the idea of women in the labor market, but they found the thought of having to do housework themselves even more repellant. They went to extreme lengths to argue that it was women's natural duty. When Lourdes attacked him, Rafael's response was to defend himself in earnest. He played fair, although he must have been furious inside. He tried hard to prove, in calm words, with factual reporting from their daily life, that he was not a bad husband. He helped. Clearing the table after lunch! One must conclude then, that he really did not do much else. I am sure he needed his leisure, but I wonder about Lourdes' situation, keeping house for seven persons with little help.

The tertulia illustrates some common asymmetries in men's and women's ways of discussing and possibilities of making each other listen.

First of all, as Matilde noticed, most of the discussion was about women, not men. But that happened more often than not around these issues, and this tertulia treated men's activities in a more critical mode than was common. (The otherwise much more expansionist discussion in chapter 13 did not contemplate taking anything out of the male role, only what might be added to it.)

The women participants agreed, without any need to negotiate with each other, what a woman's needs and duties were, whereas the men concentrated on women's duties and nature, showing little insight into practical matters.

Víctor and José kept mostly quiet. Rafael and Fernando, however, were unusually interested in these "women's issues". They talked a lot, they offered interesting arguments and personal examples. But what they did not do was to listen to the women's examples and arguments. They did answer a few of them, but not the crucial ones, like what a housewife is supposed to do when the children grow up and she has no merits for the labor market, or how one can expect an exhausted woman with a double workday to "have patience" until the children grow up.

At no time did the men say they might be willing to take on real responsibility for half of the domestic tasks. Nor did the women suggest that. But the women's arguments were crowded with hints about the men's shortcomings in family life. I think the men, under their polite façades, must have experienced the tertulia as an uncomfortable occasion for their wives to expose them to a barrage of complaints. Yet at no time did the women seriously threaten the men's position in the gender hierarchy. They did not suggest different practical arrangements, for example, so the men did not have to answer any concrete questions about what they would be willing to do.

Nor did the women have any arguments against the men's ideological statements. The biological argument, which was basic for the men, was something the women believed in, too, although with certain doubts they found difficult to express. Personal strength and merit were values both genders believed even more firmly in, so when Fernando placed the blame squarely with the women themselves, if they did not attain good careers, the women protested rather feebly. Only Lourdes tried to give concrete examples of her complaints, but she did it in such a personal and bitter way that it backfired, leaving her in the role of an unfair attacker.

Lourdes was not a skilfull debater, but the discussion in general makes a good example of appreciated verbal skills and love of argumentation. (Cf appendix C.) The critical mode of management of meaning stands on fertile ground in old and deep dispositions. This might be one reason that a critical discourse never died out even under the long period of dictatorship and why it was able to reconquer hegemony in a short time. However, the cautious mode of management of meaning must not be confused with the opposite of verbality. The cautious ladies at Club Aguafría did not usually discuss as freely as the participants in this tertulia did, but if pressed they, too, would defend their positions with verbal agility and emphasis (cf chapter 16). And Matilde and her friends tended toward a cautious mode in general. It was the issue of gender relationships that forced them to cast about for new arguments. The men stayed mostly within their normal cautious mode, but were forced to negotiate more openly after a while. The women took their time before they dared to come out of their initially cautious remarks, but the dynamics of the discussion made them critical as far as this issue was concerned.

One reading of this tertulia is as an illustration of a double bind related to women's acceptance of the gender order. The women must not work outside the home, because if they do, they will be considered unfeminine and rejected as unworthy; but they must work, because otherwise they are at material risk and also rejected as oldfashioned and perhaps not strong enough for modern times. The third alternative is to try to be a super-woman, but that is not only dangerous, as well, but unattractive. Work is not only valuable, pleasure also counts. So there is really no way out of the double bind as culturally constructed. The sacrifice required to break its hold was seen as too great, while the sacrifice imposed by things as they were was accepted – by this type of women – as inescapable.

Appendix B: Theory and Methods

This appendix gives the interested reader a larger framework in which to place this study. The piece of knowledge that I have built may have its intrinsic value, but I also want to contribute to a larger accumulation of knowledge about gender. To make that possible, it is necessary to define my epistemological points of departure.

Making descriptions of gender orders comparable

If, as a general rule, we want to understand the social processes that produce differences in power, the anthropological contribution ought to be to give empirical descriptions of situations where one category of human beings is defined in contrast with another category of human beings within the same society, whatever the criterion for the categorization is. The fact that there is a categorization indicates that something important happens along the border, i.e. at the place of the defined difference. It is quite probable, albeit not necessary, that it has to do with the distribution of resources of some kind. So the anthropologist should describe the categorization and the consequences of it, both as they are interpreted in the society in question and as they might be interpreted looking in from the outside. Studying only one of the categories can give other kinds of information, but no information on why the categorization exists or what social effects it creates.

When we have reliable empirical knowledge about the various categorizations that occur in a given society, we can try to draw conclusions about their relationship to each other.

That is why gender, not women, should be in focus in any study with a feminist-critical intent. And that is also why any other hierarchies in the society studied should be taken into account as well.

Gender, class and other social categorizations or organizational principles can be seen as structures that limit and shape social practice. They can also be seen as results of social practice. The theory of practice (Bourdieu, Giddens, Connell) is making it unnecessary to choose between these two ways of seeing.

I start out from the assumption that any and all circumstances become the accumulated experience of individuals and groups by way of their practice. Human beings interpret and work with what they have around them, and their interpretations, actions and products immediately enter and form part of the mass of circumstances. Experience is stored in the form of dispositions (Bourdieu's term), which are simple but widely applicable schemes for interpretation and action on different levels of awareness. And since experience in this indirect way shapes all action, all actions are related to all circumstances that the groups or the individuals have experienced. A habitus (Bourdieu's term) is the set of dispositions that a group or a category or an individual has.

Since individuals always belong to several groups and categories (for instance a family, a village, a gender, a class, a profession, a political party, a sports club...) their habituses are more or less unique collages of the collective habituses in which they partake. Inside each individual habitus, different and sometimes contradictory dispositions influence each other in a constant dynamic. Likewise, each collective habitus is constantly moving due to the interactions between its dispositions and the dispositions of other collective habituses in which individuals of the category also share. Plus of course the dynamism that comes from the interactions between the habitus and all circumstances and all situations in which it enters.

Habituses are changed by other habituses, by circumstances and situations, but always by way of the groups and individuals who carry them. The theory of practice emphasizes that "structures" do not directly do anything at all. People do things, it is their practice that makes things happen, but they do so starting from what they know and believe and from the material possibilities they have for action. And their ideas and resources are not distributed by chance or by individual will alone but along the lines of social structures. Therefore people of different categories have different experiences, therefore different dispositons, therefore different practice, and thus they reproduce different ideas and structures. But because of the complex intervening structures, the reproduction is never perfect. There is always change.

Class and gender can be seen as two types of experiences and therefore as separate sets of dispositions. In a class society, any individual can be classified both according to class and gender. If there are three classes and two genders, for example, we would get six possible categories. In real life, classifications are seldom clear-cut, of course.

Seen in this way, both class and gender become constantly changing entities, since they consist of accumulated experience, and since all experience is constantly changing and dispositions therefore being modified. Class and gender are formed in social process. They are products. But they are also powerful structures with heavy inertia. They cannot be changed through individual acts of will, and they are not the result only of interaction in observable situations.

The classical debates in socialist feminism on whether class or gender causes the greater part of observed inequality for working class women, and whether women of dominating classes are also oppressed or not, are moot in this light. Any individual in a complex society belongs to several hierarchical structures and can have different positions in each, and her or his total experience, practice and possibilities depend on all of them. The interesting question becomes instead just how various structures interact in specific contexts. This is what I set out to describe for the Madrilenian middle class. Since the object was too large for one study, and since it was a moving situation, I concentrated on the cultural negotiations around gender, against the background of circumstances of middle class life.

The cultural negotiations take place through many kinds of symbolic expressions, but verbal behavior is an important part of them and lend themselves well to anthropological description. Since what one hears is an important part of experience, one's habitus will be influenced by discourse, and since one's further practice will be based on one's habitus, and the gender order will be influenced by the practice of all individuals taken together, discourse around gender issues is one thing that should be described in order to describe a gender order, and a strategic one.

By middle class, here, I mean a category of persons who would be defined as workers if we use a narrow Marxist definition of class, i.e. their relationship to production is that they sell their labor. But they do so at a price that permits them a higher living standard than manual workers, higher even than most small businessmen. Within this broadly defined category, this study concentrates on people who obtain this good salary thanks to their high education. Since this is not a study of class conditions as such, the exact class concept used is not very important. What is important is that for Madrilenians, class was an inescapable experience in everyday life. [275] The frontiers may not be distinct, but the nuclei of the class categories, their approximate levels of income and education and their symbols and histories were, both subjectively and objectively. This study concentrates on people who were situated in the middle class according to the definition given and who had no doubt that they were. They kept a social and symbolic distance to the manual working class and to the less well paid parts of the middle classes. They tried to emulate the upper classes, the aristocracies of birth and capital, but they could not be confused with them, because they had little or no inherited capital of their own, and their salaries did not enable them to approach the palaces, the fashion houses or the high society social events that defined affiliation to the uppermost social sphere.

To the extent that the gender categories are placed so that they have access to different kinds of possibilities and are constrained by different kinds of limitations, some sort of hierarchy becomes the almost inevitable outcome. It is possible to imagine perfect balance in a complex system of differences, but even if the idea is a logical possibility, it is not very probable in reality.

If a description of a gender order focuses on the issue of power, all factors producing differences of power must be taken into account. All hierarchies and their interaction with each other in individual lives should be described, including those based on kinship and age, even in Occidental industrialized societies where class and gender are usually more evidently decisive. [276]

Therefore, I set out to do two studies of the Spanish urban gender order, with similar questions and methods, for two different classes. As it turned out, it was not possible to use exactly the same methods nor to ask the same questions, because the circumstances to be described were not similar enough. Reality tends to destroy systematic research plans, that is not surprising. With all due consideration of the differences, however, the results of the two studies do speak to each other.

To describe a gender order is to find out, first of all, how many gender categories the society in question recognizes (usually but not necessarily two) and what criteria are used to differentiate them and what differences between them are invested with what significance. Then one must describe which constraints and possibilities work differently for these categories, whether these causes and effects are recognized or not in that society as related to gender.

This is difficult to do without falling into ethnocentric traps. The questions must be sufficiently abstract to be applicable in any society, yet give relevant and comparable information. We need a ladder of questions that enable us to move back and forth between lofty abstractions and concrete empirical material.

A set of questions on gender orders

Connell (1987) has taken a first important step in creating basic terms with which we can describe gender-relevant circumstances. He proposes the term gender order for everything that has to do with gender in a given society. To look closer at reality, we need to subdivide this in some way, an Connell proposes the term gender regime for that which has to do with gender in any institution within the society, for instance the labor market, or the family. The amount of hierarchy or the symbols for gender, and so on, need not be the same in each gender regime. In this way the whole gender order can be described in a more dynamic way than if we speak only of "the position of women" or similar.

Just how extensive the "society" is, for which one wants to describe the gender order, is a question to be decided for each study. It is just as possible to say interesting things about "the Western world ' as about a group of people where the individuals can be easily counted. What is important is to be clear about the extension chosen and to realize that independently of the size of the population, there may be many institutions and therefore many gender regimes. One must also be careful, of course, to choose the level of abstraction (distance from empirical detail) that corresponds to the amount of generalization necessary. I have chosen "the Madrilenian middle class".[277] If I had chosen to focus on one part of it, for instance Club Aguafría, it would have been possible to make many more detailed empirical observations. But I consider that an extreme micro level is not the most useful if the purpose is to illuminate power relationships between large structural entities, such as the genders.

To avoid the rigidity of some former theoretical constructions that saw gender as something to be found within certain places in a society (for instance the socialist feminist proposition that "production" is governed by other rules while gender is relevant only in "reproduction"), Connell suggests three structures (as first approximations; there might be more than three): labor (the division of tasks, any kind of tasks), power (the distribution of resources and possibilities to participate in decisions), and cathexis (desire, emotions). All structures can be found in any gender regime, i.e. structures and regimes intersect. This is important in order to avoid simplistic descriptions that focus on love only inside intimate relationships and division of tasks only in places that are defined as places of work. There is labor, power and cathexis in any gender regime, and it is the combination of their effects that makes the gender regime into what it is.

In this way, the decriptions can also be made dynamic. We can look for contradictions in many spaces, for instance between the way two structures work inside one gender regime, or between the effects of various gender regimes on the gender order as a whole.

I use Connell's and Bourdieu's terms to arrange and illuminate my empirical data to produce a readable picture of the study object. Other pictures are of course possible.

If we follow Connell's suggestions, then, we have come closer to concrete reality, but we still need to formulate more detailed questions. And they should be stated in such a way that they avoid as far as possible taking for granted what Western feminism has usually taken for granted about what causes gender hierarchy. Anthropology needs to build generally applicable models that make gender orders comparable.

What follows is my provisional formulation of such questions. They should be applicable to any level of generalization. They constitute a way to sort the empirical material in such a way that other more abstract questions can then be asked, for instance about the relationships between different hierarchies (e.g. class-gender), about comparisons between different gender regimes within one gender order (e.g. family-school), about comparison between different societies (e.g. the gender order in Madrid – the gender order in Tokyo), and so on.

Differences between women and men (and other gender categories whenever present): How similar/different are the worlds of women and men? Do women and men have the same or different evaluations of good and bad, of goals in life? And how great is this degree of similarity/dissimilarity in comparison to the degrees of similarity/dissimilarity that exist for other categorizations in that society (for instance class, age)?

Differences of degree in cultural dilemmas: It is probable that all human beings house irreconcilable goals and values. But the irreconcilability, and therefore the difficulties of making crucial decisions in life, might be greater for one gender category than the other. Where in the cultural edifice are such dilemmas located, how do they affect each category, and what consequences do they have for individual lives? Do they have consequences for the possibilities (and possible wishes) of one gender category to obtain vital resources? Do they have consequences in the form of uneven competition for vital resources between the categories?

Role dilemmas for women and men: What do the gender norms look like and are the various recognized gender roles compatible or not? What are the norms for motherhood and fatherhood, for example? Are women's different roles (both gender-specific and general) compatible or not? Are men's? How are the possible contradictions for each gender conceptualized? How are the possible differences between women's and men's dilemmas interpreted? Is anything practical done about them? Which dilemmas are most visible or most controversial. Are there dilemmas that serve as metaphors for other things?

Ideologies (in the sense of elaborated ideas expressed in more or less stable discourses, especially institutionalized ones like religious or political thought): What major ideologies incorporate ideas about gender? Are there major systems of ideas that do not have anything to say about gender? Is there a need for legitimation of certain aspects of the gender order? If so, what are those aspects and how are they legitimized? Are there interesting similarities or differences between these legitimations and those for other aspects of social life that might be comparable? (For example, if the gender hierarchy is conceptualized as unjust, and this must be justified, is the justification the same, similar or different from the justification used for other hierarchies conceptualized as unjust, for instance class?)

Goals and possibilites: Can women and men obtain to the same extent whatever they themselves define as desirable goals in life? Can women live up to what men define as good and can men live up to what women define as good? And if the cultural goals in life are different for the genders, how do they relate to each other? Is it for example a good thing for a woman to reach a male goal and bad for a man if he should happen to reach a female one? Or vice versa? Are there any overarching criteria for what is best that are valid for both (all) gender categories? How well can the female goals be adapted to the male ones and vice versa? What need does each category have of adapting its goals to the ones of the other category? What happens when goals do not coincide?

Distribution of resources: Which resources are more or less evenly distributed between the gender categories? Which ones are unevenly distributed and how? How is this justified? What other social circumstances, apart from the construction of gender, contribute to uneven distribution of resources between the genders?

Distribution of duties and tasks: Which tasks are more or less evenly distributed between the gender categories? Which ones are unevenly distributed and how? How is this justified? What does the total burden of tasks/privilege of action look like? Which category works most, measured in objective terms like time and effort? How is the work related to material resources and social power? Which tasks are strongly associated with one gender category, which are more or less gender neutral, and to what extent are such prescriptions lived up to in practice? Are there some special tasks that seem to play a special role in the demarcation of the categories, creating gender identities?

Gender and other categorizations: Which culturally visible categorizations exist in the society, and how are they valued? What part does gender play in the total picture? Is the categorization according to gender seen as a cause of other categorizations, a consequence of them, or unrelated to them? Is the differentiation between the genders as such valued positively or negatively? Is it perhaps quite unimportant? Close to invisible? Are some of its effects invisible, even if the categorization as such is not?

This is not a complete list, but it indicates a way of formulating the descriptive questions in such an abstract way that they should be applicable to any type of society while retaining the goal of comparison. The description should give a total picture that makes inter-society comparison possible on at least three major counts: how hierarchical a gender order is, how broad a scope it has (if few or many situations, institutions, etc. are organized by gender in some way) and what its force is (if improvisations and norm-breaking is strongly sanctioned or just shrugged off) (Thurén 2008).

Obviously the task is momentous. To answer the list of questions even just for the Madrilenian middle class, one would have to compare the data from innumerable studies, some of which exist but many would have to be carried out. The aim of this book is to contribute to such a collection of data, a contribution where the emic interpretations occupy the foreground. It would be presumptuous and unscientific to offer authoritative descriptive answers to all the questions at this stage. But the contribution of this book should be seen against the background of the larger aim. Chapter 21 contains a summary of the situation in the Madrilenian middle class with reference to the Mediterranean area in space and to the 1990s in time.

Feminist anthropology

This is a feminist book. This is not the place to discuss what feminist anthropology can be and what my position is on its many issues. But since misunderstandings around the word are rampant, I need to explain what I mean by feminism.

Experience tells me that the following statements are called for: By feminism I do not mean any essentialist defense of the female sex in general. I do not think women are intrinsically better than men, and the fact that I am a woman does not give me scientific or political licence to speak for all women. Nor are women and men, as far as I can tell, similar to each other across all time and all space. Other differentiations of human beings according to class, religion, ethnicity, etc. affect women as well as men, albeit usually in different ways. And those differences are more related to the specifics of time and place than to biological determinations.

For me, feminism means, first, to recognize that gender is not sex and that therefore there is a gender order in any society, i.e. a specific way of handling the biological fact that our species has sexual reproduction and approximately two sexes. It also means that since these specific ways vary across time and space, they should be described and then scrutinized for what they do to individuals and collectivities.

By feminism, I also mean the corpus of theory and empirical research that has been carried out under that label since the 1970s (or for centuries, depending on definitions). I use the word as a general label for that corpus, not any single one of its many hypotheses or standpoints.

To be a feminist anthropologist means to consider gender as something more than a curious fact. Gender is an inescapable fact that shapes lives. But it can be changed by collective effort, and in so far as its effects are negative, it should be changed. Anthropological studies of gender are descriptive and theoretical. Feminist anthropology has the added goal of using the theory and the descriptions for political purposes, i.e. to take a stand.

What is good and bad about the gender orders of the world is difficult to specify. But even anthropologists possess the human right to have opinions on their own society. I believe the general gender order in Europe is not good for us, neither women nor men, but that it has been more negative for women, so that it is logical that women should have initiated the critical appraisal of it. I am a feminist because I believe that continued appraisal and change is necessary and possible and will improve the quality of life for everyone, and above all for women. Exactly what factors have caused suffering is a matter for both debate and research.

Anthropological knowledge can contribute to the feminist effort, but it can do so only if it is good anthropology, objective to the extent that any social science can be objective. After all we study ourselves as human beings. This book is written in the hope of contributing to that effort. It is a feminist book in the sense that its point of departure is a critical stance toward reigning gender orders, and it is an anthropological book because it is meant to be relevant not only to the time and place described but to the understanding of human societies in general. (Thurén 1998, 2000, 2002a, 2002b, 2005, 2008, 2013)

Studying up

Anthropologists have usually studied categories of people who have been poorer and less powerful than they themselves, or at least than their societies of origin. Laura Nader argued the case for "studying up" already back in 1972, and some efforts have been made since then, but much too little. If anthropology wants to gain knowledge of all types of human societies, it obviously cannot exclude the study of the rich and powerful, and if we are interested in questions of power, the exclusion is even less defensible.

However, there are good reasons why few have turned their enquiring searchlight upwards. The powerful often do not want to be studied, and they have ways of protecting themselves. Even when they do not put up barriers on purpose against researchers, there are always strong social barriers, so for a researcher that does not belong to the category to be studied, it is difficult to be admitted, or, if admitted, to behave in a way that is acceptable enough to establish the rapport needed for anthropological methods to work well.

The Madrilenian middle class was not an extremely inaccessible social world. But many of its members were well placed in society. They had means of hiding from view. Many of them were also interested in erecting symbolic and social barriers against people from lower strata. Statements about "the greater sensitivity", refinement, of the upper classes were acceptable to many of them. The key word "education" was used very frequently and in a conveniently slippery way, so that it came to mean both "formal learning" and "good behavior" and even "nice dress". Contacts with members of lower classes could then be avoided arguing that they were uninteresting, ignorant, clumsy and insensitive in interaction, perhaps dirty and ugly. Among my most conservative informants, the feeling was of rejection and fear. The fear was mostly expressed in the constant talk about burglaries and street robberies, and many would not contemplate riding the metro. Some acted as if social problems were contagious, so that people associated with them, for instance social workers, had to be avoided.

I had lived a middle class life myself in Madrid during the 1970s. That afforded me opportunities of access that I experienced as close to a moral obligation to do research in this context. I had also lived through the dramatic social and cultural changes of the end of the Franco regime and could give some time depth to the ethnography. Finally, this middle class seemed like the logical context for my continued investigation of the gender orders in Spain.

But the challenges of studying up had to be met. Since education was such an important symbol, my academic qualifications helped to compensate for my lack of money and personal contacts, but only up to a point. The project financing was not sufficient for me to fit into the life style of the informants in the way that is usually the very basis for participant observation. It was not even sufficient to enable me to be generous with informants in exchange for their time and help, and that felt very awkward and somewhat unethical. I had to ask the usual favors from informants without being able to behave in return with even the minimally expected reciprocity. This fact limited access and skewed it somewhat in favor of the most tolerant and the least well-off.

The greatest difficulty was the high rents in Madrid. The project would have been impossible if I had not already had an apartment of my own in the city. But it was a small apartment in a not very reputable quarter. From there I had to move by bus, metro and taxi, so traveling took a lot of time, and only on about half a dozen occasions did I dare to invite informants to my home. And these occasions did not always turn out well. Some informants took it naturally, for others I was a quaint bohemian who could be permitted any extravagancy, but others again turned up their noses. The safest thing was to not even tell people exactly where I lived – I used the vague phrase "near Plaza España" which made the neighborhood sound respectable. Inviting people to one's home is not all that common in Madrid, so it was not considered strange that I did not. But rapport and interviews might have been a lot better if I had had the possibility of inviting people. To live among the people you study is also basic for the usual type of anthropological fieldwork. I could not count on running into people while they were going about their daily business.

The methods of data gathering had to be adapted accordingly. And it was not just an instance of the old anthropological wisdom of doing the best with the situation at hand. If we are to take seriously the goal of studying up, more work must be done on developing methods that allow us to circumvent the high costs involved. Discourse analysis is one.

Field techniques

I was in Madrid from June 1990 to January 1992. The first two months were spent searching out old acquaintances, trying to extend the network of contacts and planning research activities. From September 1990 to July 1991, fieldwork was centered on a social club, which I call Club Aguafría. After that, and to some extent during that period, too, I widened the scope and moved all over the city in order to get acquainted with as many different kinds of middle class contexts as possible.

At Club Aguafría, the principal method was ordinary participant observation. I had been introduced at the club by long-time friends, who had been members since the club was founded, some twenty-five years earlier. Their backing gave me access and some prestige, but it also limited my freedom of movement somewhat. Their group of friends at the club became my group, also The insight into the conservative type of discourse that prevailed at the Club was a boon that would have been very difficult to obtain in any other way.

The restriction to my friends' group was not absolute. There was an ideology that all club members should feel free to socialize with all. This was far from actual practice, but it made it possible for me to establish contacts with other groups and individuals.

Outside the club, I also practiced participant observation, if one can call it that when one does not follow one group of people over a long period of time in all their doings. The important thing was to find out what kinds of contexts middle class Madrilenians participated in and what happened there. Some of the contexts are described in the empirical chapters: a book club, a gym class, a friendship group. These were contexts with which I had contact throughout fieldwork. I also stayed in touch with a feminist group, to which I had belonged for many years. I socialized as much as possible with old and new friends, not always able to distinguish between friends and informants. Because of my previous knowledge of Madrilenian life, I did not feel I needed to study family life up close, but I did take every chance to spend time in people's homes for different reasons. I went to the cinema, to the theater, to restaurants and other places where my informants went. I had some contacts with university people. I tried to watch the television programs and read the newspapers and magazines my informants talked about. I participated in the popular "cultural" activities for housewives. I made a few trips outside Madrid in the company of friends and informants.

All of this gave me the necessary general overview of activities, categories, discourses. It gave me good knowledge of spontaneous conversations – what things are talked about in what contexts and how, and what happens if norms are broken.

But I also wanted to tape conversations, in order to be able to analyze details. To this end I interviewed individuals, asking them to tell me about their lives, and I arranged group discussions.

In Benituria, I had begun to use the life story method, and I had planned to use it very much more in Madrid. But unlike Beniturians, middle class Madrilenians were not seduced by the idea of telling their life stories. Some did, and they enjoyed the exercise and talked freely. Some others said they would love to do it but found innumerable excuses and in the end never did. Most found polite ways of refusing from the start. They had no time, they had nothing interesting to say, they thought such interviews would make my research too psychological (with educated informants, one receives many comments on one's methods!), they could not see any reason why I could not ask them what I wanted to ask while sitting with the group at the club...

There is one life story in chapter 15; altogether I did twenty-three life story interviews but only ten could be taped.

After a while I gave up trying. Instead I asked other informants why they thought the idea was not appealing. They said it was perfectly understandable; people have to keep up appearances. Most people have something they want to hide. They may not be as rich as they try to appear, or they may come from humble backgrounds, or perhaps they have family trouble they don't want anyone to know about. In other words, the status insecurity of this new class translated into psychological and social insecurity and a fear of all sorts of shameful involuntary revelations.

In contrast, the other major method I had planned to use was received with enthusiasm. Group discussions fitted the dispositions for talk as entertainment, and it gave the women who offered to be hostesses a good excuse to invite people to their homes, which was thought to be a correct and even elegant thing to do but was in fact not often done.

I used the term *tertulia*, which covered the idea very well and at the same time gave it a flavor of something traditional, intellectual and prestige-laden. Tertulia can mean just a group of friends chatting together ("my husband has a group of friends visiting, they are having a tertulia in the diningroom"), or getting together regularly to chat ("we used to have a really nice Sunday tertulia at the club"), but it can also mean a group of artists or intellectuals meeting regularly at some bar or café to discuss, a sort of informal seminar ("he was a member of the writers' tertulia at Café Gijón"; "Doctor X participated in the most prestigious tertulia of his town"). To organize a tertulia, then, sounded like the right thing to do for a middle class person with social ambitions.

For these occasions, six to twelve persons sat in someone's home, usually having coffee, sometimes food, and after an initial period of general chatting, I explained the purposes of the method, suggested a few topics to get the discussion started, and placed a tape recorder on the table. There were predictable jokes about the recorder, but it was soon forgotten, and the discussions always gave me good material and the participants a good time.

Two lightly edited but complete discussions are presented as examples in appencix A and chapter 13. Chapter 19 also presents a group discussion, but more abbreviated. Altogether, I did twenty-two taped group discussions and a number of untaped, more or less improvised, ones. Most of them were with people I also knew in other ways.

Appendix C. Conversations in Madrid: Method

Ethnography of talk as a means, not as an end

While writing this book, I was tempted for a while to call it "Conversations in Madrid". I resisted the temptation, because the title had already been used, in Spanish, for a volume of political interviews in the 1960s (by Salvador Pániker), and also because it does not really cover what the study is about, which is gender.

It is a phrase that covers a method. No more. But no less. The material for this book is in great part precisely conversations. This is so first of all because an ethnography should describe what the studied people do, and a large part of Madrilenian life consisted of conversations. Second, because all ethnography is in fact based on talk in one form or another, not exclusively but to a large degree, whether or not this is recognized by the anthropologist. Third, because studying a dispersed category of people in a big city makes classical participant observation of one locale unsatisfactory. The anthropologist is caught in a dilemma: either she spreads herself thin, and runs the risk of making superficial observations, or else she concentrates on one locale anyway, and runs the risk of not understanding even that, since it is connected to so much else that she cannot observe. Fourth, in middle class Madrid, everyday life, including work done for a living, in itself consisted to a great extent of talk.

A fifth reason might be to strive for "polyphonic ethnography",[278] letting the informants speak for themselves. Such a goal is slightly naïve, since the reader would then have as hard a time to understand what is being meant as the anthropologist has the first day in the field. But from an ethic point of view, the goal is valid. The informants should be allowed to speak as much as possible but with such explanation from the anthropologist in the presentation as becomes necessary to make the message carry through to the reader. In the case of this study, this ethic point is especially important, since I cannot sympathize with the viewpoints of some of my informants. I want to be fair to all of them, and I would have liked to be able to respect all their opinions, yet I cannot but consider some of them racist, sexist and elitist – all ugly words in my vocabulary. The solution must be to let them speak for themselves as much as possible, with comments from me to aid the reader to interpret the utterances as the speakers intended them.

In other words there are culturally specific and methodologically strategic reasons for building this study around talk. Another type of reason could perhaps be called epistemological. What I wanted to describe about the Madrilenian gender order had to do with deep-seated ideas, dispositions, habitus. These are never easily visible in talk, but neither were they evident in action, in a historical moment where change, fragmentation and improvisation are key words for the informants themselves as well for observers. I have developed a method for catching in talk glimpses of that which is not said but meant (i.e. doxa, cf chapter 4, note 56).

This method was used in an earlier work (Thurén 1988) and also in this one, with modifications. It consists in finding special places in what the informants say, places where the speaker makes references to what goes without saying. In such places, what is not said, because it is not considered necessary to say and perhaps because it cannot be said, is at least hinted at and can be fished out of its dark hole and reconstructed. One such place are *accounts:* what people directly or indirectly refer to as causes of, excuses, legitimations and justifications for, or interconnections between events. *Metaphors and jokes* are another kind. They are good windows on doxa, because they rely for their effect on the presence of something unsaid that all participants in the conversation must agree to, or the metaphor would become uninteresting, the joke would fall flat. Other places are what I have called *holes, semi-holes* and *marked holes,* i. e. places where an outsider thinks some link in the chain of phrases is missing for the utterance as a whole to make sense, but the speaker does not think so (hole), or only hints at it indirectly (semi-hole) or points deliberately to something left out (marked hole). The marked hole often comes in the form of *expressions of self-evidence,* such as: of course, as everyone knows, as I am sure you realize, inevitably, as always, etc.

Of all the reasons for doing ethnography of conversations in Madrid, the first one is the most decisive. A large part of Spanish reality lies in the spoken word, so the spoken word must be described.

Spaniards talk a lot. Any Spaniard reading that phrase will probably protest, saying it depends on personality, region, class, and so on. Certainly, it is relative matter. But it is relative on a wider scale than Spain, too. In comparison to Northern Europeans, for example, they all talk a lot.[272]

Most Mediterranean cultures are in fact quite verbal. In this part of the world, reality is in the word in many ways, and this fact makes verbal action a focus for cultural elaboration. One not only talks, one talks about talk. One gossips about who is a gossip; one makes speeches in the honor of the art of rhetoric; one invents academies and parliaments; in communication with gods one prefers praying to sacrifice; one can call a god the Verb; and one creates a moral system of honor and shame where a word can be a matter of life and death and a word about a deed can count for more than the deed itself. And so on.

In case these examples themselves smack of rhetoric, let me give a few ethnographic examples. Reality is in the word, among other things, in the sense that if something is not talked about it does not exist. Witness for instance the many precautions against talking about what is uncomfortable or what is against the norms in traditional Spanish culture, both rural and urban. In Valencia, a young female informant told me that her father probably suspected that she slept with her boyfriend, but as long as he did not officially know it, i. e. as long as noone said so in so many words, he did not feel required to take any action.[280] Everyone knows that many uncomfortable things happen; and everyone knows that the action that would be required if those uncomfortable things were recognized might be disruptive and even more uncomfortable. The solution is to pretend not to know. As long as there is silence about something, it is as if that something did not exist.[281]

Reality is in the word also in the sense that spoken words are actions. They might bring a fact into existence in the way just explained. They might also create reality in other ways. In some sense, all speaking is illocutionary.[282] A statement in a discussion on almost any topic creates a place for the speaker in relationship to that topic and therefore to the other participants in the discussion. Other dispositions convert most conversations into discussions. Therefore almost all statements effect changes in the social map. An insult or a declaration of friendship, including indirect ones such as inviting someone for a drink or for a walk for more talking, are obvious examples. But utterances that look like mere affirmations often, even usually, have similar intentions and effects. A statement such as "I would never go to the falla party in street X" might translate as "I am not a member of the falla movement" which in turn probably means "I do not like the falla movement" and that in turn might well mean "I am politically radical", which finally would mean different strategic things according to the setting.[283]

Not only do all statements have some immediate consequences for the social map of the setting where it is pronounced, but the repercussions can spread to other settings and events. To continue the example, if the statement about the falla party was pronounced in a bar, in a group of friends, it had effects there, for instance placing the speaker politically in relationship to the others in a new way or confirming an old position. But it would also have effects in all other settings where the speaker was involved in some interaction where her political opinions might be relevant – a job interview, a dinner with relatives, the next fight with her husband, or whatever – at least if there had been other intermediate speech actions spreading the information. And each speech act spreading this piece of information would also have effects for each speaker, so that, for instance, the report "A says she does not like the falla world" by B to C might make C act in special ways not only towards A but also towards B, considering B more of a friend or less so, trustworthy or a gossip, etc. and it might influence the feeling of B for C according to C's reactions to the news, etc.

There are even wider repercussions. The daily talking, discussing, conversing, joking, quarreling, story-telling, arguing, embellishing, covering-up and so on, together make up a cultural negotiation, a constant process of shaping ideas and attitudes. And discourse – what is usually said about something in a given social context – becomes Discourse, a decontextualized mass of ideas, a great river, through the flowing together of thousands of rivulets of everyday talk. Furthermore, any given topic is shaped both through discourse on that topic and discourse on other topics that are related in some way. For instance gender is shaped, among many other things, by discussions about the biological determination of gender characteristics versus the social construction of them. Therefore gender is also shaped by discussions about any nature-culture-topic, even if gender as such is not mentioned.

This is how cultural negotiation works everywhere. But it is perhaps more so in very verbal societies. Perhaps Swedes used to shape their ideas and attitudes more in solitary ruminations while walking in the woods, and nowadays more in imaginary dialogues with mass media; at least they do not have anywhere near as many opportunities to thrash out their ideas in face-to-face verbal interaction with a number of different kinds of others as most Spaniards do. It is a matter of different dispositions and also of different organization of everyday life.

Because reality is created in talk (but not only in talk, of course), participation in talk is one dimension of power. This book is about what is said, but also about where it is said. The gender principle sorts women and men differently in social space, and this means (among other things) that they have access to different types of discourses, and this in turn means that they do not participate equally in creating social and cultural reality. And the contexts in which individuals participate shape their experiences and cause differentiation among them.

Anthropology houses a certain skepticism towards the ethnography of conversation. Verbal expression and social reality are sometimes described as if they were opposites. They are certainly not automatically synonymous, but neither are they opposites. They are connected in intimate ways.

Madrilenians themselves often talk about talk as if it was the opposite of reality. "Don't trust what people say," might well be a basic survival lesson that all children are taught from an early age. This just confirms my contention, however. A verbal culture breeds verbally skilled individuals, and verbally skilled individuals by definition can do many things with words, including lying, cheating, fooling and manipulating. To survive in a verbal culture, therefore, one must be skilled in seeing through the verbal fireworks of others, no matter how seductive. The verbal surface most certainly does not coincide with individual or collective depths. But that does not make the surface uninteresting nor devoid of clues about the depths. Actually the very image of surface versus depth is misleading.

To understand the meaning of the conversations presented in this book, it is necessary to keep the love of talk in mind. A Northern European or a North American might react with skepticism: Did those people really say all of those things? What did the anthropologist do to make them? Do all those words really mean anything to the people who spoke them? (I have had such reactions to my material.) My general answer is Yes, they said all of those things, and they did it because they wanted to and had fun doing it, and they really meant what they said if all factors of the setting are taken into account (which means an infinite hall-of-mirrors of determinations, of course). Among other things it is in order to prove this that I have included a couple of only lightly edited transcriptions of taped conversations (appendix A and chapter 13).

Naturally my presence influenced what happened, that is inevitable in all fieldwork. The anthropologist cannot observe without being there, and the way of being there must be adapted to the dispositions and norms of the informants. Since my informants talked a lot, I could hardly keep quiet. This is another reason for including some long transcripts – I want the reader to have a chance to see for herself how I intervened in the action, and how I was sometimes forced to when I did not want to, and how I tried to keep my own talk as neutral as possible.

Not all of my informants wanted to talk to me, or not all the time or in any company, or not about all issues. Of course. Examples of this and reasons for it are included. But overall they were verbal people who enjoyed any excuse to talk some more, including the strange excuse that an anthropologist asked them to. That did not make much of a difference. In Valencia, my working-class informants stressed that talking in itself was a major source of pleasure in their lives, and to be forced to be alone and therefore without conversation, a major punishment. The same was true for the middle class Madrilenians. Therefore, there were plenty of natural conversations of different kinds for me to tap as data, and my suggestions for arranged conversations were in general well received and the arranged conversations not substantially different from the debates that occurred spontaneously all the time. (For details on conversational interaction, cf below.)

I think that an ethnography of conversation should exist and should be something more than a description of forms and contents of the conversations in a given society.[284] For anthropologists it can be a methodological tool to try to draw closer to subtle cultural matters. For example, in gender studies, to find out how ideas about gender look, whether directly or indirectly verbalized, and also to find out how verbalized ideas about gender are used in conversation as tools in the social process, whether concerning gender or other aspects of social organization.

Doing and saying is not the same thing. I know that, and Mediterranean people know it. But saying is a kind of doing, and Mediterranean peoples know that, too, and anthropologists of Mediterranean societies ought to.

What did middle class Madrilenians do about and with their gender order? They did many things, but whatever else they did, they also talked about it. And this was a social fact in its own right. Therefore, the informants' own words have been reported in this book as much as space will allow. In this way, the reader gets a picture of their verbal actions, and they are given a voice, so that the book becomes in some sense polyphonic. But since most of the readers will probably not be middle class Madrilenians, I must translate and comment, i. e. present the talk I heard in forms the speakers themselves might not approve of in order to make it understandable for non-Spanish readers. I will also add my own voice in a more obvious way, constructing an anthropological narrative about what is happening to the gender order in Spain. That is my verbal action and a scientist's special privilege.

Conversational habits

Let us look at the dispositions that shape conversations in Madrid. I do not pretend an exhaustive analysis, just an exposition of what the reader needs to know in order not to misunderstand the intentions of the speakers. There are five major factors to be kept in mind. Finer details are explained as the occasions arise throughout the book.[285]

1. Turn-taking:

The first thing that will probably strike the reader is that the informants interrupt each other constantly. This must not be taken to signal impatience or aggression or lack of courtesy. On the contrary, to interrupt is the normal way to take turns.[286] If you are not interrupted, it is probably because the others find what you say uninteresting. If they hear something they want to comment on, whether to agree or to disagree or just to offer varying examples, they will try to interrupt. They will not interrupt until they are reasonably sure they have understood what you say, so vague speakers or expositions of complicated lines of thought may be allowed to go on for a longer time than a normally understandable and yet interesting one. But boring expositions will also be interrupted, usually with a joke or a put-down. On the other hand, when a person wants to hold the floor, he or she may re-interrupt, go on with a raised voice, or otherwise refuse to cede the floor. This may or may not work – the tolerance for several voices speaking simultaneously is high.

In the group discussions I arranged, I always told the host/ess to forewarn the guests about the activity. They did, telling the guests that I was to be there and who I was. But when I got out the tape recorder and asked if everyone knew what the whole thing was about, the answer was inevitably no, not much. The host/ess may or may not have explained enough for their tastes, but the participants always wanted my personal explanations, too.

So I talked about the project, about my general aims and how an anthropologist does long periods of fieldwork. I said this in as abbreviated a way as possible, since most informants thought this was boring and I risked being interrupted too soon if I gave details. Then I explained the reasons for the group discussions, also very briefly, and went on to suggest topics for discussion. I never reached the end of my prepared list of topics. As soon as I had mentioned three or four, and the participants understood that I was giving them a list, they prepared to start talking themselves, and as soon as someone had an opinion on how interesting some topic might be, she or he interrupted me. I then re-interrupted in order to introduce a few more topics, and after a couple of turns of this, a decisive interruption usually occurred: some topic struck several informants as so interesting that they would not let me re-interrupt, or they would interrupt each other with comments on how the topic should be handled, and in this way the debate would already be under way.

From there on, my strategy was to remain as peripheral as possible to the debate, intervening only if the discussion became too repetitive or if some informant became very uncomfortable with a topic for some reason, or if someone suggested we switch to some new topic. Or if the participants insisted that they wanted to hear my opinions. This happened regularly, since my silence did not fit the Madrilenian conversational norms at all. If the discussion was unusually interesting or provocative, or if I felt I was among informants who would accept my own opinions, I sometimes slipped into a more normal participation. I cannot see any real differences between these discussions and those where I stayed closer to the research role. Informants of other conversational cultures might be more influenced by the attitude of the observer than these, who were much too interested in the topics, in each other and in the pleasure of conversation to pay much attention to me. It is also relevant, of course, that they were not overly impressed by my professional status (similar to their own or those of their husbands), so that did not interfere with their interaction either.

In sum, turn-taking is quick and energetic. There is no norm that one should wait until other speakers have finished their turns. Norms that one should speak only one at a time exist, but they are weak, and if a conversation is too orderly and overly polite in the turn-takings, it will be experienced as boring. The techniques for holding the floor or for taking it from others involve mainly making fast points, preferably humoristic or dramatic. The side-effect of this is to increase the entertainment value of the conversation, which is a conscious value to strive for, too.

2. Rhythm:

Not just turn-taking, but the conversation as a whole is quick and energetic. Long pauses are easily interpreted as social failures and become uncomfortable. But since the participants are skillful, the pauses are not allowed to become long; before they do, someone has invented a way to break it, usually a pertinent joke.

The rhythm is not uniformly fast, however. It is rather used for good effect. (Cf note 289) Dramatic pauses and dramatic lowering or raising of pitch are used when appropriate, that is as often as a speaker feels she wants to make a special point. Which is often, cf below on self-affirmation.

Now, these norms are in full effect only in relaxed amicable conversation (including almost all of the arranged group discussions). At Club Aguafría, at least in some groups, the style was more sober and controlled. One reason for that was that a measured style, verging on the monotonous according to the general criteria, could be a sign of distinction for some sectors of the middle class. It was thought to be elegant because it went against the grain of general ('vulgar") styles. Another was probably the obligation to aparentar, i. e. to present oneself in as favorable a light as possible, and that meant especially never to reveal lack of money or lack of knowledge. This was a psychological shackle, of course, that inhibited normal dispositions for fancy conversational footwork. Finally, there was a reason that had to do with change. In some contexts the bewildering cultural and social changes were handled with great caution. Club Aguafría was one such cautious place. And when one has to be very careful with what can and what cannot be said, one cannot always give free reins to one's aesthetic dispositions. The need for caution, restraint, control, etc is problematic and self-contradictory in a culture which emphasizes self-affirmation (cf below).[287]

3. Emotional tone:

The conversations are punctuated by laughter. I have signalled this here and there, when the laughter might have some meaning for the content of what is said, but there was much more than what I can report. This does not mean that the participants did not take the discussions seriously. Laughter is a normal part of normal conversations in Madrid. Since conversation is social pleasure, one laughs because one feels good. And one laughs to show the others that one appreciates their company and their communicative creativity.

In none of the conversations did anger or sadness or other negative emotions disrupt the interaction. There were certainly such emotions, but they were not allowed to disrupt the flow of the discussion. Sometimes purposeful expressions of such emotions were used to underline speakers' points. Emotional expressions could be used like rhythm and other aesthetic features for dramatic effects. When they were not purposeful but involuntary, the speaker did not have to feel ashamed and/or be reassured by the others, but she or he would usually keep quiet for a while to recover.[288]

The emotional variations are part of what makes a conversation enjoyable. A Madrilenian conversation is not just an exchange of viewpoints. It is a composition of varying rhythms, combining attacks and defenses, collaboration and spying, rebuking and explaining, lying and revealing lies, joking and protesting, giving and demanding, learning and teaching, etc.etc. and all of it for intellectual and aesthetic pleasure and for the emotional pleasure of taking part in this kind of social interaction. None of the conversations reported in this book crossed the limits of what is normal Madrilenian social interaction, and only once during the fieldwork did I worry that an arranged discussion might have caused some personal trouble for the informants (and this was denied by them). (Cf end of appendix A.)

But of all these emotional expressions, laughter dominates. To be too serious is to give others a boring time or to show lack of mental agility.[289] Laughter and joking are as normal and necessary ingredients of serious debate as of inconsequential small talk.[290]

4. Self-affirmation:

One of the goals of the social interaction, if we see it as a game, is to express one's self: Here I am. This is what I am like. You must see me, and you must see me correctly, the way I want you to see me.[291]

Since Madrilenians are verbally skilled, one must never commit the mistake of believing that there is a direct channel from what they mean to what they say. Many interesting things happen along that way. But the need for strategic behavior is always balanced by the need to give a forceful presentation of Self. Correctly interpreted, this gives the anthropologist a fair chance to approximate informants' true intentions. Most of the time the participants in the group discussions tried hard to express their opinions clearly. To express it in game terms again: if one does not manage to show clearly who one is, creating interest and preferably even convincing others of the truth and importance of what one has to say, then one has lost one round or perhaps the whole game.[292]

5. Cultural negotiation:

Apart from all of these good reasons for enjoying conversations, reasons that are very general in Spanish culture, there was one that was more specific at the time of fieldwork, the 1990s, and probably more acute in Madrid, or at least in big cities, than in the rest of Spain. It was the need to negotiate meanings in times of social and cultural change and increasing complexity. This is a major theme of this book, so I will not expand on it here, just point out that it was another important factor that contributed to shape to my ethnographic material and motivated people to talk a lot and to seek out certain topics and handle them in certain ways. Cultural negotiations go on always and everywhere, inevitably, but they can be more or less central to social behavior.

This description of the main features of Madrilenian conversations may make someone think that those conversations must have been nervous and superficial events. It is true that individuals were not allowed to hold the floor long enough to delve deeply into subtle matters. The requirement to show a sense of humor perhaps did not limit the individuals very much in their thinking, since it came easily to them. But the fast rhythm did set a limit to how much could be said in each individual turn. However, collectively, the conversations covered ample ground and scrutinized all suggestions that came up. Since there was no norm against repeating what had already been said, each new idea was taken up by many individuals and varied in both major and minor ways. Since there was a predilection for contributing personal examples, all ideas were tried against varied empirical evidence.

What usually happened was that when a topic had been under consideration for a while, there was a tendency towards consensus. This was not because the participants strove for consensus. Quite the contrary, consensus was considered boring. When consensus approached, voices were raised for changing the topic. The establishment of consensus was not a social goal but an intellectual result that occurred, threatened or drew close when all angles the participants were capable of verbalizing had been exhausted.

Feminists and informants.

The wider relationship between the informants and myself is described elsewhere; but a few words on the way we met in the interview situations are necessary here.

The impersonal style that is the model for ideal interviewing in much social and psychological research has been found wanting by feminist researchers.[293] It is not a natural way of behaving for women in the countries where academic feminism has developed. In these parts of the world, women usually interact in more personal ways than men. And in so far as all women belong to a devalued social category, it is contradictory for them to interact in a way that implies a distance that is not experienced as the most relevant aspect of the relationship between two women, even if one of them stands with a notebook in her hand on the doorstep of the other.

Anthropologists have criticized the impersonal model, too, since their concern is to draw closer to something unknown, and in that effort emotional distance is not always a useful attitude. The professional jargon phrase for what must be done is "to establish rapport". But the need to avoid ethnocentrism sets a limit to closeness. If one becomes too involved, one may fall into the trap of interpreting things according to the categories of one's home culture and thus preclude correct understanding.

I believe it is necessary to understand and use the local norms for speaking, especially for questions and answers. One should try to establish a non-hierarchical friendly relationship to the informant in order for the situation to be comfortable and mutually honest. So far, most anthropologists would agree (cf Briggs 1986). The feminist touch is added mainly in that the researcher permits herself to tell illustrative anecdotes from her own life, compare her own opinions to those of the informant, show her reactions to what the informant says, and in other ways act more as she would in a normal situation. This was possible in Madrid, because Spain is a Western country, where feminist thinking applies, and because I am Spanish enough myself not to have to worry very much about the danger of ethnocentrism; it was also necessary because Spanish interactional styles are personal in themselves for all, and more so for women.

One must not speak too much oneself, of course, but one should speak enough to establish the kind of relationship that feels natural and comfortable for both parties and which guarantees that one does not place oneself outside the object of study in a misdirected and actually unscientific effort of objectivity. (If the object of study is gender, and we are all gendered persons, what would true "objectivity" require?) What exactly constitutes a respectful and relaxed attitude is of course culture-specific. In Spain it translates to quite a lot of speaking, including own examples and confessions, interruptions, laughter and counter-arguments, as we have just seen. Anything different would be construed as cold and manipulative. And that in turn would influence the informant's behavior much more and in more unpredictable ways than "normal" behavior from the interviewer.

The extent to which this holds true depends obviously on time and place. But in Spain it holds true to a high degree, because of the dispositions around interaction I have just described. It held even more true for my work in Madrid, since I truly had a similar background to my informants. Furthermore, other dispositions around interaction in Spain, such as self-affirmation and tolerance of contrasting opinions, also counterbalance the influence this personal behavior might have on an informant.

To give the reader a chance to monitor my possible influence on the informants, I have included my own actions in the description of all situations in the empirical chapters. A good example is chapter 15 (Esperanza's story).

I sometimes had to ask questions to which I knew the answers or on which I had personal opinions. This was especially so around the key topics of work and sexuality. But I also suggested topics for debate that honestly confound and worry me. For example: What degree of similarity between the genders is possible and desirable? And if men's and women's experiences make them into very different sorts of people, how can they get along with each other? Is love possible, in that case? What sort of love? How can unintentional harm be avoided in the personal relationship between such different beings? And how can social justice be guaranteed? How can it even be defined?

I placed such questions on the agenda in spontaneous conversations as well as in group discussions. I did so especially when other participants refused to allow me the degree of non-participation or neutrality that I had adopted. Wherever possible, however, I avoided defining the situations, since I wanted to know what topics informants themselves would bring up. After all, there are interesting research questions that can be addressed only if some portion of deviousness is allowed between researcher and informant. To balance the personal, ethical and scientific desirability of closeness and honesty against the long term scientific need for certain types of data is no easy matter and I do not pretend to have resolved it. What I am saying is that I think the balance should be found closer to the non-hierarchical pole than has been the rule in Western social science.

Conversations as data

I hope it has become clear why it is not a bad idea to use conversations as data for anthropological purposes. But they constitute data that must be most carefully contextualized.

First of all they must be interpreted correctly in the light of local habits, norms and dispositions. And the field techniques used to elicit them must be described and their relationship to the local dispositions analyzed.

The data must also be understood against the background of the modes of management of meaning (cf chapter 4), of which there may be many in a society, and in some societies they can well vary more situationally than they do in Spain. Each conversation is probably dominated by one mode of management of meaning, and the way this shapes it must be made clear. There may also be conflicts between or references to different modes of management of meaning.

For each conversation, the whole situation must be described: time and place, purposes of gathering (implicit and explicit ones), number and statuses of participants, their relationships to each other, their possibly conflicting interests and purposes, and so on.

The whole social situation in a much broader sense must also be taken into account for the influence it might have on what happens in the specific conversation. Participants belong to one or several of socially meaningful categories, such as gender or class, and this places them in specific ways in relationship to each other, to the larger society and to the topics treated. Economic, demographic, political, etc. processes and the information about them that the participants probably have and what they mean to them in general and what they mean to them more specifically in relation to the topic of the conversation must never be forgotten. The historical moment is also an essential part of the context; in the case of this study especially the fact that the introduction of a democratic regime was only 12-15 years old.

To describe all of this in an anthropological report easily becomes tedious. Perhaps it is logically impossible, involving a meta-meta-meta...n communication. Perhaps only literary techniques of writing can convey everything the reader needs to know. A scientific text must strive for transparency, leaving as little possible between the lines for the reader to fill in, but using such complex techniques as analysis of conversation for anthropological purposes, one runs up against a limit of what is reasonable.

What I want to underline here is that the anthropologist needs to know a lot in order to use conversations as data. It is not a recommendable method in a field that is new to the fieldworker. But it yields rich data to a fieldworker with longer experience of the field; and for a fieldworker doing anthropology "at home" or in a context that may be a little too close to home for comfort, the careful analysis of conversational data can be a means to obtain a degree of objectivity and analytical distance.

This is so even if space limits the presentation of all the steps of the analysis. The use of a lightly impressionistic style in the empirical chapters of this book does not mean that the analysis has not been made or that the selection of situations to be described is haphazard. The non-Spanish reader may run the risk of misunderstanding some of the things that are hidden between the lines in these chapters, but I hope this is compensated for in the more analytical chapters. And the reason for using such a separation in the presentation is to allow for both analytical distance and some intuitive closeness. Only if I am allowed to hint at things between the lines, can I feel satisfied that I have done what I could to communicate the subtler aspects of my tale.

References

ABELLAN, José Luis: *Los españoles vistos por sí mismos. La visión que los españoles han tenido de sí mismos a partir de los años en que se constitutyó la unidad nacional.* Turner, Madrid, 1986

ABRIL NAVARRO, Ma.V., FARO, C., MARTINEZ DE CASTILLA, A., OLIVA. A. (eds): *Jornadas de trabajo sobre sexualidad. Por un proyecto global de actuación.* Instituto de la Mujer, Madrid, 1986

ABU-LUGHOD, Lila: The Romance of Resistance: Tracing Transformations of Power Through Bedouin Women. In P. R. Sanday, R.G. Goodenough (eds): *Beyond the Second Sex. New Directions in the Anthropology of Gender.* University of Pennsylvania Press, 1990

ACEVES, Joseph B: *Social Change in a Spanish Village.* Schenkman, Cambridge, Mass., 1971

AGAR, Michael: Stories, Background Knowledge and Themes: Problems in the Analysis of Life History Narrative. *American Ethnologist,* 7, 1980

AGAR, Michael: Themes Revisited: Some Problems in Cognitive Anthropology. *Discourse Processes,* vol 2, no. 1, 1979

AGUILA, Rafael del, y Ricardo MONTORO: *El discurso político de la transición española.* CIS/Siglo veintiuno, Madrid, 1984

ALBA, Víctor: *Transition in Spain. From Franco to Democracy.* Transaction Books, New Brunswick, NJ, 1978

ALBERDI, Inés: *Historia y sociología del divorcio en España.* Centro de Investigaciones Sociológicas, Madrid, 1979

ALCOBENDAS TIRADO, Pilar: *Datos sobre el trabajo de la mujer en España.* Centro de Investigaciones Sociológicas, Madrid, 1983

AMBJÖRNSSON, Ronny: *Mansmyter. Liten guide till manlighetens paradoxer.* Fischer & Co., Stockholm, 1990

AMELANG, James S. y Mary NASH (eds): *Historia y Género: Las mujeres en la Europa Moderna y Contemporánea.* Edicions Alfons el Magnànim, Valencia, 1990

Anthropological Journal on European Cultures. Special issue: The Mediterraneans. Reworking the Past, Shaping the Present, Considering the Future. Nr 10, 2001

Anuario El País, Madrid, 1992

APTER, Terri and Elizabeth GARNSEY: Enacting Inequality. Structure, Agency and Gender. *Women's Studies International Forum,* 17:1:19-31, 1994

ARADILLAS, Antonio: *Piedra de escándalo: La iglesia en el cambio.* Plaza y Janés, Barcelona, 1986

ARDENER, Shirley (ed): *Perceiving Women.* Halsted Press, New York, 1977

ARDENER, Shirley (ed): *Defining Females. The Nature of Women in Society.* Croom Helm, London, 1978

ARDENER, Shirley (ed): *Women and Space. Ground Rules and Social Maps.* Croom Helm, London, 1981

Asociación Madrileña de Antropología (ed): *Malestar cultural y confllicto en la sociedad madrileña.* Comunidad Autónoma de Madrid/Asociación Madrileña de Antropología, Madrid, 1991

AUSTIN, John L.: *How to Do Things With Words.* Oxford University Press, London, 1962

BATESON, Gregory: *Steps to an Ecology of Mind.* Granada, London, 1973

BELL, C.: *Middle Class Families.* Routledge & Kegan Paul, London, 1968

BELTRAN, M. et al.: *Estudio sobre la familia española.* Ministerio de Trabajo y Seguridad Social, Madrid, 1987

BENERIA, Lourdes: *Mujer, economía y patriarcado durante el período franquista.* Anagrama, Barcelona, 1977

BENHABIB, Seyla and Drucilla CORNELL (eds): *Teoría feminista y teoría crítica. Ensayos sobre la política de género en las sociedades de capitalismo tardío.* Edicions Alfons el Magnánim, Valencia, 1990 (Original title: Feminism as Critique. Essays on the Politics of Gender in Late-Capitalist Societies)

BERMAN, Marshall: *Allt som är fast förflyktigas. Modernism och modernitet.* Arkiv, Lund, 1987. (Original title: All that is solid melts into air. Penguin Books, 1982)

BERNIS, Cristina, Violeta DEMONTE, Elisa GARRIDO, Teresa G. CALBET, and Isabel DE LA TORRE (eds): *Los estudios sobre la mujer: de la investigación a la docencia.* Actas de las VIII Jornadas de Investigación Interdisciplinaria. Universidad Autónoma de Madrid, Madrid, 1991

BETZ, Hans-Georg: *Postmodernism and the New Middle Class.* Theory, Culture and Society, 9, 1992

BORREGUERO, Concha, et.al. (eds): *La mujer española: de la tradición a la modernidad (1960-1980).* Tecnos, Madrid, 1986

BOURDIEU, Pierre: Marriage Strategies as Strategies of Social Reproduction. *Annales,* E.S.C. 27:1105-25, 1972

BOURDIEU, Pierre: *Outline of a Theory of Practice.* Cambridge Studies in Social Anthropology, Cambridge, 1977

BOURDIEU, Pierre: *Distinction. A social critique of the judgement of taste.* Routledge, London, 1989/1984

BOURDIEU, Pierre: Hederskänslan. I *Kultursociologiska texter.* Salamander, Stockholm, 1986

BOURDIEU, Pierre: *Practical Reason: On the Theory of Action.* Stanford University Press, Stanford, 1998

BRANDES, Stanley H.: *Migration, Kinship, and Community: Tradition and Transition in a Spanish Village.* Academic Press, New York, 1975

BRANDES, Stanley: *Metaphors of Masculinity. Sex and Status in Andalusian Folklore.* University of Pennsylvania Press, 1980

BRAVO, Diana: *La atenuación de las divergencias mediante la risa en negociaciones españolas y suecas.* Stockholm: Stockholm University Library. Stockholm University Tryck AB, Stockholm, 1993

BRENAN, Gerald: *The Spanish Labyrinth.* Cambridge University Press, 1943

BRIGGS, Charles L.: *Learning How to Ask. A Sociolinguistic Appraisal of the Role of the Interview in Social Science Research.* Cambridge University Press, London, 1986

CALERO FERNANDEZ, María Angeles: Los sexos y el sexo en los tacos, una cuestión etnolingüística. In Bernís et al, 1991

CAM (Comunidad Autónoma de Madrid): *La mujer en la Comunidad de Madrid.* Dirección General de la Mujer, CAM, Madrid, 1990

Cambio 16, nr 1 132, August 1993

CAMPBELL, J.K.: The kindred in a Greek mountain community. In Julian Pitt-Rivers (ed): *Mediterranean Countrymen: Essays in the Social Anthropology of the Mediterranean.* Mouton & Co., Paris/La Haye, 1963

CAMPO, Salustiano del, and Manuel NAVARRO: *Análisis sociológico de la familia española.* Ariel, Barcelona, 1985

CAMPO, Salustiano del: *La "nueva" familia española.* Eudema, Madrid, 1991

CAPEL MARTINEZ, Rosa Maria (ed): *Mujer y Sociedad en España (1700-1975).* Instituto de la Mujer, Madrid, 1986

CAPLAN, Pat (ed): *The Cultural Construction of Sexuality.* Tavistock, London, New York, 1987

CARTER, Bob: *Capitalism, class conflict and the new middle class.* Routledge & Kegan Paul, London, 1985

CASTELLS, Manuel: *La cuestión urbana.* Siglo XXI, Madrid, 1974

CASTELLS, Manuel: *Crisis urbana y cambio social.* Siglo XXI, Madrid, 1981

CATEDRA TOMAS, María: *Los españoles vistos por los antropólogos.* Júcar Universidad, Madrid, 1991

CHAFETZ, Janet Saltzman: *Gender Equity. An Integrated Theory of Stability and Change.* Sage, Newbury Park, London, New Delhi, 1990

CLIFFORD, James and George E. MARCUS (eds.): *Writing Culture. The Poetics and Politics of Ethnography.* University of California Press, Berkeley, Los Angeles, London, 1986

COLLIER, George A.: *Socialists of Rural Andalusia. Unacknowledged Revolutionaries of the Second Republic.* Stanford University Press, Stanford, 1987

COLLIER, Jane Fishburne: *From Duty to Desire. Remaking Families in a Spanish Village.* Princeton University Press, Princeton, 1997

387

CONNELL, Robert W: *Gender and Power. Society, the Person and Sexual Politics.* Polity Press and Blackwells, Cambridge and Oxford, 1987

CRENSHAW, Kimberlé Williams: Mapping the Margins: Intersectionality, Identity Politics, and Violence against Women of Color. In K. CRENSHAW et al. (eds.): *Critical Race Theory: The Key Writings That Formed the Movement.* New Press, New York, 1995

CUCO, Josepa and Joan J. PUJADAS (eds): *Identidades colectivas. Etnicidad y sociabilidad en la península ibérica.* Generalitat Valenciana, Valencia, 1990

DAVIDOFF, Leonore: *The Best Circles. Society Etiquette and the Season.* Croom Helm, London, 1973

DAVIES, Charlotte Aull: *Reflexive Ethnography.* Routledge, London, New York, 1999

DAVIS, Kathy, Monique LEIJENAAR, Jantine OLDERSMA (eds): *The Gender of Power.* Sage, London, 1991

DEL VALLE, Teresa, et al: *Mujer vasca. Imagen y realidad.* Anthropos, Barcelona, 1985

DELPHY, Christine: *Por un feminismo materialista. El enemigo principal y otros textos.* Cuadernos Inacabados, 2-3. LaSal, Barcelona, 1985

DENICH, Bette S.: Sex and Power in the Balkans. In M.Z. Rosaldo and L. Lamphere (eds): *Woman, Culture and Society.* Stanford University Press, Stanford, 1974

DENZIN, Norman K.: *Interpretive Biography.* Sage, Newbury Park / London / New Delhi, 1989

DIAZ DEL MORAL, Juan: *Historia de las agitaciones campesinas andaluzas.* Alianza Universidad, Madrid, 1967 (Original 1928)

Di LEONARDO, Micaela (ed): *Gender at the Crossroads of Knowledge. Feminist Anthropology in the Postmodern Era.* University of California Press, Berkeley, Los Angeles, London, 1991

DOUGLAS, Mary: Jokes. In: *Implicit meanings.* Tavistock, London, 1975

DUBISCH, Jill (ed): *Gender and Power in Rural Greece.* Princeton University Press, Princeton, New Jersey, 1986

DuBOULAY, Juliet: *Portrait of a Greek Mountain Village.* Clarendon Press, Oxford, l974

DURAN, María Angeles (ed): *De puertas adentro.* Instituto de la Mujer, Madrid, 1988

ESCRIVA DE BALAGUER, José Maria: *Camino.* Rialp, Madrid, 1988

ESTEBANEZ ALVAREZ, José (ed.): *Madrid, presente y futuro.* Akal, Madrid, 1990

EVERS ROSANDER, Eva: *Women in a Borderland. Managing Muslim Identity where Morocco meets Spain.* Stockholm Studies in Social Anthropology, Stockholm, 1991

FAGOAGA, Concha and Petra María SECANELLA: *Umbral de presencia de las mujeres en la prensa española.* Instituto de la Mujer, Madrid, 1984

FANT, Lars: Cultural mismatch in conversation: Spanish and Scandinavian communicative behaviour in negotiation settings. *Hermes*, 3:247-265, 1989

FANT, Lars: "Push" and "Pull" Moves in Hispanic and Swedish Negotiation Talk. *Hermes Journal of Linguistics,* 11, 1993

FERRANDIZ, Alejandra and Vicente VERDU: *Noviazgo y matrimonio en la burguesía española.* Cuadernos para el diálogo, Madrid, 1975

FOLGUERA, Pilar (ed): *El feminismo en España: Dos siglos de historia.* Pablo Iglesias, Madrid, 1988

Forskningskommittén i Uppsala för Modern Svenska: *Könsroller i språk.* FUMS rapport nr 49, Uppsala Universitet, Uppsala, 1977

FOUCAULT, Michel: *Historia de la sexualidad. 1. La voluntad de saber.* Siglo XXI de España, 2006 (Original: Histoire de la sexualité. 1. La volonté de savoir. 1976)

FOWERAKER, Joe: *La democracia española.* Arias Montano, Móstoles (Madrid), 1990

FRASER, Nancy: *Unruly Practices. Power, Discourse and Gender in Contemporary Social Theory.* Polity Press/Blackwell, Cambridge/Oxford, 1989

FRASER, Nancy and Linda NICHOLSON: *Social Criticism without Philosophy: An Encounter between Feminism and Postmodernism.* Theory, Culture and Society, 5, 1988

FRAYSER, Suzanne G.: *Varieties of Sexual Experience: An anthropological Perspective on Human Sexuality.* Human Relations Area File, 1985

FREEMAN, Susan T.: *Neighbors: The Social Contract in a Castilian Hamlet.* Chicago, Chicago University Press, 1970

FREEMAN, Susan T.: The Municipios of Northern Spain: A View From the Fountain. In R. Hinshaw (ed): *Currents in Anthropology.* Mouton, The Hague, 1979

FUSI, Juan Pablo, Sergio VILAR and Paul PRESTON: *De la dictadura a la democracia. Desarrollismo, crisis y transición (1959-1977).* Historia 16, extra XXV (Historia de España nr 13), Madrid, 1983

GALLEGO, Juana: *Mujeres de papel. De ¡Hola! a Vogue: La prensa femenina en la actualidad.* Icaria, Barcelona, 1990

GALLEGO MENDEZ, María Teresa: *Mujer, Falange y franquismo.* Taurus, Madrid, 1983

GARCÍA SAINZ, Cristina: *Mujer y empleo en la Comunidad de Madrid.* Dirección General de la Mujer, Comunidad de Madrid, Madrid, 1990

GAVIRIA, Mario J. (ed): *Gran San Blas.* (Offprint from *Arquitectura,* 113-114, 1968

GEERTZ, Clifford: *Islam Observed. Religious Development in Morocco and Indonesia.* The University of Chicago Press, Chicago, 1968

GEERTZ, Clifford: *The Interpretation of Cultures.* Basic Books, New York, 1973

GEMZÖE, L, T. HOLMQUIST, D. KULICK, B-M THUREN and P. WOODFORD-BERGER: Sex, genus och makt ur antropologiskt perspektiv. *Kvinnovetenskaplig tidskrift,* 1, 1989

GIDDENS, Anthony: *Central Problems in Social Theory. Action, Structure and Contradiction in Social Analysis.* Macmillan, London, 1979

GIDDENS, Anthony: *Modernity and Self-Identity. Self and Society in the Late Modern Age*. Polity Press/Blackwell, Cambridge/Oxford, 1991

GILMORE, David D.: Anthropology of the Mediterranean Area. *Annual Review of Anthropology*, 11:175-205, 1982

GINER, Salvador (ed): *España. Sociedad y Política*. Espasa-Calpe, Madrid, 1990

GINER, Salvador & Luis MORENO (eds): *Sociología en España*. CSIC, Madrid, 1990

GODDARD, Victoria A.: From the Mediterranean to Europe: Honour, Kinship and Gender. In V. Goddard et al (eds): *The Anthropology of Europe*. Berg, Oxford, 1994

GOETHE, Johann Wolfgang von: *Faust*. Bonniers, Stockholm, 1932

GURREA, José: *La sexualidad: sexo, embarazo y contracepción en la adolescencia*. Montesinos, D.L., Barcelona, 1985

GOULDNER, A.W.: *The Coming Crisis of Western Sociology*. 1970

HAMPSON, Norman: *The Enlightenment. An evaluation of its assumptions, attitudes and values*. Penguin, London, 1990 (1968)

HANNERZ, Ulf: *Exploring the City. Inquiries Toward an Urban Anthropology*. Columbia University Press, New York, 1980

HANNERZ, Ulf: *Cultural Complexity. Studies in the Social Organization of Meaning*. Columbia University Press, New York, 1992

HARDING, Sandra (ed): *Feminism and Methodology*. Indiana University Press, Bloomington, Indianapolis, 1987

HEATH, Shirley Brice: *Ways with Words. Language, Life and Work in Communities and Classrooms*. Cambridge University Press, Cambridge, 1983

HELLER, Agnes and Ferenc FEHER: *The Postmodern Political Condition*. Polity Press, Cambridge, 1988

HERNES, Helga Maria: *El poder de las mujeres y el estado de bienestar*. Vindicación feminista, Madrid, 1990

HOBSBAWM, Eric: *Primitive Rebels*. Manchester University Press, 1959

HOBSBAWM, Eric and Terence RANGER (eds): *The Invention of Tradition*. Cambridge University Press, Cambridge, 1983

HOLLAND, D. and N. QUINN (eds): *Cultural Models in Language and Thought*. Cambridge University Press, Cambridge, 1987

HOOPER, John: *The Spaniards. A Portrait of the New Spain*. Penguin, London, 1987

IMBERT, Gérard: *Elena Francis, un consultorio para la transición. Contribución al estudio de los simulacros de masas*. Península, Barcelona, 1982

IMBERT, Gérard, and José Vidal Beneyto: *El País o la referencia dominante*. Mitre, Barcelona, 1986

INGOLD, Tim: Becoming persons: Consciousness and sociality in human evolution. *Cultural Dynamics*, 4, 1991

INNER – Investigación Cuantitativa de Mercados: *Los hombres españoles*. Instituto de la Mujer, Madrid, 1988

INSTITUTO DE LA MUJER: *Jornadas de trabajo sobre sexualidad. Por un Proyecto Global de Actuación*. Instituto de la Mujer, Madrid, 1986

IZQUIERDO, María Jesús: *Las, los, les (lis, lus). El sistema sexo/género y la mujer como sujeto de transformación social*. La Sal, Barcelona, 1983

JämFo: *Makt och kön. Rapport från ett seminarium, oktober 1985*. Delegationen för jämställdhetsforskning, Stockholm, 1985

KENNY, Michael: *A Spanish Tapestry: Town and Country in Castile*. Macmillan, New York, 1966

KRIEGER, Laurie: Negotiating Gender Role Expectations in Cairo. In T.L. Whitehead and M.E. Conaway (eds): *Self, Sex and Gender in Cross-Cultural Fieldwork*. University of Illinois Press, Urbana, Chicago, 1986

LACALLE, Daniel: *Clases sociales y capitalismo*. Endymion, Madrid, 1990a

LACALLE, Daniel: *La estructura de clases en la España de hoy*. Comisión de Formación Política y Teórica del PCE, Madrid, 1990b

LAKOFF, Robin: *Language and Woman's Place*. Harper and Row, New York, 1975

LANCASTER, Roger N. and Micaela di LEONARDO (eds): *The Gender/ Sexuality Reader*. Routledge, New York and London, 1997

LANDES, Joan B.: *Women and the Public Sphere in the Age of the French Revolution*. Cornell University Press, Ithaca, London, 1988

LEVER, Alison: Honour as a Red Herring. *Critique of Anthropology*, vol 6, 3:83-106, 1986

LINDISFARNE, Nancy: Variant masculinities, variant virginities. Rethinking 'honour and shame'. In A. Cornwall and N. Lindisfarne (eds): *Dislocating Masculinity*. Routledge, London, 1994

LISON TOLOSANA, Carmelo: *Invitación a la antropología cultural de España*. Adara, La Coruña, 1977

LISON TOLOSANA, Carmelo: Estrategias matrimoniales, individuación y ethos lucense. In J.G. Peristiany (ed): *Dote y matrimonio en los países mediterráneos*. Centro de Investigaciones Sociológicas, Madrid, 1987

LISON TOLOSANA, Carmelo: Las Españas de los españoles. *Revista Española de Investigaciones Sociológicas*, 40, 1987

LOFLAND, Lyn H.: *A World of Strangers. Order and action in urban public space*. Waveland Press, Prospect Heights, Illinois, 1985

LOIZOS, Peter and Evthymios PAPATAXIARCHIS (eds): *Contested Identities. Gender and Kinship in Modern Greece*. Princeton University Press, Princeton, 1991

LOPEZ PINTOR, Rafael: *La opinión pública española: Del franquismo a la democracia*. Centro de Investigaciones Sociológicas, Madrid, 1982

LUNDGREN, Britta: Vila, empati, realism – om kvinnlig vänskap. *Kvinnovetenskaplig tidskrift*, 2: 3-14, 1992

LYKKE, Nina: Nya perspektiv på intersektionalitet. Problem och möjligheter. *Kvinnovetenskaplig tidskrift*, 2-3, 2005

MADRID, Juan: *Días contados*. Alfaguara, Madrid, 1993

MALO DE MOLINA, Carlos, Jose M. VALLS BLANCO, Antonio PEREZ GOMEZ: *La conducta sexual de los españoles*. Ediciones B, Barcelona, 1988

MARCUS, George E. and Michael M.J. FISCHER: *Anthropology as Cultural Critique*. University of Chicago Press, Chicago, London, 1986

MARIAS, Julián: *La mujer en el siglo XX*. Alianza, Madrid, 1980

MARKUS, Maria: Mujeres, éxito y sociedad civil. Sumisión o subversión del principio de logro. In S. Benhabib and D. Cornell (eds): *Teoría feminista y teoría crítica. Ensayos sobre la política de género en las sociedades de capitalismo tardío*. Edicions Alfons el Magnánim, Valencia, 1990 (Original title: Feminism as Critique. Essays on the Politics of Gender in Late-Capitalist Societies)

MARSE, Juan: *La oscura historia de la prima Montse*. Seix Barral, Barcelona, 1990

MARTIN GAITE, Carmen: *Usos amorosos de la postguerra española*. Anagrama, Barcelona, 1987

MARTINEZ CUADRADO, Miguel: *La burguesía conservadora (1874-1931)*. Alianza Editorial Alfaguara, Madrid, 1973

MASCIA-LEES, Frances E., Patricia SHARPE, Colleen BALLERINO COHEN: The Postmodernist Turn in Anthropology: Cautions from a Feminist Perspective. *Signs*, 15:1-2, 1989

McCALL, Leslie: Intersektionalitetens komplexitet. *Kvinnovetenskaplig tidskrift*, 2-3, 2005

McDONOGH, Gary Wray: *Las buenas familias de Barcelona. Historia social de poder en la era industrial*. Omega, Barcelona, 1989

MELHUUS, Marit: A Shame to Honour, a Shame to Suffer. *Ethnos*, 1-2, 1990

MERNISSI: Fatima: *Beyond the Veil. Male-Female Dynamics in Muslim Society*. Al Saqi Books, London, 1985

MICHENER, James A.: *Iberia. Spanish Travels and Reflections*. Random House, New York, 1968

MOI, Toril: Appropriating Bourdieu: Feminist Theory and Pierre Bourdieu's Sociology of Culture. *New Literary History*, 22:4, 1991

MOORE, Henrietta: *Feminism and Anthropology*. Polity Press and Basil Blackwell, Cambridge and Oxford, 1988

Mujeres, 4, 1991. (Magazine published by Instituto de la Mujer, Madrid)

MUKHOPADHYAY, Carol C. and Patricia J. HIGGINS: Anthropological Studies of Women's Status Revisited:1977-1987. *Annual Review of Anthropology*, 17, 1988

NIELSEN, Harriet Bjerrum & Monica RUDBERG: Kön, modernitet och postmodernitet. *Kvinnovetenskaplig Tidskrift,* 1, 1991

OBREGON, Enrique de: *La otra historia sexual de España.* Martínez Roca, Barcelona, 1990

ORGAZ, Ana I.: Uncovering cultural models of gender in the discourse of high-school peer groups about male/female relationships. *First Conference of EASA*, 1990

ORTNER, Sherry and Harriet WHITEHEAD (eds): *Sexual Meanings. The Cultural Construction of Gender and Sexuality.* Cambridge University Press, Cambridge, 1981

PATEMAN, Carole: *The Sexual Contract.* Polity / Blackwell, Cambridge UK / Oxford, 1988

PEREZ DIAZ, Víctor: *El retorno de la sociedad civil. Respuestas sociales a la transición política, la crisis económica y los cambios culturales de España 1975-1985.* Instituto de Estudios Económicos, Madrid, 1987

PERISTIANY, John (ed.) *Honour and Shame: The Values of Mediterranean Society.* University of Chicago Press, Chicago, 1966

PERISTIANY, John G.: Prólogo. In J.G. Peristiany (ed): *Dote y matrimonio en los países mediterráneos.* Centro de Investigaciones Sociológicas, Madrid, 1987

PETERSSON, Olof (ed): *Maktbegreppet.* Carlssons, Stockholm, 1987

Peuples Méditerranéens, 44-45: Les femmes et la modernité. 1988

PITT-RIVERS, Julian A.: *The People of the Sierra.* University of Chicago Press, Chicago, 1972 (1954)

PITT-RIVERS, Julian A. (ed): *Mediterranean Countrymen. Essays in the Social Anthropology of the Mediterranean* Greenwood Press, Westport, Conn., 1977 (Originally Mouton, Paris, 1963)

POSADAS, Carmen, de: *Yuppies, jet set, la movida y otras especies. Manual del perfecto arribista.* Ediciones Temas de Hoy, Madrid, 1987

PRAT, Joan, Ubaldo MARTINEZ, Jesús CONTRERAS, Isidoro MORENO (eds) *Antropología de los pueblos de España.* Taurus, Madrid, 1991

QUINN, Naomi: Anthropological Studies on Women's Status. *Annual Review of Anthropology,* 6, 1977

QUIROS, Constancio Bernaldo de: *El espartaquismo agrario andaluz.* Ediciones Turner, 1974 (1919)

RAMOS TORRES, Ramón: *Cronos Dividido. Uso del tiempo y desigualdad entre mujeres y hombres en España.* Instituto de la Mujer, Madrid, 1990.

REITER, Rayna R.: Men and Women in the South of France: Public and Private Domains. In R. REITER (ed): *Toward an Anthropology of Women.* Monthly Review Press, New York, 1975

REIS (REVISTA ESPAÑOLA DE INVESTIGACIONES SOCIOLOGICAS): 56:18: *Datos de opinión. XII años de Constitución y Democracia en España.* Nr 56, 1991

RIERA, J.M. and E. VALENCIANO: *Las mujeres de los 90: El largo trayecto de las jóvenes hacia su emancipación*. Ediciones Morata, Madrid, 1991

RODRIGUEZ RAMOS, Luis, Francisco Javier ALVAREZ GARCIA, Pilar GOMEZ PAVON: *La justicia ante la libertad sexual de las mujeres*. Instituto de la Mujer, Madrid, 1988

ROSALDO, M.Z. and L. LAMPHERE (eds): *Woman, Culture and Society*. Stanford University Press, Stanford, 1974

ROSALDO, Michelle Z.: Woman, Culture and Society: A Theoretical Overview. In M.Z. Rosaldo and L. Lamphere (eds): *Woman, Culture and Society,* Stanford University Press, Stanford, 1974

SACKS, Karen: *Sisters and Wives. The past and future of sexual equality.* University of Illinois Press. Urbana, Chicago, London, 1982

SALCEDO, Juan: *Madrid culpable.* Tecnos, Madrid, 1977

SALLE, María Angeles and José Ignacio CASAS: *Efectos de la crisis económica sobre el trabajo de las mujeres.* Instituto de la Mujer, Madrid, 1987

SANCHEZ LOPEZ, Rosario: *Mujer española, una sombra de destino en lo universal. Trayectoria histórica de Sección Femenina de Falange (1934-1977).* Universidad de Murcia, Murcia, 1990

SANCHEZ PEREZ, Francisco: *La liturgia del espacio.* Nerea, Madrid, 1990

SANCHIS, Norma and Susana BIANCHI: *El partido peronista femenino.* Biblioteca Política Argentina no 208, Centro Editor de América Latina, Buenos Aires, 1988

SAVILLE-TROIKE, Muriel: *The Ethnography of Communication.* Blackwell, Oxford UK / Cambridge USA, 1993 (1982/1989)

SCANLON, Geraldine M.: *La polémica feminista en la España contemporánea (1868-1974).* Siglo XXI, Madrid, 1976

SCHNEIDER, Jane: Of vigilance and virgins: honor, shame and access to resources in Mediterranean societies. *Ethnology*, 10:1-24, 1971

SCHNEIDER, Jane and Peter SCHNEIDER: *Culture and Political Economy in Western Sicily.* Academic Press, New York 1976

SCIAMA, Lidia: The Problem of Privacy in Mediterranean Anthropology. In S. Ardener (ed): *Women and Space. Ground Rules and Social Maps.* Croom Helm, London 1981

SERRANO VICENS, Ramón: *La sexualidad femenina.* Júcar, Barcelona, 1975

SHUBERT, Adrian: *A Social History of Modern Spain.* Unwin Hyman, London / Boston / Sydney/ Wellington, 1990

SMITH, Dorothy E.: Femininity as discourse. In *Texts, Facts and Femininity. Exploring the Relations of Ruling.* Routledge, London, 1990a

SMITH, Dorothy E.: *The Conceptual Practices of Power. A Feminist Sociology of Knowledge.* Northeastern University Press, Boston, 1990b

SORRIBES, Josep: *Crecimiento urbano y especulación en Valencia.* Almudín, Valencia, 1978

SOU 1990:44: *Demokrati och makt i Sverige.* Maktutredningens huvudrapport. Statens offentliga utredningar, Stockholm, 1990

SPRADLEY, James P. and Brenda J. MANN: *The Cocktail Waitress. Woman's Work in a Man's World.* John Wiley & Sons, New York, 1975

SUNDMAN, Kerstin: *Women are Persons too. Gender and Personhood in the Abortion Debate in Post-Franco Spain.* SANS nr 4. Socialantropologiska institutionen, Göteborgs universitet, Göteborg, 1994

SUNDMAN, Kerstin: *Between the Home and the Institutions.* Acta universitatis gothoburgensis. Gothenburg studies in Social Anthropology 15. Göteborg, 1999

TAMAMES, Ramón: *La República. La Era de Franco.* Historia de España, Alfaguara VII. Alianza, Madrid, 1980

TAMAMES, Ramón and José Manuel REVUELTA (eds): *Anuario El País 1992.* Ediciones El País, Madrid, 1992

TANNEN, Deborah: *Prat från 9 till 5. Om kvinnors och mäns samtalsstilar på jobbet.* Wahlström & Widstrand, Stockholm, 1996 (Original title: Talking from 9 to 5) 1994

THERBORN, Göran: *Vad gör den härskande klassen när den härskar? Statsapparater och statsmakt under feodalism, kapitalism och socialism.* Zenit/Rabén & Sjögren, Stockholm, 1980 (Original title: What Does the Ruling Class Do When it Rules? New Left Books, 1978)

THUREN, Britt-Marie: Utveckling och genus: två kulturella konstruktioner i en storstad i Spanien. In D. Kulick (ed): *Från kön till genus.* Carlssons. Stockholm, 1987

THUREN, Britt-Marie: *Left Hand Left Behind: The Changing Gender System of a Barrio in Valencia, Spain.* Stockholm Studies in Social Anthropology 1988

THUREN, Britt-Marie: Nuevos esquemas, viejas seguridades: Variaciones en el grado de continuidad en la reproducción cultural del sistema de género. VIII Jornadas de Investigación Interdisciplinaria sobre la Mujer. In Bernís et al (eds): *Los estudios sobre la mujer: de la investigación a la docencia.* Universidad Autónoma de Madrid, Madrid, 1991

THUREN, Britt-Marie: *El poder generizado. El desarrollo de la antropología feminista.* Instituto de Investigaciones Feministas. Universidad Complutense de Madrid, Madrid, 1993

THUREN, Britt-Marie: Opening Doors and Getting Rid of Shame: Experiences of First Menstruation in Valencia Spain. *Women's Studies International Forum,* vol.17, 2/3:217-228, 1994

THUREN, Britt-Marie: Att erövra barerna. Former och platser för kulturell förhandling kring genus i Spanien. *Kvinnovetenskaplig Tidskrift,* 3-4, 1998

THUREN, Britt-Marie: On Force, Scope, Hierarchy. Concepts and questions for a cross-cultural theorization of gender. Paper at *4th European feminist conference,*

Bologna, 2000 (Also available at https://bmthuren.files.wordpress.com/2008/12/force-scope.pdf)

THUREN, Britt-Marie: *Genusforskning inom socialantropologin – antropologiska bidrag till genusforskningen.* Högskoleverket, Stockholm, 2002a

THUREN, Britt-Marie: Conquerint els bars: plaer i poder en l'accés a espais de negociació cultural. *Revista d'etnologia de Catalunya*, 21:132-143, 2002b

THUREN, Britt-Marie: ¿Cómo hacer etnografía feminista "hacia arriba"? Dilemas éticos y políticos para la antropología crítica. In C. Díez Mintegui and C. Gregorio Gil (eds): *Cambios culturales y desigualdades de género en el marco local-global actual.* Fundación El Monte/ Federación de Asociaciones de Antropología del Estado Español/ Asociacion Andaluza de Antropología, Sevilla, 2005

THUREN, Britt-Marie: La crítica feminista y la antropología: una relacion incómoda y fructífera. *Ankulegi 12*: 97-114, 2008

THUREN, Britt-Marie: *Making barrios, making persons. Grass roots politics and gendered change in urban Spain.* https://bmthuren.wordpress.com/english, 2013

THUREN, Britt-Marie and Kerstin SUNDMAN (eds.): *Kvinnor, män och andra sorter.* Carlssons, Stockholm, 1997

TILLION, Germaine: *The Republic of Cousins. Women's oppression in Mediterranean society.* Al Saqi Books (Zed Press), London, 1983

VALE DE ALMEIDA, Miguel: Gender, masculinity and power in southern Portugal. *Social Anthropology* 5,2:141-158, 1997

VAN MAANEN, John: *Tales of the Field. On Writing Ethnography.* The University of Chicago Press, Chicago, London, 1988.

WETHERELL, Margaret and Jonathan POTTER: *Mapping the Language of Racism. Discourse and the Legitimation of Exploitation.* Harvester Wheatsheaf, New York, 1992

WIDERBERG, Karin: Vi behöver en diskussion om könsbegreppet. *Kvinnovetenskaplig tidskrift* 4: 27 – 31, 1992

NOTES

1 This is not the place for a long analysis of the term middle class. I use it in an approximate sense to refer to people that depend on a salary (i.e. not capital) for a living, but who do not do mainly manual work and whose salaries permit a relatively comfortable lifestyle.

2 Gender is of course also a term that can mean a lot of things. I use it in the common academic and feminist manner to refer to how people are categorized according to cultural understandings of what sex means. The term gender order refers to the whole set of categorizations, criteria for categorizations, and social and cultural structures based on these categorizations or the consequences of them, e.g. through the distribution of power and labor. See appendix B for a summary of the theoretical grounds of the study.

3 These terms are elaborated in appendix B.

4 There is more on the fieldwork and methods in appendix B.

5 There are many summaries in English, e.g. Quinn 1977, Moore 1988, Mukhopadhyay and Higgins 1988. Cf Thurén 1993 for a summary in Spanish.

6 However, anthropologists usually have better access to informants of their own category, and this is definitely so in segregated societies, like the Mediterranean ones. Therefore, this book is mainly on the gender order as it looks from women's point of view. This is a methodological imposition, not a theoretical preference. To the extent that I have information on men, I include it. But the ideal thing would be for a male anthropologist to apply similar questions to field material from mainly male informants.

7 As it is being worked out especially by Bourdieu and Giddens. Connell offers good summaries of it (1987). Human beings are formed by the social and cultural structures in which they live, and they reproduce them in their daily practice. But change happens, because social reproduction goes via habitus, and habitus cannot be static, as Bourdieu has so well demonstrated (Bourdieu 1977; Thurén 1988:36-39) .

8 One reason for the avoidance is a sensitivity for rank, which makes rank difficult to talk about; to talk of "lower classes" can be interpreted as if you disparage others, people feel; to talk about "higher classes" makes it sound as if you disparage yourself. Another reason is that the middle classes are unsure of where they themselves stand. A third reason is that it was not fashionable while I was in the field, at least not among conservatives, to recognize the empirical validity of the concept of class.

9 The term is from Gouldner 1970.

10 This abbreviated piece of social history will be elaborated in chapter 2. Some figures on which these generalizations are based will also be presented there. Most of the data come from LaCalle 1990 and Giner 1990. Historical and journalistic narratives of the period usually make similar interpretations, e.g. Hooper 1987, Shubert 1990.

11 The Bourdieuan terms used in this book will be discussed in chapter 4. Briefly, doxa means that which is taken so much for granted that it becomes invisible in a given culture. There is always doxa, but there can be more or less of it and it can cover different things.

12 That is to say, they consist of such a combination of ideas as to convince even those members of the society that lose out that the hierarchy is necessary and perhaps even good. The idea is similar to that of Gramsci's hegemony, but I prefer Bourdieu's term, symbolic violence, because it focuses more on the process than on the result. The hierarchy can be more or less reinforced by physical and/or economic kinds of violence, but the symbolic violence is usually a necessary component, too, and it becomes more necessary when physical and economic violence become less viable. As I see it, then, it is hardly surprising that there is more stress on women's and men's "nature" in a situation where the gender order becomes less doxic and physical violence and economic differences between women and men less legitimate. This was the case in Madrid.

13 Unlike the fields Bourdieu has described, however, the field of Madrilenian gender debate was not clearly delimited. I agree with Moi (1994:3-24) that the relationship between a field and a whole society is under-theorized by Bourdieu, and that gender can perhaps best be seen as an aspect of the whole social field, not a specific field.

14 More on the concept of management of meaning in chapter 4.

15 This concept of discourse is inspired by Dorothy Smith (especially 1990a). I use this notion of discourse because I find it a useful and critical way of concretizing Foucault's less empirical work on discourse and power, but I combine it with a theory of culture based on Bourdieu and Hannerz (cf chapter 4) and a theory of practice based on Bourdieu, Giddens and Connell (cf appendix B). I do not subscribe to Smith's standpoint feminism, which I find essentialist even though not biologist.

16 As Smith points out (1990b), both knowledge and action in contemporary society are largely mediated by texts. Utterances of all kinds, both oral and written, make up a virtual reality, an objectified but non-material world that influences opinions and decisions and actions at all levels from micro to macro. In such societies, it becomes strategically necessary to investigate the social organization of knowledge. She does not refer to the traditional sociology of knowledge, which concentrates on what circumstances in the lives of the knowers that give them

certain perspectives. There is no "pure" knowledge without any perspective at all, she points out. What is interesting is instead to describe who takes part in the shaping of which texts or discourses. I have concentrated on personal encounters, but there are many studies on textual gender-related discourses in Spain. Examples: Fagoaga and Secanella 1984, Ferrandiz and Verdu 1975, Folguera 1988, Gallego 1990, Gallego Mendez 1983, Imbert 1982, Scanlon 1976, Sundman 1994.

17 Rereading these paragraphs in 2024, they strike me as very much addressed to a specific discourse, namely Swedish anthropological debates on "post-modernism" and "reflexivity" in the 1990s. They concerned the need – or not – for anthropologists to reflect on what their own personalities and perspectives meant for how they analyzed their data and how they obtained them, what degree of objectivity is ever attainable or even theoretically possible, etcetera, and to what extent this personal relation to one's field ought to be reported.These debates are no longer in focus in the same way, but I let the text stand as I wrote it thirty years ago as a belated wink to them.

18 For details of demography, migration, urban development and urban speculation, see Beltrán et al 1987, Castells 1977, del Campo and Navarro 1985, Estébanez Alvarez 1990, Gaviria et al 1968, Salcedo 1977, Sorribes 1978.

19 The development of one area, Las Rozas, is representative. During its years of strong growth, 1981-1985, 6.000 new inhabitants arrived, converting this former village into a suburb of Madrid. 73% of these came from downtown Madrid, 59% from upper middle class districts. Most of them said the major motive for moving was to find a better dwelling. Of all inhabitants over 25 years of age in Las Rozas in 1985, 35% had university degrees (Estébanez Alvarez 1990:253). The general figure for Madrid (population over 10 years of age, in 1986) was 8.8%.

20 Urbanización is the Spanish word, and it stands for a residential area that has been developed as a unit, usually by one company and often without any immediate connection to other inhabited areas. A typical urbanización near Madrid consists of any number of one family dwellings arranged along winding streets, plus an area club with swimming pools, tennis courts and a clubhouse. The residents form an association to arrange for the upkeep of the club and the streets, pay for street lighting and sometimes a private bus line, and discuss other collectively defined necessities, such as how to get rid of a nearby gypsy camp. Some urbanizations are built near old villages, which gives the urbanization residents some extra facilities. Cf María and Enrique in chapter 3.

21 Ambiente translates literally as environment, milieu or atmosphere. But it is a culturally focused concept, meaning also good feelings, social richness, interesting contexts with lots of people. "Good vibes" is one possible translation, except that ambiente is devoid of slang connotations. Cf Thurén1988, where I have also suggested that the importance of ambiente is related to a general Mediterranean preference for having people around, having things happen (as opposed for example to the Scandinavian preference for solitude, "calm"). Cf chapter 5.

22 The kinds that are spontaneous, collective, not too orderly, more entertaining than intimate. I have called the disposition for them philia. The concept is explained in chapter 5.

23 Madrilenians did go out a lot, but not all. Even fewer participate in so called cultural activities. Especially women do not. According to sociological data 4 out of 10 women in Madrid never go to the cinema, more than half never go to the theater. 4 out of 10 never go out at night with their husband or with friends, 3 out of 10 never go out for a meal in a restaurant. 7 out of 10 (under 65 years of age) practice no sports. 24% never read books, 23% never read magazines, 31% never read the daily newspapers. One out of four women belongs to some association, but less than 2% belong to a political party or trade union. Public office is very masculine. Only 3% of the mayors of the Madrid region are women. But 17% of the members of the regional parliament are women, which is a much higher figure than for any other region. The average is 7% (CAM 1989:91-95).

24 In 1964 it constituted 62% of the active population, in 1970 65%, in 1979 close to 70% and in 1987, after the relative economic slowdown, just over 70%.

25 There were few illiterate persons, only about 130.000 in Madrid, but of these more than 3 out of 4 were women. Cf note 28 on demography. At university, women were now 48% of the students. In elementary and secondary schooling, girls and boys are about half each. Teaching was a female occupation, especially in private schools and in pre-school centers.(CAM 1989:49-62).

26 Note 2015: This contradiction has not become as acute as I predicted. The reason is that women have chosen – or been forced to – establish their careers first, before having children. That means that the age of childbearing has risen. And that in turn means that the grandmothers are also older by the time their daughters become mothers. So as grandmothers many of them are able to help, in spite of having had careers before retirement.

27 In the upper middle class, one solution was to buy help from agencies that specialized in obtaining official documents. In effect, they stood in line for you. Some government offices had special desks for such agencies.

28 Some relevant demographic figures (from CAM, 1989): 70% of the Madrilenians who got married did so in church, 25% contracted civil marriage, 4-5% had other ceremonies. Civil marriage was more common in Madrid than in the rest of the country. There was a slight tendency to get married younger now than a few years earlier, but the age difference between husband and wife was about the same, around 2,5 years. Most children were born when the mother was between 25 and 29 years old. Like in the rest of Europe, the fecundity was diminishing; it was now between 1.3 and 1.8 children per woman in other European countries. In Spain the drop occurred a decade later, falling from 3 or more children per woman in the 1960s to 2,1 in 1981 and in 1985 only 1,5, one of the lowest

figures in Europe. In Madrid it was even lower: 1,45. The drop had become possible because of increasing access to contraceptives and abortions. Both were still a problem for most Spanish women, but middle class urban women had better access than others. Only about half of Spanish women of fertile age used contraceptives. In 1988 there were 11.000 legal abortions inside Spain (more than twice as many were still performed abroad); 30% of these were performed in Madrid, but less than 7% in public hospitals. The life expectancy had gone up dramatically during this century, from 35,7 years for women and 33,9 for men at the beginning of the century, to 79,8 for Madrilenian women in 1980, which was then higher than either Sweden or Japan.

29 I will follow normal English usage and say housewife when I mean women without any economic activity outside the home. The Spanish expression *ama de casa* can mean the same thing, but it is more common for it to signify "a woman who has the responsibility for the management of her home and family." Rather like the English term "homemaker". Many Spanish women will say that they are amas de casa, even though they work outside. They may mean that they are responsible women at home, in spite of their outside duties. Or they may mean that they do have a family. Or they may mean that their husband and children do not help very much. Or they may mean that they have no paid domestic help. It is also possible for a young unmarried woman living with her parents to describe herself as ama de casa, namely if she is in charge of the household, perhaps because her mother is ill or deceased. All of these meanings overlap with each other and also with the normal English one. To say that one has no economic activity, common phrases are "*me dedico a la familia*" (I dedicate myself to the family) or "*no trabajo*" (I do not work). But these phrases are going out of style under the pressure of feminist criticism. The first one is seen as old-fashioned, associated with self-sacrifice, and the second one is seen as plainly wrong, since household tasks are also work.

30 Durán 1987, López-Pintor 1982, Giner 1990, Giner and Moreno, 1990.

31 A Catholic lay organization that is known in Spain for its secretiveness, its conservative positions on gender and social organization, its liberal views on economics and its defense of market mechanisms. During the Franco regime, it had considerable power through well-placed members.

32 The concept "mode of management of meaning" will be further elaborated in chapter 4, where modes such as cautious and expansive will also be described.

33 But even they varied, and the pattern of hours of meals, schools, stores, offices, etc. was another issue of differential possibilities for women and men to organize their lives according to their own wishes. Cf note 35.

34 In fact, "unrepresentative" individuals are even more "representative" for the purpose of showing that certain structural constraints affect everyone . The aspects of life that affected Carlota and María in similar ways were also aspects that were similar in the life of almost all middle class women in Madrid. Such aspects are pointed out in footnotes throughout this chapter.

35 For instance pre-schoolers usually attended play school between 10 AM and 5 PM; the common school day was from 9 AM to 1 PM and 3 PM to 5 PM; usual office hours from 9AM to 2 PM and 5 PM to 8 PM, but in big cities the "intensive" day was becoming very popular, from 8 AM to 3 PM with no lunch break; food stores were usually open from 10 AM to 2 PM and 4 or 5 PM to 8 or 8:30 PM; stores for clothing and other objects opened around 10 or 11 AM and closed at 1 or 1:30, to open again from 5 PM to 8 or 9 PM; bureaucratic offices had erratic hours, so if one had an errand (and in Madrid one often did, inevitably, since few matters could be solved by telephone), one should go between 11 AM and 1 PM when the probability was greatest that they were open; universities and some secondary schools had double shifts in order to save on space, so then the morning shift could be between 8 or 9 AM and 2 or 3 PM, while the afternoon shift could be between 4 and 8, like María's, but there were afternoon shifts in secondary schools that ended much later. Food schedules were complex. Breakfast was very light and many did not have any at all, but at mid-morning people liked to have a substantial snack; lunch was between 2 and 4 for most grown-ups, but school children had theirs earlier, because it used to be that parents and children ate separately; this custom was now widely criticized by the middle class, but school hours required them; soon after lunch a mother had to prepare the afternoon snack for the toddler back from play school and right after that the afternoon snack for older school children as they came home. Some families had dinner around 9, but executives usually came home very late, and school children must be in bed earlier, so Carlota's double dinner was a common predicament, and few middle class fathers could help with evening baths or homework. The classical dinner hour was 10 PM. Movies and theaters offered one show starting around 7 PM and another one starting around 11 PM. In many middle class families it was impossible ever to sit down for a common family meal on weekdays. The issue of working hours was controversial for families in which the woman worked or wanted to work outside the home. Cf appendix A.

36 Domestic help in Spain is divided into two types: Live-in maids are *called muchachas, chicas de servicio* or *criadas; asistentas* are usually older, married women who work for hourly pay. They are called asistentas independently of the number of hours a week they work for a given family.

37 Cf chapter 4.

38 After writing this chapter, I sent it to María for comment (as I did to Carlota). One year had passed and her situation at the University had changed for the better: "I am now the central point of reference. The classes often turn into debates. Most of the students are women, and more and more of them have begun to wait for my

arguments in order to second me; at other times they initiate the polemics, but they know I am there and that I will help them if they don't know how to go on. The University is the same, but in class, teachers and students have created a dynamic of debate, and they can hardly repress us at all. I do not share the ideology of the University, but what is happening inside the group is extremely interesting, there are even a few nuns with an incredibly critical spirit."

39 In her letter, María commented two aspects of her day, comments that are worth quoting, I think, even though they fall outside the theme of this chapter. They illustrate the importance of family and friendship, two of the themes of this book, and they show clearly how demanding the norms are. "I live several contradictory lives and I try to live them all with my true self and be successful and attend to the personal relations in all of them sufficiently. (…) As Enrique's companion, I want to dedicate my time and personal energy to him enough for the relationship to work. In this my criteria are demanding, I know that if one does not work hard at it, a couple relationship will not work, and I want to and I do dedicate my attention and my time to him. As mother of my five children, I want them to know that I exist for them and I want to have space for each one so that when the occasion arises the communication will flow easily and I will be able to give them what I know they need from me. I can't always do this, and this fills me with guilt. (…) My mother is living with me now, and one of the things that makes her most happy is for me to sit down beside her and chat with her. I give her too little of my time, and I know that perhaps in a short while her passage through this life will end and I will not be able to give her that satisfaction nor will I be able to enjoy her company. You know I have lots of friends (…). To each person one has to dedicate time. They call me, they say they want to have lunch with me, and I don't have the time (...). I always have the feeling that the most important thing I have, which is the human warmth of friends and family, is what I abuse because I want to do too many things. (…) Besides, you know that to take care of a house, with outside help for only six hours a week, is sufficient work so as not to do anything else." She goes on to talk about her studies and her political dreams and professional ambitions and finishes: "I feel very atypical in the context where it has been my fate to live." I agree. María was not like the majority of the women I met during this field work. But neither was she unique. Her wishes and her personality were products of her sociocultural context, as much as the women of Club Aguafría were. Like Esperanza (chapter 15), she was a good example of the wide range of lifestyles possible in Madrid at the time, and both María and Esperanza felt that their way of life was really that of the future.

40 He used to go by train, that was his plan when they moved out to the urbanization, but he now usually preferred the car in spite of the traffic. He said he might need it, for instance if he had to meet clients at the airport, and he had no parking problems, the office had a garage.

41 El País was the most important newspaper in Spain. Its circulation was the largest, by far, and it had been the paper of general reference almost since it was launched in 1976. (Imbert and Vidal Beneyto 1986, Hooper 1987:130 ff) It had been considered progressive, but in 1991 many of my informants complained that it kow-towed too much to the government. Conservatives did not usually read it. At Club Aguafría, the ABC was the major reference. It was the second largest in circulation in the country, and it had narrowed El País' leadership during the 1980s. It is not only politically but also culturally conservative. Even its layout had looked about the same for at least thirty years. In 1990, El País had an average daily circulation of 375.875 and close to 12% of the readership, while the figures for ABC were 290.517 and just over 9%. Together they dominated the market totally. Only three other dailies reached over the 5% mark, and two of these contained only sports news. (Anuario El País 1992:244) Only one in ten persons bought a daily newspaper at all (Hooper 1987:130), many of these bought only the sports papers. Of the readership of El País, only 4% were categorized as lower class or unidentifiable, while 48% were upper or upper-middle class. 62% were men. (Anuario El País 1992: 230)

42 This is a common phrase, used to express the harsh contrasts of opinions and life styles among Spaniards. The reference is to a poem from 1912 by Antonio Machado. Cf note 78.

43 Cf chapter 4.

44 Cf chapters 9, 10 and 11.

45 Cf Fagoaga and Secanella 1984. Their study of the presence of women in Spanish press shows that El País is one of the newspapers that most often mentions women as actors. 9% of actors with names in El Pais were women in 1983. They give no figures on first page mentions; it is a good guess that that percentage would be much lower. On the other hand the percentage might have increased slightly between 1983 (their sample) and 1991 (my study).

46 Hooper (1987) comments on the impressive variety in Spanish newsstands. Spaniards read a lot more magazines than dailies. Whereas only seven newspapers have an average circulation of over 100.000, thirty-one magazines do, and of these six sell over half a million copies of each issue and one over one million. If we set the limit at 10.000 copies, fifty-three newspapers make it – but one hundred and eighty-six magazines! (Anuario El País 1992:244-246)

47 This sketch of what is on the covers is based mainly on my own impressionistic observations. The report mentioned in note 41 and the study of the feminine press in Spain by Gallego (1990) have also been taken into account.

48 While writing this book, in 1992, I met my first ever woman taxi driver in Madrid. She told me that there were only fourteen in all. She had been driving for ten years and was quite tired of having to comment on the fact with

each and every customer. But, she said, "at least now it hardly ever happens anymore, as it did in the beginning, that a customer refuses to ride with a woman driver."

49 Cf above, note 41, about the popularity of sports dailies. The soccer pools were immensely popular and given much media space. Middle class men did not have the same passionate relation to sports as working class men, but they did keep up to date. At Club Aguafría, the television room was filled with men, and men only, whenever important games were played.

50 I had some access to them for instance through reading business news in the press. But for the purpose of a critical analysis of this discourse in and of itself, a different kind of empirical study would obviously be necessary, including participant observation in those contexts where it is mainly produced, i.e. where the decisions are made, and to which I had no access in this study.

51 I heard no woman do it at Club Aguafría, for example. But, as always, it varies, and people who tend to manage meaning in an expansive way will refuse to accept the existence of such norms. María commented my interpretation thus, "I think it is important for you to understand that I have absolutely nothing to do with that «club world«; my world is different, the men I know listen to my opinions and do not think there are "women's things" and "men's things", at least not rationally."

52 Like María, Carlota commented my analysis in a letter: "I think women who like that kind of discourse take part in it, and I know some who are crazy about it. But I don't like it as a theme for conversation nor to participate. I am a romantic, I don't like to live with my feet on the ground, I like to talk about feelings, sensations, experiences, music, nature, colors... About everything beautiful. The other things are necessary, but I leave them to those who enjoy them. But I don't think this is because I am a woman. Arturo does not like to talk about his work except with three or four persons at work. He thinks that he works all day, and when he leaves the office he does not want to even remember it. I don't think it is interesting to talk about work. Nor did I like to talk about the problems I had when I worked. Not that I never said anything at all, but it was not a pleasure to talk about it. Can you understand how I feel? Perhaps I am deeply influenced by the principle of my religion that says that work is a punishment!" (The last sentence was meant as a joke.)

53 But she thought women influenced it indirectly. In her letter, she said, "I don't think that men whose work implies decision-making are influenced in their decisions by what their wives may comment. What I do think is that depending on the kind of wife a man has, he will tend towards one side or another, he will be in one way or another."

54 The comments I received from Carlota, María and others to whom I tried to explain my interpretations met with reactions that showed that my descriptions of structural effects and cultural patterns were interpreted as accusations of conscious prejudice. I mention this in order to underline that that is far from my intention. I hope the attentive reader will find this remark unnecessary. Some of my informants certainly had sundry prejudices, but that is beside the point of my argument.

55 Some of the terms and the general framework for the arguments in this chapter are inspired by Hannerz' (1992) discussion of cultural complexity. Cf note 72.

56 The culturally complex world is the opposite of a highy doxic world. Doxa, according to Bourdieu, is a set of ideas that are not conscious as ideas, because they are never contradicted (unlike orthodoxy, which can be debated). It is what "goes without saying because it comes without saying." (Bourdieu 1977:167) In a highly doxic world, all ideas are coherent or at least not visibly in conflict, and social and material circumstances support them and are supported by them to such a degree that debate is not called for. Debate as such may even come to be considered a negative phenomenon. At the very least, in a doxic society, it seems inconceivable that debate might be a procedure applicable to certain areas of life, the most doxic ones. A highly doxic set of ideas extending over many aspects of life can evidently only exist in a very stable context. Wherever there is change, some ideas are made visible and probably contradicted. This means that perfect doxa may never exist, but ideas and contexts and whole societies can be more or less doxic. "Common sense" can be understood as a similar concept, but its hazier everyday meaning makes it a less suitable term, in my opinion.

57 See the many monographs by foreign anthropologists of village life from different parts of Spain produced between 1950 and 1975, approximately, e.g. Pitt-Rivers 1954, Kenny 1966, Aceves 1971, Freeman 1970 and 1979, Brandes 1975. The details are different, since the villages are different, but the sense of doxic and rather self-contained worlds is recognizable in all of them. The same is even more true of most monographs written by Spanish anthropologists. They tend to generalize less about ideas and social organization and concentrate more on detailed description of local customs, but the atmosphere of self-contained village worlds comes through very clearly; perhaps due to their studying in their own country, Spanish anthropologists tend to see more differences than similarities between villages and also between themselves and their informants. Cf the discussions in Cátedra 1991. The impression of self-contained worlds could also be an effect of the anthropological paradigm of community studies. I am sure this is true in part, but only in part. I myself had this impression of Spanish village life long before I became an anthropologist.

58 Cf e.g. Diaz del Moral 1929, Quirós 1919, Hobsbawm 1959.

59 Cf Brenan 1943, Martínez Cuadrado 1973, Tamames 1980.

401

<u>60</u> Much of Spanish fiction and autobiography from the 1950s on testifies to the sensation of opaqueness of life – incomprehensible contradictions between words and deeds, even more incomprehensible contradictions between observed conditions and official descriptions of them, plus mysterious obstacles to all efforts to understand – see for example novels by Marsé, Fernández Santos, Grosso, Juan and Luis Goytisolo, Sampedro, Martín Gaite, Martín-Santos, Rodoreda. The doxic quality of rural and small-town life in Castile is a central theme in all the works of Miguel Delibes.

<u>61</u> Over 300.000 were born in Andalusia, according to the census of 1986 (CAM 1989), but the big waves of immigration were in the sixties, so the children of those immigrants were born in Madrid but obviously had Andalusian my-villages. And those were big cohorts.

<u>62</u> This can be seen for instance in the proliferation of bars, clubs and associations with regional references. Asturias, Galicia, Catalunya, Euskadi, Extremadura...

<u>63</u> The Spanish rate of illiteracy in 1930 was between 30 and 40%. During the Second Republic (1931-1936) there were intense programs of school building, but they did not reach the whole country, and they were discontinued after 1936 (Tamames 1980:132-138). According to another source, the illiteracy rate in 1930 was 38% for women and 23.6% for men (Shubert 1990:37). By the 1970s adult women still had much lower education than men, even though equal proportions of girls and boys now attended primary and secondary school. In Madrid in 1986, three out of four illiterates were women. But the total numbers were small by then, only 2%. On the other hand 33% of the women said they had "no studies" (*sin estudios*), a phrase that usually meant that a person knows how to read a little and write minimally but has no formal schooling. Most of the illiterates and many of those with no studies were over 65 years of age (CAM 1989:50-57). Primary schooling was made compulsory for all children in 1970, but at that time there were still not enough schools to enforce the law. By 1974 most children between 6 and 14 were in school, in spite of all the difficulties (Fusi et al 1983), but the quality of education was low and continued to be. Of all comparable countries, Spain spent the least per capita on education throughout the 1970s, and had one of the highest failure rates, too (Hooper 1987:99).

<u>64</u> But there was preparedness for illiteracy in many institutions. For example, banks in poor areas of the city kept an ink-pad by the counter so that illiterate clients could sign with their finger-prints. Illiterates used not to have bank accounts, but by the 1980s they could not avoid it. Pensions were paid through banks, for example.

<u>65</u> In Bourdieu's terms, this is a hysteresis effect. A previous disposition for doxic thinking, developed and maintained in a world which was highly doxic, survives for a while in a world which is much less doxic and where therefore it does not fit. And where it will therefore, in all probability, not survive for ever. But as long as it lasts, the hysteresis effect will be fertile ground for conflicts and discomfort.

<u>66</u> Club members used that word in an unselfconscious way. They used it a lot when they wanted to explain to me and to each other what was good about the club. I do not think they meant to refer to fascist ideology. But it is a fact that "sound" or "healthy" (*sano*) was one favorite word in the vocabulary of the Franco regime and can be interpreted as the regime term for doxa, but with an ideological twist: sound is that which does not call for reflection and is therefore good, safe. Safe ideas or actions or social contexts where questioning was absent were called sound. Critical or expansive thinking was considered a dangerous germ. "Sound" things were for instance sports (especially if segregated by gender), religious activities, folklore, and traditional funmaking like village fiestas. "Unhealthy" things were for instance films or books about social problems, discussions and debates without a "trustworthy" leader such as a priest, unusual apparel, and any occasion for unsupervised contacts between the sexes. Many of the other key metaphors in the Franco regime vocabulary could be analyzed as related to "health": vitality, gaiety, strong spirit, natural instincts... Cf analyses of regime ideology and metaphors in e.g. Sánchez López 1990, Imbert 1982, Ferrándiz and Verdú 1975, Gallego Méndez 1983.

<u>67</u> Members'children belonged to the club as children, included in the family membership. When they became adults they must take out a membership of their own. How then to define "becoming an adult"? The club defined it for men as being over a certain age and/or married and/or economically autonomous, and for women as being married only. Unmarried daughters, that is, continued as daughter-members, no matter what their age and independence. One unmarried daughter of just over thirty, with a profession and an apartment of her own, told me she had asked the club administration, in writing, to be allowed to take out a membership in her own name, but she had received no answer.

<u>68</u> These thoughts about the Club are further developed in chapter 5.

<u>69</u> I am thinking e.g of films by J.A. Bardem or Luis García Berlanga, or with the popular actor Alfredo Landa whose specialty was to portray traditional ignorant characters suddenly placed in complicated urban situations that called for creative solutions.

<u>70</u> Especially "*Pepi, Lucy y Bom*"; "*Entre tinieblas*"; "*Laberinto de pasiones*"; "*Qué he hecho yo para merecer esto*"; and "*Mujeres al borde de un ataque de nervios*". His later films are of a different kind.

<u>71</u> In view of the fact that the types of absurdity, the types of common sense and the wording of the sayings are all culturally specific, it is difficult to explain the popularity of Almodóvar's films outside Spain. The reasons must be different from the reasons for their popularity at home.

72 The two modes apply in all social classes and probably all regions of Spain. Cf Thurén 1988 for a description of a working class version of them. At the time of that study, the early 1980s, those who used mainly the expansive mode called themselves progressives and called their adversaries reactionaries, and I described them with these words, albeit with care to show that they were emic terms, not mine. Those terms were not in wide use any longer in 1991, but the battlelines were still firmly in place. The mode-of-management term takes us beyond the emic vocabulary and beyond the emic interpretation. I have taken it from Hannerz (1992).

73 Cf Thurén 1988, chapter 6 on the European woman, and chapter 12 on progress as a cultural construction The progressives had a lot in common across class borders.

74 This state of things may be a consequence of the dictatorship, which was in one sense an attempt to keep Enlightenment ideas out of Spain. To oppose Francoism, then, became a struggle for the Enlightenment. It may also be the independent result of a process of modernization similar to that which produced the original Enlightenment in other European countries. I will come back to this. NB that the "Enlightenment" in this context must not be seen as it has been by e.g. 19th century romantics or present-day anti-positivists. The criticism expressed by them was necessary, and Enlightenment ideas may not be an eternal panacea. But in Spain the Enlightenment must be understood as it was seen in its own times, i.e. in opposition to an ancien régime of ascriptive social structure and a world view based on religious categories, both considered by its adepts to be universal and unquestionable. (For a description of the major ideas of the Enlightenment in the context of its own times, see Hampson 1968.)

75 Another way of seeing this would be as hierarchical nesting of cultural themes or models. Cf Holland and Quinn 1987: 3-40.

76 The clearest example, for outside observers and for the participants themselves alike, was bodily restraint. Cf chapters 6 and 17.

77 NB that this is not the same thing as sincerity! Almodóvar's films can again serve as an illustration. His protagonists are usually open-minded and expressive, but thought/feeling and expression are seldom directly linked. And part of the delight for the audience is to fill in that gap with their own interpretations. Quite another thing is the fact that expansivist Madrilenians thought that people ought to be sincere. That follows logically from their mode. And they did complain frequently and bitterly about "hipocrisy" as a widespread and serious social problem.

78 Spain has been a divided society for a long time. The civil war and dictatorship of the 20th century were consequences more than causes; the division goes further back in time. The expression "the two Spains" is often used in Spain to express this. It was Antonio Machado who wrote in a poem in 1912 "to a newborn little Spaniard" that he should look out because "one of the two Spains will always freeze your heart." He probably referred both to the bitter class divisions of his times and to the ideological divisions that had caused so much trouble ever since the failure of the Spanish attempt at a liberal revolution in 1812. Cf note 42.

79 I have found no figures on numbers of viewers of debating programs. According to some statistics and my own impressions, football and entertainment shows were the most popular programs (Anuario el País 1992:235). Even so, I dare say that in such a competitive context as the Spanish media market, the large number of debating programs, and their ubiquity across channels, was a good indication of real popularity. And Hooper (1987:141-42) affirms that the Spanish "thirst for learning" is reflected in television tastes, too, so that documentaries, current affairs and debating programs would be among the most popular. The format of the debating programs was quite uniform: a moderator and six to ten debaters would sit in comfortable chairs in a circle; the moderator would ask provocative questions but moderate as little as possible; and the debaters, chosen for their diversity of opinions on the topic at hand, would interrupt each other freely and often passionately. Perhaps that which was too difficult, for most people, to debate face-to-face could be safely handled via electronic media and stand-in debaters. There were plenty of programs on recent controversies of public life: corruption, abortion, divorce, homosexuality, unemployment, the defense budget, military service, married priests, rape, biased judges... All of them themes of intense interest but also themes that were difficult to discuss in earnest with friends and acquaintances. And among the debaters in each program, one could always discern persons using the different modes of management of meaning I have proposed. But, according to their dispositions for doxa, the debaters, whatever their persuasion on the specific topic, used debating techniques more designed to enthuse the already convinced than to take on the arguments proffered by their adversaries. And the television viewers tended to find the debaters they did not agree with arrogant and evil. Debates were popular, but more as spectacular verbal war games in which one could root for one's own team, than as exchanges of ideas from which to learn something new. The popularity of debating programs may also have something to do with the cultural disposition for verbal arts, cf appendix C.

80 The best example in this book of an Enlightenment type of discourse, as used in middle class Madrid, is Esperanza's story, chapter 15. One example of a situation in which the cautious mode dominates is that of the winter Sunday afternoon at the Club in chapter 5, another is the opposition to my attempt to organize a debate at the club, chapter 16. The summer Sunday conversation at the Club, also in chapter 5, is an example of a situation where a moderate expansivism makes inroads in a cautiously defined context. A situation in which an expansive mode of management of meaning was taken for granted as a common framework, even when opinions differed, is

the group discussion in chapter 13. In that type of context, a reference to this framework as the only acceptable one could even be made part of an argument. In the group discussion in appendix A, on the other hand, the participants believed they had similar attitudes to the management of meaning (moderately cautious but including certain Enlightenment value words, especially "rationality"), but the specific issue discussed forced men and women to adopt opposite ones, and this in itself caused confusion and deepened the conflict that the issue as such created. Chapter 19 is an example of a social context where the cautious mode dominated, but where the topics that came up constantly threatened a dilution, so that the most cautiously minded participants took it upon themselves to reign in those who deviated too far towards expansivism. And they, in turn, not being convinced expansivists, allowed themselves to be led back to safe territory. This happened, in other words, at two levels, both at the level of mode of management of meaning and at the level of opinions expressed.

81 In 1990, the value of one U.S. dollar was around 100 pesetas. The monthly salary of an unskilled worker was between 60.000 and 100.000 pesetas. Because income level was a sensitive thing, I could not ask about it, but judging from what salaries were offered in employment ads to the professions that club members had, I estimate that there might have been some who earned as little as 200.000-300.000 pesetas a month, while others certainly earned over 1.000.000.

82 Instead of disposition one could call it cultural principle or similar. But I prefer the concept disposition, since it is one of several connecting concepts defined by Bourdieu that form part of his theory of practice, along with other terms I also use, like habitus and doxa. For a description of philia in the Valencian working class, see Thurén 1988:218-223.

83 In Thurén 1988 there is a description of just how these tasks were arranged in order to give room for sociability.

84 *Tertulia* is the general Spanish word for sitting down with friends for a chat. It can mean any form of get-together with few or many participants, but it used to refer mainly to a regular meeting at a café or bar where male friends met at an approximate given hour on a given day of the week, or perhaps every day, to exchange views on politics or literature or whatever the specialty of the group members. When women friends met to chat, that was called gossip and did not count as a *tertulia*. However, in recent decades the traditional form of *tertulia* has become less common and the term has become more inclusive. As long as the focus is on exchanging viewpoints, almost any gathering can be called a *tertulia*. Regular or irregular continuity is often desired but does not have to be for the word to apply.

85 Cf note 13 about Opus Dei.

86 Cf for example chapter 3 on Maria's older children.

87 Of interest are both the specificity of the behavior the rules referred to and the vagueness with which most norms were expressed, a vagueness interpreted as courtesy and elegance. Some examples: In the ball courts, "it is forbidden to play with a naked upper body, with inappropriate shoes or in general wearing anything that does not adjust to the norms dictated by the Royal Tennis Federation." The players "should try to maintain an adequate tone of voice so that co-players or players at adjacent courts are not disturbed." Breaches of norms at the courts were classified into light, serious and very serious and the corresponding sanctions for each category were specified. Among light breaches were non-payment for use of courts, wrong clothes and "expressions of bad taste". Among serious breaches were destruction of facilities and "serious defects in education, provocative vocabulary or gestures." Quarrels were classified as very serious breaches. In all areas of the club, members and visitors were reminded "that they are in a place destined to the stay and play of children, therefore it is forbidden to show any behavior that is not appropriate for their age." The careful monitoring of voice level and vocabulary was again insisted upon for the salons. Men were reminded that they had to wear "correct shoes, long trousers and buttoned shirt". Women's dress was not specified, supposedly because women would not voluntarily dress in a way that would be considered out of place. Silence was imposed in the TV room when there was a program on. In the children's TV room, children's programs had the right of way. In both TV rooms, food was prohibited. Sports clothes could not be used in the game rooms. Drinks and snacks, but not food, could be consumed in the game rooms but must not be placed on the game cloths. In the pool area, the main prohibitions were: no eating at all, no drinking from receptacles made of glass, street clothes were forbidden, especially hard shoes (and it was just as forbidden to walk barefoot outside the pool area), radios were not allowed, one must shower before entering the pool, and finally, the rules prohibited "any act of nudism; even children of young age must at all times wear a "slip" or similar piece of clothing." Boys over five years must use the male dressing area. The dressing areas were for dressing and washing only, so games and consumption of food and drinks were forbidden there, and "it is forbidden to walk about naked in the halls", i.e. between a shower and a dressing room. "Minors" were not allowed to consume tobacco or alcoholic drinks inside the club, but the age limit was not specified.

88 The Opus Dei is a Catholic lay organization, cf note 31. There is more on its views on sexuality in chapter 17. Members have many children since they do not approve of any kind of birth control.

89 *Mus* is played with Spanish cards. The common international cards are called French in Spain. At Club Aguafría there were some who preferred the better known Spanish cards, and I did hear a person or two confess as much, but it was considered more elegant to use "French" cards.

90 In general in Spain, the use of *tú* is easy and common as soon as there is any link between two persons. The only exception at the club (as in society in general) was the respect for age which made most people use the formal pronoun *usted* to people over a certain age, between sixty and seventy, depending on the attitude of that person, and this was very logical since many persons in that generation had made their own children call them *usted*. However, the anti-hierarchy ideology of the general *tú* was restricted to members and served as a clear symbol of hierarchy between members and personnel. The only club employee usually addressed by members as *tú* was the administrator, but he was also a member himself. All the others, from a venerable elderly door watchman to the most recently employed teenage kitchen help, were always addressed by members as *usted*. The usage was always reciprocal, except in the case of the elderly, who would address young people (if members) as *tú*, even when addressed by them as *usted*.

91 *Tapa* is the Spanish word for a small plate of food to go with a drink. It used to be that they were served automatically and for free with any drink, even with a normal small shot of the cheapest wine at the cheapest tavern. In some corners of Spain this was still so, but the custom was fast disappearing. In Madrid you often got nothing at all or just an olive or two. In some elegant places, on the other hand, a waiter would walk through the room every half hour or so with a tray full of little delicacies from which each customer could choose one. However, in most bars, of any economic level, one could order *raciones*, portions. That was basically the same thing, only the quantity was larger (without being anywhere near a normal meal) and the customer paid for it In daily usage in Madrid, the word *tapas* could mean *raciones*, also. To go for *tapeo* was a beloved activity which consisted in going from bar to bar, having a glass of wine or beer in each, to taste their specialties in *tapas* or *raciones*.

92 This discourse is described in chapter 18.

93 Isabel Preysler was a famous woman of Philippine origin. Being beautiful and rich and having been married to a hit singer and to a government minister, she was a favorite celebrity of gossip magazines.

94 Cf chapter 11. One of the "values" suggested as topics for discussion in the "Nosotros" group was "coherence". That word was often heard in Madrid in the 1990s, and it usually expressed worries about the personal experience of harboring incompatible ideas and feelings.

95 E.g. Goodenough's propriospect, Schwartz's idioverse, Hannerz' perspective. (Cf e.g. Hannerz 1983:143-185 or Hannerz 1992:62-99.) They are similar in meaning but not identical. I prefer Bourdieu's habitus because it is linked to a set of other concepts that work together to handle culture as something in constant movement, transcending the dichotomy between actors and structures, and because it links individual sets to collective ones without presupposing any identity between the two. It is also a concept that includes "ideas" that are so deeply entrenched in mind and body that it would be confusing to call them ideas, but that are part of culture, not nature, since they vary between societies. A habitus can be defined as the accumulated experiences of an individual or a category, as interpreted in the light of the whole experience of that individual or category.
I have developed my view of these concepts in an unpublished lecture which can be found on my blog: https://bmthuren.wordpress.com/wp-content/uploads/2013/02/bourdieulacc88sning.pdf

96 There was social pressure to this effect. For example, one couple who had formed part for many years of a circle of conservatives seemed to be loosening their bonds with the group while I was in the field. They did go to the club, they did invite the group members to their family functions and attend those of the others (weddings, baptisms, birthdays, etc), and they assured their loyalty verbally. But they did not come as often as they used to, and the group realized that they were seeing other friends in other places. This was not openly criticized – the couple had high prestige inside the group – but the group members questioned each other: "Have you talked to X?" "Were they here last week? I did not see them!" "Oh, did X call you? Why, she has not called me since I don't know when..." and so on. There was clear irritation in the voices when such phrases were pronounced, even if the faces smiled, and whenever the topic arose, everyone concentrated on it.

97 One such individual was Sofía (chapter 5), who was seen as a somewhat suspect character by the others. And this was so in spite of her economic means, which were beyond doubt. In other words, group loyalty was a stronger criterion for acceptance than money, even in this money-conscious context.

98 I was not given access to membership files but according to both the president and the administrator, only about half of the members lived in the surrounding residential area of Aguafría.

99 See chapter 5 for a definition; examples are found throughout the ethnographic chapters.

100 *Krausismo* is a Spanish brand of thought based on the German philosopher Karl Christian Friedrich Krause (1781-1832) and very popular among anti-dogmatic thinkers, especially educators, in the early decades of the 20th century.

101 See the section "A summer afternoon – another kind of women" in chapter 5.

102 Or, to be more exact: I never heard it. Perhaps they were discussed in small groups of intimate friends of a less conservative persuasion than those I came to know best. Perhaps they were discussed in groups of men only. I cannot know that. But I do not think it very probable, to judge from the attitudes that could be openly demonstrated.

103 There is a short summary of the meeting at which Marías' book was discussed in chapter 17.

104 So I honestly tried to become a "real" member. It was an ethical necessity, and it was possible because of my past life in Madrid and because their experimental style appealed to me and the issues that were important to them were important to me, too. But it was one fieldwork context that made my ambivalent insider-outsider position painfully clear. My membership was inevitably temporary and I had reservations about some of the activities.

105 But Alberto was certainly right – in most other Madrilenian middle class contexts it would have been sensitive, since marriage would be seen as distinct from friendship, and a man is thought to be most comfortable with male friends. To have a wife as one's best friend could be construed as a lack of virility or as being dominated by the wife.

106 I have translated "*viaje fin de carrera*" as "class trip". Literally it means "the trip to mark the end of college studies." It used to be that each group of university students arranged a trip to celebrate the end of their studies before they dispersed into professional life. This idea has spread, so that now the final year classes in both primary and secondary education also make class trips. Quite an expense for the parents, even though the youngsters try to earn part of the money themselves, typically by selling lottery.

107 For example, the atmosphere of Club Aguafría did fulfill all these conditions, in spite of all the caution, all the limitations, all the complaints to the contrary.

108 In chapter 12 there is an example of how good companionship can even be seen as an almost-synonym of or a replacement for love.

109 In phrases like "My friends respect me the way I am." "One should always respect the opinions of others, of course." I.e. "respect" had no hierarchical overtones; it meant just "accepting and letting be as is."

110 I have described it for Valencia (Thurén 1988:212-218), and other students of Spanish reality usually also have something to say about it, using different terms. Its importance and its expressions vary according to class, gender, age and region, but it is a general phenomenon. Cf Appendix C.

111 In comparison to Beniturian women, middle class Madrilenian women felt much less timidity about using bars and restaurants, but they did prefer cafeterias, and they were selective in their choices, always considering carefully if a place was or was not appropriate for women of their class.

112 Of any kind – no special differentiation was made between alcoholic and non-alcoholic drinks.

113 This is a common disappointment for traveling Spaniards, especially the first time they go abroad. They tend to be optimistic about their linguistic proficiency.

114 A very large majority of young Spaniards live with their parents until they get married. If they study, they depend economically on their parents, and the parents are not usually willing to pay for their children's upkeep outside the home unless they have to move to another city to study, which is hardly ever the case for Madrilenians. The few Madrilenian students who move out from their parents' home have to find part time jobs, which is extremely difficult, and a cheap place to rent, which is almost as difficult. After finishing their studies, it usually takes some time before they find a job, and once they do, they often prefer to go on living at home for yet a while in order to save money to be able to buy an apartment of their own. And "to have dinner served at the table," as they often express it. And the mothers are usually happy to provide the service. Especially the many women whose whole personal value hinges on motherhood fear the moment when the children will move out, so they do what they can to postpone it. The only clearly acceptable reason to move is marriage.

115 The rest of this chapter is based on the transcription of the tape. It is edited, because it would have been much too long otherwise, but the quotes are verbatim. I have added indications of major topics treated.

116 To be an elementary school teacher, nowadays, one has to attend a university level three year course. But that is recent. When these women were young, one would proceed to teacher's college directly from elementary school. It was often seen as an alternative to secondary schooling. For many, especially in rural areas, it was even seen as the female version, whereas the normal secondary school, *instituto*, was seen as male.

117 The fact that all these expressions are common female names, and all of them include the most common of them all, María, was not discussed, nor have I ever heard it discussed. My interpretation is that the expressions all connote "a woman like all others, the most common type". This would mean that the contempt is directed, at some level of consciousness, not just at certain women but at all women.

118 The word she used was *compañero*. It means literally companion or friend but is generally used by left-leaning persons to signify common-law husband (and common-law wife, *compañera*). It is not usually used as a synonym for husband, as Nati did here, but that is a possible use and marks the speaker as even more "progressive" since such a usage downplays the, for others, important difference between marriage and other couple relationships. It is also a word with a certain political tint, not as strong as *camarada*, comrade, but with similar uses in social movements and political parties.

119 She did not mean that there was no difference, just that the difference was not decisive.

120 This was a "progressive" key value, of course. Cf appendix A, where the most rebellious person, Mary Cruz, also emphasized choice as a key criterion for justice but had to fight an uphill battle to get it accepted. The others opposed it mainly by passing over it in silence, since it was a value that was difficult to argue against in Madrid at that time, unless you aligned yourself with very clearly "reactionary" ideas of order and discipline, and Matilde's

guests did not want that. But neither were they ready to embrace choice as a key value the way Mary Cruz proposed, especially not talking about women's choices.

121 This was a point debated in some radical circles at the time, including some feminist groups. In such contexts the issue was whether some alternative to employment could be found, seeing that most women could not enter the labor market and seeing the heavy toll taken by the double workday. But in less radical circles, the point was easily confused with a "traditional" standpoint which opposes women's leaving the home for any reason. In this group, there could be little doubt what Emilia meant. but apparently the others wanted to make sure.

122 The remarks on the drawbacks of paid help sounded much like what one can often hear in less progressive contexts as an argument against women's working outside the home. "Everybody will suffer" is the implication, then, whereas Nati's intention was to defend herself against the possible implication of what Emilia had said. namely that she was too "traditional" to leave everything to the maid. That implication was not acceptable to her.

123 In Benituria, the food stores were almost totally female territory and seen as such. And what I saw there in 1983 was what I had also seen in middle class Madrid throughout the 1970's. Of all domestic tasks, men shunned especially the public ones, because even if they "helped", they were ashamed of it and did not want to be seen in public e.g. shopping or hanging laundry

124 The word "even" here implied that it took more bravery for a man to do it in a village than in the city. This was not explicated, since everyone took it for granted. They probably thought of two things (which were also heard in Benituria): Shopping in a village is more difficult, because there are fewer wares to choose from, no quality control and probably no super-markets, so one has to know more about cooking and choosing; and it is more shameful for a man, since village men tend to take the division of labor by gender more for granted and interpret a man in a food store as non-virile, since they also relate the division of labor to sexuality much more directly than urban men do.

125 "To come into the home" is a common phrase that perhaps should be translated with "to become engaged." In this generation, a couple relationship was usually kept secret until the couple felt sure they wanted to get married. Once the parents knew about it, it was too late to break it up, at least not without great scandal. Sometimes the acknowledgement was made into a ceremony of "asking for her hand" with exchange of gifts. But this was a matter of class; for most "ordinary" people the moment was not ritually marked, it was just that each young person was admitted into the home of the other.

126 Spanish hospitals, including private ones. do not offer much service beyond the purely medical. Therefore it is considered necessary for each patient to have a relative accompanying him or her at all times. Private medical insurance plans usually include an extra bed for the accompanying relative. When a child is born, for example, it is the accompanying relative who bathes and diapers the baby. And it goes without saying that the accompanying relative is a woman, for all ages and reasons for hospitalization, except if there is no woman available. What man would have the time, the patience and the practical knowledge? Ignacio's and Emilia's stress on couple togetherness in this context was therefore truly revolutionary.

127 These comments were not just due to my presence. Sweden was often mentioned in discussions about almost any kind of social and political issues in Spain. There was, at least in middle class radical circles, quite a lot of knowledge of Swedish social legislation and it was often talked of not as one possible model among many but as the most "evolved" model of gender relations in Europe and towards which Spain had just begun to move.

128 Cf again appendix A. The two groups were opposites in almost every way, but on this point they were similar.

129 *Sociedad de derechos* – a common phrase in Spain to indicate the opposite of a dictatorship, or more concretely the kind of dictatorship that the Franco regime was, where status and arbitrariness counted for more than any abstract rights.

130 I must leave the original word untranslated, because Nati was playing on words here. *Señorita* means "miss", in the sense of the title of an unmarried woman, "*señorita* López", as opposed to a married one, and like "miss" in English it can also be used to address a school teacher, and even talk about her ("my *señorita* is very pretty"). But there is also a completely different meaning with class connotations (and in this meaning there is also a masculine form, *señorito*, which does not exist for the first two meanings). It is a diminutive of *señora*, which means "Mrs" but also "the lady of the house", e.g. the employer of a maid. Diminutives can be used to indicate a respectful familiarity. Maids talk about their employer as "la *señorita*" and also address her as *señorita*. *Los señores*, in the plural, are the mister and mistress of the house, and this too can be put in the diminutive, to indicate intimacy, closeness, or (one expression of the constant Spanish tendency to irony and inversion) lack of good feelings. *Los señoritos* in a wider sense are people with means. Example: "The *señoritos* in this village are not as rich as the *señoritos* of the city, but they still treat us ordinary people like dirt." So what Nati was doing was to expose the contradictions between her professional prestige (*señorita*=teacher) and her prosaic duties as a housewife (*señora*=married woman) via the implication of class difference (*señorita*= upper class woman, which she was in class but not at home).

131 This is not the place for me to take a stand on the controversial issue of the gender order of traditional Basque society. Teresa del Valle and other contemporary students of it contend that it has never been matriarchal (del Valle 1985). What is important here, however, is to note that there is a stereotypical image of Basque women as powerful, and that this is used as an argument against feminist criticism.

132 The scientific discussions and the popular stereotypes about a possible matriarchy in Galicia are similar to the ones concerning the Basques.

133 The Spanish word tertulia used to refer to a group of friends or acquaintances, usually meeting in a bar to discuss something more or less regularly. In certain periods they were mostly political, in other periods mostly literary. Some tertulia groups were open to participants who just happened to pass by, others were more rigid, but never as stable as a formal association. But the word could always be used for a group of friends getting together to discuss something, and that is the most current use today. I chose it to explain to my informants what I wanted from them, and it certainly helped to establish the right atmosphere for my collective interviews. Cf note 84.

134 They would have been quick to catch – and oppose – the normative intent of the phrase as used in certain other contexts, as for instance I did when Yolanda showed me around in the Opus Dei residence and said that even students have to learn what all women have to know. Cf chapter 17. She referred to the division of labor according to gender as taken for granted, and implied that if some women, e.g. students, do not automatically accept it, they must be corrected.

135 Since Rosaldo (1974) suggested that this might be a universal feature of human societies and also universally related to women's subordination, there has been much criticism of this idea. (See e.g. di Leonardo 1991 or Moore 1988 for overviews.) It is probably not a universal phenomenon. At least anthropological studies have shown that it is very difficult to define the terms in a universally applicable way. It may even be difficult to define them reasonably well for Western usage (Thurén 1993). However, in the Mediterranean area, there are many old cultural constructions that refer to such a division. As Mediterranean ideas, they are well established, if conveniently ambiguous. In Spain, for example, there is a common saying that women are of the house, men of the street. The degree to which this corresponds to actual activities varies. In Spain it was probably more true in the cities in the 1990s than in the villages or formerly, in spite of the emic impression of change in the opposite direction. Cf Thurén 1988. For a good description of how the divide works (or used to work) in a representative Andalusian village, see Sánchez Pérez 1990.

136 The numbers are from Instituto Nacional de Estadística, downloaded from Wikipedia, February 12, 2016. https://es.wikipedia.org/wiki/Demograf%C3%ADa_de_Espa%C3%B1a

137 All the figures are from García Sainz 1990. They refer not to the city itself but to the whole region (Comunidad de Madrid), but it is a small region and the city of Madrid dominates it in every way. It is a big city (around 4 million inhabitants) surrounded by a scattering of small villages and a few medium-sized cities that in practice function as suburbs of the city of Madrid. In other words, the figures for the city itself would be almost identical.

138 Cf Carlota in chapter 3, and cf the analysis of family corporateness in chapters 2 and 4.

139 Durán (1988:392) has made an interesting comparison of the time Spanish women spend on housework, according to whether they work outside the home or not, and according to the level of family income. The pattern for women who work outside the home is complicated. At the lowest income level they spend around ten hours a day on housework and seven at their job. Consequently, they have no leisure. The leisure increases slowly and the time spent on domestic tasks decreases irregularly but steeply as family incomes rise, while the time spent on outside jobs first drops and then rises sharply. In other words, when the husband's income reaches a certain level, the first luxury the family permits itself is a housewife. But at higher income levels, women get new opportunities to work, and with the money they earn they buy appliances and food products that liberate them from some domestic tasks. Their time for leisure hardly increases, however, until a certain point near the highest end of the income scale. At this point all three curves veer dramatically. Domestic tasks drop to four hours a day, job time plummets from its high of nine to between four and five, and leisure time climbs from three to eight hours. Evidently, this is the point where women find it is not worthwhile to work outside the home, at least not full time, because their husbands earn much more money than they could, but even though they stay at home, they do little housework, presumably because they have servants.

These curves are even more interesting when compared to the two curves for housewives. They are practically level. At all income levels, the women without outside employment spend between ten and eleven hours a day doing domestic tasks. Leisure stays between three and five hours except for the highest levels of family income where it drops to between two and three, i.e. the same level as for working women at low income levels. Even remembering women's duties of representation and distinction at the high income levels, it is hard to avoid thinking that there is some make-work going on here.

140 The men of the upper sectors of society bought personal services – drivers, secretaries, meals, etc. – while their wives had to attend to themselves and often also to others. And they did so in similar conditions as working class and peasant women, says Durán. That is an exaggeration, because they did have much better working locales and tools. But I agree with her general conclusion: "With more or less clarity, this comparative process between the work she actually does and the one she could do leads the housewife to an inevitable evaluation of her working conditions, and this evaluation is the more negative the farther away she feels from her possibilities in the non-domestic sector and her professional and personal ambitions." (Durán 1987: 308. My translation.)

141 A good illustration is a shopping diary, collected by Durán. The woman who wrote it had an exacting job outside the home and a full time maid; her family consisted of six persons and belonged to the upper middle class. She and the maid each did about half of the weekly shopping, she reported, and the maid did all of the daily shopping. On April 18, 1987, a Saturday, the day of the diary, the woman spent three hours at the market, and two of the children came along and helped, mainly by standing in line in front of the various stalls while their mother shopped somewhere else. In this way they saved a lot of time. They bought six kinds of fruit, in two different stalls, eighteen kinds of vegetables in three stalls, three chicken and two dozen eggs in the chicken stall, one leg of pork and a piece of bone in the meat stall, three products from the entrails stall, two products from the fish stall, six products from the drug store and twenty products from three different grocery stalls. She also bought some flowers, but had no time for the pharmacy. Afterwards, the wife and the maid worked together for two hours, cleaning, cutting and packaging products to be stored and cooking some of them so that they would be usable at short notice during the week (Durán 1988:263-265). Such shopping can be called traditional, because it was done at a traditional market, where one has to stand in line in front of many different stalls, and where one has to use cash, and also because it included entrails and bones, and because coming home she used some of the products to make such things as sauces and bouillons, instead of buying semi-prepared products. Most working women have to cut more corners. The example is non-traditional in that the children helped, in that so much was bought on one day and taken home by car and in that vegetables were bought for a whole week at a time.

142 "In the course of a quarter century () middle and upper class women have witnessed the disappearance of the traditional organization of the household economy: their co-ownership of family property has become socially devalued, because the earnings obtained from property, shared with the husband, are ever more irrelevant in comparison to the husband's income from work; and as to inheritable property () the increase in life expectancy has robbed her almost totally of its importance as an element of social definition, because it arrives not only diminished but in a moment of the life cycle when the important steps in her social and econonomic biography have already been taken." (Durán 1987:307. My translation.)

143 E.g. Emilia in chapter 13.

144 And available evidence indicates they really did very little. See e g Durán 1987/88, Inner 1988, Ramos Torres 1990.

145 From the perspective of the 2020s, thirty years later, there are discussions around such opting out strategies as changing one's gender. But in middle class Madrid in the 1990s, it was never mentioned in non-academic contexts.

146 The conversation could evidently not be taped, but I took notes immediately afterwards in the club library. The quotes are not verbatim, but my possible bias or bad memory had little time to skew the narrative. I wrote down only what had been said. The analysis was done later.

147 Left hand (*mano izquierda)* is an expression that means a talent for seduction and manipulation, getting one's way without having a recognized right to decide. In Spain by the 1990s, everyone agreed that this is how women used to defend themselves, and everyone agreed that the use of left hand was now seen by many as illicit. But opinions differed on which women used it, for what purposes, in whose eyes it was illicit, etc. and above all on whether women should go on using it or not. Opinions differed so much, and "left hand" was such a central and necessary factor for the gender order to work, that in the Valencia study I used the expression as a symbol for the kind of "traditional" gender order that many Spaniards thought was being "overcome".

148 This was evident above all from the results: families were smaller, and women had their children earlier and closer together and thus more time for other activities after the children were grown. All research agrees on this point (del Campo and Navarro, 1985, Beltrán et al 1987, Riera and Valenciano 1991, Schubert 1990). The regular surveys on "fertility" also showed that ever more women knew about and used contraceptives. Even though, as late as in 1969, sociologists could be arrested for asking questions about contraception (del Campo and Navarro 1985: 122), as early as in 1977, 91% of Spanish women had heard of at least one method. Among young people, the percentage was 98 (del Campo and Navarro 1985:123). The most popular method was coitus interruptus, followed by preservatives, but they were superseded by the pill during the 1980's. All these surveys, furthermore, consistently indicate that the persons who knew least about contraception are of low social class, low education and living in small villages in peripheral regions. Highly educated middle class persons in Madrid in the 1990s therefore could be presumed to be those who knew most and also, probably, practiced most, even though the difference between knowing about and practicing contraception continued to be wide.

149 The Church graded films according to their "moral danger".

150 And in the working class, too, of course.

151 *Perito* is the colloquial word for *ingeniero técnico,* an engineering degree that requires only three years of studies, compared to the five needed to be a full engineer.

152 These phrases were common in the interviews. "No luxury and no problems" means approximately that the family neither belonged to the category who can afford to go on vacations or buy high quality consumer goods, nor to the category where food and health are daily problems. A woman who "dedicates herself to her children" is a woman without any economic activity outside the home. The phrase is vaguely normative (implying that a woman who works outside the home is not a good mother) and sometimes defensive (i.e. that raising children is full time

work, so a woman should not have to do anything else), but Esperanza's use of it was purely descriptive, as will become clear.

153 To describe oneself as rebellious was very common and meant to give a fittingly energetic image of self.

154 "Liberal" here means that the school was not dogmatically Catholic, not restrictive of student's personal freedom and not manipulative with their consciousness – the implied contrast is with some religious schools where "character formation" is a major educational purpose.

155 In Spanish discussions on religion this distinction was always made. Quite a few people said they believe "in something" or perhaps "in God and the Virgin but not in the priests" and did not go to church; they were called believers (*creyentes*) or non-practicing Catholics (*católicos no practicantes*). These two expressions are usually synonymous in practice, but a few individuals might specify that they were believers but not Catholics. Practitioners (*practicantes*) were those who attended mass and observed other Catholic rules. Most of these usually defined themselves as believers, too, (and to them the word practitioner automatically included that and was synonymous to "a good Catholic"), but a few confessed to practice without belief, usually for social reasons: the pressure of public opinion, the pleasure of sociability or both. This was especially true of atheists or agnostics talking about the past, their own or others'.

156 By sixth grade she is referring here not to the sixth year of her total schooling but to the sixth year of secondary schooling. This was at a time when primary schooling was very varied, so the courses only started to count when you began secondary schooling, usually around ten years of age. After four years there was a lower examination for those who did not plan to go on to university. The others went on to fifth and sixth grade and after that PREU, or *curso pre-universitario*, the university preparation course she mentioned earlier. To pass the university entrance examination, *selectividad*, a further year or more was required, usually in private evening schools. From the dates and ages given by Esperanza, we can see that she passed *selectividad* right away after PREU, and this must mean that she was a very good student indeed.

(Since the early 1970's, primary schooling, EGB, *Educación General Básica*, had begun at age six (with one or two not required previous years of *pre-escolar*, pre-school) and the grades were numbered one through eight. After the eighth year, those who planned to go on, took three years of BUP, *Bachillerato Unificado Polivalente*, and one further year which was supposedly preparatory for university, COU, *Curso de Orientación Universitaria*, but which was to all effects taught like another school year. All in all there would be twelve years of schooling before university. *Selectividad* was still a university entrance examination that must be passed, but most students now did pass it without further studies after COU. The problem centered rather on how to obtain good grades on it, since that determined access to many studies. For youngsters who did not want to go on to secondary schooling after eighth grade, there was something called FP, *Formación Profesional*, originally meant to be a practical preparation for manual jobs combined with some general education. For various reasons, FP had become rather a sort of second-rate secondary schooling for those who failed or got very bad grades in eighth grade. Middle class children never took FP.) Note 2024: This long parentheses describes the school system in the 1990s. It has continued to change since then.

157 The grey ones, *los grises*, was the common nickname for the armed urban police corps, Policía Armada, that had grey uniforms. They were the ones in charge of putting down political unrest in urban areas during the Franco regime. There were several other police corps.

158 *Formación del espíritu nacional*, the ideological education that was compulsory at all levels of schooling during Franco times.

159 Esperanza makes the common contrast between two sets of opinions, where all ingredients in each set usually go together, and when they do not, people call it contradiction. On one side are conservative politics, religious faith and practice, conservative gender opinions and a carefully managed life style in search of social prestige and a high income. On the other side are leftist politics, religious indifference or atheism, a belief in gender equality and a life style where a critical attitude is what gives prestige.

160 Ever since freedom of religion was proclaimed in Spain, already in Franco times, non-Catholics had been allowed to stay out of class during lessons in religion. Since these children had one subject less and therefore not as many grades to compete with for entrance into prestigious schools and universities, a substitute subject called ethics was introduced. The idea was that it would be required for schools to offer both subjects, but this varied in practice. Students (or their parents) had to choose; they must take either ethics or religion and they could not take both. Usually the children's choice was quite a good indication of the parents' politico-cultural opinions.

161 The first communion was an important day in all social classes. Most children got new clothes, their portrait taken by a professional photographer, a celebration in which all relatives took part and above all lots of presents. Printed cards were made, usually with a color photo, and the celebration was often held in a restaurant.

162 Cf note 165 on maternity leave. Esperanza referred to the kind called *excedencia*, maternity leave without pay.

163 23 F is short for February 23rd 1981, the day of the attempted coup d'etat in the Spanish Parliament, the moment when many thought the young Spanish democracy would collapse. Some significant days in recent Spanish history have come to be designed in this way, with just a number and the first letter of the name of the

month. Other famous dates are 15 J, June 15th 1977, when the first elections were held, and 14 D, December 14th 1988, when the unions withdrew their support for the PSOE government and called a general strike.

164 All university studies in Spain were until recently organized in five year "careers". There were no subjects that could be freely elected outside of these "careers" and most of the subjects of a career were required, even though there were a number of choices within each. After a reform in 1991, some careers took only three or four years while some others took longer than five. Esperanza's journalism studies, then, must have meant five full time year-length courses.

165 There were two kinds of maternity leave in Spain. One was established by law: the employer had to allow the woman 14 weeks of leave (during which time she did not receive a salary from the employer, but 75% of her salary was paid by social security) and her position was reserved for her. What Esperanza was talking about here, however, was the other kind, called *excedencia* (leave without pay), the right to which was also established by law but which was rather risky for the woman, especially in times of unemployment. During *excedencia*, one received no economic compensation at all, nor did one have a right to return to the previous position. The only thing that distinguished it from quitting was that if the woman decided, within three years, that she wished to return, she should be given a job, provided there was a vacancy.

166 Throughout the whole tale of lack of time, she did not say a word about any contributions from her husband to childcare and household work. One can surmise that he did not take part at all, for seeing Esperanza's progressive opinions, she would surely have liked to tell me about it, had it occurred.

167 Spanish card game. Cf note 89.

168 The issue of telling one's parents about a love relationship was a thorny one at that time. There were no clear-cut rules. With variations according to region and social class, the common traditional pattern was that young people should not see each other in private at all. Boys and girls met in groups. As soon as a couple talked to each other in private (even if that meant only walking as a couple, surrounded by their other friends, during the daily socializing hour), they were a recognized couple and ought to have their parents'permission. Already in the 1960s this pattern was considered old-fashioned and rural by Madrid middle class youth, but their parents did not approve of other patterns, so most relationships were kept secret until the couple had decided to get married. By the 1990s, parents were aware that youngsters had fleeting relationships, but in the conservative sectors of the middle class this was not talked about, and the parents seemed to believe that their children would not have a serious relationship without telling them, which was far from the truth.

169 Esperanza had told me more than enough of her opinions for me to surmise that she would include contraceptives in what she saw as a rational management of her life. Her reply shows that she appreciated my understanding.

170 In saying this, Esperanza communicated an even more progressive attitude than the one I had taken for granted. She not only accepted the use of contraceptives, as against people who considered them immoral, but she took a critical stand against them from a feminist point of view. She probably wanted to make certain that I placed her correctly, not just in the progressive camp but in the radical sector of it.

171 Since rented apartments were very expensive in Madrid, and since most couples now rejected the (never pervasive) solution of living with her or his parents, marriage was practically always postponed until a couple could afford to buy an apartment. Usually the parents helped with the down payment.

172 I used the Spanish expression *ama de casa*. It can mean different things, cf note 29. But as I phrased it and in this context, it was clear that I referred to women without paid work outside the home.

173 "*Bachillerato*" they said. What that means in years of study depends on the person's age. When these middle aged women were young, there were two levels of bachillerato, *inferior* and *superior*, and since the club respondents seldom specified which, and specified "*superior*" if they did, one may assume that most of them had the lower kind, which means that they quit school around age fourteen. Cf also note 56.

174 As I said, this number is probably a bit too high, because of the social dynamics around the selection of respondents. And naturally the total number of interviews is too small to make the results statistically reliable. They give only an approximate idea. The president of the club was surprised about the results. "That many? I wonder... Perhaps a lot of women have opened boutiques lately! I would have guessed 20% at most. Now, of course, we have gotten a lot of young married couples as members recently, and those women work..." (Women's professions were not entered into the membership files. Nor were the men's: "We ask about them when they sign up, but we don't write them down. We don't want anyone to be able to use the files for advertisement or anything like that.")

175 It was obviously impossible to tape or take notes during the debate, so what follows are approximate quotes, written down after dinner, late that same night.

176 I never received any excuse from the board, so I do not know if this was an intentional slight or just an oversight. The board had organized the debate, after all, and told me that the dining-room would be available. There were many other small tell-tale signs that the board probably had not realized how controversial the debate would be. Informants from various groups said they thought the board had received criticism, got cold feet and decided to do what they could to make me uncomfortable, not in order to stop me but to defend themselves against

their critics. It is possible, because their attitude was decidedly ambivalent. They continued to support the project, being courteous and helpful in many ways throughout my period at the club.

177 Carlos' outburst in chapter 16 is one example. It was of the joking variety, cf below. It is interesting, too, because it was proffered as a way of closing that other controversial topic, women's work. To close one strong theme, he proposed an even stronger one.

178 As an English observer phrased it, "the occasional excesses of Spain's sexual revolution are a measure of the intensity of the repression which preceded it." (Hooper1987:186)

179 Like so many other changes, the change in attitudes on sexuality in Spain can be seen as an especially concentrated and therefore more visible and dramatic, but largely parallel process to what has happened in other Western countries (Frayser 1985:419-420).

180 It did not dominate the judiciary, however, which led to contradictions between the law and judicial practice. For example, there were some widely discussed sentences on rape while I was in the field. In these cases, the victims had behaved in ways that the judges saw as provocative (in one case wearing a mini-skirt to the office where she worked, in another case accepting a lift with two male friends to get home from a discotheque) whereas the victims considered it normally accepted behavior. According to present legislation on rape, the "moral" standing of the victim is irrelevant, but that was not so when these judges had their training. One of them went on television to argue for what he saw as his "defense of public morals". He did not accept the law as it stood.

181 But only after negotiating an ambiguous clause about special attentions: "No confession will have state character. The political powers will take into consideration the religious beliefs of Spanish society and will maintain the consequent cooperative relations with the Catholic Church and other confessions." The Spanish Constitution of 1978, article 16, §3. (My translation.)

182 A polemic priest and writer has even suggested that a document from the bishops on this issue was partly to blame for the attempted coup d'etat in February 1981 (Aradillas 1986:272).

183 I will concentrate on divorce to abbreviate my argument, but it could easily be complemented by a similar analysis of two other big controversies: abortion and married priests. In these, too, other themes were apparently decisive (definition of life, professional dedication), while an analysis would show that the constant underlying the arguments was a clash between different views on sexuality. See e.g. Sundman 1994 and 1999.

184 From the "Exhortation on the Divorce Law" signed by the Permanent Commission of the Spanish Bishops' Conference on February 3rd, 1981, in other words probably the most representative document in the whole controversy. It is also the document the publication of which Aradillas calls unfortunate, cf note 182.

185 It is extremely difficult to know how many Spaniards really looked to the Church hierarchy for moral guidance. It was the belief that they were many that made Church pronouncements so sensitive politically, but one can have reasonable doubts about the numbers. One common estimate was that some 75% of the population defined themselves as Catholics but less than half practiced their religion (Giner 1990:573). Another article in the same study shows that the number of practicing Catholics had shrunk from 83% in 1965 to 41% in 1988 (Giner 1990:64) – a very significant drop whatever doubts we may harbor about such self-descriptive survey answers. (The well-known tendency for respondents to adjust their answers to what is considered "right" is, naturally, greater under conditions of dictatorship.) What exactly constitutes "practice" should also be specified. Durán (1988:126) uses the criterion of frequency of visits to church. Of the respondents who said they go to church at all, 41% said they go every or almost every Sunday, 14% go about once a month and 24% go "several times a year". Only 6% go more than once a week. This relativizes the concept of "practicing" and brings the total of weekly visitors to church to below 20% of the population, but it still says very little about the moral authority of the priests or the Church as an institution. Another relevant fact is that the proportion of non-believers and indifferents grows with rising levels of education, with rising levels of income and with rising levels of social prestige. This says something about the probable future trends, as does the fact that, asked about their most important values, Spaniards placed health, family, love, money, and work ahead of religion (Durán 1988:127). Interesting figures also in Pérez Díaz 1987:457-461. A further complication is the relationship between a practicing believer and the Church as a moral authority. References to Church positions are conspicuous by their absence from most conversations heard in Madrilenian middle class life. Cf e.g chapter 11.

186 And such protection had in fact been very slow in coming into Spanish legislation and was still ineffective.

187 Giner 1990:541. Kaplan 1992:203.

188 E.g. Castán Lacoma, bishop of Guadalajara: "Even natural marriage contracted by non-baptized persons is indissoluble." The quote is from 1980 (Aradillas 1986:186-187).

189 Cf the bishops' document quoted above, which calls its own interpretation objective fact. Cf also the fact that during the Franco regime civil marriage was even more indissoluble than ecclesiastical marriage. Civil marriage was only permitted if both spouses declared themselves non-Catholics, so it was a rare occurrence, since declaring oneself a non-Catholic had grave repercussions for all aspects of one's life in Franco's Spain. Those who did contract civil marriage were subject only to civil law, which totally forbade divorce, whereas those who contracted religious marriage were subject to canon law, according to which there was a possibility of annulment. And canonical annulment had automatic civil effects, according to the agreement between Church and State. It is also

relevant here that the main valid reason for obtaining an annulment was to "prove" (the corruption which made proof easy was well-known) that the marriage had not been consummated, i.e. that it was not a marriage in the sexual sense. If there had been no sexual relations, it had never been a marriage. Therefore annulment, not divorce. A marriage is indissoluble, but what has never been joined cannot be separated, one only recognizes a fact. What makes a marriage into a marriage in Catholic thinking is "conjugal reality", i.e. coitus.

190 But in a sociological sense, the minister was right. A national survey in 1979 found that 71% of all Spaniards thought that legal separation by mutual consent was acceptable, 65% thought divorce should be permitted after two or three years of legal separation, and varying percentages above 60% thought a divorce should be granted on grounds of abandonment, non-compliance with duties, adultery and homosexuality (López Pintor1982:119).

191 Any number of examples of the construction of sexuality as disorder could be adduced. One well-informed English observer has a chapter on it (Hooper, 1986:185-195). A Spanish classic is Ferrándiz and Verdú 1975. Pérez Diaz 1987:431-432, 441ff, discusses it. Much critical-minded Spanish fiction is also about the issue of order-chaos and its sexual symbols. In contrast to the Church, these writers usually equate order with repression and treat the consequent problem of ambivalence towards freedom. For example, in their various styles, Luis Martín-Santos, Carmen Martín Gaite, Rosa Montero, Francisco Umbral, Juan Marsé and even Camilo José Cela. "El caballo desnudo" (The Naked Horse) by José Luis Sampedro is a masterpiece in the genre, if a genre it be.

192 Imbert (1982) has reached the same conclusions analyzing a radio program, the very popular Elena Francis counselling program for women broadcast from 1951 to 1984. The program contained very little explicit talk of the body, he says, yet worry about the body, especially sexuality, was the outstanding topic, present in all the others: marriage, infidelity, love, "purity", beauty, health...

193 Virility has been a positive virtue and a strong theme in Spanish fascism, from the early 1930s and on.

194 Giner 1990:453-454. Hooper 1987: 175 ff. Other writers say similar things about its emphasis on achievement but also point out that it is rooted more in Crusade Catholicism than in any kind of aggiornamento. E.g. Schubert 1990:244-245.

195 We had met at an international feminist conference.

196 Opus Dei members seldom call the organization by that name, which is latin for the Work of God. They usually call it "la Obra", the Work in Spanish.

197 According to its own figures, the organization had 75.000 members all over the world and 1.400 priests. (El País, July 28, 1991)

198 Pope John Paul II was considered by some commentators (e.g. Aradillas 1986, El País July 28, 1991) to be very favorably disposed towards Opus Dei. It was under his reign that the Founder was canonized and the Opus Dei attained a certain administrative independence – facts which made detractors accuse it of being a parallel church hierarchy. Pope John Paul II was not considered by so-called progressives to be favorably disposed towards the emancipation of women, or, for that matter other progressive causes, quite to the contrary (Giner 1990:453-455).

199 All quotes from Marías' books are translated by me. The numbers in parenthesis refer to the pages in the 1980 edition of "La mujer en el siglo XX."

200 One of Ortega y Gasset's key ideas, to which his disciple Marías often refers.

201 And perhaps this could help explain an otherwise curious phenomenon: In the Spanish progressive discourse, transvestitism, even transvestite prostitution, has been considered exciting and positive, a step "forwards" towards freedom. It has in fact been a favorite topic in films, magazines, night life... I have seen no remark about the contradiction between this and the fact that this discourse otherwise criticizes prostitution as exploitation and criticizes traditional feminine coquetry, which is what Spanish transvestites especially imitate. But the paradox could be resolved as follows: the transvestites play dramatically with gender categorization. Therefore they question rigid dualism, therefore they question a central precept in traditional sexuality. So transvestites become an appropriate symbol of "sexual anarchy" and therefore of opposition to the conservative discourse. Their existence loosens the conceptual rigidity of conservative dualism..

202 This may seem contrary to what most ethnography of the Mediterranean area has described: that it is women's sexuality that is most feared and that women must therefore be controlled. The theme of honor and shame has been a major one in anthropological discussions. As I see it, there are two different perspectives that in the end concern the same thing: Women are seen as temptresses and must therefore be controlled. But the active part is considered to be the male. Men act, but they are forgiven because it is women's innate capacity for seduction that cause them to act. In some areas, mainly the southern shore, the emphasis has been on women's identification with chaos (see e.g. Evers Rosander 1991, Pitt-Rivers 1963), while in others, especially Catholic countries, the emphasis has been on the protection of monogamy and on forbidding sex that is not put into the service of reproduction (for Spain see e.g. Ferrándiz and Verdú 1975, Gallego Méndez 1983, Imbert 1982, Martín Gaite 1992). In either case, men are seen as actors, women as objects of desire. The penis is seen as the main instrument of sexuality (and therefore male homosexuality is doubly dangerous while lesbianism becomes almost invisible, cf Serrano Vicens 1975).

203 This idea was quite often expressed in spontaneous conversations that touched on sexuality-related issues. Cf for example María José's comments at her dinner party (chapter 12) about not wanting to talk to her daughter as if

sexuality existed, because that would be like encouraging her to practice it. Cf also the discussion at Club Aguafría about the government condom campaign: it is fine to inform, but very bad to entice, and the line between the two is thin. (Seeing how young Madrilenians actually live today, such discussions take on an ostrich-like quality.)

204 For examples, see e.g. Ferrándiz and Verdú 1975, Martín Gaite 1987 and myriad novels from the period. In the critical literature it is almost always pointed out that precisely things like locked parks and fierce sermons in church against swimming in the river served to remind everyone of what was behind the prohibitions. Much joking brought home the same point.

205 Unlike similar discourses in other European societies, the Spanish one does not reserve emotions for women. On the contrary, (certain kinds of) emotions are seen as constitutive of virility.

206 Carlos' joking during the dinner in chapter 16 can serve as an example.

207 One common type of joke plays on the phonetical near-identity of the words *sexo* (sex) and *seso* (brains). One can for example slap one's forehead, exclaiming: "I (you, he, she, they...) have my (your, etc) *sexo/seso* here!"

208 Camilo José Cela is one of Spain's great writers. His first book came out in the early 1940s and he has published extensively since then. In 1989 he was awarded the Nobel prize. His main interest in writing, or at least the feature he is most famous for, is his explicit, extensive and enthusiastic treatment of sexuality. He questions, or at least illustrates, every conceivable "taboo" except the exclusiveness of the male perspective.

209 This translation is mine as are all the rest in this chapter.

210 The word in the original is *cachondo* which means both fun and horny; a rather telling word in itself. The battle metaphor is also telling, as we will see.

211 And sometimes this fact floats to awareness. Michener (1968) describes the effects on Spanish men of the sudden invasion of female foreign tourists in the 1960s. He quotes one young man who said that he was overwhelmed at first but soon tired of the whole thing, because if the woman did not risk eternal hellfire, there was not much excitement left. No one would say such a thing today, and the new hegemonic discourse looks down on such feelings, but the joking discourse still depends on them.

212 There are and have been many other kinds of joking about sex in Spain, of course. Brandes 1980 offers examples from an Andalusian village.

213 It would be worthy of a study in itself, but this is not the place for it.

214 Hooper's observation is pertinent: "Leaving aside the British, the people who spend most time glued to their TV sets are the Spanish, followed by the Portuguese and the Italians. Almost every home in Spain has a television set – even those which lack other, more useful, amenities. Andalusia, for example, is the hottest region in Europe, yet there are more televisions there than refrigerators. The influence of television in Spanish society is further increased by the fact that Spaniards, as we have seen, take only a relatively small proportion of their information and opinion from written sources. It is no exaggeration to say that whoever controls television in Spain stands fair to control the mood and outlook of the nation and this explains why successive governments have taken such an intense interest in who controls it and what they use it for." (1987:137-8)

215 It is daring not just because it is about condoms, but also because it suggests that it is fun to use them and that women can play an active role. It can even be read to refer to a relationship between two men. None of these implications were acceptable to conservatives.

216 And still was for many. Cf Thurén 1994.

217 A fourth factor to make the spot daring might be the fact that not only young girls but also mature women in Spain found it difficult and scary to use tampons. The reason might be, as one informant told me, that it is "too similar to penetration." Cf Thurén 1994.

218 One proof of the change in attitudes: The magazine Cosmopolitan, which sells an image of "modern" "liberated" women, including sexuality, tried to launch itself in Spain in 1976. It was a total flop and the effort was given up after only a few months. "The ideal woman that was proposed in 1976 was unacceptable, but it is consumed ever more from 1986 on, to such a degree that Cosmopolitan plans its return." (Gallego 1990:88) The new attempt was successful; Cosmopolitan sat prominently on the newsstand racks during my fieldwork period.

219 The Women's Institute, *El Instituto de la Mujer,* was an organization within the Ministry of Culture. Its responsibility was to foment, interpret and publish facts about women's lives and women's needs and wishes in all of Spain. There were also Women's Institutes in several of the autonomous regions. Typical activities were: conferences on controversial issues, subsidizing feminist groups, awarding scholarships, monitoring legislation, building data bases. They had libraries and lectures and they offered courses for women who wanted to enter the labor market late in life or who wanted to go into business. (Cf Cristina in chapter 13.)

220 68% were in favor of it, and curiously even more, 75%, thought it necessary. In the age groups over fifty-five, more women than men were against the campaign, and the numbers were rather high (35% and 26% respectively) but in all other age groups women and men had similar opinions, and below thirty-five years of age the acceptance of the campaign was around 90%, slightly higher for women. The fact that most of my informants at Club Aguafría were middle age coincides with these results, but their class and educational level should have given the opposite result. According to the Women's Institute, only 15% of the population with secondary or higher schooling were against the campaign (Mujeres 1991:4:28). Once again, Club Aguafría stands out as an ideological extreme.

221 The difference between women and men was not very significant, but age was. Many kinds of surveys show that age discriminates much more than gender or education when it comes to opinions on sexuality. Among women over sixty, only 37% thought the sexual relationship important, while 64% of women under twenty-four did. Similar results, but with greater differences, were obtained in a similar survey in 1986. The question was about "sufficient causes for divorce". Of ten suggestions, an unsatisfactory sexual relationship placed sixth, after violent behavior, infidelity, loss of love, too much drinking and lack of personal harmony. 33% of all men and 25% of all women thought it sufficient cause for divorce. In the age group over sixty, 23% men and 8% women thought so, while among the under-twenty-fours, 45% of the men and 41% of the women did. In other words, not only did the younger generation place much greater importance on sexuality, but the difference between women and men had diminished dramatically (Durán 1988:72-73).

222 To judge from what people say about their own practices, there had been a substantial increase. 12% of the population said they practiced some sport in 1968, 26% in 1980. But according to another survey from the 1980s, 87% of Spanish women did not practice any kind of sport, not even gymnastics. Now, the tendency was probably for practice to increase, since the total non-practice was somewhat lower for urban women (82%), even lower for the highest income groups (60%) and for housewives with university education (56%) (Durán 1988:44-47). As to the ascetic and hedonistic traditions, feminist sociologist Durán summarizes thus: "In the present moment, the demands of the body are openly contradictory between two tendencies: the hedonistic tendency, which strives in every way for bodily pleasure (including the consumption of stimulants in contexts that recall old bacchic and orphic rites) and the ascetic tendency, with its severe diets, rigorous exercising, etc, imposed as a means of controlling one's own body, and that make some women into new Spartans." (Durán 1988:35) And later, about eroticism: "In the in-depth interviews (...) one can observe a profound rupture between the generations that are now around forty years old: the rupture has not come through eroticism but with natural science education (...) in primary and secondary schooling, but perhaps there is another rupture beginning now, with postmodernism, a rupture of permissiveness and search for hedonistic experiences through the body and in which mainly the new urban generations will participate." (1988:42)

223 It was in fact true that in survey after survey, young people independently of gender, region, class or education, expressed more "progressive" attitudes than older people. We saw that on sexuality above but it was true for almost any issue. And the dividing line could usually be placed as low as around thirty-five years of age during the 1980s, while around 1990 forty was mentioned more often. I do not think this was an effect of age as such (i.e. the experience of different stages of the life cycle). It is more logical to hypothesize that it was a matter of cohorts. Spaniards born during the 1940's or earlier were educated in harshly repressive times, and when times changed and new thoughts and more information became available, in the late 1970s, these persons had already shaped their opinions and organized their adult life. Spaniards born after 1960, on the other hand, may have received the same type of early education, but the new ideas reached them while they were still malleable. The in-between cohort, for whom other personal circumstances may be more determinant than age, are the ones born approximately between 1950 and 1960.

224 Cf Thurén 1988.

225 María Angeles Calero Fernández: "Los sexos y el sexo en los tacos, una cuestión etnolingüística." In Benís et al, 1991. Argot can be seen, among other things, as one expression of a joking discourse. If argot can also be an oppositional language, it had not happened in Spain in the field of gender. To judge from Calero's data, at least, and also from my own knowledge of Madrilenian argot, it was subversive from the point of view of the most serious and ascetic conservative discourse on sexuality in that it vindicated sexual activity and portrayed it as fun (for men), but it coincided with and reinforced the conservative discourse in every other way.

226 Cf Orgaz (1990) on this among middle class youth in Madrid. This dilemma was certainly not unique for Spanish young girls. Stated in general terms, it might be true for all of Europe; similar descriptions have been made for several European countries. The interesting thing for Spain is, first, that the dilemma was now similar to that of other European young girls, and not as "different" as it used to be; second, because the attitudes to sexuality in Spain had changed so recently and in such a short period of time, they were still different in flavor and emotion, even if their verbal expressions were similar to those of other European countries. There was more personal drama and more social confrontation.

227 Cambio 16, nr. 1.132, August 2, 1993:18-23

228 Most people did not know the figures, of course, but there was an approximate awareness of what statistics show. While the total number of pregnancies diminished from 662.000 in 1965 to 593.000 in 1979, the number of pregnancies for women younger than nineteen increased from 15.000 to 41.000. Over 12% of the teenage pregnancies occurred outside marriage in 1979, and teenagers were close to 30% of all unmarried mothers. To this figure one can add a good part of the 20% of children born in wedlock but before one year had passed after the wedding plus an unknown but high number of teenage abortions, most of them illegal still, and all of them illegal in 1979 (Gurrea 1985). On the other hand, in Madrid and during the next decade, the proportion of teenage mothers decreased. For each one hundred women between fifteen and nineteen years of age, there were 2,7 births in 1979 and only 1,7 in 1986. The total number of births in Madrid was almost halved from 1975 to 1987 (CAM

1989:25). As to AIDS, Spain was the third most affected country in Europe with 10 101 recognized cases in October 1991, or a proportion of 251 per million inhabitants. In Madrid the proportion was 391 (Anuario El País 1992:200). According to the press, the total number had increased to 17.000 by March 1993 (El País, March 4, 1993). In other words, the worries were not unfounded, but the figures could be variously interpreted.

229 Cf appendix C about how the group discussions usually began.

230 This was not an instance of exaggeration for rhetorical effect but a literal statement. It was a very common example women told in order to illustrate how little they used to know about sexuality.

231 Naturally she did not share living quarters with her boyfriend before they got married. She was from another part of Spain and moved to Madrid to work. At the time – in the 1960s – it was considered very risky for her parents to allow this, knowing that her boyfriend also lived in Madrid, even though he lived with his mother and Alicia in a religious residence. Her point was not that she broke taboos, quite the contrary: Her parents were right in not suspecting the worst. The – as she saw it – occasion did not create the crime. She went camping, too, but that was just an innocent thing, and the presence of her brother was proof of that, in her view. As a whole, the reader may find Alicia contradictory throughout the discussion, because she spoke out for a tolerant and understanding attitude towards youth while also being careful to uphold a normative stance whenever the discussion threatened to veer towards authentically new values. But she was not contradictory; she spoke from a middle of the road Catholic position in middle class Madrid: gender conservatism in a new language. For example, as to sexuality, she refused the traditional choice between permissiveness and repression; she thought there was a third alternative, an education that creates self-discipline, which makes people abstain without having to be forcefully held back, and she found this alternative "modern" without "undermining values".

232 The transition was the usual way of referring to the period between Franco's death in 1975 and the new constitution approved in 1978. Or sometimes a longer period, until around 1983, when the new democratic regime was considered reasonably stable. The women in this tertulia were young before the transition and mothers of teenaged or adult children by 1983, so the phrase "women of the transition" obviously referred to their generation. They lived through the transition from dictatorship to democracy in parallel with their personal transition from youth to maturity.

233 She did not refer to the age of forty but to the forty years of dictatorship under Franco. "These forty years" is a common expression. But this speaker took a certain risk in pronouncing it, because it is not often heard in situations where presumably some of the people present supported the regime. This was one such context. In Alicia's living room there was a framed color photograph of her husband shaking hands with Franco.

234 Perhaps one reason for this was that Alicia set the tone. She was conservative, her moral standing was well established, but she had an expansionist style of thinking and very polite manners.

235 For example, the non-card players in the ladies' group at Club Aguafría criticized the card players because they had destroyed their regular sessions of talk, and they considered this an important loss – even though these women were so particular in their aparentar that they complained that it was difficult to find acceptable themes for conversation. Another example is when Lupe and her friends criticized the "majority" of the club members for playing cards in order not to have to talk. This was scathing criticism, since it implied that they were stupid and boring and had no idea of good sociability. (Cf chapter 5.)

236 "Cultural centers" were being established in some residential areas. They sometimes housed a small library, usually a bar, always a lecture room. The activities varied widely, and perhaps these centers were more used by the working class than by the middle class, but I had information on one such cultural center in an upper middle class area which organized popular series of lectures on current issues. A sociologist, Isabel Ruiz, sent me tapes of four lectures she gave there in 1992. They were attended by about twenty-five women, and the discussions were very lively. The lectures were on marriage, the middle age crisis for women and the International Women's Day, but even so the discussion centered on the usual themes: married women's work outside the home, what is femininity, is formal equality possible, how can women learn self-confidence, how to get husbands and children to respect a wife/mother as a person, and what about youth and sexuality. The style was the usual one, too, with much joking and laughter and constant interruptions and many personal examples. This was so even though most of the women in the audience did not know one another and even though there was probably some class mixture.

237 I know of no surveys to corroborate this generalization, but it is my own impression based on many years of participation in the movement, and it is also the impression of an anthropologist who studied the movement in Madrid in the late 1980s. (Kerstin Sundman, personal communication.)

238 Except for a small number of feminist superstars who got invited to TV debates. But they represented their own individual opinions or offered a generalized feminist argument. That was all there was room for. They did not and could not report on the subtleties of the internal debates.

239 The description of discourse arenas in Benituria was developed in Thurén 1988. The data come from the fieldwork period in 1982-83, i.e. 7-9 years before the Madrid study.

240 The only exception was perhaps the feminist movement, and the fact that it did not usually admit men to its activities was used as one strong argument to delegitimize it.

241 The semi-recognition of it in form of gifts of roses at the Christmas luncheon (cf chapter 7) felt awkward. Some women felt flattered and saw the rose as a symbol of the sexually tinted gender contrast between them and the male club board. Others laughed derisively. Some left their roses on the table. Most smiled, thanked the administrator, and shrugged uncertainly, looking at each other in search of an acceptable reaction.

242 My observations in Madrid coincide with the results of sociolinguistic research on gender patterns in conversation in other Western societies, e.g. Lakoff 1975, Spradley and Mann 1975, Tannen 1996, Holland and Quinn 1987.

243 This was the reason most feminists referred to in order to defend the exclusion of men from many feminist meeting places.

244 Cf Bourdieu's concept of hysteresis.

245 The concepts of scope and force will be further elaborated in the next chapter. I have also discussed them in Thurén 1993, 1998 and 2000.

246 Let me clarify these concepts so that the cultural contradictions stand out: Feminine submission used to be expressed as seductiveness and manipulation instead of autonomous personal decision-making; dependency was seen as more valued than personal autonomy for women, even though traditional ideas valued personal autonomy very highly for both women and men; repression of sexuality was taken as necessary, even though traditional ideas placed sexuality center stage, for good and for bad.

247 The word "ignorance" referred to lack of formal education as well as lack of interest in things that have nothing to do with housewifely duties, especially current events and intellectual issues. The image of the housewife was that of the "María" discussed in chapter 13, a woman who stays physically at home most of the time, who has little social life beyond kin, who never watches news programs or documentaries on TV, who gossips about neighbors and about the famous but who may not even read the text underneath the pictures in the gossip magazines, etc. It was a negative image for all and it was very common. In other words, the most feminine type of all was negatively valued whenever the ideological guard was lowered.

248 As it was during the Franco regime when gender segregation was everywhere: schools, sports, work places, domestic arrangements, children's play... It is remarkable that this practice, uncontestable during forty years, had disappeared so completely in just 10-15 years

249 In some quarters, it was even considered antifeminist to take an interest in men's situation; "they must solve their own problems."

250 Cf e.g. Chafetz (1990) on division of tasks and its relation to power.

251 One example of remaining cultural barriers is the tension between "Madrilenians" and "villagers" in chapter 3.

252 This is the argument of Nielsen and Rudberg, 1991. The authors are inspired by and criticize several analyses of modernization that use the Faust myth, especially Berman 1982. See also Ambjörnsson 1990. Nielsen and Rudberg discuss how women and men have related in different ways to the process of modernization and how this is reflected in the myth of Faust. The process of modernization is the historical condition for the birth of the individual. Capitalist society requires free individuals, rebels, movement, renovation. Nielsen and Rudberg draw parallels to male psychology: for a man ("European" or "Western"), the building of identity is about autonomy but simultaneously about an ambivalent relationship to paradise/mother/the world of emotion for which he longs and from which he has been excluded, and which he must repress and therefore detests and fears. In his homelessness, however, he finds a new home, as does Faust after rejecting the comforts of religious certainty. His new home is the public sphere, agency, knowledge, creation – not emotions. And just as for Faust, this attitude liberates an enormous amount of energy and gives great results but also leads to human costs on the same scale.
The male's inner split can be resolved with the help of gender polarization, and that was what was brought about in Europe from the early 19th century on, say Nielsen and Rudberg. Life was divided into a public and a private sphere, production and reproduction, and men took charge of the former. The exclusion of women from the public sphere meant that men could have their cake and eat it too. Women were to represent and more or less keep alive that which had been lost. Faust could afford to be cynical, because Gretchen loved him and cared for his child. The result, however, was that Gretchen was cut off from participating in the new world. This was a very general process which naturally varied according to country, region and class, among other things. Perhaps it was especially clear for middle class women (Cf e g. Davidoff 1973). But as many others have argued, the separation of spheres became a sign of masculinity for men of all classes, so that working class men even went on strike to obtain "family wages", i.e. the possibility of having their wives stay at home. (Cf e.g. Markus 1990.) In Spanish literature and folklore, there is no equivalent to the Faust figure. This is logical, since the intense phase of modernization happened later and is still recent.

253 The clearest examples are in appendix A, and chapter 13.

254 None of the features are unique to the Mediterranean area. The combination of them probably is. The purpose of this model here is not to compare with other possible gender orders, in other places, but to summarize what in Spain is called "traditional" and point out that this does have consequences in reality and that that reality is not unique to Spain but connected to a larger geographical area. In order for the model to be sufficiently abstract, the

417

features are expressed in very general terms, without empirical content. This may make them look as if they might have universal application. That is not so, and to show how, I have added possible contrasts in parentheses.

255 The clearest expression of this in Spain was the phrase "Men are more noble than women." It was a very common phrase and one heard it in cities and villages, in different social classes and pronounced by both women and men.

256 Whether this is universal or not is an issue for debate. It was the great issue debated by feminist anthropology in the 1970s. However that may be, it is clear that there are different kinds of hierarchies and different degrees of asymmetry. And please note that saying that women are placed lower than men in a hierarchy is not saying that they do not defend themselves. Of course they do.

257 The terms "force" and "scope" and the idea to use them to compare the variations in a similar phenomenon across time and space come from Geertz (1968), who applied them to religion. I have written more on this, see Thurén 1993 and 2000.

258 Cf the man in chapter 16 who, talking about women's work load, blurted out an accusation of their, for him, insufficient interest in sexual activity: "Do you do what you should?"

259 Serrano (1975) tells how he, during decades of work as a rural gynecologist in Spain, ran into many cases of women who had lesbian relationships but did not consider them sexual. Since there was no penis involved, what they did was not sexual, as they saw it.

260 And this is what the honor-and-shame syndrome is largely about, as has been amply debated by anthropologists. References are too many to be listed here, but several of the texts in note 266 are relevant.

261 But one might think there is a logical contradiction here. If women's bodies are dangerous, because they are attractive to men, and men are defined as the people who can act on their desires, then men ought to be considered more dangerous than women. The fact that men are not separated from public space is one piece of proof that they are the ones who are doing the defining, i.e. that whatever opportunities women have of obtaining influence, men hold ultimate power.

262 Cf for instance María José's musings about her situation in chapter 12. She felt she had become "like a man" in many ways after her separation. This made her both proud and worried. She wanted the guests to reassure her of her sexual attractiveness, which for her, in accordance with the Mediterranean gender logic, was the same thing as her gender identity. But it was she herself who brought up the subject and underlined the male-like aspects of her present life. On several other occasions, she broached the subject with me in order to make sure I understood that she was very much a "person" in spite of never having had a paid job and not subscribing to very many of the ongoing changes in the gender order. She felt she had stopped being a "woman", to her own surprise, but she was and wanted to be a woman as well as a person. I see her as an example of the personal insecurities and ambivalences growing in the fertile ground of the liminal situation of "change" in the early 1990s Madrid.

263 Examples: Only women used makeup; women wore slacks to be "sexy"; men never wore skirts; men of all persuasions preferred dark colors even in festive dress.

264 Examples: Cafeterias, bars to some extent, transportation, office work.

265 The similarity to racist thinking is obvious, and many informants who argued in this vein also expressed racist convictions. It was not unusual, for example, to express the idea that the poor nations of the world are victims of their own inherent backwardness. Vicente in chapter 7 was an extreme example, but the woman who talked about the adopted children from Nicaragua was representative. On a couple of occasions, when I countered the argument of nature in gender debates by describing societies with different kinds of gender orders, the informants asked me where those societies were located, "in Africa or something like that, right?" and when I admitted that, they took it as proof that they, not I, were right: it is only logical if such backward people have unnatural gender orders, they thought.

266 One reader wondered why I used the Mediterranean area as the relevant geographic reference. I understand that one might think Europe would be a better choice. It is certainly the immediate area of reference for most Spaniards and has been for many decades. When Spain joined the European Union, it was widely celebrated as a recognition that Spain was no longer "different" but a "normal" Western European, democratic country. I agree that this was an emotionally valid symbol of having overcome the long-lasting dictatorship. But my anthropological reading has convinced me that "the Mediterranean" is more than a geographical area around a common sea. It shares millennia of history, and its economic systems based on sheep, olives, wine and wheat, plus commerce, are recognizable, with minor variations, around the area and through the centuries. The gender orders are likewise varied but recognizable on a high level of generalization. There are more similarities between the northern and the southern shores of the Mediterranean, I would say, than between the southern and northern European gender orders. To develop fully this argument would need a longer text, but some references from my reading are: Bourdieu 1972, 1986, Brandes 1980, Campbell 1963, Denich 1974, Dubisch 1986, Evers Rosander 1991, Gilmore 1982, Goddard 1994, Krieger 1986, Lisón Tolosana 1987, Loizos and Papataxiarchis 1991, Peristiany 1987, Schneider 1971, Schneider and Schneider 1976, Sciama 1981, Vale de Almeida 1997.

267 I am thinking of such material changes as pressure from Spain's democratic neighbors, the growth of the European Union, the global currents of the economy, the increasing requirements of modern education for economic success on both individual and collective levels, etc.

268 And this is not trite. Things that are now called constraints, etc. were easily legitimated during the Franco regime, in both official and unofficial discourses, by calling them discipline, self-sacrifice, order, etc. or by reference to divine will. The word freedom itself, *libertad*, was then often said to be in need of careful circumscription in order not to lead to chaos and moral disorder, and other key words that are today self-evidently positive were similarly treated.

269 For the sake of readability, I write "Beniturian" and "Madrilenian" as abbreviations for "working class Beniturians in 1983" and "middle class Madrilenians in 1991".

270 What was considered conservative or progressive was substantially the same things. The conservative side and the progressive side had a similar weight in the middle class discourses, whereas the working class discourses leaned more towards the progressive side. If we look at the extreme poles of the continua, the middle class ones were further apart than the working class ones, and the conservative pole was much more conservative.

271 University degrees in Spain used to require five years of study. There was a lower degree obtainable after three years, but that was always a second best solution for students who did not have the grades or the money to continue and get a full degree. The organization of superior studies was thoroughly reformed after this book was written, and most degrees now only require four years. But in this conversation ,"to be in fourth" meant to have one more year to go.

272 I translate the word *oposiciones* with official competition. *Oposiciones* is an old and widespread institution in Spanish society. It is one way of choosing employees/obtaining employment, ideally as an objective method to ensure fair play. Most but not all *oposiciones* are for state and municipal employment, most but not all employees of state and municipalities have passed *oposiciones*. Banks and other big companies tend to use *oposiciones* too. To "do *oposiciones*" means the following: 1. Find out about calls for *oposiciones*, dates and themes. 2. Find a night school specialized in that kind of *oposiciones* and study for about one year. 3. Pass a written examination, sometimes combined with an oral one. 4. Wait for your turn. The people who have passed the examination are ranked according to the results and given employment in that order as openings arise. The details vary according to type of employment and the objectivity is often questioned. Still, people think of *oposiciones* as reasonably fair. Women do have a statistically demonstrable better chance of obtaining employment through this method than through any other.

273 All of this was not a breach of good anthropological method but just what the situation required according to local norms of interaction. Cf appendix C.

274 The word he used was *confianza*. It means literally confidence or trust, but it is hard to translate. It can mean approximately what those words mean in English, but it is someting more, a cultural key symbol for a good relationship as opposed to a distant or cold one. It is rather the opposite of indifferent human relationships. There is a longer discussion of the concept of *confianza* in Thurén 1988: 222-223.

275 This is illustrated in the section "To arrive in another world" in chapter 6.

276 Saying "all" here does not imply that there is a fixed, known number of factors and hierarchies, but rather, "all that we can find" or "all that might be construed as relevant."

277 Originally I formulated it as "the Madrilenian upper middle class." I still think that is the correct term that excludes other middle class categories such as small businessmen or well educated but poorly paid sectors (e.g. teachers). But unfortunately, the term "upper middle class" was often confused with "upper class" and this led to complications around the project and my fieldwork. So I chose the less precise alternative and hope that readers interested in theoretical class analyses will discern my intentions anyway.

278 I am thinking of the discussions in Clifford and Marcus 1986 and in Marcus and Fischer 1986. Van Maanen discusses some pros and cons (1988:136-138). The idea is also an old theme in the literature on life stories. And feminist methodology has analyzed the issues of the privilege of interpretation and the hierarchical relationship between interviewer and interviewed long before it became a postmodernist fad. (E.g. Fraser 1989, Mascia-Lees et al. 1989-1990, and many others.)

279 Irish hispanist Ian Gibson is reported to have said, "When did you ever meet an inarticulate Spaniard!"

280 "If my father knew I had gone to bed with my novio, he would feel obliged to do something drastic, that is why I don't tell him; and it is for his own sake, mind you; he would feel forced to do something. As it is, he suspects the truth, but as long as he has not been told, he can pretend not to know and that way he does not have to do anything." (Thurén 1988:241)

281 This old disposition is part of, but not the main reason for, the cautious mode of management of meaning (cf chapters 4 and 8).

282 In his theory of speech acts, Austin,1962, defines as illocutionary a speech act that fulfills its affirmation by the act of speaking itself, e.g. a promise, a declaration of war or a bet. My use of the term here is intentionally wider. I say that an utterance creates a reality by its very being uttered – but what is created is not necessarily that which the utterance affirms.

419

283 The example is authentic, from my work in Valencia. The "falla movement" or "falla world" is the citywide organization that works year round to prepare the great city festivities *Fallas* in March. It is officially apolitical but has conservative overtones.

284 My ethnography of conversation is not about code-switching or any of the other common issues in what is usually called the ethnography of speaking. Nor is it about gender differences in speech. Nor is it about how any given idea is expressed in different contexts. I do not take speech as a false surface which must be penetrated to reach some sort of truth that lies hidden behind or beneath it, or rather, not only that. Nor is this an ethnography of genres of word-handling (cf e.g. Shirley Brice Heath, 1983). All of these possibilities are tempting, and there are probably traces in my thinking of them all. But my object of study is something else: a view of sociocultural reality. I do ethnography, not linguistics.

285 What I say here is based on my own observations, not on literature, but it can be confirmed with the methods of linguists. For a Scandinavian, the work of Lars Fant comparing Scandinavian and Spanish communicative behavior and describing sources of misunderstandings when they meet is illuminating. According to Fant, the major features that differentiate Spanish conversational styles from Scandinavian ones are: higher toleration of disagreement among speakers, more stress on contrastiveness in the content of what is said, more attention to the aesthetic aspects of discourse, less emphasis on economy of expression and an appreciation of small talk, talk without a specific purpose (in contrast to its lack of legitimacy in Scandinavian discourse), more stress on the activity of speaking as pleasure. These differences are related to the more general cultural dispositions for self-assertiveness and group membership. Both exist in both countries, but are channeled in different ways in communicative behavior (Fant 1989).

286 Fant differentiates between "floor-taker" cultures, such as the Hispanic ones, and "floor-giver" ones, such as the English and Scandinavian ones. A piece of evidence: "For an average fortuitous sample of ten minutes of conversation with three or four participants, the speakers of a Spanish group will commit 50.7 interruptions, as contrasted with 10.7 interruptions for the Swedish group, that is, almost five times as many." (1989:259)

287 Cf for instance chapter 19 where the two dispositions clash openly.

288 Only once was this pattern disrupted. At one social gathering of women only, a woman of about 55 years of age chanced to start talking about her life. She told of how she had been very beautiful when young and a brilliant student, but how she had married and never worked in her profession, how her children had now married and she was alone with an uncommunicative husband and felt old and unappreciated. At first her story was treated as just another interesting example, a contribution to the general discussion. But as she went on talking too long, and the attempts to interrupt her did not work, the others at first felt she was boring, and tried to stop her with increasingly heartless joking, and then, as this did not work either and tears started rolling down her face, a distinctly uncomfortable air settled over the gathering. This was resolved changing the atmosphere into one of reassurance. The other women told of similar feelings and gave her well-meaning advice on things she could do to make her life more interesting, such as going for walks with her friends more often. She could not stop crying nor would she stop talking. She definitely lost control. This was unusual and so were the interactive techniques to break the impasse. This shows that even though emotions form part of the normal conversational pattern, too deep and uncontrollable emotions will disrupt the rhythm of turn-taking and there is little preparedness to deal with that. In middle class Madrilenian contexts it did not happen often. What foreigners might experience as an emotional style of interaction was in fact quite controlled. For an example of a minor (and more common type of) loss of self-control, see chapter 19, Rosa María's tale of what she saw on the beach.

289 T*ener gracia,* literally to have grace, is the emic term for the desired agility. It has a much wider referent than joking humor. It can even be said to be the label for skill in the use for good effect of all the norms I have just described. A person with *gracia* may not tell a single joke but yet make people laugh with her sense of rhythm, drama, etc. A person with *gracia* also knows how to make people experience other emotions. A person with *gracia* is never boring. A person with *gracia* is appreciated for having *gracia* . A person with *gracia* knows when to joke and when not to, when to talk and when to keep quiet, etc. A person with *gracia* never overdoes self-affirmation to the point of occupying the space others need for the same thing, and is never the clumsy clown, yet never selfishly keeps her or his graces hidden. (NB, however, that the phrase "*tiene gracia*" about a thing or an event has a narrower meaning of "it is funny." The phrase "*hace gracia*" means that something makes you laugh and the meaning can be both straightforwardly positive and sarcastically negative. To say that a person is *gracioso/graciosa* likewise can be both a compliment and its opposite.)

290 Cf again Fant (1989, 1993), whose work centers on interactional style in business negotiations. In such situations, Spaniards give greater importance than e.g. Mexicans or Swedes to moves that strengthen a person-orientation and a good feeling among the participants. But they do so in ways that may be misunderstood if judged from the horizon of other dispositions. Bravo (1993) shows how Spaniards use laughter to create a climate of intimacy and fun, while Swedes use laughter more to mitigate the, for them, threatening aspect of unavoidable differences of opinion.

291 This is a very general disposition in Spain, and probably in the Mediterranean region as a whole. It has many other expressions apart from conversational style. Cf Thurén 1988:212-218. Cf also Fant (1989), who calls it self-assertiveness.

292 Whereas – to continue the comparison – in Swedish culture the real loss, what everyone fears, is the opposite: to lose control and reveal too much of one's true self. The main goal in Swedish interaction is not to show one's self nor to create pleasurably aesthetic interaction, but rather to prove to the other participants that one takes them seriously, respects their autonomy and engages in the interaction with the legitimate purpose of solving some problem or increasing mutual understanding. To listen carefully is an important sign of courtesy, whereas interruptions or too much self-affirmation signal the opposite. (Consequently an average Spaniard in Sweden and an average Swede in Spain will both be seen as great bores.)

293 Cf for instance Ardener 1978, Harding 1987, Lundgren 1992, Widerberg 1992.